The LONGMAN HANDBOOK *for* WRITERS AND READERS

SECOND EDITION

CHRIS M. ANSON
NORTH CAROLINA STATE UNIVERSITY

ROBERT A. SCHWEGLER
UNIVERSITY OF RHODE ISLAND

LONGMAN

An imprint of Addison Wesley Longman, Inc.

New York • Reading, Massachusetts • Menlo Park, California • Harlow, England
Don Mills, Ontario • Sydney • Mexico City • Madrid • Amsterdam

English Editor: Lynn M. Huddon
Development Editor: Meg Botteon
Supplements Editor: Donna Campion
Marketing Manager: Renée Ortbals
Project Manager: Bob Ginsberg
Design Manager: Wendy Ann Fredericks
Text Designer: Dorothy Bungert/EriBen Graphics
Cover Designer: Kay Petronio
Cover Illustration: © Stockart.com
Art Studio: ElectraGraphics, Inc.
Electronic Production Specialist: Sarah Johnson
Senior Marketing Manager: Hugh Crawford
Electronic Page Makeup: York Production Services
Printer and Binder: RR Donnelley & Sons Company
Cover Printer: The Lehigh Press, Inc.

For permission to use copyrighted material, grateful acknowledgment is made to the copyright holders on pp. C1–C3, which are hereby made part of this copyright page.

Library of Congress Cataloging-in-Publication Data

Anson, Christopher M., date
 The Longman handbook for writers and readers / Chris M. Anson, Robert A. Schwegler. — 2nd ed.
  p. cm.
 Includes index.
 ISBN 0-321-05804-6
 1. English language—Rhetoric Handbooks, manuals, etc.
2. English language—Grammar Handbooks, manuals, etc. 3. Reading comprehension Handbooks, manuals, etc. 4. Report writing Handbooks, manuals, etc. I. Schwegler, Robert A. II. Title.
 PE1408.A61844 1999   99-30574
 808'.042—dc21   CIP

Please visit our website at http://www.awlonline.com/ansonlhb

ISBN 0-321-05804-6

12345678910—DOC—02010099

CONTENTS

Part 3 REPRESENTING YOURSELF: CREATING YOUR PLACE IN A COMMUNITY 127

Part 4 EDITING AND PROOFREADING: MEETING COMMUNITY EXPECTATIONS 183

Part 6 USING CITATION STYLES 647

All writers, whatever their skills and experience, need at least occasional advice—sometimes even more. We've designed the second edition of *The Longman Handbook for Writers and Readers* to provide answers to specific questions as well as extended help.

The handbook offers advice about writing strategies and critical reading; answers to questions about grammar, punctuation, and style; and help in research, analysis, and documentation. In addition, it highlights the expectations of various communities of writers and readers—academic, work, and public—and it outlines the kinds of writing typical of each community.

The Longman Handbook differs from other composition handbooks in several important ways:

- It places readers and reading—especially critical reading—at the center of the writing process and helps writers develop an understanding of readers' expectations and their responses to error.
- It emphasizes the social nature of writing, especially the way different communities of writers and readers—academic, work, and public— shape written texts and the writing process, and it offers strategies for recognizing and meeting the needs and expectations of various communities.
- It treats correctness and an understanding of written conventions as essential to accomplished writing yet goes beyond a simple focus on the avoidance of error to help writers develop the ability to recognize effects of errors on readers as well as the ways conventions may vary from community to community.
- It treats writing, critical thinking, and research as processes often best conducted through collaboration, either with fellow writer-readers or with imagined audiences, and it includes numerous examples of collaborative writing and research along with numerous strategies for collaborating at all stages of the composing process.

Over the past two decades, composition teaching has changed dramatically in response to research and theory. Teachers and scholars now know much more about the processes of reading and writing, the causes of error and the remedies, and, above all, the importance of different communities of readers and writers, with differing needs and expectations. These new perspectives have led to a growing awareness of writing and reading as social acts. Yet composition handbooks, with their roots in earlier modes of teaching, have often lagged behind these advances. We have written *The Longman Handbook for Writers and Readers* out of a belief that composition instruction will benefit from an innovative approach, one that responds directly to recent theory and practice.

We know that even if a handbook is at once authoritative, flexible, and up to date, it still must be easy to use. We have paid special attention to the handbook's design, indexes, and glossary to help users locate the advice they need. We provide concrete techniques for recognizing and revising errors rather than simple statements of abstract, inflexible rules. And we offer specific writing strategies and detailed examples rather than broad, unhelpful generalizations.

What's New?

Before producing the second edition of *The Longman Handbook,* we surveyed many students and teachers to find out what features were working well for them and what we could improve on. This new edition thus represents some of the most current and innovative approaches and material for the teaching of writing while retaining those elements of the book that have served students so well in the past. Among the changes in this edition are:

- **Communities of writers.** A more diverse focus on communities for writing relies on examples and strategies illustrating the way writers work in academic, business, and public or civic contexts. While the text recognizes—and highlights—the importance of the academic setting, students also need to understand writing as a tool essential for occupational success and for participation as an involved citizen in our democracy.
- **Writing and technology.** A stronger orientation toward writing in technologically enhanced environments offers practical advice for students working with computers. The vast majority of college students now use computers and routinely access the Internet. The second edition includes many more examples and suggestions for writing on and with computers and for making the best use of the World Wide Web and other online resources.
- **Language variation.** A new chapter, "Presenting Yourself Through Language Choices" (Chapter 10), focuses on the issue of language variation, home or community language varieties, oral and written dialects, code shifting, the importance of "standard" English in text written to diverse audiences, and the effect that particular choices of personae can have on an audience's reception of a text.
- **Document design.** A new chapter, "Designing Documents" (Chapter 13), demonstrates the contexts and purposes for using visual information in texts designed for diverse audiences. In part because of the advent of multimedia technology and the new capabilities of computer graphics and design programs, many colleges and universities

have raised their expectations for well-designed documents. This chapter features four full-color annotated model documents from standard and online media.

- **Online style guide.** A new chapter, "Documenting Sources: COS" (Chapter 53) gives students an essential reference (from the Columbia Online Style Manual) for documenting online sources and citations. COS style can be adapted to both MLA and APA formats, as well as other styles of documentation.
- **Critical reasoning and progressive argumentative strategies.** Chapters 12 and 54 provide students with crucial support for academic writing in different college courses.

Continuing Features

We have retained—and enhanced—those features that helped make the first edition of *The Longman Handbook for Writers and Readers* a success.

- **Attention to readers.** Writing often takes place in private—in our minds, at our desks, on our computer screens—so we may tend to think of it as something that takes shape in the absence of readers. This perspective, however, is a mistake. Because writing is a form of communication, our real or potential readers are present (or ought to be) from the earliest stages of writing to the final editing and proofreading. In *The Longman Handbook* we emphasize the importance of readers and reading in a number of ways.
- **Reading and the writing process.** Throughout the book, we stress the many important roles that critical reading and awareness of audience play in the writing process. In addition to devoting entire chapters and parts of chapters to critical reading and to focusing on readers, we offer concrete strategies for incorporating reading into writing— even as part of the editing and proofreading processes. Of particular usefulness are those strategies (and accompanying exercises) that help writers develop the ability to keep communities of readers and their likely responses in mind during planning, drafting, revising, and editing.
- **Critical thinking and reading.** We believe that reading, critical thinking, and an awareness of audience expectations and needs are intertwined. For this reason, we have emphasized the importance of critical thinking in our discussions of analytical, interpretive, and critical reading—and we have emphasized the roles of reading and readers in our discussions of critical thinking. We also provide numerous strategies for developing these skills in tandem, supported by examples and exercises.
- **Research and reading.** Our discussions of research and writing pay considerable attention to critical reading, both analytical techniques such as summary and paraphrase and critical techniques such as synthesis and critical response. We also pay attention to the special roles

critical reading needs to play with electronic resources and discuss the special demands of readers in electronic communities.

- **Collaboration and feedback.** We believe that one of the best ways to understand how readers respond to a text and for writers to learn how others view their texts is to collaborate with other writer-readers. Many writing courses recognize the importance of collaboration by making use of peer response groups and similar activities. For these classes and for writers who wish to develop an ability to read others' work analytically and helpfully, we offer practical advice about giving and receiving constructive criticism, and we include a collaborative activity in virtually every set of exercises in the text. We also go beyond the classroom by highlighting the roles collaborating plays in work and public settings.

Writing and Reading as Social Processes

We believe that writing and reading are social processes, characterized by constant transactions between writers and readers and by the context within which these transactions occur. To emphasize this relationship, our discussions throughout the text highlight the role of audience and social setting in shaping the purposes of effective writing and in determining which forms of expression are likely to be most useful. In the current edition of *The Longman Handbook,* we have extended this focus by highlighting communities of writers and readers—academic, work, and public—as well as the interactions that characterize electronic communities.

- **A fresh approach to correctness.** We believe that correctness in writing—employing the conventions appropriately and effectively—is to a considerable extent a matter of social awareness. Errors can undermine the writer's relationship with readers or impede effective, persuasive, and imaginative interaction within a community of writers and readers. Utilizing appropriate conventions of grammar, sentence structure, punctuation, and style is an important part of being able to guide the way readers respond to writing.

  Correctness does not begin with abstract rules, however; it begins with a recognition of specific features of grammar and style and the effect of these features on individual readers and communities of readers. It continues though the development of strategies for revision and effective expression.

  Throughout the text, therefore, our treatments of error and correctness begin with an emphasis on recognizing specific features of grammar, sentence structure, mechanics, diction, and style, always keeping in mind the effects errors have on readers. We give concrete advice for revising errors and developing writing that is not only correct but also effective, persuasive, and imaginative.

  Research tells us that conventions of grammar and expression vary greatly over time and from group to group. At the same time, the members of any particular community of writers and readers are likely to place considerable importance on following certain conventions, generally with good reason. Effective writers are aware both of the importance of following conventions and of the ways in which conventions are likely to vary. Throughout the handbook, we try to develop this dual awareness through examples, through discussion of written conventions and the rules of grammar, and through specially highlighted Writer's Tips and Writer's Alerts.

- **An emphasis on concrete writing and reading strategies.** We believe that writers turn to a handbook most often for concrete advice: for ways to accomplish a writing task; for answers to questions about grammar and punctuation; or for advice on finding, reading, and documenting research sources. Even when they want to know about a relatively general subject, such as how to write a research paper or the most useful ways to revise and edit, writers are often best served by learning about specific strategies they can employ.

- **Strategies.** *The Longman Handbook* places special emphasis on concrete, practical strategies that writers and readers can employ in their work. One innovation in the text is the use of Strategy sections to present techniques that writers and readers can apply immediately. The Strategies are detailed and specific, and they suggest ways to employ the advice offered in the more general discussions that precede them.

- **Recognize and revise.** We believe that knowing the definition of an error such as a sentence fragment, a problem with pronoun reference, or misused punctuation is often not sufficient. Writers need to be able to recognize such errors as they draft, revise, and edit, and then they need to be able to correct mistakes. Each of the chapters in Part 4 of the handbook ("Editing and Proofreading") is built around a recognize-and-revise pattern and offers concrete suggestions for identifying errors and avoiding or revising them. Many of the Strategy and Writer's Tip sections in these chapters pay special attention to common errors that readers find particularly distracting and confusing. In addition, the innovative Chapter 14, "The Editing and Proofreading Process," offers useful advice for recognizing errors and other problems.

Organization of the Text

Because it is organized around the process actually used by writers, this handbook shows students how to become successful writers, how to correct and improve their writing, and how to follow conventions expected by readers. One important feature of the text is that it treats recognizing and revising errors as an integral part of the writing process (Part 4, "Editing and Proofreading: Meeting Community Expectations"), not as an activity only loosely related to the process.

In Part 1, "Writing, Reading, and Thinking: Joining Communities," we introduce strategies you can use as a writer and reader, including the journal. We then explain how to develop a paper, moving from planning strategies to defining a purpose, considering readers, and drafting.

Part 2, "Drafting and Revising: Shaping Your Writing for Your Community," first explains and illustrates the process of revision, both major and minor. The next chapters focus on ways to develop effective paragraphs and sentences and to revise these elements so that they successfully link writers and readers.

Part 3, "Representing Yourself: Creating Your Place in a Community," discusses language choices, writing online, critical reasoning, and document design.

Part 4, "Editing and Proofreading: Meeting Community Expectations," treats editing and proofreading as part of the writing process. Chapter 14 gives an overview of the process with concrete suggestions for keeping readers in mind. Part 4 includes five full sections: "Editing Grammar" (Chapters 15–19); "Editing for Sentence Problems" (Chapters 20–27); "Editing for Word Choice" (Chapters 28–31); "Editing for Punctuation" (Chapters 32–37); and "Proofreading for Mechanics and Spelling" (Chapters 38–43). These chapters concentrate first on how to recognize a problem and then on how to revise, edit, or proofread it.

Part 5, "Using Research Strategies: Reading and Writing Within a Research Community," devotes five chapters to the research process, emphasizing the writer's role as a researcher; search strategies; library, field, and electronic resources; and critical reading.

Part 6, "Using Citation Styles," discusses the MLA, APA, CBE, CMS, and COS documentation systems.

Part 7, "Writing Strategies," explores the purposes and functions of other kinds of writing, including argument and other forms of point-driven writing (Chapter 54); writing about literature (Chapter 55); informative writing (Chapter 56); and business writing (Chapter 57).

Ancillaries

The ancillary package for *The Longman Handbook,* Second Edition, is designed to bring helpful resources to both instructors and students.

Print Resources for Students

Researching Online, Third Edition, by David Munger, gives students detailed step-by-step instructions for performing electronic searches, using email, listservs, Usenet newsgroups, IRCs, and MOOs to do research, and assessing the validity of an electronic source.

Literacy Library Series. These brief supplements—Public Literacy, Workplace Literacy, and Academic Literacy—offer additional models and guidelines for writing in three different communities.

Visual Communication, by Susan Hilligoss (Clemson University), introduces document design principles and features, practical discussions of space, type, organization, pattern, graphic elements, and visuals.

The Longman Guide to Columbia Online Style is a 32-page booklet that includes an overview of Columbia Online Style, guidelines for finding and evaluating electronic sources, and many examples for citing electronic sources.

The *Documentation Guide* with sample student papers is a fast and easy reference for students writing research papers in any discipline. Adapted from the research and writing chapters in this book, the guide provides coverage of MLA, APA, CMS, CBE, and COS styles in a pocket-sized format. The Documentation Guide includes a full sample MLA paper and a full sample APA paper.

Model Research Papers from Across the Disciplines, Fifth Edition (Diane Gould, Shoreline Community College), is a collection of student papers illustrating the most recent MLA, APA, CBE, Chicago, and Columbia Online Style documentation systems. Annotations highlight important considerations for writing in each field.

A Guide for Peer Response, Second Edition (Tori Haring-Smith, Brown University, and Helon H. Raines, Armstrong State University), offers students forms for peer critiques, including general guidelines and specific forms for different stages in the writing process and for various types of papers.

The *Merriam Webster's Collegiate Dictionary,* Tenth Edition, a desktop-sized hardcover dictionary, is available with *The Longman Handbook for Writers and Readers,* Second Edition. Also available with the handbook is *The New American Webster Handy College Dictionary,* Third Edition, a briefer paperback dictionary.

The Penguin Program: In conjunction with Penguin Putnam, Inc., Longman is proud to offer a variety of Penguin titles at a significant discount when packaged with any Longman title. Popular titles include Mike Rose's *Lives on the Boundary* and *Possible Lives,* and Neil Postman's *Amusing Ourselves to Death.*

Print Resources for Instructors

The updated *Instructor's Resource Manual* is an excellent resource for both new and experienced instructors. Besides containing chapter-by-chapter coverage of *The Longman Handbook for Writers and Readers,* the *Resource Manual* includes course design strategies, sample syllabi, writing assignments, classroom and online activities and resources, and much more.

An *Answer Key* prepared by Chris M. Anson and Robert A. Schwegler, which provides answers to the exercises in this handbook, is available separately.

Other notable supplements from the *Longman Resources for Instructors* package:

- *Comp Tales,* edited by Richard Haswell (Texas A&M, Corpus Christi) and Min-Zhan Lu (Drake University), is a collection of stories that college writing teachers tell and re-tell, organized around current topics of debate in composition studies and on key issues for new writing teachers. *Comp Tales* is a timely, witty, warm resource for introducing graduate students and teaching assistants to a community of fellow teacher-scholars.

- *Teaching in Progress: Theories, Practices, and Scenarios,* Second Edition, by Josephine Tarvers (Winthrop University)
- *Teaching Writing to the Non-Native Speaker,* by Jocelyn Steer
- *Teaching Online: Internet Research, Conversation, and Composition,* Second Edition by Daniel Anderson (University of North Carolina, Chapel Hill), and Bret Benjamin, Chris Busiel, and Bill Paredes-Holt (all, University of Texas at Austin)

Media Resources for Students and Instructors

Daedalus Online is the next generation of the highly regarded Daedalus Integrated Writing Environment (DIWE), uniting a peer facilitated writing pedagogy with the inherently cooperative tools of the World Wide Web. This writing environment allows students to explore online resources, employ pre-writing strategies, share ideas in real-time conferences, and post feedback to an asynchronous discussion board. *Daedalus Online* also offers instructors a suite of interactive management tools to guide and facilitate their students' interaction.

Specifically, instructors can:

- Effortlessly create and post assignments
- Link these assignments to online educational resources
- Tie these lessons to *The Longman Handbook*
- Customize materials to fit with any instructional preference

The Longman Handbook Online at ⟨http://www.awlonline.com/ansonlhb⟩. This new companion Web site includes practice exercises for every chapter; helpful links to academic, workplace, and public sources, as well as more general writing advice links; brief writing samples illustrating key concepts of many chapters; complete annotated student papers; an interactive writing checklist to help students evaluate their completed essays; and an interactive module on internet searching methods, including a few Web source evaluation exercises. Teachers will also find sample syllabi, teaching suggestions, downloadable transparency masters, PowerPoint presentations, and more, at this site.

The English Pages at ⟨http://www.awlonline.com/englishpages⟩. *The English Pages* Web site provides professors and students with continuously updated resources for reading, writing, and research practice in four areas: Composition, Literature, Technical Writing, and Basic Skills. Features include simulated Internet search activities to help students learn the process of finding and evaluating information on the WWW and annotated links that provide the best information on the widest variety of writing issues and research topics.

Acknowledgments

If we incurred debts of gratitude over the six years it took us to produce the first edition of *The Longman Handbook for Writers and Readers,* our thanks are no fewer for the help we received producing the second edition.

First we wish to thank those who contributed directly to the writing of some of the chapters in the book. In particular, we wish to acknowledge the editorial work of Linda Stern, who kept our ideas direct and our prose lean. A community of special consultants worked closely with us on the development of new chapters and the revision of existing chapters: Victor Villanueva offered us great wisdom as we created our new chapter on language variation. Margaret Barber, University of Southern Colorado, wrote the new Chapter 53 on the COS citation style. Jim Dubinsky of Virginia Tech contributed the new Chapter 13 on document design. Mick Doherty and Sandye Thompson, writing, editing, and internet consultants, are the authors of the new Chapter 11, "Writing in Online Communities." Christina Haas, Kent State University, has been a thoughtful and generous contributor of workplace-related examples and an excellent reader and reviewer for workplace relevance. Elizabeth Ervin, University of North Carolina, Wilmington, contributed her expertise and her creativity in writing for public communities to both the content and the philosophy of this revision. Tom Maeglin helped us update the MLA, APA, CMS, and CBE chapters, and contributed new electronic examples as well as each style's guidelines for citing electronic sources. Gladys Vega Scott, Arizona State University, was a sensitive and creative reviewer of the book's ESL coverage, and suggested many new examples.

In addition, many of our colleagues have advised us, reviewed our drafts, and provided general response to our ideas. Our special thanks go to the following people: Edward Armstrong, University of Arkansas; Jennifer Bullis, Whatcom Community College; Bonnie Cox, San Jose State University; Carolyn Craft, Longwood College; Katherine Dallen, Whatcom Community College; Marcia Dickson, Ohio State University; Barbara Fein, New Hampshire Community Technical College, Stratham; Cynthia Galivan, Hudson Valley Community College; Pam Helberg, Whatcom Community College; Sandra Jamieson, Drew University; Anita Aukee Johnson, Whatcom Community College; Brian Johnson, University of Oklahoma; Millie Kidd, Mount St. Mary's College; Daniel Kies, College of DuPage; Beth Gordon Klingner, Dyson College of Arts and Sciences; Joe Law, Wright State University; Mike Little, Texas A&M University; Jane Long, Southwest Oklahoma State University; Kathy McClelland, Auburn University; Rich Meyers, Owens Community College; Roark Mulligan, Christopher Newport University; B. Keith Murphy, Fort Valley State University; Kaylene D. Nelsen, Lorain County Community College; Amy Pawl, Washington University–St. Louis; Teresa Pinney, Whatcom Community College; Dean Rehberger, Michigan State University; Robert Ronger, Whatcom Community College; Barabara Saez, Three Rivers Community Technical College; Betty Scott, Whatcom Community College; Sherrie Sawicki California University, Fullerton.

We thank especially Marcia Muth, the developmental editor of the first edition and now co-author on another project, who offered constantly sage advice about critical decisions relating to the book.

An extensive team of editors, producers, and managers at Longman were instrumental in the development and publication of the Second Edition: Anne Smith, Publishing Partner, English; Lynn Huddon, English Editor; Meg Botteon, Developmental Editor; Bob Ginsberg, Project Manager; Donna Campion, Supplements Editor. Sharon Balbos was also an invaluable resource.

Chris Anson once again expresses his appreciation to his wife Gean for her patience, love, and support; and to his sons Ian and Graham who have never lived a day without this book staring their father in the face—and who have now proudly installed it on the shelves of their second- and fifth-grade classrooms. To this little "community," Chris dedicates the new edition. Chris also expresses heartfelt appreciation to his new colleagues at North Carolina State University, who patiently awaited his arrival so that he could complete work on this edition, and whose good cheer inspired him to be quick about it.

Bob Schwegler would like to acknowledge above all Nancy Newman Schwegler, who tolerated with grace and wit the far too many years it took to prepare the first edition of this book. Her understanding of readers, reading, and the creative ways writers can represent themselves has been essential to many of the new features that characterize the second edition. "And I'll be sworn upon't that he loves her; / For here's a paper written in his hand, / A halting sonnet . . . ." He would also like to thank Ashley Marie Schwegler for arriving in the middle of the second edition, demonstrating that the writing of books is far from the most important thing in life. Brian and Tara Schwegler—though far away—added an important anthropological perspective on communities and language. And Christopher added smiles.

CHRIS M. ANSON
ROBERT A. SCHWEGLER

Finding What You Need

A handbook is of little use unless you can turn quickly to the page containing the information you need and then locate it on the page without confusion. *The Longman Handbook* offers you a variety of ways to locate the information and advice you need.

- **Index.** The detailed index at the end of the text covers all the topics, large and small, discussed in the book and gives the page number on which the discussion appears. The index also indicates related topics that may be of interest or use, introducing them with the phrase *See also.* As an additional resource, the index also includes terms that may be familiar to you from other places, such as high school courses or other textbooks. For example, the term *run-on sentence* is widely used, though it seldom appears in college handbooks. It is included in the index, however, followed by the suggestion *See also* Fused sentences.

Topic ──▶ Telnet-obtained sources
Subtopics ──▶ COS documentation style for, 784 ◀── *Page*
 ──▶ MLA works cited list format for, 678
Tense(s). See Verb tenses ◀─── *Cross-reference to another index entry*
Tense sequence, 269-270, G-41
Tentative thesis statements, 630, G-41
Testimonies, reasoning from, 813
Text analysis, G-42 ◀─── *Cross-reference to glossary entry*
  commentary on, 859
  examples of, 845-859
  for meaning in a short story, 850-855
  for technique in films, 855-858
  for technique in poems, 845-850
than, as, 242-243
than, then, G-42
that, 201, 202
  in misplaced modifiers, 355
  in nonrestrictive clauses. See Nonrestrictive
    (nonessential) clauses
  pronoun reference and, 342, 348-349
  in relative clauses, 226-228
  as relative pronoun, 315
  in restrictive clauses. See Restrictive (essential) clauses
  subject-verb agreement and, 290, 295
that, which, G-42

- **Table of contents.** The table of contents at the front of the book outlines the seven sections into which the book is divided: Part 1, "Writing, Reading, and Thinking: Joining Communities;" Part 2, "Drafting and Revising: Shaping Your Writing for Your Community"; Part 3, "Representing Yourself: Creating Your Place in a Community"; Part 4, "Editing and Proofreading: Meeting Community Expectations"; Part 5, "Using Research Strategies: Reading and Writing Within a Research Community"; Part 6, "Using Citation Styles"; and Part 7, "Writing Strategies." It also indicates the topic and major sections of each of the chapters.

The table of contents appears in detailed form on pages iii–x and in summarized form inside the front cover.

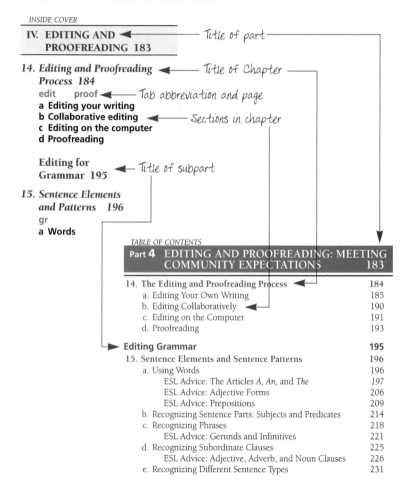

- **Revision and Editing Symbols and Reader Response Symbols.**
  Inside the back cover, on the left, is a list of correction symbols commonly used by instructors commenting on a paper. You can use this list to locate relevant sections of the handbook. On the right is a list of reader response symbols, shortcuts for responding to another writer's paper.

REVISION AND EDITING SYMBOLS

abbrev	incorrect abbreviation, **42**	**no ¶**	no new paragraph, **8**
agr	error in subject-verb or	**p**	error in punctuation, **32–37**
Abbreviation	pronoun-antecedent	**punc**	error in punctuation, **32–37**
	agreement, **18**	^	comma, **32a-32i** *Name of problem*
apos	lack of (or incorrect)	**no** ^	no comma, **32j** *or issue*
	possessive apostrophe, **34**	;	semicolon, **33a**
art	article used incorrectly, **15**	:	colon, **33b**
awk	awkward construction	˅	apostrophe, **34** ◄——— *Handbook section*
cap	capital letter needed, **38**		

- **Recognize and Revise Ten Serious Problems.** This chart, located just before the Revision and Editing Symbols, illustrates ten significant problems, identifies each problem, and directs you to the appropriate section of the handbook for advice.

RECOGNIZE AND REVISE TEN SERIOUS PROBLEMS

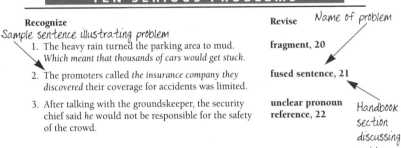

Recognize   **Revise**   *Name of problem*
Sample sentence illustrating problem

1. The heavy rain turned the parking area to mud.   **fragment, 20**
   Which meant that thousands of cars would get stuck.

2. The promoters called *the insurance company they*   **fused sentence, 21**
   discovered their coverage for accidents was limited.

3. After talking with the groundskeeper, the security   **unclear pronoun**   *Handbook*
   chief said *he* would not be responsible for the safety   **reference, 22**   *section*
   of the crowd.   *discussing*
                                                                             problem

- **Glossary.** The "Glossary of Usage and Terms" (pp. G-1 to G-45, just before the index) provides concise definitions of key terms and concepts, along with cross-references to chapters and sections with extended discussions of the topics. The terms explained in the glossary are in boldface type in the text so that you can easily turn to the glossary if you need to check the meaning of a term. In addition, the glossary answers commonly asked questions about word choice and correct usage, including definitions of frequently confused words such as *accept* and *except*.

- **Tabs, Titles, and Abbreviations.** On the pages of the text, headings on the top left supply the chapter titles and those on the top right describe the specific topics covered in the section. Tabs at the sides of the pages identify the chapter and section numbers so that you can quickly thumb through and find a particular section. Abbreviations of topics appear within the tabs and also in the brief table of contents. The ESL notation above some of the tabs marks sections particularly useful for students whose native language is not English. Throughout the text, cross-references link sections and will lead you to related or more detailed explanations.

Finding Information on a Page

Each page of your handbook includes a heading at the top of the page, a tab, and other features to help you find material quickly.

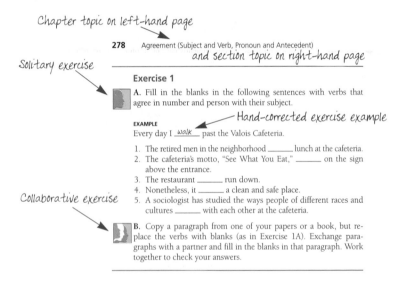

Chapter topic on left-hand page

278   Agreement (Subject and Verb, Pronoun and Antecedent)

and section topic on right-hand page

Solitary exercise

Exercise 1

A. Fill in the blanks in the following sentences with verbs that agree in number and person with their subject.

EXAMPLE — *Hand-corrected exercise example*

Every day I _walk_ past the Valois Cafeteria.

1. The retired men in the neighborhood _____ lunch at the cafeteria.
2. The cafeteria's motto, "See What You Eat," _____ on the sign above the entrance.
3. The restaurant _____ run down.
4. Nonetheless, it _____ a clean and safe place.
5. A sociologist has studied the ways people of different races and cultures _____ with each other at the cafeteria.

Collaborative exercise

B. Copy a paragraph from one of your papers or a book, but replace the verbs with blanks (as in Exercise 1A). Exchange paragraphs with a partner and fill in the blanks in that paragraph. Work together to check your answers.

Tab identifying chapter and section

18a
agr
ESL

Topic abbreviation

ESL Advice: Subject-Verb Agreement

Watch out for the following troublesome verbs that change form according to person or tense. Be sure to select the correct verb form so that your subject and verb agree.

Specific advice for ESL writers

- *Be* verbs (present and past)

I	**am, was**		
You (sing., pl.)		He	
We	**are, were**	She	**is, was**
They		It	

Your handbook also supplies headings, and special features throughout each chapter so that you can refer to information efficiently.

Chapter number and section letter

Heading for main topic

23a   Recognizing and editing misplaced modifiers

If you do not make the relationship between a modifier and its headword clear and specific, you may mislead or confuse readers. To recognize a **misplaced modifier**, look for a word that fails to modify its intended headword and instead appears to modify some other word or phrase in the sentence. Sometimes a misplaced modifier modifies *both* the word before it and the word after.

Boldfaced term explained in Glossary

STRATEGY

Explanation emphasizing first recognition and then editing alternatives

Strategy with specific technique for immediate application

To correct a misplaced modifier, either move it closer to its headword or rewrite the sentence so the connection between modifier and headword is clear.

MISPLACED MODIFIER	After you have installed the fan, follow the directions for the wiring connections on the back of the cover plate.
	READER'S REACTION: Are the wiring connections on the back of the cover plate?

`23a`
`mm/ dm`

MOVED NEXT TO HEADWORD	After you have installed the fan, follow the directions **on the back of the cover plate** for the wiring connections.

Reader's Reaction showing how a reader might respond

Labels for problems and solutions

MISPLACED MODIFIER	People who abuse alcohol frequently have other problems.
	READER'S REACTION: Does *frequently* refer to the rate of alcohol abuse or the likelihood of problems?

REWRITTEN	People who abuse alcohol tend to have other problems as well.

Writer's Tip ◄── *Writing advice or caution*

Stating your point in a thesis is a good start, but many promising papers still get bogged down in details, losing focus and losing the reader. One way to avoid this problem is to remind readers of your overall thesis each time you move to a new part of your essay, letting them know what section or technique you will discuss next and what you plan to conclude about it. This strategy can guide your drafting and your revision, helping you check the focus of your essay and pay attention to the needs of your readers.

`55c`
`lit`

Did You Know? providing information about writing.

► Did You Know?

The conjunctions *because* and *for* offer you two different ways to arrange sentences dealing with causes and effects. *Because* creates subordination; *for* creates coordination. Here is what one authority on style and usage has to say about these words and ways to use them.

BECAUSE/FOR
Often interchangeable. *Because* clearly indicates cause or reason: "They stayed at home because it was snowing." *For* (after a comma) normally joins two independent statements and may suggest cause, reason, or evidence. Cause or reason: "They stayed at home, for it was snowing." Evidence: "They may have decided to drive into town, for faint tire tracks remain in their driveway."
—J. N. Hook, *The Appropriate Word* (Reading, MA: Addison, 1990) 34.

`27b`
`sub`

Special Features

The following special features appear throughout the handbook, emphasizing valuable and engaging information for student writers. As you use your handbook, look for the special features that supply the help you need.

- **Writer's Tips** and **Writer's Alerts** highlight advice and cautions, including practical suggestions for students writing with computers.
- **Reader's Reaction** notes link writer and reader by supplying reader reactions to unedited examples.
- **Strategy** sections identify specific techniques that student writers can immediately apply in their own writing.
- **Did You Know?** boxes supply lively historical, comparative, or research-based insights about language and composition.
- Icons set off the **solitary** and **collaborative exercises,** emphasizing the social context for writing.

 Solitary exercises, designed as individual work, supply thematically linked discourse for immediate reinforcement and practice.

 Collaborative exercises translate the writer-reader relationship into activities for pairs and small groups of students.

- **Integrated ESL sections** are tailored for students whose first language is not English.
- **Paper-in-Progress** sections follow one student through planning, drafting, revising, and editing a paper.
- **Research-in-Progress, Argument-in-Progress,** and **Informative-Writing-in-Progress** sections use student examples to illustrate key phases of the research and writing processes for these special assignments.
- MLA, APA, CBE, CMS, and COS styles are explained. Two **sample research papers** illustrate MLA and APA styles.
- **Sample student papers** (three complete plus selections from two others) illustrate argumentative and other forms of point-driven writing.
- Selections from sample student papers illustrate seven types of informative writing.
- Three student papers illustrate the analysis of literary texts (a poem, a short story, and a film).

WRITING, READING, AND THINKING: JOINING COMMUNITIES

1

Readers, Writers, and Community Expectations

Someone created the Web page you browsed yesterday—writing the text, designing the arrangement, and anticipating readers' reactions. Someone else wrote your housing contract, your student loan forms, and the waiver you signed before the technician X-rayed your ankle. Several writers worked together to produce the community newsletter you found in your mailbox last Saturday.

In all these cases, the writers were fulfilling a need to communicate something. Sometimes this "need" can be quite direct: a psychology professor admonishes you to make sure you include summaries of your interviews in your research paper, or a boss expects you to explain contradictory figures from the northwest region in your sales analysis. On other occasions, your need to write will come from the goals of a group you belong to, or it will come from within you, as a desire to be heard on an issue. Your writing gives you voice; it lets you do things, express ideas, share your knowledge, and participate in a conversation about issues that matter to you and to our society. Just as your writing helps to create others, building their knowledge and opinions, so it also creates you in the process.

Writing and reading surround us, shaping our lives, choices, responsibilities, and values. This book looks at the roles writers and readers play in contemporary culture. It offers concrete strategies for writing, for critical reading and thinking, and for understanding your readers' expectations. Even more, however, it emphasizes the role of writing as a way to understand experience and share that understanding with others.

1a Recognizing communities of writers and readers: Academic, work, and public

Why would an instructor in a physiology course have little patience with a student paper written in the breezy style typical of a health care column from *Cosmopolitan* or *Men's Health?* Why would a corporate executive or a city council member frown on a detailed theoretical explanation of a problem but welcome a much shorter report that gets right to the point and proposes a solution?

These readers' sharply differing needs and expectations are typical of the challenges writers face in knowing what style to use, in deciding what structure their writing should have, and in determining what to include or not include in its contents. How can you recognize and respond to these many differences in your own writing? First and foremost, you need to envision a *community* of writers and readers. A **writing and reading community** consists of people with shared—though not necessarily identical—goals, settings, preferences, and uses for both verbal and visual texts.

In this book we focus on three broad and important writing/reading communities: academic, workplace, and public. We suggest ways you can participate in these communities and in other writing situations you may encounter. We also pay special attention to writing in **electronic communities,** the many intriguing sites that constantly form (and re-form) on the Internet and World Wide Web.

1 Writing/reading communities in action

What do people in a particular writing and reading community want? Their preferences and expectations usually reflect their shared goals: to give information to each other, to debate an issue, to find a solution to a problem. Communities may overlap as well, which means that as a writer, you need to be able to participate in more than one community—just as you move from a classroom to a football game or from a book club to a protest rally.

Consider the following example.

> In Greenwood Village, a wealthy suburb of Denver, pets have been disappearing. The culprits have been coyotes and other predators, increasingly crowded by new homes and industrial parks. These disappearances are certainly alarming to local residents—will a young child be the next victim? Will the wild animals become even more aggressive?

Much of the real problem solving that takes place in a situation like this starts with the production of written materials. City council members and concerned citizens looking for explanations and solutions turn to discussions produced within the **academic community:** detailed, complex scientific studies reporting the effects of development on the habitat and feeding habits of coyotes and other predators. Wildlife experts, for example, prepare reports that show the effects of development on the habitat and feeding habits of coyotes. A line from one of their documents looks like this.

> This report summarizes and compares the data from two studies of the habits of predators in areas that have experienced significant population growth and urbanization over the past ten years.

While such scientific information is useful, it has a focus and a goal (how do coyotes behave in a shrinking habitat?) different from the concerns of parents, pet owners, and others making up the **public community:** how can we protect our children and pets without harming local wildlife? Drawing on scientific detail and knowledge of residents' perspectives, the Colorado Division of Wildlife creates a set of tips directed at a public rather than an academic audience.

If you see a coyote:

- **Leave it alone; do not approach it.**

If a coyote approaches:

- **Use an animal repellent such as pepper spray to ward off the coyote.**
- **Throw rocks or sticks at the coyote to scare it away.**
- **Use a loud, authoritative voice to frighten the animal away.**

How to coexist with coyotes:

- **Keep your pet on a leash.**
- **Do not let pets out between dusk and dawn, when most predators are active. . . .**
- **Don't feed wildlife.**

(The Denver Post)

A neighborhood action group, which represents a more specific public community, distributes leaflets to residents, urging discussion of the problem.

COYOTE ALERT!

How safe are your children in their own backyards? In the past three months, two dogs and five cats have been attacked by coyotes. What's next? What can we do? Join the Committee to Safeguard Our Children on Tuesday, October 2, at 7:00 p.m. in the JFK High School gym.

Business leaders, meanwhile, also have views to express. Local officials address the problem with writing directed at several **work communities,** in reports to the city council, the environmental management department, and municipal development offices. The reports consider options for altering the pace and scope of new developments and for designing educational and management programs to help people, pets, and coyotes live in balance. The Construction Contractors Consortium, for example, sends out a memo to its membership calling attention to the ways that zoning and development restrictions sponsored by environmental groups could hurt their construction businesses.

As you can see from this example, writing varies in purpose, organization, and style across these different communities, each piece reflecting the different expectations of the community's writers and readers. Informed by scientific and analytic work, persuaded by business leaders, and galvanized by concerned citizens, local government officials and the entire community will seek a solution that works for all these communities. They do so by *participating* within and across these communities: talking, reading, and, especially, writing.

2 Recognizing a writing/reading community

To participate effectively in a writing/reading community, you need to recognize both the ways it limits your work and the choices or possibilities it provides. As you start to write—and again during the process—stop to consider the roles, goals, forms, and characteristics that help you recognize the particular community you're addressing and the choices your writing situation offers.

- **Roles** that you and your readers occupy
- **Goals** for writing that you and your audience share
- **Forms** that your audience will look for in writing directed toward a particular goal
- **Characteristics** typical of writing that fulfills a particular set of goals and meets readers' expectations

(For further advice, see the discussion of audience in 5b.)

Three Major Communities of Writers and Readers

ROLES	GOALS	FORMS	CHARACTERISTICS
ACADEMIC			
Students	Create or	Analysis of text	Detailed reasoning
Teachers	exchange	or phenomenon	and critical analysis
Researchers	knowledge	Interpretation of	Fresh insights or
Committees		text, artwork,	conclusions
gathering expert		or event	Extensive evidence
opinion		Research proposal	and accurate detail
Readers interested		or report	supporting
in specialized		Lab report	conclusions
knowledge		Scholarly article	Balanced treatment
		Annotated	acknowledging
		bibliography	other viewpoints
		Grant proposal	Thoughtful,
			stimulating
			exploration of topic

ROLES	GOALS	FORMS	CHARACTERISTICS
WORK			
Immediate co-workers	Provide information	Factual description of object or event	Focus on task, problem, or goal— "getting things done"
Other colleagues	Analyze problems	Detailed description of situation or problem	
Supervisors	Propose solutions	Proposal	Focus on accuracy and efficiency
Other groups within work organization:	Promote organization	Report of findings	Accurate presentation of problem or issue
Management		Memo	
Personnel		Guidelines or instructions	Promotion of product or service
Accounting			
Public relations		Promotional materials	Concise, clear, direct prose
Clients		Letters, memos, minutes of meetings, applications	
Government agencies			
Target groups within the public			
Potential clients		Texts with headings, sections, overt organization	
PUBLIC			
Residents or group members	Persuade people on an issue	Guidelines	Focus on shared values and goals
Possible supporters		Position paper	
Public officials or agencies	Provide information	Informative report or article	Advocacy of cause or policy
Local groups	Participate in local/ democratic decision making	Letter to agency, organization, or publication	Fair recognition of others' interests and goals
Readers interested in an issue		Flyer or pamphlet	Relevant evidence supporting positions or claims
		Action proposal	
		Grant proposal	
		Guidelines	Focus on point of view or on need for information
		Charter or statement of principles	Action- or solution-oriented

Exercise 1

In groups of four or five, draft a "class charter," that is, a formal statement outlining the principles, purposes, or rules that you think should govern your class. Before you start drafting, discuss the roles, goals, forms, and characteristics of this writing situation. Which members of the class do you need to address? In what ways might their values or interests be similar or different? What do you hope to accomplish with the document you produce? What does a charter look like?

1b The writing process: Realities and myths

Successful writing is almost never a matter of just setting down your thoughts on paper in finished form. Instead, it begins with a *response:* to an idea or experience, to reading or an issue, to a problem or a situation. It calls for planning; for definition of purpose and thesis; for awareness of readers; and for a careful attention to drafting, revising, editing, and proofreading. These various elements of the writing process are explored in the chapters that follow.

Usually, your writing process won't move in a straight line. When you revise, you may need to go back to more planning or reconsider your first response to the task. Or, in some projects, you might need to work collaboratively with other writers and interact with potential readers.

Some ways of viewing the writing process can lead to self-defeating habits. Test your knowledge by exploring some common myths and realities about the writing/reading process. How many of these statements are true?

1. People can easily succeed in the "real world" without needing to write.
2. Writing is easy for people who have the knack.
3. You can be a good writer without doing much reading.
4. It's cheating to ask other people to look over your writing before you turn it in.
5. Good writing is effective for all readers.

They're all myths. Here's why.

Myth: People can easily succeed in the "real world" without needing to write.

Reality: It's a popular myth that executives don't need to write because their assistants write for them. That's not what the executives themselves say. In Fortune 500 companies, over half of the employees spend between eight and forty hours writing each week. This shows that the ability to write is crucial for success in the work community. Although the amount of writing on the job varies by type of employment and rank, many workers say that they write more at work than they expected they would when they were in school. The same is true in public life and in civic activities.

Myth: Writing is easy for people who have the knack.

Reality: Few of us get to look over the shoulders of good writers. If we did, we would know what researchers know: good writers draft and re-draft. They work hard to create effective prose and to consider their work from a reader's perspective. They have become good writers through learning and hard work, not because they were born with a knack for writing.

Myth: You can be a good writer without doing much reading.

Reality: It's not likely. The more you read, the more experience you have with writing. Reading gives you models of writing that work in specific communities; it helps you learn how to adjust your writing to the needs of your readers; and it increases your options for sentence variety and precise words.

Myth: It's cheating to ask other people to look over your writing before you turn it in.

Reality: It certainly is cheating if you have someone else write a paper or parts of it and you then claim the work as your own. But successful writers always depend on readers for feedback. Readers' opinions can tell you how an audience will interpret your writing and can help you anticipate responses and concerns. Especially at work and in the community, important documents are likely to be written in groups for this reason.

Myth: Good writing is effective for all readers.

Reality: When it comes to good writing, one size doesn't fit all. While all good writing is clear, coherent, and correct, what works in one community may not work as well in another. The term paper you write for Psychology 265 will have a very different tone, style, and content from the email you write to your cousin or the proposal you write at work.

1c Entering electronic communities

The three general communities illustrated in the coyote example in 1a-1 all cohabit the fascinating world of the Internet. As you click from Web site to Web site exploring a topic or seeking information, remember that numerous electronic *communities,* large and small, are organized around a shared interest in a topic, point of view, or issue. Immersed for a while in a highly academic treatise from a university researcher, you can, with a click of the mouse, suddenly find yourself skimming a page at a site sponsored by a major corporation. Many political or nonprofit organizations circulate petitions online. People can register their support of gun control, dolphin-safe tuna, or a favorite TV show simply by typing in their name and email address.

To recognize the electronic community to which a site belongs as well as the conventions and expectations you may need to observe in contributing a Web page or posting of your own, examine one or more sites using the strategy of TASALS.

Topic: On what subject(s) does the site focus? Do contributors belong to any organization or share any other kind of affiliation?

Attitude: Does the site have a clear point of view or set of values? Do contributors have similar perspectives or values?

Strategies: Does the site use particular writing or visual strategies (see Chapter 13 for examples)? Does the writing have a particular tone or style? Does the design of the site have a particular style or emphasis?

Authority: Does the site try to be authoritative, giving support for claims it makes or information it provides? Do contributors reason carefully and offer evidence, or do they give unsupported opinion and supposed "facts"?

Links: Is the site linked to similar sites? Do postings refer to related online documents, lists, or resources?

Summarize: On the basis of your answers to these questions, summarize the qualities of the electronic community you encountered and are considering entering with a contribution of your own.

Exercise 2

A. Find the official Web site of your school or city or of an organization to which you belong. Examine the Web site carefully using the TASALS strategy. How would you characterize the community that sponsors the site? What opportunities, if any, are there to participate in the site—to send comments, to get on a mailing list, or to ask a question of an expert? What kinds of writing or participation would be inappropriate for this site, and why?

B. Use an Internet search engine to locate several Web sites maintained by or catering to professionals in your future field of work. Evaluate the Web site using TASALS. Compare your results with those of your classmates.

2

Strategies for Critical Reading and Reflection

Reading is almost always responsive. Even when you read a road sign in a split second, you respond: by checking your speedometer, by testing your brakes, or by wondering why you never see the helicopter that's supposed to be monitoring your speed. The way you respond to writing will be shaped by your purposes for reading and by your context—say, whether you're working in a family business or in the office of a busy student organization on campus.

If you respond personally and defensively to a negative sales report or an instructor's critique, you may miss the important information and advice that a more analytical response would allow. **Analytical reading** strategies help you identify information and ideas in a piece of writing. They also direct your attention to how a writer argues for a position or policy, organizes information, or explains a problem and a potential solution.

Analytical reading also involves **interpretive reading:** reading to interpret the meanings and purposes of a piece of writing. Sometimes these meanings and purposes may be clearly and directly stated. More often, you'll need to sift through a text looking for aims and ideas that are presented indirectly, even those that may have escaped the writer's conscious awareness. An interpretive reading is your restatement of the ideas, perspectives, implications, and purposes of a text—but a restatement grounded in the details of the text itself. An interpretive reading is not simple speculation or unfounded opinion. It represents your conclusions about the text and therefore needs to be presented in terms of evidence from the text that support these conclusions.

Analytical and interpretive reading, in turn, form the basis for critical reading. **Critical reading** helps you evaluate the ideas and information you encounter and to develop alternative points of view and interpretations. These strategies are discussed in detail in Chapter 46.

Reading critically, which puts your mind to work on a text, usually helps you to write more effectively. It gives you new ideas by helping you link what you read to your own experience, to other texts of all kinds, to issues and information, or to a problem or responsibility. Your writing then *adds* to the discussion of a topic by incorporating insights you've gained from your critical reading. Your writing may contribute to the same "conversation" going on in the community that produced the material you read, or it may start or continue a conversation happening in a different community. For example, you might read and critically analyze a dozen statements on an email listserv about the arrest of anti-pornography protesters and then contribute your own considered response to the list. You could also add some background information to your response and then send it electronically to your local newspaper to be considered for inclusion on the op-ed page. Your letter might even begin a new conversation in the community of newspaper subscribers and readers.

2a Reading analytically

1 Getting ready to read

If you're like most people, you begin reading by opening to the first page of a report, article, or book and plunging into the text. Even when you know something about the text—that a co-worker wrote it, for example, or that it addresses a subject you know well—if you "start cold" you can miss important points or information: What's the problem being described? How valid is the solution? What other issues need to be considered? Is the writer really proposing that . . . ?

Prereading strategies help you "warm up" by previewing the text and any specific situation—academic, work, public—it addresses. These strategies also help alert you to the writer's particular purpose(s).

Preview the organization. For books and long articles or reports, preread by skimming the table of contents to see how a work is organized. What appears first, second, third? In magazine articles, essays, scholarly papers, or reports without tables of contents, look first for any headings or subheadings; these road maps tell you where the reading will take you and help you to plan your time. If you have only half an hour to read before you need to do something else, knowing that the first section of a scholarly article ends on page 9 may help you plan your time accordingly.

Examine the context. Begin by skimming the table of contents and headings in a text or paging quickly through it to get some idea of its subject and focus. Then ask yourself the following questions about the social setting in which the text was produced and the audience or community it seems to address.

- Does the text reflect the concerns of an academic, work, or public community, or does it appear to address a more general, less defined community of readers? (See 5a.)
- Which of the typical purposes and concerns of a specific community (academic, work, or public) seem to characterize this text? Which do not? (For common features and concerns of writing in different communities, see the chart on pp. 5–6.)
- Did the text appear in a publication (scholarly journal or periodical) with a well-known point of view (conservative or liberal, for example)? Is it associated with a particular business or political organization? Does this information seem likely to help you in understanding and interpreting the contents?
- If the text is in electronic form, does it appear in a site with a particular point of view, purpose, or audience? Is it linked to other texts endorsing particular perspectives or with common interests?

Next, ask the following questions about the text's content and about its writer.

- Is the text by a single author or a group of people representing an organization?
- When was the text published, and how current do the information and ideas seem?
- Who are the intended readers? Are they identified in the text, and is the purpose clearly stated in the title, in headings, or in highlighted portions of the text?
- Do visuals, graphics, or the text's layout provide obvious cues to the writing's purpose(s), focus, and intended audience? (See Chapter 13 for advice on understanding the visual elements of a text.)
- If the text is in electronic form, do any other texts within the site or linked to it provide any hints about its focus, purpose, and audience?
- Is there any evidence of how popular or well received the text is? Has it appeared in numerous editions? Are there testimonials from authorities on the subject? Does a "hit counter" indicate the number of people who have visited a Web site?
- What does the back or front of a book tell you? What understanding can you glean from any abstracts or summaries at the beginning of a report or scholarly article?

Sample words and terms. Look for groups of words in the reading that are related in meaning or references. By scanning the text first, you can activate your knowledge. If you come across terms that seem unfamiliar, you'll be better prepared to interpret these in their proper context. If a few stand out as incomprehensible, you might look them up in a dictionary (or the book's or Web site's glossary) before you begin reading. Consider the following excerpt from an internal memo on market competitiveness for an air carrier.

> As per Strategic Plan 97: Two goals will require further delineation from your group. These are the goals pertaining to fleet types and to industry performance on DOT metrics. The original proposal for fleet type reduction was to reduce from 16 to 6; new proposals, based on late 1996 figures, suggest that this may need to be revised to 4 fleet types. The key DOT metrics to address include on-time performance and mishandles.

Note how the example uses a number of terms its writers assumed readers would understand: *fleet types, DOT metrics, mishandles.* By glancing through the text first and noting such terms, you'll gain a sense of what the document is about. (Note that for the actual readers of such a memo, "insider" terms like this would probably be common knowledge.)

Make predictions. Sample some paragraphs, sentences, or visuals, and try to predict what you think the text is about and where it will take you. Do your samples imply a particular direction, focus, or purpose? Jot your predictions down and note which are later confirmed as you read.

Exercise 1

 A. Locate a short article, a short electronic document, or a portion of a longer text that has no overt structure—no headings, section divisions, or other organizational signals. Then skim (preread) the material and make up headings or divisions for different parts of the reading.

 B. In a small group, compare your structural prereading and organizing with that of several other people. How successful, generally, was this strategy in helping each of you read and understand your chosen texts?

---

2 During and after reading

You've probably had the experience of reaching the end of a passage in an essay, report, Web site, or book (or the end of the work itself) only to realize that you don't have the vaguest sense of what you've been reading. To avoid this problem, try the following strategies.

Pause and assess. When you reach a place where you can stop reading without interrupting a line of reasoning or a crucial narrative, put the reading aside for a moment. Where are you? What have you learned so far? What do you think? What still confuses you? Jot down answers to these questions in your journal or on a piece of paper. Then skim what you've read. If you're uncertain about something, reviewing the text can sometimes clarify it.

Highlight important information. If you've ever bought a used text-book, you've probably seen someone else's bright yellow or pink high-lighting. Often there's so much highlighting on each page that you wonder how the person could have separated what's important from what's not.

If you're an avid highlighter *while* you read, try to change your style. Don't spend lots of time attending to tiny details the first time through your reading. Instead, read to capture the essential points of the piece. This will let you see a "bigger picture," a set of organizational or argumentative structures, without getting lost in the little details.

Do most of your highlighting *after* your first reading. Go back and write notes in the margins of your reading to identify important points and details, or use your highlighter to identify what's *really* important.

Highlighting an electronic document is more of a challenge. Sometimes it helps to print a copy and highlight this paper record of what you've read. You might also find it easier to read analytically when the text is on paper rather than on a screen. If your computer software allows, you may be able to print out selected portions of a document. This can be a form of highlighting, though it detaches the highlighted text from the original, making it more difficult for you to consult the entire document at a later date. You can also try to save electronic documents in a word processor and then add boldfacing or underlining to especially important sections or passages.

Annotate. At one time, students were punished for writing in books (even their own copies). For some people, this history has turned to habit. If you own the book or document you're reading, go ahead and annotate it using whatever white space is on the page. If you don't own it, consider making a photocopy of relevant material, perhaps reducing it to give you more marginal space for your notes. If you're reading a Web page or other electronic document, consider downloading and printing it so you can make annotations—unless your software allows you to open a note-taking document you can link to the text you're reading. Remember that your annotations of important information, ideas, insights, opinions, sources, and persuasive or particularly effective statements can be useful later when you want to remind yourself of those things in a text that you considered most important.

After reading, you might also consider taking a file card or creating an electronic file and writing down some of the main ideas from the text. These records are especially useful when you are creating research papers, reports, or documented position papers; they offer a convenient way to review several readings without leafing through dozens of pages of books, articles, or photocopies or having to reconsult electronic documents (a time-consuming task even if you have "bookmarked" the various sites).

Read with your audience and purpose in mind. Often we read in order to write: to gather information and ideas or to develop insights and solutions that we plan to share with readers. If this is your goal, highlight or make notes on those sections of a text that are relevant to the community of readers you plan to address or to your specific purposes for reading.

Reread and review. If you're learning sophisticated concepts, studying complicated issues and problems, or working through difficult arguments, you may need to read material more than once. Every time you read something again, you'll find more information or new ideas.

Rereading doesn't have to take the same shape as the initial reading. Try reviewing, skimming the reading more quickly, and then sampling some of the passages you highlighted on your first pass through the text. The idea is to read from different perspectives—once from afar, once closely. Skim the material quickly once; then study it meticulously.

Exercise 2

 A. Find a relatively challenging article, electronic document, or book chapter, or choose one that you've begun to read for a specific purpose, perhaps as a course assignment or in preparation for a report or another writing task. Then try several of the reading strategies outlined in this section, taking note of which best aided your understanding and which seemed most likely to be useful to you as a writer.

 B. Share your observations and readings in a small group. Explain why you think particular strategies aided (or failed to aid) understanding. Tell why you considered specific strategies likely (or not likely) to be useful for your writing.

2b Reading interpretively

What's the central idea a writer is trying to convey? What new insights does a piece of writing offer you? Can you say what the writer's opinions, generalizations, or attitudes are toward his or her subject matter? What underlying themes begin to surface from the text? When you read interpretively, these are some of the questions you try to answer. Clearly, this kind of reading is *active* and *engaged*—you're not ruffling a newspaper; you're focusing energetically on the pages or screen in front of you. It's also obvious that careful reading takes time. Skimming and scanning should give way to focusing, questioning, rereading, and note taking. The following strategies can help you hone your interpretive reading skills.

Make responsive annotations. Use the following kinds of annotations and leading questions to arrive at an understanding of a text's meanings and purposes.

- Interpretations: What does the author or speaker mean in the text as a whole or in each part?
- Confusions: At what points are readers likely to become puzzled, and why?
- Questions: What more will readers need to know about the subject, issue, or problem?
- Communities: What will different communities of readers perceive as the most important ideas and information in the text? Why would people in two different settings, who may be affected by or interested in the subject, respond in different ways?
- Restatements: How can you state the text's key ideas in your own words?
- Evaluative response: What do you like or dislike about the text as a whole or about specific parts?
- Disagreements: What disagreements does the text (writer) seem to anticipate (or fail to anticipate)?
- Memories: What experiences, memories, or related issues/problems come to mind as you read, and is it likely that the writer anticipated such reactions?
- Retentions: Which details, insights, or opinions from the text are most likely to stick in readers' minds after they have finished reading, and why?

Clint Graff made some responsive annotations to a passage from a document about the information provided to consumers on food labels.

What were they asked? And do people really read the info?

A recent review on communication of food, nutrition, and health messages did not include dietary supplement labeling specifically but did address consumer understanding of nutrient content and health claims on food labels (80). In an appendix to this report, Levy (83) indicates that <u>consumers in focus groups were interested</u> in having information about the relationship between diet and disease. Some commissioners interpret this study as <u>suggesting that consumer research has not yet established a "mandate"</u> for having health information on food labels as opposed to obtaining such information from health care providers, books, or the print and telecommunications media. Moreover, considering that food labels are viewed by consumers as reflective of the manufacturer's interest in selling the product, consumers are skeptical <u>about the veracity of health messages on food labels.</u>

How does this study lead to this conclusion?

Points to tension between consumer desire for info & fear that it's just hype.

Note repetition and emphasis. Words, phrases, ideas, and details that appear repeatedly in a text may shape its meaning and its effect, even if the writer didn't fully intend to provide such emphasis. Devices for creating emphasis—headings, thesis statements, topic sentences, vivid detail, sentence structure, and parallelism or other stylistic strategies—also highlight and create meaning and focus a text's purpose. Underline, highlight, or take notes on repetition and emphasis as you read, and use your observations to arrive at and support your interpretation of the text's meaning and aim.

Summarize in chunks. Most texts have natural "resting points," often marked with road signs like headings and subheadings, or shifts in focus. After reaching one of these natural stopping points, write an abstract or summary of what you're thinking at that point, glancing back over what you've read if necessary. This can help you to monitor your comprehension and begin interpreting the piece. Ask yourself what the main point or gist is so far. See whether you can guess or predict where the reading will go next. Developing tentative interpretations now can help you arrive at more convincing ones later.

Share interpretations and insights. Go public with the "conversation" you're having internally with a piece of writing. If other people have read the same piece, their responses can help you to formulate and test your own interpretation. Consider working in a small group to discuss what you noticed about the content, language, or structure of an article, book, or Web site. Compare your responses with those of your fellow readers. Are there differences? Did you miss something? Do any of the other readers' responses puzzle you? Skim back over the reading to see how the others might have arrived at their interpretations.

Respond in writing. If you're keeping a journal, jot down your conclusions about the writer's purpose(s) and key ideas. Be ready to reread the text to check your perceptions and understandings. By struggling to put the text's ideas into your own language, you are already developing your interpretation—and working toward ideas you might develop later in your own writing.

Exercise 3

A. Obtain a copy of the minutes from a recent city council or other public meeting (these may be available online). Read the minutes carefully, making responsive annotations as you read; then, summarize the document for a partner. Once you have done this, speculate about how different communities might read this document. Is there any specialized terminology that might be confusing to some audiences? Did any one issue seem like an ongoing problem or controversy? If so, were solutions proposed? Can you tell, from the minutes, who the most influential or powerful participants were?

B. Compare interpretive reading of an academic text to one used in a workplace. Select a challenging excerpt from some of your course reading, and locate a text from a workplace context. (You might use a document from a current or former job, ask individuals you know in the working world to share a text with you, or locate a relevant document from a work- or profession-related Web site.) Use interpretive reading strategies (making responsive annotations, noting repetition and emphasis, summarizing in chunks, sharing interpretations, and responding in writing) as you actively read the two pieces. Then reflect, in writing, on the differences between your interpretive readings of the two texts: Does one lend itself to this kind of reading more easily? Which strategies were most useful with each text? Which text elicited the strongest response?

2C Journals: Bridging reading and writing

A **working journal** is a place to explore ideas, develop insights, experiment with your prose, write rough drafts, and reflect on your reading. Entries in a working journal may be organized by a particular writing or reading task, or they may be dated and involve sequential observations. A working journal, however, is not a diary. Diaries record people's daily activities, thoughts, and personal lives. Working journals are places where analytical, interpretive, and critical reading take place in the form of written responses. Your journal is also where your own writing begins to murmur and find voice. Unlike a carefully crafted essay or report, a journal is a clearinghouse for ideas, speculations, first starts, notes and jottings, drawings and doodles, plans, occasional insights—anything that helps you to learn more fully and begin writing.

1 How to keep a journal

At first, keeping a journal may feel strange or artificial. After all, you're writing mainly to and for yourself, with no concern about your spelling, no worry that you're using the first person pronoun (*I*) when you're not sure whether this is acceptable. Here are some suggestions for getting started.

What kind of journal should you use? The actual shape and size of your journal is less important to its success than what you do in and with it. It helps to have a journal from which you can remove pages or reorganize them. An electronic word-processing document will allow you to do this, as will an inexpensive ring binder. Many avid journal writers like to keep several different electronic files or notebooks, each for its own purpose or subject.

How much and how often should you write? The more you write, the greater your chance to think about a subject, respond to your reading, and develop interpretations you can use in your own writing. The length of journal entries will (and should) differ. Working half a day in the library or searching the Internet might yield ten or fifteen pages of notes, speculations, quotations, references, and interpretations, but an idea that comes to you late at night might yield just a few lines of drowsy prose sufficient to jog your memory the next morning. Be disciplined, but don't hold yourself at gunpoint in order to scratch something out on the page or screen.

The "rhythm" of your journal writing will depend on your schedule and how comfortable you are writing at certain times of the day. If you miss a day, don't despair. But at all costs, *write regularly*. Journals abandoned for more than a day or two soon wither up and die from lack of nourishment.

Did You Know?

In a study comparing two groups of students in a high school science course, the group that wrote about their learning remembered more than the group that didn't keep a journal. Similar findings have been reported in several other studies.

Robert Tierney, "Using Expressive Writing to Teach Biology," *The Teacher-Researcher*, ed. Miles Myers (Urbana: NCTE, 1985) 149–99.

**2c
jrnl**

2 How to use a journal

Writing in a journal *makes your thoughts visible*. When you use a journal effectively, you create a cycle of connections among thinking, writing, and reading.

Translate new knowledge. Most new knowledge comes to you prepackaged in the form of someone else's words. A journal can help you translate this knowledge into your own terms, so that it will make sense to you and take a shape appropriate for your own writing and thinking. After reading or hearing about new ideas or information, imagine one or more people who know little about the topic. Explain your new knowledge to them. As you do this, two things are likely to happen. First, you'll be forced to *speculate* about the meaning of the information and concepts at places you find difficult to understand. Second, you'll often *clarify and resolve* your confusions in the process of writing.

Brainstorm. Instead of staring at a blank piece of paper or screen, waiting for perfect sentences to roll off your pen or keyboard, use your journal for **brainstorming.** When you brainstorm, you think associatively, letting one idea lead to another or exploring the connections among ideas. You create an exploratory, tentative, and often messy set of responses to reading, issues, and experience that can point the way to a focus and plan for a draft of a paper. (See Chapter 3.)

Extend your thinking. Imagine that you learn this fact from your reading in a sociology article or textbook: Human aggression increases in hot weather. Recording such an observation in your journal may take a few seconds. But imagine *extending* this idea a little, seeing its implications, wondering about possible solutions and applications. Are people more aggressive in hot regions than in cold regions? If discomfort causes aggression, why aren't people just as aggressive in uncomfortably cold weather? Are workers in hot factories more aggressive than workers in chilly factories? Do Northerners become aggressive on vacations to hot places?

Take issue with ideas. Although your journal may feel comfortably informal, it can also be an excellent place to argue with someone else's point of view or criticize a position. Many writers at first react in a combative way to ideas or beliefs that challenge their own. Journals let them "have it out" with an opponent without risking actual confrontation. The result can be a more balanced view of the controversy.

Exercise 4

 A. The following working journal entry was written by Kelly Odeen, a student in a course on literacy in America. Read Odeen's entry, and then identify specific functions for which she is using her journal. What characteristics of her entry suggest these functions?

Reading on the Amish community left me with very mixed feelings—not sure what to make of them yet. I really admired the family support of Eli's literacy development. Sounded like the older family members did just what we've been encouraged to do as tutors. They gave him positive feedback, etc. Focused on accomplishments rather than failures. But the setting looked sort of ideal. Everyone in Eli's family reads and writes, even more than in my family. I don't think it's possible to make learning totally individualized in the public school system. Choices have to be made that are better for some children than others. I don't have a solution, but I think the author is being too idealistic to think there can be this match like the Amish have. I'd like to look into this more for my project, maybe. Because I do agree that there are many ways of perceiving literacy, each valid, and we have to be sensitive to where kids are coming from *compared* with the school system they're going into.

 B. Should animals be used in laboratory experiments for the advancement of scientific, medical, and behavioral knowledge? Write a page or two in your journal on this question, considering as many issues and angles on the topic as you can. Then compare your journal writing in a small group. What ideas did the writing yield? How helpful was it? How would you describe the style, organization, and other characteristics of your writing? Which of the purposes described in the preceding section did your writing serve?

3 How to write in a journal

Like taking a walk alone, you write in a journal mainly for *yourself*. Your pace can be fast or slow, meandering or purposeful. Here are some tips for finding a comfortable voice and style in your journal.

Use a personal voice. Many academic, work, or public writing tasks require you to remove yourself from your writing. Use your journal writing to express your beliefs, opinions, and reactions in personal terms. Speculate. Get to know what you—personally—think about an issue or subject. Instead of writing in abstract terms and formal language, go ahead and use a more **personal voice.** Use phrases like "I wonder if . . . ," "I think it's wonderful that . . . ," or "I can't understand why . . . ."

Be conversational. In formal writing, you're advised not to use colloquial expressions, not to sound "talky." In your journal writing, try a chattier kind of language, as if you're carrying on a conversation with yourself. A sentence like "Hmmmmm . . . I guess I never figured zoning board members would get so ticked off about something so silly" would cry out for revision in a formal report. In a journal, you can feel safe using such a casual tone.

2c
jrnl

Use shortcuts. Try writing quickly. Use abbreviations if you're sure you will remember what they mean. Don't worry at this point about underlining titles, correcting commas in a series, or looking up the spelling of every difficult word. Make informal reference to the article or Web page to which you are responding, but provide enough information so you can identify the source later.

Experiment with language. Journals encourage the free play of language and thought. Let the poetry emerge, if you wish, from your writing. Be as expressive as you want. Try out ideas that may at first seem outrageous, or write in a style you've never used before. Try imitating or parodying other writers. All such experimentation not only helps you explore your thinking but also makes you more flexible as a writer.

Exercise 5

A. Choose a short reading about a current controversy. First try writing a journal response to the reading, following the suggestions in the preceding section. Next, write a brief letter to the editor of a local, campus, or company newspaper about the same controversy. Try *converting* your journal writing into more formal prose suitable for a general audience.

B. In a small group, discuss your "journal conversions" from Exercise 5A. What information carried over from your journal writing into your letter? On what basis did you select the information? In what ways, if any, did you make changes in style, word choice, sentence structure and rhythm, organization, and the use of evidence to support your assertions? What uses can you see for such "conversions" in writing papers for your courses?

3

Planning Strategies for College, Work, and Public Writing

Imagine trying to build a house without having any plans drawn up beforehand, or going into the playoffs without a team strategy, just to "see what happens." Success would depend on luck, not design. The same is true for writing. In almost any formal writing project, whether in college, in your community, or on the job, you need to discover and "rough out" your ideas before you can really get started. Planning before you write—often called **prewriting**—helps you to move your project forward more smoothly and confidently by giving you a map of where you want to go. Some planning strategies work well at the earliest stages of writing; others can help you later on as you fill gaps in your knowledge, work out patterns and relationships among ideas, and make some tentative decisions about structure.

3a Generating ideas and information

Whatever the writing task, you'll want to ask, "What do I know about what I'm writing? What else do I need to know?" Instead of talking or thinking through these questions, try writing about them quickly and informally. You'll get warmed up for more formal drafting, and you'll generate some crucial ideas and plans for your project.

1 Try freewriting

Write quickly for five or ten minutes. Concentrate entirely on *writing without stopping,* even if you think you have nothing to say. Simply writing "I'm stuck, I'm stuck" will at least force you to begin writing. Curiously, such empty or rambling prose will soon begin to bore you, and you'll find yourself almost magically slipping into more interesting ideas.

3a plan

2 Try focused freewriting

Focus on an idea or topic you already have in mind or on one that you began developing through freewriting. Continue writing as you freely associate ideas, especially if you start with a general topic. Your first few sentences could start, "I don't know what to say about anti-gambling laws. I can't think of anything to say, except I'm in favor of them generally." As you continue to write, you'll again find yourself exploring what you know or feel about the topic. Consider stating your topic as an assertion so that you can systematically question that assertion, anticipating a spark that ignites your interest.

Exercise 1

 A. Think of something you'd like to persuade someone or some group to do. Write down an assertion that might be the start of a persuasive paper. (You may want to do this in your working journal.) Consider either an academic audience for your paper (such as a class), a public audience (such as a city council member or public department official), or a work audience (such as co-workers and direct supervisors trying to decide on a course of action). Then use writing as a way of *considering* your assertion. First, write at least five questions about the assertion. Next, review the questions and decide which of them you could answer by doing some sort of research, such as reading, observing your subject, or interviewing someone.

 B. In a focused freewrite, note any case in which writing down one question in Exercise 1A *led* to another question. Share your questions and focused freewriting with a group of writers or readers, and ask them to identify ideas and information they find particularly interesting.

---

3 Try listing

Lists can draw out knowledge already in your mind and *create* new ideas through association. Write your topic at the top of a piece of paper and then list ten thoughts, facts, or ideas about the subject. As he started working on his proposal requesting permission to allow local bands to perform in the basement of the community center, Morgan Scott listed some of the subjects the report needed to cover.

Space isn't used for anything else during the evenings.
Will give teenagers a safe place to go, especially on weekends.
Need plans for cleaning the space up and maintaining it.

Noise wouldn't bother neighbors.
Plenty of parking for those old enough to drive.
Recreation department and police could easily provide supervision.
Will provide a creative outlet for local residents.
Low cost.
Will have the support of parents.
Add to the city's reputation as a good place to live.

4 Tease out details

Good writing is often detailed. A plea to increase funding in a public school district will be more effective if it includes facts about teachers' low salaries, out-of-date books in the classrooms, and the disrepair of the buildings. Searching for details to particularize general statements can also lead you to new ideas and associations.

To help you increase the level of detail in your writing, make a **detailing list.** For each general idea, opinion, or impression, list specific examples, features, or facts that particularize it. This will give you a rich resource to draw on as you develop your essay. Heather Strong began writing an account of her trip to the Grand Canyon for her travel club's newsletter.

> When we first looked out over the Grand Canyon, we were just amazed. What a beautiful sight! It was like nothing we had seen before—so impressive and marvelous. It was simply incredible to gaze out over such a spectacle of nature.

This paragraph cries out for specifics. Figure 3.1 shows part of a detailing list Strong created to help develop her ideas. These details found their way into her revised draft.

> The view from the North Rim was just as breathtaking. From Tiyo Point we could see Shiva Temple. To its east was the flat-topped formation of Buddha Temple, with its red sandstone lit up like a flaming torch. The effect of these varied red, brown, and gold formations is almost religious. It felt like we were standing in a cathedral of stone, looking down into a million years of spires, statuary, and domes, all bathed in soft, stained-glass hues of light.

5 Ask strategic questions

You can generate important information for many writing projects, especially proposals and recommendations, if you try answering the questions *what, why,* and *why not (where, who,* and *how* may also be important

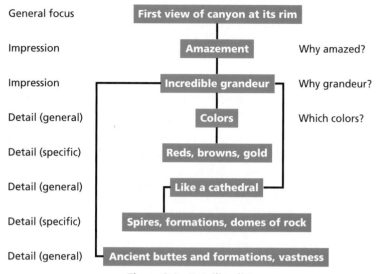

General focus	First view of canyon at its rim	
Impression	Amazement	Why amazed?
Impression	Incredible grandeur	Why grandeur?
Detail (general)	Colors	Which colors?
Detail (specific)	Reds, browns, gold	
Detail (general)	Like a cathedral	
Detail (specific)	Spires, formations, domes of rock	
Detail (general)	Ancient buttes and formations, vastness	

Figure 3.1   Detailing list

questions, depending on your writing project). Brian Corby used this strategy in prewriting for his report arguing that the city council should not allow a high-rise apartment to be built adjacent to a public park.

WHAT?
- Proposed high-rise apt.
- 18 stories, 102 units plus 3 penthouses
- Overlooking east side of Piedmont Park between Sunrise Ave. and Claremont St.
- Proposal approved by Feb.; Planning by Feb. next yr.; groundbreaking by June
- Finished structure by Aug. of following year

WHY?
- Developers' profit
- Brings jobs to Lake Walton
- Raises property tax base-supposed to funnel money back into the city and parks
- Provides medium-cost housing in growing area
- Develops ugly vacant property by park

WHY NOT?
- "Citifies" one of the few green patches in Lake Walton
- Increases traffic, crime rate, park use
- Adds to waste; pollution from proposed garbage incinerator in building

- Opens the door to other high-rise development because of new zoning ordinance
- Blocks public access to park
- Raises property taxes for longtime and elderly residents

ESL Advice: Developing Clear and Forceful Details

Readers will usually expect your writing to say something *specific* about a topic, problem, or event. If you provide too little detail, your readers may consider your approach too broad, vague, indirect, or poorly supported. You may be accustomed to other expectations, especially ones requiring less detailed support for assertions. If so, examine effective examples of writing addressed to your audience. Also, you may question specific readers about the kind of support they would like you to include in your writing assignment. College instructors, professors, and even supervisors in the workplace

- Generally expect writers to request such information
- Find it useful that writers request such information
- Are willing to provide writers with such information
- Are used to providing writers with such information

Exercise 2

 A. Begin with the topic, issue, or problem for a writing project you are working on, or choose a topic that interests you. Then try the listing procedure with your topic. Begin by listing ten things you know about your chosen topic. Then choose one item and generate another sublist beneath it. If you can, keep going to a third or fourth level.

 B. Working in a group of three, exchange topics (issues, problems) with your fellow writers. Try to generate a list of ten ideas for each partner's topic. If you have time, generate sublists of five items from one of the original ten items in each list. Then compare your lists as a group, and see which items overlapped and which were unique.

3b Structuring ideas and information

Ideas and information alone won't lead to successful writing unless you can find ways to structure them. Some writing tasks, such as business and research reports, need to follow familiar structures. For many other kinds of writing, including essays about personal experience, position papers, critiques, informative pamphlets, and proposals, you'll often need to identify relationships within the information and ideas you've generated.

1 Draw a cluster

When you create a **cluster,** begin by writing a concept, idea, or topic in the center of a page, and circle this kernel topic. Then, as in listing, randomly jot down associations with this central idea, circling them and connecting them with lines to the center, like the spokes of a wheel. (See Figure 3.2.) As you continue to generate ideas around the central focus, think about the ways the subsidiary ideas are connected, and draw lines to show those connections. You can also create clusters in cycles; each subsidiary idea becomes the central focus on a new page. The nodes or pieces of the cluster will become a visual representation of how your text might be "chunked" into paragraphs or sections.

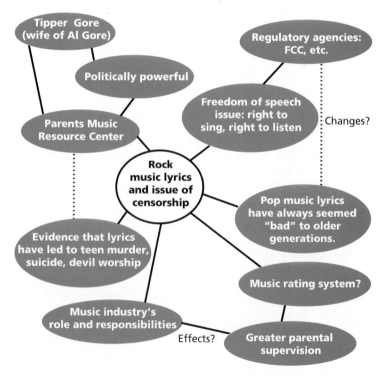

Figure 3.2   A simple conceptual cluster

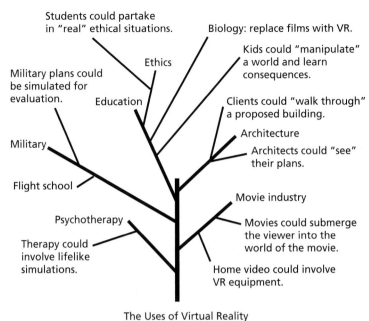

The Uses of Virtual Reality
Figure 3.3 A simple tree diagram

2 Create a tree diagram

Tree diagrams resemble clusters, but their branches tend to be a little more linear, with fewer interconnections. (See Figure 3.3.) Develop your tree diagram as a hierarchy: Each larger branch can lead to smaller and smaller branches. For this reason, tree diagramming can provide a useful way to visualize the components of your paper. You can even "revise" a tree diagram into a sort of preliminary outline to use when deciding what to place in each paragraph of your paper.

3 Build a time sequence

If you're writing a paper organized chronologically or involving sequences of time, you may find a **time sequence** useful. Begin by framing each event along a line. Then, if you wish, draw vertical lines of thicker or thinner widths depending on how closely connected one event is to the next. In planning materials for a self-guided tour of a special museum exhibit on the artist Andy Warhol, James Christenfeld drew a time sequence detailing the history of Warhol's artistic life. With thick connecting lines, he showed how certain pivotal events led to or caused other events or works in Warhol's career. Connections with thin lines were simply chronological.

Exercise 3

 A. Choose a simple topic (issue, problem) whose details are familiar to you. Then try creating a cluster or a tree diagram. Does the result suggest a possible structure for a paper? What problems might arise in "translating" the cluster or diagram into an outline for the paper?

 B. In a small group, describe your cluster or tree diagram and explain its nodes or branches. Then collaboratively try generating more branches for each writer's diagram.

3c Creating generalization-support patterns

For many writing tasks, you will need to arrive at a **generalization** (an interpretation, conclusion, or thesis) about your subject, identify appropriate **support** for your generalization, and arrange these two elements in a pattern that will help convey their relationship to readers. The following strategies may prove helpful.

1 Draw principles and look for generalizations

Any writing task that asks you to draw conclusions about (interpret) the meaning of a situation, text, phenomenon, or experience will require arriving at a generalization about the particulars that make up your subject. First, list as many facts or ideas about your subject as possible, using the listing technique described in 3a. Then ask yourself whether you can draw a generalization (conclusion, interpretation) about these facts or ideas. This strategy is illustrated in Tim Pagenhart's planning for a paper on teenage boys' gang membership. Once his list of facts led him to a generalization, he could look for other facts to support it. (See Figure 3.4.)

2 Create a problem-solution grid

Some of your writing, especially position papers, business reports, editorials, and other kinds of persuasive writing, will need to focus on a problem and propose a solution. Writing that begins by outlining a problem and then offers workable solutions or shows the advantages of one solution over another follows a **problem-solution sequence.** If your

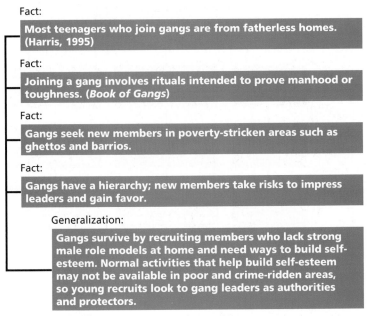

Fact:

Most teenagers who join gangs are from fatherless homes. (Harris, 1995)

Fact:

Joining a gang involves rituals intended to prove manhood or toughness. (*Book of Gangs*)

Fact:

Gangs seek new members in poverty-stricken areas such as ghettos and barrios.

Fact:

Gangs have a hierarchy; new members take risks to impress leaders and gain favor.

Generalization:

Gangs survive by recruiting members who lack strong male role models at home and need ways to build self-esteem. Normal activities that help build self-esteem may not be available in poor and crime-ridden areas, so young recruits look to gang leaders as authorities and protectors.

Figure 3.4   Generalizations from particulars

writing project calls for this kind of approach, you can use a simple but powerful technique for exploring ideas and information and revealing organizational options for your paper or report: a **problem-solution grid.** As Figure 3.5 shows, Paula Masek identified three temporary solutions to the problem of hunger among the homeless. Using a grid to guide her planning and identify a structure, Masek discussed each boxed item in a separate section of her draft paper.

3 Invent an outline

The best-known traditional prewriting technique is the trusty **outline,** complete with Roman numerals. Unfortunately, the traditional outline doesn't do much to help writers *generate* ideas before they decide how these ideas should be arranged. As a prewriting technique, however, a **working outline** can be useful. The trick is to use the outline to generate new categories of information rather than to label ones you've already discovered.

Try beginning with a simple topic as the main heading of an outline. Commit yourself to three second-level subheadings by writing the letters

Figure 3.5   A problem-solution grid

A, B, and *C* beneath the main topics. Leave a lot of space between each pair of letters. Then try filling in the blank subheadings. Once you've "discovered" three main subheadings, commit yourself to three third-level headings by writing *1, 2,* and *3* beneath *each* of your letters *A, B,* and *C.* Then try filling in the new blank headings. Mitch Weber tried this strategy when he began planning a brief history of the nonprofit organization in which he held a summer internship.

CREATION OF THE FAMILY HEALTH CENTER
I. Founding work of Susan and Roger Ramstadt
    A. The "vision"
    B. Finding the money
    C. The involvement of the Crimp Foundation
II. The Early Years (1972–80)
    A. Building momentum
    B. The great financial disaster
    C. Rebirth
III.Toward Maturity
    A. Fund-raising in the 1980s
    B. State recognition and the big award
    C. Health and sustenance
IV. The Future
    A. The new board of directors
    B. The new vision

Did You Know?

A study of planning discovered that older, experienced writers made complex, condensed, and often diagrammatic notes that the writers later expanded in draft papers. In contrast, younger, less experienced writers made notes that were simply first drafts of their composition. These observations suggest that certain kinds of planning, especially brief references to larger, complex chunks of information, may help writers more than just trying to write out the text.

P. J. Burtis, Carl Bereiter, Marlene Scardamalia, and Jacqueline Tretoe, "The Development of Planning in Writing," *Explorations in the Development of Writing*, ed. Barry M. Kroll (New York: Wiley, 1983) 153–74.

Exercise 4

A. Create a list of five topics, issues, or problems. Choose the one that most interests you. Then briefly try out three of the planning techniques discussed in 3b. After experimenting with them, jot down some notes about which one(s) worked worst and best for you. Why do you think this was the case? What sort of topic did you choose, and how did the technique you used affect its development?

B. Compare your general impressions of your three chosen planning techniques in a small group. Which ones seemed to work best for everyone? Were certain strategies more useful for certain topics?

3d Planning in electronic environments

Computer programs and the Internet offer many kinds of help to writers exploring ideas and information or planning an essay or report. Using a computer's word processing or note taking program to help plan your essay can in itself be a useful strategy because you can easily save your planning materials for later reference when you're drafting, revising, or reenvisioning your writing. Electronic planning can take other forms as well.

1 Explore question sets and thought collectors

Sets of questions you can use to explore a topic and identify patterns of ideas and information are available on many Web pages and as part of some word processing programs. Such programs provide interactive questions and prompts that help you gather your thoughts and develop plans for organizing a report or essay. One such "thought collector" at ⟨http://www.usc.edu/dept/ LAS/writing/⟩, for example, offers help in planning an argument by asking a writer to type in responses to the following statements.

> In my paper I wish to prove that:
> I believe my thesis is true because:
> Someone who disagrees with me might argue:

The program then lists the responses, allowing the writer to check those she wishes to keep. These lists, in turn, can act as an informal plan for writing a first draft.

2 Try summaries and keywords on search engines

Search engines are programs that help you identify Web or Internet sites relevant to a topic or issue. Typically, search engines provide brief summaries of potentially useful sites. Some also provide lists of keywords and key phrases.

Select a word or phrase that identifies the topic or purpose of your writing task or that is related to a subject or issue you wish to explore. For example, if you were preparing a pamphlet on avoiding sports injuries to be distributed at a health and fitness center or to athletes in an intramural sports program, you might begin searching with the words "sports injuries." When the summaries appear on your screen, read them and list any words, phrases, and sentences that suggest ideas or information you might wish to explore in your writing. Here are some notes that Rick Lopata took from links on jogging and running injuries that he found at a Web site on sports medicine.

Runner's knee	Tendinitis
—most common knee prob. for runners	—several forms
—30% of runners suffer from it	—symptom: aches that go away with exercise
—symptoms: aching/swelling behind kneecap	—runners suffer from Achilles tendinitis
—more common in women	—tendons swell and become sore
—more common in those who have abnormalities in how foot hits ground	

Foot info:
- —Human foot has 26 bones, 33 joints, 112 ligaments, network of tendons, nerves, blood vessels
- —In a 10-mile run, foot makes 15,000 strikes at force of 3-4 times body weight
- —Normal pronation (look up) can be affected by tightening of heel cord or running on angled surface

3 Follow links

World Wide Web sites contain highlighted words and phrases that provide **links** to sites discussing related issues and ideas. You can use these to survey subjects, develop ideas, and identify possible sources for a report or essay.

Identify a Web site that discusses ideas and information relevant to your writing task or to a subject you might wish to explore. List any highlighted words or phrases (links) that suggest material worth exploring or possible focuses for your writing. Then click on the links and scan the linked Web sites, writing down words, phrases, and ideas you might develop in your own work. Continue until you have filled a page or two with notes and are ready to look for patterns (see 3b–3c) in the material you've gathered.

3e Planning: Paper in progress

Jessica DiGregorio was assigned a paper in a college course focusing on literacy and its consequences for individuals and societies. The task required her to identify a public or official document (such as a charter, certificate, law, set of guidelines, or official publication) and to discuss its consequences for individuals or groups of people. Other people in the class analyzed the effects of documents such as housing contracts, NCAA regulations for college sports, a parent's death certificate, and a "driving while intoxicated" citation. Jessica had always been interested in sports, perhaps because her father was an accomplished basketball player. She decided to do some preliminary listing to see what specific kinds of documents affect participants in sports—amateur, college, and professional (see 3a). Here is a list of questions and ideas she created.

- Injury reports can shape an athlete's participation, the outcome of games, and the emotions of fans and players. Who gives the documents such power?
- Game rules—breaking some rules has serious consequences, but others are less important. Why? Who decides? How do players and fans know?
- Some sports specify the shape, size, weight, etc., of equipment. Does this make a difference? What about the sports that have few regulations on equipment? Do the differences reflect something about the nature of the sports or their roles in society?
- Professional sports contracts seem to be in the news often (major league baseball, National Basketball Assn., NFL). Can they really determine the success or failure of teams? How do they shape the lives of players? My father's contract.

- Following the box scores. What happens when people regard games as box scores?
- Drug regulations. Laws or informal rules. What's the difference?

After deciding on the consequences of professional contracts on players' lives as a focus for her work, Jessica made the following list.

- Contracts in the news—what kinds of things they cover.
- Odd things that some sports stars request.
- My father's NBA contract. What's in it?
- What he had to do as a result of the contract. What the team had to do.
- What it meant for his life. My family. Me?
- Similar to other contracts at the time?
- What if you break a contract?
- What is a contract? Legally. What exactly can contracts do and not do?

Exercise 5

 A. Study Jessica DiGregorio's two planning lists. What other topics on the first list do you think would have been worth developing in ways that addressed her assigned task? What questions would you ask her about the terms on the second list? What advice would you give her for either elaborating her second list or choosing specific items on it to include in or exclude from her paper?

 B. In a small group, compare your responses to Exercise 5A. Work together to generate a list of additional particulars that DiGregorio could use to develop her topic.

CHAPTER

4

Defining Your Purpose and Thesis

Think about what writing on the job, in school, and in civic activities actually *does*. It gives you a way to communicate new ideas and information. It helps produce commodities, provide services, make things work well, or streamline the flow of information. It can be coolly informative or passionately persuasive. It can sell things, buy things, or negotiate things. It can do public good or make private profit. And it can produce new knowledge that will delight and entertain people, lead to personal wisdom, or save lives.

Each time you write, you're also fulfilling specific purposes related to the task at hand. If you're writing to entertain your readers with a rich, interesting description of a personal experience, this purpose will also help you to choose an appropriate style, structure, and content. Thinking about your general and specific purposes can give you a sense of direction for your writing and an organizational plan for carrying it out.

4a Analyzing your purpose

Think about your last substantial piece of writing. No doubt someone else handed you a task or assignment, and it was your job to produce a decent piece of prose. In the business world, almost no one escapes such writing tasks, whether they're actually assigned ("Please reply to this request for information about product X") or you're just expected to do them as part of your job. In most cases, you're writing for several audiences, including co-workers, clients, and others in your organization—not just for your direct supervisor. Likewise, even though a teacher doles out your writing assignments in college to get you thinking about a problem or issue or to teach you something, he or she will read your writing as a representative of a subject area or a general community of educated adults.

Your purpose is less to "write for the teacher" than to "write for the academic community we share." One of your early steps in planning for any piece of writing, therefore, should be to analyze the task and setting, taking time to figure out what you're being asked (or what you're motivated) to do.

1 Define the focus of the task or assignment

In many writing tasks, your focus or topic may be defined for you in advance. In a memo to the YMCA volunteer tutoring staff, for example, your topic might be an upcoming training session. In an email message to the members of your ski club, your topic might be the results of a recent fund-raiser. (These topics may be announced in the "subject" line of your memo or email message.) On other occasions, you may need to identify the topic in a task that's given to you, or even come up with a topic on your own. In all these cases, it helps to articulate for yourself just what it is you're writing about.

Look for Noun Phrases. When your focus appears in a written assignment or task description, look for any nouns or noun phrases and underline them. In your planning notes, write these nouns and then, by freewriting or writing conceptual maps (see 3a–3c), begin inventing possibilities for your paper's contents. In analyzing a writing assignment in his child development course, Dennis Buehler underlined three key noun phrases.

> The purpose of this assignment is to integrate what you have learned in the area of <u>cognitive development</u>. Focusing on the second year of life, what are the most important <u>skills that emerge in different domains</u> (attention, language, and perception)? Give specific examples from the studies we have read so far.

The underlined topics can be stated more simply as *cognitive-developmental skills in the second year of life*.

Create a Focus Statement. When your writing task isn't an assignment given to you by someone else—that is, when it comes from your own need to get something done on the job or in a community setting—it helps to write your own focus statement to be clear about what you need to do. Be sure to include key nouns or noun phrases (as above) to identify the main focus of your writing. This can help you to keep your writing from straying from the point. Karla Spellman, for example, was asked to write a page of text for the Web site of a city project called "Green Chair," explaining how volunteers made green Adirondack chairs that were sold to raise money for creating play spaces in inner-city parks. She wrote the following focus statement and underlined the noun phrase in it.

In a page suitable for placement on the City Projects Web site, write a <u>description of the Green Chair project</u>, including its goals and how people can volunteer to build the chairs or where they can buy one.

2 Define the purpose of the task or assignment

Identifying nouns—topics or focuses—gives you a clear sense of what your writing is *about*. But nouns don't act: they're just things that sit, inert, on the page. Your writing doesn't just need to say something; it also needs to *do* something. This "doing" is the rhetorical action—the purpose—of your writing, and it usually appears in a verb or verb phrase.

Look for Verb Phrases. In an assignment someone else gives to you, underline any verbs or verb phrases that can tell you what to do with your writing. Then use one or more of the planning techniques (see 3a–3c) to generate material for your writing. In analyzing the second writing assignment in her composition course, Corinth Malletas underlined two phrases that seemed to get to the heart of the assignment.

> Assignment 2: Find an advertisement that catches your attention in a popular magazine. Then <u>analyze the ad for its hidden cultural assumptions</u>, being sure to <u>describe exactly what is happening in the ad.</u> Include techniques of camera angle, coloration, focus, and so on, paying attention to what is in the ad versus what is cut off, not shown, or partially shown. Be sure to go beyond description into analysis, showing how features of the ad reflect our selves and our culture.

Create a Purpose Statement. For unassigned and self-motivated writing occasions, create your own purpose statement that contains a verb or verb phrases; underline the verb(s) or verb phrase(s) to help you identify the main actions your writing will accomplish. In planning an announcement recruiting acoustic bands for a new coffeehouse, Ty Brown wrote the following purpose statement and underlined a key verb phrase.

> Create a flier directed at band members and leaders to <u>encourage their application to audition</u> for the X-Tra Coffee House and <u>explain the process</u> to them as well as details about the coffeehouse.

Notice that these verb phrases contain important assembly instructions for Ty's flier. "Encourage" implies "getting attention," "being positive," and "advertising." "Explain" implies "giving information," "being clear," and "avoiding deception." Here are some of the more common verbs used in writing situations, especially in college writing assignments, along with brief definitions and examples.

VERBS USED IN WRITING SITUATIONS

Describe. Show how something might be experienced in sight, touch, sound, smell, or taste. *Example:* "Describe the obstacles experienced by wheelchair-bound or vision-impaired visitors to historic homes in the area."

Analyze. Divide or break something into its constituent parts so you can analyze their relationships. Begin with careful description and observation. *Example:* "Analyze the causes of increased wildlife roadkill in a nearby suburb."

Synthesize. Combine separate elements into a synthesis, producing a single or unified entity. *Example:* "Synthesize this list of disparate facts about energy consumption."

Evaluate. Reach conclusions about something's value or worth. Substantiate all evaluations with evidence based on careful observation and analysis. *Example:* "Evaluate the proposals submitted by three different groups who each want to organize this year's charity auction."

Argue. Argue to prove a point or persuade a reader to accept or entertain a particular position (see 54a–d.) *Example:* "Write a letter to the college senate arguing your position on the campus-wide ban of indoor smoking."

Inform. Present facts, views, phenomena, or events to inform your reader. *Example:* "Inform homeowners about the hazards of lead paint in older homes."

Extend. Apply an idea or concept more fully. *Example:* "Extend the production figures to take into account the mechanics' work slowdown."

Trace. Map out a history or chronology, or explain the origins of something. *Example:* "Trace the development of Stalinism."

Discuss. Provide an intelligent, focused commentary on a topic. *Example:* "Discuss citizens' primary objections to the proposed tax hike."

Show. Demonstrate or provide evidence to explain something. *Example:* "Show how specimen transport problems contribute to operating room delays."

Exercise 1

A. Below are two writing tasks, one in the form of a college writing assignment, the other in the form of a work assignment to a writer working in an internship at a local nonprofit agency. Locate the noun(s) that indicate the *focus* of each task, and find the verb(s) that indicate its *purpose*. Restate the focus and purpose in your own words if necessary.

Sample Assignment: Everyone at some point recognizes a prejudice against another person or group. These prejudices often come from stereotypes—inaccurate generalizations made on the basis of limited experience, rumor, or what others tell us. Choose some past action in your life that came out of a prejudice. What was the cause of the action? If the same circumstances arose today, would you behave differently?

Sample Task: Draft a proposal to the State Board on Aging on our planned ElderHelp Transport System. Refer to the current guidelines for contents of the proposal, length, and format. It would be useful to include some information on actual beneficiaries of our plan, so you will want to conduct a few informal interviews with some seniors—possibly ones who use our center. Rose has written successful proposals to the state board in the past, so get her input early. Of course, you should also run your draft past Jim.

 B. Compare your analyses in a small group. What aspects of the task do you agree on? Where do you differ? How might you go about writing each of these texts?

> ## Did You Know?
>
> In a study of legislative analysts' writing, when the researchers substituted single words in the writers' documents and then asked them whether these changes were acceptable, the writers often agreed or disagreed with the substitutions on the basis of what they were trying to *do* with their writing. This research reveals how often writers' purposes guide even the smallest of decisions as they compose.
>
> Lee Odell, "Beyond the Text: Relations Between Writing and Social Context," *Writing in Nonacademic Settings,* ed. Lee Odell and Dixie Goswami (New York: Guilford, 1985) 249–80.

4b Using rhetorical purposes to guide your decisions

Now that you've analyzed the general purpose of a writing task or assignment, you can begin to consider more specific effects you want your writing to achieve. These effects are your **rhetorical purposes** for writing: what you want your writing to *do* at each stage. Do you want your first paragraph to grab your reader's attention with something really alarming, or is it more important to begin on a cool note of academic objectivity? Should you use a personal anecdote in the middle of your document to show how you understand a problem, or would it be better to launch into a description of research studies? Do you want to leave your reader hanging at the end by suggesting unexplored questions, or will you wrap everything up with a really strong, opinionated conclusion?

1 Rough out a purpose structure

As you think about how you want to affect your reader, it helps to plan a general **purpose structure** for your paper's contents. This is more primitive, at this early stage, than an outline or detailed description of parts; it's merely a blueprint to help you get started.

In planning to write about housing options for a section of her school's student guide, Carol Stotsky first defined her general purpose (to describe as objectively as possible the benefits and drawbacks of various housing options). But then she needed to get more specific. Did she want to suggest one option over another? For the rhetorical purpose in her beginning, Stotsky decided to *persuade* students that it's important to think carefully about where they want to live while in college.

> **Beginning: Why consider housing options?**

Stotsky decided that after showing why this question is so important, she would discuss each housing option (dorms, fraternities/sororities, off-campus houses and apartments, living at home) in detail, analyzing the advantages and disadvantages of each. For her rhetorical purpose in the middle section, she planned to *explore* the options objectively.

> **Middle: Explore housing options in detail.**

She then decided to move her final section toward a recommendation by presenting a scheme in which "traditional"-aged students (17–19 years old) start college by living in a dorm or at home and then move toward greater independence in their third or fourth years by considering off-campus housing. Since she'd already analyzed the options, she stood a better chance of demonstrating her point.

> **Ending: Recommend that students start secure, then move toward independence.**

This informal purpose structure gave Stotsky a tentative order and direction for her contribution to the student brochure.

2 Particularize your purposes

Rhetorical purposes work at all levels of your writing, from the most global reasons for writing to the most specific aims you want to achieve by using a particular word or adding a particular sentence. You can further specify each of the rhetorical purposes that have led to a sense of your essay's parts, listing ways to develop those purposes. Carol Stotsky decided, for example, that the beginning of her contribution to the student guide would try to grab the attention of readers who might not understand why housing options are an important topic. She listed three possibilities.

1. I could begin with a true-to-life description of two students who have made different housing options, one wise and one not so wise.
2. I could begin with a string of quotations from parents concerned about their children's well-being while in college.
3. I could begin with the results of a study by Breland on the consequences of housing choices for first-year college students.

As she considered her specific rhetorical purposes for her opening sentences, Stotsky realized that neither research results nor parents' quotations were likely to grab students' attention. She chose her first option and tried some drafting strategies (see Chapter 6), eventually weaving in the research results after she had "hooked" her readers.

Exercise 2

Roz Dane is a nurse practitioner in a family clinic. Clinic physicians often refer patients who have gum disease or who are at risk of developing gum disease to a local hospital's outpatient clinic for periodontal surgery. Such surgery has a high success rate, little risk, and a relatively low complication rate, but Roz knows that many patients are reluctant to have this surgery because most clinical descriptions of it are intimidating or even frightening to patients. After some discussion, the physicians who own the clinic have asked Roz to produce a short pamphlet for patients, describing the surgical procedure in more understandable, and less intimidating, terms.

Roz understands the surgical procedure, of course, as well as its benefits, risks, and complication rate. She is also well-informed about the kinds of patients and conditions for which this procedure is best suited. In addition, Roz has had a great deal of personal experience discussing the periodontal surgery with dozens of patients over the past few years and hearing their worries and fears about the procedure.

Write a purpose statement for Roz's task, and plan a multipart structure for her pamphlet based on that purpose.

4c Defining a main idea or thesis

Most writing has a point, but if that point isn't clear within the first page or so, readers may become frustrated and give up reading. In the work community, for instance, an executive summary might appear first, before a full report, to clarify the point right away and give readers a sense of what's to follow. In contrast, academic readers may have more patience as the writer gives background information that leads up to a main point.

One way you can be clear about your purposes and avoid bland, generalized prose is to develop a specific **thesis** for your writing that you then explore, support, or illustrate using specific examples or arguments. Although you'll hear the term *thesis* almost exclusively in college (with terms like *main idea, message,* or *point* being used more often in business and community writing), the principle of the thesis remains the same: a thesis is the controlling idea of a piece of writing. Many college papers contain a thesis statement, usually a single sentence, that appears somewhere early in the text, most often at the end of the first paragraph. In other writing, the thesis may be more subtle, but it still has the effect of telling the reader what the writing will say and do.

Depending on your writing situation, you can begin a paper with a clear thesis in mind or discover your thesis later on and revise accordingly. You can also begin with a clear thesis and then modify it as you look for evidence or **supporting ideas** to back up your assertions.

1 Turn topics into theses

When you begin a piece of writing, do you think about large areas of knowledge or experience that often appear as nouns or noun phrases? These usually take the form of *topics*: "conservation versus jobs in the timber industry," "the use of laser surgery in female infertility treatment," "death penalty by lethal injection in the state of Texas." Developing a thesis means *narrowing* one of these topics into something more specific and verbal, some statement of principle, action, or belief.

To develop a thesis from a topic, first try **narrowing** the topic to some specific angle or perspective. Then begin turning the topic from a noun (a "thing") into a statement that contains a verb, as Lynn Scattarelli did in an informational pamphlet she designed for a community parenting group.

VAGUE TOPIC	Ritalin
STILL A TOPIC	The use of Ritalin for kids with attention deficit disorder
STILL A TOPIC	The problem of Ritalin for kids with attention deficit disorder
ROUGH THESIS	Parents should be careful about medicines such as Ritalin for kids with attention deficit disorder

The topic became sharper in the second and third versions, but Scattarelli brought the fourth version to life by expressing an assertion about it, seeing it from a specific perspective.

2 Complicate or extend your rough thesis

Early thesis statements often beg for some clarification or elaboration. In Scattarelli's rough thesis, it's not clear what she's suggesting to parents about Ritalin: that it shouldn't be used? that it should be used judiciously? that it's inappropriate for kids with ADD? Answering these questions led her to a more complex and interesting thesis.

FINAL THESIS   Although Ritalin is widely used as a drug treatment for children with attention deficit disorder, parents should be careful not to overrely on such drugs until they have a complete picture of their child's problem and have explored all the options for its treatment.

Scattarelli complicated her final thesis by accepting Ritalin as a legitimate treatment for ADD. The main point—a caution about overreliance and the exploration of other options—*qualified* or *extended* her rough thesis.

More complex theses often lead to writing that your readers will find interesting and enlightening. In working on a short speech to be delivered at a local PTA meeting, Stephanie Cox turned a vague topic into a complex thesis by connecting the lack of a dress code at her children's school with the concept of social competition.

TOPIC   Lack of a dress code at Morgan County Middle School

ROUGH THESIS   The lack of a dress code at Morgan County Middle School is a problem.

COMPLEX THESIS   The lack of a dress code at Morgan County Middle School has allowed our children to compete over clothing styles and fashions, taking them away from the true social and educational purposes of being in school.

3 Expand your thesis with specifics

Think about how a thesis or main idea helps your reader. Knowing something about what you're going to say, your reader can organize the information that follows in chunks, fitting paragraphs and sections into the larger statement of purpose. But you need to decide on these ideas in the first place. Consider using the outlining processes described in Chapter 3 to create a series of points or ideas that extend, support, or illustrate your thesis. Start with a simple list—three items, for example—and then work from there. Joel Kitze, contributing an essay to a special library publication on computer literacy, created the following thesis-governed outline.

THESIS	In spite of the popularity of CD-ROM technology, computers will never take the place of books as the primary medium of written literacy.
SUPPORTING IDEA **1**	Books will always be more democratic, since only the middle and upper middle class can afford personal computers.
SUPPORTING IDEA **2**	Books can be transported and enjoyed everywhere—on a bus, on a beach, in bed.
SUPPORTING IDEA **3**	Children enjoy the physical comfort of reading with adults, a comfort harder to achieve with computers.

Each idea formed a kind of "minithesis" for its paragraph or section, guiding the ideas and focus of that paragraph. At the same time, each idea also provided support for the overall thesis or claim of Kitze's paper.

4 Modify your thesis

Don't force yourself to stick too closely to your original thesis. As you plan, you may find yourself entertaining other ideas, especially those that seem to contradict your main idea or thesis. In such cases, your writing may be more interesting if you can qualify your earlier position or perspective, revising your thesis and its supporting ideas. For example, in searching for good reasons to favor books over CD-ROM, Joel Kitze thought of some distinct advantages of CD-ROM technology, including ease of storage (CDs are much smaller than books), huge memory capacity (hundreds of book pages can be stored on a CD-ROM), and the ability to be searched or manipulated by a computer. A CD-ROM can show color and graphics, weakening the argument about the visual appeal of books. After thinking about four or five reasons like these, Kitze went back and modified his thesis, making it more complex and subtle.

ORIGINAL THESIS	In spite of the popularity of CD-ROM technology, computers will never take the place of books as the primary medium of written literacy.
MODIFIED THESIS	Although CD-ROM technology allows masses of information to be stored on small, easily shelved discs, it will never replace the bound books as the most convenient, affordable, and magical medium for print.

Kitze's revised thesis acknowledges that CD-ROMs have certain advantages, yet he still makes a case for books. Readers of this new thesis have more to think about than in the earlier version.

Exercise 3

 Turn each of the following topics into two different thesis statements or main ideas. Be as inventive as you like.

EXAMPLE

TOPIC   Saw-blade sabotage in the timber industry.

THESIS   Spiking trees to sabotage the saw blades of timber workers is both illegal and extremely dangerous but should be understood as a subversive act to stop further depletion of virgin forests.

THESIS   Protests that include the illegal spiking of trees to sabotage the saw blades of timber workers actually help the timber industry by suggesting to the public that conservationists are less concerned about human safety and human life than about trees.

Topic 1: Grandparents' rights
Topic 2: On-site day-care centers in corporations
Topic 3: Metal detectors used at public school entrances
Topic 4: "Truth in advertising" laws
Topic 5: Laws declaring English the official language of the United States

CHAPTER

5

Considering Your Readers

Imagine that you're writing a short article for one of the in-flight magazines found in the seat pockets of most commercial airlines. What and how you might write for such a magazine would depend on your knowledge of its readers—people locked into a pressurized cabin 35,000 feet above the earth. What do you know already about such readers, at least generally?

- Your readers are likely to include travel-minded vacationers and businesspeople.
- Your readers' physical circumstances (restrained in a seat, stressed by travel) may make them bored, tired, or uncomfortable.
- Your readers are likely to be impatient to get somewhere.

Potentially bored, tired, and impatient readers will not warm to a deeply theoretical reading. They'll want short, lively pieces they can read in ten or fifteen minutes, preferably on topics of human or geographical interest. They're not likely to enjoy graphic accounts of disasters or articles on the risks of airline travel. Yet they'll certainly want to be informed and entertained, if only as a distraction.

Already you can see how just a few thoughts about your readers can help to limit the infinite choices you face when you write—choices of style, content, or length. In most of your writing, plan to spend some time consciously focusing on your readers until such analysis becomes second nature to you.

5a Defining your reader

Many writing experts use the term **audience** to refer to actual or implied readers. An audience may be one person, such as the city official you address in a letter complaining about the poor condition of the neighborhood sidewalks, or it may be dozens, hundreds, or thousands of people, such as the readers of the newspaper that publishes your letter about the same problem.

Your first question in any analysis of audience will be "Who am I addressing?" Is it a flesh-and-blood person you know intimately? Or is it a shadowy, unknown reader, with only a faint silhouette to guide your thinking? Is your reader a single person or a large group?

To begin answering these questions, study Figure 5.1. This illustration shows an audience continuum, beginning with the most intimate reader on one end (yourself) and ending with the remote and amorphous "general community of unknown readers" on the other.

The self. Writing for the self can be an excellent way to learn and to plan for formal writing (see 2c). In more formal writing, the self can also act as a critic or interested reader.

The specific, intimately known reader. *Example:* a close friend, a lover, a family member. Such people make up an audience very different from people you've never met. Letters directed to intimately known readers usually don't have to be very formal, yet you can still carry on an academic conversation with such readers.

The specific, personally known reader. *Example:* A teacher, supervisor, acquaintance. Your knowledge of a personally known reader accumulates through a social, scholastic, or occupational relationship. Just as you might talk a little more formally to such a person than you would to a close friend or relative, the style and tone of your writing will also be less casual and chatty.

The specific community of known readers. *Examples:* your writing class, members of a team or club you have joined, a small electronic listserv you're on, co-workers where you have a job. Such *groups* of readers often can be characterized socially or geographically. While you can no longer describe this audience's unique personality, you can think of it as a *community* whose members may not all think, act, dress, or live exactly the same way but are bound together by some shared situation.

The specific, publicly known reader. *Examples:* Oprah Winfrey, Mariah Carey, your senator or congressperson. You come to know public audiences indirectly through news, gossip and rumor, speeches, interviews, or published works. While you don't personally know someone like Oprah Winfrey, you know *of* her; you may have seen her on her TV talk show, watched her perform in one of her TV or movie roles, or read one of her books. What you know of her largely depends on what's been made available for you to know.

The specific, unknown reader. *Examples:* Mr. Ed Walters, director of personnel at CompuGraphics, Inc.; Sondra Teisch, president, local chapter of

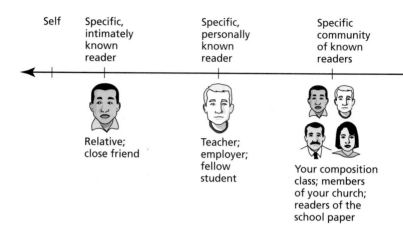

Figure 5.1   The audience continuum

Students Against Driving Drunk. Such readers live in the shadows. Often you know only their names and affiliations. Your knowledge usually comes not from any specific actions, words, or direct experience but from what these people *do,* what *context* they're in when you write to them, and what your relationship is to them. Because you know them neither personally nor publicly, you should usually address such an audience using a formal style.

The specific community of unknown readers. *Examples:* the hundreds or thousands of undergraduates at your college or university, citizens in your hometown, readers of *Mademoiselle* or *Bon Appetit,* members of a listserv dedicated to antique furniture, worldwide employees of an international corporation. The larger the group, the less direct knowledge you'll have of its individual members. While it might only take a few weeks to get to know the members of a school club, sorority, or fraternity, it might take months or years to become acquainted with everyone who reads the school paper or alumni magazine. Yet even large communities can still share the same social, academic, or work context and are tied together by mutual goals, circumstances, and knowledge or by allegiance to common symbols, mottoes, or slogans.

The general community of unknown readers. *Examples:* Americans, the public. At this end of the continuum is the most abstract and faceless audience of all. Be careful assuming that you are ever writing for such an amorphous audience. *What* you're writing about already slices away lots of potential readers; how your writing *reaches* your audience slices away many more. (Even the medium of communication—written text—already

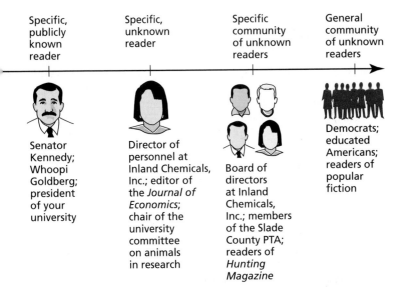

Specific, publicly known reader	Specific, unknown reader	Specific community of unknown readers	General community of unknown readers
Senator Kennedy; Whoopi Goldberg; president of your university	Director of personnel at Inland Chemicals, Inc.; editor of the *Journal of Economics*; chair of the university committee on animals in research	Board of directors at Inland Chemicals, Inc.; members of the Slade County PTA; readers of *Hunting Magazine*	Democrats; educated Americans; readers of popular fiction

eliminates all illiterates, most citizens and residents who do not speak or read English, and many people who are homeless or destitute.) When you decide to write for "the general public," think carefully about what this means, and consider the more specific context of your writing.

Audiences themselves can also shift positions over time. A co-worker you might address formally at first can become a friend, then a close friend. Some specific, personally known readers might, by virtue of their position or your relationship, be addressed more casually than others. Further, workplace texts are often read by very different audiences. A memo requesting personal leave will be read not only by your direct supervisor but by her supervisor as well. Members of your working group will probably receive a copy of the memo, even though they can't make a decision about your request. Other upper management might read the memo as well, and they will probably make the ultimate decision about your leave request. Further, if your request is approved, the payroll and personnel departments will also probably see the memo.

Exercise 1

A. Imagine that you're living on Shell Island, a small estuary along the coast of Florida. A favorite winter vacation spot, the area boasts some excellent shelling beaches. But now, after years of ravenous beachcombing, fewer shells appear at low tide, and the area is attracting a more limited variety of birds and other wildlife. During the summer, the local city council has proposed a general ban on beachcombing and plans to pass an ordinance that would require visitors to obtain a beach permit, at a cost of $30, to use the public beaches. The money would be channeled back into the study and preservation of the local environment.

You're planning to write a position statement on the proposed ordinance. Choose one of the three contexts below. Then, referring to the audience continuum, analyze the audience for your position statement. Take a position on the issue, and consider which readers will disagree with your position and why.

Context 1: Surfriders is a small organization for active surfers who visit Shell Island almost daily and are interested in keeping the area clean and safe. Write a letter to Todd Gray, president.

Context 2: Winter Birds is a newsletter sent to retired people who live in Northern states but have properties on the island and migrate there for two or three months during the winter. It is published and mailed by a local association for retired people. Write a letter to the editor.

Context 3: Nan Brown is the director of the Shell Island Chamber of Commerce. Business owners, rental agents, and tour operators rely heavily on the Chamber of Commerce for support. Write to Ms. Brown.

B. Compare your letters in a small group. Discuss the ways in which your audience analysis influenced your letters.

5b Characterizing your readers

Although you might identify actual people as readers (your mother, your rabbi, the First Lady, the owner of the gas station down the street), at some level your writing is shaped by how *you* think of your audience. Constructing audiences also draws on your social and cultural knowledge. If you know very little about feminism, for example, and you write to an audience of feminists, you may stereotype them wrongly. Knowing that there are many varieties of feminism complicates your audience, but the result is a richer and more accurate picture that leads to a better-informed and more incisive piece of writing.

Use the following list to think critically about the nature of your readers when you plan and revise your writing.

1. **Size and Relationship.** How large is your audience, and how generalized? How intimately do you know your audience? What sort of relationship do you share with your audience?
2. **Prior Knowledge.** How much does your audience know about the subject of your writing? Are your readers complete novices or just

short of being experts? Do they share your prior knowledge of the subject? Are they young or old? Are they worldly-wise or inexperienced and naive?

3. **Physical Context.** Where are your readers situated geographically? Is it possible to pinpoint their location? If not, can you generalize about their location (Florida State University, San Francisco, Capitol Hill)?

4. **Social Context.** What characterizes your audience socially and culturally? Are your readers educated? poor? middle class? Do they spend their time watching TV or reading books? Do they listen to Brahms? Do they go to tractor pulls? Do they spend time at singles bars or PTA meetings?

5. **Intellectual Disposition.** How would you characterize your readers' way of thinking? Are they highly conservative? radical? apathetic? Where would they stand on certain major issues? Are they more likely to read and enjoy the *National Enquirer* or the *National Review*? *Science* or the *Christian Science Monitor*?

6. **Conditions of Reading.** Under what conditions will your audience be reading your writing? Will readers be at home? at school? at the office? at the breakfast table? Will they be studying your writing closely at a desk or reclining in an easy chair after a good meal? Will they be busy or distracted? Will time be on their side, or will they be wishing they could buy a few extra hours?

7. **Power.** What is your status relative to your reader? Are you expecting the reader to get something done? Is your writing getting something done for someone else, such a supervisor? Is that person also going to read your writing?

In specifying these characteristics, be aware that you're dealing with *tendencies*. Ask yourself whether you are unfairly stereotyping your reader(s). Sitting on any given airplane, for example, may be a relaxed person deeply engrossed in a dense philosophical treatise or a complex analysis of trends in computer programming. Are your generalizations accurate and helpful?

Exercise 2

 A. Imagine that your longtime next-door neighbors take a temporary position in another country and rent their house. Soon after the renters move in, they begin piling up their yard and driveway with junk cars, old refrigerators, tires, and other debris. The situation becomes so intolerable that you decide to write to the renters, calling attention to the problem. You also decide to write to the local city inspections office, which is responsible for enforcing various codes on yard debris. Write the two short letters, addressing the first to

John and Susan Valentine and the second to Ms. Betsy Lewis, City Inspections Office.

 B. In a small group, compare the style, tone, and content of your pairs of letters. In each case, you were writing to a specific audience. How did their positions on the continuum influence your decisions? What general principles can you draw about the relationship of audience analysis to certain choices in your writing?

Did You Know?

In a study of audience, one group of students was assigned specific audiences to write for, and another group was not. Students in the audience group were more interested in the assignment, put more effort into the work, and used more audience-based writing strategies than students in the group without an assigned audience.

T. M. Redd-Boyd and W. H. Slater, "The Effects of Audience Specification on Undergraduates' Attitudes, Strategies, and Writing," *Research in the Teaching of English* 23 (1989): 77–108.

5c Adapting your content, structure, and style

Imagining readers of your writing means more than gathering isolated facts about them (average age, occupation, and so on). In analyzing your audience, stopping at facts is like lining up the cumin, coriander, oregano, and basil without knowing which spice you should add to the stew. Analyzing an audience can influence many decisions you make as you plan and revise your writing. In particular, consider how audience influences your *genre*, *content*, *structure*, and *style*.

1. **Genre.** What sort of text you choose for your writing—its **genre**—will depend in part on your audience. Imagine that you are an interior designer commissioned to plan the redecoration of someone's living room. Your reader will be expecting something akin to a proposal, not a poem, an editorial, or a letter. Genres are especially important because they often give you guideposts for other decisions regarding length, style, structure, and purpose.
2. **Content.** What specific information you put into your writing also depends on your audience. Your decorating proposal would probably assess the present design and its limitations; propose a redeco-

rating plan with details about wallpaper, furniture, and lighting; and estimate the work involved and the expense to carry it out. It would be inappropriate to include other kinds of information, such as instructions for hanging wallpaper (since your reader is hiring you to arrange this) or a description of your own living room (since your reader doesn't expect a comparative analysis).

3. **Structure.** How you arrange and organize your ideas will likewise depend on your audience. A utilities operations manager proposing a solution to a water utilities problem that he knows his audience (city council and city manager) will find expensive and controversial might acknowledge the problem itself early but lead gradually to his proposed solution and its benefits. In an essay for a professor of philosophy who doesn't like unsupported generalizations, it might be wise to establish some points first to lessen the risk of hearing the question "How do you know this?" In some genres, such as APA-style research reports (see Chapter 50), your structure may be inflexible; you need to know what that structure is and follow it.

4. **Style.** How you think about your audience will influence the style of your writing. How informal or formal should your writing be? how clinical or emotional? how friendly or hostile? how embracing or adversarial? Most teachers of physical anthropology reading a student's formal essay will not accept statements like "Leakey's stuff is awesome," just as most parents reading a strep warning sent from their school wouldn't expect it to begin "It has been determined that the environment of P.S. 46 contains clinical cases of *Streptococcus* bacilli in specific human organisms with whom your offspring may be in routine contact or physical proximity as a consequence of their attendance and participation in academic and extracurricular activities."

Did You Know?

Audiences from different countries can vary in what they consider desirable traits in writing. In one study, 84 percent of U.S. students and 75 percent of Finnish students preferred essays with a personal approach while only 60 percent of Australian students did so. In addition, Australian students and U.S. students tended to prefer simple language and sentences while Finnish students preferred language using metaphors and other figures of speech.

R. Elaine Degenhart and Sauli Takala, "Developing a Rating Method for Stylistic Preference: A Cross-Cultural Pilot Study," *Writing Across Languages and Cultures,* ed. Alan C. Purves (Newbury Park: Sage, 1988): 79–106.

5d Addressing communities of readers

While it may seem as though you've almost always written for a teacher, you actually participate in conversations in many communities through both your reading and your writing. Your college, work, and public communities give you a rich assortment of audiences to address. A campus alone consists of a loose confederation of scholars and teachers, students, administrators, club or team members, and people serving in many public and private capacities. In some circumstances, you may need to address or think of more than one of these readers, which complicates your task. Strategies for addressing different communities of readers depend partly on your relationship to your reader(s).

1 Writing for authorities

In some ways, writing for people in positions of authority can be especially challenging; after all, your performance and reputation may be on the line, and the stakes (such as a grade or the renewal of a contract) can be high. In academic settings, for example, a common first-day activity is figuring out the teacher. Is she tough or easy, rigorous or undemanding? Does she expect flawless, highly polished papers, or is she more concerned with the messy, exploratory side of writing? Does she seem to welcome diverse views, even if they don't match her own? In business settings, knowing what a supervisor expects can be just as daunting—and important.

Always attend to the specific guidelines for completing a writing task (see 4a). If these are provided orally, write them down carefully. Reread all directions several times. Above all, *ask questions*. Most teachers, supervisors, or superiors are willing to elaborate on their expectations. Their answers often tell you how they will evaluate your writing in light of its purposes.

2 Writing for communities of peers

Many public and civic contexts in which you might write are organized democratically. You don't have a supervisor as much as a series of self-appointed roles (such as membership on a committee), so you are on more or less equal footing with others in your group. (In other public settings, of course, power takes more complicated forms: a city council member has a certain kind of authority in her work above an ordinary citizen, but citizens themselves hold the power to vote such a person out of office.)

Many writing classes today also use peer groups as a way to encourage more diverse responses to your writing than you might get only from your teacher. Peer groups can give you support during stages when you're uncertain about your writing and can provide valuable "test runs" of audience response after you've completed a rough draft. You can also ask a peer group to read *as if* they were a specific audience, testing how well you've achieved your purposes. (For more on peer groups during revision, see 7c.)

During the planning stages of your writing, be sure to discuss your ideas with members of a peer group. If you're writing something collaboratively or with certain community goals in mind, as might be the case in a community organization, your peers will no doubt see your text and give you feedback or even contribute to it themselves. If, however, you're writing for another context, ask members of your peer group to role-play your intended audience.

3 Writing for broad public communities

A rather murky and ill-defined audience, but one often alluded to in directions for or evaluations of writing assignments, is the "general reader." Although no one yet has defined this audience very clearly, it usually refers to reasonably educated people—for example, most people in your college or university. Many teachers favor the undefined "general academic audience" for classroom writing for the very reason that opinions among this group will vary widely and require more thought, hence, deeper learning.

Readers in broad public communities are themselves very diverse. Some are well educated, well informed, and interested in the pursuit of knowledge (often for its own sake). Others read very little—just a daily newspaper, for example—in order to keep up on current events. Some readers have incisive, critical minds and like to be entertained with new and stimulating ideas; others read only when they have to and prefer not to spend much time talking about ideas.

In reading your writing, teachers often allude to various public communities with statements like "How would the audience for this piece react to so radical a statement?" or "Are you sure you've considered the opposing views your audience might raise here?" or "How would people opposed to gun control respond to this?" Such statements assume different audiences with different dispositions. Interestingly, academic readers will take you seriously if you can show, through your prose, that you've considered a range of public responses to an issue or idea. That sort of awareness of audiences can make your writing in work and nonacademic communities stronger and more convincing.

In your planning notes, circle any assertions or points that readers in various public communities could challenge. Then brainstorm to develop several responses to the challenges. Are the challenges well reasoned? If so, then consider acknowledging or incorporating them in your paper.

4 Writing for yourself and forgetting about audience

Writing for yourself can help you to formulate or explore new knowledge. If you're responding to a task or an assignment given by a teacher or supervisor, ask yourself what the writing process can do for *you*. What sort of learning is implied by the design of the project? How can you maximize your own interest in the subject? What will *you* get from your efforts?

Writing to or for yourself can also help you in the early stages of your writing, when "audience paralysis" can set in. Tough-minded audiences can make you so self-conscious that you can hardly produce a word that will survive your scrutiny. The result is frustration, procrastination, and anxiety.

Audience analysis isn't something you do once, in planning your writing, and then put aside during the later stages. While drafting and revising, keep thinking sharply about your readers. Once you've marked the general outlines in the clay, you can continue to define the features more sharply as you work your way toward finished sculpture.

Exercise 3

 A. Pick a specialized magazine with which you are very familiar (such as *Road and Track, Ski Magazine,* and so on). Get a recent copy of the magazine and glance through it, noting the topics, lengths, and formats of its articles, its advertisements, its layout, and its writing style. Then, using the advice outlined in this chapter, select one method for analyzing the magazine's audience. If you can't answer a question definitively, make as educated a guess as possible, and state what further information you'd like to have.

 B. Join a group of three or four other students. Briefly describe and compare your magazines, and then discuss your audience analyses. What issues surface about the relationship between the writing and the audience? What problems or questions about audience would you like to discuss?

DRAFTING AND REVISING: SHAPING YOUR WRITING FOR YOUR COMMUNITY

CHAPTER

6

Drafting

Drafting means stringing words together into sentences and paragraphs that will begin to make some sense to a reader. All the planning, purpose setting, and audience analysis you do for a piece of writing will prepare you to write. But don't expect to sit down and immediately draft a smooth, coherent paper simply because you've accumulated a lot of material. If you are writing collaboratively as part of a work team or a community or academic group, you will probably meet to plan the drafting process and divide the responsibilities. Whether you are working with others or by yourself, the process of pulling your information together and *writing* will always be intellectually challenging: drafting is hard work.

When you write a **rough draft,** you create something that begins to resemble a fully elaborated text. If planning can be likened to thinking up the script for a movie, then drafting means actually filming it, always realizing that later you may want to retake scenes, add new material, and let lots of footage fall to the cutting-room floor.

6a Moving from planning to drafting

Your use of various planning strategies should produce more than enough material to begin drafting. The problem you face at this stage is knowing how and where to begin writing your draft. You need to assess what you have and start turning your material into sentences that move your ideas forward.

1 Draft in manageable parts

Outlines of various sorts do more than simply help you generate ideas. A good cluster, for example, will also show you relationships among connected ideas and ways you might think about organizing your paper.

The items in your outline or other materials will usually suggest chunks of text that you can draft in one sitting. For example, a financial analyst hired to give investment advice might initially find a ten-page report on strategies for the upcoming year to be a daunting task. He might begin by writing a fairly easy section of the longer report—for example, a two-page analysis of market trends.

S T R A T E G Y

In your planning notes, look for specific ideas that suggest paragraphs or sections of your paper. Then choose one idea and write about it, either in draft form or in the form of lists, notes, or sentences.

**6a
draft**

Albert McCann, a symphony manager in a midsize city, generated the following tree diagram as he was preparing documents about his symphony's 2000–2001 tour schedule. Note how the diagram not only helps Al structure his document but also may help him determine the kind of case to make for including (or excluding) particular destinations from the tour schedule.

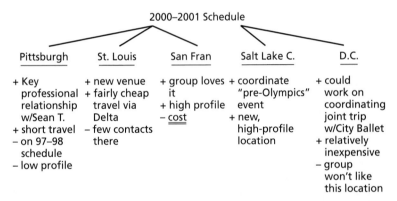

2000–2001 Schedule

Pittsburgh	St. Louis	San Fran	Salt Lake C.	D.C.
+ Key professional relationship w/Sean T.	+ new venue	+ group loves it	+ coordinate "pre-Olympics" event	+ could work on coordinating joint trip w/City Ballet
+ short travel	+ fairly cheap travel via Delta	+ high profile	+ new, high-profile location	+ relatively inexpensive
− on 97–98 schedule	− few contacts there	− <u>cost</u>		− group won't like this location
− low profile				

2 Develop a general structure

The kind of material you're writing may determine the way you organize it. A narrative, for example, will probably be arranged *chronologically* (each event following the previous event in time); an argument may be organized *logically,* by paragraphs supporting some assertion. Much of the writing done in the workplace or the public arena is highly structured. Whatever you're writing, you need to think about what should come first, second, and third in your paper.

Most academic writing will contain at least three parts: an **introduction,** a **body,** and a **conclusion.** This simple structure can help you to make some preliminary decisions about how to group your ideas.

S T R A T E G Y

Look through the material you have. Group some of your specific ideas, topics, or terms into one of the three categories of introduction, body, and conclusion. Tentatively organizing your ideas in this way will help you to develop a stronger focus when you begin writing.

By thinking about this three-part organizing scheme, Amy Burns was able to generate some ideas for a paper on superstition and develop a preliminary structure.

INTRODUCTION   Fear; people who believe in superstitions; origins

BODY   Examples of superstitions (black cat, #13, crossing fingers, ladder, rabbit's foot)

CONCLUSION   Truth and falsity of superstitions; mystery surrounding them; concepts of reality

When she began drafting her paper, Burns used the ideas from this preliminary plan to write an introduction about how superstitions originate in a fear of the unknown.

Many people are superstitious or at least practice some of the bizarre rituals of superstition, but very few know why or have thought about the reason. A lot of people practice superstitions without realizing that what they are doing is superstitious. The biggest percentage of people practice superstition because of a fear of the unknown. You might have heard some superstitions from parents or grandparents, been influenced by school or religion, or perhaps even read about them in books. However or wherever you heard of them, you practice superstitions because you are afraid of what will happen if you do not.

Although the introduction-body-conclusion structure can be helpful, much of the material you will write outside the academic community may require another approach. Petitions, newsletters, sales letters, problem descriptions, status reports, and some Web sites, for example, do not follow a rigid structure with set headings; however, readers do have expectations about how such pieces should be organized, and as a writer, you would need to understand and satisfy those expectations.

Writer's Tip: Using a Computer

Open separate files so that you can work on shorter parts of your paper, one section at a time. You can later cut and paste these separate files together into a single text, using block moves or file imports. Moving paragraphs or sections of your paper in this way can help you to see larger organizational possibilities.

---

3 Assess your purpose and redraft

Even before you've written a full draft, you may want to stop to think about whether the material is achieving your general purposes for writing (persuading someone of a position, telling a story, explaining how to do something) or your more specific purposes for different parts of your paper (providing information, livening up a paragraph with an anecdote, illustrating a point with an extended example). (See Chapter 4.)

**6a
draft**

STRATEGY

Read your early material, and extend, cut, or redraft it to more adequately reflect your intended purposes.

In her paper on superstition, Burns's broad purpose was to inform her readers about the nature of superstition and to encourage some enjoyable reflection. Her first specific purpose statement was "I want to grab my readers' attention and get them thinking about the nature of superstition." From this statement, she realized that her introduction was informative but too dull. She drafted some new sentences and then followed them with her earlier material.

> Do you knock on wood after making a prediction? Shiver when a black cat crosses your path? Consider the number 13 unlucky? If so, then you have already been swept into the fantasy world of superstitions. Many people are superstitious or at least practice some of the bizarre rituals of superstition, but very few know why or have thought about the reason.

Exercise 1

A. Thinking about your experiences as a writer, give some advice about drafting to an imaginary audience of high school students. Feel free to include personal experiences, tips, and specific techniques. You might, for example, give advice about the best times to write, how to get started, what to avoid, or how to handle difficult writing tasks.

B. Share your "advice papers" in a small group. Are any behaviors typical? Is any advice consistent?

> ## Did You Know?
>
> The word *draft,* used in the sense of creating a preliminary form of a written document, comes from a word originally related to *draw.* A drafter is a professional drawer, planner, or sketcher—someone skilled in designing. When you draft a document, you're essentially being your own designer or sketcher, roughing out the basic ideas and contents, which you can later refine into an effective text. Many related senses of *draft* suggest a sort of drawing out, in which something is extracted or pulled out from a larger mass: cattle from a flock or herd, chips from a sculptor's stone, or, for that matter, ideas from a writer's head.

6b Using drafting strategies

What makes drafting so challenging? Partly, it's the need to get a complicated job done, finding the right words while you're still figuring out where to begin. Partly, the challenge also comes from dealing with apprehensions, such as feeling the focus slipping away, or thinking your writing isn't working, or perhaps finding that you're revising every sentence instead of moving quickly ahead.

The challenge of drafting can be made much less daunting if you practice some useful techniques for getting words down on the page.

1 Write about your writing

Worrying about your writing probably won't ever go away—even the pros do it. Worrying yourself into avoidance or confusion, however, won't help you get your draft written.

A very common fear is the deadline. Strangely, many writers react to deadlines by putting off the writing until the specter of doom is practically breathing down their necks (often in the few late-night hours before the writing is due). For these procrastinators, just about any other task, even the most onerous, will take precedence over sitting down and actually starting to write.

STRATEGY

Begin drafting not by writing your paper but by writing *about it.* What's foremost in your mind about your paper? What do you hope to do with it? What possible ways might you start it? As you make these notes, you'll soon find yourself a little less anxious about starting—after all, you *have* started. As your anxiety lessens, you'll find yourself more willing to take some risks and try out a few lines.

2 Draft quickly

Another source of frustration comes from the struggle to find the right words. Sometimes every sentence seems to tangle you in a mess of contradictions, until you're no longer sure what you want to say. In this situation, you want to gain momentum, to feel that your ideas are smoothly giving way to words.

S T R A T E G Y

Draft quickly. As you begin, don't worry about writing perfect sentences and paragraphs. Just aim to get as much material on paper as you can, right from the start. Writers often find that when they write quickly, they feel a momentum developing, a kind of "flow." If you can type faster than you can handwrite, using a computer may encourage this momentum.

6b
draft

Writer's Tip: Using a Computer

If the automatic spelling and grammar checking features of your software distract you from writing quickly, turn them off. Run these applications only when you are ready to proofread your document.

---

3 Semidraft

Writing a first full draft in one sitting, especially of a major document, may be too ambitious, and you will need to divide the task into several drafting episodes. Some writers, however, can't seem to continue drafting anything for more than a few minutes before they stall out. They can't come up with the words to describe a particular idea, often because they're tired or haven't thoroughly considered their ideas.

S T R A T E G Y

Semidrafting refers to the process of writing full sentences until you feel you're about to stall out. At that point, you simply write the word *etc.* and then continue on to your next point. Or you insert a brief direction to yourself in brackets to remind you what to do when you return to the draft to push that section a little further along.

Did You Know?

In a study of college students with serious writing problems, Mina Shaughnessy found that the more they worried about the correctness of their prose while writing, the more paralyzed they became and the less coherent their drafts turned out to be. "Some writers," Shaughnessy wrote, "inhibited by their fear of error, produce but a few lines an hour or keep trying to begin, crossing out one try after another until the sentence is hopelessly tangled."

Mina P. Shaughnessy, *Errors and Expectations* (New York: Oxford UP, 1977) 7.

In a paper on the histories of "wild children" (lost children raised by wolves or other animals in the woods), Kavita Kamal semidrafted the following paragraph.

The first case to be examined was that of Victor, the "Wild Boy of Aveyron." Victor first appeared in a village in southern France in January 1800. His age was estimated to be about eleven or twelve years. [Explain how he was adopted by Jean-Marc Gaspard Itard and Madame Guerin; discuss their subsequent studies.] People assumed that he was a mute when they first dealt with him because he did not speak. Nor did he show any evidence of hearing. [Now go into the stuff from Roger Shattuck's *The Forbidden Experiment* on the fact that he had no malformation of the tongue, mouth, etc., then into Itard's paper in 1801 on Victor.] This selective deafness lasted until January of 1801, when Victor showed the first signs of hearing human voices.

Notice how Kamal suspended what may amount to several paragraphs or even pages while she pushed her draft forward into new areas. This gave her a sense of its form—a kind of flow—without forcing her to flesh out every detail. Later she was able to return to the paragraph and simply add the missing material to an existing structure.

Writer's Tip: Using a Computer

Remember that drafts are perishable. Power outages or damaged disks can spell the end of all your work on a draft. *Always* make copies of files and disks. To avoid losing material while you draft, also save your file frequently—certainly every page or every ten minutes—or set your computer to save your file automatically at reasonable intervals.

4 Talk it out or take a break

Sometimes nothing works. You simply can't, at that moment, put coherent sentences together on the page, and your frustration can cause you to lose interest in the project.

Writing is not like breathing, something you do as a matter of course. It's more like eating, which depends on your appetite. If you simply can't write, no matter how many techniques you try, then don't. Put off your writing until a little later. Just set a time to return to the task—preferably on the same day, but no later than the same time the next day. In the meantime, try this final Strategy to keep going.

6c
collab

S T R A T E G Y

Talk with or send an email about your writing project to someone you know well. Explain what you're trying to do. Expressing your concerns may help you alleviate tension and may even show you some solutions. Your listener may also have suggestions to help you get started.

Exercise 2

 A. Try out any one of the Strategies for drafting described in this chapter. Jot down some notes about how well it worked to get you started drafting and keep you moving forward.

 B. Compare the results of your experiment in a small group. What worked? What didn't? How could you modify or add to the Strategy to make it work better for you? What other problems did you encounter as you drafted, and how might you solve them in the future?

6c Drafting collaboratively

Different groups work together in different ways depending on the composition and purpose of the group. A committee formed to revise production standards at a manufacturing plant might consist of department managers who each have an area of expertise, while a Sunday school parents' committee might include people who have no experience in running a school but share the goal of increasing enrollment. Each group will distribute writing tasks in the way that seems most efficient for its resources and purposes. If your group is uncertain how to proceed, consider one of the following suggestions.

1 Do parallel drafting

In **parallel drafting,** your group divides the proposed document so that each member is responsible for drafting a particular section. Members can exchange drafts as they revise and edit. This strategy allows writers with different specializations to work comfortably together yet draw on individual expertise, but it may require one person to act as editor, integrating the drafts.

2 Do team drafting

To do **team drafting,** the group agrees on first and second authors for each section. The first author begins drafting and continues until he or she gets stuck. Then the draft passes to the second author, who begins where the first writer stopped. This method works well when various writers share similar ideas and approaches. The drafts are recirculated when the group is ready to revise and edit.

3 Do intensive drafting

Intensive drafting is most successful if you are working with a close friend or colleague. You need to find a location where you can assemble your materials and work undisturbed. Decide where each person will start, begin drafting together, and exchange sections at a certain time or as each of you finishes a segment. You continue your intensive, undisturbed work—exchanging drafts and reworking the document—until you are both satisfied with the result.

Exercise 3

 A. Imagine you are part of a student organization that is raising funds for a community project in which volunteers read to children in school libraries. Your organization intends to submit a grant proposal to a local foundation or philanthropic group. Plan how the members might use the following equipment to draft the proposal collaboratively: telephones, email, computers, fax machines. What steps would be involved in your plan?

 B. Meet with a small group of students to discuss the plans developed in Exercise 3A. How do the plans differ? How are they the same? How comfortable do students in your group feel with the idea of drafting collaboratively? What obstacles do they see? what advantages?

Writer's Tip: Using a Computer

Some software programs include a "red underlining" feature, which allows changes to your draft to appear in a different color on your monitor. Drafts can be circulated by disk or email, edited by group members using the underlining feature, and returned to the writer. Every member's changes will appear (color-coded by editor in some software) on the draft for review.

6d
collab

6d Drafting: Paper in progress

After Jessica DiGregorio listed possible examples to support her generalized topic of the consequences of professional contracts on the lives of sports players (see 3e), she tried freewriting for a few minutes on selected items in her list. Here is her freewriting passage on the item "What he [her father] had to do as a result of the contract."

- Keep himself fit for five years (meaning?)
- Not indulge in bad habits
- Not stop playing basketball
- Stay clear of ice-skating, skiing, other strenuous activities to avoid injury

Exercise 4

A. Examine DiGregorio's freewriting. At this point, she had not yet written a full first draft of her paper, but she wanted to use some ideas in her freewriting as she planned her drafting. What advice would you give her about the ideas she has begun to explore here? What other details on the subject of the contract requirements could she include in her rough draft? Is there anything in the freewriting that suggests a good place for this passage in her paper (beginning, middle, or end)?

B. In a small group, compare your responses to Exercise 4A. What did the members of your group agree could be profitably expanded from the freewriting as DiGregorio drafts her paper? Was there any consensus in your group about where to place this section of the paper?

CHAPTER

7

Revising

Because so much of what we read is in a final, published form, we often forget how much work goes into a piece of writing. Invisible to us are the hours the author spent in the process of **revision**—considering and reconsidering the content and structure of the writing, tearing out whole sections and redrafting them, honing and refining the paragraphs, polishing the style, and finding just the right words to express a thought.

Revision is not simply **editing,** a fine tuning for style, grammar, and problems with sentences and wording. Neither is it **proofreading,** a final-stage cleaning up of typographical errors or search for missing commas and apostrophes. When accomplished writers use the word *revision,* they mean making principled, effective changes in the draft.

The act of revision involves mentally "stepping outside" your draft to assess its strengths and weaknesses as if you were reading it for the first time; deciding what parts need to be expanded, clarified, elaborated, illustrated, reworded, restructured, modified, or cut; and then actually making the changes. The kind of work you do during revision takes concentration, determination, and, at times, a sort of ruthlessness with cutting and reworking your prose.

7a Making major revisions

When you begin revising, concentrate on major concerns. A **major revision** is a large-scale change in your draft. For example, if you decide that your paper's tone is too sarcastic, you may end up deleting a negative paragraph or adding several paragraphs exploring more sensibly a position you had earlier trivialized. Or if you've left out a major point, you may need to draft some new material and change your conclusion.

When you make major revisions, you'll perform at least four large-scale operations on your draft: *redrafting, reorganizing, adding,* and *deleting.*

1 Redraft unworkable material

When you read and reread your rough draft carefully, thinking critically about its content, structure, tone, style, appeals to audience, and purpose, some parts may seem inappropriate, illogical, or unworkable. You may need to **redraft** these parts entirely.

S T R A T E G Y

Read through your draft as if you were seeing it for the first time. It helps if you have left your draft alone for a short while so that you can see it afresh. As you read, place a question mark next to sections that seem confusing or garbled. After you are done, go back to the parts you've marked, and bracket the specific places where your writing seems to lose its vitality, meaning, or style. Ask yourself what you are trying to accomplish. Then, without even looking at the draft, try again on a new sheet of paper to write what you mean.

7a
revise

Jessica White shared with her classmates a draft of her essay reflecting on her cheerleading experiences. They felt the first paragraph didn't capture much tension or excitement. After changing a few words, White realized she really needed to redraft the entire paragraph. She placed brackets around the weakest sentences to help her identify areas in need of revision.

ORIGINAL DRAFT

I was a cheerleading captain and I loved basketball. [I put a lot of work into my cheerleading season] We had a great team spirit between the cheerleaders and the teammates. [We stood behind our ? team from the beginning to end] We led our crowd to great enthusiasm and spirit which I believe had a terrific effect on our team.

REVISED DRAFT

There we were, a bunch of cheerleaders packed into Rebecca's car. Everyone's spirits were soaring; we had won the quarter-final game of the state basketball championship. It was a bitterly cold night, but none of us felt the chill. Surrounded by blaring music, we laughed, joked, and endlessly replayed the highlights of the game. Talk then turned to the upcoming finals. Would the team keep up its level of intensity? What were our chances of winning? What would we do if we lost?

2 Reorganize poorly arranged paragraphs or sections

Structural problems are common in early drafts. Often you find that you've written your way "into" your main point, discovering what you want to say in the process of drafting. It may be more graceful or logical to move that material into your introduction. Or you may recognize that two different paragraphs are making the same point and should be consolidated.

S T R A T E G Y

Number each paragraph in your draft. Then, on a clean piece of paper, explain in a phrase or a single sentence what each numbered paragraph says—its main point. When you've finished, look back at your list of statements. Could any paragraphs be consolidated? Are any paragraphs ineffectively ordered? Could you arrange the paragraphs or parts of the paper to yield a clearer, smoother flow of ideas?

7a
revise

Keyshawn Williams drafted a memo of recommendations from a committee looking for ways to cut his company's expenses and losses. Reading over his draft, he noticed that the parts seemed out of order. Background information came at the end, where it did little to prepare readers for the recommendation. The most important paragraphs—description of the problem and recommendation—came at the start, with little explanation or preparation.

Williams began revising by identifying the main points of the paragraphs—background, problem statement, recommendation. Having done this, he was able to arrange the paragraphs in a more logical order, from background to problem to recommendation. He also added the phrase *in addition* to help make the organization clearer to readers.

ORIGINAL

Over the past 12 months, the company has lost more than $33,000 in sales as a result of missed delivery dates. Moreover, we have suffered returns of defective merchandise amounting to a loss of $18,000 in revenue.

A consultant should help us uncover the causes for the production delays and problems. Retraining to correct these causes should help us avoid further losses in the future.

The committee has formed a subcommittee to investigate consultation firms and make a recommendation. *In addition,*

At our January 24 meeting, the Executive Committee recommended hiring a consultant to work with the Production Department to establish more cost- and time-efficient procedures.

the
~~The~~ committee suggested a budget of $25,000 to cover consultation and retraining costs.

REVISION

At our January 24 meeting, the Executive Committee recommended hiring a consultant to work with the Production Department to establish more cost- and time-efficient procedures.

The committee has formed a subcommittee to investigate consultation firms and make a recommendation. **In addition,** the committee suggested a budget of $25,000 to cover consultation and retraining costs.

Over the past 12 months, the company has lost more than $33,000 in sales as a result of missed delivery dates. Moreover, we have suffered returns of defective merchandise amounting to a loss of $18,000 in revenue.

A consultant should help us uncover the causes for the production delays and problems. Retraining to correct these causes should help us avoid further losses in the future.

**7a
revise**

Writer's Tip: Using a Computer

Make a backup copy of your early draft so you can keep an original version. Open the copy, and experiment with broad, global revisions. You can, for example, mark, cut, and move large chunks of your writing to see how major organizational changes might work. Any sections you cut can be pasted into an auxiliary file so that you can recover them if you decide you need them.

---

3 Add new material

Because you may write your first draft quickly, just to get it down on the page, you may find places where something is missing. Added material can enliven a dull description, clarify or extend a point, or provide essential information that your readers will need in order to make sense of your ideas.

S T R A T E G Y

As you reread your paper, look at how your sentences and paragraphs relate to each other. Mark any cases in which a paragraph doesn't connect clearly enough to the one before it. Also note any gaps (in information or detail) within and between paragraphs. Try making a detailing list if you need to add information to your draft (see 3a-4).

7a
revise

Looking over her draft Web page telling employees how to transfer to a new email system, Gina DiGiacomo noticed some gaps and filled them in.

Your new email address is listed below. It should be easy to remember **because it consists of the first four letters of your name and the last four numbers of your social security number.** Our company's address is the same: @Wishfactory.com. You may send your new address to people or discussion groups that send you frequent email, but you don't need to. **Our server will automatically forward any mail directed to your old address.**

DiGiacomo added an explanation of the address as a way of helping people remember it. She included mention of the forwarding process to help ease people's worries about lost mail.

4 Delete unnecessary or redundant material

Too much prose can be just as distracting or frustrating to a reader as too little. But cutting can be hard. Once your words are on the page, they seem almost sacred. Don't be afraid to slash away large portions of your draft if it's clear that they're unnecessary, distracting, illogical, or redundant.

S T R A T E G Y

Reread your draft as if an editor has accepted it for publication in a magazine with the stipulation that you trim at least ten percent. What can you cut? Could some paragraphs be eliminated altogether, perhaps by merging just the essential material from them into another paragraph?

Jim Noka decided to cut two sentences from a petition he was preparing because they didn't add important information or make the petition more persuasive.

At twenty-four stories and six apartments per floor, Regency Towers will cast a long, wide shadow over Coulter Park for much of the day. ~~The building will be quite tall and very wide.~~ From ten to four o'clock most days, the infant and toddler play area will be darkened, depriving both parents and children of a sun-filled playtime. Late in the afternoon the shadow will cut across the baseball diamond. Players will lose track of swiftly thrown pitches and balls hit directly at them. ~~This could be dangerous.~~ People will not want to spend their leisure time at the park.

7a
revise

Exercise 1

A. Compare the following first-draft and revised versions of Maureen Lagasse's paper on racism. Describe the nature of Lagasse's changes—did she redraft, reorganize, add, or cut? What do you think motivated her revisions?

FIRST DRAFT

In setting out to write this paper my concept to explain was racism, and in doing some reading and thinking, I realized that racism can't be defined or explained in one simple definition. In the dictionary the definition of racism is "the practice of racial discrimination or segregation, etc." Although this is what racism is, this definition doesn't fully explain racism. What exactly are races, and how do people actually develop these discriminations against people of different races?

REVISED DRAFT

Have you ever wondered why people view interracial relationships as unacceptable? Have you wondered whether there really is a difference between you and someone of another race? In the dictionary the definition of racism is "the practice of racial discrimination or segregation." Although this is a legitimate definition, it doesn't fully explain racism.

B. In a small group, compare your responses to Exercise 1A. Were there any revisions you didn't notice? What other major revisions might you suggest for Lagasse's first paragraph?

Did You Know?

In a study of skilled versus unskilled writers, the skilled writers spent more of their time in various kinds of revision than the unskilled writers, who tended not to look back over their drafts when they had finished writing them. This suggests that, contrary to popular myths about writing, better writers spend *more* of their time, not less, revising.

Nancy Sommers, "Revision Strategies of Student Writers and Experienced Writers," *College Composition and Communication* 31 (1980): 378–88.

7b Making minor revisions

Minor revisions are fairly small changes, mostly in the individual sentences of your prose. Like major revisions, minor revisions involve redrafting, reorganizing, adding, and cutting, but now you have the goal of refining and polishing. Most minor revisions are made for three reasons: *sense* (how clear and understandable is your prose?), *style* (how elegant and smooth is your prose?), and *economy* (how much can you say in the least space?).

1 Revise for sense

Too full an immersion in your writing can sometimes make you forget what your reader *doesn't* know, and that can lead to illogical, contradictory, or puzzling statements.

S T R A T E G Y

Read each sentence of your paper individually and test its clarity: does the statement *make sense* in the context of the paper? Don't let your mind float back into your own construction of ideas; instead, imagine yourself as your intended reader. If you have peer readers, ask them to place question marks next to any statement or group of statements they find confusing or garbled.

---

2 Revise for style

When you revise for style, you're concerned with the way your prose "sounds"—that is, with its rhythm, complexity, and diction or word choice (see 28b). When you read a rough draft, some parts will usually sound better to you than others. Use your intuition as a reader.

Many workplaces have their own stylistic conventions. As a new employee, you will need to learn the "house style" or "company style."

S T R A T E G Y

Place an asterisk in the margin next to any paragraph that seems to need polishing. Then go back to the first paragraph you marked and code each sentence according to what you feel about it: + (positive), ✓ (neutral), − (negative), ? (unsure). Now concentrate on revising the sentences you do not like in that paragraph. Move on to revising the questionable sentences. Reread the entire paragraph. When you are satisfied, go to the next paragraph you marked with an asterisk. If you're still uncertain about any sentences, ask peer readers for their impressions. *When in doubt, try an alternative.*

7b
revise

In his report on the environmentally threatened wild mustangs of Nevada, Paul Tichey placed an asterisk next to a paragraph he had already revised for sense. Something still bothered him about the paragraph, so he looked carefully at each sentence. Tichey liked the clarity of his revision, but the end of his new sentence seemed awkward because so many words began with a *d* ("dehydration and death during the duration of the drought"). He also thought that "during the duration" seemed redundant. Here's his further revision.

The Air Force, which was partly responsible for the demise of the wild mustangs on the Tonopah missile range, has now joined forces with the Bureau of Land Management and a group of wild-horse preservationists to help save the mustangs from **fatal** dehydration and death during the duration of the drought. **while the drought persists.**

3 Revise for economy

To revise for economy, read your writing and think about what you can cut from it *without causing it to lose sense or coherence.* In the middle of Tichey's paper, one paragraph included too much material. He decided that half of it could be cut.

SECOND DRAFT

A serious problem confronting groups who want to manage wild mustangs on military sites in Nevada is the relative inaccessibility of the sites, since many require security passes or are fenced off, and environmentalists can't come and go as they please, as they can on public or even some private land. It's simply harder to study or help horses on restricted military installations. Open rangeland has easier access, and inspectors can simply move in and out at will.

THIRD DRAFT

Restricted access to Nevada military sites presents a serious obstacle to successful horse management. In contrast to open rangeland, where inspectors can come and go as they please, military sites are often fenced off and require security clearance.

In the revised paragraph, Tichey said essentially the same thing in 38 words that he had said before in 78—a cut of over 50 percent! Note, however, that he had to reword the sentences remaining after his first cuts.

Exercise 2

A. Examine the following paragraphs from Anita Jackson's paper on Buddhism. Then characterize the sorts of minor revisions Jackson made. Did she revise for sense, style, or economy? What sorts of changes did she make?

EARLY DRAFT

The man who became the first Buddha was named Siddhartha. Siddhartha was a prince in northern India who lived in a large palace. His father didn't allow him outside the palace because he wanted to spare Siddhartha from the miseries of the world.

Siddhartha became curious and one day he went riding outside the palace. What he saw would forever change his life and influence the lives of many thereafter. That which Siddhartha saw has since been named the Four Sights.

REVISED DRAFT

The man who became the first Buddha was Siddhartha, a pampered prince of northern India who lived in a lavish palace. Yet for all his riches his father would not allow him to venture beyond the castle walls because he wanted to spare Siddhartha the miseries of life. Siddhartha grew extremely curious about the outside world and one day went riding beyond the limits of the palace. What he saw that day would forever change his life and influence the lives of many thereafter.

What Siddhartha saw has since been named the Four Sights.

 B. In a small group, compare your analyses of Jackson's revisions. How successful were her changes? Why?

7C Revising collaboratively

Professional writers rarely produce a good piece of writing without getting responses from many readers along the way. Follow their lead: *make sure to ask at least one person you respect to read your papers and give you some honest feedback, and promise you'll do the same in return.* Here are some tips for getting and giving helpful feedback in **collaborative revision.**

1 Respond helpfully

When you're reading someone else's writing in order to offer constructive criticism, remember that your most helpful role is not as proofreader or editor but as real, warm-blooded *reader.* But because you may not be a part of the intended audience for your partner's work, you need to get some background information before you start.

- Find out the writer's purpose for the piece. What is the writer trying to accomplish? What sort of paper is this?
- Who is the writer's intended reader?
- What are the writer's main concerns at this point? What would the writer most like to find out from you?

Once you have reasonable answers to these questions, read the paper through, jotting down some comments in the margins and keeping track of your thoughts and impressions as a reader.

When you convey your responses to your partner, remember that you'll need to balance praise with helpful criticism. Don't simply say "I liked it. It was really good," or give directions like "You should move this paragraph up to page 3." Instead, offer diplomatic advice; ask, "What would happen if you moved this paragraph?" or suggest, "I wonder whether that paragraph would fit better on page 3."

2 Make the most of response

Remember, you're not out to collect a dozen pats on the back for a job well done; you want the most useful, constructive commentary you can get from astute, honest readers. This will mean accepting even hard-hitting reactions and suggestions with grace and diplomacy. If you react defensively to a peer reader's criticism, that person is not likely to keep giving you much feedback. If a reader questions something you especially like in your draft, *remember that no one can force you to make a change*. You have the final say.

Take note of these tips.

7c
collab

- Give your readers a list of specific concerns you have about your draft. What do you want them to comment on? tone? style? structure? logic?
- Keep your apologies to a minimum. You may feel anxious about sharing a first draft with your classmates, but as writers you're all facing the same situation.
- If you and your group members are short on time, consider giving them each an inexpensive cassette tape for their reactions. You'll get far more response than if you ask for something in writing. A group meeting, of course, is always preferable. If all of you are working on papers at the same time, forming a writer's group and spending time on each of your drafts can be an especially valuable experience.
- Using your readers' responses, *spend some time planning your changes*. If no one liked the description of your grandmother, do you want to change it? If so, how? Do you want to delete it completely, or find another way to describe her, or show what she's like by portraying her more completely in the action of your narrative? A few minutes planning your revisions may save you lots of time experimenting.

Writer's Tip

Give names to your drafts: "Hamlet.d1," "Hamlet.d2," and "Hamlet.fin" for your first, second, and final drafts. Make collaborative suggestions on a computer file by using bold-face and brackets within the text, as in this example:

Alexander the Great was tutored by one of the world's greatest philosophers. **[Who?]** However, he learned military strategy from his father, Philip of Macedonia.

---

3 Workplace collaboration

Collaborative revision is often the norm outside the school setting. However, workplace collaboration may be somewhat different from sharing your draft with classmates.

- In the workplace, many people will have a stake in your text. They are more likely than fellow students to be willing—even eager—to review it for you.
- Supervisors, in particular, may be direct and insistent about changes they suggest.
- Since, in many workplaces, individuals share experiences, you will want to solicit responses from individuals with a range of perspectives and with different kinds of knowledge about your topic or problem.

7c collab ESL

ESL Advice: Revising with a Peer Reader

If you are worried about your grammar or spelling, you might want to review these items quickly before sharing your rough draft. Look for a peer reader who is willing to ignore these details. Ask this reader to focus on specific issues (such as the order or development of your ideas) or on problems you often have in your papers (such as weak first paragraphs). Consider sharing your draft with several readers, including native speakers of English, to get a range of responses.

Exercise 3

A. If you haven't done so, form a small revision group, and circulate rough drafts of your papers in progress. Using the tips in this section as well as the techniques for major and minor revision described in 7a and 7b, comment on your partners' drafts. Then meet in a revision group to discuss your drafts. Keep track of the group's comments on your own paper.

B. Analyze your group experience. What was helpful? What comments will lead (or have led) to specific revisions? What comments did you choose not to act on? Why?

7d Revising: Paper in progress

After freewriting several paragraphs about items on her list of particulars, Jessica DiGregorio was prepared to write the following rough draft of her paper about her father's sports contract.

First Draft of Sports Contract Paper

Jessica DiGregorio

A few days ago I decided to go through the musty old cedar chest in my living room and dug up some of the old documents that I had read years earlier. I came across the Contract marked NBA (National Basketball Association) that I had looked at before, but remembered that it was very confusing. It contained words such as: hereunder, however, notwithstanding, and hereof, but when I read this over for the second time it made me realize that my father, for a total of five years was bound to this document, and chose to live his life according to what it had said. This twelve-page "AGREEMENT" caught my attention from the time I was young, but it did not make sense to me until now.

When I was younger I never took interest in my father's past mainly because I was tired of hearing people telling me "Did you know your father was the best basketball player?!" and "If you could have seen him play!" I used to just smile and not say anything because I never thought my father could be an athlete as good as Michael Jordan or Larry Bird. My perspective on his basketball career changed as I got older, I became interested in watching videos of him and asked him questions on what it was like to be a basketball legend.

"CLUB DOES HEREBY EMPLOY PLAYER AS

A SKILLED BASKETBALL PLAYER"

This statement which was said on the first page
of his contract set the setting for all of the other
statements that followed. Since the NBA decided that
my father was good enough to play the sport, a
contract was made to fit the needs of both the Club
(the Buffalo Braves) and the Player (my father).
After my father read the first line he was honored
and knew that all of his hard work and determination
had paid off. The Club which drafted him in 1973
knew that he was a person of great charisma and
talent including basketball legend Red Auerbach.
This contract was the beginning of a five-year long
agreement which was taken very seriously.

"HE WILL TO THE BEST OF HIS ABILITY MAINTAIN

HIMSELF IN PHYSICAL CONDITION SUFFICIENT

TO PLAY SKILLED BASKETBALL"

This rule stated in the contract meant that my
father had to keep himself fit for the next five
years, and not allow himself to overindulge in bad
habits. The Club made up this rule to insure
themselves that they were signing someone who was
serious about the game. This meant that my father
had to stay physically fit and never stop playing
basketball. He was advised to stay clear of skiing,
ice-skating, or any other strenuous activity not
related to basketball so that he would not get
injured. If my father, or any other player disobeyed
this part of the contract it stated that, "the club
shall have the right to suspend the player for a

**7d
collab**

period of one week . . . and will be examined by a physician."

"IN THE EVENT OF THE DEATH OF THE PLAYER PRIOR
TO THE TERMINATION OF ANY SEASON . . .
THE CLUB SHALL PAY TO THE PLAYER'S HEIRS . . ."

7d
collab

This particular part of the contract interested me the most. It stated that if my father had died, all of the money which was already promised to my father within the contract went to my mother. This was very important to my father since my mother was a housewife and stayed home with my older sisters. The Club added this statement to the contract to give the player's family the proper amount of financial help after the loss of their loved one. Basically after the death of a player the money which was promised throughout the five year term is terminated and the family only received what the player lived for. If there was to be a breach in the contract then lawyers would have had to be appointed to the family of the deceased, and determining where money goes can be a sticky situation if it is not written down and documented properly.

"THE CLUB SHALL HAVE THE OPTION IN ITS SOLE
DISCRETION TO TERMINATE THIS AGREEMENT
AND RENDER IT NULL AND VOID"

This final part in this contract stated that the Club had the final say in any of the decisions that would have come along. This meant my father had to follow all of the requirements made within the document which he had signed. If he or anyone else did not follow any of the regulations, then they

would have no say if their contract was to be null
and void. This left the final power up to the Club
and gave them the upper hand in everything that
dealt with the players. This was an important part
of his contract because it allowed the Club to
demonstrate how powerful it really was in the make
or break of a person's professional basketball
career.

Contracts and legal documents shape our
everyday life. Some people underestimate the power
of legal documents which bind and connect us to
different things. A single piece of paper can
determine where we live or how we live our lives.
The contract which bound my father to the NBA shaped
his life in a major way. For five years he lived by
rules and regulations created by the Club to which
he belonged. He became a basketball legend and lives
in the memories of some people, but to me he is just
my dad.

7d
collab

Exercise 4

 A. Study DiGregorio's first draft. Assuming that she has drafted with a loose structure in mind, how would you describe that structure? What is your impression of the draft as a whole, and what suggestions would you make for its organization and its supporting points relative to the main goal of examining her father's NBA contract?

 B. In a small group, compare your analyses of DiGregorio's first draft, and try to reach some consensus about what she should focus on in her revision.

CHAPTER

8

Focusing, Linking, and Developing Paragraphs

Every time you begin a new **paragraph,** you send a signal to readers: you tell them to watch for a shift in topic, a different perspective, or a special emphasis. You make promises, too: you will develop ideas and details in ways appropriate to your writing task, and you'll link sentences and ideas in ways that make their relationships clear.

Whether you're writing a short documented essay for a history class, a business letter at work, or a grant proposal for the soccer team you coach, you need to create paragraphs with a clear *focus (unity), coherence* among sentences, and adequate *development* of ideas and content. If you fail to do these things for your readers, they may have trouble deciding what a paragraph is about and following your reasoning from sentence to sentence, as in this example.

> The caffeine in popular beverages comes from natural sources: coffee beans (coffee), coca leaves (hot chocolate), tea leaves (tea), evergreen leaves (maté), and kola nuts (colas). Tea comes from the leaves of bushes native to Asia. Maté comes from a South American shrub similar to holly. More caffeine is found in coffee or tea than in maté. Tea and maté are made in similar ways except that the water for maté is heated in a gourd. People often drink the beverage through a straw stuck into the gourd. In Paraguay, Argentina, Chile, and the southern regions of Brazil, many people find refreshment in a maté-filled gourd.
>
> **READER'S REACTION:** What is the topic of this paragraph: tea and coffee? caffeine? caffeinated beverages? maté? Every time one sentence focuses on a topic, the next sentence suddenly changes direction.

By making the relationship among paragraphs clear, you can help readers keep track of a line of argument or the logic of an explanation.

8a Recognizing and revising paragraph focus

By making a paragraph's topic, main idea, or perspective evident and by maintaining this focus throughout, you can create a paragraph that is focused or unified. A **focused paragraph** is effective because it doesn't confuse or mislead readers by straying into unrelated or loosely related details and statements. A **unified paragraph** is one in which all the sentences are clearly and directly related to the main idea, as in the following selection.

Topic and main idea

Definition of *values*

Supporting evidence

Look at the future

Values are changing, too. Solid majorities of both women *and* men now believe that when a woman works for pay, household responsibilities should be shared. The idea that a woman's hours of employment are irrelevant for the distribution of household work no longer holds the power it once did. Of course, old habits die hard and many men who "believe" in sharing housework are not actually willing to take on much of this often-unrewarding work. Twenty-four percent of employed wives are still saddled with *all* the household work, and an additional 42 percent do "the bulk" of it. However, things are improving, especially among young people. It is likely that the future holds more, not less, household equality.

—JULIET SCHOR, *The Overworked American*

Schor unifies this paragraph by making sure all its parts develop and support the main idea: people are beginning to view housework as a responsibility shared by women and men.

STRATEGY

Use the following questions to help identify unfocused paragraphs and to guide your revisions.

- *What is my main point (or topic) in this paragraph?*
  For a paragraph lacking a central theme, decide on a focus.
- *How many different topics does this paragraph cover?*
  For a paragraph with many possible centers of interest, decide which one you will emphasize.
- *Have I announced my focus to readers? where? how?*
  Look for sentences or phrases announcing the focus or clearly implying it. Add such statements if necessary.
- *Do statements in the paragraph elaborate on the main idea? Do details fit within the topic?*
  Look for material not directly related to a paragraph's focus, and decide whether it undermines the unity or adds interesting variety.

8b Revising for focus

To bring focus to a paragraph, you need to decide what you want the paragraph to do for readers. Do you want it to announce and explain your conclusion or recommendation? Do you want it to explain a concept or process? Do you want it to support your arguments on an issue?

You can often decide on a paragraph's focus by paying attention to the needs and expectations of the community of readers you're addressing. In work settings, readers will expect paragraphs to announce and explain a decision, to analyze the elements of a problem, or to offer specific recommendations. In academic settings, paragraphs often focus on presenting an interpretation or conclusion and offering supporting evidence. In public settings, paragraphs may provide reasons for agreeing with the writer's point of view. By asking yourself what a paragraph needs to do for your readers, you can often arrive at a focus. Once you have done so, consider announcing it to readers in a topic sentence.

One way to keep a paragraph focused as you write and to help readers recognize that focus is to state your topic and your main idea or perspective in a single sentence, a **topic sentence.** As you write, you can use a topic sentence as the focal point for the other sentences in a paragraph. When you revise, you can often easily improve an unfocused paragraph by adding a topic sentence, placing it in an effective position in the paragraph.

1 Using a topic sentence at the beginning

When you want readers to grasp the point of a paragraph right away, state it in a topic sentence at the beginning. In the following paragraph, the author uses the topic-sentence-first strategy to comment on the art of comedy.

Topic sentence When writing jokes, it's a good idea to avoid vague generalizations. Don't just talk about "fruit" when you can talk about "an apple." Strong writing creates a single image for

Supporting
example everyone in the crowd, each person imagining the same thing. But when you say "fruit," people are either imagining several different kinds of fruit or they aren't really thinking of anything in particular, and both things can significantly reduce their emotional investment in the joke. But when you say "an apple," everyone has a clear picture, and thus a feeling.

—JAY SANKEY, "Zen and the Art of Stand-Up Comedy"

2 Using a topic sentence plus a limiting or clarifying sentence

If you are covering a broad topic or offering much detailed information, you can give a paragraph a sharper focus by creating a **limiting** or **clarifying sentence** (or two) following the topic sentence. The added sentence tells readers which specific aspects of the topic you will discuss or clarifies your point of view.

Topic sentence   Children on soap operas are secondary. Because they
Limiting or   serve largely as foils for the adult characters, their develop-
clarifying   ment does not follow the slow, steady pattern of the rest of
sentence   the action. Their growth is marked by a series of sudden and unsettling metamorphoses as new and older juvenile actors assume the role. On Tuesday, little Terence is cooing in his cradle . . . then one day he again emerges from the off-camera cocoon transformed into a full-fledged adult, with all the rights, privileges, pain, and perfidy of that elite corps. And so the cycle continues.

—Donna Woolfolk Cross, *Sin, Suffer, and Repent*

8b
¶ foc

3 Using a topic sentence at the end

A topic sentence at the end of a paragraph can summarize or draw conclusions from the information that comes before. This strategy can show how your perspective grows logically from the evidence, and it can tie together details with a forceful generalization.

. . . A few years ago, at an international conference held in an exotic and luxurious setting, a prestigious professor invited me to his room for what he said would be an intellectual discussion on matters of theoretical importance . . . But only minutes into the conversation—held in all-too-adjacent chairs—it emerged that he was interested in something more substantial than a meeting of minds. . . . Every time his comments took a lecherous turn, I chattered distractingly; every time his hand found its way to my knee, I returned it as if it were something he had misplaced. This went on for an unconscionable period (as much as 20 minutes); then there was a minor scuffle, a dash for the door, and I was out—with nothing violated
Topic sentence but my self-esteem. I, a full-grown feminist, conversant with such matters as rape crisis counseling and sexual harassment at the workplace, had behaved like a ninny—or, as I now understand it, like a lady.

—Barbara Ehrenreich, "What I've Learned from Men"

ESL Advice: Adjusting to Paragraph Conventions

In English, readers expect paragraphs to have a specific focus and often look to a topic sentence for guidance. In other languages, however, paragraph conventions can take quite different forms. For example, Hindi paragraphs need not focus on a sharply defined topic, do not require a clear topic sentence, and often contain discussion of loosely related ideas or information. Paragraphs in other languages, such as Thai, also differ from English paragraphs. Consequently, become familiar with paragraph conventions as you learn to write in a second language.

—Robert Bickner and Patcharin Peyasantiwong, "Cultural Variation in Reflective Writing," and Yamuna Kachru, "Writers in Hindi and English," *Writing Across Languages and Cultures,* ed. Alan C. Purves (Newbury Park: Sage, 1988) 160–74, 109–37.

4 Implying rather than stating a topic sentence

At times, the main point is so clear that you can rely on readers to recognize it without a topic statement. Omitting a topic statement is useful when you don't want to state a very obvious point or when an explicit statement might distract from examples and details. This strategy is also helpful when a topic clearly continues for more than one paragraph.

Whenever we went to my grandfather's house, he would lead the three of us to the closet stocked with toys, saying "I bought these especially for you" as his crystal blue eyes twinkled. I can remember playing with the toys outside on the lawn and running through the sprinkler he set up for me and my brothers on sunny days. Just when we started getting tired and hot, he would call us in for a lunch of hot dogs or tuna sandwiches with plenty of potato chips and soda pop. And there were always popsicles for dessert.

—Carey Braun, College Student

Reader's Reaction: **Your grandfather seems like a person who understands children and knows how to make them feel cared for and loved.**

Writer's Tip

You can often trace the explanation or argument quickly by scanning paragraphs and reading just the topic sentences. Look at your own draft essays this way to check for paragraphs with missing, misleading, or inadequate topic sentences. When you find such paragraphs, decide whether they also need revision for focus. In addition, this is a good way to identify paragraphs that take the discussion in misleading or irrelevant directions.

Exercise 1

A. Identify any topic sentence and clarifying or limiting sentence in the following paragraph. Analyze how the paragraph makes use of these sentences to create focus and emphasis.

> Kids are in the mall not only in the passive role of shoppers—they also work there, especially as fast-food outlets infiltrate the mall's enclosure. There they learn how to hold a job and take responsibility, but still within the same value context. When *CBS Reports* went to Oak Park Mall in suburban Kansas City, Kansas, to tape part of the hour-long consideration of the mall, "After the Dream Comes True," they interviewed a teenaged girl who worked in a fast-food outlet there. In a sequence that didn't make the final program, she described the major goal of her present life, which was to perfect the curl on top of the ice-cream cones that were her store's specialty. If she could do that, she would be moved from the lowly soft-drink dispenser to the more prestigious ice-cream division, the curl on top of the status ladder at her restaurant. These are the achievements that are important at the mall.
>
> —WILLIAM SEVERINI KOWINSKI, "Kids in the Mall: Growing Up Controlled"

B. After you have examined the paragraph in Exercise 1A to see how it uses topic, clarifying, or limiting sentences for focus and emphasis, work in a group to reach consensus on the ways the paragraph employs these strategies.

8C Recognizing and revising paragraph coherence

When your readers can move from sentence to sentence within a paragraph without any trouble following your train of thought or explanation, the paragraph displays **coherence.** Lack of coherence means abrupt changes in topic or idea from sentence to sentence. It means a lack of transitions or other devices to guide readers from statement to statement. A paragraph like the following is hard for readers to understand because it offers them little guidance.

LACKS COHERENCE

> Captain James Cook discovered the island of Hawaii in 1779. Mauna Kea, on Hawaii, is the tallest mountain in the Pacific. Cook might have noticed the many mountains on the island as he sailed into Kealakekua Bay. The island also has five major volcanoes. Mauna Loa, another mountain on the island, is a dormant volcano that last erupted

8c
¶ coh

in 1984. Kilauea is the most active volcano on earth. It continues to enlarge the land that makes up this largest island in the Hawaiian chain. The volcano sends forth lava continuously.

READER'S REACTION: This paragraph jumps from sentence to sentence without saying much about the way the ideas and details fit together. It's just hard to read and remember.

8d
¶ coh

S T R A T E G Y

Use the following questions to see whether your paragraphs create adequate coherence for readers.

- Does the paragraph highlight and repeat words naming the topic and main points?
- Do transition words alert readers to relationships between sentences?
- Do parallel words and structures highlight similar or related ideas?
- Do sentence beginnings identify a topic and stick to it?

8d Revising for coherence

1 Repeating words and phrases

By repeating words and phrases that refer to your topic and main point, you keep readers aware of a paragraph's focus and link sentence to sentence. Synonyms and related words can also be part of a pattern of effective repetition, as in the following paragraph.

"Childhood is the kingdom where nobody dies" is a line, from the poem by Edna St. Vincent Millay, that has stuck in my mind ever since I first read it, when I was in fact **a child** and **nobody died.** Of course **people did die,** but **they** were either very old or **died** unusual **deaths, died** while rafting on the Stanislaus or loading a shotgun or doing 95 drunk: **death** was construed as either a "blessing" or an exceptional case, the dramatic instance on which **someone else's** (never **our own**) story turned. Illness, in that **kingdom** where I and **most people** I knew lingered long past **childhood,** proved self-limiting. Fever of unknown etiology signaled only the indulgence of a week in bed. Chest pains, investigated, revealed hypochondria.   —JOAN DIDION, "After Henry"

Writer's Tip

To use repeated words to link sentences in a paragraph, place the words in prominent positions, often near the beginning or end of sentences. When you bury repetition in the middle of a sentence, its effect is weakened.

According to recent research, **people married for a long time** often develop similar **facial features. Younger couples** display only chance resemblances between their **faces.** Because **they** share emotions for many years, however, most **older couples** develop similar **expressions.**

2 Supplying transitions

You can use **transitional expressions,** statements, and paragraphs to alert readers to relationships among sentences and paragraphs and to highlight a paragraph's design and purpose.

S T R A T E G Y

Think about the possible connections among the ideas and information you are discussing; then decide which connections you wish to highlight. Draw on the following techniques to link paragraphs in ways that emphasize connections and that call attention to your line of reasoning.

- Use transitional words and phrases
- Announce your purpose
- Provide boundary statements
- Create transition paragraphs

Note how the use of transitions makes the following paragraph easy to read.

Many people still consider the choice of college the most important career decision you can make. **These days, however,** graduate school is the most important choice **because** the competition for all kinds of jobs has gotten fiercer. **For example,** business positions at the entry level often go to people with MBAs and law degrees. **In addition,** many good jobs require advanced training and skills. **Moreover,** employers pay attention **not only** to the presence of an advanced degree on your résumé **but also** to the program of study **and** the quality of the school. **Therefore,** think about going to graduate school, **and** choose your school carefully.

You can use a direct or an indirect statement to announce your purpose and organization near the beginning of a new section and to help readers anticipate the line of reasoning you will use to develop and support ideas.

<table>
<tr>
<td>**DIRECT STATEMENT**</td>
<td>The next section looks at the new generation of situation comedies that has taken over the top of the ratings chart in the last two years.</td>
</tr>
<tr>
<td>**INDIRECT STATEMENT**</td>
<td>Advertisers have developed sophisticated ways to identify the tastes, purchasing power, and needs of consumers. Each of these tactics needs to be examined in detail.</td>
</tr>
</table>

To help present detailed reasoning or information, consider opening paragraphs with a **boundary statement**—a sentence at the start of a paragraph that acts as a bridge from the paragraph before. A boundary statement begins with a reminder of material covered in the preceding paragraph (or paragraphs). It then presents the topic sentence of the paragraph to come. For example, in the following sentence the writer briefly mentions the subject he has just finished discussing and then highlights the main point of the paragraph itself.

> **The rise of the Sunbelt** in recent years has been accompanied by **the decline of rural America.**
>
> —BRAD EDMONDSON, "Making Yourself at Home"

In short essays, simple transitions or boundary statements generally provide adequate guidance for readers. In longer essays or complicated discussions, you may need to give readers extra guidance with one- or two-sentence transition paragraphs. Brief transition paragraphs perform the same functions as transitional expressions and statements.

3 Using parallel structure

You can link elements within a paragraph by using **parallelism**—repeating the same grammatical structures to highlight similar or related ideas (see also 26c). Note how the parallel words and phrases in the following paragraph create coherence.

> I have a place on the West Coast **where** my relatives still farm, **where I heard** the stories of feuds and backbiting, and **where I saw** that people **survived and flourished** because fundamentally

Transitional Expressions	
TIME AND SEQUENCE	next, later, after, while, meanwhile, immediately, somewhat earlier, first, second, third (firstly, secondly, thirdly), shortly, thereafter, in the future, over the next two days, concurrently, subsequently, as long as, soon, since, finally, last, at that time, as soon as
COMPARISON	likewise, similarly, also, again, in the same manner, in comparison
CONTRAST	in contrast, on one hand . . . on the other hand, however, although, even though, still, yet, but, nevertheless, conversely, at the same time, regardless, despite
EXAMPLES	for example, for instance, such as, specifically, thus, to illustrate, namely
CAUSE AND EFFECT	as a result, consequently, since, accordingly, if . . . then, is due to this, for this reason, as a consequence of
PLACE	next to, above, behind, beyond, near, across from, to the right, here, there, in the foreground, in the background, in between, opposite
ADDITION	and, too, moreover, in addition, besides, furthermore, next, also, finally
CONCESSION	of course, naturally, it may be the case that, granted, it is true that, certainly
CONCLUSION	in conclusion, in short, as a result, as I have demonstrated, as the data show
REPETITION	to repeat, in other words, once again, as I said earlier
SUMMARY	on the whole, to sum up, in short, to summarize, therefore

8d
¶ coh

they **trusted and relied** upon one another. **A death in the family** is not just **a death in a family;** it is a **death in the community. I saw people** help each other with money, materials, labor, attention, and time. **I saw men** gather once a year, without fail, to clean the grounds of a ninety-year-old woman who had helped the community **before, during,** and **after** the war. **I saw her** remembering them with birthday cards sent to each of their children.

—KESAYA E. NODA, "Growing Up Asian in America"

Exercise 2

A. In the following paragraph, increase coherence and readability by repeating words, adding transitions, using parallel structures, and making any other changes necessary.

> Heart attacks have many causes. Some heart attacks occur because a blood clot closes a coronary artery. Sometimes a mass of fatty substances (plaque) has the same effect. Heart attacks with these causes are the most frequent. A spasm in an artery may also close it and prevent blood from reaching the heart. Smoking, hypertension, and diabetes can create conditions that keep blood from reaching the heart. The blood-starved tissue may die. This will cause permanent damage to the heart's ability to pump blood. A dead portion of the heart is called a myocardial infarction.

B. Copy a paragraph from one of your own essays, scrambling the order of the sentences, and then exchange scrambled paragraphs with a fellow student. Rewrite and strengthen your partner's paragraph by putting the sentences in the most effective order and revising to increase coherence among sentences.

8e Recognizing and revising paragraph development

Suppose you encountered the following paragraph in an essay on pets. How would you react?

> Dogs and cats make wonderful pets, but certainly not trendy ones. Exotic animals of all kinds, including Vietnamese pot-bellied pigs and llamas, have begun appearing in living rooms and backyards.

You would probably respond that the paragraph has a clear main point and a potentially interesting example but seems skimpy and uninteresting. Without supporting details, the paragraph is neither informative nor convincing. **Paragraph development** provides the examples, facts, concrete details, explanatory statements, or supporting arguments that make a paragraph informative and support your ideas and opinions, as in this fully developed version of the paragraph.

Topic sentence   Dogs and cats make wonderful pets, but certainly not trendy ones. Exotic animals of all kinds, including Vietnamese pot-bellied pigs and llamas, have begun appearing

Brief examples in living rooms and backyards. About the size of beagles, the pigs are affectionate and easy to care for. Llamas require more room and care, but these gentle animals are now in demand as well—at least among people who can afford the one or two thousand dollars needed to buy one. Ferrets, Amazon parrots, pygmy goats, and dwarf rabbits have been finding places in fashionable homes as well. People who want to keep well ahead of the crowd might consider Old World chameleons or dart-poison frogs (the source of poison for blowdarts used by jungle hunters).

1 Developing paragraphs with details

The details of how you dangled from the sheer rock face when your climbing equipment failed may thrill the readers of your essay in an outdoor magazine. They'll look for long paragraphs filled with specifics. The equipment recall announcement you write for the Consumer Product Safety Commission will probably offer more compact paragraphs with relevant statistics, specific warnings, and product identifying information. Your memo for the equipment company would probably contain several concise paragraphs, each with the precise information needed to answer some key questions: How did the equipment fail? Why did it fail? How can we correct the problem?

Fully developed paragraphs give readers an in-depth picture of a subject when this is necessary for the purpose and context of the writing. Your readers will usually expect two kinds of statements in a paragraph: those presenting ideas (including your own conclusions) and those presenting information. Beyond this, however, you have many choices, depending on what you want a paragraph to do.

S T R A T E G Y

As you write and revise, it's easy to forget how many different options you have for developing a paragraph's content. Use this checklist to remember your options.

- **Examples.** Use brief, specific examples or an extended, detailed example.
- **Concrete Details.** Re-create sights, sounds, tastes, smells, movements, and sensations of touch.
- **Facts and Statistics.** Offer precise data from your own field research or from authoritative sources, perhaps in numerical form. Summarize the results or quote your sources. Facts and statistics are the kinds of evidence many readers consider convincing proof of generalizations and opinions. They also help readers understand complicated social and natural phenomena.

- **Summaries.** Summarize other people's opinions, conclusions, or explanations (46c-1). Tell how they agree with and support your conclusions. Or point out their omissions and weaknesses as a way of arguing for your own conclusions or insights.
- **Quotations.** Use statements you have gathered from field, electronic, or library research (47c-1) as ways of suporting your conclusions or as ways of making your discussion more dramatic and memorable.

8e
¶ dev

Rely on examples. Examples are among the most widely used and most effective strategies for paragraph development. Whether brief or extended, examples help you clarify difficult concepts, provide good reasons for readers to agree with your opinion, or show how widespread a phenomenon is. Extended examples can draw readers into an event and create emotional responses to it. Brief examples can play important roles, especially in work and public settings where readers will expect you to show that your opinions and recommendations are justified but will have little patience for long explanations. Brief examples can be particularly effective when blended with facts and statistics, as in this excerpt from a newsletter published by the Consumer Product Safety Commission.

> All kinds of products have been included in the fast-track recalls. For example, a major manufacturer recently recalled tens of thousands of humidifiers that could potentially overheat or catch fire. A leading manufacturer of children's products recalled tens of thousands of baby monitors that could smoke and flame. A prominent clothing retailer recalled more than 100,000 children's jackets with zipper pulls containing unacceptable levels of lead. A well-known company recalled tens of thousands of gas grills because a defective hose could leak gas or cause fires.
>
> —"Fast-Track Recalls," *Consumer Product Safety Review*

Interpret for your readers. When you develop a paragraph with examples, details, facts, and statistics, you can make them more persuasive and easier to understand by providing interpretive statements of your own to link them to a paragraph's main point.

> Breakfast cereals can differ radically in serving size even though most cereal boxes define a single serving in the same way, as a one-ounce portion. A one-ounce serving of Cheerios is 1¼ cup, for example, while a one-ounce serving of Quaker 100% Natural Cereal is ¼ cup. Weight

Interpretive statement   measurements can disguise the differences between products; measurement by volume reveals the contrasts. For dieters, volume can be as important a measure as the number of calories per serving because the volume indicates how much cereal you will have to appease your appetite: two bites or a bowlful.   —SARA BRILLIANT, College Student

Exercise 3

A. First, examine the paragraph in Exercise 2A and identify the various strategies of development used by the writer. Which seem particularly effective, and why? Which, if any, seem ineffective?

Next, for each of the following topic sentences, explain which kind or kinds of supporting information (examples, concrete details, facts and statistics, or supporting statements) you believe would create the most effective paragraph.

1. The fall promotional campaign increased sales of our October and November issues.
2. Upgrading our computer software would result in more efficient handling of our customer accounts.
3. Increased funding would enable us to extend our after-school basketball program for preteen boys and girls.
4. Should our budget surplus be used to fund additional hours at the senior center or to assist meal-delivery programs for the homebound?

B. Working in a group, compare your responses to Exercise 3A. Record both agreements and disagreements about the paragraph in Exercise 2A. Then continue to work together to develop one of the topic sentences into a paragraph. Be ready to explain why you chose to develop the paragraph in the way you did. Feel free to revise the topic sentence.

2 Creating paragraph structures

An important part of paragraph development is deciding on the arrangement you will use to present its content. **General patterns of development** such as narration, comparison, and cause-effect offer you ways to develop a paragraph's content as well as its arrangement. **Specific patterns of development** reflect the outlook of readers and writers in specific settings (academic, work, or public) on useful ways to develop paragraphs.

8e
¶ dev

General patterns of development.   Each of the general patterns enables you to accomplish a different writing task, as the following chart indicates.

Patterns for Paragraph Development	
TASK	**DEVELOPMENT STRATEGY**
Tell a story; re-create events; present an anecdote.	Narrating
Provide detail of a scene or object; portray someone's character; evoke a feeling.	Describing
Explore similarities or differences; evaluate alternatives.	Comparing and contrasting
Provide directions; explain the operation of a mechanism, procedure, or natural process.	Explaining a process
Separate a subject into parts; explore the relationships among parts.	Dividing
Sort things or people into groups; explain the relationships among the groups.	Classifying
Explain the meaning of a term or concept; explore and illustrate the meaning of a complicated concept or phenomenon.	Defining
Consider why something happened or might happen; explore possible causes and consequences.	Analyzing causes and effects

You'll often turn to **narration** to present events in the past, the present, or even the imagined future. In academic writing, for example, narratives can provide historical background, and in public settings, narratives can help readers understand how an issue or disagreement came about. In work settings, narratives can provide information necessary for understanding a problem or challenge, but their focus generally needs to be limited to details relevant to the current situation.

Description helps you create images of a place or object (often using a spatial organization), sketch a person's character, or evoke feelings. In a technical or business report, however, description can convey important details of a product or physical setting.

You can use paragraphs built around **comparing** and **contrasting** to evaluate alternative policies or products. In arranging comparison paragraphs, you can employ a **point-by-point organization,** examining each comparable feature for first one subject and then the next.

Topic sentence
Feature 1

Feature 2
Feature 3

Feature 4

But biology has a funny way of confounding expectations. Rather than disappear, the evidence for innate sexual differences only began to mount. In medicine, researchers documented that heart disease strikes men at a younger age than it does women and that women have a more moderate physiological response to stress. Researchers found subtle neurological differences between the sexes both in the brain's structure and in its functioning. In addition, another generation of parents discovered that, despite their best efforts to give baseballs to their daughters and sewing kits to their sons, girls still flocked to dollhouses while boys clambered into tree forts. Perhaps nature is more important than nurture after all.

—CHRISTINE GORMAN, "Sizing Up the Sexes"

8e
¶ dev

Or you can use a **subject-by-subject organization,** considering each subject in its entirety, as in the next example.

Topic sentence
Subject 1

Subject 2

For everyone, home is a place to be offstage. But the comfort of home can have opposite and incompatible meanings for women and men. For many men, the comfort of home means freedom from having to prove themselves and impress through verbal display. At last, they are in a situation where talk is not required. They are free to remain silent. But for women, home is a place where they are free to talk, and where they feel the greatest need for talk, with those they are closest to. For them, the comfort of home means the freedom to talk without worrying about how their talk will be judged.

—DEBORAH TANNEN, "Put Down That Paper and Talk to Me!"

To explain a **process,** you may need to provide readers with a paragraph of **directions** or an **explanation** of how a mechanism or procedure works. You can also divide or classify. When you divide a subject, you split it into parts. A **division** paragraph offers you a chance to explain a subject in detail and to highlight the relationship of its parts. When you classify, you sort several subjects into groups based on their similarities. A **classification** paragraph is an opportunity for you to identify the groups and explore similarities within them or the differences and relationships among them.

When you need to introduce a term or concept to your readers, you may need to write just a phrase or sentence to define it, or you may need to create a **definition** paragraph if the term is complicated.

When you hear the word crystal, many people think of a mineral dug from the ground. But the lead crystal used to make beautiful plates, glasses, and vases does not come from this source. The crystal in these objects—artworks, actually—is glass with a high lead content. The glass is made from a mixture of sand and other ingredients like potash (potassium) or soda that help the mixture melt. The various minerals also effect the color and clarity of the glass. Lead crystal must contain at least 30 percent to 35 percent lead oxide (by weight) in its ingredients. The resulting materialis easier for artists to work with as they gring intricate facets into the surface to create designs that sparkle and intrigue like a finely cut diamond.

—ANDREA HERRMANN, College Student

8e
¶ dev

When you wish to explain why something has occurred, you might focus a paragraph on causes; to explore consequences, you might focus on effects. Or you might combine them, to create a **cause-effect** paragraph.

Specific patterns of development. In work settings, writers and readers often focus their attention on problems to be solved and recommendations for dealing with the problems. In reports, writers often devote separate paragraphs to problems and recommendations. In shorter documents such as letters and memos, however, writers often turn to **problem-solution** paragraphs like the following, from a memo.

Background	While the risks of periodontal surgery to repair or replace gum tissue are low and the recovery times less than a week, *we have a disproportionate number of patients who*
Problem Description	*refuse the surgery; many even refuse to visit a dentist or periodontist to have their condition evaluated.* Many of these patients do not have adequate information, but our minutes
Causes	per patient guidelines do not allow extended conversations about periodontal procedures. *I propose that we de-*
Proposed Solution	*velop a short two-page fact sheet to give to patients about the procedures.* The sheet would provide information on the
Details about Solution	procedure itself, costs, expected recovery times, complication rate, and the names and number of are a periodontists. The fact sheet would be distributed to at-risk patients and could be made available to family members as well.

Another paragraph structure that addresses problems and recommendations is the **question-and-answer** pattern. This pattern is particularly useful in public settings because the question segment allows writers to raise questions of mutual concern they share with readers while the answer segment allows writers to explore possible policies or recommendations for dealing with the concern. Writers can even extend the answer segment to consider and reject possible answers until they provide the most reasonable and useful alternative. The following paragraph from a Web site on athletic nutrition (http://www.athleticnutri-tion.com/stjohns.html) uses the question-and-answer pattern to share research relating the use of St. John's Wort, a herbal antidepressant, to athletic workouts.

What research has been done on St. John's Wort?

The active derivative in St. John's Wort is called hypericin. This active ingredient . . . has been shown to increase the half-life of certain neurotransmitters and thus, by extending the time that these neurotransmitters are in the brain, extend and enhance their positive effects. Most studies done on St. John's Wort have explored its possible antidepressant activity. These double-blind studies indicate that indeed, St. John's Wort does possess these antidepressant capabilities and can stave off mild depression. Finally, some studies have shown that St. John's Wort may inhibit cortisol secretion, as well as possibly block the release of other catabolic hormones. This is of particular significance to weight-training athletes as this can lead to better gains and increased strength and size.

Paragraphs in public discourse often begin by stating or summarizing facts or information (such as statistics, quotations, events, or studies) and then moving into interpretation, critique, or application of information; a statement of need; or a plan or request. This is especially true of the first paragraph of a public document, such as this grant application.

Recent research in gerontology suggests that nursing home residents benefit from regular contact with animals. Such benefits include enhanced motor skills, increased interest in physical activities such as walking or dancing, decreased loneliness and stress, and increased appetite. Despite these benefits, no nursing homes in the tri-county area have made "therapeutic animal" programs available to their residents. In the hope of putting our facility at the forefront of senior care in this area, I am requesting $300 to purchase a therapy dog from the local organization Paws with a Cause.

Often, in workplace contexts, you are not required to make a case for a certain course of action or policy but rather to simply lay out a set of alternatives. Sometimes, such sets of alternatives will be the basis for managers' decision making. Other times, such sets of alternatives can become the basis of group discussions, as in the following example. This memo was produced by Al McCann, a symphony manager, before a meeting of the symphony's board of directors.

To: Symphony Board of Directors
From: Al McCann, Symphony Manager

8e
¶ **dev**

At Friday's meeting, we need to make a final decision about the Salt Lake City visit, the last on the 2000–2001 travel schedule. Our options for scheduling this trip are possible dates in March, April, and May. Since we do not complete the winter *Porgy and Bess* performances with the City Opera until the first week of March, we need to consider how much time symphony members will need between these two major events. The last two weeks of March are a possibility, but airline fares will begin to rise in late March because of spring break. The percussionists will be conducting workshops at the community college between April 14 and 24, so those dates are out. Starting in mid-May, the costs and demand for halls at Tabernacle Center and at the University of Utah will begin to increase as pre-Olympic events begin in earnest. Of course, any decisions we make need to be coordinated with Matthew Gomez, the manager of the Utah Symphony, so we should plan on a conference call with Mr. Gomez either during or immediately after the meeting.

8e
¶ dev

Exercise 4

A. Choose one of the following pairs of topics. Drawing on your own knowledge, develop each topic into a paragraph, using the pattern of development indicated in brackets.

1. A paragraph about finding a part-time or summer job [process] and a paragraph on an unusual or memorable person [description or narration]

2. A paragraph exploring different outlooks about the relationships of parents and children [comparison-contrast] and a paragraph providing advice about dealing with a difficulty in parent-child relationships [question and answer]

3. A paragraph identifying the differences between educational requirements, expected income, and working conditions for two jobs such as restaurant manager and doctor or teacher and chemical engineer [comparison-contrast] and a paragraph exploring a common work or college problem and offering possible solutions [problem-solution]

4. A paragraph identifying the reasons some students do well (or poorly) on tests [cause-effect] and a paragraph describing a good way to study for tests [process]

5. A paragraph exploring different views people hold about taking buses and driving cars [subject-by-subject comparison] and a paragraph identifying differences between educational requirements, expected income, and working conditions for two jobs [point-by-point comparison]

B. Working in a group, identify the patterns of development in the following paragraph. There may be a single dominant pattern or more than one. Explain how each pattern or combination is used.

> None of the foreign geologists had ever encountered anything quite like the disaster at Lake Nyos. Our earliest hypotheses seemed to be almost as numerous as the scientific teams present. Some workers, impressed by the accounts of survivors who reported smelling rotten eggs or gunpowder and hearing explosions, were convinced that a volcanic eruption beneath the lake had released sulfurous gases. Others, including me, suspected that the gas had come from within the sediments on the lake bed. Eventually, though, geological and chemical investigations made it obvious that the lake had released carbon dioxide from within its own waters— independent apparently of any other process. Like an enormous bottle of soda water, it belched and fizzed gas from its depths.
>
> —SAMUEL J. PREETH, "Incident at Lake Nyos"

8f
¶ dev

8f Using special-purpose paragraphs in academic, work, and public settings

Beginning a piece of writing, concluding it, and presenting dialogue are challenges you can meet with some useful special-purpose paragraphs.

1 Creating introductory paragraphs

In the opening paragraphs of an essay, report, or public document, you invite readers to learn about a subject, explore ideas, address a problem, or examine a line of argument. You need to build a relationship with your readers so they will want to continue reading. Try the following strategies to create strong introductory paragraphs.

Strategies for Introductory Paragraphs

PROVIDE BACKGROUND
Provide background information on a topic or problem; present an issue in context; give the history of the subject.

TELL A STORY
Open with a brief anecdote or story.

OUTLINE A PROBLEM
Outline a problem, danger, or challenge.

continued

8f
¶ dev

Strategies for Introductory Paragraphs *(continued)*

EXPLAIN AN ISSUE
Present the different sides of an issue, along with any particularly well-known or controversial events relevant to the topic.

PRESENT A SITUATION
Describe a situation, a set of relationships, or recent events that require some response from readers or an organization to which they belong.

OFFER A DEFINITION
Define an important concept or term that will recur throughout the paper.

ASK A QUESTION
Present provocative questions or opinions that require further discussion.

USE AN EXTENDED EXAMPLE
Start with an extended example related to the topic and main idea.

PRESENT A QUOTATION
Quote from an authority or from someone whose opinion leads into the topic or highlights key ideas.

MAKE A COMPARISON
Highlight the importance of a topic or issue by comparing it to another situation, historical period, subject, or issue; offer an intriguing analogy.

PROVIDE STATISTICS
Supply facts and statistics that introduce the topic or that help define an important issue or problem.

DESCRIBE A MYSTERY
Present a mysterious or interesting phenomenon worth exploring or explaining.

Here are examples of introductory paragraphs employing different strategies.

ANECDOTE   It was advertised as the biggest non-nuclear explosion in Nevada history. On October 27, 1993, Steve Wynn, the State's official "god of hospitality," flashed his trademark smile and pushed the detonator button. As 200,000 Las Vegans cheered, the 18-story Dunes sign, once the tallest neon structure in the world, crumbled to the desert floor.
—MIKE DAVIS, "House of Cards"

Davis introduces the environmental threat posed by Las Vegas culture.

DEFINITION   It used to be that a diner was a lowly place to eat. It was known as a greasy spoon, a hash house, or—in trucker lingo—a choke and puke. Diners were where the city's fallen angels went for a cup of mud (coffee) and a sinker (a doughnut) beneath fluorescent lights; where night hawks and wandering hoboes whiled away the wee hours. As for the food at diners, it was strictly for the crude of palate— heavy on the starch, grease, and gristle.
—JANE STERN AND MICHAEL STERN, *Roadfood*

The Sterns are about to review a different kind of diner: clean, with good food and more fashionable customers.

PROBLEM   A candle-lit Christmas tree at Grandmother's house may be a thing of the past, but fire hazards still loom in American homes, ready to turn this season's joy into holiday tragedy.
—"Fire Safety Tips for a Safe Holiday Season,"
www.sema.state.mo.us/firexmas.htm

8f
¶ dev

2 Creating concluding paragraphs

Paragraphs that conclude essays should generally remind readers of key ideas and encourage them to think about information you have presented or actions you have proposed. The following paragraph illustrates one strategy used in concluding paragraphs.

SUMMARY OF MAIN POINTS
So if it's any consolation to those of us who just don't manage to fit enough sleep into our packed days, being chronically tired probably won't do us any permanent harm. And if things get desperate enough, we just might have to schedule a nap somewhere on our busy calendars.
—DANIEL GOLEMAN, "Too Little, Too Late"

Strategies for Concluding Paragraphs

SUMMARIZE MAIN POINTS
Review the main points briefly; a detailed summary will seem repetitive.

RESTATE THE THESIS
Put the thesis in different words to drive home the essay's main point.

RECOMMEND ACTIONS OR SOLUTIONS
Repeat, for emphasis, the specific solutions, policies, recommendations, or actions proposed in the text, perhaps summarizing them in a list.

continued

Strategies for Concluding Paragraphs *(continued)*

PREDICT FUTURE EVENTS OR SPECULATE
Look at relatively clear consequences, not those requiring explanation; keep speculations interesting but not so provocative that they require extensive discussion.

USE A QUOTATION
Provide a quotation that makes key ideas memorable or supports your conclusions.

OFFER A STRIKING EXAMPLE, ANECDOTE, OR IMAGE
Supply a mental picture or brief narrative to reinforce an essay's message.

ECHO THE INTRODUCTION
Use this echo to create a sense of completion.

RESTATE IMPLICATIONS
Review the implications of any actions or policies discussed in the text.

Exercise 5

A. Revise the following concluding paragraph to make it more effective.

I probably have left out some of the arguments for and against gun control, though I think I have covered the main ones. The point I really want to stress most is that gun control is a difficult question. Simple proposals such as banning all handguns or getting rid of all regulations won't work. We need new ideas that balance the rights of gun owners with the right to be free from violence and crime. Though I have not explained it in detail, we probably need a program like the national registration and education system that has been recently proposed. And we certainly need to do something about the many handguns readily available to teenagers.

B. Have each of the members of a writing group bring in a popular magazine containing relatively long articles. As a group, examine the articles, and choose three openings and three conclusions that you consider successful. Identify the strategies used in each.

CHAPTER

9

Creating Clear, Emphatic, and Varied Sentences

Most people would find the following sentences hard to read and understand.

> Our ski club president did not, because he was embarrassed by his lack of advanced skiing experience, sign us up for the University Ski Clubs Association trip to Utah.

> It is suggested that employee work cooperation encouragement be used for product quality improvement.

You can make sentences like these clearer and easier to read with some simple revision strategies.

SIMPLE AND DIRECT   Because he was embarrassed by his lack of advanced skiing experience, our ski club president did not sign us up for the University Ski Clubs Association trip to Utah.

CLEAR   We will try to improve the quality of our products by encouraging employees to work cooperatively.

But you don't need to stop with sentences that are simply clear and direct. You can also use a number of strategies to create appropriate emphasis and pleasing variety and meet the demands of different writing situations: academic, work, and public.

9a Creating clear sentences

Generally, the clearest sentences readily answer the question "Who does what (to whom)?"

		subject	verb	object
CLEAR		The research team investigated seizure disorders in infants.		
		Who?	does what?	to whom?

		subject	verb
CLEAR		The seizures often become harmful	
		Who?	does what?

Of course, many sentences in good writing are more complicated than those that move directly from subject to verb (to object), yet you can still make them clear by making answers to the question "Who does what (to whom)?" easy for readers to identify.

**9a
sent**

1 Use significant subjects

Sentences whose subjects name important ideas, people, topics, things, or events are generally easy for readers to understand. You can create sentences with significant subjects by asking, as you write, "Who (or what) am I talking about in this sentence?" and "Is this the subject I want to emphasize?" You can also use these questions to identify and revise sentences whose subjects are not significant. Consider this sentence from an essay titled "Should You Try to Get a Tan?"

UNFOCUSED You run the greatest risk if you expose yourself to a tanning machine as well as the sun because both of them can damage the skin.

READER'S REACTION: I thought this essay was about the dangers posed by sunbathing and tanning salons. Why are these subjects buried in the middle of the sentence?

POSSIBLE REVISION Either **the sun or a tanning machine** can damage the skin, and you run the greatest risk if you expose yourself to **both** of them.

2 Avoid unnecessary nominalizations

When you create a noun from some other kind of word, the result is a **nominalization.** A verb like *complete* can become a noun like *completion;* an adjective like *happy* turns into a noun like *happiness.* Some nominalizations play important roles in effective sentences; others act as stumbling blocks for readers.

Nominalizations may name ideas and issues essential to a discussion. As subjects, they can serve as focal points for clear sentences.

USEFUL NOMINALIZATION **Distractions** like television, the VCR, and electric lights (for reading or conversing) keep us up at night, robbing us of the hours of sleep previous generations enjoyed.

Distractions, a nominalization, comes from *distract*, a verb.

VAGUE	Dissatisfaction among employees often leads to shoddiness in products.
	Nominalizations created from adjectives may lead to vague statements, as is the case with *dissatisfaction* and *shoddiness* in this sentence.
REVISED	Dissatisfied employees often make shoddy products.
	The new verb, *make*, specifies the action more clearly.

Used inappropriately, nominalizations may obscure important information from your readers or cause you to omit it entirely.

STRATEGY

As you write or as you review a draft, pay special attention to nominalizations that

- Draw readers' attention away from a sentence's proper focus
- Lead to vague sentence subjects or objects
- Cause you to leave important information out of a sentence

Revise sentences with these nominalization problems by making sure every sentence indicates clearly who did what (to whom). To do this, replace an inappropriate nominalization with a word indicating a clear and significant subject (or object), and name the sentence's action (did what?) in the verb.

**9a
sent**

Writer's Tip

Spotting nominalizations can be difficult at first, but you can quickly turn this search into a useful habit. Words ending in *-tion, -ence, -ance, -ing,* and *-ness* are often nominalizations. Here is a list of some common nominalizations to watch for.

NOUN	VERB	ADJECTIVE
analysis	analyze	
appropriateness		appropriate
beginning	begin	
calculation	calculate	
comparison	compare	
convenience		convenient
delivery	deliver	
denial	deny	
guidance	guide	
investigation	investigate	
opening	open	
openness		open
preference	prefer	
solution	solve	
suggestion	suggest	

3 Consider using *I*, *we*, and *you* as subjects

Although *I*, *we*, and *you* are often inappropriate in academic and professional writing, there are many settings in which these pronouns can act as clear subjects in effective sentences. Workplace documents such as reports, proposals, and memos; writings in the public sphere, such as election campaign materials, posters, reports, petitions, and magazine articles; and even an occasional academic text—all these can benefit from careful use of *I*, *we*, and *you*.

Using I. When you are the subject of an essay, when you are speaking directly to readers, or when you are reporting on your own investigations or conclusions, *I* is an appropriate subject.

> In designing the survey, **I** avoided questions likely to embarrass respondents.

On the other hand, adding statements like *I think* and *I feel* when you are already clearly stating your point of view makes your writing more wordy but not more effective.

Using We. *We* is appropriate when you use it to report the actions of a group or to discuss experiences you as a writer share with most readers.

> **We** [North Americans] consume a large portion of the world's resources.

Using You. *You* is appropriate when used to mean "you, the reader." Consider using *people, individuals,* or a similar word if your reader will incorrectly assume you are referring to him- or herself and not to people in general.

APPROPRIATE   Before asking a large number of people to complete the survey, **you** should test it on a few individuals to identify any major flaws in the design.

INAPPROPRIATE   According to an article in *Rolling Stone,* **you** were less drawn to the 1960s British rock invasion if **you** lived in the Midwest than if **you** lived on the East or West Coast.
READER'S REACTION: I was born in 1982. Is the author writing to my parents?

REVISED   According to an article in *Rolling Stone,* **people** were less drawn to the 1960s British rock invasion if **they** lived in the Midwest than if **they** lived on the East or West Coast.

4 Be careful with strings of nouns

In a **noun string,** one noun modifies another.

NOUN	NOUN	NOUN
hip	joint	replacement
computer	network	server

Or nouns plus adjectives modify other nouns.

ADJECTIVE	NOUN	NOUN	NOUN
triple	bypass	heart	surgery

Familiar noun strings can help you create concise yet clear sentences. Un-familiar noun strings, however, can make sentences hard to understand. Readers may have trouble deciding which noun represents the focal point.

**9a
sent**

CONFUSING   The team did a ceramic valve lining design flaw analysis.
READER'S REACTION: Did the team analyze flaws or use a special procedure called flaw analysis? Did they study ceramic valves or valve linings made of ceramic material?

One solution is to turn the key word in a string (usually the last noun) into a verb. Then form the other nouns into prepositional phrases.

REVISED   The team **analyzed** flaws **in** the lining design **for** ceramic valves.

Another strategy involves turning one noun into the subject.

REVISED   **Flaws** in the lining design for ceramic valves were ana-lyzed by the team.
This version highlights the subject being analyzed.

Exercise 1

A. Revise the following sentences to create clear subjects and make the sentences easier to understand.

EXAMPLE

We expect
~~Our expectation is that~~ athletic shoes, ~~will~~ *to* look good as well as feel comfortable.

1. Our expectation is that our elected officials will look like the populations of people they represent.
2. Fifty years ago, election of only one gender of people, male, and of only one race, white, was possible.

3. Today, politicians boast of every level of our government's racial and gender diversity.
4. Choice between candidates is on the basis of their stand on the issues, their media savvy, and their ability to communicate.
5. Choice of candidate is not always on the basis of race, in other words.

 B. In a group, collaboratively revise each sentence in Exercise 1A in two ways. Then decide which (if either) is better, and why.

5 Use clear and specific verbs

Clear, specific verbs can make sentences forceful and easy to understand. Overuse of the verb *be* (*is, are, was, were, will be*) can lead to weak sentences. Always consider replacing forms of *be* with more forceful verbs.

WEAK   Our agency is responsible for all aspects of disaster relief.

STRONGER   Our agency **plans, funds, delivers,** and **monitors** disaster relief.

Look for predicate nouns (nominalizations) you can turn into clear, specific verbs (see 9a-2). Eliminate general verbs (*do, give, have, get, provide, shape, make*) linked to nouns by turning the nouns into verbs.

WEAK   Our company **has done a study** of the new design project and **will provide funding** for it.

STRONGER   Our company **has studied** the new design project and **will fund** it.

6 Keep subjects and verbs clearly related

Clear subjects and verbs play key roles in effective sentences. When subject and verb are separated by long phrases, readers may have trouble identifying these elements and may find the sentence difficult to understand.

The veterinary association *in response to concern about the costly facilities required by new guidelines for animal care and disposal of medical waste* has created a low-cost loan program for its members.

Separating the parts of a verb phrase (see 15a-3) with a long phrase or other group of words can also make sentences difficult to read.

Manufacturing companies **can** if they wish to improve product quality, cost, and reliability, **contact** the university's Design for Assembly program.

9b Creating direct sentences

A direct sentence structure moves from subject to verb (to object). An indirect sentence structure uses an **expletive construction** (*there is, there are,* or *it is*) to control the arrangement of the words. An expletive construction does not name the subject until well into a sentence. Much of the time, expletive constructions make your sentences wordy and hard to understand.

EXPLETIVE   It is important for us to increase community awareness of our services in order to reach target audiences.

REVISED   We should increase community awareness of our services to reach target audiences.

An expletive construction may also enable you to withhold information about the doer, the person or thing responsible for an action. You need to decide whether this is appropriate, given your context and purpose, or whether you are omitting details important to your readers.

DOER NOT NAMED   There was considerable debate over whether to build a new library or renovate the old one.

DOER NAMED   Members of the fund-raising committee debated whether to build a new library or renovate the old one.

MORE SPECIFIC   Veit, Gould, and Clifford, the three members in charge of studying the issue, debated whether to build a new library or renovate the old one.

In rewriting, you can replace an expletive construction with a significant sentence subject.

STRATEGY

Review something you have written, looking for expletive constructions (*there is, there are, it is*). Decide which are justified and effective. Rewrite to eliminate any that are needlessly wordy, vague, or confusing.

You can sometimes use expletive constructions to good effect. By waiting until late in a sentence to name the subject, you can create suspense and surprise. And you can use expletives to introduce topics that will be taken up in following sentences. (See 9d-3.)

A sentence with an expletive construction may also be the clearest and most precise way to make a statement.

9b sent

Historians used to believe that a sudden invasion by shepherding tribes caused major changes in the region's culture. Now, however, **there is** new archaeological evidence that the "invasion" was actually a gradual resettling that took about a century.

Exercise 2

A. Rewrite the following sentences, using clear verbs to make them easy to understand.

EXAMPLE
Speaking in public, ~~is a frightening experience for~~ *frightens* many people.

1. Public speaking, regarded by many experts as an important element in successful business careers, especially on the executive level, is no longer a required course at many colleges.
2. Included among the programs offered by our consulting company is a course in public speaking. It is considered to be very useful.
3. We also give demonstrations of how to prepare effective graphics for a presentation.
4. Our consultants can, if a company wishes, provide training for both small and large groups.
5. It is generally agreed that the training program is a confidence builder for many people.

B. Work with several other writers to turn the sentences in Exercise 2A into a clear, forceful paragraph that a consulting company might include in a pamphlet advertising its services. Add material if necessary to produce an effective paragraph, and combine or rearrange sentences as appropriate.

9c Creating emphasis

You want your readers to notice the most important ideas and information in a sentence. In drafting and revising, you can highlight this material by placing it at the beginning or end of a sentence, by presenting it in a special sentence pattern, or by using the passive voice in a careful manner.

1 Use sentence beginnings and endings

A reader's attention gravitates toward sentence beginnings and endings. You can take advantage of this phenomenon by shifting the material you wish to emphasize to a sentence's opening or closing.

UNEMPHATIC	Gases produced during the cheese-making process by the "eye former," a bacterium, create the holes in Swiss cheese.
REVISED	**The "eyes,"** or the holes in Swiss cheese, are created during the cheese-making process by gases produced by a bacterium, **the "eye former."** **Words at the beginning and end emphasize the unusual names. The verb shifts from active to passive voice (see 9c-3).**
REVISED	**Called "eyes" and produced by gases from a bacterium called the "eye former,"** the holes in Swiss cheese are created during the cheese-making process. **Phrases at the beginning emphasize the names.**

**9c
sent**

2 Create emphatic sentence patterns

Inverted sentence order, climactic order, periodic sentences, and cumulative sentences all offer ways to create emphasis. You have undoubtedly encountered these sophisticated sentence patterns in your reading. During revision, you can make a conscious effort to use them to add interest or vary emphasis.

Inversion. By inverting the normal subject-verb-object/complement word order, you can shift the focus of a sentence. **Inverted sentence order** often calls attention to the element you have moved to the initial position.

INVERTED	**From the darkness near the rear of the auditorium thundered the director's voice** with criticisms of our acting.
NORMAL	**The director's voice thundered** from the darkness near the rear of the auditorium with criticisms of our acting.

Because inversion creates emphasis in part by disrupting a reader's expectations for sentence order, overuse of it or other exotic sentence orders will confuse or irritate readers.

Climactic order. Using **climactic sentence order**—in which elements build to a climax—can create powerful emphasis, especially on the last item in a series.

What every truly modern home has, she said, is a dishwasher, a gas grill, a Jacuzzi, **and a divorce.**

Periodic sentences. A **periodic sentence** piles up phrases, clauses, and words at the beginning, delaying the main clause of the sentence. The suspense casts a spotlight on the main clause.

Because she knows that inspired designs often spring from hard work, because she loves perfection yet fears failure, and because she believes that risk-taking does not eliminate attention to detail, Jennifer is working eighteen hours a day on her fall clothing collection.

The risk, of course, lies in delaying so long that the reader loses track of the meaning, as in the following example.

CONFUSING   Having begun the business as much to escape from boredom as to make a profit, and also suffering from a lack of skill in accounting and an unwillingness to listen to the good advice of the professionals they hired to review the management and recordkeeping procedures that were causing dissension among employees, Sheila and Stefan decided to declare bankruptcy.

Cumulative sentences. To build a **cumulative sentence,** you start with the main clause, then add details and statements in the form of modifying phrases, clauses, and words. The main clause provides a firm base to which you can add details and ideas, bit by bit.

A cumulative sentence allows you first to emphasize the main clause, then the successive words, phrases, and clauses that work cumulatively to build a detailed picture, an intricate explanation, or a cluster of ideas and information.

Main clause   Varna stumbled down the stairs,
Details   the flowerpot falling from her grip,
Details   spilling dirt into the air,
Details   shattering on the linoleum floor just seconds before she landed among the shards of pottery and fragments of geranium,
Details   the loud thud bringing everyone in the house to attention.

3 Use the passive voice with care

When a sentence's verb is in the active voice (see 17h), the doer (or agent) is also the subject of the sentence.

doer   action   goal
The outfielder caught the towering fly ball.
subject   verb   object

When you choose the **passive voice** (17h) for the verb form, you turn the sentence's goal into the subject and make naming the doer optional.

goal   action   [doer]
The towering fly ball was caught [by the outfielder].
subject   verb   [prepositional phrase]

Using the passive voice, you de-emphasize the doer by placing it in a prepositional phrase or by dropping it altogether (see 17h). In addition, you create sentences that are generally wordier than corresponding versions in the active voice. Note how emphasis and length differ in active and passive versions of the following sentence.

ACTIVE VOICE
    doer (subject)
The Centers for Disease Control interviewed three thousand people affected by the toxin.

PASSIVE VOICE
    subject
Three thousand people affected by the toxin were interviewed by **the Centers for Disease Control.**
    doer

**9c
sent**

S T R A T E G Y

Review your writing, looking for sentences that use verbs in the passive voice (see 17h). Recast in the active voice any sentences that are unnecessarily wordy or that create inappropriate emphasis. Consider naming the doer in any sentences that fail to provide this information.

If you wish to emphasize the *doer,* use the active voice. If you wish to draw readers' attention to the goal or outcome of an action rather than its doer, consider using the passive voice.

ACTIVE
Poorly trained contract workers caused the explosion and fire at the refinery.
Subject emphasizes cause.

PASSIVE
The explosion and fire at the refinery were caused by poorly trained contract workers.
Subject emphasizes result.

You can also use the passive voice to highlight significant elements in a discussion.

Refineries are potentially dangerous workplaces. **Most accidents** can be prevented, however, by careful training of workers.
Passive voice in the second sentence keeps attention on the dangers.

You can choose whether or not to name the doer in a sentence written in the passive voice.

Requirements for the term paper were distributed in all sections of the psychology course [by the individual instructors].

Did You Know?

Advice on using the passive voice has changed radically during the last hundred years. According to Dennis Baron, experts on grammar and writing style during the eighteenth and nineteenth centuries had few objections to sentences using the passive voice. By the middle of the twentieth century, however, they had begun criticizing the passive voice for encouraging wordiness, vagueness, and even deception (by allowing writers to avoid naming the person or group responsible for an action). Now, editors and writing teachers regularly advise writers to eliminate passive voice whenever possible.

Dennis Baron, "The Passive Voice Can Be Your Friend," *Declining Grammar and Other Essays on the English Vocabulary* (Urbana: NCTE, 1989) 17–22.

When the doer is unknown or unimportant, you can appropriately omit it.

Federal income tax forms will be mailed on January 1.
By the IRS, of course.

But when leaving out the doer would omit important information or mislead readers, include it.

Consumers were not informed of their right to sue for damages.
The sentence doesn't say who withheld the information.

Exercise 3

A. Revise the following sentences to eliminate passive voice.

EXAMPLE

Grocery stores sell many
~~Many~~ different kinds of ice cream ~~are sold by grocery stores.~~

1. The superpremium ice cream brands are chosen by many people.
2. More butterfat and less air is contained in superpremium ice cream than in regular ice cream.
3. The high fat content ought to be considered before the ice cream is purchased.
4. The rich, tasty ice creams are being challenged by the new frozen dessert products.
5. Frozen yogurts with candy and nuts mixed in have been heavily promoted.

B. Examine the following passage carefully, and identify the strategies the author uses to create emphasis. Then share your responses.

> There was a time when people who wanted to keep the peace and keep the crockery intact held to a strict dinner-table rule: Never argue about politics or religion. I don't know how well it worked in American dining rooms, but it worked pretty well in our schools. We dealt with religion by not arguing about it.
>
> Children who came out of diverse homes might carve up the turf of their neighborhood and turn the playgrounds into a religious battlefield, but the public classroom was common ground. Intolerance wasn't tolerated.
>
> In place of teaching one religion or another, the schools held to a common denominator of values. It was, in part, the notion of Horace Mann, the nineteenth-century father of the public-school system. He believed that the way to avoid religious conflicts was to extract what all religions agree upon and allow this "non-religious" belief system into schools.
>
> I wonder what Mann would think of that experiment now. Was it naive or sophisticated? Was it a successful or a failed attempt to avoid conflict in a pluralistic society?
>
> —ELLEN GOODMAN, "Religion in the Textbooks"

Working with a group of fellow writers, try to agree on answers to these questions about the Goodman passage: Which sentence strategies do you think add to the effectiveness of the passage, and why? Which, if any, detract from its effectiveness?

9d Revising for variety

Too many sentences of similar length, type, and structure can create unemphatic writing that bores readers. Variety, carefully constructed, can make your writing more lively. Many of the strategies that create emphasis (see 9c) can also create variety, and the two qualities often go together.

1 Vary sentence length

Revision is a good opportunity to pay attention to varying the length of sentences. Use short sentences for dramatic contrast and for emphasis. Create longer sentences to explore relationships among ideas and to add rhythmic effects to your prose. Use middle-length sentences as workhorses, carrying the burden of explanation and description, but don't use too many of them at once.

9d
sent

Note how variety in sentence length helps make this explanation easy to read and interesting.

> The real country ham may or may not be smoked after curing. Smithfield, Virginia, hams are smoked over hardwood or hardwood sawdust. Unscrupulous producers use smoke flavoring. But Mac Pierce, who runs the country's largest retail pork market, Nahunta Pork Center in Pikeville, North Carolina, says less than 1 percent of his hams are smoked, and most of those are bought by northerners. "Smoke masks a good ham's flavor," says Mac.   —BILL NEAL, "How to Cure a Pig"

9d
sent

S T R A T E G Y

Vary sentence length as you revise. Combine some draft sentences to highlight relationships; compress others to emphasize ideas.

DRAFT   Political conventions used to be occasions for selecting among rival candidates. They are no longer serious contests. The likely winners are known well in advance. Conventions are now simply places for political strategists and campaign workers to meet. They are also ways of getting attention from the media.

REVISED   Political conventions used to be occasions for selecting among rival candidates, but no longer, for the likely winners are now known well in advance. Conventions are now simply meeting places for political strategists and campaign workers. They are media events.

---

2 Vary sentence types

It's easy to get into the habit of using only **declarative sentences,** sentences that make statements (see 15e-2 sentence types). An occasional exclamation (**exclamatory sentence**), a mild order (**imperative sentence**), or a question (**interrogative sentence**) can vary the pace of your prose effectively, making it more lively and memorable.

Some community-based texts, however, may call for what seems to be repetitive sentence structure. The budget narrative in a grant proposal, for example, often consists of a series of short, simple sentences. Readers of such documents expect this kind of structure.

VARIED   Some of the less familiar sports offer good opportunities for entertainment and exercise. Are you looking for fast-paced, thrilling events? Go see a soccer game, a lacrosse match, or a bicycle race. Do you want strenuous exercise and vigorous competition? Sign up for a rugby team, a badminton class, or a squash league. To benefit from these activities you need only take a simple step: Get involved!

A **rhetorical question** is one that requires no answer or that you plan to answer yourself in the course of an essay.

These are all ways you can get more time for sleep, even in the midst of a busy schedule. **But is it really important for most of us to get more sleep?** It is, and staying healthy and staying alert aren't the only good reasons for doing so.

9d
sent

3 Vary sentence structures and patterns

You can create variety by blending sentence structures in your writing (use simple, compound, and complex sentences; see 15e-1) and by varying the kinds of coordination and subordination you employ (see Chapter 27). You can also create variety by using periodic and cumulative sentence patterns and inversion (see 9c-2). By trying different sentence openings (see 9c-1), you can make sure your sentences vary in arrangement.

EXPLETIVE   Then there was the time we painted our house.

PHRASE   **To our neighbor's eyes,** the house looked like it belonged somewhere else.

PHRASE   **Looking for a bargain,** we bought paint at a discount store.

PHRASE   **The paint having been cheaply made,** the house began peeling within a year and a half.

DEPENDENT CLAUSE   **If you want to be happy with a paint job,** spend the money for quality materials.

TRANSITIONAL EXPRESSION   **In addition,** choose the color carefully.

Exercise 4

A. Rewrite the following passage to add variety. You may wish to rearrange the order of statements, to cut or add words, or to combine some sentences and separate others.

Psychologists have been studying what events people remember. People from middle age on remember events from their early years more clearly than they remember more recent events. People in their seventies have clear memories of their thirties but less clear memories of their fifties. Most of us remember very little about childhood. Almost no one remembers events from before four years old. Researchers think that we tend to remember events that are new or exciting to us and to forget routine events. Memorable events are most likely to occur early in life. Infants probably have not developed the mental abilities necessary to create memories, however.

 B. Compare your rewritten version of the passage in Exercise 4A with those produced by other writers. Working in a group, produce one version of the passage that draws on the best parts of each version.

4 Create surprise

Good writing often employs strategies that intrigue readers. **Summative modifiers, resumptive modifiers,** and **antithesis,** which change—or seem to change—the direction of a sentence, are particularly effective at creating surprise and interest.

A **summative modifier** summarizes the preceding part of a sentence and then sends it off in a new direction.

To protect your vegetables against harmful insects, you can use soap sprays, scatter insect-repelling plants among the beds, or introduce "friendly" insects like ladybugs and praying mantises—**three techniques** that will not leave a harmful chemical residue on the food you grow.

A **resumptive modifier** extends a sentence that appears to have ended, adding new information or twists of thought.

People who are careful about what they eat may lead healthier lives, **healthier,** though not necessarily longer.

The advertising campaign is a surprising failure, **surprising** because it worked so well with test audiences.

Antithesis—the use of parallelism to emphasize contrast—can be witty, dramatic, cynical, ironic, or memorable.

To err is human, to forgive divine.

—ALEXANDER POPE

Can an honest politician be smart, or a smart politician honest?

Exercise 5

A. Browse through the current magazines at the library, looking for one that contains relatively long essays with varied and often surprising writing style. You might look at *Vogue, The New Yorker, Rolling Stone, Business Week, GQ, Vanity Fair, Advertising Age, Utne Reader, Commentary, Tikkun, Scientific American,* or *Details.* Choose two paragraphs whose style you admire, and identify any of the sentence strategies discussed in this chapter. Be ready to discuss why the sentences can be considered effective in communicating the author's ideas.

B. Although correct, carefully crafted sentences are important for writing in most communities, sometimes complex sentences are unnecessary or even distracting. Make a list of types of writing that don't require complete sentences (for example, classified ads). Then speculate about when sophisticated or complex sentences are necessary and appropriate and when they are not.

**9d
sent**

REPRESENTING YOURSELF: CREATING A PLACE IN A COMMUNITY

10

Presenting Yourself Through Language Choices

How do you talk at home, at school, at work, or in your neighborhood? Do you find yourself using language differently when you're with friends, teachers, and bosses? Are there groups of people you feel more comfortable speaking with, and do they share your way of speaking?

In an area of Miami, José Barrientes, a college student, notices how he changes his language choices the moment he walks into his physics lab or his Western civilization course. In those settings, he uses a more formal style compared to the way he speaks to people in his neighborhood. This academic way of speaking feels a little uncomfortable to him, especially because he has to avoid slipping Spanish words and phrases into his speech that help him to express himself. But he also knows that in his classes, there are other students who unfortunately aren't bilingual and who may not even understand the variety of English he speaks at home. José is not alone: his situation is also true in varying degrees for Solita Johnson, an African American student from Camden, New Jersey; for Karl Buccanan, who comes from a rural farming community in central North Dakota; and for Steve Thibodeaux of Baton Rouge, Louisiana. From the northern tip of Maine to the Mexican border of San Diego, people speak in hundreds of different ways in their homes and communities. These differences define who they are and give them a sense of personal history and group identity.

Every speaker of the English language uses a variety shaped by his or her region, culture, exposure to other languages, and home community. Where they're used, these varieties seem natural; they may even show up in the way members of the community write to each other. Not so, however, in most business, academic, and broader public settings. Unfortunately, such variations in those settings aren't seen as acceptable standards for a group or culture but as "errors." Except for very casual and personal occasions, writers substitute more general standards for their regional, cultural, and home language varieties. Members of your reading community, even those in your local area, expect most of your writing to conform to these generalized standards, in part because writing can move beyond your own surroundings and into other settings. Becoming a flexible writer means developing an awareness of the differences between the habits and standards of your own community and the biases or expectations of a more general reading public.

10a Understanding home and community language varieties

Every language in the world is spoken in a variety of ways called *dialects*. English has hundreds of dialects that vary in obvious ways between different countries, like England and the United States, but also within these countries. The American English spoken in Natchez, Mississippi, differs considerably from the American English spoken in Bar Harbor, Maine, and speakers in Fort Wayne, Indiana don't, as a group, share the same dialect as Hoosiers who live just a few hours south in Bloomington or Evansville. Dialects can also vary by culture, ethnicity, and nationality. Not only do Cuban Americans and Puerto Rican Americans speak different dialects of American English in New York City, but their dialects may vary between the Bronx and Brooklyn. Similar people may have different dialects even though they live just a few miles from each other—or a few blocks.

1 Learn to see dialect variations as "rules"

Linguists point out that all dialects have rules. What counts for a rule in one dialect may break a rule in another. This is how all language works—the rules are really structures and conventions that people within a group unconsciously agree to use in their speech. Pronouncing the word *pen* to rhyme with *hen* is a rule of Northern and much Midwestern speech, but the rule in large parts of the South is to rhyme *pen* with *tin*. Many British speakers pronounce the *t* in the word *butter* but leave off the *r* at the end ("buttah"), whereas Americans generally turn the *t* into a *d* and pronounce the *r* "budder" except in the South and in parts of New England. Who's right? Each group follows the rules of its own community. To break them is to be an outsider.

2 Understand standard English as a function of power and social prestige

If every community has its own language rules, then who's to say why the so-called standard language should be the "better" language? Why *should* it be any more correct to say "There isn't anyone who can tell me anything about what I haven't seen" than to say "Ain't no body gon' tell me nuffin' bout what I ain't see"? After all, double negatives are acceptable in hundreds of languages around the world, so there isn't any logical reason why they should be incorrect in English. In fact, they were once perfectly acceptable, used by Chaucer and Shakespeare.

The answer to this question doesn't come from something in the language; it comes from something about the people who speak it. Around the world, languages have a prestige dialect that is thought to be more "correct" or "proper" than other dialects. How this dialect came to be the "right" one is almost always a matter of historical, political, and social forces. Some group of people came into power. They used language in a certain way. Because they had power, they also controlled things like schools, information, and books. Before long, their language became associated with correctness; grammarians then simply described that form of the language *as* correct, and people who wanted to be thought powerful or educated tried to learn its rules.

If your home dialect differs from the standard, you may be unfairly stereotyped or discriminated against by people in positions of power. Even unbiased people still may not listen to you because they can't: they aren't part of your dialect group. You're leaving them out of the conversation. Before deciding what, if anything, you want to do about differences between your community dialect and the standard, it's important to reflect on this issue of power. Some people believe that the society must begin accepting more varieties of language. Others believe that if such acceptance occurs, it will happen very slowly; but meanwhile, people will still discriminate against certain language varieties. If that's true, people without power will stay powerless if they can't communicate in the language of the powerful. But if they can gain positions of power, maybe they can then help to change public prejudices about language and culture.

**10a
lang**

Did You Know?

Language scholars have described several approaches to dealing with the issue of language variation. One approach is *eradication:* try to wipe out all language differences by teaching people to use only one standard. But whose? A second approach is *appreciation:* celebrate the diversity of differences in our speech, and accept all dialects as reflections of culture, heritage, and community. A third approach is *biloquialism* or *bidialectalism:* help people to learn more than one variety, so they can express themselves equally well in different situations and not give up their linguistic identities and ways of relating to their own communities.

Exercise 1

A. Briefly describe any features of your own home or community language you're aware of in your speech or writing. What kinds of features are they: words? accent? grammar? What are their sources? Have you ever felt stereotyped or discriminated against because of your home or community language, or have you ever felt awkward in a situation in which your speech differed from the speech of others? Is there disagreement within your own community about what's correct? How do you feel about the issue of language authority? Do you want to hold on to your community language? Do you want to get rid of all traces of that language? If you did, how would people in your home community respond?

B. In a group, compare your reflections from Exercise 1A. Focus specifically on the problem of power, prestige, and language prejudice.

3 Recognize the difference between accents and written variations

Different *accents* get stigmatized all the time, but they're more likely to be accepted than differences in *grammar.* While Americans don't usually mind differences in our leaders' accents, most people would balk at a president who said, "Them senators ain't ready for this-here veto" or "The First Lady, she all d'time be givin' me good advice on foreign policy."

In writing, the most glaring (and least forgiven) variations are *grammatical,* followed by *lexical* differences (word choice, including slang, jargon, and the like). People form unfair stereotypes on the basis of these language features, thinking they're signs of ignorance or laziness. To avoid such negative stereotypes and to succeed in your most important goal—having your readers listen to and respect your ideas—you'll need to recognize and edit any home or community language variations that may not be shared by a wider reading public. Knowing these differences will make you a more flexible communicator, able to move effectively between a home or community dialect and a broader public form of language.

4 Learn how to code-shift

One way speakers adjust their language to meet the expectations of particular communities is through what's called **code-shifting.** Some situations compel you to talk in ways that meet the expectations of your home or community language variety, while other situations—less personal, or more broadly public—beg for a different kind of speech. In other words, talk the talk and walk the walk.

10a
lang

Code-shifting is also a characteristic of writing. Many people write in a home or community language to their friends, but they shift into formal language in an essay, a letter to an elected official, or a corporate report. University of Pittsburgh assistant dean Barbara Mellix, for example, tells of her own code-shifting in an essay, "From Outside, In." Annoyed by her daughter's persistent interruptions while she's writing, she tells her, "Looka here, Allie, you are too old for this kind of carryin' on. I done told you this is important. You wronger than dirt to be in here haggin' me like this and you know it. Now git outta here and leave me off before I put my foot all the way down." Yet to make her points about language difference, in her writing Mellix feels compelled to use a different code.

> Now that I know that to seek knowledge, freedom, and autonomy means always to be in the concentrated process of becoming—always to be venturing into new territory, feeling one's way at first, then getting one's balance, negotiating, accommodating, discovering one's self in ways that previously defined "others"—I sometimes get tired.
> —BARBARA MELLIX, "From Outside, In."

In some formats, such as personal letters or an academic journal designed to help you think about course material (see 2d), you should feel at ease writing in a home or community variety. In other, typically more formal situations, where certain home or community variations can be stigmatized, most writers play it safe and adopt a style for their writing that will work across many different communities. In the United States, this variety is often called standard edited American English.

**10a
lang**

S T R A T E G Y

Seek out a member of your home language community who also has good facility with standard edited American English. Ask this person for advice about how to edit one of your papers for readers who expect this from what they read. As you work with this reader, see if you can figure out his or her techniques for managing to use several language varieties successfully.

---

5 Become aware of the grammatical variations in your home dialect

Grammatical variations in your home or community dialect can be tricky to notice in your writing; after all, they may not look the least bit odd or problematic—to you. But someone who isn't a member of your dialect community will see them right away.

HOME VARIETY	Miss Brill know that the lovers making fun of her, but she act like she don't care.
EDITED	Miss Brill knows that the lovers are making fun of her, but she acts as if she doesn't care.
HOME VARIETY	The FDA guy said to Dougherty could he borrow him the test kit, but Dougherty said he would bring it with.
EDITED	A member of the FDA asked whether Dougherty could lend him the test kit, but Dougherty said he would bring it with him.
HOME VARIETY	The minutes of the last meeting state that unless if Ray-Corp had ordered the resistors, the shipment was sent out on accident.
EDITED	The minutes of the last meeting state that unless RayCorp had ordered the resistors, the shipment was sent out accidentally.

S T R A T E G Y

**10a
lang**

If you see variations in your home or community language as rules or patterns, it may be easier for you to match them up against the rules of a standard. What are the rules of your community language? Keep a list in a notebook. On the left side of each page, record examples of rule differences in your community language; on the right side, write down the corresponding examples in standard English. Then try to write an explanation of the differences in your own terms, as in the following example written by a student from Kentucky.

Rule in my part of Kentucky: The lawn needs mowed.
Rule elsewhere: The lawn needs to be mowed.

Everyone in my part of Kentucky leaves out the *to be* and just puts in the verb after *needs*. It's always seemed natural to me, but I learned that it is only done in certain parts of the United States. I can use the "search" function on my computer to look for the word *needs* and then make sure I fix the mistake.

Exercise 2

A. Consider the following exerpt from *Their Eyes Were Watching God,* a novel by African American author Zora Neale Hurston. This conversation between two characters, Phoeby Watson and Janie

Stark, represents the language variety used in the characters' home and community and is therefore the most expressive way for them to relate to each other.

> [Phoeby] found [Janie] sitting on the steps of the back porch with the lamps all filled and the chimneys cleaned.
>
> "Hello, Janie, how you comin'?"
>
> "Aw, pretty good, Ah'm tryin' to soak some uh de tiredness and de dirt outa mah feet." She laughed a little.
>
> "Ah see you is. Gal, you sho looks *good*. You looks like youse yo' own daughter." They both laughed. "Even wid dem overhalls on, you shows yo' womanhood."
>
> "G'wan! G'wan! You must think Ah brought yuh somethin'. When Ah ain't brought home a thing but mahself."
>
> "Dat's a gracious plenty. Yo' friends wouldn't want nothin' better."   —ZORA NEAL HURSTON, *Their Eyes Were Watching God*

The second passage is a letter requesting that a local YWCA suspend the writer's membership until she is able to exercise again. The passage contains features of the writer's home community dialect that are not considered standard. The letter is aimed at a general reading public, because the YWCA may employ people who do not share the writer's language variety.

**10a
lang**

Dear Mrs. Voit,

Like I explain to you when I call last week, I ain't been use my YWCA membership since November because I am pregnant and my doctor be telling me not to work out. Please stop my membership now and I call you when I want it start up again.

Sincerely,

Loretta Saunders

Edit both passages to make them conform to standard written English. Now reflect on the consequences of your changes. Has anything been lost from either passage? Has anything been gained through editing? How appropriate are the changes made to each passage?

 B. In a group, compare your changes and your reflections from Exercise 2A. What does this exercise suggest about the principle of standard English and the idea of flexibility?

10b Understanding how dialect influences writing

Along with dialect differences, all speakers of English also use differences in **register** in both their speaking and their writing. Register is the form that language takes in a particular context. The variations can be in pronunciation, grammar, or word choice. You might use a *formal* register when being interviewed for an important job, an *informal* register at a ballgame, a *technical* register when explaining to a colleague how a piece of electronic equipment works, or a *simplified* register when talking with a toddler.

In writing, you want to make sure you get the register right. That will depend on your intended readers and their knowledge, your context, and your **persona,** or who you want to "be" in your writing. You may need to shift registers if aspects of your home or community language are thought to be too informal for broader or more formal settings. (See also 10a-5.)

1 Become aware of oral language influences

Most of the language we produce is spoken. If you haven't been a very avid reader, there may be expressions, terms, and constructions that you *hear* often but haven't *seen* much in print. Your knowledge of sound can trick you into making an error when you turn that sound into print.

10b
lang

Consider one of the most common mistakes in writing: spelling the phrase *a lot* as one word (*alot*). Why do so many people do this? Partly because they're smart: spoken, this phrase really does sound like one word, with little or no pause between *a* and *lot*. Or they may not have noticed *a lot* spelled again and again as two words. These sorts of transcription errors show up often in unedited prose.

I should of signed the check	for	*I should have signed the check*
excetera	for	*et cetera*
expresso	for	*espresso*

The way language sounds in your home or community variety can also end up in your writing, and this may unfortunately (and often unfairly) lead your reader to judge you negatively or doubt your credibility or intelligence. In the first example below, the omission of *-ed* from *ask* is clearly an intelligent mistake: the *-ed* of *asked* is pronounced as a *t,* and the *t* of *Trish* swallows it in speech. In the second example, illustrating the influence of Spanish, *this* sounds like *these* to the writer, leading to another intelligent mistake, while the repetition of *either* is a common feature of the Chicano English of Southern California.

DRAFT   The personnel department ask Trish Walters could she expedite the request.

> **READER'S REACTION:** Why is *ask* in the present tense? Also, when I get to *could*, I'm thrown off track. The writer seems careless.

EDITED   The personnel department asked Trish Walters whether she could expedite the request.

DRAFT   Either the character cause all this events, or either they are coincidental.

EDITED   Either the characters cause all these events, or they are coincidental.

2 Consider your word choices

Usually, writers consciously choose their words to make them appropriate for the occasion—formal or informal, complex or simple. But sometimes writers unknowingly use words that are part of their home or community language but are not shared by a broader community of readers. In such cases, readers may think the text is too informal because it uses "local" words. These words can usually be spotted with a careful editorial eye and the help of a good dictionary.

DRAFT   Our interoffice mail is consistently slow because the mailboy has to schlep the large packages along with the memos and letters.

> **READER'S REACTION:** "Schlep?" Is that some sort of corporate term?

EDITED   Our interoffice mail is consistently slow because the mailboy has to carry the large packages along with the memos and letters.

DRAFT   Some of the budget surplus should be used on our public parks, which need new play areas and working bubblers.

> **READER'S REACTION:** What's a bubbler?

EDITED   Some of the budget surplus should be used on our public parks, which need new play areas and drinking fountains that work.

STRATEGY

To gauge the appropriateness of your word choices, first consider the intended audience and occasion of your writing. In something directed to members of a specific community, it may be acceptable to use "local" words such as *homeboy, mazeh,* or *happa.*

10b
lang

If your writing occasion and audience are broader and more formal (for example, a corporate memo or an academic paper), skim through your writing looking for word choices that strike you as questionable or problematic. Circle or underline those words as you encounter them, but keep reading to the end of the paper.

Finally, work back through the text, stopping at each underlined or circled word and listing or trying out alternatives that seem more in keeping with the level of formality, audience, and occasion of your writing.

---

3 Distinguish between slang and dialect

Words that are part of a dialect have usually been around in that dialect for some time. People of all ages may use them, and they are known by much or most of the dialect community. Sometimes these words even blend into the standard language—for example, the word *jazz.*

When groups within a dialect community (often young people) begin creating new words that aren't shared by the entire community, those words will be considered **slang.** Many older members of a dialect community express negative attitudes toward the use of slang by younger people, even though all of them may be using a language variety considered to be nonstandard. Although slang is an important way to show membership in a group and is often very creative, you should avoid using it in writing, except perhaps for informal journal writing or learning logs. Some people may not understand it; others may feel alienated from your prose. Still others, both within and beyond your language community, may not trust your ideas or take them seriously.

SLANG   The battle scenes in *The Iliad* are phat. Just when Agamemnon chill, someone diss him or jack something up and he wage another war.

(For more on word usage, see Chapter 28.)

4 Recognize cases of hypercorrection

People who use a nonmainstream or stigmatized dialect may become aware of certain language habits that are not considered the norm. When they shift registers in formal situations, they may unconsciously try to "repair" their speech. Sometimes they may unwittingly create a new error in trying to be correct. Linguists call this phenomenon **hypercorrection.**

In speech, for example, some New Englanders who don't pronounce their *r*'s at the end of words after vowels (*mothuh, fathuh, cah* for *mother, father,* and *car*) may hypercorrect themselves by putting an *r* at the end of a

**10b
lang**

word where it doesn't really belong. Some Cockney speakers in London incorrectly put *h*'s at the beginning of words with vowels (*howl* for *owl* or *hasked* for *asked*) in formal situations because they tend to drop the *h* from words where there really is one (*'e* for *he*, *'asn't* for *hasn't*, *'ad* for *had*).

Certain kinds of hypercorrection can affect writers, especially in the area of grammar. But instead of being too informal, writers create hypercorrection because they're *trying* to be formal. In an urge to be correct, the writer guesses that a construction is wrong and ironically substitutes an error for it.

HYPERCORRECT   Stuart will give the petitions to Mary and I.

EDITED   Stuart will give the petitions to Mary and me.

The concept of hypercorrection can also apply to the style and structure of your sentences. If you try too hard to be formal and sophisticated, you may end up writing tangled prose. Don't be fooled into thinking that complex words and sentences alone will create an "impressive" register; your readers won't be impressed, just frustrated.

CONVOLUTED   That the girl walks away, and the showing of the parrot to the restaurant owner who, having closed shop, is not about to let her inside, is indicative of that which characterizes the novel throughout, i.e., denial and deception.

EDITED   The central theme of denial and deception is illustrated when the girl tries to show the parrot to the restaurant owner and is turned away.

Hypercorrection can also affect the use and spelling of words. For example, when a writer spells the phrase *Adam and Eve* as *Atom and Eve,* she's assuming the *d* in *Adam* works like the *t* in *writer* or *batter* (which is pronounced like a *d*), so she hypercorrects the word to *Atom.*

10b
lang

S T R A T E G Y

When you feel uncertain about a construction or grammatical rule in your formal writing, circle the words in question or put an asterisk in the margin. Then check the rule in this handbook or another grammatical resource, or ask someone for advice. Keep a running list of any cases of hypercorrection you identify, and explain them to yourself in your own words. Do the same for any cases of hypercorrection that are identified for you by a peer reader, teacher, or collaborator.

Writing in Online Communities

Written in collaboration with Michael E. Doherty and Sandra Thompson,
Writing, Editing, and Internet Consultants

Even with the advent of multimedia Web sites, audio players, and video feeds across the Internet, the most common form of online communication is the written word.

Many types of online writing environments now foster communities in which individuals with common interests meet electronically to exchange ideas and information. Whatever your academic interests, civic concerns, or personal hobbies, you will almost certainly be able to find an online group that shares your enthusiasms. As a newcomer, you must pay attention to an online community's language, customs, and accepted standards and learn to represent yourself in appropriate ways. In order to find your own personal or professional online voice, you need to learn how to meet each community's needs.

11a Writing online

Whether you are writing an email message to classmates about a collaborative project, building a personal Web site to supplement your résumé, or participating in an online "bulletin board" discussion about a local environmental issue, you need to consider the specific needs of your online audience, your purpose, how you wish to represent yourself to others, and the conventions of online language.

1 Finding your audience online

Membership in online communities is usually determined by topic of interest. Fans of the Dallas Cowboys can chat daily about the latest trade rumor or game story. Students in a course on African American literature and culture might design a Web site featuring interviews with local

African American artists and activists. Opponents of a bill in Congress can use email to gather "electronic signatures" on petitions to their legislative representatives. In each instance, online writers must tailor their messages to the specific community to achieve their purposes.

As you use search engines (45c) or suggestions from print resources or friends to explore the various online resources available to you in your field of interest, pay particular attention to the **format** of the information. Is it long and technical, brief and informal, argumentative or conversational? Are there many links to other sites and sources, or is the site self-contained? The format reveals the type of writing typically used in an online community as well the type of writing the community will expect from you. In addition, writers in an online community must be aware of the expected **decorum** (or conduct) of the community's members.

A brief period of "lurking" (reading without participating) is a good opportunity to determine whether the audience for a particular email discussion, Web forum, or other online community is appropriate to your own talents and expectations. It's also a good time to note who else frequently participates and to learn the rules of participation or pick up any terms or ideas commonly employed.

2 Defining your purpose for writing online

Defining your purpose for writing online is similar to defining your purpose for writing in any other situation; however, your potential audience is generally larger. Before you commit to publishing your work on the Internet, consider carefully your readers and, above all, what you want to tell them. Remember that online communication has created so much more information for the average computer user that your audience may be irritated if your message doesn't really contribute anything new or have a clear purpose. If you quickly send an email response to a discussion you've just joined, without taking the time to see what messages have already been sent, you may seem to be "out of the loop" and lose credibility.

S T R A T E G Y

Before sending messages or posting information, ask some questions about your purpose.

- What's the context of my message? How does my information extend, amplify, or clarify prior information?
- Why will readers find my information helpful or interesting?
- What do I want readers to *do* with the information or ideas: respond? take action? think more deeply about the issue?

3 Creating an online persona

When you participate in an online community, your **persona,** or how you define yourself to others, can be developed indepth because you can make repeated contributions in response to what others say. Nonetheless, this aspect of online communication differs from face-to-face communication in important ways.

- You can remain anonymous.
- You can represent yourself in as many styles or voices as you wish.
- You can use your real name or choose a made-up name.
- You can choose not to identify your gender or ethnicity.
- You can choose to be a "silent" type and contribute rarely, or you can contribute often.
- You can "lurk," itself a choice of persona.

While these choices can be useful as you join new online communities, also be careful not to abuse them. It's your right to represent yourself as you wish, but do so honestly. Be cautious not to accept too blindly the way others represent themselves to you.

Of course, you may not always have this level of anonymity, especially in academic settings. If you're writing an email message to your instructor, you need to tailor your persona to suit your purpose. If you're asking for a letter of recommendation, you'll want to do so respectfully and formally in a way that reminds your instructor not only of your grades and accomplishments but also of your classroom contributions and attitude. If you're contributing to an online peer review of a classmate's paper or presentation, you'll want to be supportive and friendly—but neither too casual nor too harshly critical.

11a online

4 Recognizing community standards: Netiquette

Online communities vary widely in the kinds of language and behavior they tolerate and expect from members. It's your responsibility to familiarize yourself with commonsense guidelines (known as **netiquette**) that apply across nearly all Internet communities and to learn the standards of the specific group you want to address. Otherwise you may create a negative persona: brash, hypercritical, bossy, insensitive, or crude. As in any social situation, members will discount or ignore such participants or "expel" them from the group. Here are some guidelines.

- **Think before you act.** You can't take back a sent email. Never put anything in an email message you wouldn't want your mother to read in the newspaper. The same goes for Web pages: while you can always take them down, you never know how many people have already seen them—including potential employers.
- **Learn before you act.** Lurk and learn the norms of the community. Don't post to a group to ask what something means if you can find

the answer on a FAQ (frequently asked questions) page at the group's site.

- **Act, don't react.** Avoid posting "flames" (personal attacks) to contributors you disagree with.
- **Don't "spam."** Spamming is sending unsolicited email to large groups. The practice is rude and, in some cases, illegal. Avoid sending off-topic messages.
- **Don't use ALL CAPS.** Like shouting, this practice is rude.
- **Attend to grammar.** Even if online messages seem informal, bad grammar, spelling mistakes, and poor word usage still convey a feeling of sloppiness or a lack of concern for readers.
- **Cut the fat.** Include only *relevant* information from previous messages. When you reply to a message, delete everything from the original that's not necessary.
- **The Golden Rule of netiquette.** Don't forget that there are real people behind every computer that receives your email or loads your Web site. Be forgiving of other people's grammar or spelling errors.

Where to Find It

- *FAQ.org* ⟨http://www.faq.org⟩
  This site bills itself as "the ultimate starting point for frequently asked questions."
- *The Netiquette Homepage* ⟨http://www.albion.com/netiquette/index.html⟩
  This site includes the complete text of Virginia Shea's book *Netiquette,* a quiz, a mailing list, and more.

11b email

11b Communicating with email

Email is a popular means of communication primarily because it is *fast.*

1 Writing email for different communities

There are two main types of electronic mail: individual mail and list-based mail. When you are writing individual mail, you decide exactly who will receive your message. When you are writing list-based mail (see 1c-1), you are addressing a predetermined audience of subscribers to a list, all of whom will receive what you write.

Do not assume, however, that individual mail is more "personal" while list mail is more "professional." Many lists are chatty with informal conversation between friends, and individual mail might be written as an introduction to a potential employer or to complain about a rent increase. As in any other type of writing, you have to adopt the appropriate tone for your audience. If you don't adjust your persona to suit your purpose for writing, your message will likely not be communicated to your audience in the way you intended.

STRATEGY

Emoticons (*emotion* + *icon*) are a kind of shorthand code that allows writers to add a jolt of feeling to their text. Emoticons are faces drawn with keyboard characters; tilt your head to the left as you look at these.

:-)	grin	:-/	ambivalent
:-(	frown	:-0	shouting
;-)	wink	8-0	bug-eyed surprise

Internet writers also frequently use **acronyms,** abbreviations for common phrases that are used to speed up communication.

BTW	by the way	FYI	for your information
F2F	face-to-face	HTH	Hope that helps!
FAQ	frequently asked questions	TIA	thanks in advance
		IMHO	in my humble opinion
FWIW	for what it's worth	WYSIWIG	what you see is what you get

Emoticons and acronyms are generally considered to be appropriate for casual communication but not for professional or academic writing.

**11b
email**

2 Using the elements of email

Every email message has elements that convey a specific kind of information and help you effectively communicate your purpose or create your persona.

From. State your identity in the "from line" of each email message you send. While some email programs show a sender's address in the "from" section, others display a chosen **screen name,** a self-identifier the user chooses for herself. A screen name like *LeoFan* might entertain your friends, but it will not make a positive impression on a potential employer. Your screen name creates an important part of your online persona.

Sent. This line displays the date and time your mail is sent.

To. This line identifies the recipient of your email, either an individual or a group. Two other lines—"cc:" (carbon copy) and "bcc:" (blind carbon copy)—enable you to send mail to people who are not part of the primary audience, but who might be interested in the subject matter. With blind carbon copy, you can send copies without the main recipients knowing because the addresses for the copies will not appear in the texts sent to the main recipients.

Subject. Use this line to draw readers into reading the actual message. Short and clear subject lines are best. If you are adding commentary to a continuing "thread" or (discussion), the reply function of your mail program will usually automatically dictate the subject line: "Re: ⟨Original Subject⟩."

Message body. Long messages are more likely to be deleted, left unread, or only partially read. If you are replying to someone, make clear what it is that you are replying to, but do not include entire previous messages.

Signature or sig file. Sign your email. Differences between email programs mean that your message might not always be easily identified by the recipient. If you have a mail program that allows you to automatically attach a signature file, write out your full name and some contact information. Many people include clever quotations, song lyrics, and jokes in their signature files. Be aware of how such additions affect your online persona.

**11b
email**

Domain Names and Types

A **domain name** locates an organization or other entity on the Internet. For instance, the National Association for the Advancement of Colored People maintains the domain name naacp.org as part of its Web site address and in its email addresses.

A number of suffixes used by American Web sites can tell you a great deal about what you are reading.

.com	commercial sites	.net	network sites
.edu	educational sites	.org	nonprofit organizations
.gov	government sites		

You can identify email as originating from a country outside the United States by looking at additional suffixes. For example, email with the suffix *.ca* is from Canada, *.uk* is from Great Britain, and *.no* is from Norway.

3 Using the functions of email

Just as each email message has certain elements (see 11b-2), every email program has buttons or commands that allow you to manage your correspondence in a variety of ways.

Reply and **reply-all.** When you respond to a posting or email using the *Reply* function, your message will go to the person who sent you the message. When you use the *Reply-all* function, it will go to any other people who received the original communication. (To determine who they are, check both the "To:" and "Cc:" lines.) Be careful when you use the *Reply-all* function so that you do not accidentally post a personal note to a public space.

Forward. It is very easy to forward email; this is the reason Internet urban legends messages are so prominent. Remember that what you have written can be forwarded to anyone who has an email account. Also, think twice before forwarding information such as birth announcements, jokes, or press releases that you have received. They may not be intended for universal release.

Attach. Most mail programs allow you to attach and email documents such as word-processed files, spreadsheets, and video clips. Not all mail programs support attachments, so you cannot assume your recipients will be able to read your document.

11c
web

11c Participating in online communities

The four most common formats for online communities are listservs, newsgroups, Web forums, and "real-time" writing. Each format plays host to communities engaged in writing on a variety of topics.

1 Listservs and newsgroups

Listservs *come* to you. You *go to* newsgroups. The writing format and style concerns of each are similar. To join or subscribe to a **listserv,** the most common type of subscriber-based mailing list, you send an email message to the service that hosts the listserv. You then automatically receive all the messages from the listserv at your email address. When you post a message to a listserv, usually it is first reviewed by the list moderator (some lists are not moderated). If it passes the moderator's standards, it is emailed to the personal addresses of all the people subscribed. It is important, then, to adapt to the community's standards, or your messages will never be made available to your peers.

You can access **newsgroups** without having email messages sent to your personal address. You can scan the topics and threads for a subject that interests you and choose the individual posts you wish to read. The message you send to a newsgroup is immediately posted and available for reading by anyone. Newsgroups are usually not moderated.

As you consider your writing strategies for participating in these forums, you should keep in mind that there is one significant difference between them: newsgroup postings are generally archived and made accessible to anyone with an Internet connection, whereas listserv postings are seen only by subscribers to that list (unless the message is forwarded elsewhere by a subscriber). It is easy to become careless in newsgroup postings because they usually are not moderated and they often have an informal tone. You must always remember that someone, perhaps one of your instructors or a colleague, may read your poorly constructed message; this message can influence this person's impression of your credibility.

Listservs are more popular than newsgroups in the classroom because privacy may be required for class discussion, and readers external to the course could interfere or take the discussion off track. Conversely, newsgroups are popular resources in community and social action initiatives; groups like alt.activism.student welcome outside participation and growth.

11c
web

2 Writing in Web-based forums

Web-based forums allow users to easily access sites where they can participate in conversations with others who share interests. More than a quarter of a million Web forums are already in existence, covering topics that range from current events to entertainment.

These Web forums are a refined version of the early text-only bulletin boards, which required special software. Unlike listservs, which are mailed only to those who request to join, anyone with the proper software could read these bulletin boards. Some Web-based forums are moderated. Many, such as the popular CollegeEdge forums, ask you to set up a user name with a password; a few charge a fee for participation.

Writing in Web-based forums has adopted most of the now-traditional conventions associated with those early bulletin boards: the use of informal language, frequent use of emoticons and abbreviations, and the citing of previously written material to provide context.

3 Real-time writing

The Internet now supports a variety of ways for people to participate in "real-time" electronic discussions and communities. **Real time** means that the discussion takes place without delay; your words appear on the screen of every user involved in the discussion as soon as they are typed. Such conversations can take place between participants who are in the same classroom or scattered around the world.

The most popular real-time communities in current use are **chat rooms** hosted by private Internet services or available via the Internet Relay Chat (IRC) network. Chat rooms are usually quite informal and have become a popular way for celebrities to "meet" their fans online. Chats open to the public, such as interviews with politicians or "town hall" meetings, are almost always moderated, so your writing will be controlled by an "editor" who decides whether you may post your questions or comments.

The real-time venue most often used in academic situations and in some corporate settings is called a **MUD,** or multi-user domain. Users learn a series of commands to communicate with each other and to "move" from room to room, or place to place, in a carefully described text environment. They may adopt permanent characters, or "avatars," to regularly interact with other participants. Writing in MUD space, while playful and informal in many cases, requires significantly more practice than chat rooms to attain a comfort level most writers need for effective participation. MUD technology is frequently used to connect classrooms on different campuses, or even in different countries, so that students can discuss a group project and post their work.

Where to Find It

- *Liszt, the Mailing List Directory* ·http://www.liszt.com/Ò
  The Internet's largest and most popular searchable list directory categorizes thousands of lists by topic.
- *eGroups* ⟨http://www.egroups.com/⟩
  More than 50,000 free Web-based email lists are hosted and archived here.
- *ForumOne* ⟨http://www.forumone.com/⟩
  More than a quarter of a million Web-based bulletin boards are cataloged by topic.
- *DejaNews* ⟨http://www.dejanews.com⟩
  More than 80,000 discussion forums, primarily Usenet newsgoups, are listed at this site.

11d Writing for the World Wide Web

There are various types of Web pages. The most common is the **personal home page,** an individual author's effort to create a place for herself online. Additionally, you will see commercial sites (including corporate pages, sites sponsored by nonprofit organizations, and online shopping opportunities), educational sites (including school and university pages, scholarly journals, and free informational presentations), and news/entertainment sites (including newspapers, magazines, and other media). **Search engines** are dedicated entirely to indexing and sorting Web pages for user convenience.

1 Establishing a purpose and persona for your Web page

If you are building a personal home page on the Web, consider what you want the general format to be. Are you fulfilling an assignment for a biology class project on coral reef preservation? You might include maps and photographs of reefs to illustrate your research, along with links to sites sponsored by environmental organizations. Are you setting up an "online business card"? Limit the material to very general information and contact listings. Will your site function like a résumé? Provide detailed information about your professional interests and abilities, perhaps with links to volunteer organizations you have worked with and classroom projects you are proud of. Are you designing a resource for people with interests similar to yours? Add links and commentary on sources you find useful. Or are you producing a kind of autobiography, so your friends and family can see what you're up to?

You need to determine your audience and what aspects of yourself you want to present to the online community. If your site is designed for your instructor and your fellow students, will you be surprised or annoyed if someone you do not want to hear from or have never met sends you email commenting on your site? If your autobiographical page shows off your keen sarcastic wit and comments on your political views, are you comfortable knowing that a potential employer may find that site using a simple search engine?

Before building any Web site, spend time studying sites with similar purposes. Make lists of what you do and do not like about these sites. Consider contacting the authors and designers of those pages to ask for advice before you start, or for feedback after you have begun. And, just as you would ask for peer feedback on a paper in progress, ask fellow students, colleagues, or friends for comments and suggestions.

Be careful naming your site. Search engines will index it based on the words that appear in the title and in text of the site. Select your words carefully, and when you are ready to publish, visit the major search engine sites to learn the process of registering and indexing your site and its title. When writing for the Web, effective search engine registration is almost as important as making sure the actual information in your site is accurate.

11d
web

2 Considering your audience

Getting feedback from your intended Web audience is the best way to make sure you are effectively participating in an online community. There are a few simple rules to remember when constructing and maintaining a site.

- **Content is key.** Most Web users are looking for information, not "cool" design and graphics. Make sure any graphics reinforce your topic rather than just take up space.
- **Update, update, update.** In many ways, outdated content is worse than none at all. Don't leave "Under construction" icons all over your site. Publish the site when it is actually ready, and update it whenever necessary. Do not include a "last update" line unless you are serious about tending your site regularly.
- **Check your links.** If your site includes links to supporting documents and data or to other sites of interest, be sure to check those links from time to time to make sure they are still accurate. Rebuild any broken links; if possible, replace any that have disappeared with links to similar sites, especially if the link provides key evidence and support to your own Web page.

**11e
plag**

STRATEGY

- Allow ample "white space."
- Test your Web pages on various platforms and browsers. Something designed using *Internet Explorer* on a PC may look significantly different in *Netscape Navigator* on a Macintosh.
- Always include contact information, preferably in the form of an automatic email link. However, *never* put your full name, address, and phone number (or other vital information) in this space.

11e Avoiding plagiarism when working online

The easy availability of so much content online can challenge the very foundation of what we mean when we talk about plagiarism. Careful documentation of sources in your work is more critical to effective communication than ever before. (For more on plagiarism, see 47d.)

1 Always document or credit information borrowed from others

It's so easy to forward electronic mail, download software programs and images, create Web pages, and copy material published online that governments worldwide are being forced to reconsider the concept of "intellectual property." Who owns the rights to words, images, or ideas? How can those rights be protected without prohibiting the free flow of information that the Internet makes possible? The issues make it important for you to document every online source you use in developing your writing.

Remember too that your credibility depends on the credibility of the community resource you choose to rely on. If you are writing a paper about diabetes, citing sources from a collection of official American Diabetes Association Web pages and a moderated listserv of endocrinologists is far more effective than citing email from a local bulletin board about a new home remedy. For all information from online sources you wish to cite, ask yourself, "Where did it come from?" If you are not confident about your answer, your instructor might be able to help you evaluate the credibility of a source. You should also be prepared to find an alternative site.

11e
plag

STRATEGY

Cutting and pasting information from Web sites and other Internet resources into a single document for later use is a good way to consolidate your research. This new form of note taking, however, can lead to accidental plagiarism. It is easy to forget where something originally came from and mistakenly convince yourself the writing is your own! To avoid this problem, follow these guidelines.

- Always write down the address of any Web site you are using, and clearly label text you copy from that site. Print the first page of each Web site you're using for easy reference in case your later drafts require further documentation. The printout should include the site's URL so you can return to it for future reference and also for citation purposes.
- Always note the date when you found the information. Web sites can be updated every day, and your cited information may disappear. In addition, you will need to provide the access date in your citation if you use the information in your final document. (For more on citation issues, see also Chapter 53.)
- If you're citing an email, listserv, or Web forum message that has not been posted to a publicly accessible location, ask the author's permission before quoting. It's a good idea to do this even if the posting is public.

- Corroborate your sources. Follow the journalist's rule: If you can't find information in at least two credible places on the Internet, don't use the material.

---

2 Acting ethically online

When working online, do so ethically and professionally. If you are new to the Internet, it will not take you long to discover paper mills—the electronic equivalent of the celebrated, illegal tradition of fraternity and dormitory "test files." Additionally, many writing classes now post their work to the Web for peer review, and you may find these papers and projects when you use a search engine. It's far too easy to find and download a completed paper on virtually any topic, change a few names and dates, and turn it in. You should carefully consider the moral implications of abusing Internet resources in this way. Also keep in mind that your instructor has access to those same sources. A common practice among teachers who suspect plagiarism is to input random phrases from student papers into a search engine and see whether those phrases appear anywhere else on the Web.

In the workplace, many employers worry that the Internet provides workers with too much opportunity to "surf," to catch up on sports scores, make vacation plans, or download inappropriate material using company equipment on company time. Keep in mind that it is now possible, and perfectly legal, for these employers to track and monitor what Web sites and other Internet resources employees are accessing and to block out certain kinds of material. If you are using an email account provided by your employer, you should be aware that in most situations, you do not have any legal expectation of a right to privacy for anything you write or post from that account.

When you are using an email account provided by a college or university—whether you are in class or even on campus at the time or not—you are responsible for adhering to the institution's policies and regulations. If you are accessing the Internet through a service provider, you are obligated to abide by the client rights and responsibilities outlined in your contract.

**11e
plag**

12

Representing Yourself Through Critical Reasoning

Every day people receive letters asking them to renew something: a magazine subscription, membership in a professional organization, a business contract, or a pledge to a charitable organization. Compare these two letters urging theatergoers to resubscribe to a series of performances. Which would you prefer as a representation of your reasoning? Which line of reasoning is most likely to persuade readers to send a check?

WRITER 1   Ready to resubscribe to the "Broadway Performances" series? Next year's shows promise to be exciting and to appeal to the whole family. We have added one show to the series for a total of five. The cost for the whole series has increased by 20 percent—still a bargain, we think.

READER'S REACTION: No, I'm not ready. I've been so busy, I forgot it was time to renew. I can barely remember the shows we saw. Did we have a good time? What about the 20 percent increase? Is it really a bargain?

WRITER 2   Remember *The Phantom of the Opera? Evita?* Remember how everyone in your family enjoyed *The Lion King* and *Cats?* This year's "Broadway Performances" series offers shows like these and more: an added performance, for a total of five. That means five chances to share the music, acting, costumes, and dance that make Broadway shows so exciting and enjoyable. What's more, renewing your subscription for the five-show package will cost only 20 percent more than last year's four-show season ticket. That's even less per show.

READER'S REACTION: Yeah, they were good shows, and it might be nice to see some more. Adding one new show is probably worth an extra 20 percent. Sounds logical.

Writer 1's reasoning appears hasty and incomplete, and she leaves many potential questions unanswered. She gives readers few reasons to answer her appeal for resubscription. She also fails to explain her conclusion that the increase in costs is "a bargain." In contrast, Writer 2 gives clear reasons and detailed evidence in favor of resubscribing—examples of previous performances and enjoyable features of the shows as well as the reasonable claim that the coming year will offer similar experiences. She justifies the rise in cost. And she makes readers feel that she has anticipated their concerns and questions.

How you represent your reasoning is a crucial element in persuading readers to agree with your conclusions and accept the information in your writing. In representing your thinking, you create an image of yourself—a persona (see 10b)—whose qualities may shape the way readers in different settings and communities respond to your writing. Your reasoning, and the persona it creates, can help you

- To negotiate your role within a community of readers and writers
- To convince colleagues or fellow citizens whose outlooks differ from yours
- To persuade readers whose knowledge and authority are in some ways greater than yours: instructors, supervisors, public officials
- To encourage people to accept your advice and to draw on your expertise
- To enable you to challenge the outlooks or values of your readers

12a What is critical reasoning?

For most of us, critical reasoning begins informally. This is true even for people like scientists, philosophers, and computer engineers, who tend to be careful, logical thinkers. We begin by posing a question, identifying a problem or an issue, or considering an experience. Then we bring together ideas, information, and opinions that bear on the matter. After considering the subject or problem from various perspectives, we arrive at a likely, though tentative, conclusion.

Good critical thinkers take the process further. They fill in the gaps between their questions and their conclusions as a way of testing their reasoning. By searching for more and better evidence, considering alternatives, and checking their logic, such thinkers (and writers) are employing critical reasoning. Sometimes they confirm a conclusion, but just as often they recognize a need to modify it or arrive at an altogether different interpretation.

Can you do this alone? Not always. Even the best critical thinkers and writers draw on the insights and perspectives of others—through discussion, reading, or critical response—for help in identifying and filling in gaps in thinking and writing. To a considerable extent, then, critical thinking is a social act, taking place through dialogue.

S T R A T E G Y

When thinking critically with others, follow this advice.

- Begin the thinking/writing process with discussions (face-to-face or online) that identify issues, conclusions, evidence, and possible objections to your reasoning.
- Put your thoughts on paper tentatively; then read what others have written on the subject, creating a dialogue between your text and the others. Use the comparison to identify gaps in your evidence and reasoning or missteps in your logic.
- Ask others to critically read drafts of your writing, focusing on your conclusions, evidence, and reasoning. Ask them to raise as many reasonable objections as they can so you can take account of them as you revise.
- Put your work aside for a day or so until you can approach it as an outsider. Read it as your readers might, paying attention to gaps, misdirections, or missing evidence that undermines your clarity, persuasiveness, or credibility.
- Use electronic discussion—either in live, chat form (see 11c-3) or in posts to a discussion list (see 11c-1)—to explore and develop your reasoning.

Here are several posts to an electronic discussion on the topic of airbag safety. Note how each succeeding post adds ideas and information while addressing gaps in the reasoning of prior posts.

#1   They are in fact mandated by law. It wasn't demand, it was governmental edict.

#2   No. . . . You still have the choice of buying a car without an airbag. You know that a vehicle without an airbag is more dangerous than one with one, and you blatantly refuse to drive the safer vehicle. You instead choose the older, airbagless vehicle which also lacks other safety devices mandated by our government. If you have a wreck and hurt someone, it's because of your lack of concern for safety devices.

#3   If someone wants to thwart the efforts to reduce health care costs in this country by disabling their airbags, then so be it. If they want to buy a new vehicle, then part of that includes airbags; [they] still have the choice to buy whatever vehicle they want.

#4   You do realize they are forced on consumers by the government? More than a few people are upset about this fact. Any parent with a two-seat vehicle and a young child is very upset since the child cannot sit in the passenger seat due to the government safety laws which require two front airbags. Now wait, you can disable them, but this brings up the most aggravating point of all. The government requires you submit a form for approval with reasons you want to disable an airbag. After waiting a while, you get the form back approved, then you have to go pay the dealer to install a switch to turn off the airbag you didn't want in the first place. . . .

#5   I am sick to death of legislators, local, state and federal, passing all of these ridiculous laws which infinge on our personal liberty, under the banner of "it's for the sake of the children." . . . You tell me which would save more children: A good education, health care, a safe place to go after school, or locking up some [guy] who forgot to turn off an airbag.

#6   That guy killed a child from his negligence. . . . It's akin to pointing a gun at a person, and pulling the trigger, and saying "whoops!" When you realized you forgot to unload it. It's serious business. Driving an auto is not child's play; it's for responsible adults. Mishandling it can result in death or injury.

12a
reasor

Exercise 1

A. Locate a site where two or more people discuss the same topic in writing, preferably directly addressing each others' reasoning: an online discussion, a newspaper opinion page with contrasting editorials, a magazine article or interview, or records of a debate. Briefly summarize the position of each participant, and then discuss how each addresses or criticizes flaws or gaps in the reasoning of the other, either directly or by implication.

B. Working with a group in class or online, begin discussion by briefly stating your conclusions on an issue and giving the most important evidence for them. Pass this statement on, asking the next person to add other conclusions, evidence, objections, and counter-arguments. Have the last person summarize conclusions, evidence, and objections and circulate the original document and the summary to the rest of the group. Discuss how your group's reasoning was changed by the serial dialogue.

12b Building a chain of reasoning

Whether you are interpreting personal experience, making a recommendation about a work-related problem, exploring an academic topic, or urging people to take a stand on an issue, the path you take in your writing and ask others to follow is called a **chain of reasoning.** A chain of reasoning may have many different kinds of links, large and small. Some links may consist of information: examples, background facts, evidence, details, and scientific or scholarly data. Others may offer ideas: reasons, analysis, logical argument, citations from authorities, or differing points of view. Chains of reasoning vary from setting to setting as well. Academic audiences expect considerable attention to scholarly discussions of a subject, for example; work audiences expect discussions of the costs and workability of a proposal; public audiences may expect comment on issues of taxation or safety.

1 Identify conclusions

To gain a critical perspective on a chain of reasoning (your own or someone else's), you need to be able to identify the conclusions it offers. The end point of the reasoning—the **main conclusion**—is, of course, the most important. But remember that a piece of writing may offer more than one major conclusion. You might recommend adding workstations *and* upgrading software in order to keep better track of inventory; you might conclude that child abuse has multiple causes, each requiring explanation; or you might prepare a pamphlet offering several different ways to have a thriving garden without excessive use of fertilizers and pesticides.

Supporting conclusions are like the links in the chain of reasoning. So, too, are related though not essential observations, interpretations, or recommendations. Conclusions can take a number of forms.

Interpretations	of the meaning of an experience, film, or work of literature
	of the importance of a current or historical event
	of the causes or consequences of a problem
Analyses	of the elements of a problem, situation, or phenomenon
	of a scientific or academic subject
	of an issue or disagreement
Propositions	about an issue, problem, policy, or disagreement
Judgments	about values—the "rightness" or "wrongness" of an action or policy
	about the quality of a performance, an artwork, or a piece of writing
	about the effectiveness of a solution or proposed course of action
Warnings	about the potential consequences of specific actions or failure to act
Recommendations	for specific responses to a problem or situation
	for guidelines or policies
Plans	for further study
	for direct action
	for involving others

12b
reason

S T R A T E G Y

Listing your conclusions can help you strengthen your chain of reasoning.

1. Reflect on what you plan to say in an essay or report, or review a draft you have already written. Then list all your conclusions (interpretations, opinions, and so on), both major and minor. When your list is finished, decide which conclusions are the main focus of your essay or report and which ones contribute to the main point(s) as part of the chain of reasoning. Create two more lists, one containing the main conclusion, another the secondary or supporting conclusion(s).

2. Review your two lists of conclusions. Do any more come to mind? Are any assertions important to your chain of reasoning missing? Did you just forget to include them, or do you need to develop them?

3. Review the lists from the perspective of your potential readers. Think of any assertions you failed to include because they seem obvious. Are they actually interpretations or judgments that would be

recognized as such by readers less familiar with the subject than you are? Specific communities of readers will expect you to provide certain kinds of conclusions. Are you presenting the kinds of conclusions your readers will anticipate?

2 Identify information and inferences

Any chain of reasoning needs to contain both information (facts of all kinds—examples, data, details, and quotations) and inferences (conclusions or generalizations based on and supported by the information). Distinguishing information from inference is an important part of critical reasoning. In general, writers provide their readers with three kinds of information.

- **Background information** helps readers understand the scope and substance of an issue, subject or problem by providing knowledge of its history, context, or consequences.
- **Evidence** gives readers reasons for accepting the accuracy, value, or importance of conclusions.
- **Subject information** provides readers with an in-depth understanding of a subject and is itself of interest to readers or may be useful at present or in the future.

12b
reason

Information—what we loosely call **facts**—consists of details or knowledge you present as confirmable and as generally undisputed, or at least as likely to be accurate and reliable. **Inferences** or **generalizations** are conclusions you reach on the basis of facts. Information (facts) turns into **evidence** when it's used to persuade a reader that an idea is reasonable. As Françoise Meltzer puts it, "facts become evidence when put in the service of a claim." ("For Your Eyes Only: Ghost Citing.")

S T R A T E G Y

As you think critically about your topic and draft, be sure to distinguish between information and inference.

1. List the key facts relating to your subject. What do you know about your subject that readers will regard as undisputed or that you can confirm by presenting your observations, offering details, or documenting a reliable source? If you are reporting what someone else wrote or said, remember that while the quotation may be exact, readers may still be inclined to question its substance. You may need to provide confirming information. Sometimes the facts themselves may be in dispute, and you'll need to give readers reasons for accept-

ing the facts as you present them, at least while readers are attending to your discussion and the conclusions you offer.
2. Create a separate list of your inferences. What do the facts imply? What *might* happen as a result of the facts? If your purpose is to convey rather than interpret information, then you may list only a few inferences reflecting your understanding of the subject.

---

3 Assess evidence and reasoning

Readers will expect you to give evidence for your conclusions. They will also expect you to join evidence and assertions in reasonable ways: they will expect you to proceed logically. At the same time, evidence that one group of readers considers persuasive may not convince another group. Even scientists disagree over what constitutes evidence of global warming. No wonder, then, that businesspeople and public officials often look for different kinds of evidence when trying to decide whether to build a highway (port, airport, stadium) or to assess its environmental (social, economic) effects. This variation in what counts as good evidence is also true for the rules of logic (54c), which writers adapt to different communities of readers or purposes for writing.

Consider, for example, how two citizens groups might respond to a proposal to build a greenway between two parks, one located in the borough of Coolidge (an economically depressed neighborhood) and the other located in the borough of Lake Stearns (a wealthy, stable neighborhood of fine older homes). Starting from the assumption that residents of Coolidge are generally a law-abiding group deprived of shopping and services that have left the area due to a high crime rate, the CCC (Coolidge Citizens Consortium) logically supports the greenway because it will give residents access to recreation and shopping in Lake Stearns. Starting from the assumption that the balance of a peaceful, low-crime neighborhood can be easily upset, PLS (Preserve Lake Stearns) argues logically that though most Coolidge residents are law-abiding, the greenway will still draw some habitual criminals who will undermine quality of life and recreational space for Coolidge and Lake Stearns residents alike. Each side reasons logically, but they start with different assumptions and arrive at different conclusions.

12b
reasor

4 Consider your assumptions and your readers' assumptions

What assumptions and values do you bring to a specific writing task? How will they shape your readers' reactions? Some of these assumptions and values may be easy to identify, others less so because they are unspoken. In a work setting, for example, you might think that readers of a report are interested only in solutions to a problem that offer ways to cut costs and increase profit. You arrive at this conclusion because you've heard your colleagues talking about being more efficient and earning a greater return on investment. A closer look, though, might lead you to see that preserving jobs and offering a high-quality product are also goals your readers share, and you need to take these factors into account in your reasoning. The success of each group's reasoning may depend on how closely its members' assumptions correspond to those of their audience.

To evaluate your assumptions and values as you begin a writing task, try freewriting or brainstorming and listing (3a) in response to questions like these: "How do I view the groups of people on each side of this issue?" "What will my readers look for in a plan that addresses this problem?" "What do specialists in this field of study value as questions worth researching?"

If you know members of your intended audience, address such questions to them. If not, your freewriting and brainstorming should take into account both your specific writing task and assumptions often shared by members of the community you're addressing.

S T R A T E G Y

12b
reason

Use this checklist to critically assess the evidence in your own writing (or in something you are reading).

1. How *abundant* is the evidence? Is it *sufficient* to support your claim?
2. Does the evidence *directly support* the claim?
3. How *relevant* is the evidence?
4. How *accurate* is the evidence? How *well documented* is it?

S T R A T E G Y

---

1. Make a list of logical relationships you identify in your writing. Look especially for assertions that identify cause-effect links, that classify and make comparisons, that link generalizations and examples, or that offer definitions (see Chapter 3). Next, scrutinize your list to see whether these relationships are weak or strong, clearly logical or possibly illogical. (To help spot flaws in logic, see 54c) Delete any assertions that are weak, or rethink how to use them to support your conclusions.
2. To help spot weak reasoning and discover ways to strengthen it, try imagining (or writing out) the reactions of a somewhat skeptical reader.

WEAK   Entrance-ramp traffic lights ease highway congestion.

READER'S REACTION: **I'm skeptical. How do you know this?**

WEAK   Violence in schools is on the rise because violence in the movies and on TV has increased.

READER'S REACTION: **Is this true? My kids watch a lot of TV, but they aren't more violent than I was as a kid when TV was far less violent.**

WEAK   Smoking leads to higher rates of absenteeism in the work-place.

READER'S REACTION: **Prove it! I heard somewhere that smoking in the workplace actually makes smokers more productive workers.**

Exercise 2

A. Locate a document whose success or failure depends on the quality of its reasoning: a proposal, a position paper, an editorial, an academic article, or a memo on an important issue. Read it carefully, and identify its conclusions and the main kinds of evidence it presents. Next, try to identify any assumptions the writer makes that differ considerably from yours or those of another possible audience. Finally, use the four questions on page 160 to assess the quality of the evidence.

B. Share your document with a group of readers, and ask them to analyze it critically as in Exercise 2A. When they have finished, share your critical analyses and account for any differences, if you can. Decide as a group why you consider the document successful or unsuccessful, and be ready to explain why.

12c Representing your reasoning

Compare these excerpts from two letters to the editor of a city newspaper. Both writers express opinions about the controversial proposal to create a greenway connecting Coolidge and Lake Stearns.

WRITER **1**   City planners must be out of their minds to cook up this crazy idea. Drug pushers and thieves will have a field day preying on the people who use Lake Stearns Park, and soon the whole surrounding neighborhood will be destroyed by crime. We must stop these insane public officials before they totally destroy our lives with their senseless fantasies.

WRITER 2   The proposal to create a greenway connecting Coolidge and Lake Stearns Parks has the appearance of bridging the gap between these two very different communities. But the greenway will not solve the existing problems in Coolidge Park. Residents near Lake Stearns are not likely to ride their bikes or jog into Coolidge, and the presence of Coolidge residents in Stearns will only create a feeling, unjustified though it may be, of anxiety and defensiveness. City funds could be used more effectively to improve Coolidge Park by adding better lighting, attractive landscaping, a new basketball court, and an updated community center.

Both these letters argue the same point: that the proposal to create a greenway is shortsighted. But consider how the two writers present themselves. Writer 1 attacks the proposers and the residents of Coolidge while Writer 2 focuses on the proposal. Writer 1 uses emotionally charged words and phrases ("insane," "crazy," "drug pushers") while Writer 2 uses more balanced language. Writer 1 comes up with vague, impractical ideas ("stop these insane public officials") while Writer 2 offers specific alternatives for the use of city funds. In addition, Writer 1 dehumanizes and stereotypes the residents of Coolidge while Writer 2 seems to believe that they deserve an enhanced quality of life. Because of these and other differences, Writer 2 represents herself as balanced, thoughtful, and convincing, and Writer 1 comes off as impulsive, shallow, and uninformed.

The way you represent your reasoning in writing is crucial to acceptance of your information and ideas by readers. The tone you use and the words you choose (diction—see 28b) should be appropriate to your audience and purpose(s), of course. Emotional language may be appropriate when you're urging a public audience to act on the basis of shared belief. The same language would probably irritate, even offend fellow workers if you were trying to persuade them to abandon familiar procedures in favor of new ones you're proposing. In most cases, therefore, you can represent your reasoning most effectively by making clear to readers that you have analyzed information and ideas critically and by presenting your ideas and those of other people in balanced, thoughtful ways.

12c
reason

1 Be well informed

Whether you are creating an academic paper or a public document, preparing a report for work, or writing an essay for a general audience, you need to be well informed and make your audience aware that you are. Information, issues, and ideas are rarely "isolated"; they're embedded in social, occupational, historical, professional, or academic discipline–related contexts. As a result, writing reasonable, informed prose about a topic depends on knowing something about what surrounds it. It's difficult, for example, to give much more than an undeveloped, unsupported opinion about attempts to bar a controversial speaker from a campus or a local civic center unless you know something about local policies governing speakers, the provisions of the Constitution, the actual statements or publications of the speaker, and historical or legal cases involving freedom of speech.

STRATEGY

List what you know about your topic and what surrounds it. Rank-order your list from most to least important in light of the central purpose and focus of your writing. Now, for each of the two or three most important areas, try to define the gaps in your knowledge: What's still unclear? What *don't* you know that could help clarify your reasoning? Jot down some ideas about where you might find additional material to fill these gaps.

---

2 Acknowledge other perspectives

If you fail to acknowledge other people's points of view on some hotly contested issue, your readers will probably question your credibility, thinking: Does she know about these other arguments? Why doesn't she provide some answers to the serious questions they raise? Her whole presentation seems one-sided. You can expect reactions like these in other writing situations as well: from co-workers who wonder why you haven't discussed alternative solutions to the problem or from a research director who wonders why you haven't discussed related investigations that produced somewhat differing results.

Acknowledging and discussing other perspectives helps you avoid the suspicion that you are leaving out evidence that is not in your favor. It is also a requirement of sound reasoning. If you don't mention alternative explanations, conflicting evidence, or contrary arguments, your chain of reasoning is incomplete. Critical reasoning means considering the alternatives as well as the perspective you prefer.

3 Be balanced and reasonable

Your persona—who you are in writing—can make your reader trust and respect you, distrust and dislike you, or find you imbalanced and inconsiderate. As you decide how to present your ideas, therefore, it's important to consider your readers' potential reactions. You'll probably never write a document all readers will agree with, but you remain credible if they react by thinking, "Good point, carefully presented (even though I don't agree)" rather than "This is ridiculous, unconsidered, imbalanced."

12c
reason

UNCONSIDERED	The greenway will just become a conduit to transport the low-lifes of the Coolidge area into Lake Stearns Park and destroy its peace and quiet.
READER 1	What's a "low-life"? Is this term based on race? or class? How do we identify a "low-life"? Is everyone in Coolidge a "low-life"?
READER 2	Why is the greenway a "conduit"? Is it one-way? Where do people go when they move along a greenway? What do they do?
READER 3	What do you mean by the "peace and quiet" of Lake Stearns? Why—and how—would people from Coolidge "destroy" it?
READER 4	Doesn't everybody have access to public space? Are you suggesting that Lake Stearns should be off-limits to Coolidge residents?

4 Anticipate readers' reactions

When you're able to anticipate readers' reactions and answer their likely questions or objections in your writing, you build confidence in your reasoning and in any conclusions (recommendations, interpretations, opinions) you offer. This confidence arises both from the specific ways you respond to readers' concerns and from the sense that you understand the broader context of ideas and opinions your writing addresses.

5 Assess the appropriateness of strong bias for the occasion

The style and tone of your writing will often signal readers about your attitudes toward your subject. Some of the most colorful, interesting published writing is also admittedly very slanted, taking positions without caring too much about who might object. Such writers may feel they have earned the right to be biased because they are well known. They may even have achieved a kind of name recognition for their particular political or social dispositions.

The strength of bias in your writing will vary depending on your reading and writing community. In the workplace, some bias is expected when you represent a company and its goods or services, but you may need to be more objective when writing an internal memo about the pros and cons of a new marketing strategy. In public writing, your own devotion to a cause generally will be understood and accepted as such, especially when that cause is in the public interest. On the other hand, academic writing leans toward unimpassioned, reasoned assessments, partly because of its preoccupation with the search for truth. Learning to write effectively in these various settings means knowing when to approach your topic coolly and logically and when to show your emotional commitment to your ideas or your cause.

12c
reason

Gauge your bias according to the occasion. As you draft and revise, try to judge the appropriateness of a strong opinion for your writing occasion. To do this, imagine a scale running from the most heavily opinionated or biased writing on one end to the most objective, neutral writing on the other.

BIASED, OPINIONATED   OBJECTIVE, NEUTRAL
◄──►

Put an *X* somewhere on the scale to indicate your best assessment of your writing situation and your readers' expectations. Now put an *O* on the scale to indicate your best assessment of where your writing fits, based on a full draft. If you discern even a slight distance between the *X* and the *O,* rework your choice of words, the structure of your sentences, and the strength or breadth of the conclusions you offer until your draft is more appropriate for your situation.

Assess the strength of your bias. After writing a rough draft, read it out loud. As you read, try to gauge the strength of the bias in your writing by listening to the rhythms of the prose, the stress that you place on different words, and the way your pitch rises and falls. Underline any words that sound strong or emphatic as you read. Put exclamation points in the margins next to sentences that seem to shout or make points loudly. Use other symbols to mark the sound of your text. These marks and symbols will draw your attention to emotional or strongly felt passages. Consider revising or editing these in light of the occasion and the community for which you are writing.

12c reason

Exercise 3

A. Locate an essay, article, or report on a controversial topic or issue, and analyze the ways in which the writer succeeds or fails in representing his or her reasoning in convincing ways. Begin by deciding what community or communities of readers the author is addressing. Base your judgments on its appropriateness for the particular readers and on its purpose. Use the following questions to guide your analysis: (1) Does the writer appear well informed? (2) Does the writer acknowledge other perspectives? (3) Does the writer seem to respect his or her audience? (4) Is the presentation balanced and reasonable? (5) Does the writer anticipate readers' reactions? (6) Is the writer's bias appropriate for the occasion?

B. Share with a group of other readers the document you analyzed in Exercise 3A. As a group, prepare a revision plan addressing ways the writer could improve the presentation of his or her reasoning. Then choose one paragraph from the text and, as a group, revise it according to your plan.

CHAPTER

13

Designing Documents

Written in collaboration with James M. Dubinsky,
Virginia Polytechnic Institute and State University

What makes a research project, an essay, or a report clear? How does a document convey complex information memorably and persuasively? Why do some résumés and letters grab readers' attention? How do they build confidence in the writer's ability and knowledge? Why are some forms hard to read and some instruction manuals difficult to understand?

The answers often lie in the way a document is designed: how the writer integrates text and graphics, how visual aids (such as photographs, charts, and illustrations) are used, and how the type itself is laid out on the page to engage the reader and convey meaning clearly. This chapter is aimed at exploring document design and offering sample documents as models (see 13g).

13a Goals of document design

By using the principles of good document design, you convey your ideas and information effectively. A well-designed document helps you perform the following tasks.

- **Help readers visualize and understand information.** A chart can show readers the relationship between education and income level, for example; a photograph can bring home the terrible effects of tornadoes.
- **Help readers locate the information they want.** Headings signal the parts of a report containing specific data, providing directions, or outlining a problem. A line drawing shows which parts of a reader's community are threatened by toxic waste and which are not.
- **Emphasize key points or ideas.** Boldface or colored type can make your key recommendations stand out. Material set off from the text in a box gets special attention from readers.

- **Send signals to readers about your knowledge of a subject and your perspective.** Detailed but easy-to-read charts and tables show readers you know your subject thoroughly and that you understand it well enough to convey your knowledge simply and clearly. Well-chosen lists and drawings can help emphasize your interpretation of a subject and add weight to your opinion on an issue.
- **Let readers know you've carefully considered them as you planned and created a document.** This consideration for readers creates a positive image of you (a persona). By following the design conventions of different communities of writers and readers, you show your readers that you understand their expectations and concerns. By putting complicated information in visual form, and by highlighting key statements in complicated explanations or arguments, you project an image of yourself as someone who cares about communicating ideas in ways that readers can understand easily.
- **Make your writing persuasive.** By strategically using images and design as well as words, you show that you're aware of different perspectives on your subject and that you're skilled at the many techniques for conveying meaning. When blended with effective reasoning and clear expression, your skill at document design can encourage readers to pay special attention to your conclusions and possibly persuade them to see your point of view.

13b design

13b Principles of document design

Designing effective documents that engage readers and get your message across requires an understanding of the nature of the printed page and computer screen as well as a clear understanding of the abilities and limitations of readers to process information.

1 Presentation matters

If your document is crowded or difficult to understand, the reader will simply not take the time to read it. On the other hand, if your document is easy to understand because of your effective use of headings, graphics, and other elements of design, your readers will respond positively.

2 First impressions are critical

Often the first impression you make is based on a document you create. This is certainly the case when you're applying for a job, turning in your first essay in a class, or sending a letter to a local government official. In each of these cases, your document represents you to your readers.

3 Documents are visual

All too often people forget that their texts are also pictures. Visual elements include the letters and numbers on the page as well as any photos, charts, or other visual aids. Whether you are producing traditional paper documents or Web pages, you need to organize graphics and text on the page or computer screen to engage readers, direct their attention, prioritize information, and make the experience of reading more enjoyable and more efficient. To design effective documents, you must plan ahead (see 13c) and learn to use the various elements of design, such as layout (see 13d), type (see 13e), and visual aids (see 13f). Understanding how all these elements work will help you to create unified, attractive pages that will catch your reader's attention and achieve your intended effect.

13c Plan your documents

Designing effective documents requires planning. There is no substitute for taking the time to consider your writing task and audience before determining format, layout, and what visual aids (if any) you will use to support and enhance your presentation.

1 Consider your rhetorical situation

Your document design choices are affected by the same kinds of forces that define your writing task: audience, purpose, and context. On the basis of your knowledge of the problem you face, your understanding of your reader(s), and other considerations such as time and equipment, you must make thoughtful choices about the kind of document you will produce.

2 Consider your readers' needs and expectations

Readers need different things from different documents. The same reader approaches an essay about air pollution quite differently than a set of instructions concerning the operation of a chain saw. Equally true is the fact that two people might approach either document differently. An engineer for a chemical plant that is working to comply with EPA guidelines will read the essay about pollution very differently than will a homeowner who lives downwind from the plant.

As you participate in various communities, pay special attention to the way information is presented and received. For example, while your academic readers will expect to read a document from beginning to end, few in the work community will read that way. Eager to get to the point, readers in the work community audience are likely to limit their reading to the introduction and the conclusion. Thus, if you want to communicate effectively in that community, you need to ensure that those sections are clear, easy to access, and persuasive.

3 Determine the form and shape of your document

The following questions will help you visualize the big picture (the entire document) and move to the small but important details (the way you integrate the various design elements).

- What format or document type will you use? (See 13d.)
- How will you lay out the pages? (See 13d.)
- What highlighting devices will you use to make your organization readily visible? For example, will you use a table of contents? color? (See 13d.)
- What kind of font, typeface, and type size will you use? (See 13e.)
- Will you use visual aids? If so, which ones? Why? (See 13f.)
- If you use certain aids, such as photographs or drawings, are there any copyright issues or legal concerns you must address first? (See 13f.)
- If you use visual aids, how will you integrate them with the text? (See 13f.)

13d
design

STRATEGY

Create a mock-up version. After you answer these questions, you should create a mock-up version of your document—a quick sketch that will help with planning. Such quickly sketched versions of a document will help you visualize how the various design elements addressed in Sections 13d to 13f work together.

13d Laying out your document

Layout is a term describing the way elements such as words, sentences, lists, tables, graphs, and pictures are arranged on a page or computer screen. Laying out your document effectively involves presenting information in a way that is easy to read, access, understand, and use. All too often, student writers believe that good document design applies only to special documents such as letters of application and résumés. In fact, for every document you write, from the directions to your party to your term paper in history, careful and thoughtful attention to layout will increase your ability to get your point across and make a positive impact.

1 Use visual cues

To increase the readability of your document, use visual cues such as boldface text and color. These devices will simplify your readers' task and influence their attitudes. Always use visual cues with your audience and purpose in mind, and be careful to avoid overwhelming your text with visuals. Often, simplicity—a few well-chosen visual cues—will work best.

Use highlighting to direct the reader's eye and create emphasis. Typographic devices such as **boldface,** *italics,* shading, underlining, and boxes signal distinctions among items in a text, create impact by emphasizing a specific section, and help the reader locate main sections.

S T R A T E G Y

---

* *Italics* and **boldface type** should be used sparingly to create emphasis. Compare these examples.

  When you want to emphasize something, consider using **bold type.**

  When you want to emphasize something, consider using bold type.

* Use italics for emphasis or when irony or humor is intended. (See 39b for more on using italics.)

  His rent was late for the *third* straight month.

* Use capital letters for emphasis only, and infrequently. Using all capital letters in body texts becomes monotonous and hard to read, and in an email message, using "all caps" makes it seem like you're SHOUTING. (See Chapter 38 for more on using capital letters.)
* Don't overuse exclamation marks and underlining. Be **angry,** or perhaps *angry,* but not angry!!! Underlining, particularly on Web pages, can cause confusion because hypertext links are almost always underlined. (For more on exclamation points and underlining, see 36c, 39b.)

Use color to create order in a document. Effectively using color can help readers identify recurring themes (titles and subtitles), reveal patterns and relationships (charts and graphs), and speed searches. It can aid in decision making. Be aware, however, that colors have different connotations depending on the professional audience (as shown below) and that using color is not appropriate or necessary in all contexts.

COLOR	ENGINEERING	MEDICINE	FINANCE
blue	cold/water	death	reliable/corporate
red	danger	healthy/oxygenated	loss
green	safe/environmental	infection	profit

S T R A T E G Y

- Use color to accomplish specific goals (to warn or caution, for instance).
- Use color to communicate, not to decorate.
- Use color to prioritize information. Readers will go to bright colors first.
- Use colors to symbolize. Draw on your knowledge of your readers.
- Use color to identify a theme that recurs or to sequence information.
- Use color to code different symbols or sections and make searching for information easier.

**13d
design**

2 Arrange information effectively

Effective document design enables users to locate important information quickly.

Use white space to organize information into chunks and guide the reader's eye. *White space* is the term describing open space not filled by other design elements. It can be the spaces between letters, words, lines within a paragraph, or paragraphs. It also includes the margins (top, bottom, and sides) of a page, usually one or one and a half inches, and the space surrounding graphics. Used effectively, white space can guide the reader's eye from one point to another without overwhelming her. Crowded pages are never crowd pleasers; always be sure there is adequate white space on every page of your document.

Use informative headings to help readers find information. Headings are brief phrases that forecast or announce content in upcoming sections. Because they are usually larger and darker than the actual content of a document, headings work to catch a reader's eye—as they do in this handbook. Headings also move readers along, helping them to see the visual organization of a document (the big picture) and to find the information they seek at a glance.

S T R A T E G Y

- Use consistent font and style for headings.
- Use different size type to indicate different levels of headings.
- Make your headings stand out—use boldface type and/or white space between headings and text.
- Position your headings consistently (for example, if you center first-level headings, as in the example that follows, do so throughout your document).
- Make headings content-specific and task- or reader-oriented: **Saving Money on Taxes by Deducting Student Loan Interest** rather than **Student Loan Interest.**
- Make headings parallel in structure (see 26a–b, d).
- Use only those headings you need; avoid clutter.

Here is an example of an effective heading structure.

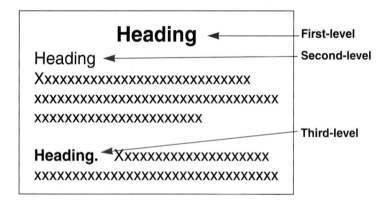

Use lists to highlight important information and to separate or group items. Lists are an effective way to present information quickly, making it easy for readers to get to your major points. They also help to break up dense text and make your document look more pleasing. Lists also help readers complete tasks (a "to do" list, for example) and are useful whenever you need to group related items (a list of healthy food groups versus not-so-healthy food groups). Consider highlighting the items in your lists with visual cues such as bullets or numbers. Remember, however, that numbered lists usually indicate a specific order: item 3 logically comes after item 2.

Rely on visual conventions. Just as our language has grammatical conventions, there are conventions for document design. Depending on the community you're in and the document you're writing, readers will expect to find certain features. Humanities papers written in MLA style will follow MLA formatting conventions (see Chapter 49); APA papers will follow APA guidelines (see Chapter 50). Letters, memos, reports, and brochures all come with a host of formatting and visual conventions. Your history teacher will expect to see a report that follows certain conventions while your prospective employer will look for others in your résumé. Learn these conventions, and use them to your advantage.

S T R A T E G Y

- Identify the conventions for the document you're designing.
- Learn which conventions are essential to follow and which are flexible.
- Use these conventions to communicate more effectively with your audience—whether your instructor or fellow students, a colleague at work, or the general public.

13e Using type

In your document, take advantage of the dramatic increase in the number and variety of fonts, typefaces, and type sizes available with today's computers and software. However, do so judiciously and based always on audience and purpose. Just because there are a lot of choices doesn't mean you should use them all. Keep in mind that using fewer is better (usually two or three fonts in a single document will suffice). In addition, always select a typeface or font that speaks to the audience in a tone that best reflects the subject matter without sacrificing readability.

- **Use proper type size and weight to influence readers and help them read the text quickly and easily.** Type size affects legibility. Standard type size is 10 or 12 point because both are easy to read (see the sample font sizes below). Type size also affects how the reader will perceive the information: the larger the type, the more important the information will appear. Twelve-point type is the most common in academic texts done in wordprocessing programs.

<table>
<tr><td>12 point</td><td>10 point</td></tr>
<tr><td>A New Deal.</td><td>A New Deal.</td></tr>
</table>

Type weight (letter width and stroke thickness) is also important in reinforcing your message levels. Because some fonts have thicker or wider letters, you can use them to highlight messages without relying on changing the type style (boldface, italics, shadow, and so on).

- **Make reading easier by using serif and sans serif typefaces appropriately.** Serif typefaces are those that have the "feet" or small strokes at the end of each letterform. Sans serif fonts lack them.

N   N

Serif   Sans serif

Readers tend to find serif typefaces easier on their eyes in long documents. Sans serif fonts are harder to read in long documents but work well in titles, headings, and labels. They also work well for material that will be presented on a computer screen. Notice how serif and sans serif fonts are used in this handbook, for example. There are many variations of serif typefaces. Examples include Times New Roman, Courier, Garamond, and Century Schoolbook. Sans serif faces include Arial, **Impact**, and Tahoma.

- **Add interesting flourishes with display or decorative fonts** such as *Mistral*, Sand, **Cooper Black**, or Harrington. Some documents, such as brochures, invitations, or posters, require special touches to catch readers' attention or sway their emotions. Decorative fonts have personality and do this well. However, these fonts are intended to be more ornamental than informative, so they should be used with discretion.
- **Add emphasis or direct attention with symbol fonts.** Used carefully, symbol fonts (such as those you find in Zapf Dingbats, Monotype Sorts, or Wingdings) can direct a reader's attention, emphasize a point, and help you add simple graphic flourishes to your documents. There are many of these special characters, which you'll often find listed under symbols in a pull-down menu in a word processing program or in a list of fonts. You may find ornamental symbols and icons like these in your font menu.

STRATEGY

- Limit the number of fonts you use. Two are usually sufficient in a document.
- Use an appropriate size for the readers; most body text is 10- or 12-point font size, although in some cases 9-point font size is acceptable. Point sizes below 8 are usually hard to read. Font sizes above 12 point should be reserved for special purposes and would be inappropriate in most academic contexts.
- Suit the personality of the type to the document and the task. Decorative type wouldn't be appropriate for a business plan or a course paper, but it might be just right for a poster, a brochure, a newsletter, or your own Web site.

13f Using visuals

Albert Einstein once said, "I rarely think in words at all." He thought in symbols and pictures; he envisioned concepts and information. This is an essential concept for writers to understand. Sometimes words aren't sufficient or aren't as efficient as tables, graphs, charts, photographs, maps, and drawings are in making a point. These visual aids, or graphics, are effective in bringing information to life.

- Graphics communicate what words cannot.
- Visuals are understood more quickly than words.
- Tables, charts, and other visuals help readers learn and retain information.
- Graphics entice readers.

Consider the needs of readers as well as your context as you decide how to use and choose appropriate graphic and visual aids (if they are needed at all for a particular project).

1 Use tables to organize information

Tables are useful when you need to present information—usually text or numbers in columns and rows—in a relatively small space. They're also helpful in depicting complex information. Tables are labeled as such and are numbered and titled, as in the example that follows; all other graphics are figures.

13f design

Table 1 Services on the Campus WWW Site (percentages, by sector)				
	PUBLIC UNIVERSITY	PRIVATE UNIVERSITY	PUBLIC 4-YR. COLLEGE	PRIVATE 4-YR. COLLEGE	COMMUNITY COLLEGE
Undergraduate application	76.3	78.8	69.4	54.1	39.1
Course catalog	86.4	91.3	75.7	62.2	54.7
Program/degree requirements	83.1	69.5	73.9	68.4	46.0
Course registration	52.5	39.1	27.0	10.7	16.1
Library catalog	84.4	95.7	83.8	68.4	37.3
Student transcripts	44.1	43.5	22.5	12.2	8.7
Instructional software	57.5	60.9	26.1	26.5	5.0
e-commerce (new)	18.5	13.0	1.8	4.1	3.1
Bookstore (new)	49.2	52.2	28.8	28.5	9.9

Source: Casey Green, *The Campus Computing Project.*

2 Use graphs and charts to represent relationships among data

If you want to emphasize trends, add credibility, interest the reader in data, or forecast future values, then graphs or charts are very useful. Graphs, like Fig. 1, rely on two labeled axes (vertical and horizontal) to show relationships between two variables.

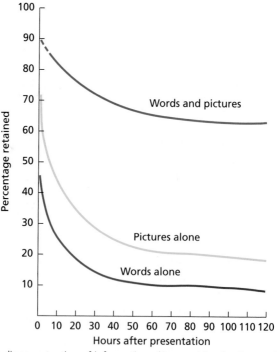

Fig. 1. Audience retention of information. (Source: Maurice Broner, "Stand Up and Be Heard," *IEEE Trans. Eng. Writing Speech* EWS-7 (1964): 25–30.)

Charts display relationships in other ways. Some, such as pie charts (see Fig. 2), show percentages of a whole; others, such as bar charts, compare items or show correlations (see Fig. 3). Graphs and charts also need to be labeled with brief captions and have a figure number (in MLA style, the word *Figure* is abbreviated *Fig.*, as in all the samples shown here).

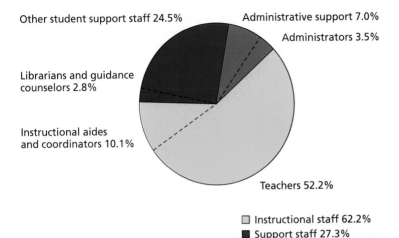

Other student support staff 24.5%

Administrative support 7.0%

Administrators 3.5%

Librarians and guidance counselors 2.8%

Instructional aides and coordinators 10.1%

Teachers 52.2%

☐ Instructional staff 62.2%
■ Support staff 27.3%
■ Administrative staff 10.5%

Fig. 2. Distribution of elementary and secondary education staff, by category. (Source: U.S. Department of Education, National Center for Education Statistics, *State Nonfiscal Survey: School Year 1993–94* ⟨http://nces.ed.gov/pubs/96213.html#figure⟩.)

**13f
design**

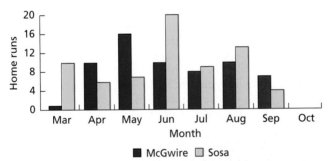

Fig. 3. McGwire versus Sosa: the run at the record (Source: "Advanced Algebra—McGwire Maps and Charts." *Mathematical Knowledge,* Robert L. Wood, Website publisher. 1 Feb. 1999. ⟨http://www.mkmath.com/MX-Adv Alg-McGwire4.html⟩.)

3 Use other visual devices

Use drawings and diagrams to present physical appearance, to show connections among parts, and to illustrate spatial relationships. Think of the diagrams you've seen in manuals for using a new car or putting together a model or that you've used to set up a priority schedule for schoolwork. All such diagrams and drawings aid readers by helping them actually *see* what to do.

You can also use photographs or illustrations to record reality, to define and provide examples, the way newspapers and magazines do. Photographs and illustrations are useful when you don't have time or expertise to create a drawing or when the external appearance (rather than the components) is the focus. But keep in mind the need to credit sources and the appropriateness of such visual devices in various contexts—and avoid overusing them.

Some word processing programs include a selection of "clip art"—simple drawings that you can easily paste into your document to enhance a point or draw a reader's attention. You can also purchase CD-ROMs of clip art and photographs (try an art supply store), which you can use to enhance your documents. There are also many Web sites that offer clip art and stock photography. In all cases, however, you should be sure that your use of images complies with copyright rules. Most disks, publications, and Web sites of clip art and photographs include information on copyright; if you aren't sure, and no contact information is given, you should look for an alternative image.

S T R A T E G Y

- Choose the appropriate visual aid.
- Use the visual to illustrate one point, and make sure it supports the point/argument. Don't use graphics as decoration or filler.
- Keep graphics as simple as possible to achieve your end.
- Set graphics off with white space. Don't crowd them.
- Use textual cues to guide the reader: label the graphics consistently, number them, and provide accurate, brief captions that explain the relationship of the graphic to the text.
- Help readers make sense of your graphics by positioning them as close to their text references as possible.
- Be sure to credit sources for borrowed graphics.

13g Model documents

The following four model documents show how the principles of document design outlined in this chapter work in action.

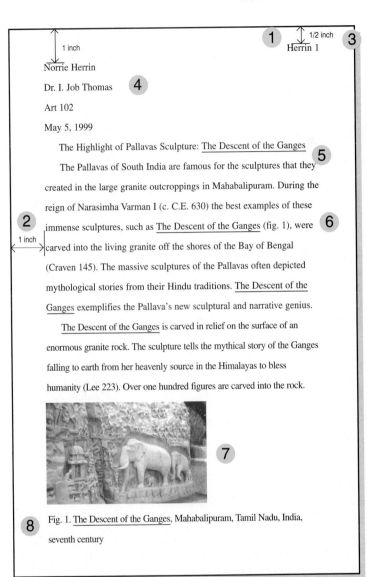

① ½ inch

Herrin 1

③

① ½ inch margin at top

1 inch

Norrie Herrin

Dr. I. Job Thomas ④

Art 102

May 5, 1999

The Highlight of Pallavas Sculpture: <u>The Descent of the Ganges</u>

⑤

The Pallavas of South India are famous for the sculptures that they

created in the large granite outcroppings in Mahabalipuram. During the

reign of Narasimha Varman I (c. C.E. 630) the best examples of these

② immense sculptures, such as <u>The Descent of the Ganges</u> (fig. 1), were ⑥

1 inch

carved into the living granite off the shores of the Bay of Bengal

(Craven 145). The massive sculptures of the Pallavas often depicted

mythological stories from their Hindu traditions. <u>The Descent of the</u>

<u>Ganges</u> exemplifies the Pallava's new sculptural and narrative genius.

<u>The Descent of the Ganges</u> is carved in relief on the surface of an

enormous granite rock. The sculpture tells the mythical story of the Ganges

falling to earth from her heavenly source in the Himalayas to bless

humanity (Lee 223). Over one hundred figures are carved into the rock.

⑦

⑧ Fig. 1. <u>The Descent of the Ganges</u>, Mahabalipuram, Tamil Nadu, India,

seventh century

13g
models

① 1/2 inch margin at top

② 1 inch margin at left, right, and bottom

③ Author's last name and page number on every page including the first, even if using a separate title page

④ Name, instructor's name, class, and date included

⑤ Title centered with no extra space before or after

⑥ Text double-spaced throughout, including long quotations and works cited list

⑦ The author decided to include a photocopy of a photo she took of the sculpture. For best quality, she used the "photo" setting on the copier.

⑧ Figures are numbered and give proper credit to the artists. In this case the artist is unknown, so the work's title and location are given.

THE POWER OF ONE
Alcohol Awareness Week
March 1 - 4, 1999 • UNC Charlotte

SPECIAL EVENTS:

MONDAY, MARCH 1ST
Alcohol Insanity Tour '99 with Wendi Foxx
Nationally renown comedienne Wendi Foxx will entertain with Alcohol Aware Educational Comedy.
McNight Hall 8pm

TUESDAY, MARCH 2ND
Copacabana Mocktail Bar
Representatives from RSA and SGA will provide refreshing alcohol-free "mocktails" in a tropical setting right here on campus!
After Hours 11:30am-1:30pm

WEDNESDAY, MARCH 3RD
DUI: Decisions Under the Influence
Campus Police will demonstrate the hazards of drinking with sobriety exercises performed on real life students.
Poplar Hall 2nd floor 8pm

THURSDAY, MARCH 4TH
Pledge Card Drive
Join the campus community in pledging not to drink and drive.
Belk Tower 11am-3pm

Sponsored by the Department of Housing & Residence Life, Resident Students Association, Student Government Association, and Campus Police & Public Safety

Mine is the Power of One
The power to make my own decisions
The power to achieve all of my goals

Mine is the Power of One
The power to create the life I want
The power to impact the lives of others

Mine is the Power of One
The power to set responsible limits
The power to drink without driving

The Power that is Mine
Comes from within

The Power that is Mine
Is the Power of One

13g
models

1 Unique font draws attention to headline.

2 Date and description of the event prominently placed

3 Original artwork adds visual interest.

4 Poem uses a more legible font that complements the headline.

5 Scheduling information presented in clear format

6 Space directs attention to key elements in poster.

RELATIVELY SPEAKING

Youth Shelters and
Family Crisis Services

Runaway/Crisis Shelter • Transition House • SafePlace • In-Home Services • Telephone
Information Line • Youth Involvement • Juvenile Restitution & Community Service

Volume 11, No. 2   *A Publication of The Relatives, Inc.*   **Winter, 1999**

1998 ENDS WITH STRONG SUPPORT FOR YOUTH AND THE RELATIVES, INC.

As we reflect on 1998, the generosity of the community becomes so vivid. All of us at The Relatives, Inc. are thankful for the sincere commitment to helping youth that so many made, especially as the end of the year and Holidays approached. Let us take a look at these last few months.

FOUNDATION GIFTS LEAD THE WAY

Special gifts from foundations led us into the New Year, beginning with a **$3,000** contribution from the **TJX Foundation, Inc.** (TJ Maxx and Marshalls stores) to support our Runaway/Crisis Shelter. Following this, a **$12,000** contribution was made by the **Mecklenburg County ABC Board** to support an outreach project of The Relatives' Youth Ambassadors—SHOUT! A Month To Be Heard, which will occur in March, 1999.

Once again, **Speedway Children's Charities** was a driving force in supporting youth through a **$6,000** donation while **Winn-Dixie** contributed **$2,000** during its annual awards luncheon from community organizations. Thanks must also go to the **Royal SunAlliance Insurance Foundation** for their **$3,000** contribution.

Additionally, **The Foundation of the Carolinas and The Duke Endowment** contributed **$5,000** respectively to assist The Relatives, Inc. in strategic planning to ensure the success of the agency in the future. More on this will be revealed in future newsletters.

A special thank you goes to **The Charlotte Observer**, for its recommendation that a **$15,000** gift be made to The Relatives, Inc. from the **Knight Foundation Endowment Fund** in support of The Relatives' follow-up services. This very important gift will help ensure that after youth leave our Runaway/Crisis Shelter, they will be offered ongoing contact and services with The Relatives, Inc. to help with their continued improvement.

Thank you to all of these wonderful groups for their support. They are helping to keep kids safe and families together, while creating a better future for the entire community. Their philanthropic efforts do not go unnoticed and certainly serve as encouragment for others to give!

(Photo by Randall Hitt)
Employees from First Union's Direct Commercial Market Group visited the Runaway/Crisis Shelter to donate holiday gifts and household items. Pictured above are volunteers who made the delivery.

WAL-MART-ARBORETUM DONATES PROCEEDS

Shopping experts say that the day after Thanksgiving is the busiest shopping time of the year. For youth and The Relatives, Inc.—we said—shop til you drop! Wal-Mart Associates at the Arboretum chose to donate a portion of their proceeds from the day after Thanksgiving to The Relatives, Inc. Altogether, **$2,795** was contributed. Thank you goes to Manager Todd Taylor, Sherry Hicks, Sue Stegall, and all the Wal-Mart Associates for their ongoing commitment to helping youth.

Continued on page 2

(Photo by Randall Hitt)
Volunteers help unload a truck load of christmas gifts donated from employees and patrons of Dilworth Billiards. Altogether, 3 familes were sponsored.

13g
models

---

1. Appealing masthead and logo repeated on every issue

2. Publication information displayed prominently without distracting from the newsletter's message

3. Large headline directs readers to most important message

4. Subheads help break up a long story.

5. Two-column format helps break up layout into manageable chunks.

6. Photos add visual interest.

7. All photos include a caption and a photo credit.

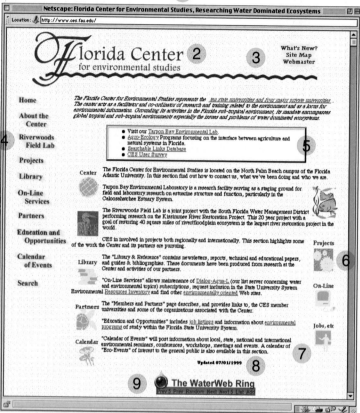

1. Descriptive title in the window frame lets users see if they're in the right place. Search engines index this title, not the one appearing on the page itself.

2. Title repeated on the actual Web page to create a visual tone for the site

3. Textured background adds appeal without diminishing legibility

4. HTML tables used to create a menu on the side of the page

5. Up-to-date information presented first so users don't have to scroll to see it

6. Icons help visitors visually scan for the information they need.

7. Textual descriptions offer another method to link to the same pages as the icons.

8. Date tells visitors how current the information is.

9. Web ring helps publicize the site and points users to related sites.

13g models

EDITING AND PROOFREADING: MEETING COMMUNITY EXPECTATIONS

14

The Editing and Proofreading Process

After making major and minor revisions in your writing (see Chapter 7), you can turn your attention to editing. **Editing** means fine-tuning your work for a reader—adjusting sentences and words for clarity, for precise meaning and effect, and for correctness. It means identifying problems in grammar and sentence structure as well as glaring omissions or repetitions. And it means looking for consistency in style, punctuation, word usage, and tone.

Finding and changing such problems should not be confused with proofreading. When you proofread a paper, you hunt for distracting or careless typographical errors such as misspelled words, transposed letters, and incorrect hyphenation or word division. Proofreading is your last chance to make sure that errors in presentation do not distract and annoy your reader.

The ability to edit and proofread is a valuable and marketable skill—so valuable, in fact, that it serves a professional role in dozens of occupations: advertising, journalism, speech writing, public relations, marketing, teaching, publishing, the law, and most scientific and technical fields. Learning how to edit your own and other people's writing can be a powerful asset in your career.

Successful editing also means recognizing and using the conventions that readers in specific communities expect you to use. Some conventions don't vary much across such communities: a spelling mistake stands out in your document regardless of its intended readers or context. Other conventions, however, may not be so rigid. For example, newspaper or magazine readers wouldn't be surprised to find only one comma in this sentence: *The suspect jumped from the car, evaded the officers and ran into the motel.* In an academic context, though, many readers would argue that a second comma ought to follow *officers,* and for evidence they might cite the well-known guides of the Modern Language Association or the American Psychological Association (see pp. 649 and 696). Likewise, a scientist would use numerals (such as *12* or *84*) for the numbers in a lab report, while an art historian might spell out *twelve* or *eighty-four* in an interpretive paper. Many workplace communities use particular "local" conventions that you'll need to learn as you adapt your writing to these contexts.

Effective writers have learned how to recognize these flexible conventions and how to assess a rule's importance to readers in particular communities. They edit carefully to meet readers' expectations, building reputations as good writers.

14a Editing your own writing

To edit successfully, you need to read your writing with an editor's eyes. Good editing demands that you focus hard on a text and read carefully and slowly. You simply can't edit well if you're skimming a paper twenty minutes before class.

Editing for style and correctness calls for a special kind of reading, one that shifts away from content (what's being said) and toward form (how it's being said). Once you've restructured confusing paragraphs or garbled sentences through major and minor revision, you can then take a magnifying glass to each sentence and scrutinize it for smaller stylistic concerns, grammar, and punctuation. Problems, inconsistencies, and errors will emerge, and you *must* fix them before your paper can be considered finished.

Often, editing requires you to hold in mind a certain concern (commas, for example, or sexist language) while you scour your entire text for specific cases. It's hard to look for too many kinds of problems at once. Sometimes you may need to read your text four, five, six, or more times, holding in mind a different cluster of concerns for each reading.

1 Final editing for economy and style

Even after major and minor revision have tightened the focus and eliminated inessential or repetitive sections (see Chapter 7), most papers can still profit from some final cosmetic surgery. If any part of a sentence adds little or nothing to style or meaning, eliminate it during a final check for redundancy or wordiness.

14a edit

NEAR-FINAL DRAFT	In actual fact, the aligned pulleys are lined up so that they are located up above the center core of the machine.
	READER'S REACTION: This seems repetitive, confusing, and tiring.
EDITED	The aligned pulleys are **positioned** above the **machine's core.**

S T R A T E G Y

To edit your draft for final trimming and styling, consider the following questions.

- Are your sentences reasonably easy to read?
  Try reading your sentences (especially out loud) from the perspective of a reader unfamiliar with their content and purpose. Whenever you stumble over a phrase or a whole sentence, try rearranging the structure for easier reading.

- Do any words stand out as odd or inappropriate for your purpose?
  Try to choose a more appropriate word. Consider turning to a dictionary or thesaurus for help (see Chapter 29).

- Have you used some sentence structures too often?
  Try varying sentence structures. For example, do almost all sentences begin with nouns or with a pronoun like *I?* Then try starting some sentences with prepositional phrases or subordinate clauses.

- If you had to cut ten words from each page, which ones could you eliminate?
  Cut the excess if you can do so without creating new problems in style (for example, short, choppy sentences) or meaning.

Exercise 1

A. In a brochure-writing assignment, Kim Francis wrote the following draft paragraph for a pamphlet describing tourist attractions and accommodations near her Wisconsin home. Read the paragraph once for meaning and then a second time for editing. During the second reading, ask some of the questions listed in the Strategy in 14a-1 (above). Then edit the paragraph to make it more effective.

> After spending a day exploring the countryside, rest and relax at a quaint country inn, relaxing by the fire and sipping on some mulled wine. After spending a quiet night in a room decorated with beautiful old antiques, wake up to a country breakfast. Then after your pleasant stay at the inn, explore the quaint towns and roads that have made Door County, Wisconsin, such an attractive vacation destination for people who like to escape and get away from it all.

B. Meet with some fellow writers and share your edited versions of the paragraph in Exercise 1A. Work as a group to prepare a single edited version of the paragraph. If you wish, make use of the individual versions produced by group members.

**14a
edit**

---

2 Editing for grammatical problems

When you edit your writing for grammatical problems, first you need to *identify* the problem, and then you must *edit* your prose to fix the problem. Many writers spend too little time identifying problems and simply correct those few they spot while quickly skimming their drafts. Don't leave it up to your reader to find errors you missed.

You'll be able to identify some problems in your writing immediately because you simply "slipped" while you were more engaged in your thoughts than in your expression. Other problems may be less obvious but still identifiable because you have a "sense" that you've made an error or because you know you have difficulty with that feature. Still others may be errors that you're not conscious of making or that you don't know how to spot. You may need to try different strategies in each of these situations.

Identifying known errors. All writers make identifiable mistakes in grammar, word choice, and other editing concerns while immersed in their thoughts during the writing process. These are the easiest problems to spot because you already know what's wrong.

STRATEGY

Read your paper slowly from start to finish. Don't become too immersed in your ideas. Instead, look carefully and deliberately at each paragraph, circling or marking any errors in grammar, punctuation, and sentence logic. If you can quickly correct an error along the way, do so. If you're not certain how to correct the error, wait until you've finished identifying problems; then refer to the appropriate sections in this handbook or other reference tools for advice.

"Before and after" paragraphs from Jim Tollefson's newsletter article on the Endangered Species Act for his local conservancy group show his circled errors (labeled in the margins) and his edited version.

DRAFT WITH ERRORS IDENTIFIED

Critics of the endangered species act think it is too broad. Because some specie's may be less vital to environmental balance than others. They want to protect species selectively, however, scientists still do not know which species are more important.

caps
fragment/apostrophe
who?
comma splice

14a edit

EDITED

Critics of the Endangered Species Act think it is too broad because some species may be less vital to environmental balance than others. These critics want to protect species selectively. However, scientists still do not know which species are more important.

Here is a list of errors that many instructors are likely to consider quite serious because they confuse or irritate readers. Refer to the chapter or section listed in parentheses for more information on these topics.

Sentence fragments (Chapter 20)
Comma splices and fused sentences (Chapter 21)
Pronoun reference (Chapter 22)
Subject-verb agreement (18a and 18b)
Comma usage (Chapter 32)
Lack of parallelism (Chapter 26)
Misplaced, dangling, and disruptive modifiers (Chapter 23)
Mixed sentence structures (25a)
Problems with verb form and tense (Chapter 17)
Spelling (Chapter 43)

You may wish to begin your editing by focusing on problems like these and then continue by checking other areas of sentence structure, word choice, spelling, and punctuation that interfere with the relationship between you and your reader.

Identifying suspected errors. Other kinds of problems in your writing that require editing will be somewhat less obvious to you. You may suspect that you've made an error but may not be completely sure. *Don't take a risk.* Check the rule or convention to be sure, and edit accordingly.

STRATEGY

Circle or mark all suspected problems or errors in your paper. Then check appropriate sections in this handbook or another reference work, and edit those that are, in fact, errors. If any suspected errors are still unresolved after a thorough check, ask a teacher, editor, or knowledgeable peer or friend to help you.

Create your own editing checklist of problems or errors that you often encounter in your writing. Apply the checklist to each paper you write. Begin by analyzing your own papers and by giving some samples of your writing to a teacher or expert writer. Ask that person to identify *patterns* of error in your writing, and also look for them on your own. Using this handbook, study the errors and try to identify their causes. Then create your own strategies for recognizing the errors, and turn these into a personalized editing checklist for your papers and other writing. As you get better at recognizing and repairing these problems, you can delete strategies you no longer need and add new ones. This process can be especially useful as you learn to write in more diverse settings.

**14a
edit**

After thoroughly editing her paper on the effects of loud music, Carrie Brehe put three more items on her editing checklist.

1. A lot—sounds like one word but is actually two. Think of an entire "lot" full of whatever. Think of the opposite of a little. From the noise paper: "Alot of teenagers have no information about how their hearing works." Search for all cases of alot.
2. Their vs. there. Sound the same. I usually write "there" for "their" when I make this mistake, but not the reverse. "Their" is possessive only, and "there" is location. From the noise paper: "Most people are not even aware that there hearing can be damaged by lawn mowers, chain saws, and even jets taking off." Search for all cases of there/their.
3. If they would have known. I say this a lot (ha!). I'm still not sure what the subjunctive means, but this problem shows up when I write "if." Correct to if they had or if they were. Search for all cases of "if + would." From the noise paper: "If they would have known what the concerts were doing to their eardrums, they might have stopped going."

Identifying unknown errors. A final category of mistakes consists of those you have no idea you're making. These are the most frustrating kind because in most cases you need to learn them through experience. Writing courses and tutoring services are designed to help you identify and edit such errors so that you can eventually avoid them in the first place. Studying handbooks and reading as much professional prose as you can may help; but by far the best strategy is to work with your own writing.

S T R A T E G Y

Read your writing, preferably aloud. Sometimes this will help you to locate problems intuitively. Or you may recognize them because you encounter difficulty reading a passage. Circle everything you question; then use the strategy on page 188 for checking suspected errors.

Ask someone to read your paper and to mark or circle any problems he or she encounters. Your reader doesn't need to be a grammarian to call attention to problems with sentences, usage, and the like. Good readers will spot errors intuitively. Since they're not as close to the text as you are, these readers may find some problems you might overlook yourself. (See 14b for more on collaborative editing.)

As you discover them, add *all* previously unknown errors to your editing checklist. Refer to your checklist when you edit all future papers. You can remove these items from the checklist when you are sure you can identify or avoid them.

**14a
edit**

Exercise 2

A. Working from a paper that your instructor has commented on (or that you have asked another teacher or expert writer to examine), begin creating your own editing checklist.

B. Share checklists with a group of your fellow writers, and create a checklist for the entire group. Do you all have the same problems? Try to explain why particular features cause difficulties for writers in the group, and come up with strategies for identifying and overcoming the problems. Then create an editing checklist for your entire class.

14b Editing collaboratively

When you edit collaboratively, you identify and talk about specific problems in a paper with one or more "consulting readers," usually friends or peers. Your goal is not just to rid your paper of errors but to learn to identify and correct errors on your own. Every time someone points out an error to you, focus on it and its effects on your reader. Identifying problems takes only a few minutes of hard, conscious attention, and the investment in time will pay off for the rest of your writing life.

S T R A T E G Y

When you are the consulting reader and one of your partners or group members is the writer, try the following suggestions for providing the best advice. Use the same principles for gleaning advice from your own consulting readers.

14b edit

- When someone asks you to read his or her paper for editorial feedback, be sure the paper is finished enough for this kind of work. If the paper still requires attention to matters of content and organization, explain to the writer that until these matters are dealt with, surface editing will be a waste of time. (You can also provide feedback for larger revisions, as explained in Chapter 7.)
- Use familiar language and symbols for your comments so the writer will readily understand them. The terminology used in this handbook is generally accepted in education and business. As you learn to identify errors in your writing, attach the appropriate labels to them.
- If you're uncertain about a feature, such as a possible spelling error, just note your uncertainty. Let the writer use a reference source (a dictionary, a style guide, or this handbook—see Chapter 29) to identify and correct the problem.

- Avoid "taking over" the writer's draft. Identify outright errors, but don't rewrite whole sentences and paragraphs. Rewriting is the author's job.
- If you think that a writer has been unnecessarily sloppy, hoping that you'll clean up the mess, don't spend much time working on the paper. The draft you're editing should be as clean a version as the writer can produce.
- Comments about style are always more helpful when they're specific. Marginal comments like "awkward," "good," or "I like this" won't always help the writer know specifically what works or doesn't work.
- If something is good or bad, tell why. But don't spend time writing long explanations.
- Try to identify patterns of error in the writer's prose. If the writer repeats the same mistakes, point the repetition out.

Exercise 3

 On the day your teacher returns drafts or finished papers with comments, look for any errors he or she has noted or identified. Working in groups of three or four, read each other's papers, looking for patterns of error. Compare these patterns and, as a group, try to write "rules" explaining how to fix them. In creating the rules, feel free to use your own terms and ways of explaining. Add any new cases to your editing checklist.

14c Editing on the computer

Editing has its share of "quick fix" remedies. Among the most attractive are computer programs that "read" a piece of prose and then tell you how to correct or improve it. Before buying such a program, learn something about what it can and can't do.

1 What computer editors can do

Each year, programs that claim to identify problems in your writing become more sophisticated. Some can be useful, depending on your goals and your writing situation. Professional contexts, for example, sometimes deceive writers into using needlessly complex or jargon-filled prose. Some editing programs can identify features like the average length of sentences and instances of the passive voice. They can also provide a "jargon index" of words not in the vocabulary of most readers. You can then use this information to edit your prose.

When examining an editing program, see whether it will meet your specific needs. Use the following questions as a guide.

- Does the program identify errors in spelling, punctuation, capitalization, and usage?
- Does it identify incorrect sentence structure?
- Does it allow you to design your own rules and add them to the program, tailoring it to meet your editorial needs?
- Will it alert you to unclear sentences, problems with subject-verb agreement or modifiers, sexist or discriminatory language, and vague expressions?
- Is it linked to a spelling checker, thesaurus, dictionary, synonym finder, or other utility?
- Will it identify clichéd or vague expressions and commonly misused words?
- Does it allow you to design and add your own rules, tailoring the program to your needs and to meet the conventions of use within your writing community?

2 What computer editors can't do

Although they may claim to answer most of your writing problems, most computerized editing programs are no match for human readers and editors. Most programs will alert you to a potential problem but leave you to identify and repair it yourself. Grammar and style checkers also take a lot of time for what they deliver, and they can check only material that has been typed into the computer. The programs provide few options for different kinds of writing or for audiences that differ in sophistication and background knowledge. Beware, therefore, of blanket pronouncements from the program. They may be inappropriate for your writing situation.

Of course, *anything* that responds to your writing can be useful, if only in increasing your awareness of the features in your text. Go ahead and try some programs. If they work for you, so much the better. But remember, computers can't do what human readers can. The challenging work of editing is probably here to stay.

**14c
edit**

Did You Know?

A recent study suggests that the activities of writers, readers, and editors are quite different. When you engage in one of the activities, it's very hard to engage in the others, because each requires a certain way of thinking and a different way of perceiving the text. Although you may be able to do all three activities fairly well, it's hard, if not impossible, to do them at the same time. This and related studies show how important it is to set aside time for each activity.

Karen M. Petit, "Communication as a Function of Writers Writing, Readers Reading, and Editors Editing," diss., U of Rhode Island, 1993.

14d Proofreading

Finally, after you've made as many conscious decisions about your writing as possible and are ready to submit it, it's time for **proofreading,** looking for errors you may have missed during the editing process. No writer produces an absolutely flawless document every single time. This book, for example, has undergone extensive scrutiny to be sure that *every* word is spelled correctly and that *every* punctuation mark is in the right place. And still, after everything the authors did, after every one of the numerous reviewers had spotted mistakes, after every editor worked on the project, there were tiny flaws only an astute proofreader's eye could find. (We hope, of course, that all of them were found, but published books often contain at least one *erratum,* a trivial mistake overlooked by the entire crew working on the project.)

You may wonder why there is so much fuss about editing. Every time a reader encounters even a tiny error, the author looks slightly less in control. One or two insignificant mistakes have little impact, especially if the work is otherwise powerful. But as the slips accumulate, the author's credibility sinks in the reader's mind.

In college, when teachers read your writing, loss of credibility can ruin the effectiveness of your ideas and lead to a poor assessment of your work. The same thing can happen at work, where good communication skills may be essential for advancement. Surprisingly, many people skip proofreading, one of the simplest of all the processes a paper needs to go through before it's finished. Before you turn in a piece of writing, submit it to a meticulous reading. Focus consciously on every word of your document. Don't let your eyes blur. Instead, move from word to word, fixing your eyes on each word to be sure it doesn't contain transposed letters, typographical errors, and the like. Or try reading your writing out loud. Treat every error you identify as if it were a prize catch, raising the credibility of your ideas.

Exercise 4

A. Two versions of a paragraph follow—one in an unedited form, the other partly edited. Without looking at the edited version, read the unedited draft like an editor. Scrutinize the passage as ruthlessly as you can, making any corrections you wish and explaining these in a notebook. Then compare your editing with the changes made in the second paragraph. What differences do you find between your own editing and the writer's editing?

UNEDITED DRAFT

At the start of her career, historian Barbara Smithey, felt forced to choose between a life of: public service vs. research. As curator of the Westville Museum of New England culture in Westville, Ct, she was passionately devoted to preserving or restoreing old houses in disrepair and seeing to it that they were entered if they qualified into the National Register of Historical Places. At the same time, she had a kean interest in research on the town of Westville which had been settled in the early 17th-Century. She manfully seized control of all public documents on the area, that were not already protected and got them housed in the local historical archives. These included, some early notes about the Indian savages that the White men encountered when they settled the land. Also some personal diaries lady settlers kept.

EDITED DRAFT

At the start of her career, historian Barbara Smithey, felt forced to choose between a life of public service vs. *and* research. As curator of the Westville Museum of New England culture in Westville, Ct, she was *Connecticut,* passionately devoted to preserving or restoreing *e* old houses in disrepair and seeing to it that they were entered *(* if they qualified *)* into the National Register of Historical Places. At the same time, she had a kean *e* interest in research on the town of Westville, which had been settled in the early 17th-Century. *seventeenth century.* She manfully seized control of all public documents on the area, that were not already protected and got *had* them housed *placed* in the local historical archives. These included, some early settlers' notes about the Indian savages that the White men encountered when *local Native Americans, as well as* they settled the land. Also some personal diaries lady settlers kept. *of women settlers*

14d proof

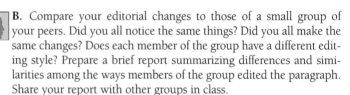

B. Compare your editorial changes to those of a small group of your peers. Did you all notice the same things? Did you all make the same changes? Does each member of the group have a different editing style? Prepare a brief report summarizing differences and similarities among the ways members of the group edited the paragraph. Share your report with other groups in class.

EDITING GRAMMAR

15

Sentence Elements and Sentence Patterns

To draft a sentence, you need not be consciously aware of its different parts. Careful revising and editing depend on such awareness, however. Most of the time, you need a basic understanding of grammatical concepts and terms in order to spot difficulties in your writing, to correct them, or to find the information in a handbook that will help you make a correction. Discussions in this handbook limit use of technical language. Some knowledge is essential, however, and this chapter provides a basic introduction to the features of sentence grammar, along with tips for identifying and using them.

15a Using words

At the simplest level, sentences consist of different types of words, often called *parts of speech:* nouns, pronouns, verbs, adjectives, adverbs, prepositions, conjunctions, and interjections.

1 Using nouns and articles

This familiar definition can help you recognize nouns: A **noun** is a word naming a person, place, idea, or thing.

Crescent Dragonwagon writes **books** for **children.**

The **pictures** capture the **beauty** of **Lake Louise.**

Nouns often require an **article:** *the, a,* or *an* (*a* before consonants, *an* before vowels).

A report proposes **an** administrative solution to **the** problem of neglected highway repairs.

Word endings often distinguish the singular and plural forms of nouns. Most nouns add -s to the singular to make the plural: *cow* + *s* = *cows; cake* + *s* = *cakes.* Some nouns ending with s-like sounds (*s, z, j, x, ch, sh,* for example) add -es for the plural: *gas* + *es* = *gases; base* (silent *e*) + *es* = *bases fax* + *es* = *faxes.* Some nouns have irregular plurals.

SINGULAR (BASE) FORM	PLURAL FORM
child	children
deer	deer
goose	geese
mouse	mice
ox	oxen

In writing and editing, you often treat count nouns, mass nouns, and collective nouns in different ways. **Count nouns** indicate individual items that can be *counted,* for example, two *chairs,* four *cups,* or a hundred *beans.* **Mass (noncount) nouns** indicate material that can't be counted, for instance, *flour, water, steel.* **Collective nouns** generally take a singular form but refer to a unit composed of more than one individual or thing, for instance, *group, board of directors,* or *family.* They may be singular or plural in meaning.

GROUP   The audience shows **its** approval in the form of applause.

INDIVIDUALS   The audience clap their hands to show approval.

You need to treat common nouns and proper nouns differently. **Proper nouns** refer to specific people, places, titles, or things. They are capitalized: *Miss America; Tuscaloosa, Alabama; Tierra del Fuego;* and *Microsoft.* All others are **common nouns** and are not capitalized (see 38b).

Nouns indicating possession (**possessive nouns**) are easy to identify because they usually add an apostrophe and -s (see 34a).

COMMON	PROPER	POSSESSIVE
school	Tollgate School	school's, Tollgate School's
people	Smiths	people's, Smiths'

15a
gr
ESL

ESL Advice: The Articles *A, An,* and *The*

In using the **indefinite articles** *a* and *an* or the **definite article** *the,* you can follow some rules and guidelines, but you need to pay attention to the many exceptions to these rules. Make sure you notice articles as you read. This will also help you to achieve a greater facility with articles. Most important, remember that the basic meaning of your sentence will still be communicated even if you choose the wrong article or if you forget to use one.

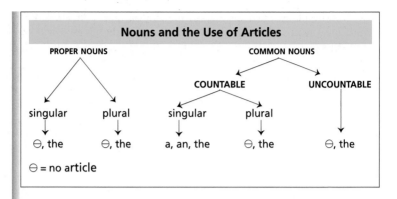

Proper nouns

Proper nouns use either no article or *the*. Proper nouns are capitalized and include names of people, places, religions, languages, courses of study, mountains, and rivers. (See 38b.) Singular proper nouns generally use no article, and plural proper nouns usually use *the*.

NOT APPROPRIATE (SINGULAR)	The Sir Francis Drake was a famous English sea captain.
CORRECT (SINGULAR)	**Rosa Parks** was an important figure in the American civil rights movement.
NOT APPROPRIATE (PLURAL)	Everglades have abundant wildlife and tropical plants.
CORRECT (PLURAL)	**The Everglades** have abundant wildlife and tropical plants.

Common nouns

Singular count nouns. Singular **count nouns** use *a, an,* or *the*. Remember, these nouns cannot stand alone.

NOT APPROPRIATE	Pig is a very intelligent animal.
CORRECT	**A pig** is a very intelligent animal.
CORRECT	**The pig** is a very intelligent animal.

Plural count nouns. Plural count nouns use either no article or *the*. You should use no article to show a generalization.

NOT APPROPRIATE	The books are the best teachers.
CORRECT	**Books** are the best teachers.

15a gr ESL

You should use *the* with plural count nouns to refer to something specific.

NOT APPROPRIATE   Books on his desk are from the library.

CORRECT   **The books** on his desk are from the library.
The prepositional phrase makes the noun specific.

Noncount (mass) nouns. Mass (noncount) nouns use either no article or *the*. They are never preceded by the singular article *a* or *an*.
General mass nouns sometimes stand alone.

NOT APPROPRIATE   A laughter is good medicine.

CORRECT   **Laughter** is good medicine.

With specific mass nouns, use *the*.

NOT APPROPRIATE   Laughter of children is good medicine.

CORRECT   **The laughter** of children is good medicine.
The prepositional phrase makes the noun specific.

Strategies for choosing *a, an,* or *the*

* Should you use *a* or *an*? When you are talking about a nonspecific, singular count noun, you use the indefinite article *a* or *an*. This means you are not referring to any specific person or thing. You use *a* before a consonant sound, *an* before a vowel sound.

    You need to have **an identification card** to cash a check.
    The identification card is unknown or nonspecific. It is any identification card.

* Should you use *the*? When you are talking about a specific, singular noun, you use the definite article *the*. This means you know the exact person or thing to which you are referring.

    You need to have **the university identification card** to borrow books.
    The identification card is a specific, known card.

    Mr. Frank was sitting on **a beach. The beach** had sand that was unusually white.
    The beach is first unknown, so the writer uses the indefinite article *a*. Then the beach is known because it has already been mentioned, so the writer uses the definite article *the*.

* Should you use *the* with plural nouns? Plural and mass nouns do not usually require any article.

COUNT   **Airline tickets** to Florida are at half price.

MASS   **Information** about flights to Florida is available.

**15a
gr
ESL**

- Should you use *the* when a plural noun is followed by a modifier? All plural count nouns and mass nouns are specific when they are followed by modifiers, and you need to use *the.*

COUNT   **The** airline tickets that you bought are at half price.

MASS   **The** information that you received about flights to Florida has changed.

In each of these sentences, the adjective clause makes the noun specific.

2 Using pronouns

A **pronoun** is a word like *them, she, his,* or *it* that takes the place of a noun and that can play the same roles in a sentence as the noun. By using a pronoun in place of a noun, you can avoid repeating the noun. Because a pronoun's meaning depends on the noun to which it refers—its **antecedent**—you need to check during editing that this relationship is clear to readers.

    antecedent   pronoun
    Jean presented **her** proposal to the committee.

(For detailed help on making pronoun-antecedent relationships clear, see 18c, 22a, and 22b.)

Pronouns usually take the place of nouns, but you can also use them as adjectives modifying a noun or another pronoun.

    pronoun noun   pronoun pronoun
    This part has been on order for four months, **that** one for ninety days.

Pronouns change form to indicate the **number** (singular or plural) or **gender** (masculine, feminine, or neuter) of the noun to which they refer. Pronouns also change form according to their role in a sentence—subject, object, or possessive (see 16a). Pronouns are used in different ways and may take different forms.

15a
gr
ESL

Personal Pronouns. Personal pronouns designate persons or things.

SINGULAR   I, me, you, he, him, she, her, it

PLURAL   we, us, you, they, them

When you use a personal pronoun as a sentence subject or object, check that you have chosen the appropriate form, or **case,** reflecting its role in the sentence (see 16a).

Possessive pronouns. A possessive pronoun shows ownership.

SINGULAR   my, mine, your, yours, her, hers, his, its

PLURAL   our, ours, your, yours, their, theirs

Some possessive pronouns take one form as noun substitutes (*mine, yours, hers, ours, theirs*) and another as adjectives (*my, your, her, our, their*).

noun
substitute   adjective
Kim bought **hers** at **her** cousin's store.

Relative pronouns. The relative pronouns *who, whom, whose, which,* and *that* introduce subordinate clauses (**relative clauses**) that modify or add information to a main clause (see 15d.) They answer the questions "What kind of?" and "Which one?" *Who* takes different forms depending on its role (see 15d).

> Cost-conscious consumers are the kind of people **who** shop at this store regularly.

> I gave Kim the coffee pot **that** I had used during four years of college.

Interrogative pronouns (*who, which*) introduce questions.

Who bought the new minivan? **Which** options did they choose?

Reflexive and intensive pronouns. Intensive pronouns (*-self, -selves*) add emphasis.

> They **themselves** did all the work on the new barn.

> They did all the work on the new barn **themselves.**

Reflexive pronouns enable the subject or doer to be also the receiver of an action.

> He paid **himself** for the work.

Indefinite pronouns. Indefinite pronouns refer to people, things, and ideas in general rather than to specific antecedents. They include *all, any, anybody, anything, anyone, another, both, each, every, everybody, everyone, everything, either, few, fewer, many, neither, nothing, nobody, no one, none, one, several, some, somebody, someone,* and *something.*

> **Nobody** has done anything to clean up the mess.

> **All** of us have a chance to win at this game.

15a
gr

Demonstrative and reciprocal pronouns. Demonstrative pronouns or **demonstrative adjectives**—*this, that, these,* or *those*—point out or highlight an antecedent or sum up an entire phrase or clause.

> **That** copier breaks down about once a week.

> She was late for the meeting. **This** surprised me because she is usually punctual.

Reciprocal pronouns (*one another, each other*) refer to individual parts of a plural antecedent.

> The two kinds of birds compete for territory by destroying **each other's** nests.

Exercise 1

A. Underline each noun in the following selection *once* and each pronoun *twice*.

> Seconds later the Help Desk received a call from another user with the same problem. The switchboard lit up. There were callers from all over the company, all with the same complaint: their computers were making odd noises. It might be a tune, one of the callers added helpfully, coming from the computer's small internal speaker. The sixth caller recognized the melody. The computers were all playing tinny renditions of "Yankee Doodle."
>
> —PAUL MUNGO AND BRYAN CLOUGH, "The Bulgarian Connection"

B. Exchange papers in progress with another writer, and identify all the nouns and pronouns in a relatively long paragraph of your partner's work. Then return the essay and point out where you agree or disagree with your partner's identification of nouns and pronouns (or lack of identification).

---

3 Using Verbs

Verbs express actions (*jump, build*), occurrences (*become, happen*), and states of being (*be, seem*). A **main verb** can stand alone or be accompanied by one or more helping (auxiliary) verbs.

main verb
Toy companies **create** many new products each year.

helping   main
verb   verb
New toys **must compete** for space on store shelves.

You change a verb's form to signal relationships in time (**tense**).

PRESENT TENSE   They **prepare** invoices.

PAST TENSE   They **prepared** invoices.

You also use verb form to indicate **person** and **number** (see 18a).

PERSON   She **restores** antique furniture.
They **restore** antique furniture.

NUMBER   The copier **makes** noise.
The copiers **make** noise.

Choice of **voice** (active or passive; see 17h) and **mood** (17f) also requires changes in form.

ACTIVE VOICE   The pump **cleans** the water.

PASSIVE VOICE   The water **is cleaned** by the pump.

INDICATIVE MOOD   The proposal **was** in the file.

SUBJUNCTIVE MOOD   If the proposal **were** in the file, I would have found it.

Helping (or **auxiliary**) **verbs** include forms of *be, do,* and *have.* **Modal auxiliary verbs** (*will/would, can/could, shall/should, may/might, must,* and *ought to*) can also act as helping verbs, though never as main verbs. (See 17d.)

helping main
verb verb
The tourist agency **is planning** to make a video of the local attractions.

modal main verb
They **might decide** to include the old courthouse.

A **verb phrase** consists of a main verb plus a helping verb.

verb phrase   verb phrase
I **am hoping** that the renovations **can be done** in time.

Use **action verbs** to indicate an action or activity, for example, *swim, analyze, dig, turn,* or *negotiate.*

The company and the union **negotiated** a new contract.

Use **linking verbs** (also known as **state-of-being verbs**) to express a state of being or an occurrence: *is, seems, becomes, grows* (see 15b-2).

Flowers **remain** my favorite decoration.
subject   verb   complement renames subject

The flowers **smelled** musky.
subject   verb   complement describes subject

Marigolds **became** popular during this century.
subject   verb   complement describes subject

15a
gr

Phrasal verbs consist of a verb plus a word that seems like a preposition but is known as a **particle,** as in *run along* (depart), *run down* (exhaust), or *look up* (improve). The meaning of phrasal verbs differs considerably from the meanings of the separate words: for example, *run by* means "consult," *fall off* means "decline," and *put up* means "preserve."

PHRASAL VERB	VERB + PREPOSITION
I **ran** the idea **by** the committee.	I **ran by** the house.
Profits are **falling off.**	My cousin **fell off** the deck.

4 Using verbals

The verb parts known as **verbals** act as nouns, adjectives, or adverbs—but never stand alone as verbs. (Word groups built around a verbal rather than a verb and punctuated as sentences are fragments; see 20c-2.) Verbals take three forms: infinitives, participles, and gerunds. (See 15c-4 for discussion of verbal phrases.) To identify an **infinitive** look for *to* plus the base form (see 17a) of a verb: *to play, to analyze, to see.*

AS NOUN	**To play** in a major orchestra is my dream.
AS ADJECTIVE	*The Naked and the Dead* is an intriguing novel **to analyze.**
AS ADVERB	They were happy **to see** the results of the study.

To recognize a **present participle** look for the *-ing* form of a verb (see 17d), such as *slipping, irritating,* or *carving.* For a **past participle** look for the *-ed* form of a verb (or its equivalent for an irregular verb), for instance, *estimated, repaired,* and *shrunken.* Participles act as adjectives to modify nouns and pronouns.

PRESENT PARTICIPLE	The **slipping** belt on the engine made an **irritating** noise.
PAST PARTICIPLE	The **estimated** cost for a **repaired** engine was more than my **shrunken** checking account could bear.

To identify a **gerund** look for the *-ing* form of a verb that is acting as a noun.

Running can be enjoyable.

The doctor tells me to restrict my **eating** to low-fat foods.

A gerund has the same form as a present participle but acts as a noun rather than an adjective.

gerund (noun)   participle (adjective)
Swimming can be a **relaxing** exercise.

15a
gr

Exercise 2

A. In the following sentences, underline each main verb once and each helping verb twice. Circle each verbal.

EXAMPLE

The new construction in Maple Valley has created some challenging problems.

1. Looking for the best way to bring electricity to the new development, the power company's engineers began studying a map of the area.
2. Because the area is heavily wooded, they thought about using underground cables.
3. A field test revealed a large rock ledge, so the engineers decided that underground lines would be too expensive.
4. They proposed cutting a path through the woods for the power lines, but the contractor claimed that potential homebuyers might not like the effect on the scenery.
5. They solved the problem by stringing the power lines on poles following the main road into the development.

B. Exchange papers in progress with a fellow student. Choose a relatively long paragraph, and underline all main and helping verbs once. Underline each verbal twice. For all verbals ending in *-ing*, indicate whether the verbal is a present participle or a gerund.

5 Using adjectives

Adjectives can modify nouns, pronouns, or word groups acting as nouns. They answer questions like "How many?" "What kind?" or "Which one?"

The **three** meetings will last all day.
how many?

Our report was the **lengthier** one.
which one?

Their proposal was **unacceptable.**
what kind?

Adjectives come in three degrees of comparison: *high, higher, highest; crooked, more crooked, most crooked* (see 19c).

15a
gr

ESL Advice: Adjective Forms

Adjectives in English never use a plural form.

NOT APPROPRIATE   Santo Domingo is renowned for beautifuls beaches.

CORRECT   Santo Domingo is renowned for beautiful beaches.

6 Using adverbs

You can use **adverbs** to modify verbs, adjectives, other adverbs, and entire sentences. They enable you to describe or limit your meaning by answering such questions as "When?" "Where?" "Why?" "How often?" "Which direction?" "What conditions?" and "What degree?"

Our committee met **yesterday.**
When? Adverb modifies verb.

We had a **very** long meeting.
What degree? Adverb modifies adjective.

I attend school board meetings **quite frequently.**
How often? Adverb modifies adverb; adverb modifies verb.

By adding *more, less, most,* or *least* to many adverbs, you can describe comparative levels: *more quickly, less clearly, most needy, least openly* (see 19c).

You can recognize many adverbs easily because they consist of an adjective plus *-ly: quickly, blindly, frequently, efficiently.* Others do not take this form, including *very, too, tomorrow, not, never, sometimes, well,* and *so.* In addition, some adjectives end in *-ly,* including *neighborly, slovenly,* and *lovely.* The surest way to distinguish an adverb from an adjective, therefore, is to see whether the word modifies a noun or pronoun (it's an adjective) or a verb, adjective, or adverb (it's an adverb).

adverb   adjective
At noon it rained **heavily,** yet by evening we had **lovely** weather.

Conjunctive adverbs, such as *however, moreover, thus,* and *therefore,* indicate logical relationships. (See 21b.)

They did not like the new administrative guidelines; **nevertheless,** they promised to implement the policies.

The commissioners approved the plan for a trash incinerator; they could not decide where to build it, **however.**

15a
gr
ESL

Did You Know?

Since the 1700s, adverbs like *frankly, strictly, regretfully,* and *basically* have been used to modify entire sentences, for example, "Sadly, they could not raise enough money to keep the bank from repossessing the farm." Clark Gable uses one of these **sentence adverbs** in *Gone with the Wind:* "Frankly, my dear, . . ." and they appear frequently in the work of highly regarded writers such as John Ruskin and T. S. Eliot. Nonetheless, some readers may react negatively to *hopefully* (meaning "let us hope" or "I hope") used as a sentence adverb.

QUESTIONABLE   Hopefully, the tests will be finished today.

ACCEPTABLE   I hope the tests will be finished today.

As Robert Burchfield points out, the ban on *hopefully* is recent but quite forceful: "Suddenly, round about 1968, and with unprecedented venom, a dunce's cap was placed on the head of anyone who used just one of the [-*ly* adverbs]—*hopefully*—as a sentence adverb."

Robert Burchfield, *Points of View* (New York: Oxford UP, 1992) 85.

Exercise 3

A. In the following passage, underline all adjectives once and all adverbs twice.

Back in Chicago, Sereno's analysis of his new dinosaur's skeleton convinces him it is indeed more primitive than *Herrerasaurus.* It lacks a flexible jaw that let *Herrerasaurus* and later carnivores snag and trap struggling prey. Thus Sereno believes this new creature is the closest fossil we have to the first dinosaur.

"I call it 'Eoraptor,'" he says. "Eos was the Greek goddess of dawn. Raptor means thief. It was a light-bodied little rascal. And it may have been a thief, dashing in to grasp scraps of someone else's kill."

—RICK GORE, "Dinosaurs"

15a
gr

B. Expand the following sentences by adding details and information in the form of adjectives and adverbs.

EXAMPLE

generally   deep, extended
The term *coma*ˏrefers to aˏstate of unconsciousness.

1. Accidents leave people in comas.
2. Comas are serious medical problems.
3. Newspapers contain reports of people awakening from comas.
4. Long comas are dangerous.
5. They cause irreversible damage.

7 Using prepositions

When you combine a **preposition** with a noun or pronoun, you create a modifying phrase known as a **prepositional phrase.** Prepositional phrases can add information that makes sentences detailed and precise. Most prepositional phrases act as adjectives or adverbs.

PREPOSITIONS

of   through   with

PREPOSITIONAL PHRASES

of grilled onions   through the window
with the musty air   of the dungeon

PREPOSITIONAL PHRASES USED AS MODIFIERS

A faint scent of grilled onions came through the window and
                    adjective   adverb

mixed with the musty air of the dungeon.
          adverb   adjective

—JIMMY BUFFETT, *Where Is Joe Merchant?*

**15a
gr**

Common Prepositions				
about	at	despite	near	to
above	before	down	of	toward
across	behind	during	off	under
after	below	except	on	until
against	beneath	for	out	up
along	between	from	outside	upon
among	beyond	in	over	with
around	by	into	past	within
as	concerning	like	through	without

Occasionally, a prepositional phrase may act as a noun.

Among friends is where I want to be.

Exercise 4

A. Underline all the prepositions in the following sentences. Circle all the prepositional phrases.

EXAMPLE

At eighteen minutes after one o'clock, the emergency number received a call from Mrs. Serena Washington.

1. From its station near city hall, the rescue truck drove to Briar Brook Avenue.
2. Along the way, it narrowly missed colliding with a bread truck that failed to pull to the side of the road.
3. Despite the near accident, the rescue team arrived at the Washingtons' home in less than five minutes.
4. Mr. Washington was complaining of pain in his chest and back and displaying other symptoms of a heart attack.
5. By its quick response to the emergency call, the rescue team may have saved a life.

B. For each of the following word groups, create two sentences, one using the words as a verb plus preposition, the other using the words as a phrasal verb (see 15a–3). Then rewrite the sentence that contains the phrasal verb, substituting another word or words for the phrasal verb.

EXAMPLE: TEAR OUT
Brian tore out the old shelving.
Brian tore out the door.
Brian hurried out the door.

cut down	hang around	run up
fill in	put up with	call up

15a
gr
ESL

ESL Advice: Prepositions

Using prepositions in English may be difficult for you, and sometimes you will need to memorize which preposition to use. However, these guidelines can help you remember which preposition to choose.

Prepositions of time, place, and location

Prepositions of time: *At, on,* and *in.* Use *at* for a specific time.

> Brandon was born **at** 11:11 a.m.

Use *on* for days and dates.

> He was born **on** Monday.
> My new job began **on** August 18.

Use *in* for nonspecific times during a day, a month, a season, or a year.

> He was born **in** the morning.
> My new job began **in** August.
> The weather becomes cooler **in** autumn.
> The book was first published **in** 1980.

Prepositions of place: *At, on,* and *in.* Use *at* for specific addresses.

> He works **at** 99 Tinker Street.

Use *on* for the names of streets, avenues, and boulevards.

> The White House is **on** Pennsylvania Avenue.

Use *in* for large areas of land—counties, states, countries, and continents.

> He works **in** Washington, D.C.

**15a
gr
ESL**

Prepositions of Place. *In, At, On,* and No Preposition

IN	AT	ON	NO PREPOSITION
the bedroom	the bottom of the stairs	a bicycle	downstairs
the car	home	the ceiling	downtown
a mirror	the office	the floor	inside
the newspaper	a party	the horse	outside
a picture	school*	the plane	upstairs
school*	work	the train	uptown

*You may sometimes use different prepositions for these locations.

Order of prepositional phrases

Use prepositional phrases in this order.

PREPOSITIONAL PHRASE OF PLACE + PREPOSITIONAL PHRASE OF TIME

place   time
The runners will be starting **in the park on Saturday.**

Writer's Alert

When you express the idea of going to a place, use the preposition *to*.

NOT APPROPRIATE I am going work.

CORRECT I am going **to** work.

NOT APPROPRIATE I am going the office.

CORRECT I am going **to** the office.

In the following cases, use no preposition.

NOT APPROPRIATE I am going **to** home.

CORRECT I am going home.

CORRECT I am going downstairs (downtown, inside).

For and *since* in time expressions

Use *for* with an amount of time (minutes, hours, days, months, and years).

The housing program has been in operation **for** many years.

Use *since* with a specific date or time.

The housing program has been in operation **since** 1974.

Prepositions with nouns, verbs, and adjectives

Some noun-plus-preposition combinations are often found together.

noun + preposition
He has a sophisticated **understanding of** global politics.

**15a
gr
ESL**

Noun + Preposition Combinations

approval of	fondness for	need for
awareness of	grasp of	participation in
belief in	hatred of	reason for
concern for	hope for	respect for
confusion about	interest in	success in
desire for	love of	understanding of

Some verb-plus-preposition combinations are also common.

verb + preposition
Vegetarians often **care about** animal rights.

Verb + Preposition Combinations

apologize for	jump into	step into
ask about	look at	study for
ask for	look for	talk about
belong to	look into	think about
care for	participate in	trust in
come out of	pay for	walk away from
go by	prepare for	work for
grow into	refer to	worry about

Likewise, some adjective-plus-preposition combinations are often used together.

adjective + preposition
Life in your country is **similar to** life in mine.

Adjective + Preposition Combinations

afraid of	fond of	proud of
angry at	happy about	similar to
aware of	interested in	sorry for
capable of	jealous of	sure of
careless about	made of	tired of
familiar with	married to	worried about

**15a
gr
ESL**

8 Using conjunctions

Conjunctions join words and groups of words. They enable you to signal relationships among these words and word groups.

Coordinating conjunctions. Use the coordinating conjunctions (*and, but, or, nor, for, yet,* and *so*) to link grammatically equal elements such as parts of compound subjects, verbs, objects, and modifiers; phrases; and clauses.

WORDS	analyze **and** discuss
	orange juice **or** grapefruit juice
PHRASES	determined to cut costs **yet** worried about harming the quality of service
CLAUSES	They put down their rackets, **and** they went to the side of the court for a cold drink from the thermos.

Subordinating conjunctions. Use a subordinating conjunction such as *because, although, while, if,* or *since* to create a subordinate or modifying clause (see 15d; see 27b-2 for a list of subordinating conjunctions).

Because <u>they were tired</u>, they missed the errors in the spreadsheet.

Remember that because the clause created by a subordinating conjunction is a modifying clause, it cannot stand on its own as a sentence. Instead, attach it to a **main** (or **independent**) **clause** that it qualifies or limits in some way.

main clause   subordinate clause
The blender still works, **although** <u>the cord needs repairing</u>.

(See 15c for discussion of main clauses and subordinate clauses; see Chapter 27 on coordination and subordination.)

15a
gr

Correlative conjunctions. Correlative conjunctions come in pairs, including *not only . . . but also, either . . . or, neither . . . nor, both . . . and, whether . . . or,* and similar combinations. You can use them to join sentence elements that are grammatically equal. (See 26c-2.)

Exercise 5

A. Underline all the conjunctions in the following passage. Indicate whether each is a coordinating, subordinating, or correlative conjunction.

Thirty-five years ago, E. R. Guthrie and G. P. Horton described an experiment in which cats were placed in a glass-fronted puzzle box and trained to find their way out by jostling a slender vertical rod at the front of the box, thereby causing a door to open. What interested these investigators was not so much that the cats could learn to bump into the vertical rod, but that before doing so each animal performed a long ritual of highly stereotyped movements, rubbing their heads and backs against the front of the box, turning in circles, and finally touching the rod. The experiment has ranked as something of a classic in experimental psychology, even raising in some minds the notion of a ceremony of superstition on the part of cats: before the rod will open the door, it is necessary to go through a magical sequence of motions.

—LEWIS THOMAS, "Clever Animals"

 B. Working with a group, rewrite the passage in Exercise 5A by employing different conjunctions (or kinds of conjunctions) than those in the original. Try to retain the general sense of the original, but feel free to add your own emphasis or perspective in the revision. Reword as necessary.

---

9 Using interjections

You can use an **interjection** to convey a strong reaction or emotion, such as surprise (*Hey!*) or disappointment (*Oh, no!*). Interjections often stand on their own or are loosely linked to the rest of a sentence.

> **Wow!** Did she really say that?

> All of a sudden, **worse luck,** I realized that my contact lens had torn.

15b Recognizing sentence parts: Subjects and predicates

Each sentence you create needs to be built around a subject, which names the doer or the thing talked about, and a predicate, which indicates an action, a relationship, the consequences, and any conditions.

1 Creating sentence subjects

In a sentence **subject** you indicate the doer or the topic being addressed. A **simple subject** consists of one or more nouns (or pronouns) naming the doer or the topic.

simple subject
Cellophane was originally made from wood fiber.

A **complete subject** consists of the simple subject *plus* all its modifying words or phrases.

A subject may be singular, plural, or compound (linked by *and* or *or*).

SINGULAR
SUBJECT   **She** put the monitor on the desk.

PLURAL SUBJECT   **Trucks** cannot use this bridge.

COMPOUND
SUBJECT   **John and Chifume** are medical students.

In an imperative sentence expressing a request or command, the subject is *you*, generally implied but not stated (see 15e-2).

[**You**] Put the insulation around the edges of the doorframe.

Subject-verb order. In most sentences, the subject comes before the verb.

subject   verb
Homeless people camped in this area during the summer.

By beginning a sentence with expletive constructions such as *there is* (*are*) or *here is* (*are*), you can delay the subject until after the verb (see 9a).

verb   subject
There **were homeless people** camping in this area during the summer.

By inverting sentence structure for emphasis or dramatic effect, you also alter the position of subject and verb (see 9c).

verb   subject
In this valley, millions of years ago, **grew plants** whose leaves are recorded in fossils.

Questions frequently place the subject between the helping verb and the main verb (see 15a-3).

helping   main
verb   subject   verb
Did dinosaurs live in this valley millions of years ago?

15b
gr

2 Creating sentence predicates

In a sentence **predicate** you indicate the action or relationship expressed in the sentence, and you may also specify the consequences or conditions. A **simple predicate** consists of a verb or a verb phrase (see 15a-3).

VERB	The engineers **met.**
VERB PHRASE	The engineers **might meet.**

The verb may be single or compound (linked by *and* or *or*).

SINGLE	The customer **slipped.**
COMPOUND	The customer **slipped and fell.**

A **complete predicate** consists of a verb or verb phrase *plus* any modifiers and other words or word groups that receive the action or complete the verb. The elements you can include in a complete predicate depend on the kind of verb you choose: intransitive, transitive, or linking.

With an **intransitive verb,** you cannot include either objects or complements in the predicate. With a **transitive verb,** you can add objects and object complements. With a **linking verb,** you can join a subject with a subject complement. (See below.)

Object patterns. With a *transitive verb,* you often include in the predicate a **direct object** that tells *who* or *what* receives the action.

subject   predicate
The bank officer approved the loan application.
         verb   direct object

Sentences built around transitive verbs can be either active or passive, depending on whether the verb is in the active or passive voice (see 17h).

ACTIVE	The bank officer approved the loan application.
PASSIVE	The loan application was approved [by the bank officer].

A sentence with a transitive verb can also include an indirect object. An **indirect object** (a noun or pronoun) lets readers know *to whom* or *for whom* the action is undertaken.

                            indirect   direct
     subject   verb   object   object
The Marine Corps Reserve gives needy children toys.
                               to whom?

You can add information to a predicate with an **object complement,** a word (noun or adjective) that renames or describes the direct object.

ADJECTIVE	Critics judged the movie **inferior.**
NOUN	His co-workers elected Jim **project leader.**

15b
gr

Five Basic Predicate Structures

1. Subject + intransitive verb
The bus crashed.

2. Subject + transitive verb + direct object
A quick-thinking passenger called the police.

3. Subject + transitive verb + indirect object + direct object
The paramedic gave everyone blankets.

4. Subject + transitive verb + direct object + object complement
Officials found the driver negligent.

5. Subject + linking verb + subject complement
The quick-thinking passenger was a hero.

Subject complement patterns. When you build a sentence around a linking verb, such as *is, seems,* or *feels* (see 15a-3), you can also include a **subject complement.** A subject complement "completes" the linking verb by describing the subject or renaming it.

                       subject
    subject   verb complement
The new store seems successful.

               subject
   subject verb   complement
The plan is too complicated.

Intransitive verb patterns. An intransitive verb does not take either an object or a complement; the verb's meaning is complete without them.

Our team **lost.**

Last week, the ferryboat **sank.**

The picture tube **faded out.**
Fade out **is a phrasal verb (see 15a-3).**

15b
gr

Exercise 6

A. In each of the following sentences, circle the complete subjects and draw a wavy line under the complete predicates.

EXAMPLE

⟨Stories about Mount Everest⟩ often mention people known as Sherpas.

1. The Sherpas are well-known guides for mountain-climbing ex-peditions in the Himalayas.
2. They are a group of about 35,000 people who live in the country of Nepal.
3. The Sherpas, who are primarily Buddhists, live in a country dominated by Hindus.
4. Before the early 1900s, most Sherpas did not attempt to scale the mountains in their homeland.
5. In the early part of this century, however, Westerners wishing to climb the mountains gave many Sherpas jobs as guides and la-borers.

 B. Exchange papers in progress with another writer. Choose two paragraphs, and identify which of the five predicate patterns (listed in the chart in 15b–2) the writer uses in each sentence. Then sug-gest revisions that vary the predicate patterns in order to provide appropriate emphasis and variety. When you are finished, work to-gether to identify those suggested revisions most likely to improve each paper.

15c Recognizing phrases

When you write sentences, you use many groups of words that can-not stand on their own as sentences yet act as contributing word groups within sentences. They may be either phrases or subordinate clauses.

A **main clause** (also called an **independent clause**) is a word group that includes a subject and a verb and can act as a complete sentence (see 15b). A **phrase** is a word group that lacks one or more elements needed to make a complete sentence. (For example, the phrase *will be climbing* lacks a subject; *the man running across the field* lacks a predicate; and *under the sink* lacks both.) A **subordinate clause** contains both a subject and a predicate yet cannot stand on its own as a sentence because it begins with a subordi-nating word (15d) such as *because, since, although, which,* or *that* (see 15a-8).

1 Creating prepositional phrases

A prepositional phrase has two parts. Look first for a preposition—a word like *at, for, in, to, according to, instead of,* or *under* (see 15a-7). Then identify the **object of the preposition**—the noun, pronoun, or word group that follows the preposition.

PREPOSITION	OBJECT OF PREPOSITION
to	the branch office
near	her
after	a city council meeting

You can use a prepositional phrase as an adjective. In this role it almost always follows the noun or pronoun it modifies.

The coupons **in the newspaper** offer savings **on groceries.**

When you use a prepositional phrase as an adverb, you may place it next to the verb being modified or elsewhere in the sentence.

Her electronic wristwatch started beeping **during the meeting.**
During the meeting, her electronic wristwatch started beeping.

2 Creating absolute phrases

An **absolute phrase** includes (1) a noun, a pronoun, or a word group acting as a noun; (2) a present or past participle and any modifiers (*the deadline approaching quickly*). You can use an absolute phrase to modify a sentence as a whole rather than a word or element within the sentence.

> **Their lungs burning from the acrid smoke,** the firefighters pressed ahead into the burning building.

> It took them several minutes to reach the fire, **the dense smoke slowing their efforts.**

3 Creating appositive phrases

In using an **appositive** you rename a noun in order to add information to a sentence. An **appositive phrase** consists of an appositive (generally a noun) along with its modifiers. You may wish to introduce an appositive phrase with words like *for example, that is, namely,* or *in other words.*

> Ken Choi and Stephanie Almano, **my classmates,** won an award for their innovative packaging design.

> They used "environmentally conscious" materials, **for example, recycled paper and soy-based ink.**

You can sometimes use an appositive to restate an adjective.

> I was tired, **not upset.**

15c
gr

4 Creating verbal phrases

Several kinds of phrases are built around the verb forms known as **verbals** (infinitives, present participles, past participles, or gerunds; see 15a-4). A **verbal phrase** consists of a verbal plus its modifiers, object, or complements.

present
participle   object   adverb
sanding the tabletop with care

infinitive   object   modifying (prepositional) phrase
to bury the roots under an inch of soil

You can use verbal phrases as adjectives, adverbs, or nouns. Verbal phrases are not complete sentences because they lack subjects and because verbals are not verbs (see 15a-4). Verbal phrases come in three kinds: participial, gerund, and infinitive.

Participial phrases. A participial phrase is built around the *-ing* (present participle) or *-ed/-en* (past participle) forms of a verbal. You can use participial phrases as adjectives to modify or limit a noun or pronoun.

Everyone **watching the show** failed to notice the commotion in the lobby.

The chef chose a cake **flavored with orange peel.**

Gerund phrases. A gerund phrase is built around the *-ing* form of a verbal and can act as a noun in a subject, object, or subject complement.

                                            object of
            sentence subject   preposition
Closing the landfill will keep it from **polluting the groundwater.**

Infinitive phrases. An infinitive phrase uses the *to* form of a verbal. You can use an infinitive phrase as an adjective, adverb, or noun.

            noun (sentence subject)
To live in the mountains of Montana was his goal.

                                              adverb
He used several books on organic farming **to help plan his garden.**

Exercise 7

A. First, identify all the phrases in the following passage, and tell whether each is a prepositional, verbal, absolute, or appositive phrase.

Without electricity, we would perish. We could learn to do without the flow of electrons that power VCRs and food processors, but the currents inside our bodies are vital. The brain needs electricity to issue its commands from neuron to neuron. When these signals reach a muscle, they set up a wave of electrical excitation in the fibers, which in turn triggers the chemical reactions that make the fibers contract or relax. The most important muscle is the heart; it shudders under a wave of electricity about once each second.

—CARL ZIMMER, "The Body Electric"

Next, combine the following sentences to create a paragraph that might follow the one above. Try to create a variety of phrases.

The heart has an electric field. The field radiates into the chest cavity. The field sends clues. The clues are about the heart's function. The clues go toward the skin. Cardiologists can get a peek at the heart. They are taping electrodes. The electrodes are taped to a person's torso. Each electrode produces a familiar squiggle. The squiggles are on an electrocardiogram. The electrocardiogram shows how the voltage changes at that single point. The point is on the body. Cardiologists spend years learning. They learn to infer heart function from these signals. They learn to recognize the telltale signs. The signs are in EKG readings. The signs tell of dangerous heart conditions.

 B. Share your revised paragraph from Exercise 7A with a group of fellow writers in order to decide which versions are the most effective.

ESL Advice: Gerunds and Infinitives

15c
gr
ESL

Gerunds and infinitives are verbals (see 15a–4).

GERUND	INFINITIVE
verb (base form) + -ing	*to* + verb (base form)

Verbs followed by either gerunds or infinitives

You can follow some verbs with either a gerund or an infinitive, though the meaning of some of these verbs may change slightly.

	subject + verb + gerund
GERUND	Developers prefer **working** with local contractors.

	subject + verb +infinitive
INFINITIVE	Developers prefer **to work** with local contractors.

Common Verbs Taking Either Gerunds or Infinitives

begin	intend	regret
can't stand	learn	remember
continue	like	start
forget	love	stop
hate	prefer	try

Writer's Alert

The meaning of some verbs will change depending on whether you use a gerund or an infinitive. For example, these forms of *remember, forget,* and *stop* have different meanings.

GERUND   I **remembered** meeting your friend.
I recall an event in the past.

INFINITIVE   I **remembered** to meet your friend.
I did not forget to do something in the past.

GERUND   I never **forget** visiting the Statue of Liberty.
I recall a past event.

INFINITIVE   I never **forget** to study for exams.
I remember to do something.

GERUND   I **stopped** smoking.
I do not smoke anymore.

INFINITIVE   I **stopped** to smoke.
I paused to smoke.

Verbs followed by gerunds

15c
gr
ESL

You can use only a gerund to follow some verbs.

subject + verb + gerund
GERUND   Children enjoy **reading** fairy tales.

Common Verbs Taking Gerunds

admit	deny	mind
anticipate	discuss	miss
appreciate	dismiss	postpone
avoid	enjoy	practice
can't help	finish	quit
consider	imagine	recommend
delay	keep	suggest

Idiomatic expressions using gerunds

You must use gerunds with some idiomatic expressions.

* After the word *go* (in any tense)

subject + *go*	+	gerund
I	**go**	shopping on Saturday.
I	**went**	swimming.

* After the expression *spend time.*

subject	+	*spend time*	+	gerund
Students	**spend**	a lot of **time**		writing papers.
Teachers	**spend**	a lot of **time**		reading papers.

* After the expression *have* + noun

subject	+	*have* + object	+	gerund
Crews		**have** difficulty		clearing streets after major storms.
Shopkeepers	**have** fun			decorating their stores.
Music lovers	**have** a great time			going to concerts.

* After a preposition

	preposition + gerund
Physicians' assistants are trained **in**	treating routine cases.
Farmers sometimes worry **about**	having an early frost.

Writer's Alert

In the following examples, the phrase beginning with *to* is not an infinitive. *To* acts like a preposition in each sentence and must be followed by a gerund ending in *-ing*.

I am looking **forward** to living abroad.
Managers are **accustomed** to receiving frequent updates.
Patrons are **used** to viewing complex exhibits.

Verbs followed by infinitives

After some verbs, you must choose an infinitive instead of another verb form.

subject + verb + infinitive
Some students **need** to work part time.

Common Verbs Taking Infinitives		
agree	hope	pretend
ask	intend	promise
choose	manage	refuse
decide	need	seem
expect	offer	venture
fail	plan	want

Verbs followed by an object and the infinitive

You must use an object and then the infinitive to follow some verbs.

subject + verb + object + infinitive
Doctors often **advise** their patients to eat well.

Common Verbs Taking an Object + Infinitive			
advise	convince	force	teach
allow	encourage	permit	tell
ask	expect	persuade	urge

Writer's Alert

The verbs *make, let,* and *have* follow a different model.
Use the infinitive without *to* (the base form).

subject + { *make* + object + base form
             let
             have }

She { **made** me   clean my room.
       let
       had }

Adjective expressions followed by infinitives

Use infinitives after certain adjectives.

subject + verb + adjective + infinitive
I   **am**   delighted   to know you.
It   **is**   easy   to understand the brochure.
Volunteers **are** pleased   to help with the food drive.

15d Recognizing Subordinate Clauses

A subordinate clause contains both a subject and a complete verb, yet it cannot stand on its own as a complete sentence because it begins with a subordinating word. This word (usually a subordinating conjunction like *because, although,* or *if* or a relative pronoun like *who, which,* or *that;* see 15a-8 and 15a-2) signals that the clause is merely a sentence element—acting as an adjective, adverb, or noun—and not a sentence in itself. For this reason, subordinate clauses are sometimes called **dependent clauses;** that is, they "depend" on the main clause to which they are attached.

SUBORDINATE CLAUSE   **because** I was very busy

AS PART OF A SENTENCE   **Because I was very busy,** I forgot to call the car dealer for a service appointment.

Do not punctuate a subordinate clause as a sentence (see 20a-2).

Subordinate clauses as adjectives.   You can use a subordinate clause to modify a noun or a pronoun.

Many people **who live in Foxwood Estates** came to the zoning board meeting.

They had questions about the industrial park **that the county plans to create near their homes.**

Subordinate clauses as adverbs.   You can use subordinate clauses as adverbs. An adverb clause begins with a subordinating conjunction such as *because, although, since,* or *while* (see 15a–8) and modifies verbs, adjectives, or adverbs.

As the workshop proceeded, many of Jeanelle's questions were answered.
The clause is an adverb answering the question "When?"

She had registered for the workshop **because she was interested in learning about tax deductions for small businesses.**
The clause is an adverb answering the question "Why?"

Subordinate clauses as nouns.   Subordinate clauses can play the same sentence roles as nouns: subject, object, or complement. Noun clauses begin with *who, whom, whose, whoever, whomever, what, whatever, when, where, why, whether,* or *how.*

sentence subject
Whoever is interested in a career in accounting ought to attend.

direct object
You should pack **what you need for the weekend.**

15d
gr

Exercise 8

A. Underline all subordinate clauses in the following passage.

Because the tax laws have gotten more complex recently, we have published a guide to tax preparation that highlights new features of the tax code. In addition, the guide provides step-by-step instruction for tax forms, which should be helpful even if a person has considerable experience filling out the forms. Anyone who plans to file taxes for a small business will be interested in the special section on business tax laws. Although many professionals and businesspeople rely on accountants when tax time arrives, they will nonetheless find that the guide provides money-saving advice.

B. Working with another writer, revise the passage in Exercise 8A by combining ideas and word groups in different ways and by using different supporting words. Retain the general sense of the passage, but feel free to add your own ideas and perspective.

ESL Advice: Adjective, Adverb, and Noun Clauses

Adjective, adverb, and noun clauses are subordinate clauses that combine with other sentence parts to form complex sentences.

Adjective clauses

Adjective clauses (also called **relative clauses**) work like adjectives in complex sentences because they modify or add more information to nouns. You also can use them to combine simple sentences and form complex sentences, thus creating a more compact writing style.

In order to form a relative clause, use a relative pronoun: *who, whom, that, which,* or *whose. Who, whom, that,* and *whose* are used to modify people. *That, which,* and *whose* are used to modify animals, places, and things. In spoken American English the use of *whom* generally is optional, but it is always used in formal writing.

Use *who, that,* or *which* to replace a **subject pronoun** with a relative clause.

SIMPLE SENTENCE   Mahatma Gandhi led India to independence.

SIMPLE SENTENCE   **He** was called the father of modern India.
                subject pronoun

COMBINED   Mahatma Gandhi, **who** was called the father of modern India, led India to independence.

Use *who, whom, that,* or *which* to replace an **object pronoun** with a relative clause.

SIMPLE SENTENCE Gandhi was a political and spiritual leader.

SIMPLE SENTENCE People admired **him.**
object pronoun

COMBINED Gandhi was a political and spiritual leader **whom** people admired.

Use *whose* to replace a **possessive pronoun** with a relative clause.

SIMPLE SENTENCE He was a great leader.

SIMPLE SENTENCE People appreciated **his** simple way of life.
possessive pronoun

COMBINED He was a great leader **whose** simple way of life people appreciated.

Use a preposition plus *who, whom, which,* or *whose* to replace the **object of a preposition** with a relative clause.

SIMPLE SENTENCE Gandhi believed in the independence of India.

SIMPLE SENTENCE He worked tirelessly **for it.**
object of preposition

COMBINED Gandhi believed in the independence of India, **for which** he worked tirelessly.

Use a quantifier plus *who, whom, which,* or *whose* to replace the *object of a quantifier* with a relative clause.

SIMPLE SENTENCE Gandhi also worked for equality for all people in India.

SIMPLE SENTENCE **Many of them** were very poor.
object of quantifier

COMBINED Gandhi also worked for equality for all people in India, **many of whom** were very poor.

15d
gr
ESL

Writer's Alert

Where (place), *when* (time), and *why* (reason) are sometimes used to form adjective clauses.

PLACE My hometown is a place **where** I long to be.

TIME The late evening is the time **when** he writes.

REASON Safety is the reason **why** seat belts are required.

Place the relative clause as close as possible to the noun (the antecedent) that it modifies.

DRAFT	The <u>attorney</u> is excellent **who advises on product liability.**
REVISED	The <u>attorney</u> **who advises on product liability** is excellent.

The relative pronoun may be dropped from the sentence if it is not the subject of the adjective clause. Either form is correct.

INCLUDED	The apartment **that** we rented was very lovely.
OMITTED	The apartment we rented was very lovely.

Adjective clauses can be changed to **adjective phrases** when the relative pronoun is the subject of the adjective clause. To change a clause with a *be* verb to a phrase, omit the relative pronoun and the *be* verb.

CLAUSE **(WITH** *BE***)**	He is the man **who is studying German.**
PHRASE	He is the man **studying German.**

To change a clause with another verb to a phrase, omit the relative pronoun and change the verb to the present participle form.

CLAUSE **(WITHOUT** *BE***)**	He is the man **who wants to study German.**
PHRASE	He is the man **wanting to study German.**

Adverb clauses

15d
gr
ESL

Adverb clauses work like adverbs in complex sentences because they modify or add more information to verbs. Adverb clauses give information about time, reason, contrast, and condition.

TIME	**When** the season changes, clients tend to want to see new colors.
REASON	It is difficult to move a previous inventory **because** the color palette has changed.
CONTRAST	**Although** many clients want the new colors, others choose the old palette.
CONDITION	We may have cost overruns **unless** we move more inventory now.

Some Words to Introduce Adverb Clauses

TIME		REASON	CONTRAST	CONDITION
while	when	because	although	if
before	whenever	since	though	even if
since	as soon as	as	even though	only if
until	after	now that	while	unless
once	as		whereas	provided that
				as long as

Noun clauses

Noun clauses work in the same way as nouns in the sentence. There are four most common uses: (1) subject of a sentence, (2) object of a sentence, (3) object of the preposition, and (4) complement of an adjective.

Some Words to Introduce Noun Clauses

who	where	however
whom	why	how much
whose	whether	how many
what	that	how long
which	which	how often

subject of a sentence
What she said was interesting.
<u>noun clause</u>
Her speech was interesting.

object of a sentence
We don't know where the ambassador is going.
<u>noun clause</u>
We don't know the ambassador's destination.

object of a preposition
His parents were concerned about how safe the car was.
<u>noun clause</u>
His parents were concerned about his safety.

complement of an adjective
They are confident that he will pass the test.
<u>noun clause</u>
He will pass the test. They are confident.

**15d
gr
ESL**

Noun clauses are also used when reporting information questions. As you transform the question into a noun clause, remember to change the word order. Note how this works.

Writer's Alert

The word order of a *wh-* question noun clause may vary.

- The word order changes when the question includes a form of *be* and a subject complement.

  QUESTION   Who **are** your friends?

  NOUN CLAUSE   I wonder who your friends **are.**

- The word order changes when the question includes a modal.

  QUESTION   How **can** I meet them?

  NOUN CLAUSE   Please tell me how I **can** meet them.

- The word order changes when the question includes the auxiliary *do, does,* or *did.*

  QUESTION   When **do** you plan to introduce us?

  NOUN CLAUSE   Let me know when you plan to introduce us.

- The word order changes when the question includes the auxiliary *have, has,* or *had:*

  QUESTION   How **have** you met so many people?

  NOUN CLAUSE   I'm interested in how you **have** met so many people.

15d
gr
ESL

Sometimes the word order remains the same as the word order in the original question.

QUESTION   Who discovered the fire?

NOUN CLAUSE   Do you know **who discovered the fire?**

QUESTION   What started the fire?

NOUN CLAUSE   Did anyone see **what started the fire?**

QUESTION	How much damage was caused?
NOUN CLAUSE	The company knows **how much damage was caused.**
QUESTION	Which firefighters came to help?
NOUN CLAUSE	He knows **which firefighters came to help.**

15e Recognizing different sentence types

You can create **sentences** with a variety of structures: simple, compound, complex, and compound-complex. You can also give them different purposes: declarative, interrogative, imperative, and exclamatory.

1 Building sentence structures

Sentences vary in structure according to the kind and number of clauses they include.

Simple sentence. A sentence with one main (independent) clause and no subordinate (dependent) clauses is a **simple sentence.**

The community development program sponsors construction projects.

The director of the program and her two assistants visited the senior center and answered questions about the proposed expansion.

Compound sentence. A sentence with two or more main (independent) clauses and no subordinate (dependent) clauses is a **compound sentence.**

main clause
Most people in the audience seemed pleased with the plans, yet

main clause
some complained about the lack of green space.

Complex sentence. A sentence with one main (independent) clause and one or more subordinate (dependent) clauses is a **complex sentence.**

subordinate clause
Because people complained about the lack of green space,

main clause   subordinate clause
the architect revised the plans. When the new plans were ready,

main clause
the director came back to the senior center to discuss them,

subordinate clause   subordinate clause
even though she was sure that most people would like the plans.

**15e
gr**

Compound-complex sentence. A sentence with two or more main (independent) clauses and one or more subordinate (dependent) clauses is a **compound-complex sentence.**

> subordinate clause   subordinate clause
> Because he wanted to make sure that work on the extension did not
>
>   main clause
> damage the existing building, the architect asked the contractor to
>
>   main clause
> test the soil for stability, and he then proceeded with the plans.

2 Choosing sentence purposes

You can create different kinds of sentences according to the relationship you want to establish with readers. A **declarative sentence** makes a statement. An **interrogative sentence** poses a question. An **imperative sentence** makes a request or command. An **exclamatory sentence** makes an exclamation.

DECLARATIVE   The motor is making a rattling noise.

INTERROGATIVE   Have you checked it for overheating?

IMPERATIVE   Check it again.

EXCLAMATORY   It's on fire!

15e
gr

CHAPTER

16

Case of Nouns and Pronouns

As you write, you use changes in pronoun form to guide readers through sentences and highlight your meaning. In the following sentence, for example, the forms of pronouns indicate their functions.

Aretha Franklin started making recordings in the 1960s, and **she** has kept on releasing **them** during the four decades of **her** career.

As you read the pronouns in this sentence, you probably noticed, quickly and unconsciously, that *she* is a pronoun indicating a subject, *them* is a pronoun indicating an object, and *her* is a pronoun indicating possession.

In writing, for the most part, you choose appropriate pronoun case as quickly and unconsciously as you recognize case forms during reading. At times, however, you may have to struggle with choices between *we* and *us, her* and *she,* and *who* and *whom.* The wrong choices can mislead readers.

CONFUSING Dr. Landova criticized the report. The other team members liked it better than **her.**

> **READER'S REACTION:** *Her* **makes the sentence say that the team members liked the report more than they liked Dr. Landova. It's possible that the writer means this, but I don't think so.**

EDITED Dr. Landova criticized the report. The other team members liked it better than **she.**

> **READER'S REACTION: This sentence makes more sense. They liked the report better than she liked it.**

Moreover, some errors are likely to irritate readers and create a negative image of you as a writer.

INCORRECT

Him and **me** will make a strong management team.

READER'S REACTION: *Him and me* sounds careless and uneducated. It's a lot easier to trust the judgment and leadership of someone who writes more carefully and precisely.

EDITED

He and **I** will make a strong management team.

16a Recognizing pronoun case

Because a pronoun's form can signal its role in a sentence, you need to choose forms that accurately reflect your meaning. Pronouns change form according to their role in a sentence. A pronoun in the **subjective case** acts as a subject. A pronoun in the **objective case** acts as an object. And a pronoun in the **possessive case** indicates possession or ownership.

SUBJECTIVE CASE   **He** designs furniture for Herman Miller Company.

OBJECTIVE CASE   The modular furniture we are using was designed by **him.**

POSSESSIVE CASE   **His** design team created the dividers forming work spaces in the sales office.

When your sentences follow a familiar order, such as subject-verb-object (see 15b-1 and 15b-2), pronoun case merely highlights roles that will also be obvious to readers from the sentence's arrangement.

> subjective   objective
> case   case
> Tanika helped them.
> subject   verb   object

When you use complicated sentence structures, your readers will depend even more on case to grasp your meaning.

With Jim, **her,** and Susan, **you** have hired three people **who** are better able to work together than **we.** In addition, as industrial engineers, **they** always pay attention to a product's ease of assembly as well as **its** appearance.

I, we, he, she, it, you, and *they,* the **personal pronouns,** take additional forms to provide readers with other kinds of information, as the chart on page 235 indicates. **First person** pronouns (*I, we*) tell who is speaking. **Second person** (*you*) tells who is being spoken to. And **third person** pronouns (*he, she, it, they*) tell who or what is being spoken about. Pronouns can also indicate **number** (*I, we, he, she, they*) and **gender** (*he, she, it*).

Other kinds of pronouns (**relative, interrogative,** and **indefinite** types—see 15a-2) change form only to indicate case.

In English, nouns vary in form only for the possessive case: *the study/the study's conclusions.* Thus the present chapter looks primarily at pronoun case.

1 Choosing subjective case

Deciding to use a pronoun's subjective form is relatively easy if the pronoun is the subject of all or part of a sentence.

She <u>wants</u> to know why the orders have not been filled.

Often, however, you need to choose the subjective case for pronouns playing other roles. (See 15b for discussion of subjects, complements, and other sentence parts.)

Case of Pronouns

PERSONAL PRONOUNS

	SUBJECTIVE		OBJECTIVE		POSSESSIVE	
	SINGULAR	PLURAL	SINGULAR	PLURAL	SINGULAR	PLURAL
FIRST PERSON	I	we	me	us	my	our
					mine	ours
SECOND PERSON	you	you	you	you	your	your
					yours	yours
THIRD PERSON	he		him		his	
	she	they	her	them	her	their
					hers	theirs
	it		it		its	

RELATIVE AND INTERROGATIVE PRONOUNS

SUBJECTIVE	OBJECTIVE	POSSESSIVE
who	whom	whose
whoever	whomever	whosever
which	which	
that	that	
what	what	

INDEFINITE PRONOUNS

SUBJECTIVE	OBJECTIVE	POSSESSIVE
anybody	anybody	anybody's
everyone	everyone	everyone's

16a
case

S T R A T E G Y

As you edit, check whether a pronoun is acting as a subject within some part of a sentence. Check also whether it renames or restates a subject. If it plays either role, use the word's subjective form.

subject of subordinate clause
Because **they** were unable to get a loan, the business failed.

subject of relative clause
Atco Manufacturers will be hiring people **who** are willing to work the night shift.

subject of implied verb
I attend class more regularly than **he** [does].

complement renames subject
The new auditor is **he,** the person at Sandi's desk.

appositives rename subject
Two of the people in the group, **she** and **I,** have experience with desktop publishing.

---

2 Choosing objective case

When you make a pronoun the direct (or indirect) object of an entire sentence, you need to use the word's objective form.

direct object
The police arrested **them** for disturbing the peace.

indirect object
The company bought **her** a spreadsheet program.

In addition, you need to choose the objective form for pronouns playing a number of other roles in a sentence. (See 15b for definitions of objects and other sentence elements.)

16a
case

S T R A T E G Y

As you edit, check whether a pronoun is acting as an object within some part of a sentence. Check also whether it renames or restates an object. If it plays either role, choose the word's objective form.

object of preposition
The rest of **them** had to wait several months for the software.

object in relative clause
An accountant **whom** the firm hired helped her out.

object in gerund phrase
Mr. Pederson's research for the report included <u>interviewing **them.**</u>

object in participial phrase
<u>Having interviewed **us,**</u> too, Mr. Pederson had a lot of material to summarize.

The report contained interviews with the two dissatisfied work-
appositive renames object
ers, **her and him.**

You may sometimes find that pronouns used with infinitive phrases are tricky, so keep the following example in mind.

Mr. Pederson asked **us** <u>to read the summaries of the interviews.</u>

You might be tempted to treat *us* as the subject of the infinitive phrase *to read the summaries of the interviews. Us* is the direct object of the sentence, however (*Mr. Pederson asked* <u>us</u>), and the objective form is correct.

3 Choosing possessive case

When you use a pronoun to show possession, choose the possessive case. Remember that the particular form of the possessive you use depends on whether you use the pronoun *before a noun* or *in place of a noun.*

BEFORE NOUN   The Topeka office requested a copy of **her** report.

REPLACING NOUN   **Hers** was the most thorough and up-to-date study available.

You should also use the possessive form before a gerund.

gerund
Their <u>requesting</u> a copy of the report pleased the project supervisor.

16a
case

Choosing Possessive Forms		
BEFORE A NOUN		**IN PLACE OF A NOUN**
my problem	=	mine
your problem	=	yours
her problem	=	hers
their problem	=	theirs
our problem	=	ours
BUT		
his problem	=	his
its problem	=	its

Writer's Tip

Do not use an apostrophe with a possessive pronoun. Readers will notice the error. (See 34a.)

INCORRECT   your's, her's, it's, their's

CORRECT   yours, hers, its, theirs

Use *it's* only as a contraction meaning *it is.*

Form possessive nouns with an apostrophe: *Luis's, cat's, Barbara's, government's.*

Did You Know?

In the 1300s and 1400s the pronoun *it* (neuter) took these forms: *hit* (subjective), *his* (possessive), and *hit* (objective). By the 1600s, *hit* lost the *h* to become *it,* but *his* remained the possessive form. As a result, one of Shakespeare's characters says, "How far that little candle throws his beams," instead of "throws *its* beams." During the seventeenth century, however, people began using several substitutes for *his* as a neuter possessive, finally accepting *its,* the form we use today.

Albert C. Baugh, *A History of the English Language,* 2nd ed. (Englewood Cliffs: Prentice, 1963) 293–95.

Exercise 1

A. In each of the following sentences, pick the correct pronoun from the pair within parentheses. Then name the case of the pronoun you have chosen.

EXAMPLE

Ruth and (*I*/me) are planning to open a children's clothing store.
subjective

1. The design for the new store was prepared by (*she/her*).
2. The city requires (*we/us*) to submit plans for remodeling the store we plan to rent.
3. Having interviewed Ruth and (*I/me*) about our marketing plan, the bank's officer approved our loan.

16a
case

4. The person who will choose the stock for our store is (*she/her*).

5. I will supervise the salespeople (*who/whom*) we hire.

Next, revise the following sentences by correcting any errors in pronoun case.

EXAMPLE

The foundation sent copies of the grant proposal to ~~she~~ *her* and me.

1. Her and three other people worked for three weeks preparing the grant proposal.

2. The original grant-writing team included two other people, Kristen and she.

3. Because I spent more time working on the grant, I think I ought to get more credit for its success than him.

4. It is me who will have to supervise research work done under the grant.

5. Responsibility for budgeting the grant money is your's.

 B. Working with a group of writers, choose a draft paper one of the group has written, and examine two paragraphs carefully. Identify all pronouns in the subjective, objective, and possessive cases, and check to see that they are used correctly. Then suggest revisions for the paragraphs, drawing on some of the sentence and pronoun patterns illustrated in 16a and 16b.

16b Editing common problems with pronoun case

All writers struggle at times with pronoun case. Many of your troubles are likely to occur at predictable places. Compound subjects and objects often cause confusion, for example, as do comparisons beginning with *than* or *as*. As you edit, therefore, pay attention to the following troublesome sentence constructions.

1 Choosing pronoun case in compound subjects and objects

When you use a compound subject or object containing a pronoun, such as *the committee and I* or *Jim and me,* you need to decide on the proper form for the pronoun. The rule is simple enough: Use the same case for pronouns in compounds that you would use for single pronouns playing the same role.

COMPOUND SUBJECT Denise or (*he/him*) should be responsible for creating the new database.

USE SUBJECTIVE CASE Denise or **he** should be responsible for creating the new database.

COMPOUND OBJECT	The coach selected (*she and him/her and him*) as team representatives.
USE OBJECTIVE CASE	The coach selected **her and him** as team representatives.

In practice, however, you may often find it difficult to decide on the correct pronoun case. The following strategy may help.

S T R A T E G Y

To choose the correct pronoun form in compound subjects and objects, use the **focus-imagine-choose strategy.**

- **Focus** on the pronoun for which you need to choose the appropriate form.

  UNEDITED Anne-Marie and **me** will develop videotapes for the sales presentation.
  I or *me*?

- **Imagine** each possible choice for the pronoun as a singular subject (or object) in a sentence.

  Me will develop videotapes for the sales presentation.

  I will develop videotapes for the sales presentation.

- **Choose** the correct form, and use it in the compound subject (or object). If the correct form is not immediately apparent to you, refer to the chart on page 235. (Choosing the form that "sounds right" can be a misleading strategy with compounds.)

  EDITED Anne-Marie and **I** will develop videotapes for the sales presentation.

16b
case

Writer's Tip

An incorrect pronoun form may pass without much notice in conversation because it "sounds right."

SPOKEN This is a private agreement between you and **I**.

You need to be alert for problems like this as you edit because readers are likely to notice the faulty choice of pronoun form.

EDITED This is a private agreement between you and **me**.

As you edit, pay special attention to pronoun forms that sound "wrong" or "unusual." Some of them may actually be correct, as in the following instance.

CORRECT Responsibility for keeping the coffee room clean is shared between **them** and **us**.

2 Choosing pronoun case for subject complements

When you follow a form of the verb *be* (*is, am, are, was, were*) with a pronoun renaming the subject, you create a **subject complement** (see 15b-2). Because you are renaming or restating the subject, choose the subjective form of the pronoun.

CORRECT   The last pharmacy graduates to get jobs at Upstate Medical Center were Rebecca Soares and **I.**

In conversation, even educated speakers occasionally use the objective case in complements.

CONVERSATION   The new traffic reporter is **him.**

In writing, however, you should aim for correctness. If correcting the problem leads to a stilted or unnatural statement, rewrite the entire sentence.

STILTED   The new traffic reporter is **he.**

REWRITTEN   **He** is the new traffic reporter.

3 Choosing *we* or *us* with a noun

When you pair *we, us,* or other pronouns with nouns, make sure the case of the pronoun—*we, they* (subjective) or *us, them* (objective)—matches the role played by the noun (subject or object).

CORRECT   **We taxpayers** ought to demand that the city fill the potholes on Pine Avenue.

CORRECT   The award went to the coach, but it really belonged to **us team members** who worked so hard during the season.

CORRECT   If a customer returns to our store because of the quality of the service, the credit belongs to **you salespeople.**

16b
case

S T R A T E G Y

Check for a correct match of pronoun and noun by imagining a sentence in alternative versions without the noun.

SENTENCE   The teaching evaluation should be conducted by (*us? we?*) students, not by the faculty or administration.

VERSION 1
(INCORRECT)   The teaching evaluation should be conducted by **we. . . .**

VERSION 2 (CORRECT)	The teaching evaluation should be conducted by **us**. . . .

EDITED	The teaching evaluation should be conducted by **us** students, not by the faculty or administration.

Us **is the object of a preposition and takes the objective form (see 16a-2).**

4 Choosing pronoun form in an appositive

When you put a pronoun in an appositive phrase (see 15c-3), it renames a preceding noun or pronoun; consequently, it must match the case of the word being renamed.

CORRECT	As an investment, the two sisters, **she** and her twin, bought a small chain of dry cleaners.

S T R A T E G Y

As you edit, look for pronouns that act as appositives in renaming a noun or another pronoun. Check for the correct pronoun form by imagining alternative versions in which you leave out the noun (or pronoun) that was renamed in the original sentence.

SENTENCE	The two children's book illustrators on the panel, (*she? her?*) and (*I? me?*), discussed all the questions asked by the audience.
VERSION 1 (INCORRECT)	**Her and me** discussed all the questions asked by the audience.
VERSION 2 (CORRECT)	**She and I** discussed all the questions asked by the audience.
EDITED	The two children's book illustrators on the panel, **she and I,** discussed all the questions asked by the audience.

The pronouns rename the subject, so the subjective forms are correct.

16b case

5 Choosing pronoun case following comparisons with *than* or *as*

When you end a comparison with a pronoun, make sure the case you choose accurately signals the information left out. A pronoun in the subjective case acts as the subject of the implied statement; a pronoun in the objective case acts as the object.

SUBJECTIVE   I rely more on computers for help with the problems than **he** [does].

OBJECTIVE   I gave her sister more help than [I gave] **her.**

You can leave out part of a sentence containing a comparison with *than* or *as* so long as your readers are able to fill in the missing part easily and accurately.

CLEAR   I have better grades in chemistry than she [*does*].

Even a sentence whose grammar is acceptable may be unclear if readers are likely to miss the grammatical signals. If there is any chance of confusion, rewrite the sentence.

POTENTIALLY   I like working with Aisha better than she.
AMBIGUOUS
READER'S REACTION: Does this mean you prefer to work with Aisha? Or that you like to work with Aisha better than someone else does?

REWRITTEN   She doesn't like working with Aisha as much as I do.

6 Using possessive case with gerunds

A **gerund** is the *-ing* form of a verb used as a noun (see 15a-4). Choose the possessive case when you put a noun or pronoun before a gerund in order to modify it.

CORRECT   **My** skidding across the wet floor frightened me.

CORRECT   **Roseanna's** skidding across the wet floor frightened me.

Why is using the possessive case important? Versions of a sentence with and without the possessive may differ considerably in meaning.

WITH   We were surprised by the principal's golfing.
POSSESSIVE
He was golfing, and we were surprised that he had taken up the sport (or that he was so good at it).

WITHOUT   We were surprised by the principal golfing.
POSSESSIVE
We were golfing, and he came up to us unexpectedly.

Admittedly, placing a possessive before a gerund can make some sentences hard to read. When this is the case, rewrite the sentence.

16b
case

INCORRECT	The new store manager was surprised by virtually **everybody** in town showing up for the sale.
	READER'S REACTION: **Does this writer mean that *virtually everybody* managed to surprise the new manager? Wasn't it the number of people who showed up that was so surprising?**
AWKWARD	The new store manager was surprised by virtually **everybody's** in town showing up for the sale.
REWRITTEN	The new store manager was surprised **that virtually everybody in town showed up for the sale.**

7 Using *myself* and other reflexive pronouns cautiously

People sometimes use *myself, yourself,* and other **reflexive pronouns** (see 15a-2) inappropriately as sentence subjects or objects, perhaps because they are not sure which pronoun form is correct and assume that *myself* and the other *-self* pronouns will stretch to fit all cases.

INCORRECT	The Nucor project led to some major disagreements between Stan and myself.
CORRECT	The Nucor project led to some major disagreements between Stan and **me.**
	Me **is the object of a preposition, so the objective case is correct; see 16a-2.**

You can use *myself, itself, themselves,* and other reflexive pronouns to refer correctly to the subject or object of a sentence.

I made the check out to **myself.**

You can also use them as **intensive pronouns** to add emphasis.

The building's design **itself,** and not poor construction, is responsible for the leaky roof.

16b
case

Writer's Alert

Forms such as *hisself, themself, theirselves,* and *themselfs* sometimes occur in various spoken dialects of English. In writing, however, use *himself* and *themselves,* the correct forms in standard written English.

Exercise 2

A. Correct any errors in pronoun case in the following sentences.

EXAMPLE
            she
Denise and ~~her~~ joined the Disney film group in our class.
               ^

1. The rest of us team members decided we should use recent animated movies as the subject of our project.
2. Because their parents own a video store, her brother and her brought in tapes of the movies we planned to study.
3. Bill and I decided to take notes on *Aladdin;* Pat and her chose to study *Beauty and the Beast.*
4. I thought the notes we took were more detailed and better than they.
5. Writing the final paper led to some disagreements between the other members and myself.

B. Working with a group, create a brief story involving three or four characters. Use at least five of the troublesome pronoun case patterns discussed in 16b, avoiding problems in their use.

16c Editing *who* and *whom*

Many writers and speakers find it hard to choose between *who* and *whom.* They will be inclined to forgive, and even ignore, an occasional misuse of *who, whom, whoever,* and *whomever.* Nonetheless, the places where you are most likely to have trouble with these pronoun forms, in relative clauses and at the beginning of questions, are also places where the pronouns can affect the meaning of a sentence substantially. To guide readers to your meaning, therefore, you need to be precise in your use of *who* and *whom.*

16c
case

1 Choosing between *who* and *whom in* relative clauses

You probably often use the pronouns *who* and *whom, whoever* and *whomever* to begin the subordinate clauses known as **relative clauses** or **adjective clauses** (see 15a-2). Choose *who* and *whomever* when you use the pronouns as subjects; choose *whom* and *whomever* when you use them as objects (see 16a-1 and 16a-2).

SUBJECT	The artist **who creates a painting or sculpture** ought to benefit from its sale.
OBJECT	The proceeds benefit **whomever** the artist designates.

Deciding between *who* and *whom* can be difficult. You need to choose the appropriate form according to the role the pronoun plays *within the relative clause.* You need to ignore the role the clause plays *within the sentence.*

INCORRECT   The fine must be paid by **whomever** holds the deed to the property.
Although the whole relative clause is the object of the preposition *by,* within the clause the pronoun acts as a subject, not an object.

EDITED   The fine must be paid by **whoever** holds the deed to the property.

If you are in doubt about either the use of *whom* or its appropriateness to your writing situation, try rewording your sentence to avoid making the choice.

EDITED   The person with the deed to the property must pay the fine.

2 Choosing between *who* and *whom* in questions

You should use *who* at the beginning of a question when the pronoun is the subject of the sentence. You should use *whom* when the pronoun is an object. (See 16a-1 and 16a-2.)

SUBJECT   **Who** is most likely to get the reader's sympathy at this point in the novel, Huck or Jim?

OBJECT   **Whom** can Cordelia trust for counsel at the conclusion of the scene?

**16c
case**

Case of *Who* and *Whoever*			
	SUBJECTIVE	OBJECTIVE	POSSESSIVE
FIRST, SECOND, AND THIRD PERSON	who whoever	whom whomever	whose whosever

Exercise 3

A. Correct any errors in pronoun case in the following sentences.

EXAMPLE   *Whoever*
~~Whomever~~ has taken an IQ test probably remembers the score.

1. In the past, psychologists assumed that whomever scored well on IQ tests was likely to succeed at school and work.
2. Recent studies of IQ tests have produced evidence of them being unable to predict success.
3. A test of constructive thinking skill may tell more about your or mine ability to meet challenges.
4. Reporting on research conducted by he and two of his colleagues, Robert Sternberg points out that "the ability to sell" is an important part of practical intelligence.
5. Other psychologists claim that personal qualities like self-confidence and optimism may by theirselves have as much to do with our mental abilities as IQ does.

 B. Working with fellow writers, identify the pronouns in the following passage, and correct any mistakes in case. Keep a record of those identifications and corrections you found most difficult, and be ready to try to explain why you found them difficult.

For we humans, yawning is a familiar activity. You and me probably yawn when we stretch, though not always. Boredom is also a likely cause for us yawning. People often think that no one yawns as much as them, but this is seldom true. We all yawn frequently during a day. We may even start yawning ourselves when we notice someone else whom is yawning.

17

Verbs

Although irregular verb forms may be accepted in many communities, they can powerfully affect the level of confidence your readers may have in your ideas. Readers might sometimes forgive a spelling mistake or two, but as soon as you write "The Dolpins done real good in the playoffs" or "The polio vaccine could have brang about some forms of cancer," you've already done serious damage to your persona and to your credibility. Learning all the nuances of the English verb system can be an arduous task; for now, it's important that you identify verb problems in your own writing and edit them before you turn in or present your final drafts.

17a Recognizing simple present and past tense

When you use a simple verb in a sentence, you will put that verb into the present or past tense depending on when the action of the verb occurred. **Present tense** indicates that the action is occurring now; **past tense** indicates it has already occurred. The **base form** of a verb is the infinitive form without *to* (as in *drive, go, bake,* or *climb*). The vast majority of verbs form their past tense with the addition of *-ed* to the base form, an addition that can be pronounced as *-t, -d,* or *-ed,* depending on the particular verb.

PRESENT TENSE (BASE FORM)	PAST TENSE	PRONUNCIATION
bake	baked	bake + **t**
call	called	call + **d**
defend	defended	defend + **-ed**

17b Editing simple present tense verbs

Most of the time, present tense verb forms will give you no trouble. You need no special endings to mark the present tense of verbs *except* in the third person singular form (when you use the pronouns *he, she,* or *it* or a singular noun).

Occasionally, however, you may need to check that your verbs agree in **number** and **person** with their subjects (see 18a and 18b). Be sure that your verbs take singular or plural forms to agree with the number (singular or plural) of their subjects (see 18a).

PLURAL SUBJECT/PLURAL VERB
Most of the people at the retirement community **eat** three meals a day.

SINGULAR SUBJECT/SINGULAR VERB
Because of his hypoglycemia, **Mr. Richardson eats** five small snacks a day.

ESL Advice: The Third Person -*s* or -*es* Ending

The present tense verbs in English are easy to write, but you must remember to add an -*s* or -*es* to verbs that are third person singular.

SUBJECT	VERB	SUBJECT	VERB + -*s*

I
you (sing., pl.)
we
they
	write	he
		she
		it (an animal,
		  a thing,
		  a concept)
			writes

Check the following points to make sure that your present tense verbs are correct when you edit your writing.

- Check the subject and the verb in a simple sentence.

UNGRAMMATICAL   The hummingbird gather nectar from flowers.
                      subject   verb

EDITED   The **hummingbird gathers** nectar from flowers.

- Check whether the subject and the verb are separated by phrases.

UNGRAMMATICAL   The hummingbird of those regions gather nectar.
                     subject   verb

EDITED   The **hummingbird** of those regions **gathers** nectar.
                Hummingbird, **not** *regions,* **is the subject.**

17b
verb
ESL

- Check for compound verbs (more than one verb) in a simple sentence.

subject   verb   verb

NOT APPROPRIATE   The hummingbird visit our garden, gather nectar, and

verb

leave quietly.

CORRECT   The **hummingbird visits** our garden, **gathers** nectar, and **leaves** quietly.

- Check for agreement between the subject and the verb in a complex sentence (see 15d-1).

adverb clause

NOT APPROPRIATE   When the **snow fall,** we enjoy the scenery.

subject verb

CORRECT   When the **snow falls,** we enjoy the scenery.

adjective clause

NOT APPROPRIATE   The young **man** that I work with **live** in town.

subject   verb

CORRECT   The young **man** that I work with **lives** in town.

Writer's Alert

Sometimes you need to be careful to match the -*s* and -*es* endings of verbs in the main clause and in the adjective clause.

adjective clause

The young **man** that **works** with me **lives** in town.

subject   verb   verb

Writer's Tip

A few irregular verbs are still undergoing change, so their usage is less certain. Should you say *sneaked* or *snuck* for the past tense of *sneak? Weaved* or *wove? Strived* or *strove? Creeped* or *crept?* Dictionaries and editors don't always agree on the preferred forms, so you may have to choose a form your audience is likely to prefer. In all cases, however, check your dictionary first to see if there is a clearly preferred form and to make sure the form you are using is acceptable and not simply an error. *Webster's New Collegiate Dictionary,* for example, prefers *sneaked* but accepts *snuck*, prefers *wove* but accepts *weaved*, prefers *strove* but accepts *strived,* and recognizes *crept* but not *creeped.*

17c Editing past tense verbs

When you form the past tense of regular verbs in writing, you will usually add *-ed* to the base form of the verb. Ordinarily, you won't make errors marking the past tense in this way. Occasionally, however, you may not "hear" the *-ed*, particularly when the verb is followed by a word beginning in *d* or *t*. In writing, make sure that every regular verb in the past tense ends in *-ed*.

DRAFT   Harold **bake** Donna a huge cake.

EDITED   Harold **baked** Donna a huge cake.

DRAFT   The company **use** to provide hard-copy documentation.

EDITED   The company **used** to provide hard-copy documentation.

About sixty or seventy common verbs are irregular—exceptions to the "add *-ed*" rule for the past tense. Most **irregular verbs** change an internal vowel in the simple past tense, such as *run* (present) and *ran* (past). A few don't change written form but are pronounced differently.

PRESENT TENSE FORM	PAST TENSE FORM
catch	caught
dive	dove
eat	ate
fight	fought
read (rhymes with *seed*)	read (rhymes with *bed*)
run	ran

Because the forms of each irregular verb must be learned independently, you may occasionally use a past tense form that is not acceptable in standard written English. Keep track of any verbs that are troublesome for you, and scan your drafts for them when you edit.

DRAFT   The movie was disappointing because the characters **sweared** at each other constantly.

EDITED   The movie was disappointing because the characters **swore** at each other constantly.

17c
verb
ESL

ESL Advice: Simple Present and Simple Past

These are the two tenses that add no helping verbs to form the verb, except for the negative and interrogative forms. No other verb forms can stand alone!

SIMPLE PRESENT   They **live** in the dormitory this semester.

SIMPLE PAST   They **lived** in an apartment last semester.

UNGRAMMATICAL   The marketing department **administering** surveys yesterday.
The writer uses the present participle as a simple predicate without any helping verb. In English this is not possible.

EDITED   The marketing department **was administering** surveys yesterday.
Now the verb form is a completed verb phrase with a helping verb and a verb form.

(For more about helping verbs, see ESL Advice: Helping Verbs.)

Did You Know?

The reason English contains irregular verbs can be traced historically to a time when the past tense and past participle forms of verbs were created mainly by internal sound changes. Most verbs, called *strong verbs,* once followed a special system of sound changes, and a smaller number (called *weak verbs*) added -ed. Over time, most strong verbs became weak verbs. Today, only about seventy strong verbs remain. A few have alternative forms, such as *dive/dived* versus *dive/dove* and *weave/weaved* versus *weave/wove*. All newly invented verbs now take the -ed ending (witness the recent *fax/faxed*).

Albert C. Baugh and Thomas Cable, *A History of the English Language* (London: Routledge, 1978).

17d Recognizing and editing problems with participles

**17d
verb**

To create complex tenses, you need to provide the main verb in a sentence with a **helping,** or **auxiliary, verb** (such as *is* or *has*) and change the form of the main verb. When linked to main verbs (see 15a-3), helping verbs can specify a range of time relationships. Consider the following sentences.

After **having eaten** up all the cake, little Jennifer **would have begun** to feel guilty **had it not been** for her father's unexpected treat—a box of delicious parfaits for the family.

Assuming he **would be going** on the trip, Terry **had started** packing when to his surprise the whole apartment **began** to tremble from a small earthquake that **will be remembered** as the July Surprise.

The complex verb forms in these sentences convey important aspects of past, present, or future time. But how can you be sure you are using the correct verb forms when creating such sentences?

The **participle** is the usual form a verb takes when it's linked to a helping verb. Verbs can take two participial forms, the **past participle** and the **present participle.** When writers have problems with complex tenses, they typically use the wrong participle.

The present participle is formed by adding -*ing* to the base form of the verb (the form with no endings or markers).

HELPING VERB	PARTICIPLE (MAIN VERB)
He was	loading the truck.
He will be	loading the truck.
He had been	loading the truck.

Chan is **greeting** the jugglers at the airport as we speak.

The past participle form of most verbs is just like the simple past tense.

HELPING VERB	PAST PARTICIPLE (MAIN VERB)
Mike has	rented the truck.
Mike had	rented the truck.

Chan has **greeted** the jugglers every year for the past five years.

Other participial forms are irregular, involving an internal vowel change or an -*en* ending.

INCORRECT	Louise lost the pie-eating contest because she **had drank** three glasses of lemonade just before it began.
EDITED	Louise lost the pie-eating contest because she **had drunk** three glasses of lemonade just before it began.
INCORRECT	By the end of the trial, the lawyers **had went** too far in their defense of the rapist.
EDITED	By the end of the trial, the lawyers **had gone** too far in their defense of the rapist.

The following list of the principal parts of some common irregular verbs should help you identify and use the correct participle.

17d verb

Common Irregular Verbs		
PRESENT	**PAST**	**PAST PARTICIPLE**
arise	arose	arisen
am/is/are	was/were	been
bear	bore	borne
begin	began	begun
bite	bit	bitten/bit
blow	blew	blown

continued

Common Irregular Verbs *(continued)*

PRESENT	PAST	PAST PARTICIPLE
break	broke	broken
bring	brought	brought
buy	bought	bought
catch	caught	caught
choose	chose	chosen
come	came	come
creep	crept	crept
dive	dived/dove	dived
do	did	done
draw	drew	drawn
dream	dreamed/dreamt	dreamt
drink	drank	drunk
drive	drove	driven
eat	ate	eaten
fall	fell	fallen
fight	fought	fought
fly	flew	flown
forget	forgot	forgotten
forgive	forgave	forgiven
freeze	froze	frozen
get	got	got/gotten
give	gave	given
go	went	gone
grow	grew	grown
hang (object)	hung (object)	hung (object)
hang (person)	hanged/hung (person)	hanged/hung (person)
know	knew	known
lay	laid	laid
lead	led	led
lie	lay	lain
light	lit/lighted	lit
lose	lost	lost
pay	paid	paid
prove	proved	proved/proven
ride	rode	ridden
ring	rang	rung
rise	rose	risen
run	ran	run
see	saw	seen
seek	sought	sought
set	set	set

Common Irregular Verbs *(continued)*

PRESENT	PAST	PAST PARTICIPLE
shake	shook	shaken
sing	sang/sung	sung
sink	sank/sunk	sunk
sit	sat	sat
speak	spoke	spoken
spring	sprang	sprung
steal	stole	stolen
sting	stung	stung
strike	struck	struck
swear	swore	sworn
swim	swam	swum
swing	swung	swung
take	took	taken
tear	tore	torn
throw	threw	thrown
wake	woke/waked	woken/waked/woke
wear	wore	worn

ESL Advice: Verb Forms

To use verbs correctly, you need to consider four things: verb form, subject-verb agreement, verb tense, and verb voice. (See 15a-3.)

In English, verbs can have the following forms.

Principal Parts of Verbs in English

PRESENT	PAST	PRESENT PARTICIPLE	PAST PARTICIPLE
REGULAR VERBS			
hope	hoped	hoping	hoped
live	lived	living	lived
want	wanted	wanting	wanted
IRREGULAR VERBS			
come	came	coming	come
eat	ate	eating	eaten
run	ran	running	run

17d
verb
ESL

Most verbs are formed by combining one or more helping verbs with a main verb (see 15a–3). The main verb plus any helping verb is called a **verb phrase.**

	verb phrase
ONE HELPING VERB	I **was walking** to school during the snowstorm.

	verb phrase
TWO HELPING VERBS	I **have been walking** to school for many years.

Exercise 1

 A. In each of the following sentences, a correct or incorrect irregular verb form appears in parentheses. Edit each sentence to make it correct, or indicate that it's already correct. If necessary, consult the list in 17d or look in a dictionary for the principal parts of a particular verb.

EXAMPLE   *had fallen*
The rain (~~had falled~~)ₐall night.

1. Jeremy (*had chose*) to work along the levee as part of the volunteer corps.
2. The floodwater (*had rised*) rapidly during the night.
3. The work team (*had heaved*) sandbags on top of the levee for almost twenty-four hours.
4. Jim O'Connor and Rebecca Gomez (*had hung*) plastic sheeting up to plug a leak.
5. By eight o'clock in the morning, people (*had woke*) up to find that the river (*had fell*) by six inches and the town was safe.

 B. Review the list of irregular verbs in 17d. Compose five sentences in which you correctly or incorrectly use the past or past participle form of an irregular verb. In a small group, exchange lists and edit your sentences. Discuss the changes you made or did not make.

**17d
verb
ESL**

ESL Advice: Helping Verbs

Helping verbs can be used as main verbs ("I am from Laos") or in combination ("I am moving to California").

Forms of the Helping Verbs

BE
am, is, are
was, were
am being, is being, are being
was being, were being

MODALS
will, would
can, could
shall, should
ought to
might, may
must
have to, has to, had to

HAVE
have, has
had

DO
do, does
did

Combinations of Helping Verbs

have	+ be	have been, has been, had been
all modals	+ be	will be
	+ have	will have
	+ have + be	will have been

In order to know which helping verb to use, you need to know which tense to use.

Verb Forms and Helping Verbs for Commonly Used Verb Tenses

The past, present, and future progressive use *be.*

PAST
subject + *was/were* + present participle
She **was** working in her studio yesterday.

PRESENT
subject + *am/is/are* + present participle
She **is** working in her studio right now.

FUTURE
subject + *will* (modal) + *be* + present participle
She **will be** working in her studio tomorrow.

The past, present, and future perfect use *have.*

PAST
subject + *had* + past participle
She **had** tried to call you all day.

PRESENT
subject + *have/has* + past participle
She **has** tried to call you all day.

FUTURE
subject + *will* (modal) + *have* + past participle
She **will have** called you by midnight.

**17d
verb
ESL**

17e Editing progressive and perfect tenses

The three tenses usually called the **present, past,** and **future progressive** allow you to show an action in progress at some point in time. When you attach a helping verb to a main verb in the **progressive tense,** the main verb must take the *-ing* ending. In the future tense, the progressive must also include the verbal element *be.*

PRESENT PROGRESSIVE	Sales **are increasing** this quarter.
PAST PROGRESSIVE	At this time last year, we **were working** for improvement.
FUTURE PROGRESSIVE	I **will be discussing** the results at the meeting.

Note that irregular main verbs are not affected in any unique way by the progressive tense; all consist of the base form plus *-ing.*

The park ranger **is catching** the injured raccoon.

The campers **will be hanging** their food from a tree at night.

Most errors in progressive tense occur when you either use the wrong form of the helping verb or omit part of the auxiliary verb.

DRAFT	The amusement park always **opening** five minutes late.
EDITED	The amusement park **is** always **opening** five minutes late.
DRAFT	The kids **was running** for the front seat of the roller coaster.
EDITED	The kids **were running** for the front seat of the roller coaster.

Three special verb tenses, the **perfect tenses,** are used to show the order in which events take place. The **past perfect tense** allows you to indicate that something had already happened before something else happened. The form consists of *had* plus the past participle (see 17b-1 for participle forms).

The general practitioner **had treated** the patient for six months before the specialist took over the case.

Carmen **had drunk** three beers and wisely gave her car keys to the designated driver.

Errors commonly occur when a writer chooses the past perfect tense but doesn't construct it with the correct form of the past participle, substituting a simple past tense form instead.

17e
verb

DRAFT   Pierre **had rode** for six years before he got injured in a rodeo.

EDITED   Pierre **had ridden** for six years before he got injured in a rodeo.

The **present perfect tense** works much like the past perfect, but the action is something that has recurred or that the writer is insisting has already occurred.

> Never **have I seen** such a commotion at an elegant party.
> But officer, **I have reported** the burglary already.

The present perfect also presents something begun in the past and continuing into the present.

> I **have lived** in St. Louis for three weeks.

The **future perfect tense** shows that something will have happened by the time something else will be happening. This form consists of the helping verb *will* plus *have* plus the past participle of the main verb.

> Nancy **will have finished** by the time the dentist is ready.
> Otto **will have eaten** all the fries before his brother gets home.

ESL Advice: Simple Present and Present Progressive Tenses

In English, both the simple present and the present progressive tenses can describe activities that happen in the present.

Simple present

Use the simple present tense to describe activities that are factual or habitual. These activities occur in the present, but they are not necessarily activities in progress.

subject + verb (with -s if third person singular)

SHOWS FACT   The planets **revolve** around the sun.

SHOWS HABIT   The museum **offers** summer programs for children.

17e
verb
ESL

Some Common Time Expressions for Present Tense Habitual Activities		
all the time	most of the time	sometimes
always	never often	usually
every day, month, class . . .	rarely	

Present progressive

Use the present progressive tense to describe activities that are in progress.

> subject + *am/is/are* + present participle
> Santiago **is testing** the formula.

In this sentence, it is clear that Santiago is in the *process* of testing a formula.

Some Common Present Progressive Time Expressions to Show Activities in Progress

at the moment	this evening, semester, year . . .
right now	today

Many present progressive time expressions can be added to the sentence to show more precisely the time of the testing.

> Santiago **is testing** the formula **this semester.**
> Now readers know that the activity is in progress over the semester.

Choosing between simple present and present progressive

When you choose between the simple present and present progressive tenses, think about which time expression best describes the activity.

**17e
verb
ESL**

NOT APPROPRIATE   All people are communicating in some language.
Is it happening only at the moment (present progressive) or all the time (simple present)?

CORRECT   All people communicate in some language.
This is a fact, so the correct tense must be simple present tense.

NOT APPROPRIATE   The students are speaking their own languages in class.
Do the students speak their own languages all the time as a habit (simple present), or is it happening at the moment or one time only (present progressive)?

CORRECT   The students speak their own languages in class.
This is a habitual activity that occurs all the time, so the correct tense is simple present.

Verbs That Are Troublesome in Progressive Tenses

VERB	EXAMPLE	OTHER USAGES AND MEANINGS
SENSES		
see	I **see** the beauty.	Also: I **am seeing** the consultant. (meeting with, visiting, dating)
hear	I **hear** the birds.	Also: I **have been hearing** about the problem for a while. (receiving information)
smell	The flowers **smell** strong.	Also: I **am smelling** the flowers. (action in progress)
taste	The food **tastes** good.	Also: The cook **is tasting** the soup. (action in progress)
POSSESSION		
have	We **have** many friends.	Also: We **are having** a lot of fun. (experiencing)
own	They **own** many dogs.	
possess	She **possesses** much knowledge.	
belong	The book **belongs** to me.	
STATES OF MIND		
be	I **am** tired.	
know	I **know** the city well.	
believe	She **believes** in God.	
think	LaShonda I **thinks** it is true. (knows, believes)	Also: LaShonda **is thinking** about relocating. (having thoughts about)
recognize	His dog always **recognizes** him. (knows)	
understand	The social worker **understands** the problem.	
mean	I **don't mean** to pry. (don't want)	Also: I **have been meaning** to visit you. (planning, intending)

continued

**17e
verb
ESL**

Verbs That Are Troublesome in Progressive Tenses *(continued)*

VERB	EXAMPLE	OTHER USAGES AND MEANINGS
WISH OR ATTITUDE		
want	We **want** peace.	
desire	He **desires** his freedom.	
need	We **need** rain.	
love	Children **love** snow.	Also: I **have been loving** this book. (enjoying)
hate	Cats **hate** getting wet.	
like	He **likes** skiing.	
dislike	Patients **dislike** waiting.	
seem	The office **seems** efficient.	
appear	He **appears** tired. (seems to be)	Also: He **is appearing** at the theater. (acting, performing)
look	He **looks** tired. (seems to be)	Also: We **are looking** at the revised maps. (action of using eyes)

Tenses of Regular and Irregular Verbs in the Active Voice

PRESENT, PAST, AND FUTURE

PRESENT

I examine/begin	we examine/begin
you examine/begin	you examine/begin
he/she/it examines/begins	they examine/begin

PAST

I examined/begin	we examined/began
you examined/began	you examined/began
he/she/it examined/began	they examined/began

FUTURE

I will examine/begin	we will examine/begin
you will examine/begin	you will examine/begin
he/she/it will examine/begin	they will examine/begin

PRESENT, PAST, AND FUTURE PERFECT

PRESENT PERFECT

I have examined/begun	we have examined/begun
you have examined/begun	you have examined/begun
he/she/it has examined/begun	they have examined/begun

17e
verb
ESL

Tenses of Regular and Irregular Verbs in the Active Voice *(continued)*

PRESENT, PAST, AND FUTURE PERFECT *(CONT.)*

PAST PERFECT

I had examined/begun	we had examined/begun
you had examined/begun	you had examined/begun
he/she/it had examined/begun	they had examined/begun

FUTURE PERFECT

I will have examined/begun	we will have examined/begun
you will have examined/begun	you will have examined/begun
he/she/it will have examined/begun	they will have examined/begun

PRESENT, PAST, AND FUTURE PROGRESSIVE

PRESENT PROGRESSIVE

I am examining/beginning	we are examining/beginning
you are examining/beginning	you are examining/beginning
he/she/it is examining/beginning	they are examining/beginning

PAST PROGRESSIVE

I was examining/beginning	we were examining/beginning
you were examining/beginning	you were examining/beginning
he/she/it was examining/beginning	they were examining/beginning

FUTURE PROGRESSIVE

I will be examining/beginning	we will be examining/beginning
you will be examining/beginning	you will be examining/beginning
he/she/it will be examining/beginning	they will be examining/ beginning

PRESENT PERFECT, PAST PERFECT, AND FUTURE PERFECT PROGRESSIVE

PRESENT PERFECT PROGRESSIVE

I have been examining/beginning	we have been examining/beginning
you have been examining/beginning	you have been examining/beginning
he/she/it has been examining/beginning	they have been examining/beginning

PAST PERFECT PROGRESSIVE

I had been examining/beginning	we had been examining/beginning
you had been examining/beginning	you had been examining/beginning
he/she/it had been examining/beginning	they had been examining/beginning

17e
verb

continued

**Tenses of Regular and Irregular Verbs
in the Active Voice** *(continued)*

PRESENT PERFECT, PAST PERFECT, AND FUTURE PERFECT PROGRESSIVE *(CONT.)*

FUTURE PERFECT PROGRESSIVE

I will have been examining/ beginning	we will have been examining/ beginning
you will have been examining/ beginning	you will have been examining/ beginning
he/she/it will have been examining/ beginning	they will have been examining/ beginning

---

17f Recognizing the subjunctive mood

Sentences can be classified according to **mood,** a term that highlights the speaker's or writer's attitude as reflected in the statement. Most of your sentences will be in the **indicative mood** (characterizing statements intended as truthful or factual) or the **imperative mood** (characterizing statements like "Stop!" or "Watch out!" which function as commands). Most of the information in this chapter focuses on verbs in the indicative mood.

Because it is not used heavily in ordinary speech, you may have trouble with the **subjunctive mood** in your writing. The subjunctive mood is used to express uncertainty—a supposition, prediction, or possibility.

Were the deadline today, our proposal would not be ready.

The subjunctive mood has faded from most casual speech and even some writing, but it is still used on occasion, particularly in formal writing. Teachers or highly educated readers may expect you to use the subjunctive. Whenever you create sentences that express desires or wishes, both positive and negative, the subjective may be required.

17f
verb

DRAFT	Jacqueline wished the news **was** not true.
EDITED (SUBJUNCTIVE)	Jacqueline wished the news **were** not true.

Many **conditional statements,** expressing the improbable or hypothetical and often beginning with *if,* require the subjunctive.

DRAFT	If Sandy **was** a person who always wore a helmet, his family would be much less worried about his riding motorcycles.
EDITED (SUBJUNCTIVE)	If Sandy **were** a person who always wore a helmet, his family would be much less worried about his riding motorcycles.

> **Writer's Alert**
>
> When you write conditional sentences (with *if*), be careful not to add the auxiliary *would* to the *had + verb* structure in the conditional clause. This error is common, in part because the clause after the conditional often does correctly contain that structure.
>
> **DRAFT**   If Sandy **would have worn** his helmet on the night of the party, he **would have hurt** himself less seriously.
>
> **EDITED**   If Sandy **had worn** his helmet on the night of the party, he **would have hurt** himself less seriously.

Finally, some clauses with *that* require a subjunctive verb when they follow certain verbs that make demands or requests. The common error here is to use the incorrect form of the main verb, which should be the same as for the past participle (see 17c-2).

DRAFT   Parents desire that their child **shows** respect.

EDITED   Parents desire that their child **show** respect.

DRAFT   The judge asked that the eyewitnesses **be swore** in before testifying.

EDITED   The judge asked that the eyewitnesses **be sworn** in before testifying.

Exercise 2

A. Rewrite each of the following sentences in the tense or mood indicated in brackets by substituting appropriate main verb forms and any necessary helping verbs for the verb in parentheses.

EXAMPLE
The airplane assembly plant ∧ (*fail*) *has been failing* for several years. [present perfect progressive]

1. First, the recession (*hurt*) the market for small airplanes. [past perfect]
2. Then a new management team announced, "We (*close*) the plant unless productivity increases." [future]

17f
verb

3. At the same time, the company (*lose*) a product liability lawsuit. [past progressive]
4. This week, the company president (*announce*), "Unless we get some new orders in a few days, we (*declare*) bankruptcy." [simple past; future progressive]
5. If the plant (*be*) closed, three hundred workers would lose their jobs. [past subjunctive]

 B. Write five sentences of your own, three using different complex tenses and two employing the subjunctive mood. Exchange sentences with a fellow writer and check that your partner has used the tenses and the subjunctive mood correctly.

ESL Advice: Conditionals

As a writer, you may at times want to express three types of ideas that are dependent on a condition or are imagined. These ideas may be (1) *true* in the present, true in the future, or possibly true in the future; (2) *untrue* or contrary to fact in the present; or (3) *untrue* or contrary to fact in the past.

17f
verb
ESL

Type I: True in the Present

IF CLAUSE	RESULT CLAUSE

- Generally true as a habit or as a fact

  if + subject + present tense verb   subject + present tense verb
  If Rafi drives to school every day, he gets to class on time.

- True in the future as a one-time event

  if + subject + present tense verb   subject + future tense verb
  If Rafi drives to school today,   he will get to class on time.

- Possibly true in the future as a one-time event

  if + subject + present tense verb   subject + modal + base form verb
  If Rafi drives to school today,   he ⎰ may   get to class on time.
                                          ⎱ might
                                            could
                                            should

Type II: Untrue in the Present

IF CLAUSE	RESULT CLAUSE
if + subject + past tense verb	subject + $\begin{cases} would + \text{simple form of verb} \\ could \\ might \end{cases}$
If Rafi drove to school,	he $\begin{cases} \text{would} \\ \text{could} \\ \text{might} \end{cases}$ arrive on time.

Writer's Alert

With the Type II conditional, when you use the verb *be* in the *if* clause, the form is always *were*.

I, *you, he/she/it, we, they + were*

NOT APPROPRIATE   If she **was** president, she would reform tax laws.

CORRECT   If she **were** president, she would reform tax laws.

Type III: Untrue in the Past

IF CLAUSE	RESULT CLAUSE
if + subject + past perfect tense	subject + $\begin{cases} would + have + \text{past participle} \\ could \\ might \end{cases}$
If Rafi had driven to school,	he would not have been late.

17f
verb
ESL

Let's look at these examples to understand the meaning of conditionals.

Type I

CONDITION   If I **study** hard, I always **get** good grades.
This is true habitual behavior.

CONDITION   If I **study** hard for tomorrow's test, I **will get** a good grade.
This is true as a prediction of the future.

CONDITION   If I **study** hard for tomorrow's test, I **might get** a good grade.
This is possibly true as a prediction of the future.

Type II

SITUATION   I **don't have** enough money to go to Canada for vacation, so I **won't go.**
This is a true situation in the present.

CONDITION   If I **had** enough money to go to Canada for vacation, **I would definitely go.**
This is an imagined condition in the present.

Type III

SITUATION   I **did not have** enough money last month to go to Canada, so I **didn't go** there.
This is a true situation in the past.

CONDITION   If I **had had** enough money last month to go to Canada, I **would have gone** there.
This is an imagined condition in the past. It refers to a situation that did not happen.

Expressing a continuous action with conditionals

If he **were living** in Hong Kong, he **would be spending** time with his family.
This is an untrue condition in the present because he is not living in Hong Kong.

If he **had been living** in Hong Kong last year, he **would have been spending** more time with his family.
This is an untrue condition in the past because he was not living in Hong Kong last year.

Writer's Alert

Sometimes you may want to express ideas about events that happen at different times, and you can shift from one tense to another to do this.

                        past
SITUATION   I **did not expect** to meet a lot of people from
                                  present
my country in the United States, so I **am** surprised.

                        past
CONDITION   If I **had expected** to meet a lot of people from my
                                  present
country in the United States, **I would not be surprised.**

17g Recognizing clear tense sequence

In conversation, we often shift from verb tense to verb tense indiscriminately, sometimes moving from past to present and back again with little warning or planning. In writing, however, such tense shifts can be annoying to readers who expect consistency. Thus you need to maintain a clear **tense sequence** in your writing, making plain the time relationships of events and ideas. In the following passage, the shift from past to present is logical and clear.

LOGICAL   In the 1950s, great ocean liners still **offered** an attractive way to travel. Nowadays, people **prefer** jet travel because it is so much faster.

When changes in tense do not reflect clear relationships in time or do so inconsistently, your readers may become confused.

INCONSISTENT   The author **begins** by giving a factual account of the storm. He **said** that if people had heeded the warnings, many lives would have been saved.

EDITED   The author **begins** by giving a factual account of the storm. He **says** that if people had heeded the warnings, many lives would have been saved.

You can shift tenses inside a sentence without creating confusion as long as you make the tense sequence logical.

LOGICAL   Although my mother and father both **loved** cats, I **dislike** them.
                                      past   present

(past) loved — *(present)* dislike

LOGICAL   People **forget** that four serious candidates **ran** in the 1948 presidential election.

(present) forget — *(past)* ran

LOGICAL   I **will accept** your report even if it **is** a bit late.

(future) will accept — *(present)* is

LOGICAL   The accountant **destroyed** evidence of the embezzlement because the police **had forgotten** to warn him of the importance of the records.

(past) destroyed — *(past perfect)* had forgotten

LOGICAL   None of the expedition's crew **had recognized** that food stored in cans sealed with lead solder **is** poisonous.

(past prefect) had recognized — *(present)* is

Putting *is poisonous* in the present tense is appropriate because the phrase is a generally true (or widely applicable) statement.

17g verb

Writer's Tip

Use the present tense to discuss events, ideas, and statements in a piece of literature, a film, an essay, a painting, or a similar creative production.

INCORRECT   In *The Mating Season,* the main character **described** an unpleasant relative as a person "who chews broken bottles and kills rats with her teeth."

CORRECT   In *The Mating Season,* the main character **describes** an unpleasant relative as a person "who chews broken bottles and kills rats with her teeth."

Exercise 3

A. Decide whether the complex verb forms highlighted in the following sentences are correct. Edit those that are not; explain why you left any as they appear.

EXAMPLE

The team leader **is planning** to ask for reports just after the production meeting ~~**will begin.**~~ *begins*

1. Kamal **is finished** testing the circuit board by the time the production meeting **had started.**
2. The team members **will ask** Kamal if he **was planning** to test the remainder of the circuit boards.
3. As I prepare this report on the project, Michelle **is assembling** the prototype using the circuit boards.
4. The other people **will assemble** the extra machines as soon as the delivery van **arrived.**
5. If our customers **will be able** to recognize the advantages of our product, they **would order** more of the machines.

B. Compose five sentences with correct and incorrect subjunctive mood and/or tense shifts. Edit each other's sentences in a small group; then discuss the changes you made.

17h Recognizing active and passive voice

Verbs in the **active voice** appear in sentences in which the doer of an action is the subject of the sentence.

	Doer (subject)	Action (verb)	Goal (object)
ACTIVE	The car	hit	the lamppost.
ACTIVE	Everyone	likes	a comedian.

To rewrite an active sentence in the **passive voice,** add a form of *be* as a helping verb, and use the participle form of the verb. Place the subject (or doer) into the object position after the word *by.* (A prepositional phrase states the doer and is optional.)

	Goal (subject)	Action (verb)	[Agent] [prepositional phrase
PASSIVE	The lamppost	**was hit**	[by the car].
PASSIVE	A comedian	**is liked**	[by everyone].

The active voice and passive voice versions of a sentence create different kinds of emphasis because they use different words as sentence subjects. In addition, a passive sentence that eliminates any mention of the doer can mask responsibility for an action.

ACTIVE VOICE	The city council banned smoking in restaurants.
PASSIVE VOICE	Smoking in restaurants was banned by the city council.
AGENT ELIMINATED	Smoking in restaurants was banned.

(For a discussion of use and misuse of the passive voice, see 9c-3.)

ESL Advice: The Passive Voice

In English you can choose to use either active or passive voice for stylistic reasons (see 17h). All transitive verbs in English may be written in the passive voice *except* the progressive forms of the present perfect, past perfect, future, and future perfect. In all the sentences in the following chart, the doer of the action is not the subject, *food,* but rather *chef.*

Verb Forms in the Passive Voice	
TENSES	SUBJECT + *BE* FORM + PAST PARTICIPLE
PRESENT	The food **is prepared** by the chef.
PRESENT PROGRESSIVE	The food **is being prepared** by the chef.
PAST	The food **was prepared** by the chef.
PAST PROGRESSIVE	The food **was being prepared** by the chef.
PRESENT PERFECT	The food **has been prepared** by the chef.
PAST PERFECT	The food **had been prepared** by the chef.
FUTURE	The food **will be prepared** by the chef.
FUTURE PERFECT	The food **will have been prepared** by the chef.

17h verb ESL

Writer's Alert

    Be sure to edit your passive verbs to check for correct forms. Each passive verb must have a form of *be* and a past participle. With regular verbs, the past participle will have the *-ed* ending. Sometimes it is difficult to hear these *-ed* endings in spoken English, so be careful to include them in your writing.

NOT APPROPRIATE   The young man was **call** by the draft board.

CORRECT   The young man was **called** by the draft board.

The verb *make* in the passive voice, unlike in the active voice, is followed by the infinitive.

ACTIVE VOICE   The council member made us **wait.**

PASSIVE VOICE   We were made **to wait** by the council member.

Exercise 4

A. Edit the following passage by rewriting unnecessary uses of the passive voice into the active voice. In rewriting passive voice sentences that do not indicate an agent (doer), fill in the names of the person(s) or thing(s) you consider responsible for the action.

    Having cash registers full of change was found to increase the likelihood of a late-night robbery. In one example, a store clerk was held up at gunpoint. It was decided by management that requiring full payment for gasoline in advance of a purchase would minimize the risk of further holdups. This course of action had been voted on by the board of directors prior to implementation. The decision was posted at each location. Following implementation, it was discovered that holdups were not minimized unless large signs indicating the clerk's lack of available cash were placed in plain view. Once this was done, fewer holdups were experienced, and the turnover of late-night personnel was decreased.

B. Compare your rewritten version of the passage in Exercise 4A with those produced by other students. Be sure you explain why you have decided to let any sentences remain in the passive voice. Working with several other students, produce one version of the passage reflecting group agreement on the best way to rewrite the sentences.

17h
verb

17i Editing troublesome verbs (*lie, lay, sit, set*)

Even for experienced writers, a few verbs can be tricky. For example, you may confuse the past or past participle forms of different verbs that "share" one or more forms. Until you can remember their correct forms, you should identify these verbs when you edit your drafts and then check them by reviewing this section. Here are the verbs most often confused (which, incidentally, also have the longest dictionary entries of any verbs in English).

VERB	PRESENT	PAST	PARTICIPLE
lie (oneself)	lie	lay	lain
lay (an object)	lay	laid	laid
sit (oneself)	sit	sat	sat
set (an object)	set	set	set

1 *Lie* and *lay*

When you use the verb *lie* to mean "lie down," you may confuse it with the verb *lay*, which means to put something down, as in "Lay the book on the table." *Lie* is an intransitive verb—it can't be used with a **direct object** (see 15b)—whereas *lay* must be used with a direct object.

DRAFT I **laid** down yesterday afternoon for a nap. I **have laid** down at around 2 p.m. each day for over a year now.

EDITED I **lay** down yesterday afternoon for a nap. I **have lain** down at around 2 p.m. each day for over a year now.

DRAFT Dr. Parsons **lay** the cadaver on the table and began the autopsy.

EDITED Dr. Parsons **laid** the cadaver on the table and began the autopsy.

A third verb, *lie,* meaning "to tell an untruth," is a regular verb whose past tense ends in *-ed* ("I *lied* to my sister"). Don't confuse it with the form for the other verb *lie.*

2 *Sit* and *set*

The verb *sit* means to place oneself on or in something, such as a chair. *Set*, however, means to place an object, such as a book, on a surface. Like choosing between *lie* and *lay*, you figure out which form to use by asking yourself whether there is a direct object in your sentence. *Sit* can't be used with a direct object, but *set* must be used with a direct object.

17i verb

DRAFT	First Erica and Steve **sat** the projector down on the table. Then they **set** down and listened to the chairperson's speech.
EDITED	First Erica and Steve **set** the projector down on the table. Then they **sat** down and listened to the chairperson's speech.

Exercise 5

 A. For each sentence, circle the appropriate verb from the two within parentheses.

EXAMPLE

A fire last Saturday (*lead, led*) to Sandy's first big assignment as a reporter.

1. Sandy (*laid/lay*) the article for the newspaper on her editor's desk.
2. To get information for the article, she (*sat/set*) in the waiting room of the fire commissioner's office for three days.
3. During the interview she (*layed/lay/laid*) on his desk a copy of the report criticizing the fire department's performance during the Brocklin Warehouse fire.
4. The commissioner looked the report over and then (*sat/set*) it next to the other report, which praised the department's performance.
5. After she had (*lead/led*) the three-hour discussion with the commissioner, Sandy was convinced that the department had done an adequate job at the fire.

 B. Write four or five sentences in which you use *incorrect* forms of *sit, set, lie,* and *lay.* Exchange your sentences in a small group, edit them, and then discuss your changes.

EXAMPLE

Mrs. Jones sat the tuna salad dangerously close to Puff, her Siamese cat.

18

Agreement (Subject and Verb, Pronoun and Antecedent)

What's wrong with the following sentence?

The Citizenship Institute and the Public Achievement Program focuses on social justice.

You probably read the opening of the sentence assuming it would be about *two* things—Citizenship Institute and the Public Achievement Program. But then you came to the verb *focuses* and no doubt stumbled a bit: are these programs really *one* program? After all, the verb is *singular* in form. The sentence sends mixed signals, unlike the version below.

CORRECT   The Citizenship Institute and the Public Achievement Program **focus** on social justice.

Readers expect you to make subjects and verbs work together grammatically—by showing **agreement** in number and person. They also expect you to make a pronoun agree with its **antecedent,** the word to which it refers. Lack of **pronoun-antecedent agreement** can cause inconsistency or confusion, thus undermining the effectiveness of a statement.

INCONSISTENT   Project status reports should address the needs, motivations, and values of its audience.

CLEAR   **A project status report** should address the needs, motivations, and values of **its audience.**

CLEAR   **Project status reports** should address the needs, motivations, and values of **their audiences.**

18a Recognizing subject-verb agreement

You need to make sure that subjects and verbs agree in **number** (singular or plural) and **person** (first, second, and third person) so that your sentences can convey consistent, clear meaning to readers.

SINGULAR	The **worker** tears down the platform.
PLURAL	The **workers** tear down the platform.
FIRST PERSON	**I** operate the air compressor.
	We operate the air compressor.
SECOND PERSON	**You** operate the air compressor.
THIRD PERSON	**He** (**she, it**) operates the air compressor.
	They operate the air compressor.

S T R A T E G Y

To edit your writing for **subject-verb agreement**, look for a subject, identify its number (singular or plural) and person (first, second, or third), and then make sure the verb agrees with it in grammatical form.

**18a
agr**

Agreement: Number, Person, and Gender

Number shows whether words are singular or plural in meaning.

SINGULAR WORDS
1. Nouns naming individual people, animals, ideas, and things
2. Personal pronouns referring to individuals: *I, you, he, she, it*
3. Indefinite pronouns *(each, someone)* or relative pronouns *(who, which, that)* referring to singular nouns or pronouns
4. Verbs in their singular forms (I *am*, she *is*; I *analyze*, she *analyzes)*

PLURAL WORDS
1. Nouns naming more than one person, animal, idea, or thing
2. Personal pronouns referring to more than one individual: *we, you, they*
3. Indefinite pronouns (*all, none*) or relative pronouns (*who, which, that*) referring to plural nouns or pronouns
4. Verbs in their plural forms (we *are*, they *are;* we *analyze*, they *analyze)*

Agreement: Number, Person, and Gender *(continued)*

Person indicates the speaker or the subject being spoken to or about.

FIRST PERSON (SPEAKER)
I, we

SECOND PERSON (SPOKEN TO)
You

THIRD PERSON (SPOKEN ABOUT)
He, she, it, they
Nouns naming things, people, animals, or ideas

Gender refers to the masculine, feminine, or neuter character generally attributed to a noun or pronoun.

MASCULINE WORDS
1. *He*
2. Nouns indicating males: *father, husband*
3. Indefinite pronouns (*everyone, somebody*) or relative pronouns (*who, which, that*) when they refer to males

FEMININE WORDS
1. *She*
2. Nouns indicating females: *sister, daughter*
3. Indefinite pronouns (*everyone, somebody*) or relative pronouns (*who, which, that*) when they refer to females

NEUTER WORDS
1. *It*
2. Nouns indicating places, things, and ideas
3. Indefinite pronouns (*everything, something*) or relative pronouns (*which, that*) when they refer to places, things, and ideas

**18a
agr**

In many cases, you will find errors in subject-verb agreement easy to spot and correct.

INCORRECT	The clients is impatient.
CORRECT	The **clients** <u>are</u> impatient.
CORRECT	The **client** <u>is</u> impatient.

At other times, however, you may need to pay careful attention to number and person in your subjects and verbs, even consulting the chart on agreement of number, person, and gender. This is most likely to be the case with the troublesome sentence constructions discussed in 18b.

Exercise 1

A. Fill in the blanks in the following sentences with verbs that agree in number and person with their subject.

EXAMPLE

Every day I _walk_ past the Valois Cafeteria.

1. The retired men in the neighborhood _____ lunch at the cafeteria.
2. The cafeteria's motto, "See What You Eat," _____ on the sign above the entrance.
3. The restaurant _____ run down.
4. Nonetheless, it _____ a clean and safe place.
5. A sociologist has studied the ways people of different races and cultures _____ with each other at the cafeteria.

B. Copy a paragraph from one of your papers or a book, but replace the verbs with blanks (as in Exercise 1A). Exchange paragraphs with a partner and fill in the blanks in that paragraph. Work together to check your answers.

ESL Advice: Subject-Verb Agreement

Watch out for the following troublesome verbs that change form according to person or tense. Be sure to select the correct verb form so that your subject and verb agree.

- *Be* verbs (present and past)

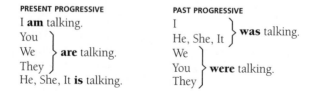

- Helping verb *be* in the present progressive and past progressive tenses

PRESENT PROGRESSIVE
I **am** talking.
You ⎫
We ⎬ **are** talking.
They ⎭
He, She, It **is** talking.

PAST PROGRESSIVE
I ⎫
He, She, It ⎬ **was** talking.
We ⎫
You ⎬ **were** talking.
They ⎭

**18a
agr
ESL**

- *Have* verbs (present)

I
You
We   **have** a new home.
They

He, She, It **has** a new home.

- Helping verb *have* in the present perfect and present perfect progressive tenses

PRESENT PERFECT

I
You   **have** been here
We   for many years.
They

He, She, It **has** been here
        for many years.

PRESENT PERFECT PROGRESSIVE

I
You   **have** been living
We   here for a long time.
They

He, She, It **has** been living here for
        a long time.

- *Do* or *does* to show emphasis

I, You, We, They   **do** want the contract!
He, She, It   **does** want the contract!

- *Doesn't* or *Don't* to show the negative

I, You, We, They   **don't** exercise enough.
He, She, It   **doesn't** exercise enough.

- Present tense for all other verbs in the third person singular. You must add *-s* or *-es* to the verb.

I, You, We, They   **check** email every day.
He, She, It   **checks** email every day.

18a
agr
ESL

Writer's Alert

In English there are many nouns, called **mass** or **non-count nouns,** which use the singular form (see 15a-1). Look out for these nouns as the subjects of your sentences, and make sure the verbs are singular.

Her **clothing** was made by hand.
Rush-hour **traffic** is always heavy.
Important **information** is found in the telephone book.
Last night's **homework** was challenging.

18b Editing for subject-verb agreement

The usually simple process of checking for agreement between subjects and verbs can become quite complicated with sentence constructions that involve plural and compound subjects, widely separated subject and verb, or subjects like *all* or *who*.

1 Choosing verb forms with plural and compound subjects

Be alert for subjects that are plural in form (*shoes, filters, children, mathematics, we, they*) and for compound subjects (*cheese and yogurt, neither Charlene nor I*). Both often need a plural verb—but not always.

Plural Subjects. Plural subjects generally need plural verbs, just as singular subjects generally need singular verbs. (See Chapter 17b.)

S T R A T E G Y

To identify plural subjects, look for *-s* or *-es* endings. Remember that most singular nouns become plural with the addition of these endings. In contrast, present tense verbs become *singular* with the addition of *-s* or *-es*.

SINGULAR   The dam prevent**s** flooding.

PLURAL   The dam**s** prevent flooding.

EXCEPTIONS
- Nouns with irregular plurals, such as *person/people, child/children,* or *louse/lice,* and nouns with the same form for singular and plural, such as *moose/moose*
- Verbs with irregular forms, including *be* and *have* (see 17d).

In a verb phrase (see 15a-3), the helping verb sometimes changes form for singular and plural, but the main verb remains the same.

	HELPING VERB CHANGES FORM
SINGULAR	The **park** <u>does</u> seem safer.
PLURAL	The **parks** <u>do</u> seem safer.

	HELPING VERB DOES NOT CHANGE
SINGULAR	The **park** <u>might</u> seem safer.
PLURAL	The **parks** <u>might</u> seem safer.

18b
agr

Subjects joined by *and*. By joining two or more subjects with *and* or *both . . . and,* you create a **compound subject.** Because *and* makes the subject plural even if one or all of the individual parts are singular, you generally need to choose a plural verb.

> **Jim and the rest of the Boy Scouts** <u>were</u> responsible for the rescue.

> **Heather, Amalia, and I** <u>contribute</u> to the Cerebral Palsy Association each year.

However, if the parts of a compound subject designate a single person, thing, or idea or if the parts should be taken as a unit, you need to choose a singular verb.

UNIT (SINGULAR)	**Ham and eggs** <u>is</u> still my favorite breakfast.
SEPARATE ELEMENTS (PLURAL)	**Ham and eggs** <u>are</u> the main ingredients in my favorite casserole.
ONE PERSON	**My fellow art teacher and friend** also <u>has</u> paintings in the show.
TWO PEOPLE	**My fellow art teacher and my friend** also <u>have</u> paintings in the show.

Subjects within phrases. When you use a phrase like *as well as, in addition to, together with,* and *along with* in a sentence, you may be tempted to treat a noun that follows it as the sentence's subject and make the verb agree with that noun rather than with the real subject.

MISTAKEN	A regular tune-up, with frequent oil **changes,** <u>prolong</u> the life of your car.

To identify the real subject, imagine the sentence without the intervening phrase: "A regular tune-up . . . prolongs the life of your car."

EDITED	A regular **tune-up,** along with frequent oil changes, <u>prolongs</u> the life of your car.

18b
agr

Because phrases like *as well as* can be easily mistaken for *and,* you may unintentionally treat a singular subject as a compound (plural) subject.

MISTAKEN	The university's **provost,** as well as the deans, <u>have</u> issued new guidelines emphasizing teaching.
EDITED	The university's **provost,** as well as the deans, <u>has</u> issued new guidelines emphasizing teaching.

If you mean *and,* use the word itself.

REWRITTEN The university's provost **and** the deans have issued new promotion guidelines emphasizing teaching.

Writer's Alert

Depending on where you place the words *each* or *every,* you can give a compound subject a singular or plural meaning.

EACH BEFORE COMPOUND SUBJECT
compound subject   singular verb
Each shift manager and unit manager **reviews** the progress logs daily.

EACH AFTER COMPOUND SUBJECT
compound subject   plural verb
The shift managers and unit managers **each review** the progress logs daily.

Subjects joined by *or* or *nor.* The words *or* and *nor* allow you to link the parts of the subject while at the same time creating a sense of separation or choice between them. When you have joined parts of a subject with *or* or *nor* (*either . . . or, neither . . . nor*), make the verb agree with the part closer to it.

BOTH SINGULAR The **mayor** or **the deputy mayor** holds a press conference each week.

BOTH PLURAL **Heads of departments** or **building supervisors** prepare monthly efficiency reports.

SINGULAR +
PLURAL **The city auditor** or **the staff accountants** review each efficiency report.

PLURAL +
SINGULAR **Incomplete records** or **dishonest reporting** weakens the review process.

In general, putting the plural element closer to the verb makes a sentence less awkward.

AWKWARD	Either members of the city council or the **mayor** drafts amendments to the city charter.
BETTER	Either the mayor or **members** of the city council draft amendments to the city charter.

When the parts of a subject differ in person and therefore need different verb forms (for example, *I have, he has*), you should make the verb agree with the part of the subject closer to it. If this strategy makes a sentence awkward, rewrite the sentence.

INCORRECT	Either the other new residents or **I** are going to file a complaint over the way our children were treated.
AWKWARD	Either the other new residents or **I** am going to file a complaint over the way our children were treated.
REWRITTEN	Either the other new **residents** are going to file a complaint over the way our children were treated or **I** am.

ESL Advice: Paired Conjunctions

Paired conjunctions like *both . . . and, either . . . or, neither . . . nor,* and *not only . . . but also* pose some problems for subject-verb agreement. *Both . . . and* always needs a plural verb, whether the elements being joined by the conjunction are singular or plural.

both . . .   *and*   +   **plural verb**
Both the president **and** her advisor **are** in Tokyo this week.

both . . .   *and*   +   **plural verb**
Both the president **and** her advisor **are** in Tokyo this week.

Either . . . or, neither . . . nor, and *not only . . . but also* may take either a singular or a plural verb. The subject closer to the verb determines the form of the verb.

singular subject   + **singular verb**
Either the president or her **advisor**
Neither the president nor her **advisor**   **is** in Tokyo.
Not only the president but also her **advisor**

plural subject   + **plural verb**
Either the president or her **advisors**
Neither the president nor her **advisors**   **are** in Tokyo.
Not only the president but also her **advisors**

18b
agr
ESL

Collective nouns as subjects. A **collective noun** is singular in form yet identifies a group of individuals (*audience, mob, crew, troop, brood, tribe,* or *herd*). When you use a collective noun to refer to a group that acts as a single unit, choose a singular verb.

> The **staff** is hardworking and well trained.
> The **number** of novelists writing mysteries is surprisingly large.

When you focus on group members and their individual actions, choose a plural verb.

> The **staff** have earned many sales awards this year.
> A surprisingly large **number** of novelists write mysteries.

If using a plural verb makes a sentence sound awkward, rewrite the sentence using a plural subject.

AWKWARD   The congregation react to Reverend Cullen's sermons in different ways, ranging from boredom to enlightenment.

REWRITTEN   **Members** of the congregation react to Reverend Cullen's sermons in different ways, ranging from boredom to enlightenment.

Nouns with plural forms and singular meanings. Some nouns, such as *politics, statistics, linguistics, news, physics, mumps,* and *athletics,* have the -*s* ending of plural nouns but are generally singular in meaning. Choose singular verbs to go with them.

> **Mathematics** is an increasingly popular field of study for undergraduates.

> The **news** about the job market for the coming year is surprisingly good.

> A measurement or number ending in -*s* may still be singular if it names a quantity or unit as a whole.

> **Four years** is the amount of time Dr. Santiago spent studying the effects of stress on lawyers.

> **One-third** of the price of books consists of production and transportation costs.

Yet when figures or measurements refer to individual elements, treat them as plural.

> **One-third** of the job trainees leave the program in the first five weeks.
> **They (plural) leave individually.**

> The **economics** of the arrangement are suspect.
> *Economics* **refers to the many different financial relationships and procedures involved.**

18b agr

Did You Know?

In 1867, William Bingham wrote, "The verb agrees with its subject in number and person: as, *I write; thou writest; he writes.*" The rule still applies, but *thou* is no longer a familiar part of the language.

Bingham taught school in North Carolina, so in giving the following example of agreement with a collective noun he might have been reflecting on the experience of the Civil War: "The army *destroys* everything in the line of *its* march."

William Bingham, *A Grammar of the English Language* (Philadelphia: Butler, 1867) 98.

Exercise 2

A. In each of the following sentences, choose the word inside the parentheses that creates subject-verb agreement.

EXAMPLE

The mayor, as well as members of the city council, (has/have) been searching for better ways to fund the zoo.

1. Several large lizards and an eight-foot python (*makes/make*) up the main attractions in the reptile building of the tiny zoo.
2. The displays as well as the building itself (*appears/appear*) well designed and well maintained.
3. The animals each (*displays/display*) good health and normal behavior.
4. Neither the zoo's overseers nor its director (*is/are*) satisfied with the reptile building and the number of animals on display.
5. Of the zoo's visitors, three-quarters (*says/say*) that the collection should be enlarged.
6. This year the Cajun and Bluegrass Festival (*features/feature*) several new bands.
7. The group *Beausoleil* (*appears/appear*) twice on the program.
8. The Cajun food, along with more familiar snacks, (*does/do*) draw many people to the refreshment tent.
9. The festival staff (*wears/wear*) buttons saying "Ask me for help."
10. Both the dancing lessons and the crafts display (*occupies/occupy*) the same tent.

B. Make up five sentences like those in Exercise 2A on any topic of your choice. Give them to a partner to complete, and work on those your partner has created.

18b
agr

2 Choosing verb forms with unusual sentence structures

When you separate subjects and verbs with other words, invert word order, or use linking verbs (*is, seems, feels*), you need to pay special attention to subject-verb agreement.

Subject and verb separated by other words. Words coming between a subject and a verb can cause an agreement error if you mistake them for the subject. This is especially true when the intervening words are nouns. You may be tempted to make the verb agree with the nearest noun rather than the actual subject.

FAULTY
AGREEMENT
The new trolley system, with its expanded routes and lower fares, are especially popular with senior citizens.
The words *routes* and *fares* are not the subject of the sentence.

EDITED
The new trolley **system,** with its expanded routes and lower fares, **is** especially popular with senior citizens.

ESL Advice: Separated Subjects and Verbs

When phrases or clauses come between the subject and the verb of the sentence, you need to check for agreement carefully.

PHRASES

NOT APPROPRIATE   A person with sensitive eyes have to wear sunglasses.

CORRECT   A **person** with sensitive eyes **has** to wear sunglasses.

CLAUSES

NOT APPROPRIATE   A person whose eyes are sensitive have to wear sunglasses.

CORRECT   A **person** whose eyes are sensitive **has** to wear sunglasses.

**18b
agr
ESL**

Inverted word order. The verb should agree with the subject even when you alter typical word order in a sentence to create emphasis or ask a question.

verb   subject

QUESTION   Are **patient satisfaction and increased efficiency** possible at the New Rockville Medical Clinic?

verb   subject

EMPHASIS   Following landslide victories comes **overconfidence** for many politicians.

In editing, pay attention to expletive constructions such as *there are* and *it is* (see 9b). They invert (reverse) the usual subject-verb sentence order, allowing you to present the subject *after* the verb. As a result, you need to make the verb agree with the subject that follows it.

verb   subject

SINGULAR   There **is opportunity** for people starting new service industries in this city.

verb   subject

PLURAL   There **are** many new **opportunities** for service industries in this city.

Although it is strictly grammatical to use *there are* with a compound subject, you may use *there is* if the first part of a compound subject is singular.

There is **a guard and an alarm system** protecting the warehouse.

Linking verbs. Examine sentences built around a linking verb such as *is, appears,* or *feels* (see 15a-3) to make sure the verb agrees with the subject. Do not mistakenly make it agree with the complement, that is, the noun or pronoun renaming the subject (see 15b-2).

subject   verb   complement

INCORRECT   The chief **obstacle** to change are the **mayor and her political allies.**

CORRECT   The chief **obstacle** to change is the mayor and her political allies.

3 Using special subjects (*all, everybody, none; who, which, that*)

Indefinite pronouns (*all, everybody, none*) as subjects. Indefinite pronouns do not refer to specific ideas, people, or things. Most have clearly singular meanings and require singular verbs.

Someone is ringing the doorbell.
Everybody has the duty to vote.

A few indefinite pronouns, such as *all, any, most, none,* and *some,* can be either singular or plural, according to their meaning.

18b
agr

S T R A T E G Y

Choose a singular or plural verb for words like *all, any,* and *none* on the basis of the noun or pronouns to which they refer. Consider whether the pronouns refer to something that *cannot be counted* (singular) or two or more elements of something that *can be counted* (plural). (See Chapter 15.)

SINGULAR   **All** of the food is for the camping trip next week.

all = singular noun

food = food in general (not countable)

PLURAL   **All** of the food supplies are for the camping trip next week.

all = plural noun

supplies = many different kinds of supplies (countable), such as flour, meat, and dried fruit

---

ESL Advice: Quantifiers

A **quantifier** is a word that indicates the amount or quantity of a subject—a word like *each, one,* or *many.*

Expressions followed by a plural noun and a singular verb

Each of
Each one of
Every one of   } the ESL students **lives** on campus.
One of   singular verb
Neither of

18b
agr
ESL

Expressions followed by a plural noun and a plural verb

Both of
Many of   } the students **live** off campus.
Several of   plural verb

Expressions followed by either a singular or plural verb

All of
A lot of   noncount noun + singular verb
Most of   } the **produce is** fresh
None of
Some of

All of
A lot of   } plural noun + plural verb
Most of   } the **vegetables are** fresh
None of
Some of

Much and **most** with noncount and plural nouns.   Look at the following examples, and be sure to watch for these errors in your writing.

quantifier + noncount noun
NOT APPROPRIATE   Much of traffic occurs during rush hour.

CORRECT   **Much traffic** occurs during rush hour.

quantifier + plural noun
NOT APPROPRIATE   Most of Americans live in the cities or suburbs.

CORRECT   **Most Americans** live in the cities or suburbs.

ESL Advice: *Other, Others,* and *Another* as Pronouns or Adjectives

When *others, the others,* and *the other* are used as pronouns in a sentence, they require particular grammatical patterns.

Pronouns

OTHERS + PLURAL VERB
Adds points about a topic; there may be more points.

I enjoy Paris for many reasons. Some reasons are the beautiful architecture and gardens; **others are** the wonderful people, culture, and language.

THE OTHERS (PLURAL) + PLURAL VERB; *THE OTHER* (SINGULAR) + SINGULAR VERB
Adds the last point or points about the topic; there are no more.

Half the members of the project team favor Mr. Chung's work Plan; **the others want** to follow Ms. Krikorian's plan.

I have two travel books. One is about New Zealand, and **the other is** about Australia.

18b
agr
ESL

Another, other, and *the other* are sometimes used as adjectives in a sentence, and they require particular grammatical patterns.

Adjectives

ANOTHER + SINGULAR NOUN
Adds an idea about the topic; there may be more ideas.

One strength of our project team is our knowledge of the problem area. **Another strength** is our excellent communication skills.

OTHER + PLURAL NOUN
Adds more ideas about the topic; there may be more ideas.

Other reasons include our prior experience and our ability to work well together.

THE *OTHER* + SINGULAR OR PLURAL NOUN
Adds the final point or points to be discussed.

There are two very important sights to see in Paris. One is the Louvre Museum, and **the other one** is the Cathedral of Notre Dame.

There are many sights to see in Paris. One sight is the Louvre Museum. **The other sights** are the Eiffel Tower, the Champs-Élysées, the Cathedral of Notre Dame, and the Arc de Triomphe.

Who, which, and *that* as subjects. The **relative pronouns** *who, which,* and *that* (see 15a-2) do not have singular and plural forms, yet the words to which they refer, their antecedents, generally have separate singular and plural forms. Choose a singular or plural verb for *who, which,* or *that* according to the number of the antecedent.

**18b
agr
ESL**

SINGULAR   He likes **a film** that focuses on relationships between characters.

PLURAL   I prefer **films** that combine action and romance.

Titles and names as subjects. When you need to use the title of a work or the name of a company as a sentence subject, choose a singular verb even if the name or title is plural.

New West Consultants **pays** staff high wages and **has** an excellent benefits package.
Think to yourself: The company pays . . .

The White Roses **is** second on the paperback best-seller list this month.
Think to yourself: The book is . . .

"Tall ships" **is** the name given to the largest sailing ships.

Writer's Alert

Watch for the phrases *one of* and *the only one of.* They can create agreement problems when they come before a relative pronoun (*who, which,* or *that*).

Dr. Gotari is **one** of those professors who help students succeed.
Who refers to the plural *professors*; consequently the verb, *help,* is plural. There are other professors like Dr. Gotari.

Dr. Gotari is **the only one** of the professors who helps students succeed.
Who refers to the singular *Dr. Gotari;* consequently, the verb, *helps,* is singular. Dr. Gotari is the only supportive instructor.

Remember that adding the -*s* to the verb makes it singular, not plural.

Exercise 3

A. For each of the following sentences, give the correct present tense form of the infinitive verb indicated in parentheses.

EXAMPLE

None of the department heads ⌃*has* (*to have*) the same administrative style.

1. Frieda O'Connor is one of those managers who (*to lead*) by example.
2. All the other department heads (*to respect*) her leadership ability.
3. She knows each of the employees who (*to work*) in her department.
4. Each year, Alberti and Campos Design Associates (*to give*) a plaque and a bonus to the employee who receives the highest rating in a company-wide survey.
5. The award, both the plaque and the money, (*to be*) given to Frieda almost every other year.

B. Working with another student, correct the errors that have been introduced into the following passage from Thomas R. McDonough's "Is Anyone Out There?" Not all the sentences contain

**18b
agr**

an error, and some may have more than one. If correcting an error results in an awkward sentence, rewrite it, but do not rewrite simply to avoid having to deal with an agreement problem. When you are finished, compare your corrections with those of another pair of students, and explain the differences.

Each of the scientists involved in the search are pretty sure something is out there. A lot of numbers, some high and some low, is thrown around to express the probability of intelligent life somewhere else in the universe. Here is some figures that are middle-of-the-road. There is an estimated four hundred billion stars in the Milky Way. Planets may be fairly common, so you can figure one out of every ten of these stars have planets, which equals forty billion stars with planets. If every such star has ten planets, that is four hundred billion planets. But how many of these places seems suitable for life? Neither too hot nor too cold is the conditions needed for life forms similar to our own. An atmosphere along with some water are also necessary. In our solar system only Earth qualifies, though Mars and Venus each comes close. Let us be conservative and estimate that only one of each solar system's planets fit the pattern. That's still forty billion habitable planets.

18c Editing for pronoun-antecedent agreement

A pronoun refers to an **antecedent.** The antecedent can be either a noun or another pronoun.

antecedent   pronoun

Campers should treat **their** tents and sleeping bags with a mildew-preventing spray.

pronoun   antecedent

Its preference for damp fabric makes **mildew** a major problem for campers.

By choosing forms of nouns and pronouns that agree in *gender, person,* and *number,* you help readers understand how the ideas in your sentence relate. **Number** refers to the forms a noun or pronoun may take to indicate singular or plural. **Person** refers to word forms indicating the speaker or the subject spoken to or about.

First person	=	*I, we*
Second person	=	*you*
Third person	=	*he, she, it, they,* and nouns naming things, people, and ideas

Gender refers to masculine, feminine, or neuter qualities generally associated with a noun or pronoun. (See detailed chart on pp. 276–77.)

1 Using antecedents joined by *and*

When you join two or more antecedents with *and* (Luis *and* Jennifer, for example), make sure you refer to them with a plural pronoun (such as *they*). The pronoun should be plural even if one or more of the antecedents are singular.

> **Luis and Jennifer** said that the tests <u>they</u> ran on the groundwater were conclusive.

> **The other students and I** admit that the tests <u>we</u> ran were not conclusive.

This rule has two exceptions.

- A compound antecedent can refer to a single person, thing, or idea. When it does, use a singular pronoun.

> **My colleague and co-author** is <u>someone</u> very skilled at analyzing soil samples.

- You can place *each* and *every* before a compound antecedent to single out the individual members of the compound. When you do, use a singular pronoun.

> **Each of the soil and water samples** <u>is</u> brought to the lab in **its** own sterile container.

> **Every soil and water sample** brought to the lab <u>undergoes</u> **its** own three tests.

2 Using antecedents joined by *or* or *nor*

When you join the parts of an antecedent with *or* or *nor* (or *either . . . or, neither . . . nor*), make sure the pronoun agrees with the part that is closer to it.

> **Neither** the project manager **nor** the engineers submitted <u>their</u> accident reports on time.

If one part of a subject is singular and the other part plural, consider putting the plural element second or rewriting to avoid an awkward or confusing sentence.

18c agr

CONFUSING   Either Jamal and Alan or **Richard** will include the sales projections in his report.

READER'S REACTION: **Does this mean that Jamal and Alan may be putting things in Richard's report? Or does it mean that there will be two reports, Richard's plus Jamal and Alan's, one of which will contain the projections?**

EDITED   Either Richard or **Jamal** and **Alan** will include the sales projections in their report.

REWRITTEN   Either Richard will include the sales projections in his report, or Jamal and Alan will include the projections in theirs.

3 Using indefinite pronouns (*everyone, any, something*) as antecedents

Many indefinite pronouns are singular. When you use them as antecedents, make sure the pronouns that refer to them are singular. (See p. 201 for a list of common indefinite pronouns.)

> **Somebody** on the team left her racket on the court.
> **Each** of the young men has his own copy of the bylaws.

Sometimes you may use an indefinite pronoun to mean *many* or *all*. When you do, it's safer to provide a plural antecedent.

INFORMAL   Everyone in the class handed in their project reports.

EDITED   **The students** in the class handed in their project reports.

To avoid sexist language (see 31a), many publishers and communities of writers accept a plural pronoun with a singular antecedent; when in doubt, however, use *both* a plural pronoun and a plural antecedent.

SEXIST   Everybody should include charts and slides in his sales talk.

INFORMAL/ SOMETIMES ACCEPTABLE   **Everybody** should include charts and slides in their sales **talks.**

SAFEST   **All presenters** should include charts and slides in their sales **talks.**

18c
agr

ESL Advice: Demonstrative Adjectives

Besides subjects and verbs, other elements in a sentence must agree. **Demonstrative adjectives** or **pronouns** (*this, that, these,* and *those*) must be either singular or plural, depending on the noun being modified. (See also 15a-2.)

INAPPROPRIATE   This agencies conduct outreach programs in local schools.

APPROPRIATE   **These agencies** conduct outreach programs in local schools.

INAPPROPRIATE   Those agency conducts outreach programs in local schools.

APPROPRIATE   **That agency** conducts outreach programs in local schools.

4 Using collective nouns as antecedents

A collective noun such as *team, group, clan, audience, army,* or *tribe* can act as a singular or plural antecedent, depending on whether it refers to the group as a whole or to the members acting separately.

SINGULAR   The **subcommittee** submitted its revised version of the report.

PLURAL   The **subcommittee** brought their different suggestions for a revised report to the meeting for discussion.

Exercise 4

A. Correct any errors in pronoun-antecedent agreement in the following sentences. You may need to change other parts of a sentence besides the pronoun or the antecedent. Each sentence can be corrected in more than one way.

EXAMPLE
People   like
A person, who likes, camping should no longer feel they are unusual.

1. In any circle of friends, several are likely to say that he or she enjoys camping.
2. Everyone who goes camping needs to pay attention to their equipment.
3. All hikers should select good shoes and socks to protect your feet.
4. A camper or a hiker needs to choose their clothing carefully, paying attention to comfort, durability, and protection as well as style.

18c
agr
ESL

5. Both regular campers and occasional campers should be willing to put his or her money into well-designed tents, sleeping bags, and cooking equipment.

6. Each store or chain of stores in the retail camping industry meets the needs of their customers in a different way.

7. A store catering to campers and the hiker usually offers him or her a wide choice of equipment at different prices.

8. Eddie Bauer or L. L. Bean provides mail-order service to his customers.

9. A camping supplies and athletic equipment store may provide a narrower range of choices to their customers because of the need to stock sporting goods as well as camping equipment.

10. Nonetheless, any of these businesses should be able to provide you and their other customers with good, safe camping equipment.

 B. Working with a group of students, compare your corrections for the sentences in Exercise 4A. Make note of any differences, and decide which version (if any) is preferable and why.

CHAPTER

19

Adjectives and Adverbs

If you use adjectives and adverbs improperly, your readers will be likely to notice the errors.

DRAFT   The new medication acts **quick.**

EDITED   The new medication acts **quickly.**

DRAFT   They **hadn't never** implemented the cost-saving program.

EDITED   They **had never** implemented the cost-saving program.

Admittedly, not all kinds of misuse are likely to irritate or confuse your readers. Some readers, for example, may not notice any difference in meaning between the following sentences.

The fumes from the mixture smelled **bad.**
The fumes from the mixture smelled **badly.**

Others, however, will recognize that the shift from *bad* to *badly* makes the second sentence say the fumes themselves have a sense of smell, but one that isn't working very well.

19a
modif

19a Recognizing what adjectives and adverbs do

Adjectives and adverbs modify other words. You use them to add to, qualify, focus, limit, or extend the meaning of words they modify.

red car	Adjective adds to meaning of the noun *car.*
cut **carefully**	Adverb qualifies the meaning of the verb *cut.*
very small crowd	Adjective *small* focuses the meaning of the noun *crowd;* adverb *very* limits the meaning of *small.*

Features of Adjectives and Adverbs

ADJECTIVES

Modify nouns and pronouns.

Answer the questions "How many?," "What kind?," "Which one (or ones)?," and "What size, color, or shape?"

Consist of words like *blue, complicated, good,* and *frightening* as well as words created by adding endings like *-able, -ical, -less, -ful,* and *-ous* to nouns or verbs (such as *controllable, sociological, nervous, seamless, careful*).

ADVERBS

Modify verbs, adjectives, and other adverbs.

Modify phrases (*almost* beyond the building), clauses (*soon* after I added the last ingredients), and sentences (*Remarkably,* the mechanism was not damaged).

Answer the questions "When?," "Where?," "How?," "How often?," "Which direction?," and "What degree?"

Consist mostly of words ending in *-ly,* like *quickly, carefully,* and *smoothly,* as well as some common adverbs that do not end in *-ly,* such as *fast, very, well, quite,* and *late.*

The table above summarizes the features of adjectives and adverbs. (See 15a-5 and 15a-6 for further discussion.)

Because the *-ly* ending does not appear on all adverbs, and because some familiar adjectives do end in *-ly* (such as *friendly, lonely*), you may sometimes have to determine whether a word is an adjective or adverb by looking at how it is used in sentences or by looking it up in a dictionary.

**19a
modif
ESL**

ESL Advice: Adjectives in a Series

When you use two or more adjectives in a series, you need to place them in the correct order before the main noun. The following chart explains the categories and the order of adjectives in English.

DETERMINER	QUALITY	PHYSICAL DESCRIPTION		NATIONALITY	MATERIAL	QUALIFYING NOUN	MAIN NOUN
that	expensive	smooth	black	German	fiberglass	racing	car
our	friendly	big	old	English		hunting	dog
four	little	round	white		plastic	Ping-Pong	balls
several	beautiful	young	red	Japanese		maple	trees

19b Avoiding confusion between adjectives and adverbs

Much of the time you will have little trouble deciding whether to use an adjective or an adverb. Nonetheless, some pairs of words, such as *real/really* or *good/well*, and some common sentence structures may need special attention as you edit.

1 Watch out for adjectives used mistakenly to modify verbs, adjectives, and adverbs

Remember that you need to use adverbs—not adjectives—to modify verbs, adjectives, or other adverbs.

INCORRECT   Write **careful** so that anyone reading the directions will be able to understand them easily.

EDITED   Write **carefully** so that anyone reading the directions will be able to understand them easily.

INCORRECT   Because of the heat, the rubber insulation underwent **remarkable** quick deterioration.

EDITED   Because of the heat, the rubber insulation underwent **remarkably** quick deterioration.

Did You Know?

Dictionary entries tell whether a word is an adjective, an adverb, or both. They also indicate the comparative and superlative forms of many adjectives and adverbs. In their introductory chapters, most dictionaries also briefly explain the forms that adjectives and adverbs take and discuss their roles in sentences.

**19b
modif**

2 Use adjectives following *is, seems,* and other linking verbs

You use a linking verb (such as *is, smells, appears,* or *becomes*—see 15a-3) to tie together a subject and a **complement** (see 15b-2). A complement can be a noun, a pronoun, or an adjective—but never an adverb.

SUBJECT	LINKING VERB	COMPLEMENT (ADJECTIVE)
The room	smelled	musty.
The procedure	proved	unreliable.

Verbs such as *look, feel, turn,* and *prove* can cause you problems because they can function both as linking verbs (indicating states of being) and as action verbs. When your sentence presents a state of being, use an adjective; when it presents an action, use an adverb.

ADJECTIVE
(STATE OF BEING)   The metal cover over the motor **turned hot.**

ADVERB
(ACTION)   The large wheel **turned quickly.**

ADJECTIVE   The movement grew **rapid.**
The motion became quick.

ADVERB   The movement grew **rapidly.**
The group got bigger, and its ideas spread quickly.

Writer's Alert

Pay special attention to *real/really, sure/surely, bad/badly,* and *good/well* as you edit. Some common uses of these words, especially *sure* for *surely,* may be acceptable in informal speech or writing but not in academic papers.

Real/Really; Sure/Surely
Real and *sure* are adjectives that often turn up in place of the adverbs *really* and *surely.*

- Use *really* to modify an adjective like *fast, accurate,* or *hot.*

  INCORRECT   The electronic timer is **real** accurate.

  EDITED   The electronic timer is **really** accurate.

- Use *surely* as an adverb to modify adjectives like *misleading, outdated,* or *courageous.*

  INCORRECT   This drawing of the mechanism is **sure** misleading.

  EDITED   This drawing of the mechanism is **surely** misleading.

Bad/Badly; Good/Well
The words in these pairs are often switched during informal speaking, sometimes without ill effect: I feel *bad* (or *badly*) about that. The project is going *good* (or *well*). Your readers, however, are likely to notice the error and be distracted by it.

- Use *bad* (adjective) with linking verbs.

INCORRECT	I feel **badly** that our group isn't working well together.
EDITED	I feel **bad** that our group isn't working well together.
	Someone who *feels badly* has a poor sense of touch.

- Use *badly* (adverb) with action verbs.

INCORRECT	The expensive new breathing apparatus works **bad.**
EDITED	The expensive new breathing apparatus works **badly.**

- Use *good* (adjective) with linking verbs.

INCORRECT	The oil and garlic dressing tastes **well.**
EDITED	The oil and garlic dressing tastes **good.**

- Use *well* (adverb) with action verbs unless it refers to health.

INCORRECT	The new pump works **good.**
EDITED	The new pump works **well.**
EDITED	After using the new medication pump for a week, the patient began feeling **well** again.

3 Use adjectives to complete direct objects

You can complete (or complement) the meaning of a direct object by following it with an adjective. (See 15b-2 on complements.)

The review panel considered the researcher **objective.**
Objective completes *researcher* by indicating the person's qualities.

You can place an adverb after the direct object, but it will modify the sentence's verb.

The review panel considered the researcher **objectively.**
Objectively describes their manner in evaluating the researcher.

An adjective that completes a direct object must appear just after or before the object; in contrast, an adverb that modifies the verb can usually appear at other places in a sentence.

COMPLETES OBJECT   The agency judged her artwork **competent.**
(ADJECTIVE)

19b
modif

MODIFIES VERB   The agency judged her artwork **competently.**
(ADVERB)

MODIFIES VERB   The agency **competently** judged her artwork.
(ADVERB)

Exercise 1

A. Rewrite the following sentences to eliminate any problems in adjective or adverb use.

EXAMPLE
I thought the band sounded ~~badly~~, though many of my friends enjoyed the music. *(bad,)*

1. Many scholars have begun studying some real surprising subjects such as rock music.
2. At first, they had trouble persuading many people to take their work serious.
3. Now they produce careful researched studies of musicians like the Beatles as well as biographies of influential figures like Sid Vicious and Johnny Rotten.
4. Remember, just because a piece of rock music sounds well does not mean that it is worth careful study.
5. At a time when the careers of many rock musicians are going bad, rock is doing quite good on campus.

B. Working in a group, decide which advice in sections 19a and 19b applies to the particular problem in adjective or adverb use illustrated by each of the following sentences. Make a note of each relevant section of the discussion, and rewrite the sentence to eliminate the problem.

EXAMPLE
Some dead rock musicians have ~~surprising~~ large and active fan clubs. *(surprisingly)*
Relevant section: 19a-1

1. Over the past year, the number of books devoted to rock groups or rock stars has grown remarkable.
2. The writer Greil Marcus has produced several high-regarded books that praise Elvis Presley as an artist and person.
3. The title of one of Marcus's books, *Dead Elvis: A Chronicle of a Cultural Obsession,* may suggest that he views Elvis "sightings" and memorabilia as humorously.
4. Some of the events he describes are undoubted weird.
5. Nonetheless, he feels surely that Elvis and his music really deserve respect.

19c Using comparatives and superlatives

You jcan use most adjectives and adverbs in three forms: positive, comparative, and superlative.

POSITIVE	COMPARATIVE	SUPERLATIVE
clean	cleaner	cleanest
shiny	shinier	shiniest
imaginatively	more imaginatively	most imaginatively
carefully	more carefully	most carefully

Use the **positive form** when you have no comparison in mind.

> This is a **quick** route.
> Rainha drove **quickly** through the circuit.

Use the **comparative form** when you are comparing two things.

> This is a **quicker** route.
> Rainha drove **more quickly** through the circuit.

Use the **superlative form** when you are comparing three or more things.

> This is the **quickest** route.
> Rainha drove **most quickly** through the circuit.

In conversation we sometimes ignore the system of positive, comparative, and superlative forms. Someone says "She is my oldest daughter," even though he has only two daughters, yet listeners grasp the intended meaning. In writing, you need to be more precise, especially if you are presenting facts and figures.

INACCURATE	The survey covered four age groups: 20–29, 30–44, 45–59, and 60+. The people in the older group smoked the least.
	READER'S REACTION: Is the sentence supposed to mean that the people in the older *groups* smoked the least or that the people in the *oldest* group smoked the least?
PRECISE	The survey covered four age groups: 20–29, 30–44, 45–59, and 60+. The people in the **oldest group** smoked the least.

**19c
modif**

Writer's Alert

Some adjectives and adverbs cannot logically take comparative or superlative form. These include *unique, impossible, pregnant, infinite, dead, gone, perfectly,* and *entirely.* If you give such words comparative or superlative form, careful readers will notice the lack of logic.

ILLOGICAL	The large painting on the far wall is **most unique.** It is the only self-portrait Gottlieb created.

READER'S REACTION: *Unique* means "one of a kind." How can a thing be *more* or *most* if it is the only one?

LOGICAL	The large painting on the far wall is **unique.** It is the only self-portrait Gottlieb created.

You can create the comparative and superlative forms of adjectives and adverbs in a number of different ways, as the following chart indicates.

Creating Comparatives and Superlatives

ADJECTIVES

ONE SYLLABLE Most add *-er* and *-est* (*pink, pinker, pinkest*).

TWO SYLLABLES Many add *-er* and *-est* (*happy, happier, happiest*). Some add either *-er* and *-est* or the words *more* and *most* (*foggy, foggier, foggiest; foggy, more foggy, most foggy*). Notice that adjectives, such as *happy* and *foggy*, change the final letter *y* to *i* when either the comparative *-er* or the superlative *-est* form is added to the word.

THREE (OR MORE) SYLLABLES Add *more* and *most* (*plentiful, more plentiful, most plentiful*).

ADVERBS

ONE SYLLABLE Most add *-er* and *-est* (*quick, quicker, quickest*).

TWO (OR MORE) SYLLABLES Most add *more* and *most* (*carefully, more carefully, most carefully*).

NEGATIVE COMPARISONS

ADJECTIVES AND ADVERBS Use *less* and *least* (*less competent, least competent; less precisely, least precisely*).

**19c
modif**

Writer's Alert

Your readers will not accept a double comparative (combining the *-er* form and *more*) or a double superlative (combining the *-est* form and *most*). Avoid using either.

INCORRECT	As the temperature dropped, the weather got **more foggier.**
EDITED	As the temperature dropped, the weather got **foggier.**
INCORRECT	Jorge is the **most agilest** athlete on the team.
EDITED	Jorge is the **most agile** athlete on the team.

Some familiar modifiers change in irregular ways to indicate comparative and superlative forms.

Irregular Comparatives and Superlatives

POSITIVE	COMPARATIVE	SUPERLATIVE
ADJECTIVES		
bad	worse	worst
good	better	best
ill (harsh, unlucky)	worse	worst
a little	less	least
many	more	most
much	more	most
some	more	most
well (healthy)	better	best
ADVERBS		
badly	worse	worst
ill (badly)	worse	worst
well (satisfactorily)	better	best

19d
modif

19d Avoiding double negatives

Negative words include *no, none, not, never, neither, hardly, scarcely, barely,* and words like *haven't* and *don't* (formed with *n't,* the abbreviation for *not*). In general, negative words do not become more forceful when more than one appears in a sentence. Instead of enhancing a statement, a **double negative** often undermines it. Readers may view the negatives as canceling each other out.

DOUBLE NEGATIVE	The state hasn't done nothing about the dangerous exit ramp on the interstate. READER'S REACTION: **If the state hasn't done nothing, maybe it** *has* **done** *something.*
EDITED	The state hasn't done anything about the dangerous exit ramp on the interstate.

19e Using noun modifiers

By using nouns to modify other nouns, you can save space. Many familiar and useful terms do this.

role model	child care
parent substitute	relief pitcher
pocket calendar	muscle pains
rain repellent	party platform

Too many nouns in a row, generally three or more, or too many clusters of long nouns can make reading difficult. (See also 9a-4.)

S T R A T E G Y

Avoid problems with noun modifiers by taking one of the following steps.

- Use the possessive forms of nouns.

AWKWARD	We need to refer to the **hospital noise reduction plan** as we design the new building.
EDITED	We need to refer to the **hospital's noise reduction plan** as we design the new building.

- Use a prepositional phrase rather than a noun.

AWKWARD	The company has developed an **employee health care financing policy.**
EDITED	The company has developed a **policy for financing the health care of employees.**

**19e
modif**

• Rewrite to break up a cluster of noun modifiers.

> **AWKWARD**   I have developed a **personal stress management program.**
>
> **EDITED**   I have developed my own way of managing stress.

Exercise 2

A. Revise the following sentences to eliminate any incorrect use of adjectives, adverbs, or noun modifiers.

EXAMPLE

I think the real difference between Necco Wafers and Skittles is that Necco Wafers last ~~longest~~. *longer*
                                            ^

1. Of the three candy bars, Snickers, Three Musketeers, and Baby Ruth, which is older?
2. Which of the two kinds of gummy bears is more sweeter?
3. Most candy companies have consumer preference research programs.
4. Trying to create a candy bar that pleases everyone's taste is a most impossible task.
5. Some people can't hardly bear the taste of sour-flavored candy.

B. Working in a group, create two different correct versions of each of the following sentences. Then decide as a group which version of each sentence you prefer and why.

1. Candy taste preference surveys are expensive.
2. They are not unlikely to be a waste of money.
3. One survey showed that consumers find a blend of hazelnuts and raspberries a most tastier combination.
4. The bar showed no profit production capability, however.
5. By adding marshmallows to the blend, the company eventually turned the bar into a most complete marketing success.

**19e
modif**

EDITING FOR SENTENCE PROBLEMS

A **sentence fragment** is part of a sentence treated as a complete sentence, with a capital letter at the beginning and a period at the end. A fragment may lack an important sentence element such as a subject or a verb, thus confusing readers by leaving out crucial information.

SUBJECT MISSING	Began pumping water out of the basement. **READER'S REACTION: Who was pumping, or what was doing the pumping?**
EDITED	**The fire truck** began pumping water out of the basement.
VERB MISSING	The insurance company responsible for the costs. **READER'S REACTION: What did the company do?**
EDITED	The insurance company **became** responsible for the costs.

Fragments may be phrases or clauses mistakenly asked to stand on their own as sentences. Such fragments make readers do the writer's job, forcing them mentally to reattach a word group to a nearby sentence.

FRAGMENT	They were able to get the pump started again. **By replacing the gas filter.** The second statement is a modifying phrase detached from the preceding sentence.
EDITED	They were able to get the pump started again **by replacing the gas filter.**

In the following passage, for example, a reader has to do extra work by either supplying a subject for the second statement or mentally combining it with the preceding sentence.

FRAGMENT   Recent immigrants from Asia and Latin America now fill many seats in elementary schools and high schools. **And have inspired many changes in curriculum and teaching methods.**

SUBJECT SUPPLIED   Recent immigrants from Asia and Latin America now fill many seats in elementary schools and high schools. **They** have inspired many changes in curriculum and teaching methods.

WORD GROUPS COMBINED   Recent immigrants from Asia and Latin America now fill many seats in elementary schools and high schools **and** have inspired many changes in curriculum and teaching methods.

Fragments that confuse readers or make them do extra, unnecessary work are serious errors. On occasion, an **intentional fragment** that causes little difficulty may effectively create emphasis or a change of pace, especially in imaginative or emphatic writing (see 20d). For the most part, however, academic, business, and professional readers will judge a piece of writing (and its writer) harshly when they encounter a fragment.

20a   Recognizing sentence fragments

Some sentence fragments are easy to identify, others less so. To edit effectively, however, you need to be able to identify word groups lacking a subject or a verb and to recognize clauses detached from sentences to which they belong.

1 Look for a subject and a verb

A **complete sentence** must contain both a subject and a complete verb, expressed or implied. If a word group punctuated as a sentence lacks either, it is a fragment (see 15b).

**20a
frag**

S T R A T E G Y   1

A good way to identify subjects and verbs is to ask *Who* (or *what*) *does?* or *Who* (or *what*) *is?*

- If a word group does not answer "Who?" or "What?" then it lacks a subject and is a sentence fragment.

FRAGMENT   Yet also needs to establish a family counseling program.
   READER'S REACTION: **This doesn't say *who* (or *what*) needs to establish the program.**

EDITED   Yet **Community Health Clinic** also needs to establish a family counseling program.

- If a word group does not answer "Does?" or "Is?" then it lacks a verb and is a sentence fragment.

FRAGMENT   The new policy to determine scholarship size on the basis of grades rather than on the basis of need.

               READER'S REACTION: This doesn't indicate anything about what the new policy *does* or *is*.

EDITED   The new policy **determines** scholarships on the basis of grades rather than on the basis of need.

In trying to identify the "Who" in a passage, remember that in commands, the subject *you* is understood and does not have to appear in the sentence.

IMPERATIVE   [**You**] Use the spectrometer to test for the unknown chem-
SENTENCE   ical ingredient.

Some familiar sentence patterns also use a clearly implied verb.

VERB IMPLIED   John went to Stanford, Regina [**went**] to UCLA.

S T R A T E G Y   2

Another way to identify a missing subject or verb is to create a question. See if you can turn a word group into a question that can be answered *yes* or *no*. If it can be, it is a sentence.

WORD GROUP   They bought a van to carry the new equipment.

QUESTION   Did they buy a van to carry the new equipment?

CONCLUSION   The word group is a sentence.

To decide whether a subject or a verb is missing, see if you need to add or alter an element to create a question.

Here are two examples of Strategy 2 at work.

WORD GROUP   Bought the building to use as a warehouse.

QUESTION   Did _____ buy the building to use as a warehouse?

CONCLUSION   The question does not have a subject, so the word group is a fragment lacking a subject.

EDITED   **Johnson Manufacturing** bought the building to use as a warehouse.

20a
frag

WORD GROUP	The company providing repairs for our computers.
QUESTION	Does the company **providing** repairs for our computers?
	Caution: Do not begin the question with *is/are* or *has/have*. In doing so you may unintentionally provide a verb for the word group you are testing.
CONCLUSION	The word *providing* cannot act as the verb in its present form. The word group is a fragment lacking a verb.
EDITED	The company **is** providing repairs for our computers.

Writer's Alert

In checking for fragments, be careful not to mistake a verbal for a verb. A **verbal** is part of a verb acting as a noun or modifier. Verbals include participles (*testing, tested*), infinitives (*to test*), and gerunds (*testing*). (See 15c-4.) A verbal alone can never act as the verb in a sentence. When combined with a helping verb (such as *is, has, can,* or *should*—see 15a-3), a verbal can be part of a complete verb (*was testing, should test*).

FRAGMENT	The laboratory **testing** the samples for traces of platinum.
COMPLETE SENTENCE	The laboratory **was testing** the samples for traces of platinum.

Did You Know?

In a survey conducted by the authors of this book, college instructors listed sentence fragments as the sentence-level error they considered the most serious. The people surveyed included teachers of chemistry, business, nursing, mathematics, literature, and psychology as well as composition. According to their answers, these instructors almost always notice sentence fragments and believe these errors confuse and irritate readers. You may be used to seeing sentence fragments in advertising and sometimes in magazine or newspaper articles. Nonetheless, sentence fragments can easily undermine whatever confidence academic and professional readers have in your authority and skill as a writer.

Chris M. Anson and Robert A. Schwegler, "A Survey of Attitudes Toward Error Among Instructors at Four Colleges," unpublished ms.

**20a
frag**

Exercise 1

Indicate which of the following word groups are sentence fragments and which are complete sentences. Correct sentence fragments by supplying any information necessary to make complete sentences.

EXAMPLE
_is_
Our job͜to find a new head for nursing services.

1. Several people applying for the job.
2. The job description in the newspaper asks for someone who is a good administrator and also an innovator.
3. Is able to convince fellow workers to develop their own innovative staffing plan and present it to the hospital administration.
4. Julie Kim, the prior head of nursing services responsible for so much turmoil during her time in the job and also so many important changes in the way nurses interact with patients and physicians.
5. A study suggesting that nursing administrators develop in-service programs to create improved morale among the professional staff and also better patient care.

2 Look for subordinating words

A word group containing both a subject and a complete verb may still be a sentence fragment if it is controlled by a subordinating word (such as _although, because, that,_ or _since_) that turns it into a modifier. Placed at the beginning of a clause, subordinators tell readers to regard the word group as part of a larger statement, as a subordinate (dependent) clause needing to be attached to a main clause that it qualifies or modifies.

**20a
frag**

MAIN CLAUSE
Potential homebuyers have learned about the low crime rate and the excellent school system.

MODIFYING CLAUSE
Because potential homebuyers have learned about the low crime rate and the excellent school system.
This clause cannot act as a complete sentence.

MODIFYING CLAUSE + MAIN CLAUSE
Because potential homebuyers have learned about the low crime rate and the excellent school system, demand for housing in the area has risen considerably in the past few years.

S T R A T E G Y

To identify subordinate clause fragments, look for a word group beginning with a subordinating conjunction such as *after, although, if, because,
unless,* or *since* (see 27b-2) or with a relative pronoun (*that, what, which,* or
who). Then check whether this word group is attached to a main clause. If
it is not, then it is a fragment.

This Strategy can help you identify subordinate clause fragments like
those that follow. Like many subordinate clause fragments, these come right
next to the main clause they modify.

FRAGMENT	Most residents love the friendly, unspoiled nature of the town. **Which has led to rapid population growth and a rise in property values.**
EDITED	Most residents love the friendly, unspoiled nature of the town, which has led to rapid population growth and a rise in property values.
FRAGMENT	Many experts think that the SAT and the ACT are some-what biased. **Although they also consider most criticism of the tests overblown.**
EDITED	Many experts think that the SAT and the ACT are some-what biased, although they also consider most criticism of the tests overblown.
EDITED	Many experts think that the SAT and the ACT are some-what biased yet also consider most criticism of the tests overblown.

Exercise 2

A. Indicate which of the following word groups are sentence fragments and which are complete sentences. Correct all the sentence
fragments by supplying any information necessary to make complete
sentences or attaching a fragment to an adjacent main clause.

EXAMPLE
Although many people think that afternoon sleepiness is caused by a
heavy lunch, Researchers say this is not true.

1. People such as interns and truck drivers often feel drowsy. Even
   though they are aware of a need to stay awake and alert.
2. Having an afternoon nap can greatly increase your alertness.
   Whether or not you got enough sleep the night before.

3. Almost accidentally, researchers started becoming aware of the importance of naps while they were mapping the cycles of drowsiness and alertness that we each go through during an entire day.
4. Almost everyone experiences sleepiness and a decline in mental alertness during the afternoon. Because our internal clocks tell us it is time to nap and get out of the sun's strongest rays.
5. Despite a widespread belief that siestas and naps are cultural customs. They actually have a biological base.

 B. Working with a group, look through one or more popular magazines, focusing on either the advertising or the articles. Identify ten sentence fragments and list them. Indicate which fragments lack a subject or a verb (or both), and indicate which fragments are modifying clauses that contain a subject and verb but are controlled by a subordinating word.

20b   Editing sentence fragments

You can correct sentence fragments in four different ways. As you edit, choose the Strategy that best suits the particular kind of fragment, your purpose for writing, the meaning you wish to emphasize, and the stylistic effect you wish to create.

S T R A T E G Y   1

Supply the missing sentence element.

FRAGMENT (LACKS VERB)

Several arguments favor allowing adopted children to contact their natural parents. **Among the most important the need to find out about any hereditary diseases.**

EDITED

Several arguments favor allowing adopted children to contact their natural parents. Among the most important **is** the need to find out about any hereditary diseases.

S T R A T E G Y   2

Attach the fragment to a nearby main clause. Rewrite the passage if necessary.

FRAGMENT (SUBORDINATE CLAUSE)

Modern trauma centers are equipped to give prompt care to heart attack victims. **Because rapid treatment can minimize damage to heart muscles.**

20b
frag

EDITED   Modern trauma centers are equipped to give prompt care
to heart attack victims because rapid treatment can minimize damage to heart muscles.

S T R A T E G Y   3

Drop a subordinating word so the subordinate clause can act as a
complete sentence (main clause).

FRAGMENT   **Although** several people argued strenuously against the
motion. It passed by a considerable majority nonetheless.

EDITED   Several people argued strenuously against the motion. It
passed by a considerable majority nonetheless.

S T R A T E G Y   4

Rewrite a passage to eliminate the fragment.

FRAGMENT   Some sports attract large numbers of participants in their
fifties, sixties, and even seventies. **For example, tennis and
bowling.**

REWRITTEN   Some sports, **such as tennis and bowling,** attract large
numbers of participants in their fifties, sixties, and even seventies.

Exercise 3

 A. Correct each of the fragments in the following passages in two
different ways.

EXAMPLE

Some innovative rock groups have been touring this year. Drawing
large crowds.

*Some innovative rock groups have been touring this year. They
have been drawing large crowds.*

*Some innovative rock groups have been touring this year,
drawing large crowds.*

20b
frag

1. Realizing that musical tastes are probably changing. Many record
    companies have decided to explore new and newly rediscovered
    kinds of music.
2. Some formerly popular musical artists no longer have recording
    contracts. Their sales of tapes and CDs having dropped drastically.

3. In recent campus concerts, jazz artists have attracted large and enthusiastic audiences. Because of their innovative melodies and sounds.

4. The rhythm section of one group consists of a single unusual
instrument. An electronic instrument making sounds like a drum
but looking like a guitar.

5. Undecided about whether to sign new groups to long-term contracts. Some companies agree to produce and sell a single CD with
an option for future recordings.

 B. Instead of doing Exercise 3A on your own, work with another
person and create *three* correct versions of each passage, rewriting
extensively if necessary. Note the ways each of you prefer to correct
fragments, especially any differences between your choices.

20c Editing troublesome constructions

Some familiar sentence structures are often mistakenly punctuated
as sentences, forming unacceptable sentence fragments.

1 Watch out for disconnected word groups

As you edit, watch for two kinds of word groups that are often incorrectly treated as complete sentences: (1) word groups beginning with phrases
like *for example,* and (2) split predicates (parts of a compound predicate).

***For Example* Fragments.** Word groups beginning with phrases like *for exam-
ple, such as,* or *for instance* are sometimes disconnected from sentences and
made to stand on their own, thus creating sentence fragments. You can identify such fragments by looking for one of these phrases at the beginning of a word
group and then checking whether the word group either is attached to a main
clause or contains all the elements needed to act as a complete sentence.

To correct *for example* fragments, decide whether the examples are
simply brief illustrations that ought to be attached to the statement they
illustrate or whether they deserve emphasis in sentences of their own.

FRAGMENT

We are trying to hire a new staff member who has skills that none of
us possess. **For example, knowledge of computer-aided design.**

EDITED (SEPARATE SENTENCE)

We are trying to hire a new staff member who has skills that none of
us possess. For example, **we need** someone with knowledge of computer-aided design.

FRAGMENT

Very few people are aware of the familiar species that are suffering from pollution or mismanagement. **Such as the striped bass and the snook.**

EDITED (ATTACHED TO MAIN CLAUSE)

Very few people are aware of the familiar species, **such as the striped bass and the snook,** that are suffering from pollution or mismanagement.

Split Predicate. A **compound predicate** contains two or more complete verbs (for example, "I *unfastened* the seat and *removed* it"), and writers sometimes split off the second (or last) element as a separate sentence. Perhaps they create fragments of this kind because they unconsciously assume that the subject in the first part of the predicate is also somehow present in the second part. To recognize a split predicate fragment, look for a word group whose verb comes near the beginning (generally following a conjunction like *and* or *but*) and whose subject is nearby—but in another sentence.

FRAGMENT

Beethoven's work as a composer began in a style similar to that of Mozart. **But soon took on its own unique style.**

To correct fragments like this, either supply the missing subject or reattach the elements of the compound predicate.

CORRECTED (SUBJECT ADDED)

Beethoven's work as a composer began in a style similar to that of Mozart. But **his work** soon took on its own unique style.

CORRECTED (REATTACHED)

Beethoven's work as a composer began in a style similar to that of Mozart **but** soon took on its own unique style.

2 Pay attention to verbal phrases

Because verbals are similar in form to verbs (for example, *swimming*—verbal; *is swimming*—verb), writers may easily mistake a verbal plus its objects and modifiers (a verbal phrase) for a complete sentence. To identify verbal phrase fragments as you edit, you need to be aware of the difference between verbs and verbals. (Sections 15a-4 and 15c-4 offer helpful advice.)

To correct a fragment consisting of a verbal phrase, attach the fragment to a nearby main clause, or turn the verbal into a verb and rewrite the passage.

20c frag

FRAGMENT (PARTICIPIAL PHRASE)

Frustrated by the meager offerings in journalism. She decided to transfer to another university.

EDITED (ATTACHED TO MAIN CLAUSE)

Frustrated by the meager offerings in journalism, she decided to transfer to another university.

FRAGMENT (INFINITIVE PHRASE)

Divorcing parents should seek advice from a counselor. **To help lessen emotional problems for their children.**

EDITED (ATTACHED TO MAIN CLAUSE)

Divorcing parents should seek advice from a counselor to help lessen emotional problems for their children.

FRAGMENT (GERUND PHRASE)

Introducing competing varieties of crabs into the same tank. He did this in order to study aggression.

EDITED (REWRITTEN)

He **introduced** competing varieties of crabs into the tank in order to study aggression.

Exercise 4

A. Correct each of the fragments in the following passages in two different ways.

EXAMPLE

Living and working in another country creates many challenges for families), For example, arranging for children's schooling.

Living and working in another country creates many challenges for families. Arranging for children's schooling is one such challenge.

1. The armed forces run elementary and secondary schools around the world. To provide education for dependents.
2. Japanese executives working in North America worry about educating their children in the Japanese language. And worry about whether they will fit into Japanese culture when they are adults.
3. Americans and Canadians working outside of North America often look for schools conducted in English. To make sure their children will be prepared to attend college when the families return home.
4. The modern world makes many demands on parents. Who must spend considerable time and energy educating their children.
5. Whoever grows up with knowledge of two different cultures. I think that person will have some distinct advantages.

B. Working with a group, identify the fragments in the following word groups. Then combine the word groups to form a paragraph made up of complete sentences. Feel free to alter the wording or to add information necessary to make the paragraph interesting and clear.

1. One store chain asks people to provide an address when cashing a check. And uses the information to create a mailing list for its advertising flyers.

2. As a result, people who buy two pairs of pants and a few blouses are going to be receiving something in the mail each week for the next few months. For instance, a colorful flyer about home furnishings or automobile accessories.

3. Some people resent this marketing strategy. And complain to the post office or the company itself.

4. Lots of people consider advertising brochures fun to read. And a way to make shopping easier.

5. I think they are just one of many small irritations we encounter every day. Such as free samples of useless products and computerized telephone calls.

20d Using partial sentences

In magazine articles, in reports, in advertising, and even in essays generally regarded as models of good writing, you are likely to encounter sentence fragments used properly and effectively. Fragments of this kind can be called **partial sentences.** Here is a concise definition of a partial sentence offered by a student.

> A partial sentence is an effective sentence fragment used for emphasis, often to call attention to a particular idea. It isn't a whole sentence and doesn't need to be.

Used sparingly, partial sentences can call attention to details, provide special emphasis for ideas, or heighten contrasts. They can help you recreate a scene piece by piece, just as a painter creates a scene with multiple brushstrokes and images. They can create emphasis or a change of pace, as in the following passage.

> Our house stood apart. A gaudy yellow in a row of white bungalows. We were the people with the noisy dog.
> — RICHARD RODRIGUEZ, "Aria"
> **By highlighting the house's color in a fragment, Rodriguez calls special attention to it, just as the yellow paint made the house stand out in the neighborhood.**

**20d
frag**

Some other appropriate uses of partial sentences include questions and answers ("Where should I put the printout?" "On my desk."); exclamations ("Wish I had time to run this experiment again!"); and transitional phrases ("Next, the results."). With the exception of transitional phrases, these uses of fragments are most common in speech and informal writing.

Even when a writing situation is one in which readers are likely to consider a sentence fragment acceptable, you need to pay attention to several important guidelines.

1. Have a clear purpose in mind, such as building a description, highlighting parallel ideas, or providing strong emphasis and contrast.
2. Make sure that your readers will recognize the purpose and not mistake the fragment for an unintentionally detached modifier or incomplete phrase.
3. Take care that your readers will be able to supply the missing elements or will be able to perceive connections between word groups without confusion.

Exercise 5

 If you have not already completed Exercise 2B, do so now, making a copy of each of the fragments you locate. Working with a group, share your different sets of fragments. Identify those fragments you consider effective partial sentences. Explain how each effective fragment fits the criteria outlined in 20d, and tell what purpose each one fulfills.

21

Comma Splices and Fused Sentences

You can easily confuse and annoy readers if you inappropriately join two or more sentences using either a comma only (comma splice) or no punctuation at all (fused sentence). Because a comma splice does not clearly specify the relationship between main clauses, readers may have to look over a sentence several times to be sure of its meaning.

COMMA SPLICE CBS was founded in 1928 by William S. Paley, his uncle and his father sold him a struggling radio network they had bought to advertise their La Palina cigars.

READER'S REACTION: At first I thought CBS had three founders: Paley, his uncle, and his father. Then I realized that the sentence probably means Paley founded CBS after buying the radio network from his relatives.

EDITED CBS was founded in 1928 by William S. Paley ; his uncle and his father sold him a struggling radio network they had bought to advertise their La Palina cigars.

Even after a close examination, readers may find it difficult to understand a fused sentence, two sentences joined with no punctuation at all.

FUSED SENTENCE The city had only one swimming pool without an admission fee the pool was poorly maintained.

READER'S REACTION: I can't decide if the *single* swimming pool in the town is poorly maintained or if the only swimming pool that does not charge a fee is in bad shape.

EDITED The city had only one swimming pool, **but** without an admission fee, the pool was poorly maintained.

Always avoid fused sentences in your writing. They are especially misleading because they do not provide readers with an indication of the boundary between the main clauses in the sentence.

Use the strategies outlined in this chapter to recognize comma splices and fused sentences and to edit them by linking main clauses appropriately.

21a Recognizing comma splices and fused sentences

A **comma splice** is the linking of two sentences (independent or main clauses—see 15c) by a comma alone.

COMMA SPLICE   Eight inches of rain fell in twenty-four hours, all the creeks swelled rapidly.

READER'S REACTION: I had to read this sentence twice because at first glance I couldn't tell where one part ended and the next began.

EDITED   Eight inches of rain fell in twenty-four hours **,** **and** all the creeks swelled rapidly.

EDITED   Eight inches of rain fell in twenty-four hours **;** all the creeks swelled rapidly.

In a **fused sentence** (or **run-on sentence**), neither a punctuation mark nor a connecting word shows where one main (independent) clause ends and the next begins.

FUSED SENTENCE   That night the river overflowed its banks and spread over the lowlands thousands of people were left homeless by the time the waters receded.

READER'S REACTION: When I first read that the river "spread over the lowlands thousands of people," I immediately imagined a mass of people being pushed over the land.

EDITED   That night the river overflowed its banks and spread over the lowlands **.** **Thousands** of people were left homeless by the time the waters receded.

EDITED   That night the river overflowed its banks and spread over the lowlands **;** **as a result,** thousands of people were left homeless by the time the waters receded.

To identify comma splices and fused sentences, be alert for situations in which they often occur.

1 Identify comma splices

As you edit, look for sentences containing word groups that could stand on their own as sentences. Make sure that the word groups are joined by more than a comma alone, perhaps by a comma with a coordinating conjunction or by a semicolon.

COMMA SPLICE   In a typical Navajo family, the husband serves as a trustee, the mother and her children are the real owners of the family's property.

EDITED   In a typical Navajo family, the husband serves as a trustee **,** **but** the mother and her children are the real owners of the family's property.

EDITED   In a typical Navajo family, the husband serves as a trustee **;** the mother and her children are the real owners of the family's property.

S T R A T E G Y

Pay attention to writing likely to contain comma splices. When you are drafting quickly, adding idea to idea and clause to clause, you may sometimes use commas to string word groups together, creating comma splices. Writing of this sort often occurs when you are working under pressure or rushing to record ideas and details. As you edit, pay special attention to sentence boundaries.

---

2 Identify fused sentences

Look carefully at long sentences. Fused sentences can be any length, but as you edit, pay special attention to long sentences without internal punctuation. Check to see if they contain freestanding (main) clauses joined without punctuation.

21a
cs/fs

S T R A T E G Y

As you edit, ask, "How many statements are there in this sentence?" A fused sentence is not a single unit but two (or more) units whose relationship is not clearly signaled to readers. If a sentence appears to contain more than one statement, check for appropriate punctuation and connecting words. For example, the following sentence makes two statements: one about the troubles encountered by the scientists and one about the nature of the skeleton. These two statements come in main clauses whose relationship is not appropriately signaled to readers.

FUSED SENTENCE   The scientists had trouble identifying the fossil skeleton it resembled both that of a bird and that of a lizard.

EDITED   The scientists had trouble identifying the fossil skeleton **because** it resembled both that of a bird and that of a lizard.

Did You Know?

Preferences in punctuation and in sentence style can change over time. Today, when you join two main clauses with a coordinating conjunction (*and, but, or, for, nor, yet,* or *so*), you must also punctuate with a comma. Over a hundred years ago, however, in *A Common-School Grammar of the English Language*, Simon Kerl recommended joining short main clauses with a coordinating conjunction but adding a semicolon for a longer clause. In *A New English Grammar for Schools* (1900), Thomas W. Harvey repeated this advice: "A clause, introduced by *for, but, and,* or an equivalent connective, is often set off by a semicolon" (294). Harvey also offered an example of a correctly punctuated sentence that highlights, by contrast, our modern taste for short, direct sentences: "The person he chanced to see, was, to appearance, an old, sordid, blind man; but upon his following him from place to place, he at last found, by his own confession, that he was Plutus, the god of riches, and that he was just come out of the house of a miser" (244).

Thomas W. Harvey, *A New English Grammar for Schools* (New York: American Book, 1900), and Simon Kerl, *A Common-School Grammar of the English Language* (New York: Ivison, 1871).

21a
cs/fs

3 Watch for sentence patterns that may lead to comma splices and fused sentences

You join sentences (main clauses) because they are related, and in joining them you emphasize the relationship. A number of relationships, however, seem to lead to more than their fair share of comma splices.

S T R A T E G Y

As you edit, look for sentences (main clauses) related in the following ways. Make sure they are not linked by a comma alone, and make sure they are joined with either the correct punctuation or a connecting word.

Sentences with the same subject
One sentence illustrated by another
Balanced sentences with contrasting ideas
Sentences with related ideas

If you have particular trouble with comma splices or fused sentences
in your writing, use this list as an editing checklist. Add to it any sentence
patterns or relationships that are problems for you. (See 21b for ways to
correct comma splices and fused sentences.)

• Sentences (main clauses) with the same subject

COMMA SPLICE The ice cream cake had begun to melt, it was dripping onto Grandmother's lace tablecloth.

EDITED The ice cream cake had begun to melt **, and** it was
dripping onto Grandmother's lace tablecloth.

FUSED SENTENCE The small commuter plane held only twelve people
it bumped and swayed throughout the flight.

EDITED The small commuter plane held only twelve people **,
and** it bumped and swayed throughout the flight.

• One sentence (main clause) illustrated by another

COMMA SPLICE Children with Down syndrome feel the same emotions as the rest of us, they get sad, puzzled, and silly.

EDITED Children with Down syndrome feel the same emotions as the rest of us **;** they get sad, puzzled, and silly.

FUSED SENTENCE Contemporary American literature no longer means
Hemingway and Faulkner it means Louise Erdrich,
Raymond Carver, and Adrienne Rich.

EDITED Contemporary American literature no longer means
Hemingway and Faulkner **;** it means Louise Erdrich,
Raymond Carver, and Adrienne Rich.

• Balanced sentences (main clauses) with contrasting ideas

COMMA SPLICE The students got good scores on the reading test, none
did well on the advanced math test.

EDITED The students got good scores on the reading test **;
however ,** none did well on the advanced math test.

**21a
cs/fs**

FUSED SENTENCE   The engineering and social work programs get the most public attention the medical technology and marketing programs get the largest enrollments.

EDITED   The engineering and social work programs get the most public attention **,** **but** the medical technology and marketing programs get the largest enrollments.

- Sentences (main clauses) with related ideas

COMMA SPLICE   She had already founded a successful company, she saw no reason to get an advanced degree.

EDITED   She had already founded a successful company **;** **therefore,** she saw no reason to get an advanced degree.

FUSED SENTENCE   Health costs are rising rapidly solutions to the problem are not clear.

EDITED   Health costs are rising rapidly **;** **moreover,** solutions to the problem are not clear.

Writer's Alert

Writers developing the useful habit of joining clauses with conjunctive adverbs (such as *however, nonetheless, therefore, consequently, moreover,* and *thus*) often forget that the technique also requires a semicolon between the clauses (see also 33a).

COMMA SPLICE   The health risks of video display terminals have not been proved, nonetheless, computer users should not sit too close to their screens.

EDITED   The health risks of video display terminals have not been proved **;** nonetheless, computer users should not sit too close to their screens.

21a
cs/fs

Exercise 1

 A. First, use the strategies discussed in 21a to identify the comma splices in the following passage.

The subarctic region provides little variety in food, therefore, Eskimo diet includes large quantities of meat such as seal and caribou. The cold weather and the available materials determine dressing habits, a loose shirt with a hood, trousers, stockings, and mittens (often made of caribou skin and fur) are a common outfit for men, women, and children alike. Social affairs are important in Eskimo communities, favorite gatherings include carnivals, Christmas parties, and feasts of game brought in by hunters. Children in Eskimo communities begin school at the age of five or six, most quit by the time they are twelve in order to go to work. Boys usually go hunting with their fathers, girls learn to sew and cook.

Next, draw a double vertical line between each of the main clauses making up the following fused sentences.

EXAMPLE
Casinos used to operate legally in only a few states‖they are now springing up all over the country as states make casino gambling legitimate.

1. The gaming industry is one of the fastest-growing industries in some areas it is a major employer.
2. Legalized gambling takes many forms bingo, lotteries, casinos, and video games are run under government supervision in many states.
3. State lotteries are popular they may also encourage people to gamble unwisely.
4. The economic and law enforcement objections to legalized gambling get the most public attention the moral and psychological objections may deserve the most attention.
5. Legalized gambling now goes beyond people in casinos betting on roulette or sports events it includes people playing bingo at a charity event or playing video poker in a family restaurant.

 B. Working in a group, decide which, if any, of the sentences in the first section of Exercise 1A follow sentence patterns likely to lead to comma splices or fused sentences, and identify the patterns.

**21b
cs/fs**

21b Editing comma splices and fused sentences

You can correct comma splices and fused sentences in many ways. Each Strategy that follows offers a different means for creating emphasis and highlighting relationships. Often, you will bring your ideas in a draft into sharper perspective through careful editing of these errors.

ORIGINAL   Ultimate Frisbee combines elements of football, basketball, baseball, and soccer it also has a few quirks that make it unique. The sport calls for a total of fourteen people (or twelve people and two dogs) divided into two teams (with one dog each), they throw a disk (called a Frisbee) up and down a football field. The object is to catch the disk in the other team's end zone and thereby score.

EDITED Ultimate Frisbee combines elements of football, basketball, baseball, and soccer**;** it also has a few quirks that make it unique. The sport calls for a total of fourteen people (or twelve people and two dogs) divided into two teams (with one dog each)**. They** throw a disk (called a Frisbee) up and down a football field. The object is to catch the disk in the other team's end zone and thereby score.

Strategies for Revising Comma Splices and Fused Sentences

1. Create two separate sentences.
2. Join main clauses with a comma plus a coordinating conjunction (*and, but, or, for, nor, so,* or *yet*).
3. Join main clauses with a semicolon.
4. Join main clauses with a semicolon plus a conjunctive adverb or transitional expression (*however, moreover, for example, in contrast,* and similar words or phrases).
5. Subordinate one of the clauses.
6. Join main clauses with a colon.

S T R A T E G Y   1

Create two separate sentences. When the ideas in two main clauses are loosely related, you can generally express them best in separate sentences.

21b
cs/fs

COMMA SPLICE Costa Rica's political life has been relatively free of damaging conflict, the same cannot be said of its neighbors. El Salvador and Nicaragua, in particular, have long histories of civil unrest.

EDITED Costa Rica's political life has been relatively free of damaging conflict**. The** same cannot be said of its neighbors. El Salvador and Nicaragua, in particular, have long histories of civil unrest.

FUSED SENTENCE Football does not cause the most injuries among student athletes gymnastics is the most dangerous sport.

EDITED   Football does not cause the most injuries among student athletes● **Gymnastics** is the most dangerous sport.

STRATEGY 2

Join main clauses with a comma plus a coordinating conjunction (*and, but, or, for, nor, so,* or *yet*). When main clauses convey ideas or information of approximately equal importance, consider linking the clauses with a comma plus a coordinating conjunction that indicates their relationship.

COMMA SPLICE   The more experienced teams use complicated strategies for offense and defense, the inexperienced teams concentrate on the basics.

EDITED   The more experienced teams use complicated strategies for offense and defense❟ **but** the inexperienced teams concentrate on the basics.

FUSED SENTENCE   Schizophrenia is a mental illness its causes may be physical.

EDITED   Schizophrenia is a mental illness❟ **yet** its causes may be physical.

Writer's Alert
Three or more closely related clauses can be punctuated as a series in order to emphasize their relationship. Be sure to include the coordinating conjunction before the last item.

We collected the specimens, we cleaned them with a mild detergent❟ **and** we measured them.

21b
cs/fs

STRATEGY 3

Join main clauses with a semicolon. You can use a semicolon to emphasize the similar importance of two main clauses.

COMMA SPLICE   During flight an airplane tends to drift up or down, left or right because of air turbulence. An autopilot is a device that detects and corrects drift, the system senses changes in the aircraft's motion and reacts accordingly.

EDITED   During flight an airplane tends to drift up or down, left or right because of air turbulence. An autopilot is a device that detects and corrects drift ; the system senses changes in the aircraft's motion and reacts accordingly.

FUSED SENTENCE   Most colleges offer alternatives to spending four years on the same campus study abroad, exchange programs with other schools, and cooperative programs are common.

EDITED   Most colleges offer alternatives to spending four years on the same campus ; study abroad, exchange programs with other schools, and cooperative programs are common.

S T R A T E G Y   4

Join main clauses with a semicolon plus a conjunctive adverb *or* with a semicolon plus a transitional expression. *However, nonetheless, therefore, consequently, moreover, thus,* and other conjunctive adverbs specify relationships between clauses. You can use transitional expressions such as *for example, in contrast,* and *in addition* for similar purposes.

COMMA SPLICE   To draw the human body, you must understand it, art schools sometimes ask students to dissect cadavers.

EDITED   To draw the human body, you must understand it ; **therefore ,** art schools sometimes ask students to dissect cadavers.

FUSED SENTENCE   Commercially raised animals such as chickens or beef cattle can reach marketable size within a matter of months or a year the American lobster must grow for an average of six to eight years before it reaches the proper size.

EDITED   Commercially raised animals such as chickens or beef cattle can reach marketable size within a matter of months or a year ; **in contrast ,** the American lobster must grow for an average of six to eight years before it reaches the proper size.

**21b
cs/fs**

S T R A T E G Y   5

Subordinate one of the clauses. Subordinators such as *although, while, when, because, since,* and *unless* and relative pronouns such as *who, which,* or *that* enable you to specify a wide range of relationships between clauses (see 27b).

COMMA SPLICE   Automobiles are becoming increasingly complex, experienced mechanics have to spend up to several weeks a year in training programs.

EDITED — **Because** automobiles are becoming increasingly complex, experienced mechanics have to spend up to several weeks a year in training programs.

FUSED SENTENCE — Margaret Atwood is best known for her novels her essays and poems are also worth reading.

EDITED — **Although** Margaret Atwood is best known for her novels, her essays and poems are also worth reading.

Writer's Alert

Conjunctive adverbs (such as *however, nonetheless,* and *thus*) and transitional expression (like *for example* and *on the other hand*) can appear not only at the beginning of a second main clause but also within it. Wherever the adverb or expression appears, it must be set off by a comma or commas, and the clauses themselves must be joined by a semicolon.

AT BEGINNING OF CLAUSE — The Great Lakes once supported a thriving fishing industry **;** **however** **,** in recent years pollution has reduced the catch greatly.

IN MIDDLE OF CLAUSE — The Great Lakes once supported a thriving fishing industry **;** in recent years **,** **however** **,** pollution has reduced the catch greatly.

AT END OF CLAUSE — The Great Lakes once supported a thriving fishing industry **;** in recent years pollution has reduced the catch greatly **,** **however** **.**

21b
cs/fs

STRATEGY 6

Join main clauses with a colon. When a clause summarizes, illustrates, or restates a preceding clause, you can join the two with a colon (see 33b).

COMMA SPLICE — The water damage under the loose roof shingles brought one conclusion to my mind, I should have hired a professional.

EDITED — The water damage under the loose roof shingles brought one conclusion to my mind **:** I should have hired a professional.

FUSED SENTENCE   Foreign study calls for extensive language preparation vaccinations and a passport are not enough.

EDITED   Foreign study calls for extensive language preparation **:** vaccinations and a passport are not enough.

Exercise 2

A. Identify and edit in *two* ways the following comma splices and fused sentences. Use the methods of revision indicated in brackets after each sentence.

EXAMPLE

Children often fight among themselves, these conflicts pose many challenges for parents. [comma plus coordinating conjunction; semicolon]

Children often fight among themselves, and these conflicts pose many challenges for parents.

Children often fight among themselves; these conflicts pose many challenges for parents.

1. Some parents refuse to become involved in their children's squabbles, they fear the children will resent the interference. [subordination; semicolon]
2. Siblings have special reasons to fight competing for space and playthings or for attention from a parent can turn playmates into rivals. [colon; semicolon plus transitional phrase]
3. Sibling fights offer an opportunity for children to become sensitive to the feelings of others, the arguments pose dangers as well. [comma plus coordinating conjunction; semicolon plus conjunctive adverb]
4. Bickering is common and normal excessive fighting can be a sign of more serious trouble. [semicolon plus conjunctive adverb; separate sentences]
5. By adolescence, most children have worked out compatible relationships with their siblings, they may still occasionally argue. [subordination; comma plus coordinating conjunction]

21b
cs/fs

B. Working with a group, edit each of the following sentences in two ways, using Strategies discussed in 21b. You may need to make changes in wording or punctuation.

1. One group claims that cattle raising is hard on the environment another group argues that raising wheat and other cereal grains causes water pollution and destroys topsoil.

2. In Central Florida, cattle waste has polluted Lake Okeechobee runoff from fertilizer has greatly increased the growth of algae in the lake.
3. The waters off Long Island's south shore are also polluted the main culprit is lawn fertilizer.
4. In my state, pesticides from potato farming have polluted the groundwater pig and chicken farming have caused problems.
5. Our large population makes a massive farming industry necessary we are going to have to deal with the problems caused by large-scale farming and livestock raising.

22

Pronoun Reference

You can often make a sentence less repetitive and easier to understand by having pronouns take the place of nouns (or even other pronouns). For the substitution to work effectively, your readers must recognize the word to which a pronoun refers, known as its **antecedent** (or **headword**). In the passage below, for example, *they* and *their* clearly refer to *kangaroos*.

CLEAR REFERENCE   **Kangaroos** normally walk on four feet unless **they** wish to move quickly, at which time **they** make large leaps using only **their** hind legs.

When **pronoun reference**—the connection between a pronoun and its antecedent—is not clear, however, readers may be confused.

AMBIGUOUS REFERENCE   Much of my supposedly glamorous life with the circus consisted of leading the elephants from their cages and hosing **them** down.
      READER'S REACTION: What got hosed down? The elephants? The cages? Both?

In contrast, by creating clear pronoun reference you help tie ideas and sentences together, clarifying their relationships and guiding your readers.

EDITED   Much of my supposedly glamorous life with the circus consisted of hosing the **elephants** down after leading **them** from **their** cages.

22a Making pronoun reference clear

Make sure each pronoun in your writing refers *clearly* to a *single* antecedent. The antecedent can be one word.

Freud claimed that slips of the tongue reveal subconscious thoughts and desires. **He** offered no real evidence to support the claim, however.

Or it can be a **compound antecedent,** a group of words acting as a unit.

Calvin Klein, Liz Claiborne, and **Donna Karan** started out as clothing designers. **They** now head major corporations bearing their names.

Watch out for pronouns that can easily refer to more than one possible antecedent (ambiguous reference) or that are widely separated from their antecedents (remote reference). Both of these can confuse your readers.

1 Watch for pronouns with several possible antecedents

Look for sentences containing two or more words to which a pronoun might possibly refer. If readers cannot easily identify the appropriate antecedent, you need to correct the **ambiguous reference.**

AMBIGUOUS REFERENCE
> Detaching the measuring probe from the glass cylinder is a delicate job because **it** breaks easily.
>
> READER'S REACTION: **Which is especially fragile, the probe or the cylinder?**

You can correct this problem in two ways: (1) replace the troublesome pronoun with a noun, or (2) reword the sentence.

REPLACED WITH A NOUN
> Detaching the measuring probe from the glass cylinder is a delicate job because **the probe** breaks easily.

REWORDED
> Because the measuring probe breaks easily, detaching it from the glass cylinder is a delicate job.

22a
pr ref

In addition, watch for pronouns that can refer to each of two or more subjects in earlier sentences.

AMBIGUOUS REFERENCE
> Robespierre and Danton disagreed over the path the French Revolution should take. **He** was convinced that the Revolution was endangered by its internal enemies; **his opponent** believed the Revolution had been won.

EDITED
> Robespierre and Danton disagreed over the path the French Revolution should take. **Robespierre** was convinced that the Revolution was endangered by its internal enemies; **Danton** believed the Revolution had been won.

You can use more than one pronoun in a sentence if readers can readily identify the antecedent for each.

CLEAR REFERENCE   The Reign of Terror began when **Robespierre** led the **Jacobins** as **they** guillotined over two thousand supposed opponents of the revolution and ended with **his** being led to the guillotine **himself.**

Writer's Tip

You may sometimes create confusion with **indirect quotations** using *said* or *told* to report in a general way what someone has said.

UNCLEAR
REFERENCE
When the project was finally completed, Jennifer's supervisor said **she** needed a few days off because **she** had been working so hard.
READER'S REACTION: **Who needs the time off, Jennifer or her supervisor?**

To correct this problem, report the person's words exactly (**direct quotation**).

REWRITTEN
WITH DIRECT
QUOTATION
When the project was finally completed, Jennifer's supervisor said, "**You** need a few days off because **you** have been working so hard."

Or rewrite the indirect quotation, using one or more nouns rather than pronouns.

REWRITTEN
WITH NOUN
When the project was finally completed, her supervisor said that **Jennifer** needed a few days off because **she** had been working so hard.

22a
pr ref

---

2 Pay attention to pronouns widely separated from their antecedents

When you place a pronoun at a distance from its antecedent (**remote reference**), your readers may have a hard time recognizing the connection between the two. This problem can occur even though no other possible referent comes between them. In editing, therefore, you need to look for pronouns preceded by detailed information that draws the reader's attention away from the antecedent.

REMOTE REFERENCE   James Van Allen designed an instrument that the first American space satellite used to detect what are now known to be two doughnut-shaped rings of high-energy particles extending from between several hundred to fifty thousand kilometers above the earth. The belts were eventually named for **him.**

To correct the problem, either bring the pronoun closer to its antecedent, or drop the pronoun and repeat the noun or pronoun to which it refers.

EDITED   James Van Allen designed an instrument that the first American space satellite used to detect what are now known to be two doughnut-shaped rings of high-energy particles extending from between several hundred to fifty thousand kilometers above the earth. They were eventually named **the Van Allen belts after the man instrumental in their discovery.**

   Keeping pronouns and antecedents close together is especially important for the relative pronouns *who, which,* and *that.* Avoid confusion by placing the relative pronoun right after its antecedent.

CONFUSING   As I lay on the carpet in my old bedroom, I noticed two stale pieces of the bubble gum under **the dresser that I loved to chew as a boy.**

EDITED   As I lay on the carpet in my old bedroom, I noticed under the dresser two stale pieces of **the bubble gum that I loved to chew as a boy.**

Exercise 1

 A. Rewrite each of the following sentences to create clear pronoun reference.

**22a
pr ref**

EXAMPLE
Someone needs to pick up the weekend shipment ~~at the airport~~ that
                                                                      at the airport
may arrive ∧ late Saturday night.

1. Both Carlo and Andy agree that he will be responsible for getting the cartons of replacement parts from the air terminal.
2. The accountant has told his client that he will be answerable for any problems with billing.
3. Airfreight offers weekend shipment and is cheaper, which means that work doesn't have to stop on Monday morning while workers wait for delivery of the replacement parts.

4. The van used to pick up shipments is the old one the company's owner purchased right after her divorce which is covered with rust spots.
5. The sales projections used to order supplies are often inaccurate because the sales manager calculates them using a formula on a spreadsheet that is overly optimistic.

 B. Working with a group of fellow students, compare the choices each of you made in editing the sentences in Exercise 1A.

3 Create clear reference chains

You can connect sentences by creating a chain of pronouns whose antecedent is stated in the opening sentence. Such a **reference chain** guides your readers through the passage and reminds them of the topic you are addressing. In this way, some of the pronouns can be relatively remote from their antecedent, even three or four sentences away, for example, but the reference will still be clear.

S T R A T E G Y

To create effective reference chains, take the following steps.

- State the antecedent clearly in the opening sentence.
- Make sure no other possible antecedents interrupt the links in the chain.
- Make sure you do not interrupt the chain and then try to pick it up again after several sentences.
- Call attention to the links by giving the pronouns prominent positions (usually at the beginning of sentences); vary their positions only slightly.

22a
pr ref

UNCLEAR

Sand paintings were a remarkable form of Pueblo art from the Southwest and Southern California. An artist would sprinkle dried sand of different colors, ground flower petals, corn pollen, and similar materials onto the floor to create **them**. The sun, moon, and stars as well as animals and objects linked to the spirits were represented in the figures **they** contained. **Their** purpose was to encourage the spirits to send good fortune to humans.

Because the pronouns *them* and *they* are buried at the ends of sentences in the middle of the paragraph, readers can easily lose sight of the paragraph's topic, sand paintings.

EDITED TO CREATE A REFERENCE CHAIN

Sand paintings were a remarkable form of Pueblo art from the Southwest and Southern California. To create **them,** an artist would sprinkle dried sand of different colors, ground flower petals, corn pollen, and similar materials onto the floor. **They** contained figures representing the sun, moon, and stars as well as animals and objects linked to the spirits. **Their** purpose was to encourage the spirits to send good fortune to humans.

Did You Know?

According to research conducted by the authors, college instructors view problems with pronoun reference as among the most irritating and potentially confusing errors they encounter in student writing. The instructors believe that problems with pronoun reference are likely to arise more frequently as the content and ideas in an essay become more complex. They also think that appropriate and careful use of pronoun reference is a key tool for writers who wish to guide and focus the attention of readers.

Chris M. Anson and Robert A. Schwegler, "A Survey of Attitudes Toward Error Among Instructors at Four Colleges," unpublished ms.

Exercise 2

A. Revise the following sentences so that they form a reference chain giving appropriate emphasis to the information provided in the passage. You will need to give some ideas and details more emphasis than others.

When it comes to reading material, Americans have some clear favorites. In terms of circulation, the top five newspapers in the country are the *Wall Street Journal, USA Today,* the *New York Daily News,* the *Los Angeles Times,* and the *New York Times.* Sales of softbound books far outnumber sales of hardbound books. Our favorite subject areas for books are medicine, history, fiction, sociology and economics, religion, and technology. The top three magazines in terms of revenue are *Time, Sports Illustrated,* and *People.* More people subscribe to *Modern Maturity* and the *AARP Bulletin* than to any other magazines, including *Reader's Digest,* which is number three on the subscription list. *1,001 Home Ideas* and *The Elks Magazine* have larger paid circulations than *Vogue, Rolling Stone,* and *Mademoiselle.*

22a
pr ref

B. Working with a group of writers, share your versions of the passage in Exercise 2A. Choose two versions that give the information different emphasis. Identify the ways each writer has created a reference chain, and indicate which ideas and details have been highlighted and which have been moved to the background.

22b Making reference specific

If readers say they "get lost" reading your work or "can't quite figure out what you are saying," part of the problem may be vague pronoun reference. **Specific pronoun reference** points out for readers the precise relationships between statements. **Vague pronoun reference,** however, makes pronouns refer to antecedents that are implied rather than stated. It does not clearly indicate the part of a preceding statement, if any, to which a pronoun refers.

You need to be alert, therefore, to contexts in which you are most likely to create vague pronoun reference: (1) with certain troublesome words like *it, which, this,* and *that;* and (2) with antecedents that are implied rather than stated.

1 Use *it, which, this,* and *that* with care

Some very useful pronouns are also easy to misuse. For example, writers often use *it, which, this,* or *that* to refer broadly to a preceding passage but end up giving readers only a vague idea of the antecedent. Or writers may ask a word like *it* to refer to several different antecedents within a short passage.

Overly Broad Reference. You are most likely to misuse words like *it, which, this,* or *that* when you want to refer to the entire idea of a preceding sentence, sentence part, or group of sentences. When you use the pronouns effectively to refer to an entire idea, you create **broad prounoun reference.** In the following pair of sentences, the writer uses *this* and *that* clearly and appropriately for just such a purpose.

> Every few million years an extremely large asteroid collides with the earth. **This** has not happened in historic times, so we have no experience of the consequences of **that** event.
>
> — ROBERT JASTROW, *Journey to the Stars*

Used carefully, broad reference can help you sum up ideas in order to comment on them, as in the preceding example. On the other hand, you can easily confuse readers if you fail to make clear the *specific* antecedent of *it, which, that,* or *this.* Consider the following example.

VAGUE REFERENCE Redfish have been heavily harvested for years, but in the last decade they have been subjected to oil pollution and to the destruction of their mangrove swamp habitat by waterfront building. **That** has led to a recent and rapid decline in the redfish population.

READER'S REACTION: Does *that* refer to the destruction of habitat, to oil pollution, to overfishing, or to some combination?

To edit for vague or overly broad reference, look for words like *it, which, this,* and *that,* and then see if you have provided a specific word or group of words to which the pronoun clearly refers. If not, correct the problem using one of the following Strategies.

S T R A T E G Y   1

Specify. Right after *this, that,* or another troublesome word, add a word or phrase that specifies (or explains) the pronoun's referent.

EDITED (SPECIFIES) Redfish have been heavily harvested for years, but in the last decade they have been subjected to oil pollution and to the destruction of their mangrove swamp habitat by waterfront building. That **combination** has led to a recent and rapid decline in the redfish population.

EDITED (EXPLAINS) Redfish have been heavily harvested for years, but in the last decade they have been subjected to oil pollution and to the destruction of their mangrove swamp habitat by waterfront building. That **increasingly serious set of challenges** has led to a recent and rapid decline in the redfish population.

**22b
pr ref**

S T R A T E G Y   2

Replace. Drop the pronoun, and use a noun or noun phrase in its place.

VAGUE One test conducted by the Mars lander discovered some evidence of life on Mars, but the other uncovered no evidence whatsoever. **This** led many scientists to conclude that there is no life on the planet.

REPLACED One test conducted by the Mars lander discovered some evidence of life on Mars, but the other uncovered no evidence whatsoever. **The reliability of the second test** led many scientists to conclude that there is no life on the planet.

S T R A T E G Y   3

Reword. Rewrite the sentence or sentences so that the pronoun is no longer needed.

REWORDED   One test conducted by the Mars lander discovered some evidence of life on Mars, but the second and more reliable test uncovered no evidence whatsoever, leading many scientists to conclude that there is no life on the planet.

It Used in More Than One Sense.   You can employ *it* in many ways.

PERSONAL PRONOUN
I threw the blender out after **it** broke for the third time.

WAY OF POSTPONING SUBJECT
It is the lack of sunshine in winter that often causes depression.

IDIOMATIC EXPRESSION
It is raining.

By using *it* in more than one sense in a single sentence or a short passage, however, you risk confusing readers.

CONFUSING   When I was young, I always found **it** surprising that my father would come home from a hard day at his job and go out to the garden to work in **it,** even when **it** was raining.

EDITED   When I was young, I was always surprised when my father came home from a hard day at his job and went out to work in the garden, even when **it** was raining.

**22b
pr ref**

2 Be alert for antecedents that are implied rather than stated

In the following sentence, the writer has an antecedent in mind but fails to communicate it to readers.

IMPLIED   In the West, **they** often prefer Japanese cars; in the center of the country, **they** drive mostly Detroit-made autos; and in the Northeast and Southeast, **they** often choose European models.

Most readers would guess that *they* refers to people in general, because that is the antecedent words like *drive* and *cars* suggest. But *they* might also mean rich people, people under forty, or some other group. By stating the antecedent directly the writer could have eliminated both guessing and possible misunderstanding.

STATED   In the West, **people under forty** prefer Japanese cars; in the center of the country, they drive mostly Detroit-made autos; and in the Northeast and Southeast, they often choose European models.

As you edit, check that you have provided readers with a *stated* antecedent rather than an *implied* one. Watch out, as well, for the following troublesome words and contexts that may lead to implied or missing antecedents.

***They* or *It* Without an Antecedent.**   In most writing, especially academic writing, you need to make sure readers can identify an antecedent in your text so your statements are precise and clear. If you *imply* an antecedent but do not actually *state* it, your writing becomes vague and often confusing.

IMPLIED   In February, a deep frost damaged most of the citrus groves in the state, but **it** has not yet been determined.
                 READER'S REACTION: I can't be sure what *it* is.

STATED   In February, a deep frost damaged most of the citrus groves in the state, but **the extent of the loss** has not yet been determined.

***You* Without an Antecedent.**   When you intend to address the reader directly, *you* is acceptable in most writing. It means "you, the reader." In effect, *you* makes the reader the antecedent, that is, the person to whom the pronoun refers. (See also 24a.)

ACCEPTABLE   In implementing the recommendations of this report, **you** may find that staff members resist some of the suggestions for long-term patient care. The following statistics should help **you** convince them that the new procedures will be useful.

When *you* refers indefinitely to experiences, situations, and people in general, it is not appropriate and often leads to wordy and misleading sentences.

MISLEADING   In Brazil, you pay less for an alcohol-powered car than for a gasoline-powered one.
                 READER'S REACTION: Who is *you*? After all, I'm not likely to be buying a car in Brazil.

22b
pr ref

EDITED   In Brazil, alcohol-powered cars cost less than gasoline-pow-
          ered ones.

EDITED   In Brazil, consumers pay less for an alcohol-powered car
          than for a gasoline-powered one.

Possessive Noun or Modifier as Antecedent. In academic writing, using
a possessive noun as an antecedent will seem like an error to most readers
(unless the pronoun is also possessive), even though the pattern appears
often in informal writing.

INAPPROPRIATE   In William Faulkner's *The Sound and the Fury,* he presents the
                 first part of the story from the point of view of a mentally
                 retarded person.

EDITED   In *The Sound and the Fury,* William Faulkner presents the
          first part of the story from the point of view of a mentally
          retarded person.

Because a modifier may *suggest* an antecedent, you may sometimes
mistakenly use an adjective as the referent for a pronoun. In doing so, you
confuse readers by forcing them to guess at your intentions. To avoid this
problem, supply a specific antecedent.

CONFUSING   Whether or not a product is successfully marketed may
             depend on how many demographic studies were conducted.
             As a result, people trained in **it** often get good jobs in major
             corporations.
             Demographic is an adjective. It is not the name of a field of study,
             as the writer seems to assume.

EDITED   Whether or not a product is successfully marketed may
          depend on how many demographic studies were conducted.
          As a result, people trained in **demography** often get good
          jobs in major corporations.

**22b
pr ref**

Noun Implied by Another Word. If you make a pronoun refer to a noun
that is not in a sentence but is merely implied by some other word, your
sentence is likely to be clumsy or hard to understand. Make sure a pronoun
refers to a noun or phrase that is actually stated, not implied.

CLUMSY   Growing up in the Southwest, Alice dreamed of studying
          oceanography, though she had never seen **one.**

EDITED   Growing up in the Southwest, Alice dreamed of studying
          oceanography, though she had never seen **an ocean.**

UNCLEAR	Rosalind Franklin participated in the discovery of DNA's molecular structure, though she is seldom given credit for **it.**
EDITED	Rosalind Franklin participated in the discovery of DNA's molecular structure, though she is seldom given credit for **her contribution.**

Writer's Alert

When you use a possessive noun, you must pair it with a possessive pronoun, for example, *Kristen's . . . hers.*

UNCLEAR	The **company's** success with a well-known jazz fusion artist led **it** to contracts with other musicians.
EDITED	The **company's** success with a well-known jazz fusion artist led to **its** contracts with other musicians.

Another way you can correct the problem is to rewrite the sentence to eliminate the possessive noun.

EDITED	Success with a well-known jazz fusion artist led the company to contracts with other musicians.

Exercise 3

A. Revise the following sentences to eliminate vague pronoun reference and provide specific antecedents.

EXAMPLE   *The committee's report*
~~In the committee's report it~~ ∧points out that students generally benefit from participating in a music program.

   (or In its report, the committee points out . . .)

1. Many people study a musical instrument in high school though few students intend to become one.
2. At most secondary schools they offer a variety of music programs.
3. Last February, the town began investigating the quality of its high school band program, but it has not yet been completed.
4. In many regional high schools in the West, the band's large size mirrors the role it plays in the school's social life.
5. In the Northwest you quickly get used to marching and playing in the rain.

B. Compare your revised versions of the sentences in Exercise 3A with those of other writers. As a group, choose the best version of each sentence, and state the reasons for your choice.

22b
pr ref

22c   Matching *who, which,* and *that* to antecedents

Who refers to people and may refer to animals with names.

Branford and Wynton Marsalis, **who** are brothers, rank among the top contemporary jazz musicians.

Which refers to animals and things (including ideas).

Quantum theory, **which** includes the work of Einstein, Planck, Bohr, and others, was the chief contribution of early twentieth-century physics.

That refers to animals, to things, and to anonymous people or people viewed collectively.

Rheumatoid arthritis is a disease **that** affects the entire body, though it appears mainly in the form of joint inflammation.

The patients **that** this hospital serves can make use of the institution's Part-Time Patient program for extended physical and occupational therapy.

22c
pr ref

> ### Writer's Alert
>
> Many readers will expect you to use *which* or *who* with **nonrestrictive clauses** and either *that, which,* or *who* with **restrictive clauses** (see 32c for a discussion of restrictive and nonrestrictive modifiers). Though other readers may pay little attention to the distinction between *that* and *which* or *that* and *who,* you should generally maintain the distinction in formal writing.
>
> #### RESTRICTIVE (ESSENTIAL, LIMITS MEANING)
> Drugs **that** limit tissue rejection are necessary for the survival of transplant recipients.
>
> #### NONRESTRICTIVE (NONESSENTIAL)
> The license, **which** will cost you twenty dollars, permits you to fish anywhere in the state for seven days.
>
> Noam Chomsky, **who** is a professor at MIT, is a famous linguist.

Exercise 4

A. Revise the following sentences to correct inappropriate pronoun references. Indicate which sentences, if any, contain appropriate pronoun reference.

EXAMPLE

Many scholars ~~which~~ *who* are interested in Buddhism have begun to study Tibetan religious practices.

1. The gathering was addressed by the Dalai Lama, a man which is one of the spiritual leaders of Tibetan Buddhism.
2. Tibetan Buddhism is characterized by large monastic organizations who practice yoga and other spiritual and intellectual rituals.
3. It is also true that this form of Buddhism retains features that it inherited from the folk religions of Tibet.
4. Up until the recent Chinese invasion, that occurred in 1959, Tibetan life was dominated by religious practices.
5. Although Lamaism has its greatest influence in Tibet and in countries who are nearby, such as Nepal and Mongolia, it is beginning to spread its influence in the West, including North America.

B. At a library, find a magazine with somewhat complicated, information-filled articles. Choose an article that interests you, and identify several paragraphs where the author uses a variety of the pronoun reference patterns discussed in this chapter. Make enough copies of these paragraphs to share with a group of fellow students. As a group, identify each of the pronoun reference strategies and try to decide why the author used each one.

22c
pr ref

CHAPTER

23

Misplaced,
Dangling, and
Disruptive Modifiers

The following sentences leave readers with some unanswered questions.

MISPLACED MODIFIER When I was at the store last week, I only looked at the cassette tape player.

READER'S REACTION: *Only* is confusing. Do you mean you just looked and didn't try the cassette player out? You didn't have time to look at other equipment, such as the CD player? You were the only person who looked at the cassette player?

DANGLING MODIFIER Rushing to get to the post office before it closed, my bicycle nearly hit an unwary young woman.

READER'S REACTION: Who was rushing to the post office—I, the bicycle, or the young woman?

Because a **modifier** qualifies, adds to, or limits the meaning of another word or word group, the relationship between a modifier and the word it modifies (its **headword**) needs to be clear to readers. The misplaced modifier in the first sentence (*only*) and the dangling modifier in the second (*Rushing to get to the post office . . .*) cause confusion because they are not clearly related to the words they ought to modify.

EDITED When I was at the store last week, I looked only **at the cassette player.**

EDITED Rushing to get to the post office before it closed, **I** nearly hit an unwary young woman while riding my bicycle.

A misplaced modifier is one that is not placed closely enough to its intended headword and appears to modify something else. A dangling modifier is one that appears in a sentence that contains no headword or phrase to which the modifier can be reasonably linked.

A third problem you may encounter is a disruptive modifier that separates closely connected elements such as a subject and a verb, making the sentence difficult to read and understand.

DISRUPTIVE MODIFIER   The chief accountant, **even though her assistant first uncovered evidence that the company president had been embezzling funds,** assumed the responsibility of reporting the crime to the police.

EDITED   **Even though her assistant first uncovered evidence that the company president had been embezzling funds,** the chief accountant assumed the responsibility of reporting the crime to the police.

23a Recognizing and editing misplaced modifiers

If you do not make the relationship between a modifier and its headword clear and specific, you may mislead or confuse readers. To recognize a **misplaced modifier,** look for a word that fails to modify its intended headword and instead appears to modify some other word or phrase in the sentence. Sometimes a misplaced modifier modifies *both* the word before it and the word after.

STRATEGY

To correct a misplaced modifier, either move it closer to its headword or rewrite the sentence so the connection between modifier and headword is clear.

MISPLACED MODIFIER   After you have installed the fan, follow the directions for the wiring connections on the back of the cover plate.
READER'S REACTION: Are the wiring connections on the back of the cover plate?

MOVED NEXT TO HEADWORD   After you have installed the fan, follow the directions **on the back of the cover plate** for the wiring connections.

MISPLACED MODIFIER   People who abuse alcohol frequently have other problems.
READER'S REACTION: Does *frequently* refer to the rate of alcohol abuse or the likelihood of problems?

REWRITTEN   People who abuse alcohol tend to have other problems as well.

23a
mm/
dm

1 Pay attention to a modifier's location

You can choose to word a sentence in many different ways to create emphasis and rhythm. With so many choices, don't be surprised if you position a modifier inappropriately on the first try. As you edit, therefore, check that modifiers are placed closely enough to their intended headwords that the relationship is clear. For example, the following draft sentence does not accurately convey its author's meaning.

DRAFT   After a divorce, toddlers demand to be fed often instead of feeding themselves.

While editing, the writer noticed that her sentence could be read as a statement that *all* toddlers regress after a divorce by demanding to be fed *often*. She moved the modifier *often* to make the sentence state clearly that demanding to be fed is a common though not universal response.

EDITED   After a divorce, toddlers **often** demand to be fed instead of feeding themselves.

When you are drafting, you may occasionally add new ideas and details to the end of a sentence next to a word that seems to be a headword but is not the word you actually intend to modify.

MISPLACED MODIFIER   The wife believes she sees a living figure behind the wallpaper in the story by Charlotte Perkins Gilman, which contributes to her sense of entrapment.
READER'S REACTION: **This sounds as if the story itself causes a feeling of entrapment.**

EDITED (MODIFIER MOVED)   The wife **in the story by Charlotte Perkins Gilman** believes she sees a living figure behind the wallpaper, which contributes to her sense of entrapment.

EDITED (MODIFIER MOVED)   **In the story by Charlotte Perkins Gilman,** the wife believes she sees a living figure behind the wallpaper, which contributes to her sense of entrapment.

**23a
mm/
dm**

You may sometimes draft sentences that present prepositional phrases or participial phrases (see 15c-1 and 15c-4) in confusing order.

CONFUSING   It was not a good idea to serve food to the guests standing around the room on flimsy paper plates.
READER'S REACTION: **Surely the guests were not standing on their plates!**

EDITED
(MODIFIER
MOVED)

It was not a good idea to serve food **on flimsy paper plates** to the guests standing around the room.

Exercise 1

Identify and correct the misplaced modifiers (words or phrases) in the following sentences. You may decide either to move the modifier or to rewrite the entire sentence.

EXAMPLE *in pet store windows*
Puppies, spend a lot of time staring at people ~~in pet store windows.~~

1. They decided to buy the beagle puppy confused by the many exotic breeds of dogs.
2. This dog would replace the one killed by a truck running across a busy highway.
3. They forgot to buy a dog bed distracted by the crowd of people in the store.
4. Hurriedly, John sighed and began tearing up newspapers in order to begin house-training the puppy.
5. The parents could hear the children playing outside with the dog yelling and laughing.

---

2 Pay attention to limiting modifiers

You can alter the meaning of a sentence considerably by moving around words like *only, almost, hardly, just, scarcely, merely, simply, exactly,* and *even* (these are called **limiting modifiers**).

During this recession, **only** charities for disabled children are maintaining their normal levels of support.
They are the sole charities that have been able to maintain normal levels.

During this recession, charities for disabled **only** children are maintaining their normal levels of support.
The charities are for disabled children from families with one child.

During this recession, charities for disabled children are **only** maintaining their normal levels of support.
They are not increasing the levels of support.

Be ready to move a limiting modifier or rewrite a sentence to achieve the meaning you intend. Remember, a limiting modifier generally applies to the word that immediately follows, though not always.

23a
mm/
dm

Did You Know?

In some languages, words change form to indicate their role in a sentence. In Latin or German, for example, the relationship between a modifier and the word being modified is generally clear from the form or ending of the words. In English, however, modifiers tend to change location, not form, to show which words they describe. As a result, a modifier's position in a sentence can make a big difference in the sentence's meaning. Checking on the position of modifiers as you edit is a challenging job even for professionals, such as magazine editors, as J. N. Hook points out.

Should you write "Smith only wanted one" or "Smith wanted only one"? A study by Bryant reported in 1962 that 86 percent of magazines placed *only* as in the second sentence. Logic supports that placement: it was *only one* that Smith wanted. Bryant added that in spoken English, sentences like the first predominated. Her findings, although dated, still appear valid.

J. N. Hook, *The Appropriate Word* (Reading, MA: Addison, 1990) 180.

---

3 Be alert for squinting modifiers

Readers become understandably confused when they encounter a modifier that appears to modify *both* the word or phrase that comes before it and the one that comes after. As you edit, look for **squinting modifiers** that present two possible meanings to readers, and rewrite to avoid possible confusion. To edit squinting modifiers, ask yourself which word or phrase you intend to modify, then move the modifier into a position that repairs the ambiguity.

**23a
mm/
dm**

SQUINTING
MODIFIER
: People who enjoy listening to Aaron Copland's music **often** claim that he was the finest American composer of the twentieth century.

READER'S REACTION: **Does this mean that they *listen often* to the music or that they *often claim* something about Copland?**

EDITED
: People who enjoy **listening often** to Aaron Copland's music also tend to claim that he was the finest American composer of the twentieth century.

EDITED
: People who enjoy listening to Aaron Copland's music **will often** claim that he was the finest American composer of the twentieth century.

Exercise 2

A. Each of the following sentences contains either ambiguity caused by a squinting modifier or a limiting modifier that can be moved to different positions. Indicate the type of problem in each sentence.

EXAMPLE

A good car costs a lot of money often. *(limiting modifier)*

1. Five years ago, many people were interested only in buying fancy cars.
2. Today, anyone hardly has the money to buy a basic automobile, let alone a luxury car.
3. People who have big families frequently drive passenger vans.
4. Paying attention simply to a vehicle's initial price and likely trade-in value is not enough.
5. Anyone who buys cars infrequently may get a lemon.

B. Working with a group of other writers, edit the sentences in Exercise 2A by rewriting each in two different ways.

4 Pay attention to dependent clauses

You should generally place a modifying clause beginning with *who, which,* or *that* right after its intended headword. (See relative clauses, 15a-2.) If you do not, the clause may modify the wrong word, creating unintended meanings.

MISPLACED MODIFIER	The environmental engineers discovered another tank behind the building that was leaking toxic wastes.
	READER'S REACTION: I know a building can leak, but I'll bet the writer meant to identify the tank as the culprit.
EDITED	Behind the building, the environmental engineers discovered another tank that was leaking toxic wastes.

Modifying clauses that begin with other subordinators, such as *when, although, because, since,* and *while* (see 15a-8), allow you more flexibility in placement. Nonetheless, you still need to make sure the relationship between modifier and headword is clear.

MISPLACED MODIFIER	The company has decided to switch from the old health plan to one offered by a competing insurance company because premiums are rising rapidly.

EDITED   **Because premiums are rising rapidly,** the company has decided to switch from the old health plan to one offered by a competing insurance company.

Exercise 3

A. Revise the following sentences to eliminate any misplaced modifiers.

EXAMPLE
Sliding into second base, ~~my leg~~ broke.
(with handwritten edits: *I* my leg broke*my leg*)

1. The coach tossed out the practice balls to the players, wet and soft from yesterday's rain.
2. They worked on hitting and catching for fifteen minutes before the first game which was the only practice time they had.
3. The coach who was known as a strict disciplinarian of the championship Little League team invented a rigorous new set of conditioning exercises.
4. A proposal to follow the infield fly rule was defeated by the coach's committee which no one understood.
5. The coach is unable to present the award given in memory of Father Baker because he is sick.

B. Compare your edited versions of the sentences in Exercise 3A with those of other students. As a group, decide which versions you prefer and why you prefer them.

23b Recognizing and editing dangling modifiers

If you begin a sentence with a modifying word or phrase that does not mention the person, idea, or thing being modified, readers will assume that the modifier refers to the subject of the main clause immediately following. When it does not do so—at least in a reasonable way—the modifier is a **dangling modifier.**

DANGLING
MODIFIER   **Leaking in several places,** the scouts abandoned their tents for the dry cabin.

READER'S REACTION: **Surely the tents were leaking, not the scouts themselves.**

EDITED   **Their tents** leaking in several places, the scouts decided to spend the night in the dry cabin.

EDITED   The scouts decided to spend the night in the dry cabin **because their tents were leaking in several places.**

Because they are often vague, illogical, or unintentionally humorous, dangling modifiers can needlessly distract readers. A sentence with a dangling modifier can also leave out important information.

DANGLING MODIFIER	Looking for a way to reduce the complaints from non-smokers, a new ventilation fan was installed.
	READER'S REACTION: This sentence doesn't tell *who* is looking to reduce complaints, though the opening makes me expect such information.
EDITED	Looking for a way to reduce the complaints from non-smokers, **the company installed** a new ventilation fan.

S T R A T E G Y

To correct a dangling modifer, take *one* of the following steps.

1. Add a subject to the modifier.

DANGLING	While shopping for a birthday gift for my brother, the stuffed alligator caught my eye.
EDITED	While **I was** shopping for a birthday gift for my brother, the stuffed alligator caught my eye.

2. Or change the subject of the main clause.

DANGLING	Trying to decide where to hold the fundraiser, the new restaurant was attractive.
EDITED	Trying to decide where to hold the fundraiser, **the committee** was attracted to the new restaurant.

3. Or rewrite the entire sentence.

DANGLING	Having debated changes in the regulations for several months without reaching a decision, the present standards were allowed to continue.
EDITED	The commission debated changes in the regulations for several months without reaching a decision, then decided to allow the present standards to continue.

Remember that a modifier may also dangle when the word to which it should refer appears in the sentence as something other than the subject.

**23b
mm/
dm**

DANGLING MODIFIER

Jumping into the water to save the drowning swimmer, the crowd cheered the lifeguard.

EDITED (HEADWORD BECOMES SUBJECT)

Jumping into the water to save the drowning swimmer, **the lifeguard** was cheered by the crowd.

Remember, too, that a modifier in the body of a sentence dangles when the sentence contains no word or phrase to which it can reasonably refer.

DANGLING MODIFIER

The emergency repairs were completed by noon, having become aware of the problem only at ten o'clock.

READER'S REACTION: Who became aware of the problem?

EDITED (PHRASE ADDED)

The emergency repairs were completed by noon, **the telephone company** having become aware of the problem only at ten o'clock.

Exercise 4

A. Rewrite each of the following sentences in the *two* ways indicated in brackets in order to eliminate dangling modifiers.

EXAMPLE   *Marion designed her research poorly.*
Unable to meet with an advisor, ~~Marion's research was poorly designed~~.
[add subject to main clause; rewrite]
*Because Marion was unable to meet with an advisor, she
designed her research poorly.*

1. Because of a failure to gather enough data, her study was incomplete. [rewrite; add subject to modifier]
2. Lacking the money to pay skilled interviewers, minimally trained volunteers were relied upon. [add subject to main clause; rewrite]
3. Many subjects were not asked appropriate questions because of poor training. [add subject to modifier; add subject to main clause]
4. Anxious and tired, the two-day attempt to write the research report was unsuccessful. [add subject to modifier; add subject to main clause]
5. After spending over twenty hours writing at the computer, the report was still not satisfactory. [rewrite; add subject to modifier]

B. Compare your edited versions of the sentences in Exercise 4A with those of another student, and decide which versions are the most successful and why.

23c Recognizing and editing disruptive modifiers

Readers generally expect subjects and verbs to stand close to each other in sentences. The same is true for verbs and their objects or complements. However, you can add variety and suspense to your sentences by using a brief interruption that provides relevant information.

CLEAR   The researcher, **unfamiliar with chimpanzees,** was surprised when they purposely undermined the experiment he was trying to conduct.

Longer interruptions and those with less relevant information can be **disruptive modifiers.**

DISRUPTIVE   The researcher, **because he had not worked with chimpanzees before and was therefore unaware of their intelligence,** was surprised when they purposely undermined the experiment he was trying to conduct.

Disruptive modifiers make a sentence difficult to understand when they come between subjects and verbs, verbs and objects, and verbs and complements. Disruptive modifiers also cause problems when they split infinitives or verb phrases.

1 Pay attention to separated subjects and verbs

Some modifiers placed between subject and verb are disruptive; others are not. How can you recognize the difference? Modifiers that provide information related to both the subject and the verb are disruptive when they appear between these elements. Modifiers that provide information related to the subject alone are generally not disruptive even when they come between subject and verb.

                          subject   modifier
DISRUPTIVE   Work on the building, **due to problems with the construc-**
                                              verb
                tion permits, was completed three months late.

                          subject   modifier   verb
NOT DISRUPTIVE The electronics store **that opened last month** has drawn crowds of customers.

Move a potentially disruptive modifier out of its position between subject and verb so that it no longer disrupts the flow of the sentence and makes it hard to understand.

23c
mm/
dm

DISRUPTIVE MODIFIER	Contractors, **because house building is a boom-or-bust business,** should be ready to do home repairs when housing starts are down.
EDITED (MODIFIER MOVED)	**Because house building is a boom-or-bust business,** contractors should be ready to do home repairs when housing starts are down.

In contrast, modifiers that are adjective phrases or relative clauses (see 15a-2) simply add information to a subject, expanding the sentence without disruption, the way single-word adjectives work.

ADJECTIVES	**long and bitter** negotiations
ADJECTIVE CLAUSE	negotiations **that are long and bitter**
CLEAR	Negotiations **that are long and bitter** may lead to unsatisfactory contracts.

2 Pay attention to separations between verbs and objects or complements

Readers expect an object or complement to come right after the verb. If you split these elements with an adverb phrase or clause, you may create a sentence that seems clumsy or difficult, even if most readers are able to understand it.

CLUMSY	Joanne began collecting, **with special attention to survey results,** data for her study of dating preferences.
EDITED	**With special attention to survey results,** Joanne began collecting data for her study of dating preferences.

3 Be alert for split infinitives or verb phrases

If you split the parts of an infinitive (*to* plus a verb, as in *to run* or *to enjoy*), you may make it hard for readers to understand the relationship between the parts.

UNCLEAR	The office designer tried **to** respectively **address** each of the workers' concerns.
EDITED	The office designer tried **to address** each of the workers' concerns **respectively.**

Even when such a **split infinitive** is easy to understand, you might consider revising it because some readers find split infinitives irritating.

IRRITATING   When the lead Canada goose changes direction in flight, all the rest of the geese move **to** <u>very rapidly</u> **align** themselves with it.

EDITED   When the lead Canada goose changes direction in flight, all the rest of the geese move <u>very rapidly</u> **to align** themselves with it.

At times, however, you may discover that a split infinitive is the clearest and most concise way of phrasing a statement.

Our goal is to more than halve our manufacturing errors.
The alternatives are more wordy and complicated—for example, "Our goal is a rate of manufacturing error less than half the present rate."

You usually cause no difficulty for readers if you separate the parts of a verb phrase (helping verb plus main verb, as in *had been digging*) by adding one or more adverbs.

CLEAR   The archaeologists had been **carefully** digging at the site for three years.

Longer word groups within a verb phrase may be disruptive, however.

DISRUPTED   The archaeologists <u>had been,</u> **because of initial discoveries made during construction of a new house,** <u>digging</u> at the site for three years.

CLEAR   **Because of initial discoveries made during the construction of a new house,** archaeologists <u>had been digging</u> at the site for three years.

Exercise 5

A. Rewrite each of the following sentences to eliminate disruptive modifiers and to make the sentence easier to read and understand.

EXAMPLE

~~The architect,~~ ᵝbecause she was unfamiliar with eighteenth-century
the architect
interior design and furnishings,ₐhad to do some research before completing the project.

1. The overall design of a building and its interior decoration ought to thoughtfully and harmoniously work together.
2. Furniture design has at least for the past several centuries been greatly influenced by a handful of designers, including Hepplewhite, Chippendale, Sheraton, and, most recently, Eames.

3. Design in Colonial America, because of economic limitations and social customs, was generally simple and practical.

4. Americans had, by the early 1800s in what is now known as the Federalist period, developed more refined and expensive tastes.

5. Today, magazines like *Architectural Digest* and *House Beautiful* illustrate the tendency for styles in interior design to rapidly change and to add considerably to the cost of a home.

 B. Working with a group of fellow writers, compare your revisions of the sentences in Exercise 5A. Decide which versions you prefer and why.

23d   Using absolute phrases effectively

An **absolute phrase** consists of a noun or pronoun, a participle, and modifiers (for example, *the water level having risen* and *her view of market conditions changing almost daily*). An absolute phrase qualifies or limits an entire sentence rather than a specific word or group of words. (See 15c-2.)

The water level having risen, people in the valley feared that the dam was about to burst.

The absolute phrase sets the scene for the rest of the sentence.

The stockbroker began pelting her clients with urgent and sometimes contradictory advice, **her view of market conditions changing almost daily.**

The absolute phrase provides a context for the rest of the sentence.

Because absolute phrases do not modify a particular word, you may be tempted to avoid using them for fear of creating dangling modifiers. However, an absolute phrase provides its own noun or pronoun subject, so it does not dangle. Absolute phrases are expressions that can add variety and flair to your writing. Notice the difference between a dangling modifier and an absolute phrase.

**23d
mm/
dm**

DANGLING
MODIFIER

Having growled at the door for half an hour, she decided to call the police.

READER'S REACTION: Was the person growling? Or did the dog call the police?

ABSOLUTE
PHRASE

The dog having growled at the door for half an hour, she decided to call the police.

Adding "the dog" as the subject of the modifier turns the dangling modifier into an absolute phrase, thus clarifying who "growled." The absolute phrase then explains the reason why she called the police.

24

Shifts

In most kinds of writing, you are likely to ask readers to shift their attention many times. For example, you might ask them to focus first on events occurring in the past, then on those occurring in the present or likely to occur in the future. Or you might ask readers to consider your point of view ("I argue that this solution is unworkable") and then ask them to reject the perspective offered by others ("They made their proposal without considering the practical consequences").

As long as shifts such as these are consistent and are signaled clearly, your readers should have little trouble following them. You can mislead readers, however, if you are inconsistent or confusing when you signal **shifts** in pronoun form, verb form, or direct and indirect quotation. You may even cause readers to doubt your authority and ability as a writer.

24a Keeping person and number consistent

In grammatical terms, **person** refers to the ways you can use pronouns and nouns to shape the relationship involving you, your readers, and your subject.

- **First person (I, we).** Use *I* to refer to yourself as the writer or the person whose experiences and perceptions are the subject of an essay. *We* is appropriate when more than one person is author or subject. You may use *we* to refer to both yourself and your readers when you are discussing shared experiences or understandings. This use of *we* is appropriate in some academic fields, such as the study of literature ("At this point in reading the novel, we begin realizing that Amelia is not the self-sacrificing person she seemed to be in the opening chapters"). It is often inappropriate in other fields, such as chemistry or engineering.

- **Second person (*you*).** Use *you* to refer directly to the reader ("you, the reader"). In most kinds of formal writing, including academic and professional writing, readers will consider *you* inappropriate unless it is called for by the situation, as in a set of instructions.

- **Third person (*he, she, it, they; one, someone, each,* and other indefinite pronouns).** Use third person pronouns for the ideas, things, and people you are writing about. *People* and *person* are third person nouns, as are names of groups of things, ideas, and people (for example, *students, teachers, doctors*).

1 Pay attention to shifts in person

Watch out for unwarranted shifts in person in your writing. In particular, look for inconsistencies created by illogical shifts between first and second person or between second and third person.

INCONSISTENT	**I** am thinking of taking out a two-year certificate of deposit because **you** can get a high interest rate on it.
	READER'S REACTION: I don't think the writer means that *she* bought the certificate of deposit because *someone else* can get a good interest rate.
EDITED	**I** am thinking of taking out a two-year certificate of deposit because **I** can get a high interest rate on it.
INCONSISTENT	If a **person** is looking for a higher interest rate than the rate offered on certificates of deposit, **you** might consider the securities offered by stockbrokers.
EDITED	If **you** are looking for a higher interest rate than the rate offered on certificates of deposit, **you** might consider the securities offered by stockbrokers.

24a
shift

2 Pay attention to shifts in number

To keep your sentences logical and consistent, check that pronouns and their antecedents agree in number (see 18c). Writers often make shifts in number when using nouns that identify groups or members of a group, such as *business executives* or *a student.*

SHIFTED	When **a business executive** is looking for a new job, **they** often consult a placement service.
	READER'S REACTION: I think this writer had business executives in mind as a group and referred to them as *they,* even though the sentence mentions only one *business executive.*

EDITED   When **business executives are** looking for **new jobs, they** often consult a placement service.

Words like *person* and *people* often cause difficulty. Remember that *person* is singular and *people* is plural.

SHIFTED   If **a person has** some money to invest, **they** should seek advice from a financial consultant.

EDITED   If **a person has** some money to invest, **he or she** should seek advice from a financial consultant.

                READER'S REACTION: I know *he or she* is correct, but it seems more complicated than it needs to be.

EDITED   If **people have** some money to invest, **they** should seek advice from a financial consultant.

Exercise 1

A. Rewrite the following sentences to make them consistent in person and number.

EXAMPLE
Each person has ~~their~~ *a* favorite fast-food restaurant.

1. A would-be restaurant owner often fails to carefully consider the competition they will face from other restaurants of all kinds, both fancy and informal.
2. Good franchise chains survey competition, tell potential owners how much money they will need to open the business, and help you with the many problems a restaurant owner faces.
3. Admittedly, running a doughnut shop or a pizza place gives one less prestige than you get from owning a gourmet restaurant.
4. I would still rather run a successful business than one where you lose money.
5. Not all franchise arrangements are good ones, so people should do some research before he or she decides to open a franchised restaurant.

B. Working with a group of fellow students, write a brief paragraph on a topic of general interest. Choose a topic about which the group members have some knowledge, for example, finding a good summer job, developing effective study habits, or buying good clothing cheaply. Then rewrite the paragraph so it contains several nouns and pronouns that do not agree in person and number. Give a copy of the faulty paragraph to another group as a "quiz." Correct the paragraph they have created, in turn, for you.

**24a
shift**

24b Keeping tense and mood consistent

The **tense** of a verb indicates time as past, present, or future. The **mood** of a verb indicates the writer's aim or attitude (see 17e and 17f).

1 Pay attention to shifts in tense

When you change verb tense within a sentence or group of sentences, you signal a change in time and the relationship of events in time (see 17a and 17g).

> Until synthetic fabrics like nylon, rayon, and Dacron **were invented** in the 1930s and 1940s, clothes **had been made** primarily of natural fabrics. Blends of synthetics with linen, cotton, or wool now **dominate** the clothing industry and **will** probably **be** the most popular textiles in the coming decade.

Watch out for unnecessary, illogical shifts that can mislead your readers and that contradict your meaning.

ILLOGICAL SHIFT Scientists digging in Montana **discovered** nests and clutches of eggs that **indicate** how some dinosaurs **take care** of their young.
Indicate (present tense) is appropriate because the scientists and others interpret the evidence in the present. *Take care* (present tense) is inappropriate because the actions of the dinosaurs clearly occurred in the past.

LOGICAL Scientists digging in Montana **discovered** nests and clutches of eggs that **indicate** how some dinosaurs **took care** of their young.

In particular, if you begin by narrating events in the past tense, avoid shifting suddenly to the present tense under the mistaken assumption that this will make the events seem more vivid.

TENSE SHIFT We **had been digging** at the Dry Gulch site for several weeks without finding any further evidence of dinosaur bones when suddenly Tonia **starts yelling**, "Eggs! I think I've found fossil eggs!"

EDITED We **had been digging** at the Dry Gulch site for several weeks without finding any further evidence of dinosaur bones when suddenly Tonia **started yelling**, "Eggs! I think I've found fossil eggs!"

24b shift

2 Watch out for tense shifts in indirect quotation

In an **indirect quotation** you *report* what someone has said. You don't quote word for word as you do in **direct quotation.** Use the past tense for indirect quotations.

DIRECT	In 1980, a report from the state Department of Commerce said, "The region will lose one-third of its manufacturing jobs over the next ten years."
INDIRECT (TENSE INCONSISTENT)	In 1980, a report from the state Department of Commerce says that the region **will** lose one of every three factory jobs over the next ten years.
INDIRECT (EDITED)	In 1980, a report from the state Department of Commerce said that the region **would** lose one of every three factory jobs over the next ten years.

In contrast, use the present tense when you summarize or comment on events and information from a written work or from another source, such as a film or television show.

INCONSISTENT	At the beginning of the novel, Ishmael **arrives** at New Bedford with the intention of shipping out on a whaler, which he soon **did.**
CONSISTENT	At the beginning of the novel, Ishmael **arrives** at New Bedford with the intention of shipping out on a whaler, which he soon **does.**

Did You Know?

Watching for inappropriate shifts is one job done by the copy editor who reads and corrects an author's manuscript, preparing it for publication. According to Elsie Myers Stainton, one of the dangers a copy editor should look for is "mixing tenses." She says the work of any author, living or dead, may be discussed as

living, existing in the present. . . . The choice of tense usually depends upon a nearby verb: "Whitman *was* just a clerk in the Attorney General's office, but he *said,* 'I celebrate myself.'" If excerpts are quoted from the poet's work as though from the living present, the present tense can be used: "Whitman *says:* 'Sing on, there in the swamp!/O singer bashful and tender!'" (54).

Elsie Myers Stainton, *The Fine Art of Copyediting* (New York: Columbia UP, 1991).

**24b
shift**

3 Be alert for shifts in mood

The term *mood* refers to the forms a verb takes according to your purpose in a sentence: to make a command or a request (**imperative mood**), to present a statement or question (**indicative mood**), or to offer a conditional or hypothetical statement (**subjunctive mood**). (See 17f.)

If you shift mood inappropriately, your sentences will be inconsistent and difficult for readers to follow.

	subjunctive indicative
INCONSISTENT	It is essential that our small company **cut** costs and **increases** revenue.
	Sentence shifts from subjunctive to indicative.

	subjunctive subjunctive
EDITED	It is essential that our small company **cut** costs and **increase** revenue.

Watch especially for shifts from the imperative to the indicative when you give directions. If you use the imperative consistently, your directions will be less wordy and easier to understand.

INCONSISTENT	To reduce costs for office supplies, **order** reusable ribbons for printers, and **you should** encourage employees to use electronic mail in place of paper memos.
CONSISTENT	To reduce costs for office supplies, **order** reusable ribbons for printers, and **encourage** employees to use electronic mail in place of paper memos.

Exercise 2

A. Rewrite the following sentences to make them consistent in tense and mood.

EXAMPLE

I went to the video store last week, and after half an hour I still ~~can't~~ *couldn't* figure out which movies I ~~want~~ *wanted*.

1. The video store manager said that if I bought two tapes I will get a third one free, and then he tells me about several of his favorite tapes.
2. In the movie *Sacrifice for Glory,* set in World War II, a British Mosquito bomber crashes in the jungle, and only the copilot managed to survive the long walk through the tropical heat back to civilization.

3. The hot sun beat on the shoulders of the copilot as he wades through the waist-deep, crocodile-infested swamp.

4. In *The Phantom Menace,* Anakin is a child with the power of the Force, but later in the series he turned to the Dark Side as Darth Vader.

5. In *Ghoulish Lunch,* the main character was reaching into the refrigerator around the guacamole dip for the last piece of apple pie when suddenly a cockroach crawls out from under the crust.

 B. In a newspaper or magazine, locate a brief review of a movie, performance, book, or recording. Make sure the review contains numerous shifts in tense and mood. Make a copy of the review to share with a group of fellow students. After looking over all the reviews brought in by the group, choose one with particularly complex shifts. As a group, identify each shift and describe its nature. Continue working through as many reviews as you can.

24c Keeping voice consistent

When a verb is in the **active voice,** the agent, or doer, of the action functions as the sentence's subject; when a verb is in the **passive voice,** the goal of the action functions as the sentence's subject. (See 17h.)

	subject	verb	object
ACTIVE	The lava flow	**destroyed**	twelve houses.
	agent	action	goal

	subject	verb	
PASSIVE	Twelve houses	**were destroyed**	by the lava flow.
	goal	action	[agent]

In general, stick to either active or passive voice within a sentence, and be alert for unwarranted shifts as you edit. In shifting between active and passive, you risk blurring a sentence's focus and confusing readers.

INCONSISTENT   Among the active volcanoes, Kilauea **erupts** [active] most frequently, and over 170 houses **have been destroyed** [passive] since 1983.

READER'S REACTION: The first part of the sentence focuses on Kilauea, but the volcano is not mentioned in the second part. Did Kilauea alone destroy the houses, or were some of the other volcanoes mentioned at the start also responsible?

24c
shift

EDITED   Among the active volcanoes, Kilauea has erupted most frequently in recent years, and **it has destroyed** over 170 houses since 1983.

Occasionally, you may need to shift between active and passive voice to highlight a sentence's subject or emphasize your meaning.

                                    active   active

UNEMPHATIC   Volcanic activity **built** Hawaii, and the island still **has** active volcanoes.

                The sentence seems to shift subjects from *volcanic activity* in the first part to *the island* in the second part.

                        passive

EDITED   Hawaii **was built** by volcanic activity, and the island still
                active
                has active volcanoes.

                The shift between passive and active voice keeps Hawaii as the sentence's focus.

Writer's Tip

    When you write instructions, watch out for shifts between active and passive voice that make sentences hard to follow.

CONFUSING   **You can purchase** the necessary hiking clothes from any good outdoor equipment store, and picks, specimen bags, and other useful rock-collecting equipment **may be obtained** through a mail-order geological supply company.

EDITED   **You can purchase** the necessary hiking clothes from any good outdoor equipment store, and **you can obtain** picks, specimen bags, and other useful rock-collecting equipment through a mail-order geological supply company.

**24c
shift**

Exercise 3

 A. Rewrite the following sentences to make them consistent in voice.

EXAMPLE
                                  and   *much*
We enjoyed the expedition, ~~and much was~~ learned ˄ about fossils.

1. In the morning we dug in the base of the ravine, and during the afternoon the walls were explored.

2. The team found fossils of trilobites, and other fossils were also found at the site.

3. Team members learned many things about the science of paleontology, and much was learned about the geological history of our area as well.

4. A chart helped in identifying fossilized animals, and we also learned useful identifying strategies from the lecture given by Bill Gonzales, the team leader.

5. After you fill out the application for next month's dig, the form should be given to Bill or sent to his office.

 B. Working in a group, use the sentences in Exercise 3A as the basis for a brief narrative telling the story of the "dig." Add sentences to fill in the information needed to make the story believable and interesting. Make your narrative consistent in voice.

24d Avoiding shifts between direct and indirect quotation

In direct quotation you present a speaker's or writer's ideas and feelings in that person's exact words, setting the material off by using quotation marks. Through indirect quotation you report the substance of what the speaker or writer said, but you put it into your own words and do not use quotation marks.

DIRECT According to the writer Adam Frank, stars "form deep within clouds of interstellar gas and dust so dense and opaque that no visible light can escape."

INDIRECT The writer Adam Frank points out that stars develop inside thick gas and dust clouds which trap all perceivable light.

Try to avoid mixing direct and indirect quotation within sentences, and edit any mixed sentences in order to make them less confusing and easier to read.

MIXED Writing about the Teenage Mutant Ninja Turtles, Phil Patton names cartoonists Peter Laird and Kevin Eastman as their creators and says, "They were born quietly in 1983, in the kitchen of a New England farmhouse."

EDITED Writing about the Teenage Mutant Ninja Turtles, Phil Patton says, "Cartoonists named Peter Laird and Kevin Eastman dreamed up the characters," who "were born quietly in 1983, in the kitchen of a New England farmhouse."

**24d
shift**

Be especially alert for sentences that mix indirect and direct quotations without using quotation marks to indicate the difference.

CONFUSING

Before we set out on our glacier hike, the guide told us to stay in line, and you should obey all orders immediately.

EDITED TO INDIRECT QUOTATION

Before we set out on our glacier hike, the guide told us to stay in line and to follow every order right away.

EDITED TO DIRECT QUOTATION

Before we set out on our glacier hike, the guide told us, "You should stay in line and obey all orders immediately."

Exercise 4

A. Rewrite each of the following sentences twice. First use direct quotation consistently, and then use indirect quotation consistently. (Feel free to invent direct quotations in order to complete the exercise. Be sure to change direct quotations into your own words when you present them as indirect quotations.)

EXAMPLE

The article began by saying, "People often fear bees," and that this fear is a result of ignorance.

The article began by saying, "People often fear bees, and this fear comes from ignorance."

The article began by saying that the widespread fear of bees is caused by ignorance.

1. I once heard a beekeeper claim that unless beekeeping becomes more popular as a hobby, "I believe that agriculture in this country may suffer."
2. At a meeting last night, the county agriculture commissioner argued that increased beekeeping would aid agriculture in our area and "We should be willing to provide beekeepers with financial support for their efforts."
3. Having eaten honey every day for sixty years, my grandfather says, "I may not look as good as I did when I was younger," but that he feels just as good.
4. My grandfather also says that he has stayed mentally alert because "I manage a large beekeeping and honey business."
5. My neighbor told me, if you are too busy to sell your honey at a roadside stand I should see if the supermarket in town would sell it for me.

**24d
shift**

B. Share your edited sentences from Exercise 4A with a group of your fellow students. Decide which versions of each sentence are best and why.

24d
shift

Mixed and Incomplete Sentences

When someone you are talking with switches topics abruptly, you can ask for an explanation. When you are reading, however, you can't ask the author to explain a confusing shift of topic that comes in the middle of a sentence, as in the following.

SHIFTED TOPIC   One **skill** I envy is **a person** who can study despite noise and other distractions.

Clearly, a *skill* is not a *person.*

EDITED   One **skill** I envy is **the ability** to study despite noise and other distractions.

Just as confusing are sentences that begin with one grammatical pattern, then shift to another.

SHIFTED STRUCTURE   Because the new television show did poorly in the ratings **explains why** programming executives decided to move it to a slot between two hit shows.

EDITED   Because the new television show did poorly in the ratings, **programming executives** decided to move it to a slot between two hit shows.

Sentences with mismatched topics or with shifted grammatical structures (both referred to as mixed sentences) confuse readers by undermining sentence patterns they rely on. Incomplete sentences do much the same. An **incomplete sentence** either lacks grammatical completeness, in which case it is a fragment (see Chapter 20), or omits wording necessary to make a logically complete and consistent statement. For example, if you start by saying, "X is larger," you should be ready to complete the comparison: "X is larger *than Y*."

INCOMPLETE   When they are first introduced, high-definition televisions are likely to cost three times as much.

> **READER'S REACTION: Are the new TVs likely to cost more when they are first introduced than they will cost later? Or are they likely to cost more than TVs being sold now?**

EDITED   When they are first introduced, high-definition televisions are likely to cost three times as much **as the most expensive television sets currently available.**

Spotting mixed and incomplete sentences in your writing may require extra effort. Because you know what your sentences are supposed to mean, you may mentally supply missing elements or compensate for shifts as you read your own work and thus mistakenly treat your sentences as correct.

25a Editing mixed sentences

Mixed sentences shift topics or grammatical structures without warning and for no clear reason. They throw readers off the track and make illogical statements. To recognize and edit mixed sentences, you need to keep certain basic sentence patterns in mind and watch for a number of troublesome phrases.

1 Recognizing topic shifts

In most sentences, the subject announces a topic, and the predicate comments on or renames the topic.

> subject   predicate
> The Old PC Network publishes a newsletter about outdated computers.
> topic   comment

> subject   predicate
> The Kaypro 64 is an out-of-date (but useful) computer.
> topic   topic renamed

25a
mixed

You create confusion if you mistakenly make each part of a sentence address a *different* subject. In a sentence with a **topic shift** (**faulty predication**), the second part of a sentence comments on or names a topic different from the one announced at the beginning of the sentence. As a result, readers are likely to have trouble deciding on the true focus of the sentence.

SHIFTED TOPIC   The **presence** of ozone in smog is the **chemical** that causes
eye irritation.
Presence **is not a chemical, though that is what the sentence
says.**

EDITED   The **ozone** in smog is the **chemical** that causes eye irritation.

S T R A T E G Y

To identify shifted topics, try asking the question "Who does what?"
or "What is it?" If the answer is illogical, the sentence needs editing.

SHIFTED TOPIC   In this factory, **flaws** in the product noticed by any worker
can stop the assembly line with the flip of a switch.
QUESTION: **Who does what? Certainly flaws can't stop the line or
flip a switch.**

EDITED   In this factory, **any worker** who notices flaws in the product **can stop** the assembly line with the flip of a switch.

SHIFTED   An **actuary** is the **process** of determining insurance risks
and premiums.
QUESTION: **What is it? An actuary is a person, not a process.**

REVISED   An **actuary** is a **person** who determines insurance risks
and premiums.

---

2 Editing topic shifts

In general, you can eliminate problems with mixed sentences by making sure the topic in both parts of a sentence, subject and predicate, is the same.
Most mixed sentences follow one of a small number of common patterns,
and for these sentences the following tips on editing may prove helpful.

**25a
mixed**

Rename the Subject. In building a sentence around the verb *be* (*is, are,
was, were*), you may use the sentence predicate to rename the subject. When
you do, make sure the topics on each side of the verb are roughly equivalent, as in the following sentence.

Jane Goodall is a **scientist** whose work has added to our understanding of chimpanzee behavior.

If the topics are not equivalent, edit the sentence by making sure the second
part of the sentence renames the topic that appears in the first part.

SHIFTED TOPIC   **Irradiation** is **food** that is preserved by the use of radiation.

EDITED   **Irradiation** is a **process** that can be used to preserve food.

Cut *Is When* or *Is Where*. In building a definition around the verb *is*, you need to balance the topics on each side of the verb.

noun (noun phrase,   noun (noun phrase,
pronoun)   verb   pronoun)

In field events, a **hammer** is a **steel ball** (like the one used in shot put events) attached to a chain.

Is when and *is where* make this kind of balance impossible. Cut them and rewrite to balance the topics.

NOT BALANCED   **Blocking** is **when** a television network schedules a less popular program between two popular ones.

EDITED   **Blocking** is the **practice** of scheduling a less popular television program between two popular ones.

Did You Know?

Few things are as distressing to readers as a sentence that starts out in one direction, then abruptly shifts to another. In her classic study *Errors and Expectations,* Mina Shaughnessy devoted a long discussion to the ways writers and readers can be derailed within sentences containing mixed structures. The mixed and incomplete patterns described in this chapter provide a small (but useful) start at an understanding of sentence strategies to avoid or correct in your writing. Because the number of potential mixed and incomplete structures is so great, perhaps the best overall advice we can give you is to reread your work carefully (aloud, if possible), trying to view it as a reader or listener might.

Mina Shaughnessy, *Errors and Expectations* (New York: Oxford UP, 1977).

25a
mixed

Omit *The Reason . . . Is Because*. In informal conversation, the phrase *the reason . . . is because* causes little confusion. In writing, however, readers will recognize that it creates an illogical statement. A phrase opening with *because* is a modifying phrase that cannot logically rename the subject (topic) of the first part of a sentence. Its job is to modify, not rename.

| NOT LOGICAL | One **reason** for research into alternative fuels **is because** of the need to reduce air pollution. |
| EDITED | One **reason** for research into alternative fuels is **the need** to reduce air pollution. |

STRATEGY

To edit sentences containing *the reason . . . is because,* either rewrite the entire sentence or use one of these patterns.

- Drop *the reason . . . is.*

| INCORRECT | **The reason** he took up figure skating **is because** he wanted something to do during the long winter. |
| EDITED | He took up figure skating **because** he wanted something to do during the long winter. |

- Change *because* to *that.*

| EDITED | **The reason** he took up figure skating **is that** he wanted something to do during the long winter. |

Edit for Intervening Words. Watch out for words or phrases coming between the subject and the verb. Writers sometimes mistake these intervening words for the actual sentence topic.

| SHIFTED TOPIC | Programming **decisions** by television executives generally keep in mind the need to gain audience share. |

READER'S REACTION: I know that network executives can keep an audience in mind, but according to this sentence it is programming decisions that are thinking about the viewers.

| EDITED | **Television executives** making programming decisions generally **keep** in mind the need to gain audience share. |
| EDITED | When **they are making** programming decisions, **television executives** generally **keep** in mind the need to gain audience share. |

Exercise 1

 A. Rewrite the following sentences to eliminate topic shifts.

EXAMPLE

Hides ~~that are~~ treated with tanning chemicals turn ~~them~~ into leather.

1. Tanning is when animal hide is made supple and resistant to decay.
2. The first step is when the hides are thoroughly scraped and cleaned.
3. The use of diluted acid is the substance that pickles the hides to prepare them for tanning.
4. The reason leather is supple is because it is lubricated with oil after pickling, then dried and impregnated with resins.
5. The final steps are when the leather is dyed and given a shiny surface through compression.

 B. Compare your edited sentences for Exercise 1A with those produced by other writers. Decide which versions you prefer and why you prefer them.

3 Recognizing mixed grammatical patterns

Occasionally, you may begin a sentence with one grammatical pattern in mind only to shift to another partway through. The resulting sentence confuses readers.

MIXED

Because of the rebellious atmosphere generated by protests against the Vietnam war helps explain the often outrageous fashions of the time.

READER'S REACTION: When I encounter a word like *because*, I expect it to modify or qualify a main clause. But this sentence doesn't contain a main clause for it to modify. Besides, the sentence says the same thing twice: *because* and *helps explain.*

EDITED (**MAIN CLAUSE ADDED**)

Because of the rebellious atmosphere generated by protests against the Vietnam war, **fashions of the time became outrageous.**

EDITED (**REWRITTEN**)

The rebellious **atmosphere** generated by protests against the Vietnam war **helps explain** the often outrageous fashions of the time.

Mixed grammatical constructions can take so many forms that you may find them difficult to recognize and edit. The three suggestions in this Strategy may be useful, however.

25a
mixed

S T R A T E G Y

- Pay attention to the *meaning* of sentences, checking that all the elements, especially subjects and predicates, stand in clear and reasonable relationships to each other. Read aloud sentences that seem potentially confusing.

- Ask "What is the topic of this sentence, and how does the rest of the sentence comment on or rename the topic?"
- Check that the sentence clearly indicates who does what to whom.

MIXED   By wearing bell-bottom pants, love beads, long hair, and tie-dyed T-shirts was how many young people expressed their opposition to mainstream values.
This sentence ought to be edited to make clear who did what to whom.

EDITED   By wearing bell-bottom pants, love beads, long hair, and tie-dyed T-shirts, many young people expressed their opposition to mainstream values.

4 Editing mixed grammatical patterns

Because sentences can mix grammatical patterns in many different ways, you may have to study a mixed sentence carefully in order to decide how to edit it. Nonetheless, the next four Strategies for editing the following kinds of mixed sentences are relatively easy to use.

Rewrite Sentences That Begin Twice. When writers try to give more emphasis to a topic than is allowed by a sentence's structure, they often mistakenly start the sentence over again, treating the sentence's object as a second subject.

S T R A T E G Y   1

Rewrite the sentence, moving most or all of the information in one of the two main clauses to a modifying phrase or clause.

MIXED   **The new procedures for testing cosmetics, we** designed them to avoid cruelty to laboratory animals.
READER'S REACTION: It seems like the writer starts this sentence twice.

EDITED   **We** designed **the new procedures for testing cosmetics** to avoid cruelty to laboratory animals.

EDITED   **The new procedures for testing cosmetics** were designed to avoid cruelty to laboratory animals.

25a
mixed

Edit Whole Sentences Used as Subjects. Another way writers mistakenly give emphasis to a topic is to put it in a complete sentence (main clause) used incorrectly as the subject of another sentence.

S T R A T E G Y   2

Rewrite the sentence so that most or all of the information in one of the two main clauses appears instead in a modifying phrase or clause.

MIXED

In 1872, Claude Monet exhibited the painting *Impression, Sunrise* was the source of the term *Impressionism.*

EDITED (PHRASE CREATED)

The source of the term *Impressionism* was the painting *Impression, Sunrise,* **exhibited by Claude Monet in 1872.**

EDITED (CLAUSE CREATED)

In 1872, Claude Monet exhibited the painting *Impression, Sunrise,* **which was the source of the term *Impressionism.***

Rewrite Adverb Phrases or Clauses Used as Subjects. When readers encounter a phrase like "By designing the questionnaire carefully" at the beginning of a sentence, they expect it to be followed by the sentence's subject. They do not expect it to act as the subject.

S T R A T E G Y   3

Either add a new subject, or alter the form of the phrase so that it can act as a subject.

	adverb phrase
MIXED	**By designing the questionnaire carefully** made Valerie's psychology study a success.
EDITED	By designing the questionnaire carefully, **Valerie made** her psychology study a success.
EDITED	The **careful design** of the questionnaire **made** Valerie's psychology study a success.

Similarly, readers expect a clause introduced by a subordinating conjunction such as *when, because, if, while, as,* or *despite* (adverb clauses) to be followed by a main clause, not to act as a sentence subject.

S T R A T E G Y   4

Either add a subject, or rewrite the sentence by dropping the subordinating word and turning the introductory clause into a subject.

25a
mixed

MIXED

subordinate clause

Even if an audition gets off to a bad start does not mean giving up hope of getting the part.

EDITED (SUBJECT ADDED)

Even if an audition gets off to a bad start, **you** should not give up hope of getting the part.

EDITED (SUBORDINATING WORD DROPPED)

An audition that gets off to a bad start does not mean you should give up hope of getting the part.

Exercise 2

A. Rewrite the following sentences to eliminate shifts in grammatical pattern.

EXAMPLE

~~Many people used to die from infectious diseases was why~~ scientists worked hard to develop vaccinations, *because many people used to die from infectious diseases.*

1. By observing that farm workers who had had cowpox were resistant to smallpox led Jenner to develop an inoculation for smallpox in the 1790s.
2. Paying attention to Jenner's methods was why Pasteur was able to develop vaccines for chicken pox, rabies, and human anthrax.
3. Vaccinations produce antibodies are the sources of immunity.
4. Because they are not effective against all infections means that vaccinations are not a perfect solution for diseases.
5. Making sure your vaccinations are up to date, you need to do this during your regular medical checkup.

B. In a group, compare your edited sentences for Exercise 2A with those produced by other writers. Identify those edited versions you consider correct, consistent, and clear.

25b
mixed

25b Editing incomplete sentences

Incomplete sentences fail to complete an expected logical pattern, such as a comparison, or they leave out words necessary to the meaning or logic of a statement. They make readers do extra, unnecessary work. (Sentences missing a *grammatical* element are fragments; see Chapter 20.)

1 Avoiding incomplete and illogical comparisons

When readers encounter a written comparison, they expect to learn something about the relationship of the things being compared, as in the following sentence.

> The long-term costs for inexpensive, moderately reliable computers are greater than those for expensive, highly reliable computers.

If you create comparisons that are incomplete or illogical, you disappoint your readers' expectations and make them work harder to understand your writing.

Supply the Elements Missing from an Incomplete Comparison. You create an **incomplete comparison** when you omit one of the items being compared.

INCOMPLETE   The picture quality of the new DVDs, is much better.

READER'S REACTION: **They are better than what? Than they used to be? Than the old analog tapes? Than CDs?**

EDITED   The picture quality of the new DVDs is much better than **that of the older VHS tapes.**

You also create an incomplete comparison when you omit a word or words necessary to complete a comparison or make it clear.

AMBIGUOUS   The most experienced members of the maintenance staff respect the new supervisor more than their fellow workers.

READER'S REACTION: **Do the experienced staff members respect the supervisor more than they respect their fellow workers, or do they respect the supervisor more than their fellow workers do?**

CLEAR   The most experienced members of the maintenance staff respect the new supervisor more **than do** their fellow workers.

CLEAR   The most experienced members of the maintenance staff respect the new supervisor more highly **than they respect** their fellow workers.

25b
inc

To edit either kind of incomplete comparison, you must provide the missing element. However, you can omit part of the wording of a comparison when the meaning is clear without it and when the meaning can be easily inferred by readers.

CLEAR   Most customers like dealing with a bank teller better than
                        [dealing with] a machine.

                        **The second *dealing with* can be left out because the sentence
                        has only one possible meaning.**

Correct Illogical Comparisons. An **illogical comparison** seems to be
comparing things that cannot be reasonably compared.

   To make seemingly illogical comparisons reasonable, consider either
filling in the missing words or using the possessive.

   ILLOGICAL
   Even a small hamburger's fat content is higher than a skinless chicken
   breast.

   **READER'S REACTION: The writer probably wants to compare the fat content
   of two foods, but the sentence actually compares one *kind* of food (chicken
   breast) to the *fat content* of the other.**

   EDITED (WORDS PROVIDED)
   The fat content of even a small hamburger is higher than **that of** a
   skinless chicken breast.

   EDITED (POSSESSIVE USED)
   Even a small **hamburger's** fat content is higher than a skinless chicken
   breast's.

Make Comparisons Within and Between Groups Logical. When you
are comparing items belonging to the *same group,* you need to distinguish
each item (for example, field hockey) from other members of the class to
which it belongs (all *other* team sports). Otherwise, the comparison will be
illogical.

   In making such distinctions, the word *other* serves to keep the two
things separate by marking off the group as a whole from one of its members.

                        Field hockey has a higher percentage of women players than does
                        any **other** team sport.

   Therefore, if you leave out the word *other* when comparing members
of a group or class, your comparison will be illogical.

ILLOGICAL   At times, more cargo was loaded onto ships docked at New
                        Orleans than at **any** city in North America.

                        **READER'S REACTION: Do you mean that New Orleans is not in North
                        America?**

EDITED   At times, more cargo was loaded onto ships docked at New
                        Orleans than at any **other** city in North America.

25b
inc

For *different groups,* however, a comparison using the word *other* is inappropriate and illogical.

ILLOGICAL	Though he wrote in the last century, Dickens painted as vivid a picture of oppressive government and society as **any other** author writing today. **READER'S REACTION: Do you mean that Dickens is still writing even though he is dead?**
EDITED	Though he wrote in the last century, Dickens painted as vivid a picture of the ways government and society can oppress people as **any** author writing today.

2 Recognizing appropriate and inappropriate omissions

Leaving out repeated words or phrases can make a compound construction easier to read.

LEFT IN	Some presidents spend much time mastering the facts before making a major decision; others spend little **time mastering the facts before making a major decision.**
OMITTED BUT CLEAR	Some presidents spend much time mastering the facts before making a major decision; **others spend little.**

As long as they do not undermine meaning or confuse readers, **elliptical constructions** of this sort can make writing concise and effective. For example, you can frequently eliminate the word *that* from sentences where it introduces a noun clause after a verb: "Artists know [that] there is a difference between oil and acrylic paints." On some occasions, however, an omission can create confusion, so reread your sentences carefully to determine whether their intended meanings are clear.

Careless omissions of articles, prepositions, pronouns, and parts of verbs may occur when you are hurried or are focusing on the information and ideas rather than on the details of your writing. Careful editing (including reading passages aloud) is normally the best way to identify such omissions.

25b
inc

INCOMPLETE	A corporation issues common stock a way raising money. People buy stock because it can be easily converted cash and because the shares can gain in value if the company is doing well.
REVISED	A corporation issues common stock **as** a way **of** raising money. People buy stock because it can be easily converted **into** cash and because the shares can gain in value if the company is doing well.

Exercise 3

 A. Rewrite the following sentences to eliminate any incomplete or illogical constructions.

EXAMPLE

Both Shannon and Bill like tennis more than any~~ ^other~~ game.

1. His tennis serve has more speed and accuracy than Bill.
2. He also has better sense of where an opponent is going hit ball.
3. Bill's commitment to tennis is greater than his family.
4. He has more fun playing tennis.
5. Like many exercise-addicted people, Bill would be exercising than eating, and he would rather be playing tennis than doing anything else.

 B. In a small group, compare the effectiveness of your edited sentences in Exercise 3A with those of your fellow writers. Make sure the members of your group agree on what is incomplete or illogical in the original version of each sentence.

25b
inc

CHAPTER

26

Parallelism

Parallelism is the expression of similar or related ideas in similar grammatical form, as in the following sentence.

I furnished my first apartment
> with **purchases | from department stores,**
> **items | from the want ads,**
> and **gifts | from my relatives.**

Parallelism enables you to present ideas concisely while highlighting their relationships.

Parallelism can also offer pleasure and surprise. You can use it to create intriguing sentence rhythms while highlighting unexpected images and contrasts.

> According to **how** and **when** you said it, zydeco meant either **the kind of music itself,** or **the kind of two-step touch-dancing that you did at parties to the music.** In theory, this meant that you could **zydeco** to **zydeco** at the **zydeco.**
> — Susan Orlean, *Saturday Night*

> At this writing, **with** television in **more** American homes than indoor plumbing, **with more than half** of American households **possessed** of two or more TV sets, **with more than** 60 percent **possessed** of a VCR and 25 percent **possessed** of two or more VCRs, **with** the average set in use roughly seven hours a day, it is hard to recall that **for decades, for better or worse,** movies were the centerpiece of America's popular culture.
> — Todd Gitlin, "Down the Tubes"

26a Building parallelism

Readers generally find a sentence with parallel elements easy to read and understand. They also appreciate the touch of style parallelism can bring even to everyday sentences. Once you begin a parallel pattern, however, you need to complete it. Incomplete or **faulty parallelism** (with mixed structures) disappoints readers' expectations and may make sentences confusing and hard to read.

MIXED Consider swimming if you are looking for exercise that **aids** cardiovascular fitness, **overall** muscle strength, and probably **will not cause** injuries.

PARALLEL Consider swimming if you are looking for exercise that **aids** cardiovascular fitness, **develops** overall muscle strength, and **causes** few injuries.

In deciding which elements to make parallel and where to place them, you should consider each sentence's message as well as the emphasis you wish to create within an entire passage. In the following selection, for example, the poet Nikki Giovanni uses parallel structures to point out similarities between people who often see themselves as different.

> The true joy, perhaps, of being a Black American is that we really have no home. **Europeans bought** us; but the **Africans sold.** If we are to be human we must forgive **both . . . or neither.** It has become acceptable, in the last decade or so, for intellectuals to concede Black Americans **did not come here** out of our own volition; yet, I submit that just as **slavery took away our choice, so also did** the overcrowded, disease-ridden cities of Europe; **so also did** religious persecution; **so also did** the abject and all but unspeakable Inquisition of the Spanish; **so also did** starvation in Italy; **so also did** the black, rotten potatoes lying in the fields of Ireland. **No one came** to the New World in a cruise ship. **They all came** because they had to. — NIKKI GIOVANNI, "Pioneers: A View of Home"

Giovanni uses parallelism in ways that highlight and persuade. Her conclusion that African Americans and European Americans share an essentially similar immigrant experience comes up against an obvious objection: African Americans first came to the United States as slaves, and many people hold the ancestors of European Americans responsible for the slave trade. In the second sentence, therefore, Giovanni uses parallel forms ("Europeans bought," "Africans sold") to show that both Europeans and Africans shared responsibility for the slave trade. In the body of the paragraph, she points out that although African Americans came against their will ("did not come here out of our volition," "slavery took away our choice"), so did the vari-

26a
ll

ous groups of European American immigrants, a point she makes by parallel phrases beginning "so also did." The final set of statements in parallel form ("No one came" and "They all came") re-emphasizes the main point: African Americans and European Americans have much in common.

26b Editing for parallelism within the sentence

Whether you create parallelism with words, phrases, or clauses, you need to make sure all the elements employ the same grammatical forms. Your readers will also expect this consistency when you use common writing strategies such as series, paired elements (*either . . . or, neither . . . nor*), and lists.

1 Use parallelism in a series

When you place items in a series, make sure they are parallel in grammatical form. Using mixed grammatical categories can make a series clumsy and distracting.

WORDS — MIXED	To get along with their parents, teenagers need to be patient, tactful, and **to display tolerance.**
WORDS — PARALLEL	To get along with their parents, teenagers need to be patient, tactful, and **tolerant.**
PHRASES — MIXED	The singer Jim Morrison is remembered for his innovative style, his flamboyant performances, and for behavior that was self-destructive.
PHRASES — PARALLEL	The singer Jim Morrison is remembered for his innovative style, his flamboyant performances, and **his self-destructive behavior.**
CLAUSES — MIXED	In assembling the research team, we looked for engineers whose work was innovative, with broad interests, and who had boundless energy.
CLAUSES — PARALLEL	In assembling the research team, we looked for engineers whose work was innovative, **whose interests were broad, and whose energy was boundless.**

26b
//

You don't have to create word-for-word parallels. Sentence elements that differ somewhat in length and wording can still be parallel as long as they have the same structure. In creating sentences with this kind of parallelism, you need to pay attention both to the overall structural similarity and to the meaning you are trying to convey.

An effective manager must be **ready to set** goals, **willing to encourage** criticism and advice from employees, and **able to lead** by example.

The three phrases are generally parallel in structure even though they differ in length. The verb *must be* sets up the parallelism because it applies to all three phrases: *must be ready, must be willing,* and *must be able.*

Writer's Tip

In creating parallelism, make sure you repeat all words necessary to the meaning of a sentence, including all the words called for by grammatical structures or idiomatic expressions. You need not repeat a lead-in word, however, if it is the same for all elements in a series.

Mosquitoes can breed in puddles, ~~in~~ ponds, and ~~in~~ swimming pools.

If the lead-in words differ, you must include them.

You need to **chop** the cilantro, **grind** the coconut, and **grate** the nutmeg.

As you edit, read each series with the structure of the full sentence in mind so you can decide what words are necessary to the meaning.

INCOMPLETE	The main character from the novel *Tarzan of the Apes* has appeared on television, films, and comic books.
	READER'S REACTION: **Do you really mean to say he appeared *on* films and *on* comic books?**
EDITED	The main character from the novel *Tarzan of the Apes* has appeared *on* television, *in* films, and *in* comic books.

The final position in a series often receives the greatest emphasis from writers and the most attention from readers. Use this knowledge to create sentences with a strong cumulative effect, directing attention to the final element.

When VG Industries moved, the town was left with abandoned buildings, unused rail lines, and **thousands of unemployed workers.**

If you fail to make the last element in a series parallel, you undermine a potentially strong climax.

WEAK   To complete their training for the marathon, runners need stamina, courage, and, most of all, to want very much to succeed.

EFFECTIVE   To complete their training for the marathon, runners need stamina, courage, and, most of all, **ambition.**

Exercise 1

A. Underline the parallel structures in each of the following sentences.

1. We've told you about the bombs, the fires, the smashed houses, and the courage of the people.
   — EDWARD R. MURROW, "From London, September 22, 1940"
2. She looked at a man because she liked the way the hair was tucked behind his ears, or she liked the question-mark line of a long torso curving at the shoulder and straight at the hip.
   — MAXINE HONG KINGSTON, "No Name Woman"
3. But far below, in the warren of passages on the starboard side forward, in the forward holds and boiler rooms, men could see that the *Titanic's* hurt was mortal.
   — HANSON W. BALDWIN, "R.M.S. *Titanic*"
4. In that context three groups of wounded soldiers are identified: those whose survival depends on their receiving immediate treatment; those who need medical attention but will survive even if they do not get it immediately; and those who are hurt so badly they would not survive even with medical attention.
   — RUTH MACKLIN, *Mortal Choices*
5. For in each American marriage there is a special code, developed from the individual pasts of the two partners, put together out of the accidents of honeymoon and parents-in-law, finally beaten into a language that each understands imperfectly.
   — MARGARET MEAD, *Male and Female*

B. Working in a group, rewrite the following sentences to correct faulty parallelism and create appropriate emphasis. Include all necessary words. If a sentence can be rewritten in several ways, choose the version the group considers most effective.

1. What kind of job would be appropriate for a person who enjoys sailboarding, skiing, and to skydive?

2. The college's career counselor suggested that Rosalie write out her personal goals, read some materials on choosing a profession, or that she might take a career interest test.

3. Optimism, stamina, and being a good thinker are three traits of a good sales representative.

4. If you wish to choose a career at which you can succeed, you might start by making a list of the things you like to do, anything you are very good at, and also jobs or experiences you always try to avoid.

5. You can locate possible jobs in newspaper ads, friends, and employment agencies.

2 Use parallelism for paired sentence elements

When you use paired sentence elements to emphasize similarities and heighten contrasts, you should present them in parallel form.

Paired Elements Joined with Coordinating Conjunctions. Use parallel grammatical structures when you connect sentence elements with a coordinating conjunction (*and, but, or, for, nor, so,* or *yet*). The parallelism will direct your readers' attention to the relationship of the elements and make the sentence easier to read.

LACKS PARALLELISM

A well-trained scientist learns to keep a detailed lab notebook and make the entries accurately.

PARALLEL WORDS

A well-trained scientist learns to keep a **detailed and accurate** lab notebook.

26b
//

LACKS PARALLELISM

First-year chemistry courses are supposed to teach students how to take notes on an experiment and the ways of writing a lab report.

PARALLEL PHRASES

First-year chemistry courses are supposed to teach students **how to take notes on an experiment** and **how to write a lab report.**

LACKS PARALLELISM

Because she is interested in science and organizing complex information intrigues her, Lynn has decided to become a technical writer.

PARALLEL CLAUSES

Because she is interested in science and intrigued by organizing complex information, Lynn has decided to become a technical writer.

Paired Elements Joined with Correlative Conjunctions. When you wish to call special attention to a relationship or a contrast, you may wish to use pairs of connectors such as *both . . . and, not only . . . but also, either . . . or, neither . . . nor,* and *whether . . . or* (known as **correlative conjunctions**). You need to use parallel form for the elements you are joining.

> Our dilemma is clear: **either** we must reduce manufacturing costs **or** we must file for bankruptcy.

Correlative conjunctions are also effective strategies for organizing sentences with long phrases or clauses.

ORIGINAL
People in this country claim to marry "for love," yet their pairings follow clear social patterns. They choose partners from the same social class and economic level. Most marriages bring together people with similar educational and cultural backgrounds. Similarities in race and ethnic background are important as well.

EDITED (CORRELATIVE CONJUNCTIONS ADDED)
People in this country claim to marry "for love," yet their pairings follow clear social patterns. They choose partners **not only with the same class and economic background but also with the same educational, cultural, racial, and ethnic background.**

The items you link with correlative conjunctions should be clearly related in meaning and similar in grammatical form. If you fail to match the elements that follow the first and second connectors, you may create a sentence that is hard to follow or unclear in meaning.

AMBIGUOUS
Léon Blum's election represented a significant change in French politics and society because he was not only the first Socialist premier but also the first Jew.

PRECISE (PARALLELISM ADDED)
Léon Blum's election represented a significant change in French politics and society because he was not only the **first Socialist premier** but also **the first Jewish premier.**

Comparison and Contrast. Putting items to be compared or contrasted into parallel form helps you call attention to them.

26b
//

DRAFT   This new ingredient will reduce the calories in our frozen yogurt, and the yogurt will have more taste.

EDITED   This new ingredient in our frozen yogurt will **reduce the calories** and **improve the taste.**

As you edit, you may wish to create sentences built around pairs of parallel phrases and clauses (known as **balanced sentences**). This strategy is particularly useful if you wish to emphasize a sense of balance between opposing ideas. (The use of parallel structure to develop contrast is called **antithesis.**)

> If women are not always perfectly satisfied by their friendships with women, neither are all men perfectly happy with their friendships with men.   — DEBORAH TANNEN, *You Just Don't Understand*

> The only thing history teaches us, a wise man once said, is that history doesn't teach us anything.   — MICHAEL LEWIS, *Liar's Poker*

Writer's Alert

When you use two parallel clauses beginning with *who(m), which,* or *that,* check that both clauses begin with the same relative pronoun. If they do not, the clauses will lack parallelism because they will not have the same grammatical form.

LACKS PARALLELISM   The sailor embarking on hazardous voyages and who wore one earring of his lover's matched pair believed he would always be reunited with her.

PARALLEL   The sailor **who** embarked on hazardous voyages and **who** wore one earring of his lover's matched pair believed he would always be reunited with her.

Because nouns and adjectives are different parts of speech (see 15a-1 and 15a-5), the two cannot be parallel in grammatical form or perform the same function within a sentence.

                                                              adjective
LACKS PARALLELISM   Sociologists view marriage as both a **social** and a
                    noun
system of economics.

PARALLEL   Sociologists view marriage as both a **social** and an **economic** system.

Exercise 2

A. Rewrite the following sentences to eliminate faulty parallelism.

EXAMPLE

In choosing a career, you should plan carefully and ~~also~~ some research ~~is needed.~~

1. Anthony could not decide whether he wanted to be a lawyer or if investment banking was a more promising career.
2. His friends thought Anthony's career plans were not suited to his abilities and his interests didn't fit the plans either.
3. After thinking about his goals, Anthony realized that the two things he wanted most from a career were stability and an income that was reasonable.
4. The counselor suggested that he might consider either working for the federal government or a job with a large, stable corporation.
5. Anthony had been reading about corporations in financial trouble and which had been laying off employees, so he decided to look carefully at government jobs.

B. Working with a group of fellow students, gather a number of pamphlets offering advice. Campus offices, libraries, clinics, banks, and similar places usually provide pamphlets on all kinds of subjects, from health care and home safety to job hunting. Choose one of the pamphlets, identify those places where parallelism is used effectively with paired sentence elements, and edit to correct any faulty parallelism. Enhance the parallelism when appropriate in order to highlight ideas and their relationships.

26c Editing for parallelism beyond the sentence

As you write or edit, you can use parallelism beyond the sentence level to organize clusters of sentences and even paragraphs. By introducing parallelism into a draft essay, you can often clarify complicated information for readers or highlight the overall pattern of an argument or explanation.

1 Use parallelism in sentence clusters

By adding parallelism to groups of sentences, you call attention to **sentence clusters,** groups of sentences that develop related ideas or information. You can use parallel elements to link related items, guide readers through the steps in an explanation or argument, and highlight patterns like cause-effect and comparison (see 8c–8e on patterns of development).

One way you can draw readers' attention to a sentence cluster is through using parallel sentence openers. For example, in editing a draft of the following passage, the writer added parallel sentence openings to link the examples, thereby emphasizing the general applicability of the experience she is discussing.

> Each of us probably belongs to several organizations whose values are in conflict. **You may belong to** a religious organization that **endorses restraint in** alcohol use or **in** relations between the sexes while at the same time **you belong to** a social group whose activities seem to endorse a contrasting set of values. **You may belong to** a sports team **that endorses** conflict and winning and a club **that promotes** understanding among people and conflict resolution. **You may belong to** a political club whose platform contradicts the policies of your professional organization.

The loose parallelism within the sentences also helps reinforce the writer's opening point about conflicting values.

Did You Know?

Many well-known writers make frequent and skillful use of parallelism. Here is E. B. White.

The yellow squash illuminates the aging vine, the black-billed cuckoo taps out his hollow message in code (a series of three dots), and zinnias stand as firm and quiet as old valorous deeds. This is the day the farmer picks up the first pullet egg, a brown and perfect jewel in the grass; the day a car stops and a man gets out and tacks up a poster advertising the country fair. You couldn't get us to swap this one day for any six other days.

And here is Annie Dillard.

Back in New Orleans where he was headed they would play the old stuff, the hot, rough stuff—bastardized for tourists maybe, but still the big and muddy source of it all. Back in New Orleans where he was headed the music would smell like the river itself, maybe, like a thicker, older version of the Allegheny River at Pittsburgh, where he heard the music beat in the roar of his boat's inboard motor; like a thicker, older version of the wide Ohio River at Louisville, Kentucky, where at his family's summer house he'd spend his boyhood summers mucking about in boats.

—E. B. White, "Late August," in *Writings from* The New Yorker: *1927–1976*, ed. Rebecca M. Dale (New York: HarperCollins, 1990) 74, and Annie Dillard, *An American Childhood* (New York: HarperCollins, 1987) 6.

26c
//

2 Use parallel paragraphs

Paragraphs that are parallel in structure and wording can help you reinforce the overall pattern of a report or essay and alert readers to your line of argument or explanation. The parallel element can be as simple and unobtrusive as a brief opening phrase for each paragraph.

One reason for acting on this recommendation now is that the flooding gets worse every spring.

A second reason for action is that the city currently has a budget surplus that could be spent on drainage improvement.

A third, and most important, reason for taking immediate steps is that the health and safety of city residents is endangered by the floods.

You can also employ parallel elements to create patterns of repetition that clarify a complicated explanation or that convey patterns of thought such as cause-effect analysis, comparison-contrast, or classification (see 8e).

Exercise 3

A. Underline all examples of parallelism in the following passage.

Large computers have some essential attributes of an intelligent brain: they have large memories, and they have gates whose connections can be modified by experience. However, the thinking of these computers tends to be narrow. The richness of human thought depends to a considerable degree on the enormous number of wires, or nerve fibers, coming into each gate in the human brain. A gate in a computer has two, or three, or at most four wires entering on one side, and one wire coming out the other side. In the human brain, a gate may have as many as 100,000 wires entering it. Each wire comes from another gate or nerve cell. This means that every gate in the human brain is connected to as many as 100,000 other gates in other parts of the brain. During the process of thinking innumerable gates open and close throughout the brain. When one of these gates "decides" to open, the decision is the result of a complicated assessment involving inputs from thousands of other gates. This circumstance explains much of the difference between human thinking and computer thinking. — ROBERT JASTROW, "Brains and Computers"

B. Working in a group, decide what each example of parallelism in Exercise 3A contributes to the effectiveness of an individual sentence or the entire passage. Note any differences of opinion, and discuss whether these difference reveal alternative ways of viewing the meaning or purpose of the passage.

26c
//

26d Maintaining parallelism in lists

Lists can summarize key points, instructions, or stages in a process. To avoid confusing readers, edit lists to make sure the elements are as nearly parallel as possible.

UNEDITED (CONFUSING)

The early 1960s were characterized by the following social phenomena.

1. A growing civil rights movement
2. Kennedy pursued a strongly anticommunist foreign policy.
3. An emphasis on youth in culture and politics
4. Taste in music and the visual arts was changing.
5. Government support for scientific research increased greatly.

EDITED (CLEAR)

The early 1960s were characterized by the following social phenomena.

1. **A growing** civil rights movement
2. **A strongly** anticommunist foreign policy (encouraged by President Kennedy)
3. **A youthful** emphasis in culture and politics
4. **A changing** taste in music and the visual arts
5. **A marked** increase in government support for scientific research

If you present every item on a list in a different grammatical form, readers must shift expectations often and will find it difficult to concentrate on the differences and similarities between the items. Parallelism makes it easy for readers to pay attention to the ideas and information in the list, and it encourages readers to compare the items covered in the list.

Exercise 4

 A. Arrange the following materials into a list whose elements maintain parallel form.

The awards for arts and entertainment for 1985 offer an interesting picture of American culture in the middle of that decade.

Academy Award: *Out of Africa* (Best Picture); William Hurt, *Kiss of the Spider Woman* (Best Actor); Geraldine Page, *The Trip to Bountiful* (Best Actress); Don Ameche, *Cocoon* (Best Supporting Actor); Anjelica Huston, *Prizzi's Honor* (Best Supporting Actress).

The Emmy Awards went to *The Golden Girls* (Outstanding Comedy Series), *Cagney & Lacey* (Outstanding Drama Series), William Daniels and Sharon Gless (Outstanding Lead Actor/Actress in a Drama Series), and Michael J. Fox and Betty White (Outstanding Lead Actor/Actress in a Comedy Series).

Tony Awards for Broadway Theater. Best Play: *As Is* by William Hoffman. Best Musical: *Big River* by Roger Miller.

MTV Video Music Awards. Best Video: Don Henley, "The Boys of Summer." Best Male Video: Bruce Springsteen, "I'm on Fire." Best Female Video: Tina Turner, "What's Love Got to Do with It." Best Group Video: USA for Africa, "We Are the World."

 B. Compare your list for Exercise 4A with the lists of several other students. Note any differences in the ways your lists are organized.

26d
//

CHAPTER

27

Coordination and Subordination

Suppose you were asked to edit a report containing the following passage. Reading it for the first time, you notice that the sentences are short and choppy and that they fail to emphasize connections among the ideas.

> California's farmers ship fresh lettuce, avocados, and other produce to supermarkets. They never send fresh olives. Fresh olives contain a substance that makes them bitter. They are very unpleasant tasting. Farmers soak fresh olives in a solution that removes oleuropein, the bitter-tasting substance. They make sure just enough is left behind to produce the tangy "olive" taste.

How could you edit the passage to make the sentences read more smoothly and to help readers see relationships among the statements? You could *coordinate* the sentences by linking them with a comma and a coordinating conjunction (*and, but, or, for, nor, so,* and *yet*), with a semicolon plus a conjunctive adverb (like *however*), or with either a semicolon or a colon. Using **coordination,** you indicate how the sentences are related and you give equal emphasis to each of the linked statements.

COORDINATED
> California's farmers ship fresh lettuce, avocados, and other produce to supermarkets**, but** they never send fresh olives. Fresh olives contain a substance that makes them bitter**, so** they are very unpleasant tasting. Farmers soak fresh olives in a solution that removes oleuropein, the bitter-tasting substance**; however,** they make sure just enough is left behind to produce the tangy "olive" taste.

You could also make some of the sentences modify others by using **subordination.** By beginning some of the sentences with subordinating words (such as *because, although,* and *since*) and attaching these sentences to others, you specify the relationships between ideas and indicate their relative weight.

SUBORDINATED

California's farmers ship fresh lettuce, avocados, and other produce to supermarkets, **though** they never send fresh olives. **Because** fresh olives contain a substance that makes them bitter, they are very unpleasant tasting. **When** farmers soak fresh olives in a solution that removes oleuropein, the bitter-tasting substance, they make sure just enough is left behind to produce the tangy "olive" taste.

27a Using coordination

When you want to link words, clauses, or phrases and emphasize their equal weight, use coordination.

WORDS	trims **and** shapes
PHRASES	in the shallow water, near the islands, **or** in the middle of the main channel
MAIN CLAUSES	The winter freeze prevents boats from sailing**,** **but** the residents are still able to fish through holes in the ice.

When you coordinate main (independent) clauses (see 15c-d), you create a single sentence, known as a **compound sentence,** that gives equal prominence to the ideas in each clause.

Winds of almost one hundred miles per hour surge through the surrounding river valleys**,** **and** these winds create violent storms on the lake during spring and summer.

Effective coordination enables you to specify and highlight relationships between ideas.

RELATIONSHIPS NOT SPECIFIED	Cats have no fear of water. They do not like getting their fur wet and matted. Cats like to feel clean and well groomed.
CLEAR RELATIONSHIPS	Cats have no fear of water**,** **but** they do not like getting their fur wet and matted**;** they like to feel clean and well groomed.
CHOPPY	Cats are able to swim. A hungry cat will gladly jump into water to catch a fish. House cats are usually well fed. They are not willing to get soaked for an extra bite to eat.

27a coord

SMOOTHER Cats are able to swim, **and** a hungry cat will gladly jump into water to catch a fish. House cats are usually well fed; **therefore,** they are not willing to get soaked for an extra bite to eat.

Editing for Coordination

WORDS AND PHRASES

1. **Use *and, but, or, nor,* or *yet* (coordinating conjunctions).**

   cut **and** hemmed   smooth **or** textured   intrigued **yet** suspicious

2. **Use pairs like *either . . . or, neither . . . nor,* and *not only . . . but also.***

   either music therapy **or** pet therapy

   not only a nursing care plan **but also** a psychological treatment program

MAIN (INDEPENDENT) CLAUSES

1. **Use *and, but, or, for, nor, so,* or *yet* (coordinating conjunctions) preceded by a comma.**

   The psychology students observed the responses of supermarket shoppers to long lines, **and** they interviewed a number of people waiting in line.

   Most people in the study were irritated by the lines at the checkout counter, **yet** a considerable minority found the wait enjoyable.

2. **Use a semicolon (see 33a).**

   The wait provoked physical reactions in some people; they fidgeted, grimaced, and stared at the ceiling.

3. **Use conjunctive adverbs like *however, moreover, nonetheless, thus,* and *consequently* (see 15a-6) preceded by a semicolon.**

   Store managers can take simple steps to speed up checkout lines; **however,** they seldom pay much attention to the problem.

4. **Use a colon (see 33b).**

   Tabloids and magazines in racks by the checkout counters serve a good purpose: they give customers something to read while waiting.

27a
coord

Writer's Tip

Do you sometimes want to emphasize the *contrast* between two main clauses? Do you occasionally want to get readers themselves to think about the relationship between the ideas and information in the clauses? Consider using a colon to create these effects.

> People gain weight during the winter holidays ; they try to lose it before the summer holidays.

When you use a second clause to illustrate, sum up, or comment on the preceding clause and you want to give this relationship particularly forceful emphasis, you might join the clauses with a colon.

> For three weeks we used a new program of radio and television ads to invite customers to our once-a-year sale : they came in droves.

Both a colon and a semicolon alone create an abrupt stop between clauses, unlike other connectives such as *and* and *moreover*. This stop generally encourages readers to single out each clause for attention.

Exercise 1

A. Combine each of the following pairs of sentences into a single sentence using coordination. Make sure you use each of the strategies listed in the preceding table for joining main clauses, and do not use any particular conjunction (such as *and* or *however*) more than once. Rewrite the sentences if necessary to avoid awkwardness or confusion.

EXAMPLE

Winter weather makes outdoor exercise difficult ,so Winter has its own forms of exercise.

1. Ice skating can be enjoyable. It is also physically demanding.
2. Recreational skaters need to be in good shape physically. They should exercise to increase their fitness.
3. Skaters who are not in good shape get tired quickly. These skaters are also more likely to pull a muscle or fall.
4. To get in shape for skating, try a program of regular exercise for at least several weeks. Pay special attention to exercises focusing on knees and ankles.
5. Other areas to exercise are hip and leg muscles. Exercises aimed at each muscle group are best.

**27a
coord**

B. Working with a group of fellow writers, prepare a brief paragraph (five to seven sentences) offering advice on some subject: fitness, cooking, appliance repair, gardening, or the like. Make sure all but one or two of the sentences are compound sentences containing at least two main clauses. Connect the clauses using a variety of strategies for co-ordination, making sure they are appropriate for your subject and purpose.

---

1 Edit for excessive coordination

If you use words like *and, so,* or *but* simply to string together loosely related sentences, you risk boring readers with excessive coordination. This problem often arises during drafting when you jot down ideas quickly. Later on, while editing, you need to complete the job of specifying their relationships.

DRAFT	Ripe fruit spoils quickly, **and** the fresh grapefruit for sale in supermarkets is picked before it matures to avoid spoilage, **and** it can taste bitter, **but** the grapefruit in cans is picked later, **and** it tastes sweeter.
EDITED	Ripe fruit spoils quickly. The fresh grapefruit for sale in supermarkets is picked before it matures, **so** it can taste bitter. The grapefruit in cans is picked later; **consequently,** it tastes sweeter.

Even if you have specified relationships through coordination, you need to edit carefully. Too much coordination and too many conjunctions can create sentences that are "stringy" or hard to follow.

STRINGY	The toy was designed in Japan, **but** its parts are made in Brazil, **and** it is assembled in St. Louis, **so** what is the country of origin for tax purposes?
EDITED	The toy was designed in Japan, its parts are made in Brazil, **and** it is assembled in St. Louis. What is the country of origin for tax purposes?

27a
coord

Writer's Tip

You can punctuate three or more coordinated main clauses as a series, placing a coordinating conjunction only before the last clause. (See 26b-1 on using a series to create emphasis.)

The lawyers drew up the contract, the accountants checked it for accuracy, **and** we signed it in good faith.

---

2 Edit for illogical coordination

Check that clauses you have linked (or plan to link) by coordination are related closely enough to deserve equal emphasis within a single sentence. To correct illogical coordination, try adding information to a sentence or changing its emphasis.

ILLOGICAL   Antarctica is a remote continent with an unusually harsh climate, and scientists are now studying its unique animal life in detail.
READER'S REACTION: **What do the remoteness and the climate have to do with either the scientists or the animals?**

EDITED   Antarctica's remoteness and harsh climate **have made exploration difficult**, and scientists are **only now beginning detailed study** of its unique animal life.

EDITED   Antarctica is a remote continent with an unusually harsh climate **;** **therefore,** much of its animal life is unique.

Don't coordinate clauses unless they belong together logically.

ILLOGICAL   Miles Davis was an innovative musician, and record companies often made sure his album covers featured him in a dramatic pose.
READER'S REACTION: **I can't see any relationship between the qualities of Davis's music and the choice of album covers.**

EDITED   Miles Davis was an innovative musician, and the title of his album *Birth of the Cool* reflects his progressive approach.

EDITED   Miles Davis attracted many listeners because of his "star quality"; therefore, record companies often made sure his album covers featured him in a dramatic pose.

> ### Writer's Tip
> *And* connects ideas that are similar or closely related, emphasizing their likeness. *But* and *yet* emphasize contrasts and unlikeness. If you fall into a habit of using only *and,* you may miss appropriate occasions for *but* and *yet,* creating inappropriate connections in the process.

**27a
coord**

Make sure you link clauses in ways that indicate their relationships precisely and clearly.

VAGUE   Penguins swim in frigid water and stand on ice, **and** their feet never seem to freeze.

EDITED TO SHOW
CONTRAST
Penguins swim in frigid water and stand on ice **, yet** their feet never seem to freeze.

Exercise 2

A. Revise the following passage to eliminate excessive or illogical coordination. Combine short sentences with coordination when appropriate to clarify relationships and eliminate choppiness.

Working for someone else can be unrewarding, and this is also true of working for a large corporation, so many people in their early thirties decide to open businesses of their own, but they often do not have very original ideas, so they open restaurants or small retail stores, for these are the small businesses they are most familiar with, yet they are also the ones that are most likely to fail, and they face the most competition. Franchises are small businesses, and they often provide help to people getting into business on their own for the first time. Fast-food restaurants are often franchises, and they are quite expensive to start up, or they face a lot of competition. What many potential small-business owners fail to investigate are the many less familiar kinds of franchise operations. Enterprising people can own the local office of an armored car service, or they can run a regional unit of a nation-wide cleaning service for commercial buildings, and they can open hardware stores with the name of a national chain over the front door. Electronics stores, fabric stores, and real estate offices can be locally owned yet parts of a national chain, so people who want to be their own bosses have many opportunities.

B. Work with a group of fellow writers to produce two versions of the passage in Exercise 2A, each with a different emphasis.

27b Using subordination

In sentences containing subordination, one clause modifies another and in so doing helps readers perceive links between ideas or information.

1 Edit and punctuate for subordination

To create a sentence using subordination, you present a central idea in a main (or independent) clause and add a **subordinate clause** that modifies, qualifies, or comments on the ideas or information in the main clause. You signal the relationship to readers by beginning the subordinate clause with a subordinating word like *because, while, although, who, which,* or *that* (see list in 27b-2) and by attaching the subordinate clause to the main clause. (A sentence with a main clause and one or more subordinate clauses is a **complex sentence.**)

In using subordination, you create a sentence with unequal elements: one presenting the central idea (main clause), and one (or more) acting as a modifier (subordinate clause).

MAIN CLAUSES   I use a personal computer to keep track of my finances. I know how much rent I pay each year for my apartment.

SUBORDINATED   **Because** I use a personal computer to keep track of my finances, I know how much rent I pay each year for my apartment.
READER'S REACTION: Now I know how the ideas relate—one is a cause and the other an effect.

MAIN CLAUSES   Most first-time home buyers are people in their late twenties or early thirties. They have tired of paying rent.

SUBORDINATED   Most first-time home buyers are people in their late twenties or early thirties **who** have tired of paying rent.
READER'S REACTION: The second clause adds information to the statement presented in the first and ties the ideas together.

SUBORDINATED   Sales of single-family homes are up, **although** sales of the more expensive homes are still depressed.
READER'S REACTION: The second clause not only qualifies the meaning of the opening statement—it also takes the sentence in a new direction.

SUBORDINATED   I am saving money **so that** I can make a down payment **as soon as** I find an affordable house.
READER'S REACTION: I like the way the subordinate clauses add more and more focus to the opening statement.

2 Indicate relationships through subordination

As you write and edit, you can use subordination to precisely describe the relationships among ideas or information. Subordination enables you to put some information in the foreground (in a main clause) and other information in the background (in a subordinate clause). Thus, you can help readers distinguish primary statements from secondary statements, new information and ideas from old, and important information from background.

SECONDARY/ PRIMARY   **Although** energy costs are declining, costs for raw materials have more than doubled in the past six months.
READER'S REACTION: *Although* shows the declining energy costs to be less important than the rising costs of raw materials.

27b
sub

Creating and Punctuating Subordination

SUBORDINATING CONJUNCTIONS

You can use a subordinating conjunction such as *although, because,* or *since* (see list on page 409) to create a subordinate clause at the beginning or end of a sentence. (See 15d on adverb clauses.)

PUNCTUATION WITH SUBORDINATING CONJUNCTIONS

Use a comma *after* an introductory clause that begins with a subordinating conjunction.

At the end of a sentence, do not use commas if the clause is *essential* to the meaning of the main clause (restrictive); use commas if the clause is *not essential* (nonrestrictive). (See 22c.)

BEGINNING   **Once she understood the problem,** she had no trouble solving it.

END   Radar tracking of flights began **after several commercial airliners collided in midair.**
Essential

END   The present air traffic control system works reasonably well, **although accidents still occur.**
Nonessential

RELATIVE PRONOUNS

You can use a relative pronoun (*who, which, that*) to create a relative clause (also called an adjective clause) at the end or in the middle of a sentence. (See 15d on adjective clauses.)

PUNCTUATION WITH RELATIVE PRONOUNS

If the modifying clause contains information that is *not essential* to the meaning of the main clause, the modifying clause is nonrestrictive and you should set it off with commas. If the information is *essential,* the modifying clause is restrictive and you should not set it off with commas. (See 22c.)

RESTRICTIVE   The anthropologists discovered the site of a building **that early settlers used as a meetinghouse.**

NON-RESTRICTIVE   At one end of the site they found remains of a smaller building, **which may have been a storage shed.**

RESTRICTIVE   The people **who organized the project** work for the Public Archaeology Lab.

NON-RESTRICTIVE   A graduate student, **who was leading a dig nearby,** first discovered signs of the meetinghouse.

27b
sub

Expressing Relationships Through Subordination

TIME	before, while, until, since, once, whenever, whereupon, after, when
CAUSE	because, since
RESULT	in order that, so that, that
CONCESSION OR CONTRAST	although, though, even though, as if, while, as though
PLACE	where, wherever
CONDITION	if, whether, provided, unless, rather than
COMPARISON	as
IDENTIFICATION	that, which, who

OLD/NEW **Though** most biographies of Charles Dickens have spent considerable time examining his experiences as a child, his latest biographer pays little attention to these important events.

IMPORTANT/ BACKGROUND Raymond Carver, **who** died in 1990, created a stir with his "minimalist" short stories.

You can also vary the meaning of a sentence considerably, depending on the subordinating conjunction you choose.

As soon as the copier is repaired, we can print the newsletter.

Whenever the copier is repaired, we can print the newsletter.

If the copier is repaired, we can print the newsletter.

In addition, subordination can help you turn short, choppy sentences into smooth, graceful ones.

CHOPPY For each moon, the Seneca have a name. They draw the name from the season. The sixth moon is called the Strawberry Moon. Strawberries ripen in June.

EDITED For each moon, the Seneca have a name **which** they draw from the season. **Because** strawberries ripen in June, the sixth moon is called the Strawberry Moon.

27b sub

Exercise 3

A. Use subordination to combine each of the following pairs of sentences. Choose appropriate subordinating conjunctions, and create emphasis consistent with each sentence's meaning. Rewrite the clauses if necessary to produce effective sentences.

EXAMPLE

Newspapers often contain reports of car accidents. ~~The accidents~~ *that*
were preventable.

1. Comedian Sam Kinison died in a car crash. A pickup truck swerved across the road and hit his car.
2. Kinison was not wearing a seat belt. A seat belt might have saved his life.
3. Driving quickly off the road to the right is one thing you can do. This will help you avoid collisions.
4. Drive a large car. Big, heavy cars and passenger vans are much safer in crashes.
5. Buying a car with front and side impact air bags is an excellent way to reduce your chances of getting injured or dying. These cars cost more money.

B. Working with a group of fellow students, conduct some research to determine which subordinating words are widely used. Each person should locate a five- to seven-paragraph segment of a magazine article and make a list of all the subordinating words in it, tallying the number of times each word appears. (The list on page 409 and a dictionary can help you decide whether a word is a subordinator.) Pool your lists, and determine how often the various words appear in the articles you sampled.

**27b
sub**

3 Edit for illogical subordination

Sometimes the subordinating word you choose may fail to specify a relationship clearly or correctly.

S T R A T E G Y

To identify illogical subordination, state a sentence's meaning to yourself with slightly different wording. You may discover that the original sentence does not convey your intended meaning or that the subordinating word you have chosen can convey several conflicting meanings. In either case, edit the sentence by choosing a more appropriate subordinator. The list on page 409 provides alternatives.

UNCLEAR EMPHASIS	Since she taught junior high school, Jean developed keen insight into the behavior of twelve- and thirteen-year-olds. **READER'S REACTION: I'm not sure whether** *since* **here means she developed insights** *because* **she was a teacher or** *after* **she quit teaching.**
EDITED	**Because** she taught junior high school, Jean developed keen insight into the behavior of twelve- and thirteen-year-olds.

Watch out, too, for subordination that confuses readers by putting key ideas in a subordinate clause and secondary ideas in a main clause. To correct this problem, make sure the main clause presents the sentence's most important statement.

FAULTY	His training and equipment were inferior, although Jim was still able to set a school record throwing the discus. **READER'S REACTION: Isn't Jim's achievement the key point?**
EDITED	**Although** his training and equipment were inferior, Jim was still able to set a school record throwing the discus.

Did You Know?

The conjunctions *because* and *for* offer you two different ways to arrange sentences dealing with causes and effects. *Because* creates subordination; *for* creates coordination. Here is what one authority on style and usage has to say about these words and ways to use them.

BECAUSE/FOR
Often interchangeable. *Because* clearly indicates cause or reason: "They stayed at home because it was snowing." *For* (after a comma) normally joins two independent statements and may suggest cause, reason, or evidence. Cause or reason: "They stayed at home, for it was snowing." Evidence: "They may have decided to drive into town, for faint tire tracks remain in their driveway."
J. N. Hook, *The Appropriate Word* (Reading, MA: Addison, 1990) 34.

27b
sub

4 Edit for troublesome subordinators

Certain subordinators can be ambiguous, confusing, or simply incorrect and therefore irritating to your readers. These subordinators come in two groups: (1) *as* and *while,* and (2) *and which, but that,* and *and who.* Be alert for these words as you edit, and use the following discussions to help you make the correct choice.

As, While. You can use *as* correctly to create a comparison, or you can use it to indicate simultaneous events.

COMPARISON — Our team spent **as much** time on the accounting problems **as** the other, less successful teams did.

TIME — They began interviewing students **as** the semester was coming to an end.

However, if you use *as* to point out a cause-effect relationship, you will probably confuse some readers. Other readers may consider this use of *as* unacceptable in standard written English.

AMBIGUOUS — **As** the level of achievement in the morning and afternoon classes differed, the researchers looked for possible explanations.
READER'S REACTION: Does *as* mean "while" or "because"?

EDITED — **Because** the level of achievement in the morning and afternoon classes differed, the researchers looked for possible explanations.

Do not use *as* in place of *whether* or *that.* This substitution is always incorrect in writing and formal speaking.

INCORRECT — They were not sure **as** the differences in achievement were significant.

EDITED — They were not sure **whether** the differences in achievement were significant.

EDITED — They were not sure **that** the differences in achievement were significant.

While can indicate events occurring at the same time. *While* can also signal a concession.

SIMULTANEOUS EVENTS — I can get some work done at home **while** the children are at school.

CONCESSION — **While** she thinks the presentation was a success, I am not so sure.

Nonetheless, *while* may be ambiguous in some sentences, and you may need to replace it with another, clearer subordinator.

**27b
sub**

UNCLEAR	**While** they interviewed the students, the researchers did not come to any conclusions. **READER'S REACTION: Does** *while* **mean "although" or "when"?**
EDITED	**When** they interviewed the students, the researchers did not come to any conclusions.
EDITED	**Although** they interviewed the students, the researchers did not come to any conclusions.

In addition, *while* is never an acceptable replacement for *but* or *and*.

INCORRECT	One researcher claimed that teachers in the morning classes were more effective than those in the afternoon, **while** the other researcher disagreed.
CORRECT	One researcher claimed that teachers in the morning classes were more effective than those in the afternoon, **but** the other researcher disagreed.

And Which, But That, And Who. When you place *and* or *but* at the head of a clause along with *which, that,* or *who,* you add an unnecessary word and confuse readers by obscuring the relationship signaled by the subordinating word.

CONFUSING	The research was funded by the Champlin Foundation, **and which** also published the results.
EDITED	The research was funded by the Champlin Foundation, **which** also published the results.

5 Edit for excessive subordination

When you use too much subordination in a sentence, you create a pattern of relationships so intricate that it overloads readers. To clear up such confusion, separate your ideas into several sentences, and rewrite them so that readers can grasp your meaning more easily.

CONFUSING	The election for mayor will be interesting this year **because** the incumbent has decided to run as an independent **while** his former challenger for the Democratic nomination has decided to accept the party's endorsement **even though** the Republican nominee is her former campaign manager **who** switched parties last week.
EDITED	The election for mayor will be interesting this year. The incumbent has decided to run as an independent. His former challenger for the Democratic nomination has decided to accept the party's endorsement **even though** she will have

27b
sub

to run against her former campaign manager. He switched parties last week to become the Republican nominee.

Exercise 4

A. Revise the following sentences to eliminate illogical, incorrect, or excessive subordination. Combine short sentences through subordination when appropriate to clarify relationships and eliminate choppiness.

EXAMPLE

Because
~~Since~~ my doctor said I need more exercise, I have been looking for a sport I might enjoy.

1. As I am not particularly good at athletics, I want a sport that is not too demanding. I would also like a sport that is fun.
2. I enjoy volleyball, although it is a serious, highly competitive sport demanding considerable quickness and coordination. Volleyball is not the answer.
3. Since I have played tennis, I have thought about trying out for the tennis team. I have also thought about talking this idea over with the tennis coach.
4. Some of my friends think I should give the tennis team a try while others think the idea is laughable.
5. What I really want to find is a brand-new sports program, and which will give me the training I need, because I don't have the experience necessary to succeed in established sports, although I am willing to work as hard as I need to in order to bring my skills up to a competitive level.

B. Working in a group, share your revisions of the sentences in Exercise 4A. Decide which versions of the sentences are the best, and be ready to explain and defend your choices.

ESL Advice: Grammatical Structures for Coordination and Subordination

It is good composition style to use the four varying sentence types in your writing: the simple sentence, the compound sentence, the complex sentence, and the compound-complex sentence (see 15e-1).

Using coordination to form a compound sentence

When you combine two simple sentences to make a compound sentence, you can use a coordinating conjunction, a conjunctive adverb, or a semicolon.

Coordinators		
COORDINATING CONJUNCTION	**CONJUNCTIVE ADVERB**	**MEANING**
, and	; in addition, ; furthermore,	adds something
, but	; in contrast,	gives an opposite
, yet	; however, ; nonetheless,	gives a contrast
, so	; therefore, ; thus, ; consequently,	gives a result
, for		shows cause
, or	; otherwise,	shows choice
, nor		gives a negative

Notice how the different ways of creating a compound sentence offer variety and subtle changes of meaning.

	main clause + main clause
COMPOUND SENTENCE	The helicopter is a versatile aircraft, **and** it can be used for many kinds of jobs.

	main clause + main clause
COMPOUND SENTENCE	The helicopter is a versatile aircraft; **therefore,** it can be used for many kinds of jobs.

	main clause + main clause
COMPOUND SENTENCE	The helicopter is a versatile aircraft; it can be used for many kinds of jobs.

Using subordination to form a complex sentence

When you combine a simple sentence with a dependent clause to form a complex sentence, you use a subordinating conjunction.

	subordinate clause main clause
COMPLEX SENTENCE	**After** the invention of the helicopter in the 1930s, this aircraft became very useful in rescue missions.

	main clause subordinate clause
COMPLEX SENTENCE	Many rescue missions have been successful **because** helicopters take off and land vertically.

27b
sub
ESL

Using coordination and subordination to form a compound-complex sentence

When you combine two main clauses and a dependent clause, you use both coordination and subordination.

	subordinate clause

COMPOUND-
COMPLEX
SENTENCE

Because the helicopter can fly in any direction and hover in

	main clause		main clause

midair, it can maneuver in many places, **and** this versatility makes it useful for all kinds of jobs.

Subordinating Conjunctions

FOR ADJECTIVE CLAUSES

that	when
who	where
which	why
whom	
whose	

FOR ADVERB CLAUSES

TIME		**CONTRAST**	**CONDITION**
after	as	although	as long as
as soon as	before	though	if
once	since	even though	in case
until	when	while	provided that
whenever	while	whereas	unless
			whether . . . or not

PLACE	**PURPOSE**	**REASON**	**RESULT**
where	so that	because	so . . . that
wherever	in order that	since	such . . . that

FOR NOUN CLAUSES

who	where	however
whom	why	how much
whose	whether	how many
what	that	how long
which	which	how often

27b
sub
ESL

Writer's Alert

It is necessary to use coordinators or subordinators when you write different sentence types, but you must be careful not to mix the two grammatical structures.

MIXED	**Although** frogs can live both on land and in water, **but** they need to breathe oxygen. **This sentence has both a subordinator, *although*, and a coordinator, *but*. You must use one pattern, but not both.**

	main clause
CORRECT COORDINATION	Frogs can live both on land and in water, **but**
	main clause
	they need to breathe oxygen.

	subordinate clause
CORRECT SUBORDINATION	**Although** frogs can live both on land and in
	main clause
	water, they need to breathe oxygen.

27b
sub
ESL

EDITING FOR WORD CHOICE

28

Choosing Appropriate Words

When you search for appropriate words, you will want first to ask yourself whether you have used the correct word to express your intended meaning. Consider the following sentence.

Dr. Parsippani [*caused to die*] Mr. Rollet.

In this sentence, several words meaning "cause to die" could fill the slot, including *killed, slaughtered, assassinated, exterminated,* and *murdered.* Choosing the best word means first avoiding words that are incorrect or inaccurate. *Assassinate* would be ruled out unless Mr. Rollet were an important political figure; *slaughtered* is usually reserved for deaths involving brutal, deliberately inflicted bodily injury; *murdered* indicates foul play; *exterminated* applies, at least for humans, to cases of genocide. If you meant none of these more specific meanings, *killed* might be the simplest and most precise word to use.

Choosing the right words also means choosing words appropriate to your intended purpose, audience, and context. In a formal paper, writing "This guy's theories, well, I think they're just plain garbage" represents an inappropriate choice of words and phrases, or **diction.** A word like *guy* does, in fact, refer to a person (usually male), so technically it's not *incorrect.* But as slang, it would violate any reader's expectations if it were used in the context of a formal academic paper, and it is therefore *inappropriate.*

28a Thinking about word choice

Whenever you choose specific words while you write, you base your decisions partly on your writing situation, which includes your purpose, audience, context, and persona (the image of yourself that you project in your writing). Considering each of these can help you choose appropriate words as you draft and revise.

1 Adjust your diction to your readers' needs

The characteristics of your readers should play a major role in your choice of words (see Chapter 5). Whenever you write for teachers or students in college, you should maintain a fairly high level of formality in your diction (the exceptions being deliberately informal notes, responses, journal entries, or quoted speech). Avoid **colloquialisms.**

TOO INFORMAL The stock market crash didn't seem to **faze** many of the investors with **megabucks stashed** in property assets.

READER'S REACTION: This seems really colloquial; I'm not sure I trust the writer's authority.

EDITED The stock market crash did not profoundly affect investors with extensive property assets.

Writer's Tip

Because much college writing assumes an academic, sophisticated diction, it is easy to forget that not all readers are experts who will recognize complex vocabulary. College student Steven Hoecht discovered this as he edited his write-up of an activity he used in his volunteer work at a nearby elementary school.

TOO TECHNICAL In order to create effective leaf silhouettes, it is necessary first to procure several preferably truncated and partially dehydrated leaves.

EDITED To start making your leaf rubbing, first gather a few large, partly dried leaves.

---

2 Adjust your diction to your purpose

Your *purpose* for writing plays an important role in determining your diction (see Chapter 4). In much academic writing, your main purpose will be to inform your readers, providing them with a balanced, detailed assessment of a topic. Using inflammatory, highly emotional, unreasoned, or outrageous language will only subvert your own purposes.

**28a
words**

BIASED Most proponents of rock-music censorship grew up listening to pablum and thinking even wimpy bands like the Beach Boys were a bunch of perverts.

READER'S REACTION: I thought this was a paper weighing the sides of the rock-music censorship debate. This seems too biased and emotional.

EDITED   Proponents of rock-music censorship may unfairly stereo-
                type all of rock-and-roll culture as degenerate or evil.

3 Adjust your diction to your persona

Writing can portray you in many different roles. Through your choice of words, you can sound like a mean-spirited, unyielding demagogue or a reasonable, open-minded arbiter of conflicting opinion. Your **persona** as a writer refers to the public role or character you assume. Thinking carefully about how *you*, as a writer, portray yourself can help you to choose appropriate words.

For example, your persona in a clinical experiment will be objective and detached; using too many personal references may call into question the accuracy of the experiment. But using such clinical diction in a classified ad selling puppies may convey too cold and unfeeling a persona for the occasion.

TOO CLINICAL   [*in a classified ad selling unpedigreed puppies*] Three domes-
                tic canines, *Canis familiaris,* type Shetland sheepdog, @29
                centimeters, 0.522 kilograms; age: 8 weeks; normal soma-
                totype; iris: brown; coloring: burnt umber with variegated
                blond diameters; behaviorally modified for urination and
                defecation; inoculated. $25 per canine.

                READER'S REACTION: **The writer seems uncaring, treating puppies
                like laboratory specimens.**

EDITED   Three healthy shelty puppies 8 weeks old, brown with light
                spots, housebroken, all shots. $25 each.

ROBOT-LIKE   The river having been reached, it was decided to portage to
                the campsite. A camp was set, and dinner was prepared and
                eaten. The sunset was observed at the lake. Then eight hours
                of sleep ensued.

                READER'S REACTION: **This narrative lacks vitality. The characters
                seem like robots.**

EDITED   When we reached the river, we decided to portage to the
                campsite. There, we set camp, cooked dinner, enjoyed the
                sunset at the lake, and slept for eight hours.

4 Use specialized diction appropriately

If you're writing in a certain field or discipline, you need to adjust your diction to your context. For example, in a history course, readers of your papers will expect certain terms and language that might not be appropriate in a physics course.

Many specialized terms eventually find their way into general usage,

**28a
words**

two examples being *ego* from Freudian psychology and *modem* (modulator-demodulator) from computer science. When you write for general audiences, your readers will find highly specialized language inappropriate. "No shop talk allowed at this party" is a lighthearted way to stop guests from using the language of their specialized careers, boring or confusing their listeners. If you use diction too general for readers in a specialized field, however, your writing may seem naive *in that context*. Revise your drafts to include specific terms used in the field (if you actually understand those terms, and if they improve accuracy and economy).

TOO GENERAL   [*in an analysis of a painting for an art history course*] Tiepolo's *Apotheosis of the Pisani Family* (1761) is a lively painting with lots of action going on in it, with nice colors, and typical of the period when it was painted.

READER'S REACTION: The diction seems too general for a specialized analysis in my field of art history.

EDITED   Tiepolo's *Apotheosis of the Pisani Family* (1761) shows affinities with typical rococo frescoes of the period, including bright colors with characters in various highlighted actions set against dark border accents.

When you learn new words in one field, you may inadvertently use those words in another field in which they are inappropriate.

TOO COMPLEX   [*in an economics paper on the influence of sexuality in the marketplace*] Ego gratification, originating in the neo-erotic domains of the pleasure principle, remains one of the chief factors influencing the attractiveness of sexuality in marketing.

READER'S REACTION: I'm an economics major, not a Freudian psychoanalyst. Talk in my language, please.

EDITED   Freudian theory can help us to explain why sexuality sells in the American marketplace. According to Freud, humans are biologically caught in a kind of sexual rhythm. This rhythm causes us to seek certain kinds of gratification not always explicitly sexual.

**28a
words**

Exercise 1

A. Assume that the following paragraph is part of a brochure on dental hygiene found in a dentist's office. Examine the passage, and circle words and phrases you find inappropriate. Write a paragraph explaining the problems in diction that you identified in the passage. Consider its intended audience, purpose, context, and persona.

Brushing and flossing of human dentin has been shown to be instrumental in the systematic reduction of invasive caries. When brushing, it is advisable to rotate the cusp of the preventive maintenance tool at alternating angles during upward and downward motion. When flossing, it is advisable to insert and retract the flossing material several times between the dentitial spaces.

 B. In a group, compare your responses to Exercise 1A. Which choices of diction did everyone find inappropriate? As a group, try editing the passage.

Did You Know?

The insurance industry has been attacked for writing policies that the average citizen can hardly read. Policy writers were caught up in the special legal terminology of their profession and forgot their audience. Recently, the industry has tried hard to correct this problem, and now many policies are written in plain, readable English. This projects a warmer, more positive image of the industry as well.

28b Using precise diction

Because you may write most fluently when you're not weighing every word you put on the page, you'll find it helpful to work with diction during the editing process. Think of this as adjusting your prose to match your intended meaning.

**28b
words**

1 Choose specific words

Try whenever possible to edit for more specific, accurate words.

TOO VAGUE   [*in a do-it-yourself brochure describing bathroom remodeling*]
Note: Do not put any new flooring over old uneven floor or with evidence of wood rot. Remove damaged area before flooring.
READER'S REACTION: The language is vague and imprecise. What does "damaged area" mean?

EDITED   Note: Do not **install** any new flooring over **existing** floors that are **weak or uneven or show signs of wood rot.** Remove any damaged **flooring material or tiles** before **installing new flooring.**

2 Choose words with appropriate connotations

English is full of **synonyms**, words that are identical or nearly identical in meaning. When you make a choice between two words, you will often consider the words' **connotations**—"shades" of meaning, or associations that words acquire over time. For example, if someone *retreated* from a gathering, they literally left; but the word suggests that the person felt attacked, bewildered, or overcome. When editing, look for any inappropriate connotations in your choice of words.

IMPRECISE   When I **came to** on Saturday morning, Billy had already left for Chicago.
READER'S REACTION: **Was the writer knocked out? Or did he or she just wake up?**

EDITED   When I **awoke** on Saturday morning, Billy had already left for Chicago.

3 Edit for stuffy language

English is filled with Latin words that entered the language centuries ago, creating an abstract, educated way of speaking and writing that may be alluring because it sounds sophisticated. Heavily Latinized language, however, can make your writing seem unnecessarily wordy and complicated (see Chapter 30). Notice how direct the following words are compared with their more abstract synonyms.

PLAIN WORD	LATIN-BASED
bathroom	lavatory
bickering	disputatious
die	expire
drunk	intoxicated
graveyard	cemetery
split	bifurcate
stingy	penurious
think	cogitate

28b
words

In general, use simple, direct diction unless the context of your writing calls for specialized language or unless a more abstract term better reflects your intended meaning than its concrete counterpart.

LATINATE   The reflections upon premarital cohabitation promulgated by the Supreme Court eventuated in the orientation of the population in the direction of moral relaxation on this issue.
READER'S REACTION: **The diction seems stuffy. Say it more plainly, please.**

EDITED   The Supreme Court's views about living together before marriage led to greater public acceptance of this practice.

4 Edit for archaic words and neologisms

The English language constantly changes. Some words are doomed to disuse and eventual death. Other, new words enter the vocabulary by the hundreds. Still others shift their meanings, as in the case of *gay,* which used to mean "carefree" but now almost exclusively means "homosexual."

Most **archaic words**—words that are rarely used any more but are still found in older literature—will be labeled as such in the dictionary. In general, you should avoid archaic words unless you're using them for a special reason. **Neologisms**—words coined very recently—may not be in the dictionary at all. You may have a harder time recognizing neologisms because they tend to be used in casual speech. Whenever you suspect that a term is too new to be acceptable in writing, identify it as a neologism and define it, or else avoid it altogether.

ARCHAIC/
NEOLOGIC

Good reviews of our previous play had been scarce (**save** in *Fanfare*), and this time around we had to **forfend** the **trashing** of the critics again.

READER'S REACTION: *Save* and *forfend* seem old-fashioned, and what's *trashing*?

EDITED

Good reviews of our previous play had been scarce (**except** in *Fanfare*), and this time around we had to **defend ourselves against** the critics' **attacks** again.

5 Edit for idiomatic and trite expressions

Idioms are words and phrases whose meanings have changed, usually to something quite different from their literal definitions. These terms often have "forgotten histories." Here are some common idioms.

IDIOM	MEANING
bust a gut	work extremely hard
get in the fast lane	be ambitious, rise up; lead a fast-paced, self-destructive life-style
get some z's	sleep, take a nap
lose your marbles	go insane
meet your maker	die
pack it in	quit, resign
stack the deck	cheat
take a spin	go for a ride
toss cookies	vomit
wipe the slate clean	start over

In most academic writing, idioms are too informal or have become trite from overuse. Replace them with precise words.

IDIOMATIC   The winning team was **placed high upon a pedestal,** while the losers, **wallowing in a slough of despond,** reminded themselves of what a **dog-eat-dog** world it is in sports.

EDITED   The winning team was idolized and cheered by the fans, while the losers, despondent and humorless, consoled themselves over their defeat.

Did You Know?

Some idiomatic expressions have interesting histories. For example, the phrase *kick the bucket* (meaning "to die") is thought to come from a crude method of suicide in which the victim stood on a bucket, put a noose around his or her neck, and then kicked away the bucket. However, the term may have come from medieval slaughterhouses. Immediately after being slaughtered and hung on the "buckets" (or beams), the livestock would inevitably "kick the buckets" as they died. The phrase *rule of thumb* also has a disputed history, possibly coming from brewers' practice of gauging the temperature of a brew by dipping a thumb into the vat. However, others believe the word comes from centuries-old English common law and refers to the maximum size (the diameter of a human thumb) of the instrument with which women were permitted to be beaten. Some people now avoid the term because of its possibly sexist history.

Ebenezer Cobham Brewer, *Brewer's Dictionary of Phrase and Fable,* rev. ed. (New York: HarperCollins, 1963), and William Morris and Mary Morris, *Morris' Dictionary of Word and Phrase Origins* (New York: HarperCollins, 1962).

**28b
words**

Exercise 2

A. Read the following paragraph and identify as many cases as you can of inappropriate diction. Look for imprecise, misused, stuffy, or trite words, checking in a dictionary if you need to. Then edit the passage by replacing the misused words or expressions with more appropriate ones.

The inaugural time I witnessed someone parachuting from a plane was when I was in college. The parachuting establishment was located in the desert of Arizona. First we apprised ourselves on the diminutive single-prop plane and shackled ourselves into the seats. Three employees of a local business were the jumpers. We circled around until we reached the pinnacle for jumping, about 6,000 feet up. The first customer was about to detort but became lugubrious with fear and couldn't jump. The second man faced us with his back to the open side of the plane and a verecund expression on his face, then fell back deliberately and dejected himself from the craft, spinning downward toward the verdurous desert.

 B. In a small group, compare your edited versions of the passage in Exercise 2A. Discuss all your choices, and then try to reach consensus on the best substitutions.

28c Using strategies for editing diction

Having a wide-ranging vocabulary—not just *knowing* lots of words, but knowing how to use them thoughtfully—is clearly helpful for editing your diction. But even the most experienced writers will tell you that when it comes to choosing words, they are always searching for just the right flavor, testing one idea and then another, even asking other people's opinions by thrusting unfinished work at them and saying, "Read this, and tell me what you think." Use the following strategies when you think common sense isn't enough.

ESL Advice: Using Dictionaries

Sometimes you want to express an idea or concept in writing, but you do not know what word or words would express it in English. Bilingual dictionaries are usually a good starting point to find a possible translation. However, for every word, they list several options. It is important that you consult an English dictionary to ensure that you choose the most appropriate word. These dictionaries contain definitions and examples that can help you decide which word best matches your intended meaning and your diction.

1 Use the dictionary

As suggested in Chapter 29, the dictionary will be your most important tool when you work on diction. Dictionaries give you precise definitions as well as usage notes.

S T R A T E G Y

When editing your work, circle any words that you have learned fairly recently or have not used often; then look them up to be sure you've used them correctly.

IMPRECISE   Employees should know that their contracts may be terminated if they deliberately **abrogate** their usual work hours.

> READER'S REACTION: The term *abrogate* means to abolish or nullify, usually by some formal means. Do you really mean this?

EDITED   Employees should know that their contracts may be terminated if they **miss work.**

---

2 Use a thesaurus

A thesaurus provides good lists of synonyms when you're editing diction and want to replace an existing word that you question for some reason. But be careful. Be sure you are familiar with a synonym and its connotations before simply substituting it.

Writer's Tip

Some writers begin using a thesaurus and then become so addicted to it that their prose begins to suffer from "thesaurus-ese," a disease that leads to the proclivity for excessively prolix and convoluted linguistic verbiage that can stray several standard deviations from definitional accuracy. In plainer English, such writers may reject good, common words, choosing instead to pepper their prose with sophisticated-sounding synonyms, often without knowing whether they're using them correctly. When possible, stick to words that are part of your vocabulary. Jot down alternatives that are unfamiliar, and learn to use them in your speech before you use them more formally in your writing.

28c
words

S T R A T E G Y

When using a thesaurus, ask yourself whether your new word choice captures your meaning more accurately, gives more flavor, or avoids redundancy better than your original choice. When in doubt, stick with words you know.

ORIGINAL | She was **angered** to the point of frustration and could no longer hold her dissatisfaction inside.

WRITER'S REACTION: I'm not satisfied with *anger.* My thesaurus suggests the alternatives *vexed, irritated, exasperated, infuriated, inflamed, miffed,* and *enraged.*

IMPRECISE | She was **enraged** to the point of frustration.

WRITER'S REACTION: **The word is too strong and does not convey the woman's true feelings.**

EDITED | She was **irritated** to the point of frustration.

3 Use the slash/option technique

Sometimes you already have several alternatives in mind for a particular word while you're writing. Stopping to weigh the alternatives may break your train of thought.

S T R A T E G Y

Write down the alternative words and separate them with slashes. Later, as you revise and edit, you can choose which word most accurately fits your intended meaning.

DRAFT | Steve and Esme stopped their chess matches only long enough to enjoy John's delicious **culinations/cuisine/cooking/delectables/repasts/meals.**

EDITED | Steve and Esme stopped their chess matches only long enough to enjoy John's delicious **meals**.

**28c
words**

4 Fight insecurity with simplicity

Vagueness, words with wrong connotations, overused expressions—you can slice all these from your prose if you develop a keen eye for style and clarity in your writing. But the problem of overblown, deliberately complex diction—diction intended to puff up your writing with "sophisticated" language—often has its roots in insecurity. When writers worry about their intellectual status, they often toss away good, direct vocabulary in favor of gobbledygook. Professionals in advanced fields have earned the right to use words with *specialized* meanings. They sound sophisticated because, in their fields, they *are.* But using overly complex prose out of a fear of sounding naive only makes you sound more naive than ever.

Whenever you have the slightest urge to puff up your prose with jar-gon or needlessly complicated diction, *stop*. Ask yourself what kind of sales-person in an audio store you would be more likely to trust—one who talks to you in simple, honest language about the pros and cons of various CD play-ers, or one who uses dozens of alien-sounding words for acoustic features and for complex mechanisms inside the machines. Then return to your draft. Be direct; choose concrete, visually appealing words when you can.

Exercise 3

 A. Locate a short passage in a newspaper or magazine article. Rewrite the passage, substituting words that are inappropriate or inaccurate.

 B. Make several copies of your original passage and the changed ver-sion in Exercise 3A. In a group, work on each other's passages to "repair" the damage. When you finish, compare your edited versions with the original passages. How close did you come to the originals? What differences can you see between your "repaired" versions and the originals?

29

Using Dictionaries and Building Vocabulary

In cultures that have no writing, all the words in the language must be passed orally from generation to generation. The entire "dictionary" exists in the memories of the speakers. In societies with advanced literacy, such as ours, no one could hope to know all the words in the language. Most educated Americans use a working vocabulary of about 25,000 words. That's less than 4 percent of the total vocabulary of the English language, which exceeds 1 million words. Under these circumstances, it's easy to see why the dictionary is such an important tool for any writer or reader. But there are many kinds of dictionaries, for many purposes. What are your special needs as a writer?

29a Choosing dictionaries to serve your needs

As you work with your writing, you will need different kinds of dictionaries for different purposes, even beyond the typical need to check on the correct spelling, pronunciation, and definition of a word. Here are some common questions writers ask about dictionaries and their use.

What's the best kind of all-purpose dictionary I can get?

Desk dictionaries are suitable for most routine academic and professional tasks. Although they don't pretend to give an exhaustive list of English vocabulary, they are still quite substantial reference works. Desk dictionaries are often called *college dictionaries* because they represent the standard of vocabulary used by educated people. Less bulky and less expensive than full-length dictionaries, they are widely used in most homes and workplaces.

What if I don't want to lug around a huge book when I'm working on my writing away from home?

Most people use a **pocket dictionary** for quick checks on spelling or syllable division. Pocket dictionaries are **abridged dictionaries,** meaning that they contain far fewer words and much less information than standard dictionaries. They are inexpensive and convenient, but you'll still want to use a more substantial dictionary for checking definitions and etymologies (the origins of words).

What's a good place to get really full information on a word? What's the most authoritative source?

If your desk dictionary doesn't answer your questions or contain the word you're looking up, you can consult much more comprehensive **unabridged dictionaries,** which are found in most libraries and schools. These dictionaries contain many more words than desk and pocket dictionaries. They usually provide detailed information about words in common use, and they include specialized words from various fields, archaic words, words "borrowed" into English from other languages, and so on. Unabridged dictionaries often provide glosses on usage as well as complete etymological information.

The *Oxford English Dictionary* (OED for short) is the most comprehensive dictionary ever compiled in English. It takes up many volumes, but a compact version is available in two massive books of 4,116 pages accompanied by a magnifying glass for reading the very small print. There is also a new "shortened" edition of two (legible) volumes. For every word listed, the OED quotes the earliest known use of the word in a written document and explains or illustrates many uses that followed. Because they provide such complete etymological and other information, dictionaries like the OED are considered research tools.

Sometimes I feel that I use the same words over and over. Is there a book that can help me to find alternatives?

A **thesaurus** is a dictionary of **synonyms** and **antonyms**—words related or opposite in meaning to each other. A thesaurus is useful when you want to find an alternative to a word you've already considered, or perhaps to remember a word that has temporarily slipped your mind. Under the word *funny,* for example, *Webster's Collegiate Thesaurus* lists the synonyms *laughable, comic, comical, droll, farcical, gelastic, ludicrous, ridiculous,* and *risible.* Obviously, not every synonym listed means exactly what the word *funny* does; your choice of word will depend on your context. The thesaurus lists the related words *antic, bizarre, fantastic,* and *grotesque.* It gives as an idiom *too funny for words,* and it provides the contrasting words *doleful, dolorous, lugubrious, melancholy,* and *plaintive,* along with the single antonym *unfunny.*

29a
dctnry

What if I just want to check on correct spelling?

Spelling dictionaries are dictionaries without definitions. They provide spellings and information on word division (**syllabification**). Spelling dictionaries range from lists of the one hundred most commonly misspelled words (these brief lists are often preferred by secretaries because they're so easy to use) to much more substantial works with thousands of words. If you own a good desk dictionary, you probably won't need a spelling dictionary unless you're a frequent misspeller or do a good deal of your writing away from your desk.

Occasionally when I'm writing poetry I need to find rhymes for words. Is there a reference that can help me?

If you want to rhyme a word, you can consult a **rhyming dictionary.** Most rhyming dictionaries are organized into clusters of rhymed words accessible through an index.

I've often needed to know the complete history of a specific word. What reference should I use?

Most good dictionaries include etymological information, and research dictionaries, especially the OED, will give you very complete accounts. **Etymological dictionaries,** however, specialize in the history of words **(etymology)** and will often give fuller histories of some words. A few, such as John Ciardi's *A Browser's Dictionary,* make enjoyable reading.

I've noticed that some words just aren't in the standard dictionary. How can I find their proper spellings and meanings?

Most formal dictionaries don't include every word that might be heard in casual conversation, much less the sort of jargon found among drug users, avid sports fans, surfers, and the like. Dictionaries of colloquialisms, slang, idioms, and informal usage fill the gaps. They're often revised to keep up with new expressions, such as *za, undertoad,* or *mommy track.*

In some of my classes, I hear words that I can't find in the dictionary, probably because they're specialized. Where can I look them up to make sure I understand them and can use them correctly?

Many disciplines use and require complex vocabularies that sound like a foreign language to the average person. To ensure the precise use of specialized terms, these disciplines have their own academic and professional dictionaries. It's a good idea to ask a librarian or teacher to help you locate such dictionaries for your field of study. As you gain expertise in your chosen field, you may want to add such resources to your personal reference library.

29a
dctnry

Exercise 1

A. Conduct a brief "anatomy exam" of your own dictionary by answering the following questions.

1. What kind of information does your dictionary give for words?
2. How complete are the entries?
3. How have the definitions been determined?
4. How many separate entries does the dictionary include? (A good reference dictionary should contain at least 150,000 words.)

5. Are variant uses, definitions, and spellings given?
6. Does the dictionary contain acronyms (such as SIDS, ARC, NATO, FDA)?
7. Does it contain abbreviations?
8. Does it include often-used foreign words such as *tête-à-tête, pied-à-terre, calzone, karate,* and *kibosh?*
9. Does the dictionary show when to *italicize* words such as *cogito ergo sum* or *mea culpa?*
10. What is contained in the introduction or preface? Is there an appendix? Are there any special features?

 B. Compare your notes from Exercise 1A (and your dictionaries) with those of other students.

Did You Know?

Most people think of dictionaries as timeless authorities on matters of spelling, word division, and definition. But dictionaries constantly change. As you're reading this, experts called *lexicographers* are working to keep abreast of important changes in the word stock of American English. One of their jobs is to decide whether certain new words should be put into the dictionary. James Lowe, an editor of *Webster's Ninth New Collegiate Dictionary,* said that most of the new material in that edition consisted of "high-tech" terminology (such as *camcorder, CD, colorize, hard disk, icon, laser printer, LAN,* and *uplink*), but other new terms included *cash cow, Cornhusker* (a native of Nebraska), and *liposuction.* Special reference works like the *Barnhart Dictionary of New English* compile new words not yet found in conventional dictionaries. That one, in particular, includes some 12,000 entries, such as the acronyms ARC (AIDS-related complex) and CRT (cathode ray tube); abbreviations such as *veejay;* and terms such as *sick-building syndrome, sequencing,* and *wilding.*

"'Ninja' Nixed from Dictionary," *Minneapolis Star Tribune* 21 May 1991, and *Third Barnhart Dictionary of New English* (New York: Wilson, 1990).

29b Using a dictionary

In one sense, you already know how to use a dictionary. You've done this hundreds of times: flipped the book open, found the word, checked the spelling or the definition, and slapped the book shut again. But have you really *used* the dictionary to its fullest potential? If anything in an entry has seemed like so much gobbledygook to you, you may have skipped over some useful information.

The annotated illustration of the word *college* (Figure 29-1) appears in *Webster's Third New International Dictionary of the English Language* (Unabridged). As you read the annotations, note what sorts of important information are provided in the entry.

This brief example shows that deciphering the more technical and abbreviated language of dictionary entries is not difficult if you use the explanations and keys found in the front. And once you start looking *carefully* at dictionary entries, you'll find yourself thinking more critically and deeply

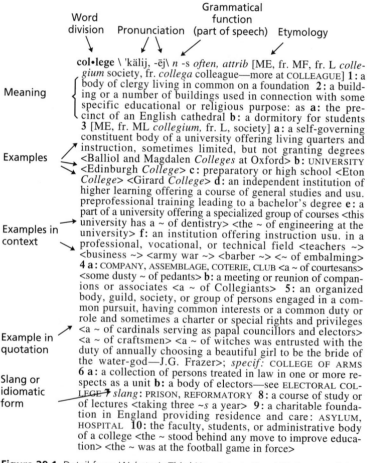

Figure 29.1 Detail from *Webster's Third New International Dictionary of the English Language* (Unabridged). Springfield, MA: G.&C. Merriam, 1993.

about the word stock of your language, especially as you choose appropriate words for your papers.

Exercise 2

A. Using a good college-level dictionary, look up one or more of the following words:

caduceus   hoist   surprise   denizen   picnic

Using the annotation of *college* in Figure 29-1 as a guide, list the types of information your dictionary provides for each word—part of speech, etymology, definitions, hyphenation for word division, and so on. Be sure to look at every piece of information given for each word. What did you learn about each of the words that you looked up for this exercise?

B. Compare your answers to Exercise 2A with those of other students in a small group. Look for differences in the kinds of information your dictionaries provide for these words and in the ease with which you can access that information.

29c dctnry

29c Using dictionaries in the age of technology

You probably already know how helpful computer technology is to college-level research and writing. A single CD-ROM disk (similar to a disk used in a CD player) can contain an entire encyclopedia. With the touch of a few keys, you can retrieve the information on a personal computer.

Several dictionaries and dictionary-like programs are currently available for microcomputers. Those used most often are actually simple spelling checkers that scan your document for any words that don't fit the spellings in the computer's memory. Most spelling checkers are little more than matching programs; they don't contain definitions or guides to usage. A few newer programs, however, do. Software versions of major dictionaries contain definitions, notes on correct usage, hyphenation information, and spelling correctors. Some have accompanying thesauruses capable of producing a million responses for as many as forty thousand entries. These programs can provide acronyms, synonyms, antonyms, contrasted words, compared words, and related words. A few programs boast average access times of less than one second and can insert a replacement word directly into a document.

Computerized dictionaries have several advantages over typical printed dictionaries. For one thing, they are far less bulky. They can be upgraded more easily and more quickly than a book can be edited, updated, and republished. You can usually also personalize a computer dictionary, unlike a standard shelf dictionary, adding your own special words to the dictionary's memory (good mainly for spelling checks).

Computerized dictionaries also have their limitations. It's difficult to browse through them. They may cost three or four times more than a good college dictionary. If you like to write in different locations, you won't be able to use your dictionary without a computer (and power to drive it). Computerized dictionaries, unlike a good sturdy book, can easily be damaged or can simply go bad. Still, many avid computer users find them a valuable resource in lieu of or in addition to standard desk dictionaries.

Did You Know?

The word stock of English has increased dramatically over the past several centuries. The vocabulary of English (spoken and written) contains an estimated 3 million words. The King James Bible, famous for its elegant prose, contains only about 7,000 different words. Taken together, all the works of William Shakespeare contain less than three times that number (around 18,000 words). Yet a single issue of the *New York Sunday Times* contains, on average, about 25,000 different words.

Bill Bryson, *The Mother Tongue* (New York: Morrow, 1990), and Joseph T. Shipley, *In Praise of English* (New York: Times Books, 1977).

29d Building vocabulary

A rich, varied vocabulary is the mark of an educated person—and is absolutely essential to effective writing and easier reading. To understand the importance of a good vocabulary, try reading the following sentences, which contain some words that may be unfamiliar to you.

The mouse debouched valiantly from the hole.
The senate engaged in an internecine feud over the bill.
Harold died by defenestration.
It wasn't so much a tome as a missal.

The point should be clear: the better your vocabulary, the more able you are as a writer, reader, speaker, and listener.

1 Vocabulary and the writing process

Without many options for word choice, you essentially put a stranglehold on your prose, limiting its variety, its accuracy, and its metaphoric potential. Consider the six versions of one line written by Johanna Vaughan in her paper about food-shelf programs.

Without the help of local and state government, the food-shelf program in Seattle will become **ineffective.**

Without the help of local and state government, the food-shelf program in Seattle will become **obsolete.**

Without the **beneficence** of local and state government, the food-shelf program in Seattle will **die.**

Without the beneficence of local government, the food-shelf program in Seattle will die **of starvation.**

Without the **financial nurturing** of local government, Seattle's food-shelf program will die of **nutritional neglect.**

Without the financial **sustenance** of local government, Seattle's food-shelf program will **slowly** die of starvation.

Many of Vaughan's changes depend on more than the substitution of individual words, but it's hard to overlook the role her vocabulary plays in her writing process. She can revise more effectively *because she has more options*—she can experiment with words like *sustenance, beneficence,* and *obsolete.*

Although it can become tedious to keep moving between your emerging sentences and that 1,500-page dictionary on your desk, there is something to be said for some modest vocabulary development during the process of completing each of your writing assignments. Especially while revising, take time to consider alternatives to some of your words, perhaps circling those that seem repetitive or bland, then listing alternatives or using a dictionary or thesaurus (as long as you're confident that you know the exact meaning of the replacements).

29d
vocab

2 Vocabulary and the reading process

Every time you pick up a book or newspaper, you're exposed to new words. If you're like most people, you probably pass over them, as long as you're not hopelessly confused without knowing their meaning. In many cases, the mere exposure to these words, in their contexts, helps you to acquire them as part of your vocabulary. But a few techniques can help.

S T R A T E G Y

Each day, select one word from something you've read, look up its definition, and check its etymology. Then, without sounding too unnatural, try incorporating the word into your speech at least three times during the day. If that's not possible, just make up sentences on your own, and say them silently to yourself. You'll find that the word stays with you, and you'll begin using it more regularly.

Keep an ongoing list of unfamiliar words, look them up, and review them periodically, crossing them out when they've become part of your vocabulary. Your journal is an excellent place to do this (see Chapter 2). This method works much more effectively than the one recommended by some self-improvement books, which advise you to cram dozens of words into your brain each day in the hope that you'll actually remember them later and be able to use them accurately. The words on your list should come directly from material you're reading and studying, from the daily newspaper to the most complex textbook chapters.

Every time you look up a word for its meaning, check its etymology. Most English words have Anglo-Saxon, Latin, Greek, or French origins. When you look up a word's roots, you will develop your vocabulary. Over time, you will become able to make educated guesses at the meanings of new words on the basis of their parts.

**29d
vocab**

Learning about a word's origins is a particularly interesting and useful way to expand your vocabulary. The word *elevate,* for example, comes to us from Latin *elevatus,* "lightened" or "lifted up." The parts of the word include a prefix, *e-;* the form *lev(is),* which means "light" (as in "not heavy"); and the suffix *-ate.* The root word *lev(is)* is found in several related words. If you didn't know the meaning of the word *levitate,* your knowledge of the etymology of *elevate* might help you, and the context of the word might do the rest to define it for you.

Many word origins will also surprise you and reveal the linguistic diversity of English, which has absorbed words from dozens of other languages. The word *cookie,* for example, comes from the Dutch spoken by early settlers of Manhattan. The word *alcohol* is from Arabic. The word *typhoon* hails originally from the Chinese *tai fung,* "great wind." *Chicago* was an Algonquian word meaning "place of the wild onion" or "foul-smelling place." The *tomatoes* you eat have their word origins in Nahuatl, an indigenous language spoken in Mexico and Central America. *Hibachi* is Japanese. *Goober* is African. *Cockroach* is Spanish. *Sauna* is Finnish.

Exercise 3

 A. To practice studying the etymologies of words, look up the following interesting ones in a good, full-length (unabridged) dictionary. The best source will be the OED in your college library. Look for anything unusual or interesting about the history of these words.

EXAMPLE: *KANGAROO*

The OED says that the word probably comes from an indigenous aboriginal language of Australia and meant "I don't know" or "I don't understand," the response given to visitors who asked the aborigines the name of the animal.

barbecue	guillotine	mesmerize	sadist
blimp	juke (box)	muscle	sandwich
blurb	ketchup	OK or okay	serendipity
dollar	laser	robot	voodoo

 B. In a group, compare your etymologies for the words in Exercise 3A. What surprised you about the origins of these words?

Did You Know?

The development of your vocabulary began in your infancy and exploded by the time you were between two and three years old. If you were a typical preschooler, you learned around ten to fifteen new words *each day,* or approximately 14,000 new words between the ages of two and six. Your vocabulary development slowed as you became older and already had a large fund of words at your disposal, but the college years are also increasing your store of words. Every course you take exposes you to dozens and sometimes hundreds of new terms. In many ways, getting a degree in a certain area or major means being able to use the specialized language of your discipline—including its vocabulary.

Mildred C. Templin, *Certain Language Skills in Children* (Minneapolis: U of Minnesota P, 1964).

29d
vocab

30

Wordiness

As a writer, you can state similar thoughts in different ways to achieve different effects on your readers. For example, you can create a short, direct sentence.

Incentive pay improves work quality.

You can then add words to anticipate readers' reactions and guide the effect of the sentence.

Incentive pay **often encourages** work **of higher** quality.

Or you can bury the message with unnecessary language that clogs the meaning and frustrates or bewilders your reader.

There is evidence that the use of pay **as an** incentive **can be a contributing or causative factor** in the improvement **of the** quality **of** work.

Wordy writing includes words not necessary to the meaning or desired effect of a passage. Of course, even the best writing often starts out wordy. While drafting, you may pay more attention to exploring ideas and conveying information than to writing concisely. Most rough drafts contain sentences that need pruning.

Avoiding **wordiness** does not always mean using the fewest words possible. It means including all the words appropriate for your meaning, purpose, and audience, but no more. Defining every medical term in an article on a rare skin disorder might seem wordy to specialists in the field but appropriate for general readers. Other aspects of wordiness are more universal, such as redundancy or overblown vocabulary. To make sure your final drafts are concise, you need to learn how to edit for wordiness, a process that involves cutting unnecessary words and phrases, substituting better words, and rewriting entire sentences.

30a Editing for common types of wordiness

Redundancy can creep into your writing when you use everyday phrases and patterns of expression. Their familiarity disguises their wordiness.

1 Eliminate empty words and phrases

Cut Empty Phrases. Empty phrases like *at this point in time, totally overcome, due to the fact that,* or *each and every* add length but little meaning to your writing. Cut them.

WORDY	**At this particular juncture,** the fire damage **makes it incumbent** upon us to decide whether **or not** to rebuild the old plant.
	READER'S REACTION: What exactly is a "particular juncture"? What does "incumbent upon" mean? Doesn't deciding "whether" imply "or not"?
CUT	The fire damage **now** forces us to decide whether to rebuild the old plant.

Reduce Redundant Pairs. English is rich in pairs of synonyms and near-synonyms. Because they say the same thing twice, **redundant pairs** are always candidates for editing.

above and beyond	free and clear	questions and problems
aid and abet	full and complete	ready and willing
any and all	kith and kin	various and sundry
around and about	one and only	way, shape, or form
each and every	part and parcel	

WORDY	To encourage innovation, the manager spoke with **each and every individual** team assigned to the project. Team One made a complex task manageable by dividing it into **bits and pieces.**
CUT	To encourage innovation, the manager spoke with **each** team assigned to the project. Team One made a complex task manageable by dividing it into **pieces.**
REPHRASED	To encourage innovation, the manager spoke with **each** team assigned to the project. Team One made a complex task manageable by **splitting it up.**

Shorten Wordy Phrases. You can shrink many familiar phrases to just one or two words. The shorter versions are easier to read, and they convey your message more effectively.

30a
wordy

WORDY	Carbon 14 can be used to date a site only **in the event that** organic material has survived. **In a situation in which** rocks need dating, potassium-argon testing is appropriate.
CUT	Carbon 14 can be used to date a site only **if** organic material has survived. **When** rocks need dating, potassium-argon testing is appropriate.

Wordy phrases are so familiar that they may be hard to recognize. Use the following list as a guide until you develop the habit of turning phrases into words.

**30a
wordy**

Common Wordy Phrases

PHRASE	REPLACEMENT
as a result of being that due to the fact that for the reason that on account of on the grounds that	because, since
has the capability of is able to possesses the ability to	can
at the present moment at this juncture at this point in time within the current time frame	now
a considerable proportion of a large number of the greater number of the substantial majority of	many, most
a case in point is an example of this would be in regard to in the case of with attention to	for example
it is evident that it should be obvious that	clearly, obviously
concerning the matter of	about

PHRASE	REPLACEMENT
circumstances dictate that	should, must
it is imperative that	
it is incumbent upon	
it is of great importance that	
there is a need for	
at a time which	when
during an occasion when	
in a situation in which	
on the occasion of	
despite the conditions that	although
even taking into consideration the fact that	
even though	
regardless of the fact that	
at all times	always

Cut Intensifying Phrases. Intensifying phrases meant to add force (*for all intents and purposes, in my opinion,* and *all things considered*) carry little meaning. Your reader will find your sentences more effective and forceful without them.

WORDY   **As a matter of fact,** most archaeological discoveries can be dated accurately.

CUT   Most archaeological discoveries can be dated accurately.

Shorten or Rewrite Redundant Phrases. Redundant phrases say the same thing twice, adding unnecessary words to your writing. Sometimes an adjective simply repeats the meaning of the noun it modifies; *true facts, free gifts,* or *final outcomes* are redundant because by definition facts are true, gifts are free, and outcomes are final.

added bonus	baby puppies	each individual
end result	fresh news	future plan
necessary requirements	past history	terrible tragedy
unintentional mistake	cheap bargain	unexpected surprise

Similar repetition occurs in redundant verb phrases (*completely finished, totally overcome,* and *revert back*).

    Some redundancies occur when you use a specific word that implies a more general term you've used with it. *Blue,* for example, clearly implies the category *color,* so it is redundant to state both (*blue in color*).

30a
wordy

<table>
<tr><td>aggressive <s>by nature</s></td><td>circle <s>around</s></td></tr>
<tr><td>consensus <s>of opinion</s></td><td>curved <s>in form</s></td></tr>
<tr><td>expensive <s>in cost</s></td><td>first <s>in order</s></td></tr>
<tr><td>handsome <s>in appearance</s></td><td><s>in a</s> clumsy <s>manner</s></td></tr>
<tr><td><s>in a</s> grumpy <s>mood</s></td><td>old <s>in age</s></td></tr>
<tr><td>plans <s>for the future</s></td><td>small <s>in size</s></td></tr>
</table>

WORDY   Because it was sophisticated **in nature** and tolerant **in style,** Kublai Khan's administration aided the development of China in the late 1200s.

CUT   Because it was **sophisticated and tolerant,** Kublai Khan's administration aided the development of China in the late 1200s.

REWRITTEN   Kublai Khan's **adept and tolerant administration** aided the development of China in the late 1200s.

Edit or Rewrite to Cut All-purpose Words. They sound serious and important, yet **all-purpose words** like *factor, aspect, situation, type, field, range, thing, kind, nature, character,* and *angle* are often fillers. By eliminating the fillers and rewriting, you can make sentences easier to understand.

WORDY   Viewed **from a** sociological **perspective,** the president's popularity **factor** might be **a type of** result of the changing **nature of** our attitude toward authority.

EDITED   Viewed sociologically, the president's popularity might be a result of our changing attitude toward authority.

   All-purpose modifiers include *very, totally, major, central, secondary, unlikely, peripheral, great, really, surprisingly, definitely, absolutely, marginal, quite, superlative,* and similar terms. They are appropriate when used precisely and sparingly but can easily become clutter.

**30a
wordy**

WORDY   In the short story, Young Goodman Brown is so **totally** overwhelmed by **his own** guilt that he becomes **extremely** suspicious of the people around him and **absolutely** destroys his relationships. [*30 words*]

EDITED   In the short story, Young Goodman Brown is so overwhelmed by guilt that he becomes suspicious of the people around him and destroys his relationships. [*25 words*]

REWRITTEN   In the short story, Young Goodman Brown's **overwhelming** guilt makes him suspicious **of everyone** and destroys his relationships. [*18 words*]

Exercise 1

A. Edit the following sentences to make them more concise. Use one of the three editing options for wordiness: cut unnecessary words, substitute better words, or rewrite the sentence entirely. Keep track of your changes.

EXAMPLE

~~In spite of the fact that~~ *Although* most ~~ordinary~~ middle-aged people ~~say they generally~~ feel ~~physically~~ healthy, ~~and in good shape~~, ~~severe physical~~ catastrophes such as ~~debilitating~~ strokes and/or heart attacks can strike ~~suddenly~~ at any time.

1. As a matter of fact, my uncle had just come back from playing nine holes of golf when he suffered the terrible tragedy of his heart attack.
2. We all thought my aunt was absolutely in the very best of health, but she also died extremely suddenly.
3. For me, the end result of these experiences has been regular visits to the doctor to check on my health.
4. On account of my last visit to the doctor, I have started exercising on a regular basis.
5. A regular exercise program helps me to a better kind of feeling about myself.

B. In a small group, compare your revised versions of the sentences in Exercise 1A. Create a "best" version of each sentence by pooling the changes in your group. Try to base your decisions on which version gets the writer's point across most concisely.

Did You Know?

Legal writing is full of redundancies, perhaps because the law is written to exclude as much uncertainty as possible. Because many legal expressions have a long history, they tend to change slowly. However, recent movements in the law have begun to eliminate such wordy expressions as *cease and desist, null and void,* and *give and bequeath.*

**30a
wordy**

2 Edit wordy and repetitive sentences

Some sentence patterns encourage wordiness, which will annoy your readers. You should always treat them as likely candidates for cutting and rewriting.

Rewrite Sentences with Expletive Constructions. Beginning a sentence with a construction like *There is, There are,* or *It is* allows you to hold off announcing the subject—a strategy sometimes useful for creating emphasis or surprise. You should use this technique sparingly, however (see 9b). Using strong verbs in the place of expletive constructions can yield shorter, more forceful sentences.

OVERUSED   **It was** between 1346 and 1350 **that** the bubonic plague struck swiftly and horribly. **There were** over 20 million deaths from the plague—one-fourth of Europe's population. **It is** not surprising that records from the period are confusing and incomplete.

REWRITTEN   Between 1346 and 1350, one-fourth of Europe's population—about 20 million people—died swiftly and horribly from the bubonic plague. Not surprisingly, records from the period are confusing and incomplete.

Substitute Active for Passive Constructions. Sentences in the active voice often strike readers as livelier and more direct than their passive counterparts. (See 17h.) This impression may come from the presence of a strong verb closer to the beginning of the sentence, tied to the subject or doer of the action. Favor the active voice in your writing unless you have good reason to use the passive.

PASSIVE   Even more unanswered questions **are posed** by Mercury, the smallest planet. Pictures of Mercury **were taken** from within 300 kilometers.

ACTIVE   Mercury, the smallest planet, **poses** even more unanswered questions. *Mariner X* **took** pictures of Mercury from within 300 kilometers.

30a
wordy

Substitute Verbs for Nominalizations. A **nominalization** is a verb transformed into a noun or an adjective.

VERB	NOMINALIZATION
analyze	analysis
combine	combination
fail	failure
move	movement
propose	proposition
recognize	recognition
vary	variable

Some professions and disciplines heavily nominalize their prose. However, you can resist this tendency and create shorter, livelier sentences if you turn nominalizations into verbs.

NOMINALIZED   The committee held **a discussion of** the new regulations for airplane safety. **A limitation on** flammable seat materials now is necessary.

EDITED   The committee **discussed** the new regulations for airplane safety. Airlines now **must limit** flammable seat materials.

Turn Clauses into Phrases and Phrases into Words.   You can often shorten clauses and phrases or reduce them to single words. Look for clauses beginning with *which, who,* or *that* and phrases beginning with *of.*

CLAUSES   The Comstock Lode, **which was a vein of high-quality silver ore**, was named after Henry T. P. Comstock, **who staked one of the first claims.**

CUT TO PHRASES   The Comstock Lode, **a vein of high-quality silver ore**, was named after Henry T. P. Comstock, **one of the first claimants**.

CLAUSES   An airplane **which is on fire** often produces fumes **that are toxic**.

CUT TO WORDS   A **burning** airplane often produces **toxic** fumes.

PHRASES   Bridge joints **covered with paint** cannot flex to relieve pressure or to avoid **fatiguing of the metal**.

CUT TO WORDS   **Painted** bridge joints cannot flex to relieve pressure and avoid **metal fatigue.**

Eliminate Unnecessary Repetition.   When you are writing quickly, you may become repetitive. Such careless repetition, which will tire and annoy your readers, can occur even when you are actually varying your wording of ideas. As you revise and edit, look for ideas *already stated or implied* elsewhere in your sentence or paragraph.

WORDY   GPS is a **navigation** system that helps sailors and pilots **navigate**. By getting information **about their position** from **orbiting** satellites, travelers can pinpoint their **global** position **on a chart.**

30a
wordy

EDITED   GPS is a system that helps sailors and pilots navigate. By
             getting information from satellites, travelers can pinpoint
             their position.

Good writing may repeat information in order to help readers keep
track of an explanation or argument. On the other hand, excessive repetition makes a passage dull and difficult to read.

REPETITIVE   **Our proposal** outlines a **three-step** program for **convert-
             ing the building** into a **research center** for the study of
             literature, film, and culture. Each of the **three steps** dis-
             cussed in **our proposal** should be complete in six months.
             We expect that **the building** will be **converted** to its new
             use as a **research center** eighteen months from the time
             work is begun.

CUT   Our proposal outlines a **three-step** program for **convert-
             ing the building** into a center for the study of literature,
             film, and culture. Each **step** should be completed in six
             months. We expect that **the building** will be **converted** to
             its new use eighteen months from the time work is begun.

REWRITTEN   We propose **three steps** for **converting the building** into
             a center for the study of literature, film, and culture. At six
             months per **step,** the project should be completed in eigh-
             teen months.

Exercise 2

Rewrite the following sentences to make them less wordy.

EXAMPLE   *My*
It was an ~~interest in ancient cultures~~ ^interest~~ that first sparked my interest in~~
~~an~~ anthropology course ~~taught by~~ (Professor Donaldsons) *attracted me to*

30a
wordy

1. There is much information and detail in this informative course
   about the civilizations of the pre-Columbian Americas.
2. Anthropologists have spent a great deal of time studying and investigating Machu Picchu, which was the center point of an advanced
   culture high in the Andes Mountains.
3. There are many excavations in the area that have received support from American universities.
4. It seems to be true that the ruins are a breathtaking sight.
5. Proposals for further exploration are now being made to funding
   organizations by several groups of anthropologists.

30b Editing for clichés, generalizations, and overblown language

Many writers in college choose language that is either overused (clichéd) or too stuffy or complicated (see 28b). They may do this because they're unfamiliar with a specialized topic or think they must sound "smart" to their reader, a teacher with considerable knowledge. But most teachers are more irritated than impressed by such language.

1 Omit clichés and vague generalizations

Much wordiness stems from a lack of the tough, careful attention to language characteristic of the best writing. **Clichés** and **vague generalizations** are like the sayings in fortune cookies, empty of meaning until the reader plugs in some concrete association. But it's a serious mistake to assume that your reader will do your work for you.

CLICHÉD
: In **today's modern world,** college graduates **stumble across a startling discovery** before they **strike out on their own.** The best jobs are not necessarily the ones that give you a **shot at big money** but the ones that **turn you on** personally.

EDITED
: Almost before they have received their diplomas, today's college graduates begin to rethink the idea of employment. The glamour of high-salary positions soon wears thin, replaced by hopes of happiness, job security, and friendly colleagues.

A passage with vague generalizations may be short but still wordy because it offers relatively little information. To revise, *add specific details* or *combine sentences* to eliminate repetition and highlight relationships.

WORDY
: Glaciers were of central importance in the shaping of the North American landscape. They were responsible for many familiar geological features. Among the many remnants of glacial activity are deeply carved valleys and immense piles of sand and rock.

COMBINED
: Glaciers carved deep valleys and left behind immense piles of sand and rock, shaping much of the North American landscape in the process.

DETAILS ADDED
: Glaciers carved deep valleys and left behind immense piles of sand and rock, shaping much of the North American landscape in the process. Cape Cod and Long Island are

30b
wordy

piles of gravel deposited by glaciers. The Mississippi River and the Great Lakes were left behind when the ice melted.

2 Edit overblown language

Overblown language consists of words too formal or technical for the writer's purpose and audience. Students often use formal language and technical terms in an attempt to impress their instructors and sound authoritative. Rein in your formal diction and technical words, using them only when you are sure of their meaning and when they contribute directly to your point.

OVERBLOWN | Under the **present conditions of** our society, marriage **practices** generally **demonstrate a high degree of** homogeneity.

APPROPRIATE | In our culture, people tend to marry others who are like themselves.

3 Eliminate excessive writer's commentary

In certain contexts, talking directly to readers can be an acceptable strategy. If you use such **writer's commentary,** do so cautiously. You can use phrases like *as previously stated* or *I intend to demonstrate* to remind your readers of a point you made earlier or to set the stage for what's to come, but such phrases can become superfluous if you use them too often.

IRRITATING | **As I have already shown,** considerable research suggests that placebos (pills with no physical effect) can sometimes lead to improvements or a cure. However, **my paper documents the tendency of** experts in medical ethics to question the ethics of placebo use, calling it a form of lying. **I intend to show** that the effects of placebos **(mentioned above)** overcome any moral concerns **such as the one I have just described.**

EDITED | Considerable research has shown that placebos (pills with no physical effect) can sometimes lead to improvements or a cure. Experts in medical ethics, however, question the ethics of placebo use, calling it a form of lying. **This paper** will argue that the effects of placebos overcome any such moral concerns.

TOO OVERT | **The thesis of my paper is that** American culture associates the pursuit of knowledge with social ineptitude and the denial of emotion. **I have chosen to focus on** Mr. Spock

30b wordy

from the *Star Trek* series as an exemplar of this unfortunate public attitude toward education.

EDITED American culture associates the pursuit of knowledge with social ineptitude and the denial of emotion. This unfortunate public attitude toward education is well represented in the character of Spock, the brilliant but only half-human Vulcan in the *Star Trek* series.

Exercise 3

A. Rewrite the following passage to eliminate overblown language, unnecessary commentary, vague generalizations, and clichés. As you revise, make the passage more concise.

The social psychologist and student of human behavior Peter Marsh several years ago published a tome entitled *Tribes* in which he set forth the challenging, and for many readers, downright revolutionary, conception that the denizens of our modern world perpetuate the primitive form of social organization known as a tribe. According to Marsh in his book, as a reaction against the tendency of our modern society to break up the social networks characteristic of the more rural life-styles of earlier decades and centuries, many people form formal and informal groups based on their preferences in food, clothing, recreation, and work. Some of these groupings are of remarkably short duration, consisting of what we might call fads. Let me point out that, in my opinion, Marsh is trying to be critical of many of these groups, particularly those that seek to raise the social status of members by excluding nonmembers from certain privileges. Yet I think that a careful reading of Marsh's book would also indicate that he is favorably predisposed toward the tendency of modern people to form tribes.

B. In a small group, compare your revisions of the passage in Exercise 3A. What specific changes did you and your peers make that were especially effective?

30b
wordy

31

Avoiding Sexist and Discriminatory Language

Prodded by the women's movement, writers and editors have begun to eliminate sexist language from published work. But what is **sexist language?** People disagree about some common terms. For example, *seminal* is widely used to mean "highly original and influencing future events or developments"—but the literal meaning of the word is "pertaining to, containing, or consisting of semen." As such, it represents a potentially sexist usage: why should originality and creativity be associated with maleness? Some people think the term should be dropped in favor of words like *important* or *influential;* others argue that it's perfectly acceptable to use the common English word *seminal* to describe an important and influential work.

No matter how you feel about the issue of gender, as a writer you *must* be concerned with the reactions of your readers to the way you represent men and women and members of minority groups. You don't want to alienate your readers, to prejudice people against your ideas, or to perpetuate unhealthy attitudes.

31a Recognizing and editing sexist language

As you edit your writing, try to read what you've written from the perspective of a person of the opposite gender or another culture. If you're male, for example, ask yourself whether women might object to anything you've said. If you're white, think about your paper from the perspective of an African American or a member of another minority group. Be especially sensitive when you're characterizing such groups, discussing occupational roles, or referring to all human beings.

1 Avoid demeaning characterizations of women

Your readers are likely to object to language that demeans women or plays into negative stereotypes of women's behaviors, roles, and attributes.

DEMEANING   Pasquale's defense attorney called on **three blonde babes** to testify that they had seen him in a bar on the night Smith was shot.

EDITED   Pasquale's defense attorney called on **three women** to testify that they had seen him in a bar on the night Smith was shot.

DEMEANING   Two undergraduates and **a co-ed** were jointly awarded the prize for the most unusual recipe.
READER'S REACTION: I'm angered by the implication that women aren't real students.

EDITED   **Three undergraduates** were jointly awarded the prize for the most unusual recipe.

DEMEANING   Driving **like a typical woman,** Susan backed her car into the shopping cart.
READER'S REACTION: This unfairly stereotypes women as incompetent.

EDITED   Susan **inadvertently** backed her car into the shopping cart.

2 Avoid gender-stereotyping roles and occupations

Our use of language has not entirely kept pace with social changes in men's and women's roles, especially in the area of occupation. Be on the lookout for unfair or inaccurate stereotyping.

STEREOTYPED   The most important thing **a mother can do** to facilitate language growth in **her** child is to read aloud to **him** as much as possible.
READER'S REACTION: I'm the father of a little girl. I object to the implication that only mothers can care for their children or that all these children are boys.

EDITED   The most important thing **parents can do** to facilitate language growth in **their children** is to read aloud to **them** as much as possible.

STEREOTYPED   Setting industry standards, the OnCall Remote Beeper is **smaller than most doctors' wallets and easier to answer than a phone call from their wives.**
READER'S REACTION: I'm a woman and a doctor. I'm insulted by the assumption that all doctors are male and the negative reference to "wives."

**31a
discrm**

EDITED   Setting industry standards, the OnCall Remote Beeper **will appeal to doctors because of its small size and ease of operation.**

3 Beware of male terms used generically

The most common form of sexist language uses *mankind* or *men* for humankind; *he, his,* or *him* for all people; and a host of words that imply male roles for occupations (*fireman, policeman,* and the like). Most cases are easily edited: *police officer* for *policeman, garbage collector* for *garbageman.* Editing out the generic *he,* however, may prove more difficult. When possible, try first to make the construction plural. For example, you can substitute *their* for *his* or for the clumsy *his or her.*

SEXIST   Every child should bring **his** lunch money to school with **him** each day.

AWKWARD   Every child should bring **his or her** lunch money to school with **him or her** each day.

BETTER   All children should bring **their** lunch money to school with **them** each day.

SEXIST   The Alejandro Restaurant serves **man-sized** portions of paella.

EDITED   The Alejandro Restaurant serves **heaping** portions of paella.

Writer's Alert

Some nonsexist style manuals suggest avoiding the use of generic *he* by making a pronoun plural even if it does not agree in number with the subject (see 18c). Some readers, however, object more strenuously to the error in agreement than to the sexist language. The solution is to avoid both problems whenever possible.

ORIGINAL   **Everyone** has at one time or another squandered **his** money at a gambling casino.

PROBLEMATIC   **Everyone** has at one time or another squandered **their** money at a gambling casino.

BETTER   **Most people have** at one time or another squandered **their** money at a gambling casino.

Everyone has at one time or another squandered money at a gambling casino.

31a
discrm

Exercise 1

A. The following list of words and proposed replacements ranges from the obviously sexist (and therefore inflexible and in need of revision) to the highly debatable and even absurd. For each word, decide whether you would accept the alternative term, and explain why. (Tip: Consult a dictionary when in doubt.)

1. *Persondible* for *mandible*
2. *People-eating tiger* for *man-eating tiger*
3. *Personic depressive* for *manic depressive*
4. *Face-to-face talk* for *man-to-man talk*
5. *Sanitation employee* for *garbageman*
6. *Actor* for both *actor* and *actress*
7. *"Our parent, who art in heaven . . ."* for *"Our Father, who art in heaven. . ."*
8. *Chair* or *chairperson* for *chairman*
9. *Waitperson* or *waitron* for *waiter* and *waitress*
10. *Flight attendant* for *steward* and *stewardess*

B. Compare your responses to Exercise 1A with those of your fellow writers. (And, while you're at it, add *fellow* to your list in Exercise 1A.)

Did You Know?

In 1990, staff administrators for the city of Sacramento decided to eliminate the term *manhole cover* from city documents, suggesting *maintenance access cover* as a suitable substitute. The access holes are used by both male and female maintenance workers, and it is misleading and inappropriate to characterize them in male terms. Such a change is not all that different from the now widespread use of *flight attendant* for *stewardess, police officer* for *policeman,* or *letter carrier* or *postal worker* for *mailman.*

Anne Rudin (former Sacramento mayor), telephone interview, 17 September 1993.

31a
discrm

4 Avoid implying sexist views

Whenever you revise your prose, read it once through paying special attention to the ways you characterize men and women and their roles and relationships. Avoid making any offhand remarks that could be interpreted as sexist.

SEXIST   **Being a girl,** Sondra was chosen to be at the top of the cheerleading pyramid.

READER'S REACTION: I'm not comfortable with what's being implied about girls' abilities here.

EDITED   **Being the lightest person on the team,** Sondra was chosen to be at the top of the cheerleading pyramid.

SEXIST   **Naturally,** Mike wrestled with the flat tire while Natasha **tried to seduce someone into pulling over and helping.**

READER'S REACTION: This stereotypes men as inherently strong and capable and women as sex objects.

EDITED   Mike **struggled to change the tire** while Natasha **tried to flag down a car for help.**

5 Avoid making unwarranted claims

Much sexism finds its energy in misunderstandings about the biological and intellectual nature of men and women. Men are assumed to be stronger, more agile, and more aggressive. Women are assumed to be weaker, worse at math and science but better at language (especially stereotypically "effeminate" forms such as poetry), and less able to manage and negotiate. Many of these assumptions either are unsubstantiated or have come about as self-fulfilling prophecies. In your writing, avoid reinforcing such unfair and incorrect notions.

STEREOTYPED   The anti-abortion protest became more heated when several people appealed to the **instinctive nurturing emotion of the women** in the crowd.

READER'S REACTION: Aren't men nurturers too?

EDITED   The anti-abortion protest became more heated when several people appealed to the **feelings of nurture among the parents** in the crowd.

STEREOTYPED   **Behaving like a wimp,** Roger chose to stay home and read instead of playing football with his friends.

READER'S REACTION: This attaches negative stereotypes to men who engage in intellectual activities.

REVISED   Roger chose to stay home and read instead of playing football with his friends.

31a
discrm

Exercise 2

  A. Examine the following paragraph. Then revise its sexist language. Add to the original if you wish.

Preschool programs for children in poor families have always been underfunded and at best only a stopgap measure for more permanent educational reform. This was the message delivered by the man-and-wife team, Dr. and Mrs. Herbert Kline, Ph.D.s, at the Eleventh Regional Conference on Preschool Education. About seven hundred elementary school teachers came to the conference to hear the Klines debunk some old wives' tales about education. The Klines also focused on what the future holds for those interested in becoming public school teachers, including the need to balance work with attending to one's husband and family. Every teacher of young children, Mrs. Herbert Kline pointed out, must not only practice her craft well but also keep abreast of new theory and research which she can then integrate into her classroom in a way rewarding to her and to her students.

 B. In a small group, compare your responses to Exercise 2A. What strategies did you use to revise the sexist language?

Did You Know?

Sensitivity to sexist language has to some extent already changed the way we write. A study examined how frequently masculine forms such as *man* and *he* appeared in print between 1971 and 1979. At the start of that period, the masculine forms were used twelve times in every 5,000 words, but by the end of the period the proportion had dropped to around four forms per 5,000 words. The steepest decline took place in women's magazines, followed by science magazines and newspapers. Congressional records came in last.

David Crystal, *The English Language* (New York: Penguin, 1988) 257.

31b
discrm

31b Avoiding discriminatory language

Members of minority groups often suffer from discriminatory practices, especially those that are manifested in language. Most readers won't tolerate racism, and as soon as they encounter **discriminatory language,** they'll stop reading or throw the material away.

1 Avoid derogatory terms

You may be used to hearing certain derogatory terms and epithets in others' speech. Now is the time to make sure that they don't appear in your writing so as not to anger and alienate your readers.

RACIST
The economic problems in the border states are compounded by an increase in the number of **wetbacks** from Mexico, some of whom are illegally trying to rip off jobs from good, taxpaying citizens.

READER'S REACTION: **I object to characterizing a group of people this way. This derogatory name is offensive.**

EDITED
The economic problems in the border states are compounded by an increased number of illegal immigrants from Mexico, some of whom are able to get jobs in this country.

HOMOPHOBIC
The talk show included a panel of **fags** who spoke about what it's like to be a **homo.**

READER'S REACTION: **Using emotionally loaded names for people doesn't encourage reasonable discussion. You'll have to be more objective than this if you want me to pay attention to your ideas.**

EDITED
The talk show included a panel of gay guests who shared their thoughts about homosexuality.

DEROGATORY
In a typically **white-male** fashion, the principal argued against the schoolteachers' referendum.

READER'S REACTION: **The fact that white men are in the majority doesn't give you permission to stereotype all white males negatively.**

EDITED
The principal argued against the schoolteachers' referendum.

DISCRIMINATORY
The Johnsons **welshed on** their response.

READER'S REACTION: **What made you think that you could say this without offending people of Welsh descent? Casual stereotyping is just as offensive as deliberate insults.**

EDITED
The Johnsons were not true to their word..

31b
discrm

2 Revise unfair stereotypes

Some racial and cultural stereotypes are so ingrained in our society that you may not notice them at first. Try to maintain a critical consciousness about these stereotypes, and then edit sentences or words that run the risk of unfairly stereotyping various groups. Don't rely on your intentions here; think first about how your reader *might* construe your words.

RACIST/ELITIST
The streets in St. Paul are so confusing that they must have been planned by a bunch of **drunken Irishmen.**

READER'S REACTION: **I object to the off-hand acceptance of this stereotype and the condescending attitude toward a group of people.**

EDITED   The streets in St. Paul are so confusing that no one appears to have done any planning.

DEMEANING   My paper focuses on the **weird** courtship rituals of a **barbaric** Aboriginal tribe living in southwestern Australia.
         READER'S REACTION: Your paper already sounds biased. How can you fairly inform me about this topic if you don't speak respectfully about this tribe yourself?

EDITED   My paper focuses on the unusual courtship rituals of an Aboriginal tribe living in southwestern Australia.

Writer's Tip

In attempts to create an ideally just world, some social critics have proposed new names and terms for various groups, such as the homeless, the physically and mentally disabled, and even the short or the fat. The terms *vagabond, bum,* and *tramp,* for example, are no longer acceptable; *homeless* is now generally preferred. More questionable, however, are the terms *differently abled* for *disabled, vertically challenged* for *short,* and *prewoman* for *girl.* Debates about such proposed substitutions don't seem likely to subside in the near future. Again, the advice on this matter is to test your choices on your readers and keep up with changes in the language.

---

3 Choose appropriate group names and terms

Just as the issue of sexism in language continues to evolve, the representation of various groups, especially minorities, cannot be seen as "finally" corrected. Making informed decisions about how to identify different groups may require some thought or consultation. The term *American Indian* is still widely accepted, but a preferred form, *Native American,* has entered the vocabulary. Some Native American groups prefer their tribal names (*Hopi, Navajo, Havasupai*). In the 1960s, the word *Negro* gradually gave way to *black,* but not without considerable overlap in usage and much debate in both the black and white communities, including whether the terms should be capitalized. The term *colored* has been out of use for some time, but *people of color* is now preferred for members of any "nonwhite" minority group. (Many people also object to the term *nonwhite.*) *African American* itself has been gaining popularity in place of *black,* though even African Americans do not agree on which is preferred. Terms for people of Hispanic descent can also be confusing, from *Chicano* (and its feminine form, *Chicana*) for Mexicans to *Latino* and *Latina* for people from South and Central America more generally.

31b
discrm

How, then, should you decide what terms to use to describe members of various groups?

1. Whenever possible, use the term preferred *by the group itself.*
2. When there is disagreement within the group itself about the preferred name or term, choose the *most widely accepted term* or the one favored by a majority of the group's members.

Exercise 3

 A. The chief editor of a large city newspaper received several complaint letters from readers about a sportswriter's use of the word *niggardly* to characterize the owner of a major football team who was reluctant to pay the salary asked by a new superstar player. In a column, the chief editor explained that the word *niggardly* means "stingy" or "cheap" (from Old Norse) and has absolutely no etymological connection with any racial terms. Yet some readers were offended. And, he argued, as long as they were simply *reminded* of a more offensive word, he had a duty to avoid it. He subsequently asked all reporters and editors to use alternative words. In your judgment, did the chief editor do the right thing? What issues are at stake here? Write a position statement.

 B. Share your position statement from Exercise 3A with your classmates.

EDITING FOR PUNCTUATION

Of all the punctuation marks in written English, the comma is probably the one you find easiest to misuse. At some places in a sentence, commas are mandatory; at others, they are optional. Moreover, unneeded or inappropriate commas can confuse your readers or disrupt a sentence's meaning. Consider the following sentence.

> During interviews avoid dominating the discussion because doing so especially with reticent subjects can affect whatever they say cut off the free flow of their ideas and contaminate your data.

Clearly, it's difficult to read this sentence with the commas missing. But where should you use them? In the following version, the correctly used commas make the sentence easier to read and understand.

> During interviews, avoid dominating the discussion because doing so, especially with reticent subjects, can affect whatever they say, cut off the free flow of their ideas, and contaminate your data.

32a Using commas to help join sentences

Whenever you wish to use *and, but, or, for, nor, so,* or *yet* (coordinating conjunctions) to link two word groups that can stand alone as sentences (main clauses—see 15c–15d), you need to use a comma *before the conjunction.*

The air was cold **,** **and** he could see his breath.

He heard the dog barking on the other side of the field **,** **so** he decided to investigate.

The ground was rough **,** **yet** the dog still ran quickly through the grass.

Linking Sentences with a Comma
Plus a Coordinating Conjunction

main clause   +   **,** + $\left(\begin{array}{l}\textit{and, but, or, for,}\\ \textit{nor, so, yet}\end{array}\right)$ + main clause

We wanted to take a hike **,** **but** the weather was too bad.

Remember to join main clauses with a comma *plus* a coordinating conjunction, not with a comma alone. If you join the clauses with only a comma, you create a **comma splice,** a serious sentence error that can distract or irritate readers (see 21a).

COMMA SPLICE   The heavy rains loosened the soil by the highway **,** the mud slide tore the guardrail away.

EDITED   The heavy rains loosened the soil by the highway **,** **and** the mud slide tore the guardrail away.

EDITED   The heavy rains loosened the soil by the highway **,** **so** the mud slide tore the guardrail away.

If the main clauses you plan to join are quite short, you can sometimes omit the comma.

The temperature dropped **and** the snow began falling.

A comma is appropriate even with short clauses, however.

Writer's Alert

When you use a comma plus a coordinating conjunction to join main clauses, make sure you do not distract readers by adding commas at the following inappropriate places.

- *After* a coordinating conjunction linking main clauses rather than *before* the conjunction

  INCORRECT   I coated the table with varnish **and ,** I sanded it again.

  EDITED   I coated the table with varnish **,** **and** I sanded it again.

32a
⌄

- Between sentence elements other than main clauses—words, phrases, or clauses—that are linked by a coordinating conjunction

INCORRECT	We sanded**,** and stained the old oak table.
	The comma splits parts of a compound verb that belong together.
EDITED	We sanded and stained the old oak table.
INCORRECT	I bought a wood stain that was inexpensive**,** and that cleaned up easily.
	The comma comes between subordinate clauses, not main clauses.
EDITED	I bought a wood stain that was inexpensive and that cleaned up easily.

Exercise 1

A. Combine each of the following sentence pairs into a single sentence, using commas and coordinating conjunctions.

EXAMPLE

Shopping by mail can be convenient.~~It~~ˏsometimes helps save money.
↑ and it

1. Jim wanted to buy paper for his copier. He went to all the office supply stores in town.
2. The stores had plenty of paper. It cost more than Jim was willing to pay.
3. Jim then heard about a mail-order office supply company. He called the company for a catalog.
4. The catalog contained more than fifty different kinds of reasonably priced copier paper. The paper was available in packs of one thousand sheets. For an even greater discount, the paper came in bulk orders of five thousand sheets.
5. He ordered five thousand sheets of medium-quality paper. It lasted for the next three months.

B. Compare your versions of the sentences in Exercise 1A with those produced by a group of classmates. Decide which versions are the most effective and why.

32b
↕

32b   Using commas to set off introductory phrases

A comma can help your readers sort sentence parts that might otherwise run together and create confusion. The simplest sentences, consisting of a noun phrase and a verb phrase, need no comma.

noun phrase   verb phrase
Jessica mowed the lawn.

When you add another layer to this basic sentence—a word or a word group—you may need to signal the addition with a comma.

Tirelessly, Jessica mowed the lawn.
On Saturday, Jessica mowed the lawn.
After running five miles, Jessica mowed the lawn.
In spite of the throbbing pain in her ankle, Jessica mowed the lawn.

S T R A T E G Y

Place a comma after an introductory sentence element when the comma makes the sentence easier to read and understand.
The following sentence needs a comma to avoid confusing readers.

CONFUSING   Forgetting to remove the hose Jessica mowed the lawn.

EDITED   Forgetting to remove the hose **,** Jessica mowed the lawn.
                The comma lets readers know where the introductory word group ends and the main sentence begins.

In contrast, the following sentences are easy to understand without a comma.

CLEAR   By noon Jessica will be finished mowing the lawn.

CLEAR   Suddenly it started raining and Jessica quit mowing.

In general, you need to put a comma at the end of a long introductory element to let readers know where the main sentence begins.

CONFUSING   When Ruane came home and saw the chopped pieces of hose she was furious at Jessica.

CLEAR   When Ruane came home and saw the chopped pieces of hose **, she** was furious at Jessica.

You should also use a comma with a short introductory element that might otherwise briefly confuse readers.

CONFUSING   By six boats began showing up.

EDITED   By six **,** boats began showing up.

32b

CONFUSING   Adamant that man kept shouting at the bank teller.

EDITED   Adamant, that man kept shouting at the bank teller.

You can insert a comma to tell readers which of two possible meanings you intend.

Curious, George went deeper into the cave.

Curious George went deeper into the cave.
Curious George is a character in a series of children's books.

Well, over there was where I saw him, officer.

Well over there was where I saw him, officer.
***Well over there* is a location.**

Writer's Alert

Sometimes the comma after an introductory word or word group is required; sometimes it is optional. When you are uncertain, stay on the safe side: use a comma.

---

1 Use a comma after an introductory clause beginning with *because, although, if,* and similar words

When you open a sentence with a subordinate clause (see 27b-1) that begins with a subordinating conjunction such as *since, although, because,* or *when* (see 27b-2 for a detailed list), place a comma after the clause to mark the beginning of the main sentence.

Although I am healthy, I see a physician for a regular checkup.

When I need to see my doctor because I feel ill, I can usually schedule an appointment within a day.

2 Use a comma after an introductory phrase

Phrases lack one or more elements necessary to form a complete sentence, such as a subject, a predicate, or both (see 16b). When you start a sentence with a phrase, you generally add a comma to signal the boundary between the phrase and the main sentence.

During the past decade, Dr. Bandola has worked for an HMO.

Growing tired of the HMO's management, she decided last year to open her own medical practice.

32b

Worried about the costs of a new office, she consulted a real estate broker specializing in medical and dental offices.

To furnish her waiting room, she went to a discount office furniture company.

Her office now furnished, she is ready to begin seeing patients.

Did You Know?

Writers sometimes claim that commas (and other punctuation) ought to appear where someone reading a text aloud would be likely to take a breath. They often use this argument to excuse their highly personal or inconsistent punctuation. As William Bridgwater points out, however, if you try to follow the punctuation marks when you read aloud, you may find yourself "panting like a dog on a hot day." Bridgwater admits that "in English punctuation there are fashions, just as there are in dress and in popular use of phrases," yet he observes that many punctuation practices are "fairly stable" while others, such as the use of commas with nonrestrictive modifiers, "are almost universally accepted by English-speaking readers." His job as a copy editor is to recognize the conventions and "promote punctuation that will aid the reader today."

William Bridgwater, "Copyediting," in *Editors on Editing,* ed. Gerald Gross (New York: HarperCollins 1985) 79–81.

---

3 Use a comma after introductory words like *however* or transitional phrases like *for example*

Words like *however, nonetheless,* and *moreover* are **conjunctive adverbs** (see 15a-6). *For example, in addition, in contrast,* and similar word groups are **transitional expressions.** Set off both of these elements with a comma when they begin a sentence.

32b

> **Nonetheless,** I do not think we should ban all use of chemical pesticides in the region.

> **In contrast,** a group of organic farmers has been urging us to rely on natural methods of pest control.

You may occasionally wish to open a sentence with an interjection, such as *yes, no, well,* or *oh.* When you do, follow it with a comma unless an exclamation mark is more appropriate as a way to express strong emotion.

Yes, I cleaned the beakers and the test tubes.

No! I do not want to attend any more meetings on the problem.

Exercise 2

A. Edit the following sentences by placing commas after introductory elements where necessary.

EXAMPLE

In the past,mailboxes usually had simple designs.

1. In contrast mailboxes today come in many surprising designs.
2. Occasionally people in the suburbs choose an unusual mailbox, but residents of small towns generally display the most imagination.
3. On a recent trip through rural Iowa I noticed mailboxes in the shape of log cabins, igloos, Eiffel Towers, cows, cats, and even parrots.
4. One morning I drove down a block on which each mailbox took the shape of a different kind of fish, including bass, trout, bluegill, shark, pike, and salmon.
5. Whenever you start thinking that people in big cities or suburbs are more creative than people in small towns remember the mailboxes.

B. Working in a group, combine each of the following pairs of sentences by making one an introductory element for the other. Insert commas when appropriate.

EXAMPLE

Because

The morning was gray and foggy. Many people woke up late.

1. People felt sleepy. They still had to go to their offices and plants for a full day's work.
2. People were trying to get to work on time. They jammed the highways and commuter trains.
3. Avi felt rested and alert. The gloomy weather did not bother him.
4. Avi worked hard throughout the afternoon. The other people in Avi's office were exhausted by two o'clock in the afternoon.
5. Avi still felt awake at seven o'clock in the evening. He went to see a movie.

32c

32c Using commas to set off nonrestrictive modifiers

Restrictive and nonrestrictive modifiers are common midsentence elements. You use a **restrictive modifier** to present information that is essential to the meaning of a passage. You use a **nonrestrictive modifier** to add information that is interesting or useful but that is not essential to the meaning (see 22c).

S T R A T E G Y

When the information in a modifier is essential to the meaning of a passage, present it without commas so that readers will regard it as a necessary, integral part of the sentence (that is, restrictive clauses need no commas).

RESTRICTIVE   The charts **drawn by hand** were hard to read.

> READER'S REACTION: This sentence implies that the other charts, presumably those that were computer-generated, were easier to read than the hand-drawn ones.

When the information in a modifier adds to a passage but is not essential to its meaning, set it off with commas so that readers will regard it as providing helpful but not necessary detail (that is, nonrestrictive modifiers require commas).

NONRESTRICTIVE   The charts**,** **drawn by hand,** were hard to read.

> READER'S REACTION: This sentence says that all the charts were hard to read. It adds the detail that the charts were hand-drawn but doesn't indicate that this was necessarily related to the problem with legibility.

Because of the difference between restrictive and nonrestrictive modifiers, you can change the meaning of a sentence considerably by deciding whether or not to set off a modifier with commas.

1 Identify nonrestrictive modifiers

As you edit, you need to identify nonrestrictive modifiers and set them off with commas. You also need to be able to identify restrictive modifiers, which require no commas to set them off.

S T R A T E G Y

To identify a nonrestrictive modifier, try eliminating the modifier from a sentence. If you can do so without altering the sentence's essential meaning, then the modifier is nonrestrictive and you should use commas

32c

with it. Remember, eliminating a nonrestrictive modifier may make a sentence less informative but will not change its basic meaning.

UNEDITED SENTENCE	Their band **which performs primarily in small venues like clubs** has gotten many fine reviews for its music.
WITHOUT MODIFIER	Their band has gotten many fine reviews for its music. **The meaning is retained, though the sentence does not offer as much interesting information. The modifier is nonrestrictive.**
EDITED	Their band **,** **which performs primarily in small venues like clubs ,** has gotten many fine reviews for its music.

If eliminating a modifier changes a sentence's meaning, the modifier is restrictive. Do not set it off with commas.

UNEDITED SENTENCE	Executives **,** **who do not know how to cope with stress ,** are prone to stress-related illness.
WITHOUT MODIFIER	Executives are prone to stress-related illness. **The intended meaning of the original sentence is that *some* executives are susceptible to stress-related problems; in contrast, the shortened sentence says they *all* are. The modifier is restrictive.**
EDITED	Executives **who do not know how to cope with stress** are prone to stress-related illness.

2 Use commas with nonrestrictive modifiers

If a nonrestrictive modifier appears in the middle of a sentence, enclose it with commas. Place a comma after one coming at the beginning of a sentence and before one coming at the end.

32c

main clause begins **,** nonrestrictive modifier **,** main clause ends
The public hearing **,** scheduled for 7 p.m. **,** will gather responses to cable TV rates.

nonrestrictive modifier **,** main clause
Unable to meet their rising costs **,** the cable companies have requested a rate hike.

main clause **,** nonrestrictive modifier
Many residents oppose the hike **,** which is larger than last year's.

3 Pay special attention to modifying clauses, phrases, and appositives

In identifying nonrestrictive (and restrictive) modifiers as you edit, keep in mind that they can be clauses, phrases, or words (see 23c).

Modifying Clauses Beginning with *Who* and *Which*. Pay special attention to clauses beginning with *who, which, that, whom, whose, when,* or *where* (see 15c-5 and 22c), and decide whether or not they should be set off with commas. These common modifying elements can appear in the middle or at the end of a sentence.

NONRESTRICTIVE   Preventive dentistry, **which is receiving greater emphasis,** may actually reduce the number of times each of us has to visit a dentist's office.

NONRESTRICTIVE   At the heart of preventive dentistry are toothbrushing, flossing, and rinsing, **which are all easily done.**

RESTRICTIVE   Dentists **who make a special effort to encourage good oral hygiene** often provide helpful pamphlets and samples of toothbrushes and floss.

Modifying Phrases. Be alert as well for phrases (word groups lacking a subject, a predicate, or both) that are nonrestrictive and should be marked with commas. These modifying elements can appear at the beginning, middle, or end of sentences.

NONRESTRICTIVE   **Occupying the daily headline of the local newspaper for the last two weeks,** our city's budget crisis now threatens to spread to the state budget.

NONRESTRICTIVE   The governor has called for a conference of the people most directly involved in trying to solve the budget problem, **including the mayor, state legislators, and the city's budget director.**

RESTRICTIVE   City services **popular with voters** are seldom cut from the budget.

Appositives. An **appositive** is a noun or pronoun that renames or stands for a preceding noun. Since most appositives are nonrestrictive, you generally need to set off appositives with a comma. Be on the lookout for an occasional restrictive appositive, however, and do not use commas with it.

NONRESTRICTIVE   Amy Nguyen, **a poet from Vietnam,** recently published her second collection of verse.

NONRESTRICTIVE   The athletic performance drink, **a concoction of electrolytes, vitamins, minerals, and fructose,** contributed to Jose's endurance in the marathon.

NONRESTRICTIVE   Stump grinding, **a method for removing old tree roots with a special machine,** is much easier than digging the roots out with a shovel.

32c
△

RESTRICTIVE   The well-known executive **Louis Gerstner** went from heading RJR Nabisco to the top job at IBM.

RESTRICTIVE   The terms **cognitive** and **neural pathways** are familiar to anyone involved in brain research.

Exercise 3

A. Edit the following sentences to set off all nonrestrictive modifiers with commas and to eliminate any commas that unnecessarily set off restrictive modifiers.

EXAMPLE
My mother͵who is ninety͵lives in the retirement residence͵called South Bay Manor.

1. Fifty years ago, a residence that served retired people, was called an old folks' home.
2. These homes which provided few services for residents were apartment buildings with dining rooms.
3. A retirement residence today offers many things to do including recreational activities, fitness programs, trips, classes, and social events.
4. The image of infirm people, sitting in rocking chairs, has been replaced by one of senior citizens, who are vigorous and involved.
5. Retirement residences often known as retirement communities are small towns, where people go to lead active lives.

B. Have each member of a small group bring in a paragraph from a magazine article, both in original form and rewritten to eliminate the commas setting off all nonrestrictive modifiers. As a group, first attempt to restore the commas to the rewritten versions; then check the originals to see if you agree with their punctuation.

32d

32d   Using commas to set off parenthetical expressions

Remember that the basic structure of a sentence can be interrupted with all sorts of words and word groups that add information or modify the sentence's various elements, including conjunctive adverbs (like *however* or *nonetheless*), transitional terms (like *in contrast*), and parenthetical remarks.

Use commas to set off conjunctive adverbs like *however* and *moreover* (see 15a-6, 21b) when they appear in the middle of a sentence or at the beginning or end. Do the same with transitional expressions like *on the other hand* or *for example* and with parenthetical remarks like *in fact* or *more importantly* (sometimes called **interrupters**).

TRANSITIONAL EXPRESSION The hailstorm last week, **on the other hand,** caused severe damage.

INTERRUPTER **In fact,** the hailstorm was so powerful that it broke a dozen priceless stained glass windows on the west side of the church.

CONJUNCTIVE ADVERB We should not be surprised, **therefore,** if someone takes up a collection for the windows' repair.

You should also use commas to set off tag questions, statements of contrast, and words indicating direct address.

TAG QUESTIONS We should be ready to contribute to the cause even if we don't attend the church, **shouldn't we?**

STATEMENT OF CONTRAST The windows' beauty touched all of us in the community, **not just the church members.**

DIRECT ADDRESS Please remember, **friends of beauty,** that your contribution will help restore the windows to their former magnificence.

Exercise 4

 Edit the following sentences to add or eliminate commas as appropriate.

EXAMPLE
Scheduling may be ⌃ in fact ⌃ the toughest job any manager faces.

1. Project schedules need to be arranged so that the job gets done on time of course.
2. Moreover meetings need to be set up so they do not interrupt people's work, unnecessarily.
3. Most staff members are cooperative however, and may even offer suggestions for scheduling.
4. Management training programs should, I think offer instruction in scheduling techniques.
5. Remember your staff's time is too valuable to be wasted.

32d

32e Using commas in a series

Whenever you list items in a series and give each roughly equal status, you should separate the items with commas. In one sense, commas take the place of a repeated *and,* which appears only before the last item in the series.

HARD TO READ   Harvey's favorite novels are *Moby Dick* **and** *The Awakening* **and** *Jane Eyre* **and** *Things Fall Apart.*

EDITED   Harvey's favorite novels are *Moby Dick*, *The Awakening*, *Jane Eyre*, **and** *Things Fall Apart.*

Note how difficult the following sentence is to read when the series lacks commas.

HARD TO READ   Tiffany's favorite novels, however, are *War and Peace Of Time and the River Heart of Darkness* and *The Color Purple.*

EDITED   Tiffany's favorite novels, however, are *War and Peace*, *Of Time and the River*, *Heart of Darkness*, and *The Color Purple.*

Placing a comma before the *and* that introduces the last item in a series helps avoid confusion. Many readers prefer this practice, especially in academic and professional writing. Editors of newspapers and some magazines, however, do not use this comma.

CONFUSING   The ingredients for the casserole are peas, potatoes, ham, caramelized sugar and bread crumbs.
READER's REACTION: **Does** *caramelized sugar and bread crumbs* **refer to some special mixture, or are they two separate ingredients?**

EDITED   The ingredients for the casserole are peas, potatoes, ham, caramelized sugar, and bread crumbs.

A numbered or lettered list that is part of a sentence should be punctuated as a series.

To make sure your analysis is complete, you should (1) check the bottom of the container for residue, (2) measure the salinity of the water, (3) weigh any organic waste in the filter, and (4) determine the amount of dissolved oxygen in the water.

32e

Writer's Tip

If the items in a list are long and complex or if they contain commas, separate the items with semicolons rather than commas (see 33a).

CONFUSING	The company is marketing a line of jigsaw puzzles of cities, like San Antonio, Texas, states, like Michigan and Montana, and countries, like Mexico, Japan, and France.
EDITED	The company is marketing a line of jigsaw puzzles of cities, like San Antonio, Texas; states, like Michigan and Montana; and countries, like Mexico, Japan, and France.

32f Separating coordinate adjectives with a comma

In a pair of **coordinate adjectives,** each adjective modifies a noun on its own. Therefore, separate coordinate adjectives with commas to indicate that they apply to the noun (or pronoun) in an equal manner.

COORDINATE (EQUAL)	These drawings describe a **quick, simple** solution to the drainage problem.

With **noncoordinate adjectives,** the first adjective modifies the entire noun phrase formed by the next adjectives plus the noun. Usually noncoordinate adjectives are of different categories. For example, one adjective may describe a quality and another a nationality, as in the phrase *friendly Dutch student* (see 19a). Do not separate noncoordinate adjectives with a comma. In the following example, the adjective *flexible* modifies *plastic pipe.*

NONCOORDINATE (UNEQUAL)	We can use **flexible plastic** pipe to carry water away from the building.

In place of a comma, you can connect coordinate adjectives with *and* or *but.*

COORDINATE	These drawings describe a **quick and simple** solution to the drainage problem.

32f

S T R A T E G Y

To identify coordinate adjectives, ask one of the following questions. If the answer is *yes,* the adjectives are coordinate and should be separated with a comma.

- Can you place *and* or *but* between the adjectives?

COORDINATE	Through irrigation, the region's farmers have turned dry infertile [*dry and infertile?—yes*] land into orchards.
EDITED	Through irrigation, the region's farmers have turned dry **,** infertile land into orchards.
NOT COORDINATE	Five percent of the budget goes to new telecommunications [*new and telecommunications?—no*] equipment.

- Can you easily invert the adjectives without creating an awkward sentence?

COORDINATE	We wanted to move from our small cramped [*cramped small?—acceptable*] apartment.
EDITED	We wanted to move from our small **,** cramped apartment.
NOT COORDINATE	We decided to move to a small Manhattan [*Manhattan small?—awkward*] apartment.

Exercise 5

A. Edit the following sentences so that any series and any coordinate adjectives are correctly punctuated. Let any correct sentence stand.

EXAMPLE
McDonald's ₐ Burger King ₐ and Wendy's are worldwide symbols of American culture.

1. McDonald's and the others offer quick appetizing meals and clean pleasant surroundings.
2. In the late 1940s, the McDonald brothers opened a restaurant serving a limited inexpensive menu, including fifteen-cent hamburgers french fries and shakes.
3. The brothers did not want to expand their modestly successful restaurant into a chain.
4. Ray Kroc, a manufacturer of milkshake machines, recognized the potential of the brothers' innovations joined their business to help it expand and, frustrated by their lack of ambition, eventually bought them out.
5. Kroc continued to develop innovative imaginative ways to serve customers, and these fast efficient practices have come to characterize today's fast-food restaurants.

32f
⌒

B. Working with a partner, exchange your current papers. Edit your partner's draft so that all series and coordinate adjectives are correctly punctuated.

32g Using commas with dates, numbers, addresses, place names, people's titles, and letters

You should separate the elements in dates, place names, long numbers, and addresses according to conventional practice. Separate the elements whether or not they appear in sentences.

1 Dates

Put a comma between the date and the year and between the day of the week and the date.

The first computer in this office arrived on August 17, 1983.

The workshop will begin on Wednesday, September 11.

In the middle of a sentence, follow the year with a comma when you are giving the full date.

On February 4, 1923, the woman destined to be my mother was born in the middle of a snowstorm.

Do not use commas when the date contains only a month and year or a month and a day.

A test version of the software will be available in January 1997. The regular version will be shipped to stores on June 1.

Likewise, do not use commas with dates stating a season and a year.

The fall 1996 issue of the magazine arrived late.

You do not need to use commas when you present the elements of a date in inverted order: 5 July 1973.

2 Numbers

In order to help your readers understand long numbers, use commas to create groups of three, beginning from the right. In numbers with four digits, you may choose whether or not to use the comma, but keep your practice consistent within an essay or report.

During the livestock census on the ranch, we counted **1,746** sheep, **835** beef cattle, and **3,589** chickens.

32g
⌄

The combined income for people in our rural town is $8**,**543**,**234.

The best personal copier available costs $1**,**525 at Electronics World.

Omit commas in addresses or page numbers of four numbers or more.

18520 South Kedzie Drive   page 2054

ESL Advice: Numbers

In writing long numbers, make sure you use commas to create groups of three. Periods are used only to indicate decimals.

1.000 = one

1,000 = one thousand

3 Addresses and place names

Separate names of cities and states with commas.

Kansas City**,** Missouri**,** is a larger town than Kansas City**,** Kansas.

For addresses appearing within a sentence, place a comma between all elements *except* the state and ZIP code.

You can order the zucchini and carrot seeds from Fredelle and Family**,** Seed Brokers**,** Box 389**,** Holland**,** Michigan 30127.

Do not place a comma after the ZIP code unless the punctuation of some other sentence element requires one.

32g
ESL

NO COMMA   Send the bill to Mr. Robert Mfume at 82 Nassau Avenue, Kenmore, New York 11327-8501 for a full refund.

COMMA NEEDED   The pamphlet can be obtained from Bradley Hospital, Veterans Memorial Parkway, East Providence, Rhode Island 02915**,** a children's psychiatric center.

4 People's names and titles

Place a comma before a title or initials that come after a person's name.

The report on possible lung damage among plant employees was prepared by **Luis Aguayo,** **M.D.**

If the name and title come at the beginning of a sentence or in the middle, use a comma after the title as well.

We hired **Crystal Bronkowski , A.I.A. ,** to design the new building.

When you give a person's surname (last name) first, separate it from the first name with a comma: **Shamoon , Linda K.**

5 Salutations and closings of letters

Use a comma after the salutation of personal or informal letters.

Dear Tiffany ,   Dear Volleyball Players ,

Use a colon after the salutation in business and formal letters.

Dear Specialty Metals Customers :   Dear Sir or Madam :

Use a comma after a letter's closing, just before the signature.

Sincerely ,   Best wishes ,   With affection ,   Regards ,

Exercise 6

A. Edit the following sentences by adding or eliminating commas as appropriate.

EXAMPLE

My mother remembers assembling her first jigsaw puzzle in autumn, 1953, several months before my birth on January 22,1954.

1. Puzzles have fascinated me for the last thirty years, and last year I spent exactly $1479.83 on them.
2. For my birthday this year, one cousin gave me a map of Chicago Illinois in the form of a jigsaw puzzle, and another cousin gave me a puzzle of a seventeenth-century print from the Beinecke Library at Yale University New Haven Connecticut.
3. I have ordered a puzzle map of Atlanta Georgia from Buffalo Games, Inc. P.O. Box 85 601 Amherst Street Buffalo New York 14207 and a puzzle of Edward Hopper's painting, *Nighthawks* from Galison Books 36 West 44th Street New York New York 10036 .
4. From January through June 1994, I assembled one puzzle a week, with the puzzles ranging from 500 to 1250 pieces each for a total of somewhere between 10500 pieces and 26250 pieces.
5. I am planning to have a business card made up with both my official and unofficial titles, Jessica Montoya Ph.D. Puzzle Assembler.

32g

B.   Working in a group, share copies of magazine or newspaper articles that contain numbers, addresses, people's names and titles, or openings and closings of letters. Check the articles to see whether they follow the same conventions for comma use as those described in 32g. If not, or if the author uses commas inconsistently, edit each article so that it agrees with the recommendations for comma use covered in 32g.

32h   Using commas with quotations

When you introduce or conclude a quotation by indicating its source or explaining the context, you should remind readers of the difference between your explanation and the quotation itself by using commas to separate them.

> At the grand opening, he said, "This facility is dedicated to the physical and mental health of the citizens of Oakdale."

> "Some books are meant to be chewed," said Francis Bacon, "and others to be digested."
> **Because the explanatory words interrupt the quotation, the first part ends with a comma.**

> "The fire doors need to be replaced before the school can be reopened," the commissioner wrote.

When a quotation ends with a question mark or an exclamation point, you should keep this punctuation even if you provide an explanation after the quotation.

> "We can't afford the $30,000 to replace the doors right away!" the school board president responded angrily.

> "Why can't you understand the paramount importance of fire safety?" the commissioner retorted.

If your explanation ends with *that* just before the quotation, do not include a comma.

> Lorene Cary begins her story by saying that "they had just come home from Woolworth's, where they both worked at the cheap-and-greasy fountain on Friday nights and Saturdays in a town they and their friends called 'Tacky' Darby."

When you quote a person's words indirectly (rather than word for word in quotation marks), do not use a comma after *that.*

FAULTY	He testified that **,** he did not damage the machinery as a protest during the strike.
EDITED	He testified that he did not damage the machinery as a protest during the strike.

Exercise 7

A. Edit the following passages by adding, deleting, or moving commas so that quotations are appropriately punctuated.

"Ice cream is virtually the only food we eat frozen, which means that its flavor, which we define as a composite of taste and smell, is only fully released upon melting" explains Arun Kilara, a 43-year-old professor of food science at Penn State and one of the world's acknowledged authorities on ice cream.

Not surprisingly, few true ice cream connoisseurs are fond of the industry's use of fat substitutes, such as the complex protein found in NutraSweet's Simplesse. "The search for the perfect fat substitute" Kilara says "is like a contemporary version of alchemy—lots of useful discoveries, but they'll never turn lead into gold." While some protein-based fat substitutes approximate fat's texture, or "mouth feel" he explains, they cannot dissolve flavor compounds in the same way.

"The smaller the ice crystals, the smoother the ice cream" says Kilara. "You get the smallest crystals when the drop in temperature is the most rapid and when agitation is most vigorous."

"There's one basic truth about ice cream—its quality begins deteriorating from the moment it is made" Kilara concludes. "Over the product's lifetime, ice cream's air escapes, its fat clumps, its ice melts, and its water freezes." —LAWRENCE E. JOSEPH, "The Scoop on Ice Cream"

B. Working in a group, write a paragraph that presents information drawn from a newspaper or magazine article. Include several quotations from the article in your paragraph. Indicate the source or context for the quotations, and use commas appropriately to introduce or conclude the quoted material.

32i
ᛆ

32i Using commas to make your meaning clear

Even if no rule specifies a comma, you may still include one in a sentence if it is necessary to make your meaning clear to readers, to remind them of deleted words, or to add emphasis.

CONFUSING	When food is scarce, animals that can expand their grazing territory at the expense of other species.
EDITED	When food is scarce, animals that can, expand their grazing territory at the expense of other species.
HARD TO READ	Anyone who can afford to buy this high-speed file management program should.
EDITED	Anyone who can afford to buy this high-speed file management program, should. **The comma reminds readers that *should* means "should do so."**
UNEMPHATIC	Stocks go up and down.
EMPHATIC	Stocks go up, and down. **The comma emphasizes the contrast.**

32j   Avoiding commas that do not belong

When they are not sure precisely where to put commas, some writers insert them at every possible point. The result is confusing and irritating to readers. Try to avoid scattering commas throughout your writing with no clear purpose in mind. If you are not sure whether to add a comma, leave it out until you have checked to make sure one is required. In addition, avoid using commas in the situations discussed below.

1 Do not insert a comma after words like *although* and *because* that introduce a clause

Certain conjunctions and other words may mislead you into thinking you need a comma. Among the most common words of this type are subordinating conjunctions like *although, when,* and *since* (see 27b-2 for a detailed list). They introduce an entire subordinate clause and should not be set off with commas. One reason writers set off subordinating conjunctions with commas is that they mistake the words for conjunctive adverbs (like *however*) and transitional expressions (such as *for example*), which should be set off with commas (see 21b).

INCORRECT	**Although,** Jim had just started to learn how to ski, we took him to the most expert slope on his first trip up the mountain.
EDITED	**Although** Jim had just started to learn how to ski, we took him to the most expert slope on his first trip up the mountain.

32j
no

2 Do not insert a comma between a subject and a predicate

Unless subjects and predicates are separated by a modifying clause, don't insert a comma between them.

INCORRECT   Cézanne's painting *Rocks at L'Estaque* , hangs in the Museu de Arte in São Paulo, Brazil.

EDITED   Cézanne's painting *Rocks at L'Estaque* hangs in the Museu de Arte in São Paulo, Brazil.

3 Do not overuse commas

Today readers generally prefer a style in which commas are not used heavily. Too many commas, even when they are correctly used, can lead to a style that is choppy and hard to read. Whenever possible, avoid sentence structures that call for a large number of commas. If necessary, edit and rewrite to eliminate excessive comma use.

TOO MANY COMMAS   Samantha, always one, like her mother, to speak her mind, loudly protested the use of force, as she called it, by two store detectives, who had been observing her while she, looking for bargains, absentmindedly slipped a pair of gloves into her jacket pocket.

EDITED   Always one to speak her mind, like her mother, Samantha loudly protested what she considered the use of force by two store detectives who saw her absentmindedly slip a pair of gloves into her jacket pocket while she was looking for bargains.

In the first passage, none of the commas are incorrect, but the comma is clearly overused. In the second passage, careful editing turns a nine-comma sentence into one with two commas.

32j
no ⌀

Exercise 8

A. Edit each of the following sentences in two ways: (1) by removing any unnecessary commas, and (2) by rewriting to create sentence structures that contain fewer commas, all of which are necesssary.

EXAMPLE
When/ they realized they had no job prospects, the five friends/ formed/ a company, which they called Home Restorers, Inc.
When they realized they had no job prospects, the five friends formed Home Restorers, Inc.

1. Because, she likes the outdoors, Sandy, a devoted gardener, takes care of landscaping, grass cutting, and outdoor cleanup.
2. Strong, tireless Jun, does roofing, paving, and similar work.
3. Interior design was, Padmaja's major, so she, everyone agrees, is the person best qualified to do interior decorating.
4. Having painted, her parents' house one summer, Rachael was, chosen, by her partners, as the company's painting supervisor.
5. Desperate, for a place in the company, Joel decided that, marketing, because it would draw on his undergraduate work in sociology, was the best thing for him to do.

 B. Exchange draft papers with another writer, and edit each other's work to eliminate unnecessary commas. When you encounter a sentence that might be rewritten to reduce the number of commas, underline it. When your partner returns your paper, check over the editorial changes and consider rewriting any underlined sentences.

CHAPTER

33

Semicolons
and Colons

Semicolons and colons help you connect words, word groups, or sentences in useful and varied ways. Compare the following brief passages.

> On April 12, 1861, at 4:30 a.m., one of Beauregard's batteries fired upon Fort **Sumter. The** Civil War had begun.

> On April 12, 1861, at 4:30 a.m., one of Beauregard's batteries fired upon Fort **Sumter; the** Civil War had begun.

> On April 12, 1861, at 4:30 a.m., one of Beauregard's batteries fired upon Fort **Sumter: the** Civil War had begun.

The first version consists of two sentences; the second and third join the sentences with a semicolon and a colon, respectively. All three examples are correct, yet each encourages readers to take a different perspective. Note, for example, that in the first version there is no *necessary* connection between the two sentences. Readers may choose whether to view the sentences as a simple statement of facts or as the presentation of a dramatic moment. In the second version, however, the semicolon connects the two statements and encourages readers to link the firing of a gun battery to the beginning of the Civil War. In the third sentence, the colon provides even more direction to readers. It encourages them to view the guns' firing as a dramatic and significant moment: the beginning of the Civil War.

33a
;

33a Using semicolons

A semicolon joins two main clauses that could act as complete sentences on their own. The semicolon indicates that the clauses are linked logically; at the same time, it creates a brief reading pause between them.

1 Try joining main clauses with a semicolon

You can use a semicolon to join two complete sentences (main clauses—see 15c–15d) into a single unit. Think of a semicolon as an alternative to using a period and starting a new sentence.

TWO SENTENCES   The demand for paper products is at an all-time high. Business and industry alone consume millions of tons of paper each year.

ONE SENTENCE   The demand for paper products is at an all-time high; business and industry alone consume millions of tons of paper each year.

You signal the relationship between main clauses by joining them with a semicolon, though you do not specify the logical link as you might by joining clauses with a conjunction such as *and, but,* or *yet* (see 27a). A semicolon can highlight the close relationship of ideas or dramatically emphasize a contrast between clauses.

> The city council wants more parks, an expanded recreation program, and a civic center; the mayor wants to cut expenses and limit services.

When you join main clauses with a semicolon, make sure readers will be able to recognize the logical relationship without having to puzzle over the sentence.

S T R A T E G Y

Remember that a semicolon joins main clauses that can stand on their own as sentences. If you can't convert the clauses on either side of a semicolon into complete sentences, the semicolon has probably been misused.

33a
;

INCORRECT   The demand for recycled paper has also increased greatly; with manufacturers rushing to develop reliable supplies of scrap paper.

TEST   The demand for recycled paper has also increased greatly.
The first clause is a complete sentence.

With manufacturers rushing to develop reliable supplies of scrap paper.
The second part is a sentence fragment.

CORRECT   The demand for recycled paper has also increased greatly; manufacturers are rushing to develop reliable supplies of scrap paper.

> ## Did You Know?
>
> ---
>
> Historically, the semicolon was often used to mark an abbreviation, indicating that something had been eliminated or cut off. The word *Esquire,* for example, was often abbreviated with a semicolon (*Esq;*), as were *Mr;* and *Mrs;*. This usage fell out of favor in the United States in the nineteenth century. Many Europeans still use the semicolon to indicate abbreviation, and some use it occasionally in formal citations where Americans would use a comma (*Dear Sir:* can become, for example, *Monsieur;* in French).

2 Use a semicolon with transition words

When you use a semicolon alone to link main clauses, you ask your readers to recognize the logical link between the clauses. When you use a transition word like *however* or a transitional expression like *on the other hand*, you create a different effect. The transition specifies the relationship of the clauses, so the effect on readers is something like the following.

Assertion → semicolon → transition → assertion
(pause)   (consider relationship)

I like apples ; **however** , I hate pears.
assertion pause contrast assertion

To specify the transition between clauses, you can choose a **conjunctive adverb** such as *however, moreover, thus,* or *therefore* (see 27b-2 for a detailed list) or a **transitional expression** like *for example, in contrast,* or *on the other hand.* The linking word or phrase can appear between clauses (just after the semicolon), within one of the clauses, or at the end of a clause. If such a transition comes between clauses, right after a semicolon, it must be followed by a comma; if it comes within a clause, it must be preceded and followed by commas; if it comes at the end of a clause, it must be preceded by a comma.

33a
;

BETWEEN CLAUSES	Joe returned from the Arctic ; **however** , Alan was never found.
WITHIN A CLAUSE	Joe returned from the Arctic ; Alan , **however** , was never found.
AT END OF CLAUSE	Joe returned from the Arctic ; Alan was never found , **however.**

> ### Writer's Tip
>
> Consider joining a series of short to medium-length sentences with semicolons when (1) the sentences are logically linked; (2) as a group, the unlinked sentences seem choppy or disconnected; and (3) commas do not separate the elements enough to encourage readers to consider each one fully.
>
> | | |
> |---|---|
> | **CHOPPY** | The shelty took first prize. The German shepherd took second. The poodle walked away in third place. |
> | **BETTER** | The shelty took first prize, the German shepherd took second, **and** the poodle walked away in third place. |
> | **MOST EFFECTIVE** | The shelty took first prize **;** the German shepherd took second **;** and the poodle walked away in third place. |

3 Use a semicolon with deleted structures

There are exceptions to the rule that semicolons must join main clauses. In some cases, elements within a second clause can be deleted if they "match" elements in the first clause. The two clauses can be joined with a semicolon even though the second could not stand on its own as a sentence.

ELEMENTS INCLUDED	In winter, **the hotel guests enjoy** the log fire in the dining room **;** in summer, **the hotel guests enjoy** the patio overlooking the river.
ELEMENTS DELETED	In winter, **the hotel guests enjoy** the log fire in the dining room **;** in summer, the patio overlooking the river.

4 Use a semicolon with a complex series

Most of the time, you can use commas to highlight and separate elements in a series, with no risk of confusion (see 32e). When some of the items themselves contain commas, however, readers may have a hard time deciding which commas mark the parts of the series and which belong within the items, as in the following example.

CONFUSING	For the project, I interviewed Debbie Rios, my roommate, Rhonda Marron, my former employer, and my calculus instructor. **READER'S REACTION: How many people were interviewed? Three, four, or five?**

To avoid confusion, put semicolons between elements in a series when one or more of the elements contain commas or some other internal punctuation, such as a dash, parentheses, or a colon.

EDITED   For the project, I interviewed Debbie Rios, my roommate; Rhonda Marron, my former employer; and my calculus instructor.

Exercise 1

A. The following passage contains some semicolons used correctly and some used incorrectly. It also contains some sentences that might be more effective if joined with semicolons and others that would be better as separate sentences. Rewrite the passage, adding or eliminating semicolons and making any other changes necessary to create a more effective piece of writing.

The Grateful Dead came back into my life recently; largely because of my children's interest. My daughter has been *associated* with the group; I find it difficult to apply the common description of a fan as a Deadhead; since she was fifteen. Her school band; the Cosmic Country Sound, was patterned after the Grateful Dead; she was its lead singer and tambourine player.

I had no idea that my son, four years younger; had any interest in the group. His room is decorated with posters of Boris Becker and Albert Einstein. But then a year ago he let his hair grow into a mane; started wearing beaded necklaces and rope wristlets, and, sure enough; turned up one day at my study door to announce, "Dad; there's this concert I'd like to go to. . . ."

Both of my children have urged me to go to a Grateful Dead concert. I hadn't taken them up on the offer until this summer; when by chance I met someone way up in the band's hierarchy who gave me not only some tickets to a concert at the Meadowlands in New Jersey; but also a backstage pass. I told my son. His eyes widened at the news. He invited three of his friends. His sister; with a job on the West Coast, was devastated that she couldn't be on hand.

— Adapted from GEORGE PLIMPTON, "Bonding with the Grateful Dead"

B. The passage in Exercise 1A can be rewritten in many ways, depending on the focus and stylistic effect a writer wishes to create. Share your version of the passage with a group of fellow students. Each group member should be ready to explain the reasons for his or her choices when they differ from those of other writers in the group. As a group, rewrite the passage, and share that version with the class.

33a

;

33b   Using colons

You can use a colon to introduce or set up an example, illustration, list, or quotation. By calling attention to what follows, a colon seems to say "Here is . . ." or "Pay attention to this." In most cases, the words coming *before* a colon form a complete sentence while those coming after take the form of a dependent clause, a phrase, or even a single word.

WORDS	Bring these things with you: paintbrushes, a drop cloth, and gloves.
WORDS, PHRASES, AND CLAUSES	Each year the river claims something that optimistic humans have built on its banks: part of a yard, a toolshed, a drive way edged with bushes, or a house that people admired for its dramatic view from the bluff.

Sometimes, however, you may wish to use a colon to join two sentences, the first providing a relatively broad statement and the second offering a sharper focus, a summary, or a change in direction.

> After searching through the house most of the day, she finally admitted the obvious: her grandmother's ring was lost.

1 Use a colon to introduce lists and examples

You can use colons to introduce examples and concluding generalizations. Commonly, a colon comes after the first part of a sentence, which offers a statement or generalization that the remainder of the sentence illustrates, explains, or makes concrete and particular.

> Mulholland believed that the growing city at the edge of the desert would have to tap another source of water: the Owens Valley, several hundred miles away.

> Remember this important selling guideline: Know your customer!

By asking readers to pause partway through a sentence, a colon calls special attention to the second half of the statement and avoids the run-together effect that a comma may create.

RUN TOGETHER	After saving for eleven years, the Cranes finally had enough money to get what they wanted, a ranch in Wyoming where they could live out their own version of self-reliance.
EDITED	After saving for eleven years, the Cranes finally had enough money to get what they wanted: a ranch in Wyoming where they could live out their own version of self-reliance.

33b
:

A colon can also introduce a more formal series or list.

> Though baseball doesn't reign in England, the British enjoy a wide variety of sports: soccer, golf, rugby, cricket, tennis, croquet, polo, and billiards, to name just a few.

> The prosecutor introduced into evidence the following exhibits: a nine-inch knife, a piece of clothing belonging to the victim, and a bloodstained rag from the suspect's car.

Writer's Tip

When a complete sentence follows a colon, you can choose to begin it with either a capital or a lowercase letter. Stick to one style or the other throughout an essay.

CORRECT
The airline lost the bag containing my insulated jacket, pants, and boots: **our** long-awaited winter hike in the Rockies was ruined.

ALSO CORRECT
The airline lost the bag containing my insulated jacket, pants, and boots: **Our** long-awaited winter hike in the Rockies was ruined.

When the word group following a colon is not a sentence, begin it with a lowercase letter.

LOWERCASE
The symptoms are as follows: **sore** throat, joint pain, fever, and headache.

---

2 Use a colon to introduce quotations

You can also use a colon as a convenient way to introduce quotations, either short ones that you integrate into your own words or longer ones that you set off from the body of your text (see Chapter 35). The word group before the colon must be a complete sentence; if it is not, use a comma instead.

> Ms. Johnson responded to criticism of the sales campaign: "For a program launched in the middle of a recession, sales were actually quite strong."

33b

3 Use a colon to separate titles and subtitles

Colons separate the main titles of books, movies, and the like from their subtitles.

Computers for the Absolute Novice **:** *An Introduction*

Freddie's Dead **:** *The Final Nightmare*

Date Rape **:** A Major Problem on Today's Campuses
The title of your own paper should not be italicized.

Colons are also used in separating hours from minutes (10:32); in certain chapter and verse notations, such as those in the Bible (John 8:21–23); and in some reference styles, such as that of the Modern Language Association (MLA) (see Chapter 49).

4 Use a colon to join sentences

A colon is one of the strategies you can use to join complete sentences (main clauses). (See 21b.) It works most effectively when the second sentence sharply focuses, sums up, or illustrates the first.

Hearing a sound like both rushing water and cloth being ripped, she knew it was too late to abandon her house in the canyon **:** The mud slide had begun.

In the middle of a week filled with heavy rain and mud slides, Joel thought of the bushes and grasses now sprouting **:** Next summer the hillside might be on fire.

5 Avoid overuse and misuse of colons

Because colons add emphasis to examples and assertions, you may be tempted to use them often. Don't. Vary your style. Remember that anything is weakened by overuse.

33b
:

COLON OVERUSED Suzanne had an obsession for books **:** there were bookshelves in her kitchen, her bathrooms, and even her closets. She read voraciously **:** in the morning, at lunch, after dinner, and late at night. Her house soon turned into a lending library **:** friends and relatives borrowed books by the dozen. And she liked everything **:** classics, mysteries, pulp romances, autobiographies.

EDITED Suzanne had an obsession for books. There were bookshelves in her kitchen, her bathrooms, and even her closets. She read voraciously **whenever she could, from morning to** late at night. Her house soon turned into a lending library, friends and relatives borrow**ing** books by the dozen. And she liked everything **:** classics, mysteries, pulp romances, autobiographies.

You can use a colon to introduce a list at the end of a complete sentence. When you introduce a list with a word group other than a complete sentence, however, do not use a colon.

INCORRECT	Her three favorite activities were **:** jogging, volunteering at the local homeless shelter, and cooking.
EDITED	Her three favorite activities **were jogging,** volunteering at the local homeless shelter, and cooking.
EDITED	**She had three favorite activities :** jogging, volunteering at the local homeless shelter, and cooking.
INCORRECT	The room had **:** a fireplace, oak floors, and an oak buffet.
EDITED	The room **had a** fireplace, oak floors, and an oak buffet.

The colon and the words introduced by it should appear only at the end of a sentence, not in the middle.

INCORRECT	Keep in mind these elements **:** introduction, body, and conclusion, while preparing your presentation.
EDITED	Keep in mind these **elements**—introduction, body, and conclusion—**while** preparing your presentation.

33b
:

Exercise 2

A. Edit the following sentences by deleting misused or overused colons, adding colons where needed, or retaining any colons that are appropriate. You may need to rewrite some sentences to correct overuse or misuse of colons.

EXAMPLE
For the Hirsches, retirement meant a trip to France.

1. They prepared for the trip by: first looking for inexpensive hotels in Paris.
2. The Residence Rivoli seemed like a good value clean, centrally located: private bath.

3. Mr. Hirsch, however, wanted to splurge: He argued that an upper-bracket hotel would be so much more enjoyable: a shining marble bath, plush dining room, and elegant meals. There would be parking as well: essential for anyone with a car.

4. But Mrs. Hirsch wasn't impressed: the expensive hotels would be comfortable, but she wanted atmosphere: and small, charming hotels would have that in abundance.

5. Finally, they reached a compromise; they would: stay in a chateau near the Loire, which would be cheaper than a fancy Paris hotel but afford plenty of atmosphere. Then they could: drive into Paris; enjoy the sights; and have a peaceful night: all without driving more than an hour or so each way.

 B. Share your edited versions of the sentences in Exercise 2A with a group of classmates. For each sentence, choose one version the group considers both correct and effective. Then share your chosen sentences with the other groups in order to see how often you have made similar and different choices.

33b

CHAPTER

34

Apostrophes

Like the dot above the i, the apostrophe may seem trivial. But without the help of apostrophes, your readers would stumble over your sentences and might have to go back to the beginning to figure out what you're saying. Misplaced apostrophes are also distracting.

MISUSED OR LEFT OUT   James horse cant canter, but two months rest and his leg's will heal, and then well see him in race's at Blueberry Down's again.

No doubt you had difficulty reading this sentence. You weren't sure which words were possessives, which were contractions, and which were plurals; the omitted and misplaced apostrophes misled you into putting some words into the wrong categories. Try reading it again.

CORRECTED   **James's** horse **can't** canter, but two **months'** rest and his **legs** will heal, and then **we'll** see him in **races** at Blueberry **Downs** again.

At first, you may need to work consciously with apostrophes in your writing, hunting for misused or omitted cases. Eventually, the correct use of apostrophes will become second nature in your writing.

34a
v

34a Using apostrophes to mark possession

A noun that expresses ownership is said to be a **possessive noun.** In writing, you must mark possessive nouns to distinguish them from plurals. In the phrase *the cats meow,* for example, a reader will assume that *cats* is plural and will expect certain kinds of structures to follow it (such as *all night* or *in the house*), to complete the sentence.

APOSTROPHE MISSING	The **cats** meow is becoming fainter.
CORRECTED	The **cat**'s meow is becoming fainter.

Without a way of distinguishing between the plural and the possessive in writing, readers would be misled and frustrated by many such constructions.

1 Add an apostrophe plus -s to mark possession in singular nouns

In general, when you write a singular possessive noun, you will follow it with an apostrophe plus -s.

Bill's coat
the dog's collar
Connecticut's taxes

When a noun ends with -s, though, showing possession may be tricky. Writers follow two different conventions in such circumstances (and editors will usually adopt one of these and stick to it).

1. Add an apostrophe and another -s, just as you would do with any other noun. This is the more common and preferred method.

   Chris's car
   Elliott Ness's next move

2. Alternatively, simply add an apostrophe to the final -s.

   Chris' car
   Elliott Ness' next move

For nouns ending in -s, choose one of these conventions and stick to it throughout an essay.

34a

INCONSISTENT	After driving closer to the **lioness'** cub, we discovered that **Hess's** camera had no film.
EDITED	After driving closer to the **lioness's** cub, we discovered that **Hess's** camera had no film.

Writer's Tip

To avoid the awkward sound of possessive nouns ending in -s ("the bass's solo part," "the pass's success"), try revising the construction ("the part of the solo bass," "the success of the pass").

Occasionally, adding a possessive -s to a word already

ending in that sound will seem awkward to say ("Hodges-es"). In such cases it may be preferable to indicate the typical pronunciation (with only one -s sound) by using only the apostrophe (Hodges').

Writer's Alert

Be careful with personal pronouns. You may be tempted to add an apostrophe plus -s to these, but they're already possessive.

INCORRECT   If the car was **your's**, why did you tell Jose that it was Lida's and then take **her's** and dent **it's** fender?

EDITED   If the car was **yours**, why did you tell Jose that it was Lida's and then take **hers** and dent **its** fender?

Be especially wary of confusing *it's* and *its*. Practice expanding the contraction *it's* (*it* + *is*) whenever you use it in writing, and you'll locate any slips more easily.

DRAFT   **Its** not the muffler shop employees who were responsible for the fraud, but **its** managers.

EXPANDED   **It is** not the muffler shop employees who were responsible for the fraud, but ~~it is~~ managers.

EDITED   **It's** not the muffler shop employees who were responsible for the fraud, but **its** managers.

34a

2 Add an apostrophe to mark possession in plural nouns

Most English nouns end in -s or -es in the plural. When you want to make a plural noun possessive, simply add an apostrophe after the -s.

PLURAL POSSESSIVE   The **Solomons'** house had its lead paint removed.

PLURAL POSSESSIVE   The **roses'** petals had begun to wither.

Some irregular nouns form their plurals differently (*mice, children, fish*). In these cases, the word will be plural without ending in -s or -es. Mark possession by adding an apostrophe plus -s, even if the word does not change in the plural (*deer/deer, fish/fish*).

IRREGULAR PLURAL	The livestock show included several **oxen.**
PLURAL POSSESSIVE	The livestock show featured the **oxen'**s plowing abilities.

Writer's Alert

Even though third person singular verbs end in *-s*, remember that these are not possessive nouns, so they don't require an apostrophe.

INCORRECT	The *Enterprise* **speed'**s out of the galaxy with the Klingons in hot pursuit.
EDITED	The *Enterprise* **speeds** out of the galaxy with the Klingons in hot pursuit.

---

3 Add an apostrophe plus *-s* or an apostrophe to only the last word in a noun phrase

Hyphenated and **multiple-word nouns** are becoming increasingly common in English. As a general rule, treat the entire noun phrase as a single unit, marking possession on the last word.

HYPHENATED NOUN	My **father-in-law'**s library is extensive.
MULTIPLE-WORD NOUN	The **union leaders'** negotiations fell through at the last minute.

When you use a compound noun phrase (two or more nouns connected by *and* or *or*) as a possessive, you'll need to decide whether these nouns function as separate items or as a single unit.

34a
⌄

SEPARATE ITEMS	**Billy's and Harold's** lawyers were ruthless.
	READER'S REACTION: Billy must have one lawyer and Harold another, since the possessive is marked on both.
SINGLE UNIT	**Billy and Harold's** lawyers were ruthless.
	READER'S REACTION: Billy and Harold must have shared the same team of lawyers, since the entire noun phrase is marked as possessive.

Exercise 1

A. Edit the possessive forms in the following sentences so that each uses possessive apostrophes correctly. You may also have to add or move apostrophes, but do not change any correct forms. Some of the possessive forms may be correct.

EXAMPLE

France's longest river, the Loire, has its source in Vivarais and winds its way some 600 miles to the Atlantic.

1. The rivers name is especially associated with the many chateaux that line its bank's.
2. Serious sightseers visits to the Loire Valley should include tours of several of this regions beautiful castles.
3. The Loires reputation is also founded on its renowned cuisine and its sophisticated wines.
4. Barton and Jone's wine import businesses have flourished in the United States ever since Jones came up with the companys award-winning advertising campaign.
5. Several other companies have found an eager market for Frances excellent wine's.

 B. In a small group, compare your corrections to Exercise 1A, and discuss any especially difficult cases.

34b
∨

34b Using apostrophes to mark contractions and omissions

You can use the apostrophe to indicate the omission of one or more letters when two words are brought together to form a **contraction.** Contractions generally suggest an informal style to which some college teachers may object. When in doubt, always err on the side of formality.

For those times when you do want to use contractions, follow a simple rule: learn exactly where the apostrophe goes. Most contractions are so common that you've already memorized them. But you still may inadvertently omit apostrophes from even simple words. For example, perhaps you've written *your* (a possessive pronoun) when you really meant *you're* (*you are*).

1 Use an apostrophe to contract a verb form

You can contract pronouns and verbs into a single unit by "splicing" them, eliminating the first part of the verb and substituting an apostrophe. Use the following chart to check your work.

it's	=	it	+	is
who's	=	who	+	is
they're	=	they	+	are
can't	=	can	+	not
you'll	=	you	+	will
you're	=	you	+	are

You can also splice nouns followed by *is*. Such forms are informal and should be avoided in most academic writing.

INFORMAL   **Shoshana's** going to the ballet, but her **seat's** in the very last row of the theater, and **she's** concerned that **she'll** miss the action.

MORE FORMAL   **Shoshana is** going to the ballet, but her **seat is** in the very last row of the theater, and **she is** concerned that **she will** miss the action.

34b
ᐯ

Writer's Tip

Edit your papers *very* carefully for contractions before turning them in. Take note of these often-confused forms.

they're	=	they + are
there	=	an adverb
you're	=	you + are
your	=	a possessive pronoun
who's	=	who + is
whose	=	a possessive pronoun
it's	=	it + is
its	=	a possessive pronoun

2 Use an apostrophe to mark plural letters

When you want to make individual letters plural, add an apostrophe plus -s.

Mind your **p's and q's.**
The **x's** mark the spots.

You can omit the apostrophe in the plurals of numbers.

I'll take two size **5s** and two size **7s.**
They walked out in **twos** and **threes.**

Writer's Tip

The apostrophe is often omitted from the plural form of abbreviations, especially if it runs the risk of making the word look like a possessive. "I took all my freshman courses from **TAs**" might be just as acceptable as "**TA's**" because the abbreviation is capitalized.

---

3 Use an apostrophe to abbreviate a year

You can abbreviate years by omitting the first two numbers of the century as long as the century is understood by your reader. Such contractions represent informal usage.

INFORMAL   Sam has a **'75** Johnson class M sixteen-foot sailboat for sale.

UNCLEAR   Victorian details on houses in our neighborhood remained popular throughout the **'70s.**
READER'S REACTION: **Does this mean the 1870s (in the Victorian period)? I'm confused.**

EDITED   Victorian details on houses in our neighborhood remained popular throughout the **1970s.**

34b
ᵛ

4 Use an apostrophe to show colloquial pronunciation

When quoting people, you can use apostrophes to indicate certain omissions and other features of colloquial speech and dialects.

DIALECT   I'm **a-goin'** to the post office first **an'** then home.

Exercise 2

A. The following paragraph contains sentences with some contracted words that require apostrophes and some "look-alikes" that do not. All these words appear in italics. Insert apostrophes where they belong.

Many medical scholars believe that the age of molecular biology *didnt* really begin until April 1953 when Watson and Crick's article on the double helix appeared in a scientific journal. These researchers *werent* sure at that time how influential their ideas would become. *Its* generally thought, for example, that if several important researchers *hadnt* immediately seen the underlying brilliance of the double helix, the whole idea *wouldnt* have gained such a quick following. "*Your* basic educator," Professor Ewell Samuels asserts, "*couldnt* have seen beyond what was already a given in biology. *Its* when *youre* presented with many scholars *whose* ideas agree that things really begin to happen. *Whos* going to argue with a whole field jumping on the bandwagon of a new theory?"

B. In a small group, compare your corrections to the passage in Exercise 2A. After reaching agreement on which cases are actual errors, try to decide as a group which contractions in the passage, if any, are too informal. Would you use no contractions in this passage? Some?

You learn about some of the many uses for quotation marks almost as soon as you begin to read.

> The three soldiers went on to the house of Albert and Louise. **"**Could you spare a bit of food? And have you some corner where we could sleep for the night?**"**
> **"**Oh no,**"** said Albert. **"**We gave all we could spare to soldiers who came before you.**"**
> **"**Our beds are full,**"** said Louise.
> — MARCIA BROWN, *Stone Soup*

And when you start reading about pets, you encounter some other uses.

> Whereas no reptile alive today can be considered aerial, we do come close with the Asian genus of **"**flying dragons,**"** *Draco.*
> — ROBERT G. SPRACKLAND, JR., *All About Lizards*

You use quotation marks in still other ways when you incorporate other people's words and ideas in your writing.

> As Ruth Macklin points out in *Mortal Choices,* however, **"**many state laws now permit involuntary hospitalizaton of mental patients only if they are judged dangerous to themselves or others.**"**

Quotation marks have many important roles, so keeping track of the various conventions for their use is both difficult and necessary.

35a Marking quotations

Use quotation marks whenever you quote someone else's words. Quotation marks tell readers which words are someone else's (and which

words are yours). Quoted material can make your writing lively and interesting while providing explanation and support for your ideas.

To use quotation marks effectively and correctly, you need to know
whether you are quoting words directly or indirectly, on their own or within
another quotation.

1 Direct quotations

Whenever you quote someone directly, use double quotation marks
(" ") both before and after the quotation unless the quotation is long or needs
special emphasis (see 35b). Make sure that the words within the quotation
marks are the exact spoken or written words of your source.

DIRECT QUOTATION (SPOKEN)
"The loon can stay beneath the water for several minutes," the
park ranger told us as we walked along the shore.

DIRECT QUOTATION (WRITTEN)
Samuel Gross has written that "every generation looks with scorn
upon its offspring's own developing culture."

As you edit, check that you have placed quotation marks around all
directly quoted material.

QUOTATION NOT FULLY MARKED
"Had it not been for the flight navigator," the pilot said, we wouldn't
have been able to make the emergency landing.
**READER'S REACTION: The second part of the sentence doesn't have any quo-
tation marks, so at first I didn't notice that it was also something the pilot
said.**

EDITED
"Had it not been for the flight navigator," the pilot said, "we
wouldn't have been able to make the emergency landing."

Make sure you use quotation marks within a sentence to separate
quoted material from the words you use to introduce or comment on it. This
is an especially important practice when your words interrupt a quotation.

QUOTATION MARKS MISSING
"I'm grateful, too, commented one passenger dryly, though I would
have gladly missed the whole experience."
**READER'S REACTION: "Commented one passenger dryly" seems like part of
the quotation.**

EDITED
"I'm grateful, too," commented one passenger dryly, "though I
would have gladly missed the whole experience."

35a
" "

2 Indirect quotations

Whenever you **paraphrase** or **summarize** someone else's speaking or writing, do not use quotation marks. Reserve the marks for cases when you quote someone's words exactly.

INDIRECT QUOTE (PARAPHRASE)
The pilot told us that if it hadn't been for the flight navigator, the plane would not have made a safe landing.

INDIRECT QUOTE (SUMMARY)
Samuel Preston believes that after just one generation, the social consequences of a major war have almost completely vanished.

3 Quotations inside quotations

Whenever the quotation you are presenting contains another quotation, use single quotation marks ('') for the inside quotation and double quotation marks (" ") for the one enclosing it.

> Goddio became interested in searching for the sunken ship *San Diego* after reading an account by De Morga who "wrote of a struggle 'obstinately and bitterly waged on both sides so that it lasted more than six hours,' until the pounding of the battle caused his ship to 'bust assunder at the bows.'"

Note how the comma is placed inside the single quotation marks and the period is inside both the single and double quotation marks. (See 32h.)

35b Using block quotations

When you quote more than four typed lines of prose, you should use a **block quotation** rather than quotation marks. To create a block quotation, begin on a new line after the sentence preceding the quotation, indent ten spaces (or one inch on a word processor), and present the quotation double-spaced without quotation marks. Do not indent the opening line of the quotation if you are quoting only one paragraph or part of a paragraph.

35b
66 99

> According to Postman, we can no longer ignore the profound effects of technology on all aspects of American life.
>
> > To be unaware that a technology comes equipped with a program for social change, to maintain that technology is neutral, to make the assumption that technology is always a friend to culture is, at this late hour, stupidity plain and simple.

In a longer quotation, indent three spaces (or one-fourth inch) for the first line of each full paragraph. In addition, include any quotation marks that appear within the original, but do not add any at the beginning or end of the block quotation.

Clifford Geertz's discussion of cockfights on the island of Bali illustrates the personal, almost informal tone of much contemporary anthropology.

> My wife and I were still very much in the gust-of-wind stage, a most frustrating, and even, as you soon begin to doubt whether you are really real after all, unnerving one, when, ten days or so after our arrival, a large cockfight was held in the public square to raise money for a new school.
>
> Now, a few special occasions aside, cockfights are illegal in Bali under the Republic (as, for not altogether unrelated reasons, they were under the Dutch), largely as a result of the pretensions to puritanism radical nationalism tends to bring with it. The elite, which is not itself so very puritan, worries about the poor, ignorant peasant gambling all his money away, about what foreigners will think, about the waste of time better devoted to building up the country. It sees cockfighting as "primitive," "backward," "unprogressive," and generally unbecoming an ambitious nation. And, as with those other embarrassments—opium smoking, begging, or uncovered breasts—it seeks, rather unsystematically, to put a stop to it.
>
> — CLIFFORD GEERTZ, "Deep Play: Notes on the Balinese Cock-Fight"

(See 49b for a discussion of parenthetical documentation with block quotations; see 33b-3 for the use of colons to introduce block quotations.)

When you are quoting more than three lines of verse, present them in a block quotation, beginning on the next line after an introductory sentence and indented ten spaces from the left margin. If the verse contains any quotation marks, include them, but do not add any of your own at the beginning and end of the quotation.

35b
" "

> Donald Hall also uses lines of uneven length and varying rhythm in his poem "The Black-Faced Sheep."
>
> If one of you found a gap in a stone wall,
> the rest of you—rams, ewes, bucks, wethers, lambs;
> mothers and daughters, old grandfather-father,
> cousins and aunts, small bleating sons—
> followed onward, stupid
> as sheep, wherever
> your leader's sheep-brain wandered to.
>
> My grandfather spent all day searching the valley
> and edges of Ragged Mountain,
> calling "Ke-*day!*" as if he brought you salt,
> "Ke-*day! Ke-day!*"

35c Writing dialogue

When writing dialogue, use the conventions for direct quotations (see 35a). Whenever a new person speaks, indent as if you're beginning a new paragraph, and begin with new quotation marks.

> Finally the old man woke.
> "Don't sit up," the boy said. "Drink this." He poured some coffee in a glass.
> The old man took it and drank it.
> "They beat me, Manolin," he said. "They truly beat me."
> "*He* didn't beat you. Not the fish."
> "No. Truly. It was afterwards."
> —ERNEST HEMINGWAY, *The Old Man and the Sea*

When a character in a written dialogue speaks for more than one paragraph with no interruption, begin each new paragraph with quotation marks, but don't end with them. End only the *last* paragraph with quotation marks.

CORRECT

> "And then that imbecile crowd down on the deck started their little fun, and I could see nothing more for smoke.
> "The brown current ran swiftly out of the heart of darkness, bearing us down towards the sea with twice the speed of our upward progress. . . ."
> —JOSEPH CONRAD, *Heart of Darkness*

Did You Know?

The most common way to quote someone's words directly is by enclosing the words with quotation marks. Writers in the past and some contemporary writers striving for special effects have used other devices to mark the start of quoted speech. For example, the King James version of the Bible uses no quotation marks, even though dozens of people are quoted throughout its pages. Instead, each quotation is introduced with a comma and starts with a capital letter:

Then cried a wise woman out of the city, Hear, hear; say, I pray you, unto Jo'ab, Come near hither, that I may speak with thee.

—2 Samuel 20:16

Other devices, including colons and semicolons, can be used for introducing quoted speech. These devices are rare, but you may encounter them in your reading.

35c
" "

35d Labeling titles of short works

You should use quotation marks to enclose titles of short works, such as articles, essays, stories, songs, and short poems; parts of a larger work or series, such as chapters in a book, episodes in a television series, or sections of a musical work; and unpublished works, such as doctoral dissertations or speeches.

Quotation Marks with Titles

ARTICLES AND STORIES

"TV Gets Blame for Poor Reading"	newspaper article
"Feminism's Identity Crisis"	magazine article
"The Idea of the Family in the Middle East"	chapter in book
"Baba Yaga and the Brave Youth"	story
"The Rise of Germism"	essay

POEMS AND SONGS

"A Woman Cutting Celery"	short poem
"Evening" (from *Pippa Passes*)	section of a long poem
"Riders on the Storm"	song

EPISODES AND PARTS OF LONGER WORKS

"Billy's Back"	episode of a TV series
"All We Like Sheep" (from Handel's *Messiah*)	section of a long musical work

UNPUBLISHED WORKS

"Renaissance Men—and Women"	unpublished lecture
"Sources of the Ballads in Bishop Percy's Folio Manuscript"	unpublished dissertation

---

35d
" "

Writer's Tip

Remember, *never* put the title of your own paper in quotation marks. This is a common mistake that irritates many teachers. If your title contains quoted material, place that material, not the entire title, in quotation marks.

INCORRECT "The Theme of the Life Voyage in Crane's "Open Boat""

EDITED The Theme of the Life Voyage in Crane's "Open Boat"

35e Indicating special meanings of words and phrases

You can use quotation marks to set off words and phrases you are using in a special sense or to indicate terms that are part of a technical vocabulary or that are unusual in some way. In using quotation marks to call attention to words and phrases, remember an important principle: Go lightly to avoid distracting readers with too many highlighted words.

Most disciplines use a host of specialized words that readers *within* the discipline readily recognize. If you are writing for a general audience, however, consider calling attention to specialized terms and phrases by setting them off with quotation marks. Quotation marks can also help you highlight a term you are defining. (Italics can be used for this purpose as well; see 39a-4.)

> The phenomenon that draws each person into the crowd's irrational and often destructive and confrontational behavior is known among social psychologists as "crowd contagion."
>
> The "FSBO" (sometimes actually pronounced as "fizbo") is generally used in the real estate industry to refer to a home that is "for sale by owner."

When deciding whether to use quotation marks to set off specialized terms, ask yourself whether the term is likely to be known to your intended readers. Ask also whether the term is unusual enough to require highlighting or will seem clear to readers. In the following sentence, for example, a well-known writer includes quotation marks that most readers will probably consider unnecessary.

UNNECESSARY

The number of these folds varies from individual to individual and each adult has a characteristic "frown pattern" of one, two, three or four lines.   — DESMOND MORRIS, *Body Watching*

READER'S REACTION: I have no trouble figuring out what a frown pattern is, so for me the quotation marks make the sentence appear cluttered.

35e
" "

Exercise 1

A. Add quotation marks to the following passage as appropriate.

The shame of illiteracy—or so Robert Cullany puts it—affects millions of adults in the United States alone, but the problem is not nearly as prevalent as innumeracy, Cullany's term that means being unable to use numbers. Cullany writes, illiteracy and innumeracy are a national blight on our intellectual landscape, and cannot be tolerated. He also points out that they cripple our productivity, lead to familial dysfunction (poor family structures), and deny people the ability to become what Cullany calls self-learners. The ALVC, or Adult Literacy Volunteer Corps, is made up of dedicated people who believe they can help this so-called mind plague.

 B.   Working in a small group, share your edited versions of the passage in Exercise 1A. Which quotation marks did you all agree on? Which ones did members of your group miss or disagree on?

Writer's Tip

Clichés and idioms, perhaps because they seem informal or slang-like, often fool writers into placing them in quotation marks. Doing so, however, only calls more attention to their presence, further weakening the prose. Instead of placing such expressions in quotation marks, simply replace them with stronger words and phrases.

DRAFT   After pulling an "all-nighter," Joe said, in the "clear light of day," that he felt like he'd just "kicked the bucket" and "cashed in his chips."

EDITED   After cramming all night for his test, Joe spent the next day complaining that he was exhausted and ached all over.

35f Indicating irony, sarcasm, and authorial distance

You can—*sparingly*—use quotation marks to indicate irony or sarcasm or to show a reader that you don't "lay claim" to a specific term or expression.

> To the people who oppose animal rights, the suffering of helpless animals is somehow justified by the "great medical advances" that are encouraged by what they view as "legitimate research" on animals.

This strategy is easy to misuse or overuse, and careful word choice is generally a more effective way of conveying disapproval (see 28a-1 and 28a-2).

Exercise 2

A. Edit the following passage by adding or deleting quotation marks as appropriate. Leave in place any quotation marks that are correctly used.

On April 12, 1633, Galileo was interrogated by the Inquisitor for the Holy Roman and Universal Inquisition. The focus was Galileo's book, the *"Dialogue on the Great World Systems,"* in which he posited the theory of a "spinning" earth that "circulated" around the sun. The theory itself was "bad" enough given the Pope's "beliefs," but one of the "characters" in the book's "dialogue" was cast as a "simpleton," and the Pope thought that perhaps it referred to him because he didn't go along with Galileo's "theory." At one point, the Inquisitor asked Galileo, "Did you obtain permission to write the book? To which Galileo replied, I did not seek permission to write this book because I consider that I did not disobey the instruction I had been given. "Did you disclose the Sacred Congregation's demands when you printed the book?" asked the Inquisitor. "I said nothing, Galileo replied, when I sought permission to publish, not having in the book either held or defended opinion. In the end, "Galileo" had to retract his "book," and was also shown instruments of torture "as if" they were going to be used—a "scare tactic," to be sure.

—Adapted from JACOB BRONOWSKI, *The Ascent of Man*

B. Working in a small group, share your edited versions of the passage in Exercise 2A. Discuss each of the changes, and note any that gave you trouble. Indicate whether all group members agreed about each change.

36

Periods,
Question Marks, and
Exclamation Points

When you speak, you mark boundaries between sentences with changes in pitch or with pauses of various lengths. When you write, however, you must mark these divisions with visual symbols because your reader can't "hear" a rising pitch in a word or a pause between sentences. When you want to mark the end of a sentence, you will use one of three symbols: a period, a question mark, or an exclamation point.

36a Using periods

Use a period when you want to mark the end of a sentence. A sentence is like a train, sometimes moving directly from one location to another, sometimes taking a few structural diversions before completing its journey. For each sentence, a period marks the end of the line. The period can also be used in abbreviations.

1 End a sentence with a period

No matter how long or complicated, all sentences that are *statements* must end with periods. However, sometimes a sentence will contain embedded clauses that appear to be something other than statements. Use a period to end a sentence when the main, or "outer," sentence is a statement.

INCORRECT   Ten-year-old Naomi affectionately kissed her little brother on the forehead but wondered whether he really knew that she was sorry for startling him**?**

READER'S REACTION: **The sentence as a whole is a statement; the question in the second half is being reported in the sentence, but the sentence doesn't ask the question.**

EDITED   Ten-year-old Naomi affectionately kissed her little brother
              on the forehead but wondered whether he really knew that
              she was sorry for startling him▪

2 Use periods in abbreviations

Periods are also used to punctuate abbreviations and to mark deci-
mal points in numbers. Most abbreviations require periods to let the reader
know that something has been eliminated from the word or term.

> Dr▪   Mrs▪   Ms▪   Ph▪D▪
> pp▪   in▪   abbr▪ (for *abbreviation*)
> a▪m▪ (or A▪M▪)   B▪C▪ (or B▪C▪E▪)

Many common abbreviations, including *a.m.* and *p.m.,* come from Latin,
and, for brevity, have been "permanently" shortened (it would seem odd to
spell out *a.m.* and *p.m.* as *ante meridiem* and *post meridiem*).

Some abbreviations, especially acronyms (see 42a), may not require
periods at all. When the entire term is capitalized, periods are generally not
used (NASA, NATO, SALT talks). (See Chapter 42.) Use of periods in abbreviations varies considerably. When in doubt, use the preferred choice in a
dictionary. Remember too that some academic disciplines have their own
styles for abbreviations. (See Chapters 49–53.)

When an abbreviation that requires a period occurs at the *end* of a
sentence, that period will also end the sentence.

CORRECT   Before he became a freelance writer, Richard Rodriguez
              earned a Ph▪D▪

If the abbreviated word occurs in the *middle* of a sentence, the period may
be followed by another punctuation mark, such as a comma, dash, colon,
or semicolon.

INCORRECT   Officials from the paper industry testified until **10 p▪m,**
              well before the meeting adjourned.

EDITED   Officials from the paper industry testified until **10 p▪m▪ ,**
              well before the meeting adjourned.

36a
▪

Exercise 1

Edit the following sentences so that periods are used correctly, adding
or omitting punctuation as appropriate.

EXAMPLE

Every two years the French department at St◦Joseph's College organizes a group trip to a foreign countr◌y   ^
                                               ^

1. On our trip to France, we visited the medieval city of Carcassonne
2. As we approached the inner city, which was surrounded by high walls and a real moat, we wondered whether we were still in the twentieth century?
3. "Have we fallen into a time warp or something" Trish said?
4. As we climbed up to the ramparts at 10 p.m, we decided that the experience was almost as good as watching a N.A.S.A. space shuttle launch.
5. Mr Siefert, the hotel manager, told us that the Bastille Day fireworks would begin at 9:30 p.m..

Did You Know?

The use of periods in pronounceable acronyms often follows a pattern of change. The common word *laser* was originally an acronym meaning "*l*ight *a*mplification by *s*timulated *e*mission of *r*adiation." The abbreviation process began with periods separating the capital letters designating each word: *L.A.S.E.R.* Soon the periods disappeared, yielding *LASER*. Then the capital letters disappeared, though in some contexts the first letter may still have been capitalized. Finally, the term became a common, lowercase, pronounceable word, which has even been clipped into the verb *to lase*. Similar processes appear to have happened for other pronounceable acronyms, including *scuba* (*s*elf-*c*ontained *u*nderwater *b*reathing *a*pparatus), *TV*, and *telex*. Keep your eye on ones in transition, like *AIDS, fax,* and *DJ* (now commonly spelled out as *deejay*).

Chris M. Anson, North Carolina State University.

36b Using question marks

A question mark indicates that something has been asked, either directly or hypothetically.

1 End a direct question with a question mark

Always end a direct question with a question mark.

DIRECT   When is the train leaving?

DIRECT   Considering all the attention given in the media to the issue of homestead tax breaks, why aren't more homeowners filing for the exclusion?

When a sentence (like the preceding example) has more than one clause, the main clause will usually determine the proper punctuation. Occasionally you may embed a direct question within an outer statement, generally using parentheses to set off the embedded question.

EMBEDDED   The telephone repair technician arrived only after the electricians had removed the power lines (did they pose a danger**?**) and disconnected the service box.

Writer's Tip

End **indirect questions** with a period. These are sentences whose main clause is a statement and whose embedded clause asks a question.

INDIRECT   Phil wondered whether to support the department's proposal to create a new program**.**

INDIRECT   Carlos asked if he could help out on the bid for the highway project**.**

When you present the exact words, your quotation is *direct* rather than *indirect*, and you need to include the question mark.

QUOTED   It was Laitan who said, "Why is the temperature in the solution rising so quickly**?**"

---

2 Watch for other uses of question marks

Question marks may appear in writing for more specialized reasons. In various kinds of informational writing, for example, a question mark may signal a date or other fact that is uncertain or that has been questioned.

36b
?

David Robert Styles, 1632**?**–1676
Meadville, pop. 196**?**

Occasionally writers will call attention to or mock other people's statements by including a parenthetical question mark. Sometimes this may come from a genuine lack of information; more often it's a device for sarcasm.

PARENTHETICAL   The veterinarian informed us that our Siamese cat had contracted a rare (**?**) ailment.

SARCASTIC   We dispute R & D's finding that the lubricant burns off (**?**) under high heat.

Such a use of question marks is usually colloquial or informal; in general, try to find other ways to convey the same message in academic writing.

Unless you're writing very informally (in a note to a friend, for example), avoid using more than one question mark for emphasis or combining question marks and exclamation points.

INAPPROPRIATE Can you believe they arrested him for parking in front of the building**?!** How can they do that**?????**

EDITED Can you believe they arrested him for parking in front of the building**?** How can they do that**?**

Exercise 2

 A. Edit the following passage by removing any inappropriate question marks or adding any that are required.

Are you bat-phobic. Although bats have been hated and feared for centuries, most species are harmless to humans and beneficial to the environment. In his article "Are We Batty Over Bats," Harlan Sneed wonders whether our destruction of bats is really justified? Should we be smoke-bombing caves that are breeding places for thousands of bats, just because we are afraid of them. Sneed also gives examples of cultures that are contributing to the extinction of bats not through fear but through excessive trapping—for food; they are a delicacy (!?) is some parts of the world. Sneed ends his article with a reminder: "Environmental protection is as much a matter of the way we think as the way we act. Maybe you have never *acted* against your environment but are you entirely inculpable in your thoughts and attitudes."

 B. In a small group, compare your edited versions of the passage in Exercise 2A. Create one collaboratively edited version.

36c Using exclamation points

When you use an exclamation point, you make your statement emphatic, alerting your reader to its importance. You can also use exclamation points to indicate commands or, in quotations, words that are shouted.

1 End an emphatic statement with an exclamation point

Exclamation points are often used to end emphatic statements such as commands or warnings.

EMPHATIC   Keep all the camp children away from the precipice**!**

Writer's Tip

Avoid overusing exclamation points to do the work that should be assigned to strong, carefully chosen words. Treat the exclamation point like a rare and powerful spice: If you don't saturate your text with exclamation points, they will carry much more flavor when you do decide to use them. When you want to make your prose more dramatic, try some revision and add vivid details.

OVERUSED	I couldn't believe it! Andrea and I were face to face with a small black bear! We were terrified! I screamed! Andrea jumped back into the tent and buried herself under her sleeping bag! That left me holding an entire bag of delicious corn chips right under the hungry creature's nose!
REVISED	Suddenly, I began to realize we were not alone. Out of the shadows, just three feet from the front of our tent, appeared the black nose and sharp, glinting teeth of a small black bear.

Also avoid using more than one exclamation point at the end of any sentence. A single exclamation point is worth exactly as much as a hundred.

INCORRECT	The bear was grunting right outside our tent!!!!!
EDITED	The bear was grunting right outside our tent!

2 Watch for other uses of exclamation points

Like question marks, exclamation points can be used parenthetically or marginally in casual writing to express dismay, outrage, shock, or strong interest. In more formal contexts, look for other ways to emphasize the word or idea in question.

INAPPROPRIATE	Emergency rescue workers spent several hours (!) trying to reach the stranded toddler.
EDITED	Emergency rescue workers spent several **agonizing** hours trying to reach the stranded toddler.

When you quote people's words directly, you can use exclamation points to indicate emphatic statements or commands.

QUOTED   Halfway to the airport, Sybil suddenly shouted, "Oh, no**!**
We forgot the plane tickets**!** "

Use exclamation points sparingly and realistically in quotations and dialogue. Few people continue to speak emphatically for very long.

    Remember that when you use an exclamation point, you are punc-
tuating the end of your sentence. Don't add another mark, such as a comma,
when you write an emphatic sentence within an outer sentence.

INCORRECT   "Stop**!** **,** " yelled Steve.

EDITED   "Stop**!** " yelled Steve.

Exercise 3

 A. Edit the following passage by removing or adding exclamation
points to make them correct and stylistically acceptable.

    Seventy-five miles (!) from anywhere, Frank's old Buick decided
to sputter and stall out on the edge of Route 61. Meanwhile, the temperature had fallen to 16 below!!!! To make matters worse, the wind
had whipped up to 30 miles per hour! That's an incredible wind chill
of around 75 below zero!!!!! "Hey," yelled Bill, "don't anyone leave
this car. If we stay put, maybe the highway patrol will spot us." "Who
are you kidding!!??," shouted Frank. "It's 3 a.m.!"

 B. In a small group, compare your edited versions of the passage in
Exercise 3A. Discuss any differences, and create one collaboratively
edited version.

37

Special Punctuation Marks

Most punctuation symbols—dashes, commas, semicolons, colons, slashes, ellipses, quotation marks, and the like—make up a kind of toolbox for writing. You can use the tools in various ways to change the style and sense of your prose and its effects on your readers. Five "special" punctuation marks—parentheses, brackets, dashes, ellipses, and slashes—can be useful strategies for guiding readers through complex sentences and for providing emphasis appropriate to your purpose for writing.

37a Using parentheses

Parentheses *enclose* a word, sentence, or clause: you can't use just one. Whatever you write between two parentheses takes on the quality of an aside—something in a "softer" voice than that of the rest of a sentence. Or it becomes information and ideas presented in the background rather than the foreground.

1 Use parentheses to set off words or sentences

With parentheses, you can set off a word, a group of words, or an entire sentence from the rest of your text. By using parentheses to place some information in the background, you can direct your readers' attention to the main assertions and details in a passage without having to omit worthwhile (though potentially distracting) secondary material.

INFORMATION SET OFF WITHIN A SENTENCE
Although most of the team always eats a hearty and varied breakfast (if also a little high in fats and cholesterol), Jim feels he performs much better with less food in his stomach. Invariably, this means only one thing: a bowl of Cheerios (without milk).

INFORMATION SET OFF IN A SEPARATE SENTENCE

Consuelo had tried for two years to get a hearing about her immigration status. (Her employer, during this time, had been unsympathetic to her pleas.) Then, in June, she finally received a letter.

Use parentheses sparingly and carefully. Too many parenthetical statements can clutter your sentences, distracting readers and obscuring your main assertions.

DISTRACTING   Handico, Inc., decided (early in 1993) to use its waste milling chips (which had been warehoused in Detroit) to manufacture pencils (described as "environmentally friendly") to donate to public schools (which gave the company a tax credit).

CLEAR   Early in 1993, Handico, Inc., decided to use its waste milling chips (warehoused in Detroit) to manufacture "environmentally friendly" pencils. These they donated to public schools, resulting in a tax credit for the company.

2 Watch for special uses of parentheses

You can use parentheses to present information that is not part of the structure of a sentence. You can also use parentheses in numbered lists.

NUMBERS AND LISTS   Harry's Bookstore has a fax number (349-0934) for (1) ordering books, (2) inquiring about the availability of specific items, or (3) requesting publication information.

3 Punctuate parenthetical statements correctly

Don't use a comma *before* a parenthetical statement placed in the middle of a sentence. *After* the closing parenthesis, use whatever punctuation would normally occur at this point in the sentence if the parenthetical statement were not there.

37a
( )

WITHOUT PARENTHESES   If you sign up for Telepick by August 15, you are eligible for one hour of free long-distance calls.

WITH PARENTHESES   If you sign up for Telepick by August 15 (and list up to four commonly called numbers), you are eligible for one hour of free long-distance calls.

When a parenthetical statement *inside a sentence* comes at the end of the sentence, always place the sentence's end punctuation *after* the closing parenthesis.

INCORRECT	People on your Telepick list can also call you at the same discounted rate (as long as they, too, use Coombs Communication as their long-distance carrier.)
CORRECT	People on your Telepick list can also call you at the same discounted rate (as long as they, too, use Coombs Communication as their long-distance carrier).

When parentheses enclose an entire freestanding sentence, however, place the end punctuation *inside* the closing parenthesis.

CORRECT	You can sign up for Telepick's "Free Hour" program until August 10. (This offer does not include international calls.)

37b Using brackets

Use brackets to indicate that you have added words of your own to a quotation or to act as parentheses within parentheses.

1 Use brackets for interpolations

Sometimes you need to introduce your own words into a quotation to help clarify a word or a statement for readers or to provide important background information. To indicate that the words are your own, and not those of the writer or speaker being quoted, enclose the **interpolation** in brackets.

INTERPOLATION	My friends Paula and Kent decided to have their wedding on a sailboat off Key West. When I asked them if the ceremony would take place at a specific place offshore, Kent said, "It's a surprise even to us. Captain Sims [the boat's owner] has chosen a special place within two hours of Key West."

2 Use brackets within parentheses

When you need to include a parenthetical statement *within* a parenthetical statement, use parentheses first, and then use brackets for the inner statement. Try to limit your use of brackets because they can make your writing seem unnecessarily complex.

> You can contact Rick Daggett (Municipal Lumber Council [Violations Division], Stinson County Municipal Center) to report violations of the rules governing logging of old-growth trees.

37b
[ ]

37c Using dashes

You can use dashes, like parentheses, to set off material within a sentence. Dashes call more attention to a word or group of words than parentheses do; use them to create emphasis or indicate a change in tone. Dashes differ in function from hyphens, which are used to connect words or to separate words into parts (see Chapter 40). On typewriters and computers, dashes appear as two unspaced hyphens, with no space before, between, or after them: --. In professional typesetting, the dash is represented by a single line: —.

1 Use dashes for emphasis

Use dashes in pairs to highlight a word or group of words in the middle of a sentence.

> **MATERIAL SET OFF IN THE MIDDLE**
> After picking out two pet mice—**one brown with white spots and one white with a brown forehead**—the little boy realized he had only enough money to buy one of them.

When the word or words you want to emphasize appear at the *end* of a sentence, however, use one dash to introduce the material. Conclude with the appropriate end punctuation for the sentence.

> **MATERIAL SET OFF AT THE END**
> Heartbroken at the thought that someone might buy the mouse, the boy offered his six quarters as a deposit—**along with his Mickey Mouse watch and his school notebook.**

You can use dashes to create contrasts in tone or structure within a sentence. When you use dashes, you don't need to make the material within them part of the grammatical structure of the sentence or make it consistent in tone with the rest of the sentence. Inside the following sentence, for example, the dashes enclose another complete sentence.

> **FULL SENTENCE SET OFF**
> The mice—**by this time they were fully domesticated**—frolicked in the cedar chips.

Remember that dashes call attention to the material within them. In contrast, enclosing material in commas provides no real emphasis, and using parentheses de-emphasizes the enclosed material.

37c

STRONG EMPHASIS
When the boy━**clutching three weeks' allowance**━returned to the store, it had already closed.

NO SPECIAL EMPHASIS
When the boy, **clutching three weeks' allowance,** returned to the store, it had already closed.

LOSS OF EMPHASIS
When the boy **(clutching three weeks' allowance)** returned to the store, it had already closed.

2 Use dashes to set off introductory and concluding ideas

You can use dashes to set off an idea or a series of items. This is a dramatic way of opening a sentence or calling attention to the assertion it makes.

ITEMS SET OFF IN OPENING
Extended TV hours, better meals, and more physical exercise━these were the inmates' three major demands for prison reform.

You can also use dashes instead of a nonemphatic colon to list a series of items at the *end* of an assertion.

ITEMS SET OFF AT THE END
Charles had learned several ways to forestall the effects of long flights **━drinking lots of water, avoiding alcohol, and moving around the cabin as much as possible during the flight.**

3 Avoid overuse of dashes

The use of dashes can become addictive, resulting in sentences and paragraphs that seem to be clusters of fragmented statements.

37c

OVERUSED   There had been some interest━chiefly by Stockton━in an automated navigation system━a way to track cars by telecommunication and let drivers know if they are going in the right direction━or give them directions.
READER'S REACTION: This sentence highlights so many points with dashes that it is hard to tell what the writer considers the most important point.

MORE EFFECTIVE   There had been some interest, chiefly by Stockton, in an automated navigation system━a way to track cars by telecommunication and let drivers know if they are going in the right direction or give them directions.

Did You Know?

During the late nineteenth and early twentieth centuries, handbook discussions of special punctuation included many symbols that rarely appear today in written texts, as in the following advice from an 1871 handbook.

*†‡   The **Star, Dagger,** and **Double Dagger;** which are used as marks of reference.

§   The **Section;** which is sometimes used to mark the small divisions of a book.

☞   The **Hand;** which directs special attention to something.

Simon Kerl, *A Common-School Grammar of the English Language* (New York: Ivison, 1871) 337.

Writer's Tip

If you find yourself using too many dashes in your writing, look over a draft and circle the dashes that seem really important—those that help emphasize the key point in an entire section of an essay, for example. Then either replace the other dashes with commas, colons, or parentheses or create emphasis through word choice and sentence structure. (See Chapter 9 for advice on creating emphasis within sentences.)

Exercise 1

A. Some dashes and parentheses have been added to the following paragraph. Edit the paragraph to make it more effective, deciding which of these punctuation marks should stay and which should be replaced. Change sentence structure and strategy if necessary.

The next morning—their donkeys carried them—to the site of the excavation. Carter and his assistant—A. R. Callender—had already begun clearing the stairway (again). As more of the doorway was exposed, the seals (of Tutankhamun) could be seen—in addition to those of the royal necropolis. When all sixteen steps had been cleared (and the entire doorway could be seen), Carter got a jolt—holes had been cut into the (upper) part of the door. The damage had been repaired—and bore the seals of the necropolis, but the question remained—had this tomb, too, been pillaged?

— Metropolitan Museum of Art, *The Treasures of Tutankhamun*, p. 13

37c

B. Compare your edited version of the passage in Exercise 1A with those created by some of your fellow students. Remember that there will be no single—or "most correct"—answer. Compare the relative strengths and weaknesses of each version.

37d Using ellipses

The **ellipsis** (from Greek *elleipsis,* "an omission") is a series of three or four *spaced* periods telling your reader that something has been left out. You will use ellipses chiefly for two purposes: to omit parts of a quotation and to suggest gaps in a sentence, either in dialogue or in quoted speech.

1 Place and space ellipses correctly

Correct placement and spacing of ellipses can be tricky. The following guidelines should cover most cases.

- Use three spaced periods ● ● ● for ellipses within a single sentence.
- Use a period before an ellipsis that falls at the end of a sentence● ● ● ●
- Leave a space before the first period ● ● ● and after the last period of all ellipses.
- When another punctuation mark occurs before omitted words, you can eliminate it if it is not necessary to the grammar of the sentence, but you must retain it if it is necessary to the grammar.

EXAMPLE   The newspapers reported that "Officer Hatt testified solemnly, ● ● ● often staring at his hands and slowly shaking his head."

2 Use ellipses in quotations with omitted words

Ellipses are especially useful when you want to quote some (but not all) words in a passage. You may wish to omit the material because it doesn't offer relevant ideas or information, because it makes the quotation too long for your purposes, or because you want to "skip" from one part of a long quotation to the next without including everything between. The following examples from a student's paper on sailing show his original draft, from which he wanted to cut the boldfaced sentence in the block quotation, and his edited draft, in which he has used ellipses to do so.

37d
● ● ●

ORIGINAL   Drummond, in his *Complete Guide to Sailing,* blames the instability of the sandbagger on its sail-to-hull ratio:

> Extremely fast, sandbaggers were very wide and shallow. They carried an enormous amount of sail area

on an expanded rig. **As a result, when they were raced, they carried twenty-five or more bags of sand in the cockpit as ballast. When a boat came about, a crew of husky men quickly shifted the bags of sand to the windward side.** The boats ran from eighteen to twenty-eight feet in length, and carried a bowsprit almost as long as the hull and a main boom that extended ten feet or more beyond the stern.

EDITED

Drummond, in his *Complete Guide to Sailing,* blames the instability of the sandbagger on its sail-to-hull ratio:
> Extremely fast, sandbaggers were very wide and shallow. They carried an enormous amount of sail area on an expanded rig● ● ● ● The boats ran from eighteen to twenty-eight feet in length, and carried a bowsprit almost as long as the hull and a main boom that extended ten feet or more beyond the stern.

You can also eliminate *parts* of a sentence. When you do so, maintain normal sentence structure and grammatical form; don't just rip out words at random. The following example from a student's interview paper shows the original quotation from his notes; the way he incorporated this into his rough draft (with ellipses); and his corrected, edited version.

ORIGINAL QUOTATION

"We've always played well against Duke. Year before last, we creamed them. Last year their defense fouled us up, but we still won. This year we've got a deep bench. I bet we'll take them to the cleaners, for sure."

INCORRECT DRAFT

When I pressed him to predict the team's performance, Coach Harms paused for a minute, then said with determination, "We've always played well against Duke. Year before last, we creamed them. Last year ● ● ● but we still won ● ● ● we'll take them to the cleaners● ● ● ● "

37d
● ● ●

EDITED

When I pressed him to predict his team's performance, Coach Harms paused for a minute, then said with determination, "We've always played well against Duke. Year before last, we creamed them. Last year ● ● ● we still won. This year ● ● ● we'll take them to the cleaners● ● ● ● "

3 Use ellipses for other gaps

Occasionally you may want to indicate a pause or a gap in your own writing, not just in quoted material. In fiction and personal narrative, for example, ellipses are often used to show suspense, hesitation, or uncertainty or to suggest continuing action.

FOR SUSPENSE   When we returned to our campsite, we were stunned. The tent was in a shambles. Our food was strewn everywhere. Our water jug was fifty yards away. Muddy claw marks were everywhere ● ● ● ●

37e Using slashes

You will use slashes mainly to indicate alternative forms of words. You can also use slashes in a more specialized way to quote lines of poetry when those lines are not already set off from your text.

1 Use slashes with alternative words

When used to indicate alternative words, the slash translates as "or" or "and." It is a shorthand often used in technical documents and manuals.

Be certain that the **on/off** switch is in the vertical position.
There is no exemption from the Composition **101/102** sequence.

Combinations such as *he/she* and *him/her* are not entirely acceptable in formal writing. Many good alternatives for these combinations are available. (See 31a.) The term *and/or* appears primarily in legal writing, but it can be used in moderation elsewhere. Different fields or professions may have particular functions for the slash or may use the slash in specific terms.

2 Use slashes when quoting lines of poetry

When you quote lines of poetry *within* your text rather than setting the material off in a block quotation, separate the lines of verse with a slash. Type a space before and after the slash.

The speaker in Sir Philip Sidney's sonnet addresses the moon by saying, "With how sad steps, O Moon, thou climb'st the skies, / How silently, and with how wan a face."

37e
/

Exercise 2

A. Find or create a short paragraph that uses as many of the punctuation marks described in this chapter as possible: parentheses, brackets, dashes, ellipses, and slashes. Choose one example of each case, and explain what purpose it serves in the paragraph.

 B. Write or type out another version of the paragraph in Exercise 2A, stripped of its special punctuation. Make two copies to exchange with classmates. Ask the members of your group to edit the two copies, which lack parentheses, brackets, dashes, ellipses, and slashes. They should insert these punctuation marks wherever they think the marks are appropriate. Then compare your original and the versions punctuated by your classmates. Decide which marks of punctuation you consider effective and ineffective, and give reasons for your judgments.

PROOFREADING
FOR MECHANICS
AND SPELLING

CHAPTER

38

Capitalization

Capital letters call attention to themselves and to words containing them. Your readers expect capitalization to signal the start of sentences or to identify specific people, places, and things. Capitalization that follows convention not only makes reading easier but also reflects a general sense that certain people and things deserve the kind of recognition that capital letters can provide. In the passage that follows, notice how hard it is to pay attention to specific details when some capitals are removed.

> Then, as i cross the state line, i remember a florence, alabama, composer named william christopher handy. After moving to memphis and writing songs about boss crump, beale street, st. james infirmary, and st. louis, he became known as "the father of the blues." Maybe i should turn north. —HUGH MERRILL, *The Blues Route*

The general rules for capitalization are easy to remember.

- Use a capital letter at the beginning of a sentence.
- Capitalize proper nouns, proper adjectives, and most words in titles of works.

38a
cap

Specific conventions are often harder to keep in mind, and you may need to consult this chapter for answers to questions: Should I capitalize a sentence after a colon? What about the beginning of a sentence within parentheses? When should I use *president* and *President*? How can I recognize when a noun is "proper" and requires capitalization?

38a Using a capital at the beginning of a sentence

Sentences begin with capital letters. This convention applies to regular sentences and sentence fragments used appropriately as partial sentences. (See 20d on partial sentences.)

Two national parks, Yellowstone and Grand Teton, are in Wyoming.
Are camping spots in the parks hard to get in the summer?
Make your reservations early!
No camping without a reservation.

1 Capitalize the opening word in a quoted sentence

When you quote someone else's words or sentences, you will ask, "When should I capitalize within the quotation?" The answer generally depends on the relationship between the main (outer) sentence and the material you are quoting within it.

Capitalize the first word in the quotation when it is a complete sentence or when it begins your own sentence.

COMPLETE SENTENCE QUOTED Speaking of *Blind Man with a Pistol,* James Lundquist says, "**T**he novel begins with an opening chapter that, without exaggeration, is one of the strangest in American literature."

If you interrupt a quotation with your own words, do not capitalize after the interruption.

QUOTATION INTERRUPTED "The novel," claims James Lundquist, "**b**egins with an opening chapter that, without exaggeration, is one of the strangest in American literature."

Also drop the capitalization if you integrate the quotation into the structure of your own sentence.

INTEGRATED QUOTATION On the other hand, James Lundquist claims that "**t**he novel begins with an opening chapter that, without exaggeration, is one of the strangest in American literature."

If you are quoting only part of someone else's sentence, capitalize the quoted material when you use it to open your sentence but not when you place it in the middle or at the end. (Indicate any changes in capitalization in brackets.)

38a cap

OPENING QUOTATION "[**O**]ne of the strangest in American literature" is how Lundquist describes the first chapter.
The first word is not capitalized in the source, so the writer indicates the change in brackets.

CONCLUDING QUOTATION James Lundquist overstates his case when he argues that the first chapter remains "**o**ne of the strangest in American literature."

2 Capitalize a freestanding sentence in parentheses

Capitalize the first word of any sentence that stands on its own within parentheses.

FREESTANDING SENTENCE   By this time, the Union forces were split up into nineteen sections. (**G**rant was determined to unite them.)

However, when you place a sentence within parentheses (or dashes) inside another sentence, do not begin the enclosed sentence with a capital.

ONE SENTENCE INSIDE ANOTHER   Saskatchewan's economy depends heavily on farming (**o**ver half of Canada's wheat crop comes from the province), though oil production and mining have also become important in recent decades.

3 Capitalize the first word of a line of poetry

Lines of poetry generally begin with a capital letter, regardless of where the initial word appears in the "sentence."

Long since, we pulled brown oak-leaves to the ground
In a winter of dry trees; we heard the cock
Shout its unplaceable cry, the axe's sound
Delay a moment after the axe's stroke.
— LOUISE BOGAN, "Old Countryside"

For special effect, however, poets sometimes ignore this and other conventions of capitalization.

new **h**ampshire explodes into radio primary,
newspaper headlines & beer—
well-weathered tag-lines from lips of schoolchildren.

we triumph by not being clear.
— T. R. MAYERS, "(snap)shots"

When you are quoting poetry, follow the author's practice.

4 Decide whether to capitalize following a colon

If a complete sentence follows a colon, you can choose to capitalize it or put it in lowercase (see 33b on colon use). Since either choice is correct, you might make your decision on the basis of style or emphasis. But be consistent.

38a cap

CORRECT   The province of New Brunswick is bilingual both by law
and in practice: **O**ne-third of the population is French-speak-
ing and the remainder English-speaking.

ALSO CORRECT   The province of New Brunswick is bilingual both by law
and in practice: **o**ne-third of the population is French-speak-
ing and the remainder English-speaking.

In general, if the word group following the colon is not a sentence, you do
not need a capital letter.

> Foremost among the educational issues in New Brunswick is another
> problem related to language: **b**ilingualism in the schools.

There are some special cases in which the word group after a colon
takes a capital letter even if it is not a complete sentence. If the word group
after a colon states a principle, for example, use a capital letter.

> Remember this rule as you go through life: **A**lways look on the bright
> side.

5 Decide whether to capitalize elements in a series or list

You can treat questions in a series or elements in a list in a variety of
ways.

Questions in a Series. You can choose whether to use capital letters to
highlight the opening of each question in a series.

CORRECT   Should we spend our limited campaign funds on television
ads? **O**n billboards? **O**n smaller signs and posters? **O**n flyers?

ALSO CORRECT   Should we spend our limited campaign funds on television
ads? **o**n billboards? **o**n smaller signs and posters? **o**n flyers?

Stick to one style throughout an essay.

**38a
cap**

Run-In Lists. If the items in a **run-in list** (a list whose items aren't placed
on separate lines) are simple, you may use commas to separate them and a
lowercase letter for the first word in each item. If the items themselves in a
run-in list contain commas or are very complex and lengthy, you may decide
to separate them with semicolons.

> In estimating the project's costs, remember that you need to pay for the
> following: (1) **l**ab facilities, (2) **u**tilities, and (3) **m**easuring equipment.

In estimating the project's costs, remember the following: (1) **l**ab facilities must be rented; (2) **l**ight, heat, and other utilities need to be charged to the project's account; (3) **m**easuring equipment should be leased.

If the list following the colon consists of complete sentences, capitalize the first word of each item.

In estimating the project's costs, remember the following: **F**irst, lab facilities must be rented. **S**econd, light, heat, and other utilities need to be charged to the project's account. **F**inally, measuring equipment should be leased.

Vertical Lists. You may choose whether to capitalize the elements in a **vertical list** when they are either words or partial sentences. You must use capitalization with complete sentences, unless they appear in an outline without periods (see 4b on outlining).

CORRECT   When you estimate the project's costs, remember the following:
1. **L**ab facilities
2. **U**tilities
3. **M**easuring equipment

ALSO CORRECT   When you estimate the project's costs, remember the following:
1. **l**ab facilities
2. **u**tilities
3. **m**easuring equipment

Use the same pattern of capitalization in all the lists in a paper, and make sure the items in each list are parallel in form (see 26d).

38a
cap

Did You Know?

In other languages, capitalization conventions can be quite different from those for English. In German, for example, nouns and pronouns are capitalized: *Ich werde Sie ihrer Blumen zurückgeben* (I will give you your flowers back). In Spanish, pronouns and the names of days and months are not capitalized: *Almuerzo con ella los lunes* (I lunch with her on Mondays).

38b   Using capitals for proper nouns and adjectives

To capitalize a word is to highlight its importance. Readers pay special attention to words naming specific people, places, and things (proper nouns) and to adjectives created from these nouns (proper adjectives). When readers come across the title of a work, they are also aided if you identify this title with capitals.

1 Capitalize proper nouns and adjectives

You should capitalize the names of specific people, places, and things (**proper nouns**) as well as adjectives derived from them (**proper adjectives**).

PROPER NOUNS	PROPER ADJECTIVES
Brazil	Brazilian music
Dickens	Dickensian portrait
Venice	Venetian architecture

Writer's Tip

An article (*a, an,* or *the*) preceding a proper noun or adjective should not be capitalized unless it begins a title or starts a sentence.

All other nouns and adjectives are **common nouns** and **common adjectives.** Do not capitalize them except in special contexts, such as at the beginning of a sentence, in titles of works, or as parts of proper nouns.

COMMON NOUN (LOWERCASE)	PART OF PROPER NOUN (CAPITALIZED)
lake	Lake Jackson
river	Danube River
park	Prospect Park
computer company	Mesa Computer Company

The following categories should help you recognize words that need to be capitalized.

CAPITALIZED	LOWERCASE
INDIVIDUALS	
President Clinton	the president
Michael Jordan	her boyfriend
Georgia O'Keefe	my teacher's father

**38b
cap**

CAPITALIZED	**LOWERCASE**

RELATIVES

| Aunt Rosa; Uncle Jack | an uncle; my cousin |
| Mother; Dad | your mother; her dad |

GROUPS OF PEOPLE AND LANGUAGES

Caucasian	black (preferred in general usage)
Japanese	
Hopi	
Negro	
African American	
Russian	
Native American	

TIME PERIODS, HOLIDAYS, AND SEASONS

Thursday; October	spring; summer; fall; winter
Easter; Ramadan;	holiday
Yom Kippur; Labor Day	

RELIGIONS AND RELATED SUBJECTS

Judaism, Jews	
Christianity, Christians	
Islam, Muslims	
Catholic	catholic (meaning "universal")
Protestant	
Hinduism	
Buddhist practices	
Talmud; Bible	talmudic; biblical
God; Jesus Christ	a god, goddess; godly

ORGANIZATIONS, INSTITUTIONS, AND MEMBERS

Chicago Bulls, the Bulls	the team
Democratic Party, Democrat	democratic (referring to democracy)
Heritage Foundation;	conservative (referring to a
Conservative Party; Tory	political philosophy)
Girl Scout; Boy Scouts of	the scout
America	
Metropolitan Opera;	the opera; the string quartet
Cincinnati Symphony	
Rolling Stones	a band
Florida State Police	the police, the state police
Coast Guard; Virginia Board	the sailors; the board
of Ethics	
House of Commons;	a member of parliament; a senator
U.S. Senate, the Senate	
Air Line Pilots Association	the union, union member

**38b
cap**

CAPITALIZED	LOWERCASE

PLACES, THEIR RESIDENTS, AND GEOGRAPHIC REGIONS

Malaysia, Malaysian	the country; the citizen
Cape Verde Islands, Cape Verdean	the state; the resident
Tibet, Sino-Tibetan	
Berlin, Berliner	the city; the resident
Erie County; Nassau Avenue	the county; the street
South China Sea; Volga River	the sea; the river
Amazon Basin; Mars	the region; the planet
the Southwest, the East; East Coast	southwest, east southwestern, eastern (directions)

BUILDINGS AND MONUMENTS

Taj Mahal; Peace Bridge	Jim's garden; our backyard
Tower of London; Busch Stadium	the tower; a stadium
Space Needle; Getty Museum	a landmark; a museum
Piazza Navona; Grant's Tomb	the piazza; her tomb

HISTORICAL PERIODS, EVENTS, AND MOVEMENTS

Thirty Years' War; Dorr's to Rebellion	the war; the rebellion
Algerian Revolution; Ming Dynasty	the revolution; a dynasty
Romantic period; Impressionism	the period or style
First Great Awakening; Postmodernism	the movement; a trend
Jazz Age; Renaissance	a cultural epoch

Writer's Tip

Sometimes a time period such as a week or season refers to a specific event. In such cases the time period is capitalized because it is part of the name of the event.

PART OF THE EVENT'S NAME

At Bardstown College, **F**all **O**rientation runs from September 3 to 5.

NOT PART OF THE NAME

The **f**all **o**rientation at Bardstown College runs from September 3 to 5.

38b
cap

CAPITALIZED	**LOWERCASE**

ACADEMIC INSTITUTIONS AND COURSES

Auburn University; Utica College	a university
English Department	an English department
Department of Chemistry	chemistry department
Sociology 203; English 101	sociology or English course

VEHICLES

Boeing 767; Pontiac Bonneville SSE	a passenger plane; my car
J Boat	a sailboat

COMPANY NAMES AND TRADE NAMES

Siemens; Monsanto Chemical	the company; the chemical company
GTE; Fuji Heavy Industries; Xerox	a manufacturer; an employer
Luvs; New Balance; Kleenex; Toblerone; Patagonia	diapers; shoes; tissues; chocolate bar; outdoor equipment

---

Writer's Tip

Some company and institutional names include both a proper and a common noun. Both parts are capitalized because together they form a proper name.

proper   common   proper   common
Sandberg **U**niversity   **R**obinson **C**orporation

People writing documents under the auspices of an institution (for example, a memo to university staff or a corporate annual report) may decide to capitalize the common noun when it is used as a shortened name for the institution.

Sandberg **U**niversity is pleased to announce plans for renovating Smith Hall. The **U**niversity has contracted with Jacksonville Construction for the project.

If the subject of your paper has a common noun as part of its name, you may wish to follow the same procedure, after first giving the subject's full name, in order to help your readers readily distinguish references to the subject from more generic uses of the word.

The Democratic **P**arty has always been the dominant **p**arty in this county. However, recently other political groups have begun to encroach upon the **P**arty's territory.

38b
cap

CAPITALIZED	**LOWERCASE**
SCIENTIFIC, TECHNICAL, AND MEDICAL TERMS	
Big Dipper; Earth (planet)	earth (ground)
Marxism	marxian theory
Heisenberg's uncertainty principle	
Alzheimer's disease; Down syndrome	tuberculosis
organ of Corti	pancreas
Pistacia vera; Gazella dorcas	pistachio tree; gazelle

2 Use capitals in titles of works

In titles, you should capitalize the first word, the last word, and all words in between *except* articles (*a, an,* and *the*), prepositions under five letters (such as *in, of,* and *to*), and conjunctions under five letters (such as *and* or *but*). These rules apply to titles of long works, short works, and parts of works as well as titles for your own papers. If a colon divides the title, capitalize the first word after the colon.

> *The Mill on the Floss*
> "Factory of the Future: A Survey"
> *Thelma and Louise*
> *Briefing for a Descent into Hell*
> "Politics and the English Language"
> *Fragile Glory: A Portrait of France and the French*
> "Just like Romeo and Juliet"
> "The Civil Rights Movement: What Good Was It?"
> "Sumer Is Icumen In"
> Developing a Growth Plan for a Small Retail Business [your own title]

(For the rules governing the use of italics and quotation marks in titles, see 39a and 35d.)

38b
cap

3 Capitalize the pronoun *I* and the interjection *O*

Whenever **I** try to argue with my parents, they make me feel as if **I'm** still a child.

Trust in him, **O** people, and pour out your heart.

Although *oh* would seem to be capitalized by analogy with *O,* convention requires that *oh* remain in lowercase unless it begins a sentence or is capitalized in material you are quoting.

"**O**h dear, no," said the housekeeper.

—WILKIE COLLINS, *The Woman in White*

Exercise

A. Add capitalization wherever necessary in the following sentences. Replace any unnecessary capitals with lowercase letters. Circle the cases that seem the toughest to figure out.

EXAMPLE

Over the next ten years, *I*ndia will become an increasingly important trading partner for *N*orth *A*merica.

1. Located on a subcontinent in the southern part of asia, the republic of india has a territory of about 1.2 million Square Miles.
2. India's population of almost 800 Million falls into two main groups, dravidians and indo-aryans, which in turn are made up of many other cultural groups.
3. Dravidians live mainly in the south, an area that is dominated geographically by the deccan plateau.
4. The religion of the Majority is hinduism, though other religious groups such as sikhs and muslims are important.
5. Recently, religious conflicts have broken out in the provinces of kashmir and uttar pradesh.
6. Indian History is long and complicated, but in Modern Times it has been dominated by the british rule over the Country and by attempts to escape that rule and found a democratic State.
7. British Rule over most of the country began after the sepoy rebellion of 1857–58.
8. It ended after world war II with the independence movement led by mahatma gandhi.
9. The move toward industrialization has been the main goal of indian leaders since Independence, though this movement has at times been complicated by the problem of overpopulation and by conflicts stemming from the hindu social (or caste) system.
10. The dominant political Party since Independence has been the congress Party, with leaders such as jawaharlal nehru, indira gandhi, and rajiv gandhi.

B. In a small group, compare your list of difficult cases from Exercise A. What did you do to figure out your answer to each difficult case? Compare your answers.

38b cap

39

Italics
(Underlining)

Type that slants to the right—***italic type***—gives special emphasis to words and ideas. In handwritten or typed texts, underlining is the equivalent of italic type: The Color Purple = *The Color Purple.*

Convention requires you to use underlining (or italics) to give distinctive treatment to titles of full-length works such as books and films, foreign words, names of vehicles, and words named as words. (Titles of shorter works, such as stories and articles, or parts of works, such as chapters, require quotation marks rather than italics; see 35d and 39a-1.)

If you write your papers out in longhand or use a conventional typewriter, you will underline all such words and phrases. A computer word processing program may give you the option of *italics,* though some readers, including college instructors, may prefer you to underline.

TYPEWRITTEN   Alice Walker's novel The Color Purple has been both praised and criticized since it appeared in 1982.

COMPUTER
PRINTOUT   Alice Walker's novel *The Color Purple* has been both praised and criticized since it appeared in 1982.

You can also occasionally use underlining or italics to add emphasis to your writing and clarify your meaning.

> Not only was he one of the captains of the Permian team, not only was he number one in his class, but now he was thinking of applying to Harvard.
> *Harvard?*
> Never in a thousand years could Tony Chavez have imagined it turning out this way. Never in a million.
> —H. G. BISSINGER, *Friday Night Lights*

39a Following conventions for underlining (using italics)

Knowing when to use underlining (italics) can sometimes be difficult. As you proofread, therefore, you may need to consult the lists and discussions that follow in order to answer your questions. For example, should Stephen Crane's novel be written as *Maggie: A Girl of the Streets* or as "Maggie: A Girl of the Streets" (in quotation marks)? Should the borrowed French word "quiche," meaning a dinner pie with a filling, be written *quiche* (italicized or underlined) or quiche (in plain type)? Should the name of the famous Star Trek vessel be written as *The Enterprise*, the *Enterprise*, "The Enterprise," or The Enterprise?

1 Underline titles of long or major works

Underline (italicize) titles of most long works, such as books, magazines, and films, and of major works such as paintings and sculptures. For parts of works, however, and for short works such as stories, reports, magazine or newspaper articles, and episodes in a television series, use quotation marks rather than underlining. Some titles, such as those of sacred books (like the New Testament, Pentateuch, or Koran), require neither underlining nor quotation marks. (See the following list.)

UNDERLINE OR ITALICIZE	USE QUOTATION MARKS
BOOKS AND PAMPHLETS	
Generations: The History of America's Future, 1584 to 2069 (nonfiction book)	"Boomers" (book chapter)
Maggie: A Girl of the Streets (novel)	"Preface" (chapter in a novel)
Beetroot (collection of stories)	"The Purloined Letter" (story)
The White Album (collection of essays)	"Once More to the Lake" (essay)
Tracing Your Family's History (pamphlet)	"List Your Relatives" (section of a pamphlet)
POEMS	
Paradise Lost (long poem)	"Richard Cory" (short poem)
The One Day (long poem)	"Whoso list to hunt" (first line of a poem, used as a title)
PLAYS	
King Lear	
'night Mother	
Fences	

**39a
und/it**

UNDERLINE OR ITALICIZE	USE QUOTATION MARKS
MOVIES AND TELEVISION PROGRAMS	
Murphy Brown (TV show)	"Is She or Isn't She?" (episode in a TV series)
Ghostbusters (film)	
20/20 (TV news show)	"Daycare Dilemmas" (report from a news program)

PAINTINGS AND SCULPTURE
Nude Descending a Staircase (painting)
Winged Victory (sculpture)

MUSICAL WORKS	
Nixon in China (opera)	"Luck Be a Lady" (song in a musical)
Nutcracker Suite (work for orchestra)	"Waltz of the Flowers" (section of a longer work)
Invisible Touch (album)	"Big Money" (song on an album)
Camille Saint-Saëns's *Organ Symphony*	Saint-Saëns, Symphony no. 3 in C Minor, op. 78

MAGAZINES AND NEWSPAPERS	
Discover (magazine)	"What Can Baby Learn?" (article in magazine)
Review of Contemporary Fiction (scholarly journal)	"From Krazy Kat to Hoodoo: Aesthetic Discourse in the Fiction of Ishmael Reed" (scholarly article)
the *New York Times*	"Asbestos Found in Schools" (newspaper article)

NO UNDERLINING, ITALICS, OR QUOTATION MARKS

SACRED BOOKS
Bible, Koran, Talmud, Bhagavad Gita

PUBLIC, LEGAL, OR WELL-KNOWN DOCUMENTS
United States Constitution
Last Will and Testament

TITLE OF YOUR OWN PAPER
The Attitudes of College Students Toward Intramural Sports
(paper for a sociology class)
The Role of Verbal Abuse in *The Color Purple*
(title of a work being discussed is italicized)

EXCEPTION   If your paper has been published and you are citing it,
enclose the title in quotation marks.

39a
und/it

> ### Writer's Alert
> A reader needs to know whether certain end punctuation (such as a question mark) is part of a title or part of your own sentence in which the title appears. Underline any punctuation *only* when it's part of the title.
>
> | | |
> |---|---|
> | **INCORRECT** | What did he think of <u>Thelma and Louise?</u> |
> | **CORRECT** | What did he think of <u>Thelma and Louise</u>? |
> | **CORRECT** | The book <u>What's Up, Doc?</u> provides an intriguing history of cartoons. |
> | | **The comma and question mark are part of the title, so they need to be underlined.** |

2 Underline names of specific vehicles

Underline (italicize) the names of specific ships, airplanes, trains, and spacecraft, but not the names of *types* of vehicles. Note that USS and SS are not underlined. (See also 38b-1.)

SPECIFIC VEHICLES	TYPES OF VEHICLES
Voyager VI	Boeing 767
Orient Express	Chris Craft
USS *Corpus Christi*	Arctic Cat snowmobile
SS *Norway*	Chevrolet Lumina
Memphis Belle	Honda 750
Enterprise	Boston Whaler

3 Underline foreign words and phrases

39a
und/it

Foreign words and phrases pass through stages of familiarity as they are first adopted and then become more and more common. When a word or phrase has not moved into common use and still seems very foreign, highlight it with underlining or italics. Extremely common words and phrases—for example, "quiche," "junta," "taco," and "kvetch"—have lost their foreignness. You need not underline such words. When you can't decide whether to treat a word or phrase as part of the language, look it up in a dictionary.

FOREIGN	The code of <u>omertà</u> supported a kind of order in the criminal world.
FOREIGN	Many lawyers contribute to their communities by doing <u>pro bono</u> work.

COMMON   I served the vegetables grilled on skewers like shish kebab.

Scientific names for the genus and species of plants and animals also require underlining; the common names do not.

SCIENTIFIC NAME   The seaweed Chrodus crispus turns up in processed form in ice cream, in nondairy creamer, and even in hamburgers.

SCIENTIFIC NAME   Anthropologists speculate about the social arrangements practiced by early human species such as Homo habilis.

COMMON NAME   Tests found algae growing in the Swansons' pool.

4 Underline words, letters, and numbers named as words

When you focus attention on a word, letter, or number by discussing it as itself, you should underline it.

DISCUSSED   In several Boston accents, r is pronounced ah, so that the words car and park become cah and pahk.

Also underline a word or phrase you are defining.

DEFINED   Electricity can also be generated from a piezoelectric crystal, a piece of quartz or similar material that responds to pressure by producing electric current.

Did You Know?

Most of this book is printed in the familiar vertical letters known as roman type. The slanted letters discussed in this chapter, however, are in *italic* type. Italic type was developed around 1500 from a kind of swift handwriting that scholars and scribes of the period used to write out manuscripts. Italic type first appeared in 1501 in an edition of the work of the Latin poet Virgil published in Venice by the famous Italian printer and print designer Aldus Manutius.

**39a
und/it**

Exercise 1

The following sentences contain words that need to be highlighted by underlining (italics) or by quotation marks. Edit each by supplying any necessary underlining or quotation marks. Star the items that seem the most difficult to decide about.

EXAMPLE
The well-known *Old Farmer's Almanac* contains information about the weather and <u>articles on various topics</u>

1. I first leaned about this famous American almanac from a newspaper article, You Can Look It Up There, that appeared in my local paper, the Record-Advertiser.
2. GQ and Cosmopolitan probably would not print an article like Salt: It's Still Worth Its Salt, which appeared in a recent edition of the almanac.
3. According to this article, the word salary comes from the Latin term for wages paid to some soldiers, salarium argentum, that is, salt money.
4. In an essay on the historic effects of weather, the author points out that freezing temperatures on January 28, 1986, led to the space shuttle Challenger disaster.
5. If you are interested in learning about the ocean, you can find out that high tides occur twice a month at syzygy, the times when the sun and moon are lined up on the same side of the earth or on opposite sides.

39b   Underlining for emphasis

By underlining (italicizing) a word or phrase, you give it special emphasis. You should make use of this strategy on a *very* limited basis, however, since readers become annoyed when you rely too often on underlining to do the work your words should be doing on their own.

EMPHASIZES CONTRAST
A letter of recommendation mixing strong praise with a few reservations seems direct and realistic; a letter filled with <u>faint</u> praise makes the endorsement seem lukewarm.

39b
und/it

ADDS FORCE
In releasing themselves from the single ideal of the dependent woman, women have more or less incidentally released a lot of men from the single ideal of the dominant male. The one mistake the feminists have made, I think, is in supposing that <u>all</u> men need this release, or that the world would be a better place if <u>all</u> men achieved it. It would just be duller.   —NOEL PERRIN, "The Androgynous Man"

HIGHLIGHTS IMPORTANT INFORMATION
Whenever you start the generator, <u>make sure there is sufficient oil in the crankcase.</u>

Exercise 2

A. For each of the following sentences, add any underlining required by convention or needed for appropriate emphasis. Circle any words that are underlined but should not be. Star any items that are difficult to decide about.

EXAMPLE

In 1957, Chevrolet produced the <u>Bel Air</u>, a model now considered a (classic.)

1. As David Halberstam points out in his book The Fifties, automobiles from the period were so hot they were cool.
2. Cars from that period, with <u>enormous</u> tailfins and <u>lots</u> of chrome, are still <u>eye-catchers</u> today.
3. The musical <u>Grease</u> is set in the same era.
4. Television shows from the period included the Ed Sullivan Show and Lassie.
5. Readers could choose from such now-defunct publications as the Herald Tribune newspaper and Look magazine.

B. In a group, compare your corrections to Exercise 2A. Which were the hardest to make, and why?

Writer's Alert

Many kinds of informal writing, such as notes, journal entries, and personal letters, rely on underlining to add a certain "oral" emphasis to the prose. Be careful not to rely on underlining for this purpose when writing formal papers and other documents.

INFORMAL	Next time, <u>hand</u> the receipts to me instead of <u>dropping</u> them on my desk.
MORE FORMAL	In the future, give the receipts to me personally instead of placing them on my desk.

39b
und/it

CHAPTER

40

Hyphens and Word Division

Hyphens divide words and tie them together as well. At the end of a line, you may need to split a word, completing it on the next line. A hyphen (-) tells readers to treat the divided word as one word, not two.

Hyphens also help to divide words that are hard to read without a break (for example, *anti-intellectual,* not *antiintellectual*), and they link familiar compound words (*three-quarters, commander-in-chief*).

40a Using hyphens to divide words

To make your readers' job easier, use a hyphen to split a word at the end of a line. Also hyphenate words that may be misleading or hard to read without a visual break. As you proofread, moreover, check that you have divided words whenever necessary and that the hyphens come at appropriate points in words.

40a
-

1 Divide words at the end of a line

When you don't have enough room at the end of a line to complete a word of *two or more syllables,* type it on the next line unless doing so will create a right margin that is very jagged and distracting. To create a reasonably even margin, split the word *between syllables,* and mark the break with a hyphen at the end of the line.

DISTRACTING   The rate of change in home appliance manufacturing
                    has accelerated rapidly over the past decade.
                    Increasingly sophisticated consumers,
                    international competition, and the need for an
                    ozone-safe refrigerant to replace CFCs
                    (chlorofluorocarbons) have provided the impetus.

HYPHENATED The rate of change in home appliance manufacturing has accelerated rapidly over the past decade. Increas▪ ingly sophisticated consumers, international compe▪ tition, and the need for an ozone-safe refrigerant to replace CFCs (chlorofluorocarbons) have provided the impetus.

If there is no space for a word at the end of a line, a word processing program will automatically move a word to the next line. This process is called *word wrapping.* In proofreading a word-processed document, you need to be alert for jagged margins created by this process and hyphenate to make margins more regular.

Writer's Alert

A hyphen is a short line used to divide words at sylla-bles or to join parts of compound words and word clusters. Type a hyphen as a *single* line (-) with no space on either side. A dash, in contrast, interrupts sentences (see 37c). Type a dash as *two* lines (- -) with no space on either side or in between.

INCORRECT HYPHEN   one ▪ fourth of the workforce

CORRECT HYPHEN one▪fourth of the workforce

INCORRECT DASH surprising ingredients ▪ peanut butter, raisins, and whipped cream

CORRECT DASH surprising ingredients ▪▪peanut butter, raisins, and whipped cream

---

Although it may seem simple, dividing words at the ends of lines can be tricky. The following tips may help you to follow convention.

40a
-

Divide Words Only Between Syllables. Readers will have a hard time recognizing words that are split at a place other than a syllable break. For example, the word *adjustable* can be correctly divided in only two places: *ad-just-able.*

CONFUSING Experts disagree about the wisdom of **adju▪ stable** rates for mortgages.

CLEAR Experts disagree about the wisdom of **adjust▪ able** rates for mortgages.

Consult a Dictionary to Determine Where to Divide a Word. If you rely entirely on your own pronunciation, you may divide some words incorrectly, especially those you encounter in reading but seldom use in conversation. For example, *irrevocable* is divided as *ir-re-vo-ca-ble,* not *ir-rev-oc-able; milieu* is *mi-lieu,* not *mil-ieu.* Your pronunciation of a familiar word may also differ from the standard one given in the dictionary and expected by readers. (For example, you may pronounce the word *nuclear* in two syllables, *nuc-lear,* rather than with the three syllables listed in the dictionary, *nu-cle-ar.*)

Writer's Tip

Some word processing programs will hyphenate words at the ends of lines for you. This feature can be timesaving and helpful, yet the programs often split words incorrectly, especially less common terms. Consequently, the programs allow you to accept or reject proposed word divisions, and effective proofreading includes checking on the accuracy of the hyphenations you are offered.

Leave More Than One Letter at the End of a Line and More Than Two at the Beginning.

INCORRECT Two designers announced they are considering an **a‒greement** to produce a line of affordable clothes for professional women.

EDITED Two designers announced they are considering an **agreement** to produce a line of affordable clothes for professional women.

INCORRECT The concert ended because a stagehand **disconnect‒ed** the power supply for the main amplifiers.

EDITED The concert ended because a stagehand **discon‒nected** the power supply for the main amplifiers.

40a
-

Divide Compound Words at Natural Breaks. Generally, divide a compound word at the break between the words making it up. If a compound already includes a hyphen, divide it at that point.

DISTRACTING If the sports car is the classic European car, the **Volkswa‒gen** is the classic California car.

EDITED If the sports car is the classic European car, the **Volks‒wagen** is the classic California car.

DISTRACTING In his new movie, the actor plays a bumbling, **acci‒dent-prone** police detective.

EDITED   In his new movie, the actor plays a bumbling, **accident-**
prone police detective.

Don't Divide One-Syllable Words. Even relatively long words such as
touched, drought, kicked, and *through* have no stopping points in pronunciation and should be left intact. If the undivided word doesn't fit on a line,
you should move it to the next line.

Avoid Confusing Divisions. When some words are correctly divided,
they form other words with meanings that may be distracting.

DISTRACTING   The school board is proposing a solution for **sin-**
gle parents unable to afford child care.

CLEAR   The school board is proposing a solution for
single parents unable to afford child care.

Don't Split Abbreviations, Numerals, or Contractions. Abbreviations
and acronymns (NATO, ROTC, NCAA), numerals (528; 100,000), and contractions (didn't, should've) can be sounded out with syllables, but splitting them will distract your readers.

DISTRACTING   Foreign policy experts disagree about funding the **NA-**
TO alliance at present levels.

CLEAR   Foreign policy experts disagree about funding the
NATO alliance at present levels.

Exercise 1

A. Look at each hyphen in the following sentences, and decide
whether to retain it, to change within the word, or to eliminate it in
favor of placing the entire word on the next line. Use your dictionary
if you need to, and keep track of the toughest cases.

EXAMPLE
Although receiving a present can be very pleasant, gift-~~giv-~~
giving
~~ing~~ can be equally rewarding.

1. Looking for a job that would be challenging, Jen thought long and hard about taking the position at Hammond's Gift
   Shop.
2. By the next Saturday, however, she was unpacking a truck-
   load of the exquisite vases and figurines that the gift shop sells.
3. Hank wanted only one thing for his birthday: an ornamental Chinese vase that was way beyond Rachel's budget.

40a
-

4. When he came home one afternoon and saw the vase on the mantle, Hank went right out to get flowers as a way of saying "thank you."

5. The bouquet was lovely, redolent of roses, tulips, and baby's-breath.

 B. In a small group, compare your edited sentences from Exercise 1A. Which were the most difficult, and why?

---

2 Divide words to prevent misreading

You can use a hyphen to help readers distinguish between words that are spelled the same but have very different meanings.

> In the spirit of **reform** politics, the party sought to **re-form** a defunct citizens' action committee.

> For **recreation,** the Prichards staged a hilarious **re-creation** of the argument between Joe and Arnold.

You should also hyphenate words that are difficult to read because of repeated letters or odd combinations of letters.

> anti-imperialism (*not* antiimperialism)
> post-traumatic (*not* posttraumatic)
> co-owner (*not* coowner)

40b   Using hyphens to join words

Instead of *dividing* whole words, hyphens are often used to *tie together* the elements of compound words and phrases. The conventions for linking compounds, however, tend to be quite mixed; should the mechanical heart regulator be written as *pacemaker, pace maker,* or *pace-maker?*

40b
-

1 Check hyphens in compound words

A compound word is made from two or more words. Some compounds are hyphenated (*double-decker, time-lapse*), some are treated as one word (*backfire, timekeeper*), and some are treated as separate words (*mail carrier, time bomb*). A dictionary will tell you how to treat a particular compound. Make sure the dictionary is up to date, however, because usage changes. Today's *baby-sitter* can quickly become tomorrow's *babysitter.*

2 Hyphenate familiar compounds correctly

Some familiar compounds generally require hyphens.

Numbers. You should hyphenate all numbers between twenty-one and ninety-nine when they are spelled out.

forty-one　　eighty-six　　twenty-five

This rule holds even if the number is part of a larger number.

fifty-eight thousand　　twenty-three million

Use a hyphen to show inclusive numbers.

pages 163-78　　volumes 9-14

Fractions. Hyphenate fractions when you spell them out.

five-eighths of the liquid in the container
two-thirds the size of last year's convention

Prefixes and Suffixes. Hyphenate a prefix attached to a capitalized word or a number.

Cro-Magnon　non-Euclidean　post-Victorian　pre-1989
mid-October　pre-Reagan　　trans-Canadian　post-1066

Hyphenate a capital letter and a word that together form a compound.

A-frame　　I-beam　　T-shirt
B-movie　　O-ring　　X-factor

Some specialized terms, such as those used in music, do not require a hyphen.

A minor　　G sharp　　C clef

The prefixes *ex-*, *self-*, and *all-* and the suffixes *-elect* and *-odd* should generally be hyphenated in compounds.

all-encompassing　self-centered　president-elect
ex-partner　　self-denial　　twenty-odd

40b
-

Writer's Tip

Writers in academic, technical, and professional fields often present detailed information by using a series of compound modifiers. When you use parallel modifiers, you can save space and reduce repetition by using **suspended hyphens**—hyphens that signal the suspension of an element that readers can find at the end of the series. In strings of three or more modifiers, always leave a space after the hyphen and before the word *and,* but don't leave any space before a comma.

> The process is equally effective with **oil- and water-based** compounds.

> The testing program calls for **sixth-, eighth-, and tenth-grade students** to submit portfolios of their work.

---

3 Hyphenate compound modifiers correctly

When you ask two or more words to work as a single modifier and you place them *before* a noun, hyphenate them.

BEFORE NOUN   The **second-largest** supplier of crude oil to the United States is Nigeria.

BEFORE NOUN   Ayn Rand's works are among the most popular **twentieth-century** novels.

When the modifiers come *after* a noun, you generally do not need to hyphenate them.

AFTER NOUN   Many of the drugs used to treat cancer are **nausea inducing**.

40b
-

Remember that modifying compounds can mean something quite different from the sum of their independent meanings. Hyphens help readers to know which meaning to assign the compound.

> The director needed three **extra wild** monkeys for the scene.
> The director needed three **extra-wild** monkeys for the scene.

> The **bird eating** spiders flew away.
> The **bird-eating** spiders have enormous fangs.

Do not hyphenate compound modifiers containing *-ly* adverbs or comparative and superlative forms.

The new products were developed by the company's **highly regarded** research team.

Nigeria is the **most populous** country in Africa.

(Compound modifiers differ from coordinate adjectives, which are joined with a comma. See 32f.)

4 Use hyphens to create new compounds

To add vividness and emphasis to your writing, you can occasionally create (or "coin") a new compound word or phrase. Join the elements in such a compound with hyphens to indicate its original, temporary nature.

She entered the program with a **prove‑it‑to‑me** attitude.

Did You Know?

Short compound words are common in English, with and without commas, but in other languages, long compounds occur quite frequently. As Bill Bryson points out:

German is full of jaw-crunching words like *Wirtschaftstreu-handgesellschaft* (business trust company), *Bundesbahn-angestelltenwitwe* (a widow of a federal railway employee), and *Kriegsgefangenenentschädigungsgesetz* (a law pertaining to war reparations), while in Holland companies commonly have names of forty letters or more, such as Douwe Egberts Koninlijke Tabaksfabriek-Koffiebranderijen-Theehandal Naam-loze Vennootschap (literally Douwe Egberts Royal Tobacco Factory–Coffee Roasters–Tea Traders Incorporated; they must use fold-out business cards).

Bill Bryson, *The Mother Tongue* (New York: Morrow, 1990) 19.

40b
-

Exercise 2

A. Insert hyphens in the following sentences wherever appropriate. Consult a dictionary if necessary.

EXAMPLE

The company hired a well‑regarded accounting firm as part of its financial reorganization.

1. Alejo enjoys painstakingly exact work, such as building scale model ships.

2. While working, he likes to listen to Francis Poulenc's jazz influenced classical music.
3. One fourth of all his model ships are sold at auction.
4. Tony, his assistant, keeps track of the profits in a pre and post auction sale log.
5. Although his creations are awesome, Alejo harbors many insecurities that are mostly selfinflicted.

B. In a small group, compare your edited versions of the sentences in Exercise 2A. Which were the most difficult decisions, and why? Did your dictionaries give all members of the group the same advice?

41

Numbers

You can convey numbers in several ways in your writing—as numerals (37; 18.6), as words (eighty-one; two million), or as a combination of numerals and words (7th, 2nd). Understanding the appropriate ways to present numbers is important because unconventional or inconsistent usage can mislead your readers. This chapter shows you how to present numbers appropriately in general academic writing. For advice about the use of numbers in business, technical, and professional writing, see the reference guides listed in Chapters 49 through 53.

41a Spelling out numbers or using numerals

Whenever you use numbers in your writing, you need to decide whether to spell them out (twenty-five) or use numerals (25). The rules that follow tell you how to use numbers in general writing, including much academic writing. Conventions for the use of numbers may vary according to academic discipline and profession, however, so check with your instructor or with one of the style sheets describing conventions for specific fields (see Chapter 46).

1 Spell out numbers of one or two words

Spell out a number if you can write it in one or two words.

CORRECT   We are ordering **twenty-seven** personal computers.

CORRECT   Folktales have been popular in children's storybooks for the past **two hundred** years.

Treat hyphenated numbers (see 40b-2) as a single word.

CORRECT   Last year, our farm produced more than **seventy-eight thousand** eggs.

2 Spell out numbers that begin a sentence

Readers expect every sentence to begin with a capital letter. To avoid unsettling your readers, spell out any number that opens a sentence, even if the number contains more than two words. If the number is long enough to be distracting, rewrite so that it appears elsewhere in the sentence.

INAPPROPRIATE   **428** of the houses in Talcottville are built on leased land.

DISTRACTING   **Four hundred twenty-eight** of the houses in Talcottville are built on leased land.

EASY TO READ   **In Talcottville, 428** houses are built on leased land.

3 Express related numbers in a consistent form

When the numbers in a sentence or passage refer to the same category, treat them consistently by sticking to either words or numerals. If one of the numbers would require numerical form on its own, expressing the rest in numerals will help you keep sentences direct and concise.

INCONSISTENT   Café Luna opened with a menu of **twenty-six** items, which soon expanded to **eighty-five** and then **104** items as word spread about the good food.

CONSISTENT   Café Luna opened with a menu of **26** items, which soon expanded to **85** and then **104** items as word spread about the good food.

Did You Know?

Although numbers might seem unimportant, they may have led to the very birth of writing as a communicative medium. The most ancient written forms (inscribed on stone tablets several thousand years ago) talked of sales, exchanges, cattle, and other possessions—subjects that required a way to represent numbers. Without a way of writing numbers, ancient people would have been unable to record and convey much of the information they considered important.

41b
num

41b Following special conventions

In using numbers as part of dates, measurements, addresses, and the like, you need to follow some special conventions.

1 Use numerals when appropriate

ADDRESSES AND ROUTES
10 East 53rd Street   Interstate 6   Route 102
2450 Ridge Road, Apartment B3, Alhambra, CA 91801

DATES
September 7, 1976   1998   1880–1910
class of '97 (informal)   the '80s (informal)   1930s
486 B.C. (or B.C.E.)   A.D. 980 (or 980 C.E.)
from 1955 to 1957   between 1872 and 1876

PARTS OF A WRITTEN WORK
Chapter 12   page 278
Macbeth 2.4.25–28 (or act II, scene iv, lines 25–28)
Genesis 1:1–6 (reference to the Bible)

MEASUREMENTS USING SYMBOLS OR ABBREVIATIONS
120 MB   55 mph   80 kph
6'4"   47 psi   21 ml

PERCENTAGES, DECIMALS, AND FRACTIONS
7 5/8   27.3   67 percent (or 67%)

TIME OF DAY
10:52   2 p.m.   6:17 a.m.
12 p.m. (noon) 12 a.m. (midnight)
EXCEPTION   seven o'clock, not 7 o'clock

MONEY (SPECIFIC AMOUNTS)
$7,883 (or $7883) $4.29 $7.2 million (or $7,200,000)

SURVEYS, RATIO, STATISTICS, AND SCORES
7 out of 10   3 to 1   a mean of 23
a standard deviation of 2.5
the Bills defeated the Packers 21 to 17

CLUSTERED NUMBERS
paragraphs 2, 4, 9, and 13–15 (or 13 through 15)
units 23, 145, and 210

**41b
num**

2 Spell out numbers when appropriate

DATES AND TIMES
the sixties   October seventh   the nineteenth century
four o'clock (or four in the morning)
times rounded to the quarter hour: half past eight, a quarter after one

ROUNDED NUMBERS OR ROUNDED AMOUNTS OF MONEY
about three hundred thousand citizens
close to eleven thousand dollars
sixty cents (and other small dollar or cent amounts)

RANGES OF NUMBERS

LESS THAN 100	Give the second number in full.
	9–13 27–34 58–79 94–95
OVER 100	Give only the last two digits of the second number unless more are needed to prevent confusion. Do not use a comma in four-digit page numbers.
	134–45 95–102 (not 95–02) 370–420
	1534–620 (not 1534–20) 1007–9
YEARS	Supply both years in a range except when they belong to the same century.
	1890–1920 1770–86 476–823 42–38 B.C.

LARGE NUMBERS
For especially large numbers, combine numerals and words.
75 million years   2.3 million new automobiles

41c Avoiding too many numbers

Using too many numbers in a sentence or passage can confuse read-ers. If numbers come next to each other, first check for any needed hyphens (see 40b).

CONFUSING	For the company picnic we can buy either **forty six packs** of soda pop or **twenty two liter** bottles.
HYPHENS ADDED	For the company picnic we can buy either **forty six-packs** of soda pop or **twenty two-liter** bottles.

41c
num

When a passage contains so many numbers that readers may have trouble keeping track of the relationships, consider organizing the numbers in a table or chart.

DETAILED DESCRIPTION	The origins of Canada's population include the British Isles (40%), France (27%), other European regions (20%), and Indian (indigenous) or Eskimo (1.5%).

CHARTED NUMBERS	**CANADIAN POPULATION**	
	ORIGIN	**PERCENTAGE**
	British Isles	40.0
	France	27.0
	Other European	20.0
	Indian (indigenous) or Eskimo	1.5

This alternative is appropriate only when the numbers identify comparable categories. In other instances, you can avoid confusing readers by rewriting in order to simplify or to separate numbers so they are easier to understand.

Exercise

A. In the following sentences, correct any errors in the use of numbers. Circle any especially difficult items. You may need to rewrite some sentences.

EXAMPLE
When the list of cities for the Rock and Roll Hall of Fame was narrowed down to *one* ~~1~~, the choice was Cleveland.

1. Of the groups and individuals elected to the Rock and Roll Hall of Fame from 1986 to 1990, 5 were female and 68 were male.
2. The Hall of Fame is increasing its membership goals from nineteen thousand to twenty-one thousand five hundred.
3. 411 of the 2000 questionnaires about favorite rockers were returned by the deadline.
4. This year the Hall of Fame purchased twenty-six articles of clothing, 127 signed memorabilia, and 232 unused concert tickets for the museum.
5. Although subscribers were told the museum would open by 10:30 in the morning on the twelfth, the personnel weren't ready for the large crowd until about 2 o'clock.

B. In a small group, compare your edited versions of the sentences in Exercise 1A. Which cases gave you the most trouble? How did you resolve them?

41c
num

42

Abbreviations

When they are understood and agreed upon by both a writer and reader, abbreviations act as a kind of shorthand, making a sentence quicker to write and easier to read.

SPELLED OUT   In her course Reporting Economic Issues, new faculty member **Doctor** Marian Hwang will be drawing heavily on her prior employment at both the **Internal Revenue Service** and **the National Broadcasting Company.**

ABBREVIATED   In her course Reporting Economic Issues, new faculty member **Dr.** Marian Hwang will be drawing heavily on her prior employment at both the **IRS** and **NBC.**

Improper or badly placed abbreviations, however, can make a sentence *harder* to read and understand.

CONFUSING   The legal theory known as Law **&** Economics has a strong advocate in **Jg. Rich.** Posner. He is a former **U of C** law **prof.** who now sits on the Seventh **U.S. Cir. Ct. of App.** in Chicago.

READER'S REACTION: Am I supposed to know all these abbreviations? What is "Cir. Ct. of App."? Is "U of C" the University of California? Cincinnati? Chicago?

CLEAR   The legal theory known as Law **and** Economics has a strong advocate in **Judge** Richard Posner. He is a former **University of Chicago** law **professor** who now sits on the Seventh U.S. **Circuit Court of Appeals** in Chicago.

Abbreviations should aid your readers, not distract them. This chapter provides some basic rules for abbreviating words and phrases in your writing.

42a Using familiar abbreviations

Many abbreviations are so widely used that readers have no trouble recognizing them. These abbreviations are acceptable in all kinds of writing as long as you present them in standard form.

1 Abbreviate titles with proper names

When people's titles come right before or after their names, you should use standard abbreviations such as *Dr., Rev., Ms.,* and *Prof.*

BEFORE NAME	**Dr.** Antoinette Plocek; **Mr.** William Choi; **Ms.** Rutkowski; **Mrs.** Stephanie Chenier; **Rev.** Richard Valantasis; **Hon.** Patricia Hacaj; **St.** Rose of Lima.
AFTER NAME	Christine Carruthers, **M.D.**; Cathy Harrington, **D.V.M.**; Angelo Iacono, **Jr.**; James Guptil, **Sr.**; Ralph Romero, **S.J.**; Jane Berger, **M.A.**; Rosemary Anzaldua, **C.P.A.**

If the person's title is preceded by *the,* the title should be spelled out.

The **Reverend** Robert Marsh

The **Honorable** Judith Loesser

When you give a person's entire name, you may abbreviate his or her title, but if you use the title *as part of your reference to the person,* spell out the entire title.

INCORRECT	The list included **Prof.** Levesque, **Brig. Gen.** Washington, and **Rep.** Schroeder.
ACCEPTABLE	The list included **Professor** Levesque, **Brigadier General** Washington, and **Representative** Schroeder.
ALTERNATIVE	The list included **Prof. Roland** Levesque, **Brig. Gen. William** Washington, and **Rep. Patricia** Schroeder.
EXCEPTIONS	**Rev.** Mills and **Dr.** Smith were not invited.

Spell out a title when it does not come next to a proper name.

INCORRECT	You should consult the **Dr.** about that knee.
EDITED	You should consult the **doctor** about that knee.
EDITED	You should consult **Dr. Boyajian** about that knee.

42a
abbre

Use only one form of a person's title at a time.

INCORRECT	**Dr.** Vonetta McGee, **D.D.S**
CORRECT	**Dr.** Vonetta McGee
CORRECT	Vonetta McGee, **D.D.S.**

Academic titles such as *M.A., Ph.D., B.S., Ed.D.,* and *M.D.* can be used on their own in abbreviated form.

| ACCEPTABLE | The university offers an **Ed.D.** specifically designed for schoolteachers who want to become administrators. |

2 Abbreviate references to people and organizations

Your readers may be more familiar with some abbreviations (3M, IBM, NATO) than with the names for which they stand (Minnesota Mining and Manufacturing, International Business Machines, North Atlantic Treaty Organization). Such abbreviations are almost always acceptable, as are those that simplify complicated names (AFL-CIO for American Federation of Labor and Congress of Industrial Organizations).

In some abbreviations the letters are pronounced singly (YMCA, USDA). In others, called **acronyms,** the letters form a pronounceable word (AIDS, NATO). Abbreviations and acronyms in which each letter stands for a word are usually written in capitals without periods.

ORGANIZATIONS	NAACP, AMA, NBA, FDA, NCAA, UNESCO, IBEW
CORPORATIONS	GTE, USX, PBS, GM, CNN, AT&T, PBS, BBC
COUNTRIES	USA (*or* U.S.A.), UK (*or* U.K.)
PEOPLE	JFK, LBJ, FDR, MLK
THINGS OR EVENTS	FM, AM, TB, MRI, AWOL, DWI, TGIF

42a
bbrev

Writer's Tip

If your reader won't recognize an unfamiliar abbreviation, you can still use it in your document as long as you give the full word or phrase once and show the abbreviation in parentheses. From then on, you can use the abbreviation without confusion.

| EXPLAINED | The **American Library Association (ALA)** has taken stands on access to information. The **ALA** |

> opposes book censorship and favors privacy for
> records of the books borrowed by an individual.
>
> This technique is especially useful in academic or
> technical writing because it enables you to shorten com-
> plicated and often-repeated terms.

3 Abbreviate dates and numbers correctly

Abbreviations of dates and numbers may be used only when they
specify a number or amount; they are not a substitute for the general term.

ABBREVIATION	MEANING
A.D. or AD	*anno Domini*, meaning "in the year of Our Lord"
B.C. or BC	*before Christ*
B.C.E. or BCE	*before common era*, used by some writers in place of *B.C.*
C.E or CE	*Common Era*, used by some writers in place of *A.D.*
a.m.	*ante meridiem*, meaning "morning"; some writers use *A.M.*
p.m.	*post meridiem*, meaning "after noon"; some writers use *P.M.*
no.	number
$	dollars

INCORRECT Because of the lack of capable leadership, the bill providing **$** for inspection of meat-processing plants was not passed
until late in the **p.m.,** just before the legislature adjourned.

EDITED Because of the lack of capable leadership, the bill providing **money** for inspection of meat-processing plants was not
passed until late in the **evening,** just before the legislature
adjourned.

You may use either *a.m.* and *p.m.* or *A.M.* and *P.M.* in handwritten
or typewritten papers. Book and magazine printers generally set the abbreviations in small capitals (A.M., P.M.). Your word processor may allow you
to do this.

42a
abbrev

> ### Writer's Tip
>
> In a hurried, informal note, you can use abbreviations
> to avoid spelling out words as long as your reader understands
> your shortcuts. In formal writing, however, use only familiar,
> acceptable abbreviations.

INFORMAL	If I'm not in the office during the **a.m.,** leave your **ID no.** and have the **$** delivered to **Dr. B.** at the Oak **Blvd.** office.
FORMAL	If I'm not in the office during the **morning,** leave your **identification number** and have the **money** delivered to **Dr. Baruti** at the Oak **Boulevard** office.

Did You Know?

Each day we use some common abbreviations without knowing that they were originally longer words or expressions (a famous example being *OK,* which has many proposed origins but most likely comes from an African word pronounced *ah-keh* or *wah-keh*). The term *good-bye,* for example, was abbreviated from the phrase *God be with you,* a kind of blessing and simple statement of departure. The substitution of *good* for *God* may have come about by association with similar phrases like *good day* or *good night.* Today we have gone a step further with the shortened form *bye* or the curious repetition *bye-bye.*

42b Using abbreviations sparingly

You can shorten many words and turn most names into initials, but the resulting sentences are likely to be hard to read and irritating. Their only real use is in shorthand notes to yourself or as a quick drafting technique (see 7b).

42b
abbrev

UNREADABLE	The descr. in the opening ch. is ~ to that in B. House except for the hum. tone and the emph. on a single char.'s pt. of view.

In most formal writing, your readers will expect words in full form except for certain familiar abbreviations (discussed in 42a). In special situations, such as research papers and scientific or technical writing, you can draw on a wider range of appropriate abbreviations to save space, particularly in documenting sources. (See Chapter 46 on abbreviations to use in documentation and in specialized writing.)

1 Avoid inappropriate abbreviations

The following lists should help alert you to inappropriate abbreviations.

DAYS, MONTHS, AND HOLIDAYS

AVOID	Thurs., Thur., Th.	Oct.	Xmas
USE	Thursday	October	Christmas

PLACES

AVOID	Wasatch Mts.	Lk. Erie	Phil.	Ont.	ave.
USE	Wasatch Mountains	Lake Erie	Philadelphia	Ontario	Avenue
EXCEPTION	988 Dunkerhook Road, Paramus, **NJ** 07652				
	Use accepted postal abbreviations in all addresses with ZIPs.				

If an abbreviation is officially part of a company name, you may use it (for example, *Newman & Son Mfg.* for *Newman and Son Manufacturing*). Otherwise, spell out the entire name.

COMPANY NAMES

QUESTIONABLE	The switches were installed by **LaForce Bros. Electrical Conts.**
EDITED	The switches were installed by **LaForce Brothers Electrical Contractors.**

Some contexts require you to use abbreviations in a particular way. The Modern Language Association (MLA) reference style, for example, requires abbreviations of publishing companies; thus, Holt, Rinehart and Winston, Incorporated, becomes just Holt (see 46a). Otherwise, spell out the entire name.

PEOPLE'S NAMES

AVOID	Wm. and Kath. Newholtz will attend.
EDITED	William and Katherine Newholtz will attend.

DISCIPLINES AND PROFESSIONS

INCORRECT	econ.	bio.	poli. sci.	phys. ed.	OT
EDITED	economics	biology	political science	physical education	occupational therapy
	Abbreviations may be acceptable in particular contexts; for example, reports in medicine or education routinely refer to PT (physical therapy) and OT (occupational therapy).				

PARTS OF WRITTEN WORKS

IN DOCU-MENTATION	ch.	p.	pp.	fig.
	Check style guide for academic field or profession (see Chapter 46).			
IN WRITTEN TEXT	chapter	page	pages	figure

**42b
abbre**

Use symbols such as @, #, =, ~, and + only in tables or graphs, not in the text of a paper. In general, spell out units of measurement such as *quart* and *mile* when you use them in sentences. You may, however, abbreviate phrases such as *rpm* and *mph,* with or without periods. You may also use @ when including an email address in text.

Write to her at jmjones@adcorp.com.

Symbols and Units of Measurement

AVOID	pt.	qt.	in.	mi.	kg.
USE	pint	quart	inch	mile	kilogram
CORRECT	Above 5600 **rpm,** viscosity breaks down.				
CORRECT	Above 5600 **r.p.m.,** viscosity breaks down.				

2 Limit Latin abbreviations

Limit your use of Latin abbreviations such as *et al.* and *e.g.* to documenting sources and making parenthetical comments.

c.f.	compare (*confer*)		i.e.	that is (*id est*)
e.g.	for example (*exempli gratia*)		N.B.	note well (*nota bene*)
et al.	and others (*et alii*)		viz.	namely (*videlicet*)
etc.	and so forth (*et cetera*)			

INCORRECT	Many products, **e.g.,** laptops, have flat-screen displays.
APPROPRIATE IN PARENTHESES	Many products (**e.g.,** laptops) have flat-screen displays.
PREFERABLE	Many products, **such as** laptop computers, have flat-screen displays.

42b
abbrev

Writer's Alert

The abbreviation *et al.* is very often used incorrectly. Meaning "and others," *et al.* comes from the longer Latin phrase *et alii.* No period appears at the end of the word *et,* but a period *always* appears at the end of *al.* because it is an abbreviation. Making the phrase possessive can be awkward; avoid such constructions as "Johnson et al.'s new book." Try "a new book by Johnson et al."

Exercise

A. Revise the following sentences, adding or correcting abbreviations when appropriate and spelling out or rewriting any inappropriate abbreviations. Assume that these sentences are all written in a fairly formal academic context.

EXAMPLE   *New York, Los Angeles,*
People think of ~~NY, LA,~~ and Montreal as international cities, but many small- to medium-sized towns are just as cosmopolitan.

1. At a drugstore in a small Montana town, I talked with a clerk who told me about the Wine Appreciation Guild, Ltd. (155 Conn. St., San Francisco, CA 94107), which publishes nonfiction books on food, wine, etc., e.g., *Wine Technology and Operations* by Yair Margalit, PhD.
2. According to a study by Ernest D. Abrams Consulting, smaller towns like Sioux City, IA, and Vero Bch., Fla., are even more likely to be the homes of inventors and innovators.
3. In one town in upstate NY, an engineer, Chas. D'Angelis, has created a device that measures rpms by counting the # of times a gear with a single tooth interrupts a laser beam.
4. While I was driving through the rural Midwest, I visited Rich. Forer, D.O., who examined my sore back, prescribed an innovative exercise rout. he had developed, and gave me an Rx for a mild painkiller.
5. In a city of twenty thou. people in eastern Tenn. I came across a health coop. that is pioneering a new phys. therapy program.

B. Meet in a small group and compare your editing of the sentences in Exercise A. Which ones seemed the hardest? Why?

42b
abbrev

Strategies for Spelling

Consider the fact that the sounds in the word *see* (an *s* and an *e*) can be spelled in at least a dozen different ways, as illustrated in the words *see, senile, sea, scenic, ceiling, cedar, juicy, glossy, sexy, cease, seize,* and *situ.* Or consider the six different pronunciations of the letters *ough* in the words *cough, tough, bough, through, though,* and *thoroughfare.* English spelling is often difficult, and unless you have been gifted with a marvelous visual memory for the way words are spelled, the best you can do is to develop some practical strategies for identifying spelling problems and choosing correct spellings.

43a Spelling as you write

Spelling errors are most likely to occur as you draft. You can deal with them immediately, during drafting, or later, as you edit and proofread. If correct spelling is hard for you, try to keep this difficulty from turning into a fear of misspelling that distracts you from what you are trying to write. Worrying about spelling can draw your attention away from the most important parts of drafting and revising—exploring ideas and expressing them in effective ways. Stopping to check every word you *might* have misspelled is a sure way to disrupt your train of thought.

Giving special attention to spelling is therefore something often best reserved for proofreading. Nonetheless, you can take some positive steps to deal with spelling errors as you write.

1 Recognize possible errors

To recognize possible spelling errors as you draft, consider the following sources of incorrect spelling.

Inattention. You know the correct spelling of a word, but you don't use it. You might make a typing mistake. You might focus so hard on what you want to say or how to say it that you let a misspelling creep in. Usually, you can recognize errors of this sort quickly when you glance back over what you have written.

Guessing. You don't know the correct spelling of a word, so you guess on the basis of reason or of similar-sounding words. You know, for example, that the words *irreconcilable, reasonable, honorable, justifiable,* and *probable* all end with *-able,* so you reason that the word you don't know, *irresistible,* must do the same—and you get it wrong.

"Sounding Out." You don't know the correct spelling of a word, so you "sound it out." Although this strategy works occasionally, it can often lead you astray because of the sound/spelling discrepancies in English. And if you mispronounce a word, your spelling will probably be wrong. Many a motel billboard has mistakenly offered "congradulations" to a graduating class. Perhaps the most common spelling error in the United States is the infamous *alot,* incorrectly spelled as one word because, when spoken, the *a* and the *lot* blend together. Sounding out a word can be helpful during the drafting process, when you need to get the word down on the page and can't, for the moment, look it up. Nonetheless, you can recognize right away that the spelling *might* be wrong.

2 Note possible misspellings as you draft

Instead of interrupting your thoughts to check every possible spelling error while you draft, try the following Strategy.

S T R A T E G Y

Circle possible misspellings as you write. As you draft, you regularly glance back over a sentence or two in order to review what you have said. When you do this, circle any obvious spelling errors that have slipped into your work as well as any words you think *might* be spelled wrong. You may want to correct some errors right away, but don't allow correcting to distract you from the more important practice of drafting and developing your ideas. Come back to the circled words later, after you have completed drafting, and check them for misspellings.

**43b
spell**

43b Recognizing and correcting spelling errors

As you edit and proofread, you can use one or more of the following methods to recognize and correct misspellings.

1 Pause to think

While you are editing and proofreading, remind yourself to pay attention to spelling. If you suspect for whatever reason that a word might be misspelled, pause to check the spelling. Think about the sequence of letters, concentrating especially on sequences that are likely to be misspelled. Correct any words whose spelling you know; look up any unfamiliar spellings (see 43b-2). Develop some way to remember the correct spelling for future use. For example, if you often misspell the plural of *quiz*, try to remember that *quizzes* has two *z*'s—perhaps by associating quizzes with boredom (*zzzzzz*).

Did You Know?

Noah Webster proposed dozens of spelling reforms in his famous dictionaries, and other American lexicographers made similar proposals. Only a few really stuck, however. Of these, the most noteworthy are words spelled with -*our* in England (*colour, humour, valour, honour*), from which Webster proposed cutting the *u*. Other differences between American and British spelling include *theater/theatre, gray/grey, center/centre, check/cheque,* and *tire/tyre*.

Chris M. Anson, "Errors and Endeavours: A Case Study in American Orthography." *International Journal of Lexicography* 3.1, 1990, 35–63.

---

2 Look it up

A dictionary will give you the correct spelling of a word, and it may even offer spelling advice. *Merriam-Webster's Collegiate Dictionary* (10th ed.), the *New World Dictionary of the American Language,* the *American Heritage Dictionary of the English Language,* or any other standard dictionary is a good place to start. If you have a general idea of how a word is spelled, especially how it begins, you can usually locate it in a dictionary with a little looking around. If you know how a word sounds but are not sure about the spelling, you can use the lists of correspondences between sound and spelling that some dictionaries offer. If you still can't find your word, you may wish to use a specialized dictionary or handheld electronic speller designed for people who have considerable trouble with spelling. These dictionaries list words both under the correct spelling (*phantom,* for example) and under likely misspellings (*fantom*). Electronic spellers work like computer spelling checkers.

As shown in the samples from *Merriam-Webster's Collegiate Dictionary* (10th ed.), a dictionary entry will tell you a word's correct spelling and also

43b
spell

in·fer \in-ˈfər\ *vb* **in·ferred; in·fer·ring** [MF or L; MF *inferer*, fr. L *inferre*, lit., to carry or bring into, fr. *in-* + *ferre* to carry — more at BEAR] *vt* (1528) **1 :** to derive as a conclusion from facts or premises ⟨we see smoke and ∼ fire —L. A. White⟩ — compare IMPLY **2 :** GUESS, SURMISE ⟨your letter . . . allows me to ∼ that you are as well as ever — O. W. Holmes †1935⟩ **3 a :** to involve as a normal outcome of thought **b :** to point out : INDICATE ⟨this doth ∼ the zeal I had to see him —Shak.⟩ **4 :** SUGGEST, HINT ⟨another survey . . . ∼s that two‡ thirds of all present computer installations are not paying for them‑ selves —H. R. Chellman⟩ ∼ *vi* : to draw inferences ⟨men . . . have observed, *inferred*, and reasoned . . . to all kinds of results —John Dewey⟩ — **in·fer·able** *also* **in·fer·ri·ble** \in-ˈfər-ə-bəl\ *adj* — **in·fer‑ rer** \-ˈfər-ər\ *n*
in·fer·ence \ˈin-f(ə-)rən(t)s, -fərn(t)s\ *n* (1594) **1 :** the act or process of inferring: as **a :** the act of passing from one proposition, statement, or judgment considered as true to another whose truth is believed to follow from that of the former **b :** the act of passing from statistical sample data to generalizations (as of the value of population parame‑ ters) usu. with calculated degrees of certainty **2 :** something that is inferred; *esp* : a proposition arrived at by inference **3 :** the premises and conclusion of a process of inferring
in·fer·en·tial \ˌin-fə-ˈren(t)-shəl\ *adj* [ML *inferentia*, fr. L *inferent-*, *inferens*, prp. of *inferre*] (1657) **1 :** relating to, involving, or resem‑ bling inference **2 :** deduced or deducible by inference
in·fer·en·tial·ly \-ˈren(t)-sh(ə-)lē\ *adv* (1691) : by way of inference : through inference

Figure 43.1 Detail from *Merriam-Webster's Collegiate Dictionary*, 10th ed. Springfield, MA: Merriam-Webster, 1993.

the spelling of its various forms (Figure 43.1). The entry will indicate pre‑ ferred spellings and alternative forms, and it will contain listings for related words. It will also provide information about the word's roots and history, and this information may help you remember the spelling.

Exercise 1

A. Assume that you've circled the following words in italics in one of your papers. You're done with your draft, and now you want to double-check your spellings. Look each word up, make any neces‑ sary corrections, and then write out one way to remember each cor‑ rect spelling. Do this whether or not you already know how to spell the word.

EXAMPLE   *pal*
school *principle*
The school principal is not always every kid's "pal."

coal *minor*   *precede* to the gate   *stationery* car
vacume the rug   she was *lieing*   *likelyhood*

B. In a group, share your devices for remembering the spellings in Exercise 1A. Write out those the group thinks are best in order to share them with the rest of the class.

43b spell

3 Be alert for common patterns of misspelling

Many words contain groups of letters that can trip up even the best spellers. Other words have plural or compound forms that may be confusing, and others add suffixes and prefixes that need special attention.

Plurals. For most words, you can form a plural simply by adding *-s* (*novel, novels; experiment, experiments; contract, contracts*). Watch out for words that end in *-o* preceded by a consonant; they often add *-es* for the plural.

ADD *-ES*	potato, potatoes	tomato, tomatoes
	hero, heroes	zero, zeroes
ADD *-S*	cello, cellos	memo, memos

When a vowel comes before the *-o,* add *-s.*

ADD *-S*	stereo, stereos	video, videos

For words ending in a consonant plus *-y,* change *y* to *i* and add *-es.*

etiology, etiologies   gallery, galleries   notary, notaries

EXCEPTION   Add *-s* for proper nouns (*Kennedy, Kennedys; Tanury, Tanurys*).

For words ending in a vowel plus *y,* however, keep the *y* and add *-s.*

day, days   journey, journeys   pulley, pulleys

For words ending in *-f* or *-fe,* you often change *f* to *v* and add *-s* or *-es.*

hoof, hooves   knife, knives   life, lives   self, selves

Remember, however, that some words simply add *-s.*

belief, beliefs   roof, roofs   turf, turfs

43b spell

Words ending with a hiss (*-ch, -s, -ss, -sh, -x,* or *-z*) generally add *-es.*

bench, benches	bus, buses	bush, bushes
buzz, buzzes	fox, foxes	kiss, kisses

A number of one-syllable words ending in *-s* or *-z* double the final consonant: *quiz, quizzes.*

Though most plurals follow these simple rules, some do not, and you need to be alert for their irregular forms. Words with foreign roots often follow the patterns of the original language, as is the case with the following words drawn from Latin and Greek.

alumna, alumnae (female)   criterion, criteria
alumnus, alumni (male)   datum, data
bacterium, bacteria   vertebra, vertebrae

Some familiar words form irregular plurals: *foot, feet; woman, women; mouse, mice; man, men.* (If you suspect that a word has an irregular plural, be sure to check a dictionary for its form.)

For compound words, use the plural form of the last word except in those few cases where the first word is clearly the most important.

basketball, basketballs   pegboard, pegboards
meadowland, meadowlands   snowflake, snowflakes

EXCEPTION   sister-in-law, sisters-in-law

Word Beginnings and Endings.

Prefixes do not change the spelling of the root word that follows.

precut   dissatisfied   misspell   unendurable

The prefixes *in-* and *im-* have the same meaning, but you should use *im-* before the letters *b, m,* and *p.*

USE *IN-*   incorrect   inadequate   incumbent

USE *IM-*   immobile   impatient   imbalance

Suffixes may change the spelling of the root word that comes before, and they may pose spelling problems in themselves.

Retain the silent *-e* at the end of a word when you add a suffix beginning with a consonant.

KEEP *-E*   fate, fateful   gentle, gentleness

EXCEPTIONS   words like *judgment, argument, truly,* and *ninth*

Drop the silent *-e* when you add a suffix beginning with a vowel.

DROP *-E*   imagine, imaginary   generate, generation
                  decrease, decreasing   define, definable

EXCEPTIONS   words like *noticeable* and *changeable*

Four familiar words end in *-ery: stationery* (paper), *cemetery, monastery, millinery.* Most others end in *-ary: stationary* (fixed in place), *secretary, primary, military,* and *culinary.*

Most words with a final "seed" sound end in *-cede: precede, recede,* and *intercede,* for example. Only three are spelled *-ceed: proceed, succeed,* and *exceed.* One is spelled *-sede: supersede.*

**43b
spell**

The endings *-able* and *-ible* are easy to confuse because they sound alike. Add *-able* to words that can stand on their own and *-ible* to word roots that cannot stand on their own.

USE *-ABLE*   charitable, habitable, advisable, mendable

> **Drop the e for word roots ending in one e (*comparable, detestable*), but keep it for words ending in double e (*agreeable*).**

USE *-IBLE*   credible, irreducible, frangible

Words Containing *ie* and *ei*. Here is an old rhyme that tells you when to use *ie* and *ei*.

> *I* before *e*
> Except after *c,*
> Or when sounding like *a*
> As in n*ei*ghbor and w*ei*gh.

Most words follow the rule.

USE *IE*   believe, thief, grief, friend, chief, field, niece

USE *EI*   receive, deceit, perceive, ceiling, conceited

There are some exceptions.

EXCEPTIONS   weird, seize, foreign, ancient, height, either, neither, their, leisure, forfeit

4 Watch for commonly misspelled words

Words that sound like each other but are spelled differently (*accept/except, assent/ascent*) are known as **homophones.** Writers often confuse them, creating errors in both spelling and meaning.

43b spell

INCORRECT   The city will not **except** any late bids for the project.

PROOFREAD   The city will not **accept** any late bids for the project.

The list on pages 579–580 of homophones and other words often confused is designed to help you recognize errors in spelling or meaning as you proofread.

5 Try alternatives to the dictionary

Sometimes when you want to use a particular word, you can't find the correct spelling in a dictionary, no matter how hard you look. Try the alternatives listed in the Strategy on pages 580–581.

Commonly Misspelled or Confused Word Pairs

WORD	MEANING	WORD	MEANING
accept	receive	elicit	draw out, evoke
except	other than	illicit	illegal
affect	to influence; an emotional response	eminent	well known, respected
effect	result	immanent	inherent
all ready	prepared	imminent	about to happen
already	by this time	fair	lovely; light-colored; just
allusion	indirect reference	fare	fee for transportation
illusion	faulty belief or perception	foreword	prefatory comment in book
ascent	upward movement	forward	advance, ahead
assent	agreement	forth	forward
assure	state positively	fourth	after *third*
ensure	make certain	gorilla	an ape
insure	indemnify	guerrilla	kind of soldier or warfare
bare	naked	hear	perceive sound
bear	carry; an animal	here	in this place
board	get on; flat piece of wood	heard	past tense of *hear*
bored	not interested	herd	group of animals
brake	stop	hole	opening
break	shatter, destroy; a gap; a pause	whole	complete
capital	seat of government; monetary resources	its	possessive form of *it*
capitol	building that houses government	it's	contraction for *it is*
		later	following in time
cite	quote an authority	latter	last in a series
sight	ability to see; a view	lessen	make less
site	a place	lesson	something learned
complement	to complete or supplement	meat	flesh
compliment	to praise	meet	encounter
		loose	not tight
desert	abandon; sandy wasteland	lose	misplace
dessert	sweet course at conclusion of meal	no	negative
		know	understand or be aware of
discreet	tactful, reserved	passed	past tense of *pass*
discrete	separate or distinct	past	after; events occurring at a prior time

(continued)

**43b
spell**

Commonly Misspelled or Confused Word Pairs *(continued)*

WORD	MEANING	WORD	MEANING
patience	calm endurance	road	street
patients	people getting medical treatment	rode	past tense of *ride*
		scene	section of a play; setting of an action
peace	calm or absence of war	seen	visible
piece	part of something	stationary	fixed in place or still
plain	clear, unadorned	stationery	paper for writing
plane	woodworking tool; airplane	straight	unbending
		strait	water passageway
persecute	harass	than	compared with
prosecute	take legal action against	then	at that time; next
personal	relating to oneself	their	possessive form of *they*
personnel	employees	there	in that place
		they're	contraction for *they are*
precede	come before		
proceed	go ahead, continue	to	toward
principal	most important; head of a school; invested money	too	in addition, also
		two	number after *one*
principle	basic truth, rule of behavior	waist	middle of body
		waste	leftover or discarded material
rain	precipitation	which	one of a group
reign	to rule; period of ruling	witch	person with magical powers
rein	strap for guiding an animal	who's	contraction for *who is*
		whose	possessive of *who*
raise	lift up or build up	your	possessive of *you*
raze	tear down	you're	contraction for *you are*
right	correct		
rite	ritual		
write	compose; put words into a text		

**43b
spell**

S T R A T E G Y

- List as many possible spellings as you can, even if they seem odd. Try looking them all up. Often you will find the right area in the dictionary and will be able to locate the word with a little more searching.
- Try a thesaurus (see 28c) if you know a suitable synonym; the word may be listed there in its correct spelling.

- Ask friends or classmates if they know the spelling, especially for technical terms; then look up the word in the dictionary to be sure you got good information.
- Check the indexes of books that deal with the topic the word relates to.
- Check your textbook, class notes, or handouts to see whether the word appears there.

6 Get help

All writers make some spelling errors that they simply can't fix because they don't know the word is misspelled. If at all possible, ask members of a revision group to identify any spelling errors you haven't caught. But first clean up all the errors you already know, even if you simply circle the words to identify them as misspelled. If someone else finds any more misspellings in your paper, you have the chance not just to fix them before sending the paper on to its reader but also to learn the correct spellings along the way.

43c Using long-term strategies to improve your spelling

Improving your spelling more generally is like improving anything that develops slowly: you need to practice. Here are three useful ways to become a more effective speller.

1 Use memory devices and pronunciation aids

The use of **mnemonics** (memory aids) can greatly improve your spelling by reminding you of odd spelling conventions that don't correspond with pronunciation. In *Beyond the "SP" Label,* Patricia McAlexander, Ann Dobie, and Noel Gregg offer a number of memory aids, including the following.

43c
spell

> *All right* is spelled like *all wrong.*
> *A lot* is like *a little.*
> *Emigrant, immigrant:* An *e*migrant l*e*aves; an *i*mmigrant comes *i*n.
> *Separate: sep*a*rate* rates two *a*'s; there's a rat in *sep*a*rate.*

Use these as models to create memory aids of your own.

Some words get misspelled because often they are *not* pronounced fully or correctly. You need to develop an ear for "careful" pronunciations equivalent to spelling. Instead of hearing *new-cue-lar,* a common pronunciation of *nuclear,* hear the word in its carefully pronounced (spelling) form: *new-clee-ar.*

Did You Know?

Experts frequently argue over just how difficult the English spelling system is. In his book *The English Language*, David Crystal tries to show that the system isn't really as bad as we think. He claims that only 400 words have "irregular" or idiosyncratic spellings and cites a study showing that 84 percent follow some sort of general (learnable) pattern, such as *purse, nurse, curse* and *hatch, catch, latch.*

David Crystal, *The English Language* (New York: Viking, 1988) 69.

---

2 Read more and attend to spellings

Nothing boosts literacy (spelling included) so powerfully as reading. The more you read, the more likely you are to see words spelled correctly. When reading, keep a list of words you might use (and might otherwise misspell) someday. Focus consciously on words with difficult spellings (if you've been doing that in this chapter, you may already have learned the spellings of *mnemonic* and *nuclear*).

3 Build your own speller

The most useful spelling aid should look like someone's personal telephone book: filled with names and numbers generally meaningless to other people. If you keep track of words you commonly misspell, perhaps in a little notebook or file, you'll find yourself looking up possible candidates for misspellings much more quickly. As you begin learning and remembering the correct spellings, you can cross some words off your list as you're adding new ones.

**43c
spell**

Exercise 2

 A. Without using a dictionary, circle the words that are misspelled in this list.

supercede	conceed	procede
idiosyncracy	concensus	accomodate
dexterous	impressario	irresistable
rhythym	opthalmologist	diptheria
anamoly	afficianado	caesarian
grafitti	judgement	liason

 B. Working with a partner or in a small group, compare your answers to Exercise 2A, and *then* resolve any debates with a dictionary.

43d Spelling and the computer

The personal computer has become for spelling what the handheld calculator became in the 1970s for routine math. If you use a word processor, you've no doubt discovered the virtues of the spelling checker, a program that searches your document for misspellings and asks you whether they're correct.

1 Understand how spelling checkers work

Most spelling checkers on personal computers work in conjunction with a dictionary that must be present in the computer's memory. Often these computer dictionaries hold several thousand basic words. When you ask the computer to screen your document for any spelling errors, it compares each word in your text with the words in the dictionary. If the word matches a word in the dictionary, the computer assumes the word is correctly spelled, and it moves on to the next word.

When the computer encounters a word that does *not* match any word in its dictionary, it asks you whether the word is misspelled. If it is, you can select an alternative spelling or type in the correction, and the computer then moves on until it finds the next possible error. A typical program also allows you to add words to its often limited dictionary. In this way, you can personalize the dictionary so that an unusual word or technical term won't be flagged every time the computer finds it in your paper.

2 Use a spelling checker cautiously

Using a spelling checker, especially on longer documents, is likely to reveal at least one or two errors. But whatever you do, don't rely *entirely* on a spelling checker to fix your writing.

A spelling checker can't reveal words that are properly spelled but used incorrectly. If it runs across the sentence "The Lakewood High quarterback lead his team to victory in the semifinals," a spelling checker will ignore *lead* because this is a correctly spelled word in the dictionary. But here, *lead* should be *led.*

The computer may flag a word as misspelled and then, on command, offer you other correct spelling options. If you're not careful, you can mistakenly choose the wrong word to be inserted in place of the misspelled one.

**43d
spell**

USING RESEARCH STRATEGIES: READING AND WRITING WITHIN A RESEARCH COMMUNITY

44

Participating in Research Communities: Academic, Work, and Public

Are you searching through books and periodicals in the library because your psychology instructor asked you to analyze recent studies on work-related stress? If so, you are doing research: bringing together ideas and information from a variety of sources, blending them with your own insights, and sharing your understanding of the subject with readers.

Perhaps you can also imagine yourself searching the World Wide Web for information to use in a proposal for company-financed daycare. Or you can see yourself planning to interview people for a newspaper article on the ways different generations view each other. These tasks involve different sources of information and ideas, address different audiences, and call for different writing strategies, yet each is a form of research. The techniques of inquiry and expression you develop in research addressed to one community of readers and writers—an academic community, for example—are also likely to prove useful when you are addressing readers in work or public communities. But truly good research involves more than reporting what is known about a subject; it involves interpreting, developing, or re-envisioning the subject in some way that adds to readers' understanding.

44a Focusing your research topic

As a researcher and writer, how can you arrive at a focus for your work that enables you to go beyond what others have to say about a subject? Begin by avoiding broad subjects. Aim for limited topics: specific elements of a subject or particular issues and unanswered questions arising from it. For example, while it might not be too difficult for you to gather and report information and ideas about subjects like "the effects of exercise" or "gender and advertising," it would be a very challenging task indeed to conduct the kind of detailed inquiry necessary to arrive at fresh insights of your own on such broad subjects.

While some people can develop intriguing research topics of their own, most worthwhile research writing grows from issues or questions developed within a research community, that is, a group of writers and readers sharing an interest in a specific subject. Typically, such people focus their reading and writing on the most puzzling, controversial, or intriguing aspects of a subject, and in so doing raise specific questions or problems that researchers can address. For example, recent academic discussions of the effects of exercise have focused on the question of whether or not regular exercise helps relieve depression, on the effects of exercise on self-image, and on the influence of exercise habits on dating and marriage. In short, by paying attention to what others are thinking and saying about a subject, you can discover ways to focus your research and arrive at a limited topic worth exploring.

For research to be productive, your research topic should be well focused and manageable and address aspects of the subject (issues, questions) that your readers will consider worth your attention and theirs. Try one or more of the following approaches to focus your topic.

1 Consider the assignment

Most of the time, your research papers in college will be prompted by specific assignments. Even when that assignment specifies a subject for research, you'll probably need strategies to help identify a focused research topic.

S T R A T E G Y

- If the assignment comes in written form, read it carefully, looking for key words and phrases that specify a topic or question and that either limit or open up your choices. If the assignment takes oral form, ask questions to identify key words and phrases or concerns you will need to address. If the project begins with an occasion or problem, write down words and phrases you or your readers are likely to associate with it.
- If a word or phrase immediately suggests a topic, write it down, followed by a list of synonyms or alternative terms. Draw on this list as you develop guiding questions for your research (see 44a-4), follow a research thread (see 44a-5), and write your paper or report.

44a
resrch

- If you can't identify a topic right away, take key words and phrases, write them down, and brainstorm (see 2c-2) related words and phrases along with the topics they suggest.
- Consider asking the person or people who made the assignment what they think of a potential topic—and for further topic suggestions. Consider asking potential readers for their reactions.

In an intermediate composition course, Summer Arrigo-Nelson and Jennifer Figliozzi were asked to "investigate the psychological or social dimensions of a local or campus problem" by drawing on print or electronic sources and field research of their own and to present their conclusions in the form of an academic research report. They underlined the words *psychological or social dimensions* and *campus problem* in the assignment and made a list of campus problems.

low class attendance	new majors	date rape
inadequate library	role of sports	student alcohol use
living conditions	canceled classes	student fees
parking	drugs	crime

They chose "student alcohol use" as a focus. The topic interested them. They also thought they could easily find some research sources and that doing field research of their own wouldn't be too difficult. Some initial reading and brainstorming led them to wonder about the role of parents in determining the drinking habits of college students, and they decided to address this question in their research.

2 Consider your audience

As you join the "conversations" that various research communities may be having about your topic, remember that readers in each community expect different things from the documents they read, so your own collection of sources won't all look alike. Academic readers look for detailed evidence from a variety of sources and expect carefully documented sources and quotations. Readers in work settings expect a clear and direct presentation, accurate information, and detail appropriate to the subject and the audience's expertise, along with less formal documentation. And readers in public communities expect information and supporting evidence that is accurate, clear, accessible, and persuasive, without quite as much attention to documentation. While college research papers typically address academic audiences, they don't have to; your own paper may take one of many forms and be addressed to one of many different communities of readers.

S T R A T E G Y

An **audience inventory**—a checklist or set of questions adapted to a specific audience—takes into account the specific concerns of your audience. An inventory works best when you know your audience well, as is often the case in work settings or when your audience is a local one such as the residents of a town, a campus community, or the members of an organization. Typical questions in an inventory include the following.

What problems or issues has the audience been facing?

What new discoveries or information might interest or be useful to the audience?

What policies or programs are causing your readers difficulty or might be helpful to them?

You can also use audience inventories to analyze readings you gather from other sources for your own research: Who were these readings addressed to? What were their audiences' main concerns?

Summer Arrigo-Nelson and Jennifer Figliozzi prepared an audience inventory to help plan their paper on the effects of alcohol consumption among college students. Below is a sample of their inventory focusing on the audience of their own campus community.

Audience Inventory Question	*What new discoveries or information about student alcohol use might benefit the campus community?*
Summer and Jennifer's Response	*Our conclusion about the relationship between student drinking behavior in college and parental permissiveness for drinking in the home could be important for a campus program aiming to reduce student alcohol use.*

3 Make connections

If you're free to choose from a wide range of subjects, create a list of topics you consider intriguing. If your writing situation limits the focus of your research, list different ways of approaching your subject matter. Then choose the topic that interests you most (or the approach that seems most likely to meet the needs of your writing situation). Freewrite (see 3a) on it for at least ten minutes, raising questions you might ask and attempt to answer. Next, read over your freewrite and underline questions your research

**44a
resrch**

project might attempt to answer (or make a list of research questions that come to mind as you read your freewrite). Finally, write down the topic that seems most promising and the questions that you think will help you focus your research.

4 Develop guiding research questions

All research is an attempt to answer questions. While you might have chosen an interesting topic to investigate, you can't move forward in your project unless you begin to ask questions about that topic. **Guiding questions** are questions that help you set goals for gathering and examining information and help you focus on the most important ideas as you comb through print and electronic sources or analyze data gathered from field research.

S T R A T E G Y

To start seeing connections among the ideas from your listing and freewriting, arrange your topics and questions into related groups. Concentrate on the most promising group or groups. Now narrow the possibilities and develop one or two guiding questions to focus your research. Your questions should be specific but reasonable; avoid questions if they will be difficult to answer or if it's not likely you'll find any existing research on them.

Summer Arrigo-Nelson and Jennifer Figliozzi developed the following questions for their academic research project on the relationship of parental behaviors to college student drinking.

> Will students with permission to drink at home show different drinking behaviors at college than those without permission to drink at home?

> Do the students feel that a correlation exists between drinking behaviors at home and at college?

Exercise 1

A. Choose one of the following general topical areas as if you were going to write a research paper on it. Using the strategies in this section, consider possible audiences for the research, make connections by freewriting, and create several guiding questions for your research.

Whole language versus phonics in reading instruction
Road rage
Cures for Lyme disease
Suburban sprawl
Rising acceptability of body piercing and tattoos
Threat of biological warfare
Massacre in the Balkans
Irradiation of perishable foods

B. Exchange work from Exercise 1A with at least two other students. How do your questions differ? Which questions identify points that need to be clarified? What possible audiences could be addressed, and in what form of writing?

5 Identify a research thread

To help you track ideas and information from source to source, identify a **research thread.** A research thread links your topic more explicitly to your research questions and gives you a kind of road map for working on your project.

Researchers and writers frequently rely on a limited set of terms, including some referring to the topic itself and others to related questions or controversies. Just as such terms helped you to identify a research topic at the start of your project, now they can help you in a more specific way to develop a research thread. (Also see the Tip box, page 592.)

STRATEGY

When you have located one or more sources addressing the question(s) guiding your research, begin a list of key words, names, and phrases these sources use repeatedly. Use this list to search library catalogs, bibliographies, databases, and the Internet or the World Wide Web as you follow your research thread. Pay particular attention to the names of people who have written on the topic or produced Web sites on it. Researchers who have written on a topic once are likely to do so again.

44b Developing your persona as a researcher

As you begin formulating your research questions and refining your topic, you'll need to ask yourself, "What do I want to gain from this research, and what role will I be playing as a researcher?" Answering this question not only will suggest the communities of research you may need to explore in

**44b
resrch**

Writer's Tip

You can also create a research thread by tracing discussions of a topic online. Newsgroups take two general forms: Usenet newsgroups and discussion lists. **Usenet newsgroups** tend to attract a diverse membership consisting of people from different regions (even countries), professions, and backgrounds. They can offer you a wide range of opinions and perspectives, and if you trace a research thread through them, you're likely to encounter fresh information, interesting or controversial ideas, and new developments. **Discussion lists** tend to have a more focused membership, reflecting the interests of specific academic, work, or public communities. Lists can help you identify the most current knowledge of a subject or the most recent state of a discussion. Tracing a research thread through a list can be especially helpful when you plan to address an academic community that will expect you to take into account the latest research or a work community that will expect you to respond to the newest developments or approaches to a problem. For more information on discussion lists and newsgroups, see Chapter 11.

your own research (and what, more specifically, you'll gather) but will also give you a sense of direction and form for your writing. The subject "cosmetics," for instance, includes a variety of more focused topics and research questions, each representing concerns of different researchers who play various roles, address different audiences, and produce different sorts of documents.

International marketing strategies for cosmetics—How much should trademarked packaging be modified for regional markets?
(Work audience; topic from *BIZZ—Business Index,* electronic index)
Animal testing of cosmetics—Is animal testing necessary? How good are the alternatives?
(Public audience; topic from *Reader's Guide to Periodical Literature,* print version)
Gender roles in cosmetics advertising—What roles (and values) for women and men are reinforced by advertising?
(Academic audience; topic from *Social Sciences Index,* CD-ROM version)

Each research community has individual concerns shaped by its setting. The boundaries of these settings are not distinct, and they share many goals; yet their special characteristics are important to writers and readers alike, as illustrated on page 593.

44b
resrch

GENERAL COMMUNITY	GOALS	TYPICAL QUESTIONS	TYPICAL FORMS
ACADEMIC	Explain or prove; offer well-supported interpretations or conclusions; advance knowledge; provide information for use in other settings.	What does it mean? What happened? How does it occur? How might it be modified?	Interpretive papers; informative papers; research reports; grant reports.
WORK	Document problems; propose a project or course of action; compare information; improve performance.	What is the problem? How can we solve it? What course of action will help us achieve our goals?	Proposals; reports; feasibility studies; memos.
PUBLIC	Support arguments for a policy or course of action; provide information of general interest; advise citizens for public good.	How can this policy be made better? What do people need or want to know?	Position papers; editorials; informative articles; pamphlets; or guidelines.

As you explore your topic and begin planning your research, remember that you may find information that represents the concerns of these various communities and also reflects the usual forms and formats of their writing. If the occasion permits, you can also choose to aim *your* research document or report toward one of the specific research communities in these general categories, following the conventions expected in that community.

Exercise 2

 A. Consider the following assignment from a journalism course. This assignment allows considerable freedom of topic. First, come up with a topic for the article. Then, using the chart in this section, invent two different research communities that your own research might explore, and describe what sort of information or perspectives you might find in those communities.

44b
resrc

Prepare a magazine feature article of 5 to 10 pages by examining contrasting stands on a specific controversial issue. Then develop your own stand on the issue. Make sure you provide detailed facts, statistics, and quotations from other sources to represent the contrasting points of view and to support your own conclusions.

 B. In a group, compare the results of your planning sketches. How did the topics you chose vary in terms of the way they might be discussed or researched in different communities?

44c Planning your research

Managing all the decisions and activities involved in research is like juggling: you need to plan your moves. To manage time and effort effectively, pay attention to three decision points.

1. **How much time do you have?** When should your report or document be in final form? Do you have to produce any intermediate assignments such as a progress report, drafts, or notes?

2. **What kind of report or document will you be creating, and for whom?** What form will your work take? What resources will you have to gather or develop in order to produce such work? What audience or community of readers will you be addressing? What will you need to learn about them and their expectations? Will you need to share or discuss the project with them while you're researching and writing?

3. **What kind of research must you do?** Will you be doing research in printed or library sources (books, articles, documents, microfilms, databases)? in electronic sources (Internet, World Wide Web, email, CD-ROM databases)? in field settings through interviews, surveys, observations, experiments, or ethnographic study?

STRATEGY

Create a research and writing plan by working backwards from the due date for a project. Even if you don't follow the plan exactly, a calendar, list of dates, or chart of activities can help you get started on a project and give you a sense of direction. It can also help you avoid the problem of leaving too many activities for the last moment. Your plan should take the shape dictated by your topic, audience, purpose, and resources.

Here is brief plan that reflects some activities you might include in your own research plan.

ACTIVITY	COMPLETE BY
Analyze task and audience; focus topic. Figure out guiding questions. Do preliminary research; look for research thread.	October 22
Do journal writing, freewriting, outlining, or sketching out of ideas to identify goals for the project and the resources necessary.	October 29
Go to library and identify print resources. Make appointments for interviews. Go online and identify electronic resources. Prepare working bibliography.	November 6
Do research in print resources and take notes. Conduct interviews; transcribe them or take notes. Do electronic research, take notes, and download information. Summarize ideas and information in notes, outlines, or preliminary drafts of parts of the report.	November 20
Create a tentative plan and thesis. Draft the report or document.	November 27
Share the draft with colleagues. Begin a list of works cited.	December 4
Revise the paper. Check citations and list of works cited. Proofread and submit final paper.	December 12

45

Using Print and Electronic Resources

When you start your research, you may be suprised to find just how many resources are available, and how many ideas and opinions on your topic you encounter. Library and electronic resources are filled with easily accessible information and also offer many strategies for locating harder-to-access sources. With a careful and thorough search strategy, you'll probably uncover plenty of sources, more than you can possibly use. This wealth of information will let you write with authority and sophistication about your research area.

45a Developing search strategies

A **search strategy** begins with your topic and research questions. It helps you select, examine, and evaluate resources most appropriate for your task, from the general through the specific. A search strategy is not a detailed plan. You can't know the specific twists and turns your research will take until you encounter them as you trace a thread of information and ideas. Still, your knowledge of a subject, of the research process, or of the kind of task you're undertaking can help you make some useful plans. As your research goes forward, you can make more specific plans, reflecting your growing understanding of your subject and the shape your report or document will take.

1 Pay attention to *where* research takes place

- **Library research** focuses primarily on print or electronic resources: books, articles, pamphlets, microfilms, databases, recordings, films, artworks, and reproductions. Your skill with indexing and reference systems will help you work with materials in library settings.

- **Electronic (online) research** focuses on information and documents on disk or available through networks: texts, data, graphics, pictures, audio, film, and email. Your skill with computer software and search engines will give you access to materials in electronic settings.
- **Field research** focuses mainly on events and oral texts gathered through observation, interviews, surveys, note taking, and recording. It requires skills in interviewing, administering surveys, observing, and interpreting.

2 Pay attention to the differences between primary and secondary sources

Primary sources consist of information and ideas in their original (or close-to-original) form: historical documents, works of literature, email resources, letters, tapes of interviews, survey data, videotapes, raw statistics, and other kinds of basic information that contain little or no interpretation by the observer or gatherer. **Secondary sources** consist of works that analyze, summarize, sort, interpret, or explain the information in primary sources. Secondary sources tell you what others have said about your area of research.

3 Move from preliminary sources, to general sources, to specialized sources

Effective research generally begins with skimming of the most general and broadly informative sources such as encyclopedias, magazine articles, ready references, general information books, or Web pages (see 45b). These **preliminary sources** are helpful in focusing on a topic, arriving at research questions, and identifying keywords to use in searching indexes and databases or with search engines on the Web and Internet (see 45c).

General sources provide background information on a topic and help identify issues, problems, and ideas you might examine more closely. They include books, articles in general-interest magazines and academic journals, online news sites, Web pages devoted to specific topics, introductions to databases, and postings to listservs or electronic bulletin boards.

Specialized sources provide information and ideas that add substance to the explanations, interpretations, and arguments you advance in a paper. They include research or project reports, technical documents, surveys, entries in a specialized database, field notes, theoretical books, specialized newsletters, electronic discussion groups and newsgroups, reports from industry or public interest groups, scholarly articles, and scientific reference works.

45a
sour

STRATEGY

- **Write.** Begin by jotting down your ideas about the directions your research might take, including notes about the resources you might consult first and those you might consult later on. Ask yourself whether you're likely to do library, electronic, or field research or some combination. Consider whether you're likely to consult primary sources, secondary sources, or both.
- **List.** Next, create a list of the steps you plan to take in your research process (consult preliminary sources, focus on topic, decide on research questions, consult general sources to identify issues, prepare and administer survey, etc.), including specific resources to consult.
- **Be prepared.** Review your research questions and search strategy whenever you do library or online research. Keep a list of key terms handy so you focus on the same research thread each time you work.
- **Stay aware of the direction of your work.** Work from broad, general sources to narrower, specific ones. Look for a variety of sources and fair, representative information. Balance online resources such as Web sites, discussion groups, and databases with traditional library resources. (In academic settings, instructors may require you to use more than one kind of resource.)
- **Revise.** Review and revise your research questions, keywords, and search strategy in the course of your research (and writing).

In her research on *Saving Private Ryan*, Sue Aquino mapped out several areas she thought would yield some useful information.

Movie reviews: Get as many as possible online and in library's periodicals holdings. These could be useful to see critics' responses and to gauge public opinion.

Biographical and work-related info. on Spielberg: Film biographies? Biographies of famous Americans and also indexes of popular culture. Try Web search.

Interviews—with Spielberg but also with actors (Tom Hanks? Matt Damon?) and others involved in the film.

Information on World War II: Too much! Narrow to representations in popular culture or the media. Comparisons to other recent war films, especially Vietnam; why did filmmakers decide to go _back_ to WWII? Or narrow to events in film.

Writer's Tip

To decide on the kinds of research appropriate for your project, ask the following questions.

1. Has your topic been frequently discussed in books, articles, Web sites, electronic discussion groups, or newspapers? (Do library and electronic research so your writing can build on what others have said.)
2. Is your subject a text (book, poem, Web page, document), an object (painting, sculpture), or an event (play, musical performance, video, film) that you need to locate in a library, museum, or theater; on disk; or through the Internet? (Obtain the material from a library or in electronic form along with the record of what others have said about it. Or do field research by witnessing a performance and observing the behavior of the audience.)
3. Is your subject a historical event that you can study only through written documents, films, or pictures? (Do research in library and electronic resources.)
4. Is your subject an event, a situation, a set of attitudes, or a pattern of behavior that has not been widely studied and that you can investigate directly? (Do field research, using observation, interviews, questionnaires, or surveys to gather data.)
5. Is your subject one of current interest to researchers and others who use electronic means of exchanging ideas, including email? (Consult electronic sources like newsgroups.)

An important caveat: It may seem easier to sit at a computer than to make a trip to the library, but this doesn't mean online research is the best method for your project. Some materials are available *only* in book or other print form in the library. As you begin your research, don't let the possible inconvenience of a trip to the library prevent you from using the material that you can obtain only there.

Exercise 1

A. Consider Sue Aquino's preliminary brainstorming plan for her research on *Saving Private Ryan*. In addition to the sources of information she has considered, what else comes to mind as potentially productive avenues for her research? How might her purpose, audience, and kind of writing help her decide which information is the most valuable? (Think up some specific purposes, audiences, and genres of writing.)

45a
source

B. In a group, compare your responses to Exercise 1A. How expansive were your additions to what Aquino had started? How much did the constraints of purpose, audience, and text rein them in?

45b Identifying print and electronic resources

Your topic, guiding questions, or search strategy will probably lead you to a rich variety of resources: books, articles, microfilms, indexes, CD-ROM databases, Web pages, Internet files, or electronic messaging. You need to be familiar with the categories in which these resources are commonly arranged, the names of some of the most useful ones, and the ways you can best consult them.

You also need to be familiar with resources that have been assembled for your use. Many universities provide access to databases and references via their library Web pages. Businesses and organizations frequently subscribe to databases; professional organizations (legal, medical, scientific, or scholarly) often maintain collections of articles and reference materials in electronic form. Government organizations provide electronic access to documents and records for public use. University, corporate, public, and government libraries make an astonishing range of printed and visual resources readily available.

1 General references

You can use general references to gain a broad overview of a topic, including background information and a sense of relationships to other subjects. General references can also provide names, keywords, and phrases useful for tracing a topic as well as bibliographies of potential resources. Commercial Internet services like America Online and Compuserve offer access to online reference works (such as *Grolier Multimedia Encyclopedia*), databases (such as *The Digital Tradition Folk Song Database*), reference services (such as *Medline*), and collections of resources (such as Electric Library).

General encyclopedias, ready references, maps, and dictionaries

The New Encyclopaedia Britannica, Grolier Multimedia Encyclopedia (CD-ROM), *Microsoft Encarta* (CD-ROM), *Compton's Encyclopedia* (CD-ROM and online), *The Concise Columbia Encyclopedia* (online), *The World Almanac and Book of Facts, Canadian Almanac and Directory, Statistical Abstract of the United States, National Atlas of the United States, National Geographic Atlas of the World, Street Atlas USA* (CD-ROM), *Webster's New Geographical Dictionary, The American Heritage Dictionary of the English Language, The American Heritage Talking Dic-*

tionary (CD-ROM), *The Oxford Dictionary of the English Language on Compact Disk, Webster's New World Dictionary of the American Language, Merriam-Webster's Collegiate Dictionary*

Specialized encyclopedias and dictionaries. Almost all fields of academic, work, or public interest are represented by specialized reference works that can be easily located in a library's catalog (see 45b-3) or by searching online. The range of resources is wide, as the following list indicates.

Encyclopedia of Advertising; Handbook of Modern Marketing; Concise Dictionary of American History; Encyclopedia of Latin American History; Reference Encyclopedia of the American Indian; Total History (CD-ROM); Encyclopedia of Pop, Rock, and Soul; Encyclopedia of World Literature in the 20th Century; International Encyclopedia of Film; International Television Almanac; Oxford Companion to American Literature; Encyclopedia of Religion; Encyclopedia of Bioethics; Religion Bookshelf CD; Dictionary of Anthropology; Encyclopedia of Crime and Justice; Encyclopedia of Educational Research; Encyclopedia of Psychology; Funk and Wagnalls Standard Dictionary of Mythology, Folklore, and Symbols; International Encyclopedia of the Social Sciences; Encyclopedia of the Biological Sciences; Encyclopedia of Computer Science and Technology; Health and Medical Horizons; McGraw-Hill Encyclopedia of Science and Technology; Current Biography; International Who's Who; Dictionary of American Biography; Who Was Who in America; Who's Who in America

Bibliographies

Bibliographic Index: A Cumulative Bibliography of Bibliographies; Film Research: A Critical Bibliography with Annotations and Essays; International Bibliography of the Social Sciences; MLA International Bibliography of Books and Articles on the Modern Languages and Literatures; United States History: A Selective Guide to Information Sources (CD-ROM)

2 Specialized indexes for periodicals, books, documents, and electronic collections

Periodicals are publications containing articles by different authors. **General-interest magazines** appear once a month or weekly, with each issue paginated separately. **Scholarly journals** generally appear less frequently than magazines, perhaps four times a year, with the page numbering running continuously throughout the separate issues making up an annual volume. Newspapers generally appear daily or weekly and frequently consist of separately numbered sections. **Online (electronic) periodicals** are available through the Internet, with past issues or selected articles sometimes available in electronic archives. **Web sites** may act like periodicals, offering a selection of articles and materials with links to

45b
sourc

other, related sites. Print periodicals generally appear at regular intervals. Electronic sites may add materials at irregular intervals, whenever new material is available or the person responsible for the site updates it.

You can locate articles in print and electronic sources like these by consulting some of the many readily available print and electronic indexes and by consulting Internet services or search engines. Many of these aids are quite specialized in coverage, provide lists or electronic links to related resources, and offer brief summaries (or abstracts) of the contents of articles and books.

General and newspaper indexes

Academic Index (online), *Article First* (online), *Current Contents* (online), *Editorials on File, IIN (Inside Information;* online), *InfoTrac* (online), *Hispanic American Periodicals Index* (online), *OCLC/World Catalog* (online), *PAIS (Public Affairs Information Services;* online), *Reader's Guide to Periodical Literature, New York Times Index, Wall Street Journal Index, Washington Post Index*

Specialized indexes. Almost every field of academic, work, or public interest has one or more indexes available, and many have collections of abstracts, which are brief summaries of articles.

INDEXES

America: History and Life (print and online), *Anthropological Literature* (online), *Art Index* (print and online), *Humanities Index, Music Index, The MLA International Bibliography* (Modern Language Association; print and online), *Government Documents Catalog Service (GDCS/GPO Index;* online), *Legi-Slate* (online), *NTIS (National Technical Information System;* online), *BIZZ (Business Index;* online), *Business Periodicals Index, CIRR (Corporate and Industry Research Reports;* online), *EconLit* (online), *Education Index, ERIC Current Index to Journals in Education* (Educational Resources Information Center; online), *Index to Legal Periodicals, Public Affairs Information Service Bulletin (PAIS), Social Sciences Index* (print and online), *Sociofile* (online), *Agricola* (online), *Applied Science and Technology Index* (print and online), *Biological and Agricultural Index* (print and online), *Compendex* (online), *Engineering Index, General Science Index, Geobase* (online), *History of Science and Technology* (online), *Index Medicus* and *Cumulated Index Medicus, INSPEC* (online), *Medline* (online)

ABSTRACTS

Abstracts of English Studies, America: History and Life, Biological Abstracts (online), *Chemical Abstracts, Dissertation Abstracts Interna-*

tional, Biological Abstracts, Historical Abstracts, Language and Language Behavior Abstracts (online), *Newspaper Abstracts* (online), *Psychological Abstracts* (*PsycInfo;* print and online), *Sociological Abstracts* (*SocioAbs;* print and online)

Electronic databases. Databases are files of information available in electronic form on disks or through the Internet. To find electronic databases covering your topic, you might consult a catalog such as the *Gale Directory of Databases,* the *Federal Database Finder* (a directory of free and fee-based databases and files available from the federal government), or one of the many other guides available in bookstores and libraries.

Many people begin searching for sources using general terms to identify their topic, only to discover that these are not the terms used in the index. Indexes, databases, library catalogs (see 45b-3), and many other reference sources are arranged by keywords. If you can identify the keyword (for a printed index) or a series of keywords (for an electronic index), you can usually locate all the resources you need.

In her preliminary search for information on *Saving Private Ryan,* Sue Aquino found several Web sites that got her off to a good start. An "official" site for the film at ⟨http://www.rzm.com/pvt.ryan⟩, for example, had options for pages on the movie, the production, and the "official book." The production page offered three more options: the cast, the filmmakers, and "behind the scenes." The filmmakers page offered several further options: the director (Steven Spielberg), the director of photography (Janusz Kaminsky), the composer (John Williams), the cast, and others. An *Encyclopedia Brittanica* site at ⟨http://www.private-ryan.eb.com⟩ offered information on "the history behind *Saving Private Ryan.*" As she explored these sites, Aquino was able to develop a list for further searches, with terms that included "Battle of Normandy" and "Omaha Beach" for historical research and "John Williams" and "Janusz Kaminsky," two famous artists she had not known were involved in the production, for research on the making of the film.

STRATEGY

Make a list of different words or concepts that could be used to identify your subject in whole or in part. Don't stop with the most obvious or the one you have become accustomed to using. Try synonyms or alternative terms. Skim something you have read on the topic in order to discover possible terms. Indexes and databases may provide cross-references, identifying them with phrases like *see also* or *related topics.* Add these words to your list.

45b
source

3 Library catalogs

Once you have a list of resources on your topic and a start for your working bibliography (see 46a), your next job is to locate the resources. For resources likely to be available in a library, the place to start is your library's catalog. The catalog will be in either printed form (a **card catalog**) or electronic form (an **online catalog**). They are similarly organized. You can search under the *author's name;* the *title of a work* or a periodical or series containing the work; or the *subject area.* You're most likely to encounter electronic catalogs, though card catalogs are still used in some libraries, mainly for older works. Here is what Sue Aquino found on her topic by using a Web-based electronic catalog at her school.

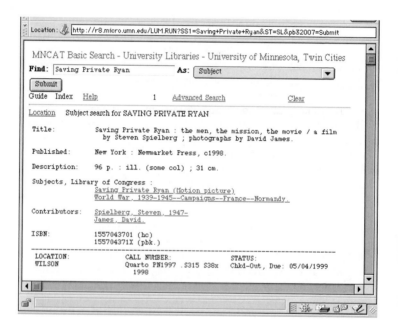

This entry indicates that the book is checked out from the library's Wilson branch. Highlighted options near the top of Sue's screen let her get help, do a more specific search, or return to the catalog search screen.

If you find that your library doesn't have a particular title, you may be able to get it through a lending service called **interlibrary loan**—ask a reference or circulation librarian. Some libraries now give you the option of requesting interlibrary loan materials electronically.

4 Government documents and other resources

Libraries, the Internet, and electronic sites have a variety of resources other than books and articles. **Government documents** include reports, pamphlets, and regulations issued by Congress, federal agencies, and state or local governments. These rich sources of information, both general and technical, are sometimes housed in separate collections in a library. The *Monthly Catalog of U.S. Government Publications* can also aid your search.

Library **special collections** include rare books, manuscripts, and documents, including those of local historical interest. **Audiovisual collections** contain videotapes, films, and audio recordings. A **microform collection** contains microfilms and microfiches of books, periodicals, newspapers, and unpublished documents.

Almost all libraries can arrange for interlibrary loans within a few days. Many have overnight arrangements with local libraries and college or university reference libraries within a region. Some library online catalogs even list the holdings of regional libraries.

45c Search strategies for electronic environments

Try to keep in mind the differences among academic, work, and public communities as you search the Internet and the World Wide Web for sources to use in a research project. The **Internet** links computers of all kinds through email, discussion groups, resource sites, and the World Wide Web. **Web sites** provide text and graphics with numerous links to related sites so that you can move quickly ("surf") from site to site following a research thread. Though the Internet and Web provide almost unlimited access to anyone with a computer and the knowledge to use it, they are nonetheless populated by distinct communities. Some examples follow.

COMMUNITY	TOPICS OF INTEREST	SITE
Academics	Music (from Tanzania; Russian panpipes; hip hop performance)	*EOL: Peer-Reviewed Multimedia Web Journal* ⟨http://www.research.umbc.edu/eol/2/index/html⟩
Specialized technology businesses	Manufacturing techniques, new technologies, especially for production	*Michigan Manufacturing Center* ⟨http://www.iti.org/mmtc/⟩
People across the United States	Drunk driving policies and related topics	*NCADD (National Commission Against Drunk Driving* ⟨http://www.ncadd.com⟩

Writer's Tip

1. Know what kinds of resources are available and how to access them.
2. Be able to locate discussions of your topic and materials related to it.
3. Evaluate whether a site meets standards of the research community you plan to address.

1 Web resources

The Web consists of documents ("pages" or "sites," which are collections of pages) that you can contact using an address known as a **URL** (uniform resource locator) or by selecting a **link** embedded in a Web document (usually a logo or a highlighted portion of text). To contact a Web site, you need a **browser** program, such as *Netscape Navigator* or Microsoft *Internet Explorer.*

Search engines. To locate sites relevant to your research, use a **search engine** like *Excite, Yahoo!, Infoseek,* or *WebCrawler,* which will provide a list of documents containing the keyword(s) you have indicated along with a brief summary of each site's contents. Here is one such entry from the search engine *Excite* in response to the keywords "aspirin research."

> ASPIRIN VS. CANCER . . .
> URL: http://www.gene.com/ae/WN/SU/aspirin_cancer.html
> Summary: CANCER By Sean Henahan, Access Excellence TORONTO-Aspirin appears to have the ability to stop the proliferation of human lung cancer cells, reported researchers at the 86th Annual Meeting of the American Association for CANCER RESEARCH. "Our new findings suggest that some of the stimulatory effects of epidermal growth factor on proliferation of non-small cell lung cancer cells may be . . .

Search engines and most electronic indexes, databases, and directories use keywords to identify material related to a topic. The computer will search for the exact word(s) you specify, so check your spelling and be ready to try synonyms or related terms if your initial search produces meager results (a common occurrence). Patience, persistence, and a willingness to be inventive are often the keys to successful searches.

Writer's Tip

Many search engines and indexes allow you to construct a **query** (a string of words) using **Boolean logic** to link terms with the operators OR, AND, and NOT to expand or limit a search.

OPERATOR	EXAMPLE	RETURNS . . .
No operator	X Z	All the words in the phrase in the exact order (i.e., documents containing the exact phrase)
OR (expands)	X OR Y	Either term (i.e., documents containing references to either X or Y)
AND (restricts)	X AND Y	Both terms (i.e., documents containing references to both X and Y, not to either alone)
NOT (excludes)	X NOT Y	X except for the part of X that includes Y (i.e., documents containing references to X unless they also contain references to Y)

When you find a Web site that could be useful for your project, check first to see whether it actually addresses your topic. Some search engines list sites in order of probable relevance based on the occurrence of keywords, but you really need to do the work yourself by looking at the summaries provided by the search engine and then scanning the sites themselves. If a site addresses your topic, check to see whether it contains the kind of information and ideas you need and whether it's appropriate to the research community you're addressing. (An extremely academic site may contain material that is not appropriate for general public consumption, for example, unless you "translate" it.)

S T R A T E G Y

Use the following questions to evaluate Web sites you locate in your search.

1. Who is responsible for the site? Does the responsible person or organization have a reputation for accuracy or expertise that will make the source acceptable to your audience? Papers for an economics

45c
source

course that cite statistics from the Federal Reserve Bank's Web site at ⟨http://www.bog.frb.fed.us/releases/⟩ will usually be on more solid ground than those citing online opinions from stockbrokers (for example, at ⟨http://www.thestreet.com⟩), though the brokers' opinions may be perfectly appropriate for a business report, especially if they come from the Web site of a source like the *Wall Street Journal* at ⟨http://info.wsj.com/⟩.

2. How much detail does the site provide? Are sources cited? Is the writing effective? A site providing detailed information and supporting evidence is likely to be more reliable than one lacking in detail, especially if it gives references whose accuracy you can check. Though good writing and high-quality graphics don't guarantee honesty or accuracy, they are evidence of the care taken in producing a site.

3. Are other opinions taken into account? If other people's perspectives are acknowledged and presented fairly, it's more likely that the conclusions offered in a site rest on careful thought and attention to evidence.

In her research on *Saving Private Ryan,* Sue Aquino found excellent preliminary information at the film's "official" Web site. This information helped set the stage for her further searches, but she also realized that she wouldn't get an entirely objective representation of the film because all the information at the site was selected and presented by the company that produced the film—a company that wants to show the film in a favorable light.

2 Commercial services

Services like America Online and CompuServe provide access (for a fee) to reference works and databases through easy-to-use sets of screens. The volume and range of information available is often astounding. If you looked up "Lithuania" in the *Travel* section of America Online, for example, you could learn about the country, its people, its politics, the current weather in the capital (Vilnius), and the day's headlines in the newspaper *Lietuvos Rytas.*

3 Email, newsgroups, and listservs

Electronic mail, or **email,** allows you to send messages to people or organizations that can provide information on a topic or answer your specific questions. Web search engines have directory services that can locate email addresses for you.

Newsgroups, or bulletin boards, are public sites where anyone interested in a topic can post a message or question and read what others have posted. **Listservs,** or discussion groups, have some access restrictions (you need to contact the list to subscribe) and are generally more focused in discussion because the subscribers tend to be people actively interested in the subject to which the listserv is dedicated. Academic discussion groups are particularly common.

Newsgroups have a reputation for unreliability and ranting; listservs are generally considered a bit more reliable. As is the case with all Internet and Web resources, however, critical reading and evaluation should be a regular part of your research. (See Chapters 2 and 46.)

As you search electronic and other resources for your research, especially for larger writing projects, you may begin to feel overwhelmed with information. Chapter 46 provides some strategies to help you read, analyze, and sort such information. It helps to do at least some preliminary organization, however, during even the early stages of research for your project. Keeping track of sources, classifying and filing information, and saving electronic materials in labeled folders or on separate disks can make the job of retrieval much easier later on, when you'll also have important issues in your drafting and revising to worry about.

S T R A T E G Y

To keep track of your research materials and begin pulling them together as you work, try the following tips.

- Gather your notes, photocopies, electronic printouts, and other relevant materials.
- Sort your resources. Make a note of missing material, and track it down.
- Using your research questions as a guide, identify major points and subtopics. Use keywords, color coding, stacks of material, or some other method to sort your resources by category.
- If one category contains little information, decide whether to drop it or do further research.
- If a category contains a great deal of information, decide whether to break it into subtopics.
- If you feel you have not found enough appropriate material, ask for help from a reference librarian, an instructor, a colleague, or a specialist in the field you are researching.
- Reexamine and regroup your resources until you are ready to plan and draft your paper.

45c
source

Exercise 2

 A. To familiarize yourself with the resources of your library, take tours or library introduction sessions offered by the staff, or locate the following resources on your own (using any maps the library provides): general and specialized encyclopedias, bibliographies, print indexes, electronic indexes and databases, government documents, and the periodical collection. Learn how to access the catalog electronically and search for books and other information, and find out whether there are any electronic resources at the library that are not accessible from computers located elsewhere.

 B. Each person in a work group should look up entries for a particular topic in one or more of the kinds of resources listed in Exercise 2A, then report back to the group. You may all research a topic someone in the group is working on, or each of you may look up the topic you are researching for a paper of your own.

46

Reading Critically and Evaluating Sources

You can't identify, gather, and use research sources without reading them. But if you read your sources in superficial ways, your research project and your writing will suffer. Careful reading—analytical and critical—adds depth and insight to your work. Approaching your sources as a critical reader also means working with them in a writerly way, reshaping and synthesizing information and ideas, experiencing insights, and accomplishing your own purposes and those of your readers. The process of critical reading begins with the creating of a working bibliography and with careful, insightful note taking.

46a Building a working bibliography

In the process of research, you'll consult various sources: library catalogs, online and print indexes, Web and Internet search engines, specialized bibliographies and encyclopedias, and similar reference material (see 45b). As the information accumulates, you don't want to end up in a tangle of confused references, photocopied pages, and printouts with no source information. To keep track of what you discover, construct a **working bibliography** that lists items likely to help you address your research question(s).

1 Decide what to include in a working bibliography

When you consult indexes, bibliographies, and other reference works listing possible resources, let your research question(s) organize the most relevant information. Write your research question(s) at the head of your working bibliography (or keep a copy close at hand), and include only those sources that will help you address the question(s).

INCLUDE

- **More sources than you expect to use for your final paper.** Some will be unavailable; others may be of little use.
- **Items whose titles or lengths suggest they will be relevant.** A descriptive title can be a good guide. A long article may contain more useful material than a short one.
- **Sources that are recent enough to provide up-to-date information.** Older sources may be useful, too, but be selective.
- **A variety of sources.** Choose some that are broad surveys and some that focus on specific aspects of your topic and research questions.

EXCLUDE

- **Sources that may be very difficult to obtain.**
- **Sources whose relationship to your topic and research question(s) is questionable.**

Writer's Tip

Many bibliographies include annotations summarizing the content of a book or article. Electronic indexes and search engines may also provide brief summaries (called abstracts). Use these annotations to decide whether to include an item in a working bibliography.

---

2 Make complete and accurate entries

Entries in a working bibliography should contain the following information.

BOOKS	ARTICLES	ELECTRONIC INFORMATION
Call number	Author(s)	Name of source
Author(s), editor(s), translator(s)	Title and subtitle	Address/URL/access route/vendor
Title and subtitle	Periodical name	Date of access or receipt of information
City of publication, name of publisher, and date of publication	Volume and issue number (if any)	Name of person responsible for writing or posting information/name of sender
	Date	
	Page number(s)	Original publication information for materials also in print

3 Choose a format to record entries

If you write out each entry on 3″ × 5″ cards, you can arrange the cards in categories appropriate for your topic and research plan, or you can put them in alphabetical order for eventual use in a list of works consulted or a list of works cited. Adding and eliminating cards is relatively simple.

Keeping a working bibliography in a notebook is convenient, especially if the notebook also has pockets for the printouts that many electronic indexes produce for you (see 45b-2). Rearranging, adding, eliminating, and alphabetizing is less convenient in a notebook, though you can organize by making marginal comments or using a highlighter.

Electronic card file systems and database programs have most of the advantages of 3″ × 5″ cards and often resemble onscreen card collections. By specifying subtopics or specific research questions on each card, you can enable a computer to sort and reorganize entries and to retrieve any on a particular subtopic. The contents of the entries can be easily transferred to a word processing program when you wish to create a list of works cited or a list of works consulted.

46b Taking notes: Analytical and critical

Analytical reading identifies ideas and information presented in a text, and often includes activities like paraphrasing (see 46c-2), summarizing (see 46c-1), and synthesizing (see 46c-3). **Critical reading,** too, begins with the careful identification of information and concepts. Above all, however, critical reading means adding your knowledge and insight to what you read by identifying unanswered questions, synthesizing perspectives, and interpreting and evaluating sources.

1 Critical reading: A checklist

Critical reading is a way of looking at and interacting with your sources. Keep this critical reading checklist in mind as you gather sources and take notes on them.

1. **Identify unanswered questions.** Look for questions or problems a text leaves partly or completely unaddressed. Are there any unexamined ideas, situations, or evidence? Can you identify any perspectives and interpretations that aren't fully considered?
2. **Synthesize perspectives.** Pay attention to the relationship among sources. How do they agree or differ in coverage? What are their strengths and limitations?
3. **Interpret sources.** Texts often reflect a writer's commitments, perspectives, and values. Make a habit of reading in these terms. How does the writer's background or advocacy of a particular perspective affect the trustworthiness and importance of a source?

**46b
source**

4. **Evaluate sources.** Look for evidence that the information in a source is accurate and complete. Are its arguments and interpretations are offered reasonably, without the aim of distorting or deceiving?

2 Informational and critical notes

The research notes you take can be informational, critical, or (preferably) both. **Informational notes** record facts, details, concepts, interpretations, and quotations from your sources, helping you focus on material relevant to your research question(s). They also help you retrieve this material easily and document its source as you draft and revise.

Whether you use note cards, a research journal, or an electronic record, make sure you *write down the complete source* for later use, including the page numbers to which the notes refer (especially the location of any quoted material). Include an annotation that says how the material is related to your topic and your research questions so you'll have an easier time following your thread of research and drawing on the material as you draft and revise your paper.

Critical notes include comments, interpretations, or evaluations of a source. They also indicate the relationship of the source to your research question(s) and include necessary information for documentation. Most often your comments will accompany information from the sources, though you may wish to devote some notes entirely to your critical observations.

3 Note cards, research journals, and electronic notes

Note cards. Many writers prefer to take notes on index cards, generally either 4″ × 6″ or 5″ × 7″ cards. Cards are easily portable and convenient for brief note taking. If you write the topic of each card clearly at the top and restrict each card to one kind of note taking (quotation, summary of facts and ideas, paraphrase), you can arrange and rearrange cards in related groups as you plan or write a paper.

Research journal. If you use a research journal (usually a notebook) instead of cards, you'll have space to record information, reflect on new knowledge, and begin assembling parts of a paper or report. Use an entry's heading or make marginal comments to show what's covered in the notes. These annotations will help you organize your notes later for use. If your research journal is a notebook with pockets or a folder, you can also use it to store photocopies of print materials or downloaded copies of electronic sources. Write the source and topic at the top of the copy (if the source title is printed on the page, circle it).

Electronic notes. You can use a computer word processing file as either a research journal or a set of note cards (one page = one note card). Some computer programs are specially designed for note taking.

Writer's Tip

   Sometimes you'll need to work with original sources (actual books and journals, not photocopies). In such situations, be extremely careful when you write quotations in your notebook or on cards. You should be *absolutely certain* that you've copied them word for word and that you've recorded the exact page number(s) where each quotation appears. Having to return to your source when you're writing and revising will use up valuable time, especially if the source is not close at hand.

46c Reading print and electronic sources analytically

   A research project calls for two types of reading, analytical and critical. Both are challenging, and they're often intertwined. When you read *analytically,* you try to understand the ideas and information presented in a source. When you read *critically,* you interact with the source, assessing its strengths, limitations, and biases; analyzing its relationships to other texts produced by a research community; and identifying questions or issues it leaves unaddressed.

   Both kinds of reading contribute in significant ways to the outcome of a research project. Analytical reading leads to the summaries, paraphrases, syntheses, quotations, and details you develop into much of the content of a research report or paper. Critical reading leads to many of the insights you contribute to an understanding of the topic. It helps you determine what use to make of information and concepts from your source, as shown below.

ANALYTICAL READING	CRITICAL READING
What does it say? (literal)	What does it mean or imply? (interpretive)
—summary	—interpretation
—paraphrase	—position of author
—synthesis	—nature of publication
—quotations	—use in one's own ideas
—details	—reception of audience

   Of course, analytical reading and note taking (see 46b) require critical thought. Selecting quotations that accurately represent a source's main points, paraphrasing and summarizing, understanding ideas and information—all these call for critical comprehension. Critical reading goes even further; it assesses and decides on the value of information and ideas, generally with an eye toward developing insights and perspectives you can develop in your own writing.

46c
source

In a **summary** you present the essential information in a text without interpreting it. A summary is shorter than the original, *compressing* the information and presenting only the key ideas and support. In a **paraphrase** you restate an author's ideas in your own words, retaining the content and sense of the original but providing your own expression. A **synthesis** brings together summaries of several sources and points out the relationships among the ideas and information.

1 Summarizing

A summary helps you understand the key ideas and content in an article, part of a book, a Web site, or a cluster of paragraphs. You can also use summaries you create as a concise way of presenting ideas and information from a source in your own writing. In an **objective summary,** you focus on presenting the content of the source in compressed form and avoid speculating on the source's line of reasoning. In an **evaluative summary,** you add your opinions, evaluating or commenting on the original passage.

S T R A T E G Y

To prepare a summary of information relating to your topic, follow this process.

- **Read** the selection, looking for the most important ideas, evidence, and information. Underline, highlight, or make note of key points and information that you think should be mentioned in your summary.
- **Scan** (reread quickly) the selection to decide which of the ideas and bits of information you noted during your first reading are the *most* important. Try also to decide on the writer's main purpose in the selection and to identify the major sections of the discussion.
- **Write** (1) Summarize *each section* of the source (each step in the argument, each stage in the explanation) in a *single sentence* that mentions the key ideas and information.
- **Write** (2) Summarize the *entire passage* in a *single sentence* that captures its main point or conclusion.
- **Combine** your summaries in (1) with your summary in (2) (above) to produce a draft summary of the main point, other important points, and the most important information.
- **Revise** to make sure your summary is logical and easy to read. Check against the source for accuracy.
- **Document** clearly the source of your summary using a standard style of documentation (see Chapters 49–53).

46c
source

In a summary, you can present the key ideas from a source without including unnecessary detail that might distract readers. Summer Arrigo-

Nelson and Jennifer Figliozzi used two one-sentence summaries of research to help introduce one of the questions for their academic research paper.

First, research has shown that adolescents who have open and close relationships with their parents use alcohol less often than do those with conflictual relationships (Sieving 1996). For example, a survey given to students in seventh through twelfth grades reported that approximately 35 percent of adolescent drinkers were under parental supervision while drinking (Dept. of Education 1993). Based on this research, we are interested in determining if students who were given permission to drink while living with their parents would possess different drinking patterns, upon reaching college, than those who did not previously have permission to drink.

2 Paraphrasing

A good paraphrase doesn't add to or detract from the original but often helps you understand a difficult work. When you want to incorporate the detailed ideas and information from a passage into your own writing but don't want to quote your source because the wording is too dense or confusing, then a paraphrase can be the answer.

S T R A T E G Y

To paraphrase part of a source, put the information in your own words, retaining the content and ideas of the original as well as the sequence of presentation. (Many paraphrases contain sentences that correspond with the original except for the changes in wording and sentence structure.)

- **Read** the selection carefully so that you understand the wording as well as the content.
- **Write** a draft of your paraphrase, using your own words and phrases in place of the original. Rely on synonyms and equivalent expressions. You can retain names, proper nouns, and the like from the original, of course.
- **Revise** for smooth reading and clarity. Change sentence structures and phrasing to make sure your version is easier to understand than your source.
- **Document** clearly the source of your paraphrase using a standard style of documentation (see Chapters 49–53).

As part of her research for an editorial supporting a new alcohol abuse program on her campus, Jennifer Figliozzi encountered the following passage in a report on current programs at various schools.

46c
source

The university also now notifies parents when their sons or daughters violate the alcohol policy or any other aspect of the student code of conduct. "We were hoping that the support of parents would help change students' behavior, and we believe it has," says Timothy F. Brooks, an assistant vice-president and the dean of students at the University of Delaware.

Because she wanted to avoid long quotations and instead integrate the information smoothly into her discussion, Jennifer paraphrased part of the passage.

> Officials at the University of Delaware thought that letting parents know when students violate regulations on alcohol use would change students' drinking habits, and one administrator now says, "We believe it has" (Reisberg 42).

Exercise 1

 A. Choose an article that interests you in a magazine such as *Natural History* or *Scientific American*. Paraphrase the first paragraph or two or any passage of a few lines or more. Do as Jennifer has done above and try to integrate the passage into an imaginary research report, putting much or most of the passage into your own words.

 B. In a group, paraphrase the same passage and then compare paraphrases. Discuss which paraphrases are the most accurate and thorough, yet the most concise.

---

3 Synthesizing

By bringing together summaries of several sources and pointing out their relationships in a synthesis, you can use your sources in some special ways: to provide background information, to explore causes and effects, to look at contrasting explanations or arguments, or to bring together ideas and information in support of a thesis.

- **Identify** the role a synthesis will play in your explanation or argument as well as the kind of information and ideas you wish to share with readers.
- **Gather** the sources you plan to synthesize.
- **Read** your sources, and prepare to summarize them.
- **Focus** on the purpose of your synthesis, and draft a sentence summing up your conclusion about the relationship of the sources.

- **Arrange** the order in which you will present your sources in the synthesis.
- **Write** a draft of your synthesis, presenting summaries of your sources and offering your conclusion about the relationship(s).
- **Revise** so that your synthesis is easy to read. Make sure readers can easily identify the sources of the ideas and information.
- **Document** clearly the sources for your synthesis using a standard style of documentation.

Many academic papers begin with a summary of prior research designed to identify a need for further research and to provide justification for the research questions. The opening section of Summer Arrigo-Nelson and Jennifer Figliozzi's academic research paper uses synthesis for this purpose.

> Research dealing with student alcohol use most often focuses on children's perceptions of their parents' actions and on the relationship between child and parent. Studies conducted with high school students have supported the hypothesis that positive family relationships are more likely to be associated with less frequent alcohol use among adolescents than are negative relationships. Adolescents model the limited substance use of their parents where there is a good or moderate parent/adolescent relationship (Andrews, Hops, and Dunkin 1997). Other factors the studies found to be associated with positive family relationships, along with substance use, were academic achievement, family structure, place of residence, self-esteem, and emotional tone (Weschler, Dowdall, Davenport, and Castillo 1995; Martch and Miller 1997).

Work and public writing often uses synthesis in a similar fashion to identify a problem that needs to be addressed or a policy needing to be examined or reconsidered.

46c
source

4 Analyzing electronic and visual sources

Print sources consist mostly of text, so that when you're summarizing, paraphrasing, or synthesizing, you're putting someone else's words into your own words. In contrast, electronic sources, especially Web pages, may include pictures, drawings, charts, and even video or sound, which convey both information and ideas. Print documents make use of graphics, too, of course. Public writing may use pictures to convey or reinforce values and may use graphs to present detailed information in accessible form. Workplace writing and academic writing sometimes use charts and drawings to present complex data and explain causes, consequences, or relationships.

S T R A T E G Y

You can "quote" pictures and graphic representations by reproducing them within your own text (with appropriate documentation). Paraphrasing and summarizing are more difficult, though not impossible. To paraphrase pictures, drawings, or graphic presentations, you need to "extract" information and concepts from them and "translate" the material into your own words. Instead of paraphrasing a paragraph reporting the results of a study on car theft in major U.S. cities, for example, you would describe the bar graph that reports the statistics.

46d Reading print and electronic sources critically

To read critically, you must be able to do four things: (1) *identify* in your sources any unanswered questions (academic), unsolved problems (work), or unresolved issues (public) that you can make the focus of your research and writing; (2) *synthesize* different perspectives among sources; (3) *interpret* your sources; (4) *evaluate* your sources.

1 Identifying questions

A final research report or essay often begins by identifying an unanswered question, an unsolved problem, or an unresolved issue in a way that highlights its importance for readers, going on to address this concern in detail. As you read and reflect on your topic, use note cards or your research journal (or even the margins of photocopies) to record and explore unanswered questions, unsolved problems, and unresolved issues. Try stating them as concisely as you can in a *question paragraph* (or a *problem* or *issue paragraph*). Such a paragraph can suggest ways for you to develop your paper or report, and you may even include all or part of it in the finished product. Here is a critical note card Lily Germaine made for a paper about bodybuilding.

Tucker, Larry A. "Effect of Weight Training on Self-Concept: A Profile of Those Influenced Most." <u>Research Quarterly for Exercise and Sport</u>, Introduction, pp. 389–91.

Tucker uses the word <u>although</u> at least four times when summarizing other <u>studies</u>, and he tends to use phrases such as <u>only a few studies have shown</u>.... He's being nice on the surface but is setting his readers up to find fault with the other studies. That basic fault is their lack of objective methodology, which he

seems to plan on rectifying by using mathematical measurements and rigid definitions of terms. A glance through the rest of the article reveals lots of equations and two tables of statistics. He seems to think he can be completely objective in determining such a slippery thing as "self-concept." I really have to question this assumption.

Lily's question paragraph begins with insights and wording from her notes.

Does bodybuilding affect self-concept? Before we can answer this question, we need to ask if we can accurately measure such a slippery thing as "self-concept." Some researchers, like Tucker, believe that self-concept can be accurately gauged using mathematical measurements and rigid definitions of terms. For several reasons, however, this assumption is questionable....

46d
source

2 Synthesizing perspectives

To offer your readers an in-depth understanding of a subject, use a **critical synthesis** to bring together perspectives, opinions, interpretations, and evidence from a variety of sources and explore their potential connections. Like an **analytical synthesis** (see 46c-3), a critical synthesis provides readers with a unified discussion reflecting your understanding of the various perspectives, but it also pays special attention to highlighting and summarizing differences and to presenting your conclusions about the sources.

Be alert to agreements and disagreements as you read and take notes on your sources, identifying and exploring the various perspectives in critical notes or a research journal. When you are drafting your paper, consider preparing a critical synthesis that may become an important element of the finished project, such as a review of prior research (academic), a consideration of alternative responses to a problem (work), or an overview of differing stands on an issue (public).

Look over your sources and notes, and then synthesize (sum up) the main ideas, positions, or facts of your sources, building on the techniques you use to prepare an analytical synthesis. To do this, imagine that you're an expert on the topic and that you're trying to give someone a quick state-of-the-art overview based on your sources. Here are some guidelines.

1. Be true to the ideas and information in your sources.
2. Suggest relationships among conclusions, opinions, ideas, and facts that go beyond those relationships discussed in your sources.
3. In a thesis statement (4c) or a statement of the central idea of the synthesis, summarize the relationships you observe.
4. Be selective. Focus on material that relates directly to your central idea.
5. Be balanced. Acknowledge facts, opinions, and alternative perspectives that contradict the central idea of your synthesis.
6. Base your synthesis on your own thinking as well as material from your sources.

Here is a critical synthesis Kimlee Cunningham used to introduce the thesis of her academic paper on three recent Disney animated feature films.

> It is probably an exaggeration to say that
> a character like Belle in <u>Beauty and the Beast</u>
> is a lot like a contemporary feminist, as one
> critic suggests: "She wants adventure and he
> wants commitment; he holds a mirror and she

46d
source

hugs a book" (Showalter). However, we should
not simply ignore an interpretation like this
by claiming "that it takes a classic fairy
tale, and turns it around and analyzes it from
a modern feminist view" (Hoffman). Even if many
people view a film like <u>Beauty and the Beast</u>
(or <u>Aladdin</u>) as "just a love story" (Hoffman),
the films nonetheless grow out of the
complicated values and roles that shape
relationships today. Disney's contemporary
portrayal of women characters shows a
willingness to change with the times but also a
reluctance to abandon traditional values and
stereotypes.

3 Interpreting sources

Most research papers or reports should present a point of view
about the topic: a conclusion about its meaning or causes, a commitment
to a particular course of action, or a stand on an issue. At the same time,
you need to share with your readers the differing outlooks embodied in
your sources and to indicate why readers should accept your interpretation as an alternative. Here are some basic questions concerning the outlook (or bias) of your sources.

1. Does the source display a balanced perspective in offering its conclusions?
2. Does the source advocate strongly, though fairly, for a particular
   point of view?
3. Does the source display one-sided bias, including misrepresentation
   of facts and distortion of others' positions?

In an **interpretation,** you build on synthesis (see 46c-3) by explicitly including your opinions and giving priority to your own ideas
and points of view. Interpreting involves **generalizing** (coming to
broad conclusions about what your research has to say about your
topic) and **extending** (going beyond this to connect your source's ideas
to your own).

S T R A T E G Y

Begin an interpretation by stating the point of view of your source(s) as accurately as possible. Add your own ideas and conclusions. Take into account any strong advocacy (or questionable bias) in the source(s).

1. Present material from your sources accurately. Select material most relevant to the point you want to make, but do not suppress contradictory, biased, or partisan material that contradicts other ideas.
2. Present your point of view, and provide supporting evidence, perhaps comparing the perspective of one source to that of another and to your own.
3. Add interpretations and conclusions of your own not present in the sources or present in a different form.

---

4 Evaluating sources

Not every source you encounter is equally valuable, accurate, or persuasive. One important part of your work as a researcher is to evaluate sources in order to decide what material to treat as authoritative and what to reject or refute. An equally important part is to share the results of your evaluation with your readers.

S T R A T E G Y
---

1. Consider the reputation of the publisher or organization responsible for the source. Does the publisher or journal have a reputation for balance and accuracy? Is the writer or organization an advocate whose views require caution?
2. Consider the reputation of the author. Is the author's reputation clear from the outset? What do other sources think of the author's trustworthiness, fairness, and importance?
3. Ask how accurate your source is, especially if it presents facts as truth. Can you spot obvious errors? Which points are detailed and well documented?
4. Find and test generalizations in the source. How does the writer support them? Do they go beyond the facts in the text? Are they consistent with your knowledge of the topic?
5. Compare the source with others. Are the ideas generally consistent with those in your other sources? If different, do they seem original and insightful or misleading and eccentric?
6. Use questionable sources with caution. Does an electronic listserv have current, exciting ideas but also contentious or half-developed notions? Does material apply only to a specific setting? Is the source's information outdated or biased? Do experts cited have particular political or financial interests?

46d
ource

7. Consider the expectations of your audience or research community. Academic audiences look for detailed explanations, evidence, and acknowledgment of scholarship on the subject. Work audiences look for precise, clear, and accurate presentation of facts. Public audiences look for fairness in presenting opinions and alternatives.

8. Look for documentation. Does the source either appropriately document information, quotations, and ideas or clearly indicate the author is responsible for them?

When you draw information from a source, use it to support your conclusions, or disagree with its perspective, you may need to share your evaluation of it with readers.

1. Support your judgments with examples from the texts or data you are evaluating.

2. Explain your judgments of one text or body of data by comparing it to other texts or data.

3. Base your evaluation on your own ideas, but feel free to draw on evaluations you have found in other sources.

Exercise 2

 A. Read an entire article, preferably one that is relevant to a writing project you're working on. First write an objective summary of the article that tries to capture its main points as clearly as possible. Next, using one or more of the strategies in 46d, write a critical commentary on the piece, identifying gaps or unanswered questions, authorial biases, or problems with the credibility or stance of the source.

 B. In a small group, share your critical commentaries and objective summaries. Discuss what you see in the relationship between the two types of writing, focusing especially on how the objective summary can help you to support (with clear, careful reasoning) some of the evaluative assertions you made in your critical commentary.

---

5 Evaluating Internet and web sources

Internet and World Wide Web sources pose special problems for evaluation. Many Web sites or Internet documents are produced without the editorial checks and balances that make books from reputable publishers or articles in scholarly journals and well-known magazines relatively trustworthy sources. You can begin evaluating Internet and Web sources using questions developed by Paula Mathieu at the University of Illinois, Chicago, as part of the *Critical Resources in Teaching with Technology* (CRITT) project featured at ⟨http://www.engl.uic.edu/~stp⟩.

46d
sourc

Evaluation Questions

1. **Who benefits? What difference does that make?**

   The Web pages accessible at ⟨http://www.whymilk.com⟩ seem dedicated entirely to the good of the Web surfer who has just accessed them: "Happy browsing—and remember, DRINK AT LEAST THREE CUPS OF MILK EVERY DAY! (Your body will thank you.)" Perhaps the three cups will indeed benefit most readers. With a little bit of critical thinking, however, these readers can easily recognize that milk producers and distributors will also benefit from sales of those three cups a day.

   > What is milk? What is its story? Why should I drink it? What kinds of milk are there? What kinds are right for me? You've got questions—we've got answers.

   Why are you willing to share all this? How do you benefit? In fact, this part of the site should tell you everything you ever wanted to know about milk (and even a bit more). But, if there's a milk-related morsel you can't find here, just call 1–800-WHY-MILK, email us, or order yourself up some free, fact-filled brochures.

   How will I benefit? Happy browsing—and remember, DRINK AT LEAST THREE CUPS OF MILK EVERY DAY! (Your body will thank you.)

2. **Who's talking? What difference does that make?**

   The "speaker" responsible for all the positive facts about milk is not clearly identified in the pages except as "we" at the bottom of some pages in the invitation to call for more information. "We" is the Milk Council, an organization of milk producers and distributors. Can

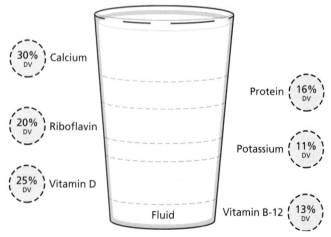

readers trust the "facts" presented by this group that goes unnamed in the pages? Perhaps. But it seems unlikely that all the "facts" will appear on the pages, especially those that might call into question an unqualified endorsement of milk's goodness.

Is there such a thing?

Think you're getting enough calcium? Well, 85% of girls and 60% of guys aren't! Calcium is one of the most essential bone-growin' nutrients, and milk is one of the best sources in the natural world for calcium. Be sure to visit the *Personal Trainer* and check your Calcium Quotient to make sure your bod isn't suffering from milk thirst.

Are you an authority? Why should I beleive what you have to say?

Also, with all of us protecting ourselves from the sun more and more, we might be missing out on one important thing (no, not a great tan). Vitamin D! Guess where you can get the D without the burn? Give you a clue—it starts with M-I-L—OK, OK, we know you're not stupid. Just make sure to drink at least three cups of milk a day and prove us right.

The Web page at ⟨http://arrs.envirolink.org/AnimaLife/fall94/milk .html⟩ provides a contrary voice, linking milk drinking to disease. The author tells us nothing about himself, so we are left to judge what he says based on the quality of his evidence and reasoning. He does seem to provide scientific support, but the reasoning seems strained and the tone a bit extreme. Neither this Web site nor "Whymilk" is entirely satisfactory as a source, but taken together they outline a topic and issue worth further research.

3. **What's missing? What difference does that make?**
Under the heading "All Kinds of Milk" appears the following: "Fat free skim, 1% lowfat, 2%, whole—there are lots of different kinds of milk to fit your fancy." Why does this list ignore soy milk, rice milk, goat's milk, sheep's milk, coconut milk? The selective nature of the presentation, its commercial purpose, and its strategies become even clearer when a reader asks what is left out and why.

**46d
sourc**

47

Turning Research into Writing

How do you know when to begin *writing* your research paper or report? Actually, there's no set time. When you've gathered enough material to begin seriously creating a draft of your research paper, you can piece together some of your preliminary and less formally written material from notes or a journal, then add significant new material to make a more complete and coherent text. Instead of trying to draft your paper by launching right into the first word of the first line, start by thinking strategically about the nature and shape of your task.

47a Moving from research questions to a plan and a thesis

The research questions that focus and guide your research (see 44a-4) should have evolved as you worked, reflecting your developing knowledge of your subject. Consider using the latest versions of your research questions to create a plan for drafting your report or document.

1 Review your research questions

Arrange your research questions in a logical *order:* in what sequence do you want to address them in your essay or report? Add any further questions you now think you ought to address. Use your list as a tentative guide for your drafting. As you answer the questions, think about the way the blocks of information connect with each other. Don't be too concerned about getting the sequence just right at this point, but keep your structure in the back of your mind as you work.

2 Envision your readers

As you begin drafting, asking questions about your audience can help you provide clear explanations, arguments, and sufficient supporting evidence. Begin by writing informally about your imagined readers. What are the interests and values of your readers? What questions do they want answered? What are their likely reactions to what you have to say? How do issues of gender, age, position, or background affect the way readers may respond to the material in your research?

3 Examine your purpose

Think about your general goals (to inform, to persuade) as well as your specific ones (to get a committee to adopt a policy; to show that your interpretation is the most plausible one). Ask yourself what you want your paper to *do*. Then ask what form it might take, given this purpose. What do you want your audience to learn, to do, or to feel? Does your research suggest an argument or position paper? Does it suggest a history, a case study, an action proposal, or a research report?

S T R A T E G Y

A **purpose structure** is a series of statements that briefly describe what you intend to do in each section of a paper and that help you begin to visualize the finished product. (See Chapter 4.) Try to create a purpose structure as you review your notes and questions.

Jim Nowak created the following purpose structure for his paper on intellectual property rights.

Beginning	Explain the importance of copyrights, patents, and intellectual property rights, especially for computer software.
Middle	Discuss questions of intellectual property rights as they evolved in three legal controversies: Sun Microsystem's Java language versus Microsoft's version of Java; Lotus 1-2-3 versus similar spreadsheets; and Apple's Macintosh user interface versus Microsoft's Windows.
Ending	Describe recently proposed solutions to the problem of establishing ownership of software designs.

4 Develop a thesis

Develop a thesis statement in a sentence or two as a way of giving your planning a focus and maintaining this focus as you draft and revise.

47a
draft

Begin with a **tentative** (or **draft**) **thesis statement** (see Chapter 4), perhaps based on your research question(s). Modify it as you draft and in your final version, perhaps breaking it into several sentences to make it easier to read. You might develop your thesis from the research questions you created earlier in the process (see Chapter 44). Consider using your thesis statement as an organizing strategy for your final draft, repeating parts of it in modified form at key points in the paper.

47b Planning and drafting your paper

The moment you begin your research, you are planning your project. But when you've collected most of the information you need, you'll need to focus more sharply on the organization and content of your paper.

Outlining. A traditional outline is often too detailed for a long research essay because writers become frustrated trying to fit into the outline all the bits of information they have gathered—information that doesn't always prove useful as they develop their reasoning in a draft. Consider making a **working outline** that shows the general sequence of information along with the relationships (transitions) between segments of information.

STRATEGY

In an informal outline, quickly block out the main parts of your paper. Write detailed transitions between the parts. Focus on the largest units of your paper first, and then work on smaller organizational chunks such as sections and paragraphs. This will give you a clear sense of how the parts fit together and how the paper will progress.

Grouping information. Grouping your information (3b) is useful if you have many bits of information but not a particularly clear idea of how they relate.

STRATEGY

Write down or describe separate pieces of information (such as major points from your sources, informal paraphrases or summaries, or thoughts and ideas you want to include) on pieces of paper. If you took notes on 5″ × 7″ cards, you may be able to use these. Now arrange the pages or cards in relation to one another. As you begin to see patterns emerge, you may think of additional information that fits into one grouping or another.

Cutting and pasting. If you've been using a research journal to record and reflect on research, you may already have the segments of your draft. Instead of spending a lot of time writing, try moving around the pieces you've already sketched.

STRATEGY

If you've written on both sides of your journal pages or don't want to cut up the original, photocopy the relevant pages. Now cut out the separate entries. Arrange the entries to reflect a cohesive relationship, and think of or draft transitions. Depending on how extensive your journal entries are, you may end up with a rough draft by the time you finish cutting and pasting.

Cutting and pasting can be done easily using a word processing program. Choose relevant passages from your journal or research notes, and then paste them into a new file wherever they seem to fit. Print out the results from time to time so you can see the overall pattern emerging.

Focusing on the introduction and conclusion. Sometimes you might want to write the introduction and the conclusion first. You'll have to consider your readers' level of interest and familiarity with your topic, and you'll have to predict your paper's design and goals. You may find your research question(s) helpful in developing your introduction or conclusion.

STRATEGY

In writing the introduction, ask yourself, "How can I engage readers from the start and make them want to read on?" Think of interesting ways to begin—even formal academic papers don't have to have dull openings. Write two or more different openings, experimenting with style and content.

In writing the conclusion, ask, "How can I make my readers want to keep thinking about the topic?" Don't hide behind a quotation. Avoid sentimental or patriotic clichés, and don't merely summarize. Try several versions.

Exercise 1

 In a group, choose one of the planning methods in 47a and collaboratively apply it to one person's project. If the group chooses to write an introduction and conclusion, everyone should prepare a separate one-paragraph introduction and a brief (one- or two-sentence) conclusion. Compare all the versions.

47b
draft

47C Integrating print and electronic sources into your writing

You can integrate sources in a number of ways: as quotations, paraphrases, or summaries; as facts, details, or statistics; or as visuals.

1 Integrating words and phrases into sentences and paragraphs

When you quote, paraphrase, or even summarize a source, you retain something of the original: the exact wording, the sequence of ideas and details, or the general point.

Quotations. Avoid stringing quotations together or using many long quotations set off in blocks (which may look like padding). Instead, use quotations for these reasons:

- To support your conclusions by showing that a recognized authority or someone who writes with style and insight agrees with your conclusions
- To show that you're accurately representing ideas that you want to challenge, modify, or extend
- To preserve an especially stylish, persuasive, or concise way of saying something
- To show vividly and dramatically what other people think
- To provide a jumping-off point for your thoughts or a change of pace

You can quote entire sentences from a source and let them stand on their own, with proper attribution.

Celebrities can also play roles in our fantasy lives. "The heavy-metal rock stars who engage in outrageous and bizarre behavior both on and off stage are presenting a model of rebellion most of us would not do but can admire because they get away with it" (Coombs 41).

Or you can use an **embedded quotation** if it is less than a line or two.

EFFECTIVE Many teenagers were "mesmerized by the cynical bite and lyric jumps" (Schwarz 124) of Bob Dylan's early vocal style.

A **block quotation** is a longer passage from a source, set off from your own prose because of length. Remember that readers expect you to *do* something with block quotations, not just insert them.

Paraphrases and summaries. To make your writing smoother and more sophisticated, be selective in using quotations. Usually, you can summarize, even combining several sources, or paraphrase rather than quoting sources directly.

2 Integrating facts, details, and statistics

You can build entire paragraphs around facts, details, and statistics drawn from your sources as long as you indicate clearly the sources of your information. You may retain some of the emphasis of your source in using these materials; more likely, you'll end up integrating these details into prose that reflects your own purposes.

3 Visuals

Visuals (drawings, photos, graphs, and the like) can sometimes present or emphasize data better than words. If you copy a visual from print or download it from an electronic resource, you'll need to cite the source, and you may need permission to use it. Whether you create a visual yourself or draw it from your research, make sure it adds to the written text and doesn't simply substitute for it. Visuals that add to a written explanation or extend it imaginatively can increase the credibility and effectiveness of your writing. (See Chapter 13.)

S T R A T E G Y

- Put the visual as near to the relevant written text as you can without disrupting the flow of the text or distorting the visual.
- Don't interrupt the writing in ways that make it hard to read.
- Make sure your visuals are of good quality and of appropriate size for the page.
- Ask one or more readers whether your visuals are easy to understand and whether they add to the text's ideas and effect.
- Label each visual (*Figure 1, Figure 2* . . . ; *Table 1, Table 2* . . .).

47d Understanding documentation and avoiding plagiarism

The biggest challenge in writing up research is to integrate other people's words and ideas into your own thinking—and your own text. To do so effectively, you need to think carefully about what information or words you should document (that is, give credit for). *When* should you cite a source? What exactly is considered plagiarism, even when a source is cited?

**47d
draft**

1 What to document, what not to document

In general, you need to document the words, ideas, and information you draw from another person's work. Bear in mind the two most important reasons for documenting sources: (1) to add support to your conclusions and credibility to your explanations by showing they're based on careful research and (2) to acknowledge another person's hard work. Decisions on what needs documenting may vary from audience to audience. If you're writing to a general audience, readers may expect you to cite sources for your discussion of subatomic particles. If you're writing for a physics professor or an audience of physicists, you can probably assume that such matters are common knowledge.

YOU MUST DOCUMENT

- Word-for-word (direct) quotations taken from someone else's work
- Paraphrases or summaries of someone else's work, whether published or presented more informally in an interview or email message
- Ideas, opinions, and interpretations that others have developed and presented, even if they are based on common knowledge
- Facts or data that someone else has gathered or identified if the information is not widely known enough to be considered common knowledge
- Information that is not widely accepted or that is disputed
- Illustrations, charts, graphs, photographs, recordings, original software, performances, interviews, and the like

BUT DO NOT DOCUMENT

- Ideas, opinions, and interpretations that are your own
- Widely known ideas and information—the sort you can locate in common reference works or that people writing or speaking on a topic usually present as common knowledge
- Commonly used quotations ("To be, or not to be")

2 Understanding and avoiding plagiarism

When you include quotations, paraphrases, and summaries in your writing, you *must* acknowledge their sources. If you don't, you are treating someone else's work as your own.

- Be sure you enclose someone else's exact words in quotation marks.
- Make sure that paraphrases and summaries are in your own words.
- Be sure to cite the source of any ideas or information that you quote, paraphrase, or summarize.

The following paraphrase is too close to the original to be presented without quotation marks and would be considered plagiarized.

**47d
draft**

ORIGINAL PASSAGE

Malnutrition was a widespread and increasingly severe problem throughout the least developed parts of the world in the 1970s, and would continue to be serious, occasionally reaching famine conditions, as the millennium approached. Among the cells of the human body most dependent upon a steady source of nutrients are those of the immune system, most of which live, even under ideal conditions, for only days at a time. (From Laurie Garrett, *The Coming Plague*, New York: Penguin, 1994, p. 199)

PLAGIARIZED VERSION

Garrett points out that malnutrition can give microbes an advantage as they spread through the population. Malnutrition continues to be a severe problem throughout the least developed parts of the world. The human immune system contains cells that are dependent upon a steady source of nutrients. These cells may live, even under ideal conditions, for only days at a time.

The writer of the plagiarized version made only minor changes in some phrases and "lifted" others verbatim.

APPROPRIATE PARAPHRASE

Garrett points out that malnutrition can give microbes an advantage as they spread through the population. The human body contains immune cells that help to fight off various diseases. When the body is deprived of nutrients, these immune cells will weaken (Garrett 199).

Because this writer's paper focused on the general threat of global disease, he also could have simply summarized the passage.

APPROPRIATE SUMMARY

It has been suggested that malnutrition can weaken the immune system and make people

47d
draft

```
more susceptible to diseases they would
otherwise fight off (Garrett 199).
```

3 Be aware of different conventions in the use of sources

Academic research usually acknowledges and draws on the work of previous scholars and researchers. The writer indicates where he or she fits in the tradition of research on a topic and explains any agreements and disagreements with previous work. In this community, much value is placed on a thorough presentation of data and evidence, along with precise, formal documentation in the style appropriate to the subject matter or academic field (MLA, APA, CMS, CBE, or COS—see Chapters 49–53). The following excerpt from Summer Arrigo-Nelson and Jennifer Figliozzi's research report shows their careful integration (and critique) of a research study.

```
First, although both questions 1 and 4
looked to determine student alcohol use within
the home, a discrepancy appeared between the
percentage of people who replied that they were
offered alcohol at home and those who said that
their parents believed alcohol was only for
those over twenty-one years of age. This
discrepancy could have arisen if the students
in the sample were not thorough in their
evaluation of their parents' views, in which
case, correlations drawn from this data should
not be relied upon (Aas, Jakobsen, and
Anderssen 1996).
```

When you read academic research, you'll find that many of the conventions for citation and for the quoting of material will be relevant to your own papers, which will most often assume a similar academic orientation. Material from other settings, however, may follow somewhat different conventions. Work audiences will expect concise treatment of things they already know and extended summaries, tables, graphs, and illustrations—all carefully documented with a recognizable citation system (see Chapters 49–53). Material designed for general public consumption may cite sources in a somewhat informal fashion; texts with many footnotes or academic-sounding references can confuse or put off some public audiences.

**47d
draft**

The following paragraphs are excerpted from the "Oil Spill Public Information Center" ⟨http://www.alaska.net/~ospic/⟩, which contains documents of public interest with special focus on the Exxon Valdez cleanup effort and that spill's impact on the Alaskan shoreline environment. Notice how several important and scientifically complex studies are condensed into a research synthesis that is readily understandable by a reasonably educated public audience.

> Harbor seals, already in serious decline throughout Prince William Sound and the Gulf of Alaska prior to 1989, showed no sign of recovery in 1994 from either spill-related effects or the ongoing decline.
>
> Pilot studies conducted in 1994 using two new techniques, however, provided surprising information which may help biologists understand the lack of recovery. Chemical tests conducted on whiskers and blubber samples from harbor seals in Prince William Sound showed that the seals ate different prey during different times of the year, that they were consuming different foods in various parts of the sound, and that adults and juveniles were eating different things.
>
> Data collected during 1992–1994 from harbor seals tagged with satellite-linked transmitters indicated that seals usually do not move far from their haulout sites. In fact, they are remarkably faithful to the same one or two haulout locations for many months. The haulout information, coupled with the new findings on feeding habits, suggests that the prey preferred by seals, such as pollock, herring or other small fish, are not all available at all sites or are available in varying amounts. This data may provide an important clue in understanding whether food availability is in some way preventing harbor seals from recovering.

If you cite such work in your own papers or projects, you may wish to "unpack" the general references into specific citations. In more informal and less research-oriented public writing, be sure that you check any quotations or material that appears to be from some other source than the public document itself. If you encounter an unreferenced quotation, try contacting the organization or author of the document to get the full citation of his or her source.

Exercise 2

A. Choose a passage from one of your secondary sources, and write a summary and paraphrase of it. Then embed a quotation from the source into a sentence of your own.

**47d
draft**

B. With a group or partner, discuss your writing for Exercise 2A. Does any of it seem plagiarized? If so, help each other to rewrite. Talk about how to improve the passages. How can you make them read more smoothly? How can you make them more concise?

Doing Fieldwork

Field research is firsthand research. As a field researcher, you gather information and ideas directly from **informants**, people you interview or survey, or from your observations of events and places. You may choose to supplement your fieldwork with data gathered by other researchers and writers. Still, your fieldwork will yield original results, meaning that the material in your paper or report is the product of your own work, not borrowed from somebody else's research, and that the information and ideas you present are more likely to be fresh and original.

Good field research also involves interpretation. Be prepared to give the data you collect the same kind of critical "reading" and analysis you give to print and electronic resources (see 46c–46d). The same secondary sources may also suggest kinds of conclusions you can draw from your data or uses you can make of it. Of course, the goals of your fieldwork and the method you employ should depend on both your writing tasks and the research community (see 44a-2) you're addressing.

- **Academic settings.** Field research in disciplines like sociology, psychology, business, education, or urban planning generally means studying people's behaviors or outlooks in order to identify patterns or causes and effects. When field research takes the form of scientific inquiry in fields like chemistry, engineering, or pharmacy, it inquires into how substances, organisms, objects, or machines work or can be constructed.
- **Work settings.** Field research in businesses or other organizations often looks at the way customers (or staff) act and interact, focusing especially on problems, programs, or future actions and choices.
- **Public settings.** Field research in public settings often aims to gather (and measure) people's opinions, attitudes, and values, especially in relationship to policies, public programs, and institutions as well as issues affecting all or part of a society.

> **Writer's Tip**
>
> If you launch into original field research too quickly, you might overlook important perspectives or miss the chance to think about your data-gathering process more carefully. It helps to do some background research before beginning field research. What have other people said or found out about your topic? What problems or unanswered questions arise from their work? Be sure to plan your fieldwork carefully (see Chapter 44) so that you won't feel you've missed something important after the field experience is over.

48a Ethnographies

You can use **ethnographic research** to interpret the practices, behaviors, language, and attitudes of particular groups that are tied together by their interests or ways of understanding and acting in the world. Such cultural analyses are at the heart of much important research on human belief and ritual. The term *ethnography* means, literally, the writing ("graphy") of culture ("ethno"). Because an **ethnograpy,** the written report of ethnographic research, aims to provide an in-depth understanding of its subject, you may need to use several methods to gather detailed information about your subject, including **observation** of people, events, and settings; **interviews** with informants (people who provide you with information about the group to which they belong); and collection of **artifacts** (material objects characteristic of a group or culture). Most full-scale ethnographies require months or even years of participation in a community; you can use the principles of ethnographic research, however, for more modest "quasi-ethnographies."

To understand your subject in depth, focus your fieldwork on a specific setting, activity, person, or group of people to which you can devote enough time and energy to arrive at worthwhile conclusions. Conduct **structured observations** in which you carefully and objectively look at a situation, behavior, or relationship in order to understand its elements and processes. For instance, in researching the ways preschoolers use language during play, you could arrange and plan in detail a series of structured observations at a day-care center.

STRATEGY

1. Choose the site, and, if necessary, get permission to conduct your observation.

2. Decide how to situate yourself. Will you move around or remain inconspicuous? How will you explain your presence to people you are observing?
3. Decide what information you want to gather and why. Consider how you will use it in your report.
4. Consider your means for recording information: tape recorder, camera, notepad, or video camera.
5. Make a list of problems that might arise, and develop strategies for dealing with them.

Take careful, detailed notes on your observations and transcribe any tape interviews. The following notes were transcribed from an interview for an anthropology class assignment to study a person with an unusual occupation.

Dave Glovsky
Palace Playland: Dave's Guessing Stand
July 8
Brian Schwegler

(Sound of game, the Striker: hammer swing in background for all of tape; background noise; greetings inaudible.)

BS: So, Dave, can you tell me a little something about how you guess? Can you tell me how you guess?

DG: Ages? I read the lower lids. I read the lower lid. It deteriorates as we get older. The more it gets darker, they get older. Even children of sixteen can fool me with the deterioration under the eyes. They can have beautiful skin, but I don't check the skin. I check the lower lid of their eyes.

BS: How about weight?

DG: Weight, well I just guess on the weight. You know, I feel the arm, I feel the stomach. Not women though. I don't touch the women. I just guess ....

[The interview continues until a female customer arrives.]

DG: Hey, come on in, have fun. What do you want me to guess?

Cust: My age.

DG: All right, that's a dollar. (Holds up one-dollar bill) A hundred-dollar bill. Step into the office here. (Points to a patch of pavement) Are you going to tell me the truth?

Cust: Yeah.

48a
field

When you present enthnographic data in a report, be precise, and make sure you go beyond simply presenting details by offering your interpretations.

First Draft: Dave the Guesser

by Brian Schwegler

"Come on in, have some fun with the famous guesser of Old Orchard," says Dave "The Guesser" Glovsky. Relying on his voice and personality to attract customers, he seems out of place in this mechanized wonderland. Hand-painted signs covered with cramped writing are his advertisement. I peer at them and try to decipher the writing that is more anxious than able.

> The Guesser Has
> Experience
> Sex Appeal
> Personality

> Try him, you'll
> enjoy his humor
> and guessing skill.

> Palace Playland's World Famous Guess
> Station: Come in, fill up with fun—
> You'll be glad you did.

As I wait in front of his stand and read his signs, a young woman approaches Dave.

"Hey, come on in, have fun. What do you want me to guess?" Dave asks.

"My age," says the young woman.

"All right, that's a dollar." Holding up the dollar bill that the woman gives him, Dave examines it the way a jeweler examines a precious stone. "A hundred dollar bill." Pointing to a space on the pavement, Dave says, "Step into the office here." Dave checks her out from all angles, looking for the clue that will let him know her age within two years, his margin of error.

48b Interviews

You can use interviews to supplement your research in print and electronic resources either by talking with experts or by contacting people whose experiences may help you test the validity of conclusions offered in your other sources. You might also decide to make interviews your main method of research. Such a strategy would be especially appropriate for research on an organization or a program such as a juvenile justice system or an emergency medical response program currently facing a number of problems.

STRATEGY

1. List possible interviewees. Begin by writing down questions you'd like to have answered; then list people who might be able to answer them. Consider whether you'll need to do a thorough, lengthy interview or just collect short answers to a few questions.
2. Write out questions you want to ask your interviewees. Arrange your questions logically; avoid those that can be answered by *yes* or *no*, unless you plan follow-ups. If possible, rehearse questions with friends to discover those that are likely to be ineffective.
3. Use your list of questions, but don't be shackled by it. Follow the train of new information and ideas as long as it serves your purpose.

48b field

Writer's Tip

Consider tape-recording your interview instead of writing everything down. This will let you focus on the content of the interview. Always ask permission to use a recorder, and bring along extra tapes and batteries. After an interview, send a thank-you note to the interviewee—both to be polite and because you may need a follow-up interview.

Exercise 1

 A. Brian Schwegler was clearly gathering more than just Dave the Guesser's responses to his questions: he was observing the scene of Dave's work, taking notes on his interactions with customers, and so on. But consider just his interview process. Make a list of questions that you might ask Dave the Guesser in order to find out more about his job, his history, and the like.

 B. Working in a group, compare the questions you generated in Exercise 1A. Which ones are likely to yield the most interesting information? Which ones are risky or potentially unhelpful? For any questions that could yield a *yes* or *no* response, what are some follow-up questions that could help Dave to expand his answers?

48c Surveys, polls, and questionnaires

Surveys, polls, and questionnaires are useful in gathering people's opinions or information about specific behaviors and the likelihood of future actions. Research in public and work settings often relies on these techniques, but they're common in academic research, too.

1 Surveys and polls

Surveys and **polls** collect short answers, often in *yes/no* form. They provide statistics you can present in charts and tables, measure against research findings, or use to support your opinions.

STRATEGY

1. Consider the people that you'll survey or poll. Do you want to poll on the basis of gender, age, or occupation? For example, if you were

comparing the opinions of college students and parents about alcohol use, you would want a large enough sample from each group to enable you to generalize about any differences.

2. Always draft, test, and revise your questions to make them as effective as possible.

3. Think carefully about where you'll conduct your survey or poll because the location you choose may determine the particular groups of people who answer your questions. Polling people in a bar about their attitudes toward alcohol use will yield quite different information than the same poll conducted in the parking lot of a health food co-op.

Here are a few of the questions Shane Hand asked people about recycling. As they answered, he put a mark on a tally sheet.

```
Do you . . .

Use coffee mugs instead of
polystyrene cups?                           (Yes)    No
Reuse plastic wrap, foil,
and plastic bags?                            Yes    (No)
Recycle newspapers and/or
magazines?                                  (Yes)    No

Are you willing to . . .
Take your own bags to the store?            (Yes)    No
Shop at a store that's harder
to get to but carries
biodegradable products?                      Yes    (No)
```

2 Questionnaires

Questionnaires allow you to gather in-depth information, sometimes from a large number of people. Because they're usually mailed, most questionnaires don't require the "live" contact time of interviews, but they need to be prepared carefully so they don't confuse respondents and ruin a project.

S T R A T E G Y

1. Consider the form of your questionnaire. Will you ask respondents to write out explanations, check boxes, or circle answer choices? Will you use a multiple-choice format or a rating scale?
2. Draft a list of questions that will yield the information you want. Scrutinize your wording carefully, and test your draft on at least two or three people. Ask them to describe points at which they were confused or needed more information.
3. Revise the questionnaire and prepare it for distribution. Try to fit your questions on one page (front and back) if possible, but leave enough room for longhand comments if you have time to analyze them.

PART

6

USING CITATION STYLES

49

Documenting Sources: MLA

The MLA (Modern Language Association) documentation style offers you a convenient system for acknowledging your sources for ideas, information, and quotations and for directing readers to these sources. It consists of an in-text citation (generally in parentheses) and a list of works cited (presented at the end of the text). (For advice on what to document and what not to document, see 46d-1.)

USE MLA DOCUMENTATION STYLE IN . . .
ACADEMIC SETTINGS

When writing in humanities fields such as English and foreign languages
When writing for publications or groups requiring use of MLA style
When writing papers for an instructor who asks for a simple form of parenthetical documentation such as MLA style

CONSIDER USING MLA DOCUMENTATION STYLE (PERHAPS A MODIFIED FORM) IN . . .
WORK AND PUBLIC SETTINGS

When readers are not expecting a specific form of documentation
When you feel your subject and audience are best served by a simple, direct documentation style that seldom uses footnotes or endnotes
When other writers in the setting use either MLA style or a similar though informal system.

If the MLA documentation style does not meet your needs, consider using these other documentation styles: APA (Chapter 50), CBE (Chapter 51), CMS (Chapter 52), or COS (Chapter 53).

For detailed treatments of the MLA documentation system, see the *MLA Handbook for Writers of Research Papers* (5th ed., New York: MLA, 1999) or the *MLA Style Manual and Guide to Scholarly Publishing* (2nd ed., New York: MLA, 1998).

49a Using in-text citations

The **MLA documentation style** uses a citation in the text (generally an author's name) to identify a source for readers. The citation helps readers locate the source in the list of works cited appearing at the end of the paper. Many in-text citations provide a page number to indicate exactly where in the source readers can find the particular information.

IN-TEXT CITATION

Although the average Haitian peasant calls himself a Catholic and views himself as such, he generally continues to call on his African ancestors' gods, or *loa,* for spiritual and emotional support. As one peasant put it, "One must be Catholic to serve the loa" (Metraux 59).
—FREDZA LÉGER, College Student

ENTRY IN THE LIST OF WORKS CITED

Metraux, Alfred. <u>Haiti: Black Peasants and</u>

   <u>Their Religion</u>. London: Harrap, 1960.

Citations may appear within parentheses or as part of the discussion itself. They may refer to a work in general or to specific parts of a source (by including a page number).

Author's name inside parentheses. You can choose to provide the author's name in parentheses. For a quotation or for specific information, include the page number to indicate where the material appears in the source, as in (*Jenkins 134*). Do not place a comma between an author's name and a page number nor use *p.* or *pp.* to indicate page(s).

> Comparing the writing styles of individual authors in classic Chinese literature is difficult because ancient China had "no concept of single authorship" (Liu 30).

Author's name as part of discussion. You can make the author's name (or other information as well) part of the discussion.

> James Liu reminds us that it is difficult to compare the writing styles of individual authors in classic Chinese literature because ancient China had "no concept of single authorship" (30).

General reference. A **general reference** enables you to refer to the main ideas in a source or to information presented throughout the work, not in a single place. It may also refer to a book, an article, or some other source as a whole. You need not provide page numbers for a general reference.

PARENTHETICAL   Many species of animals have developed complex systems of communication (Bright).

The statement summarizes one of the work's main points, so the reference cites the work as a whole, not a specific page or pages.

AUTHOR NAMED
IN DISCUSSION   According to Michael Bright, many species of animals have developed complex systems of communication.

Specific reference. A **specific reference** enables you to document words, ideas, or facts appearing in a particular place in a source.

People have trouble recognizing sound patterns dolphins use to communicate. Dolphins can perceive clicking sounds "made up of 700 units of sound per second," yet "in the human ear the sounds would fuse together in our minds at 20–30 clicks per second" (Bright 52).

The page number gives the specific location of the quotation.

According to Michael Bright, dolphins recognize patterns consisting of seven hundred clicks each second, yet such patterns begin to blur for people at around twenty or thirty clicks each second (52).

The page number cites the specific source.

Writer's Tip

Punctuation and abbreviations are kept to a minimum when you use in-text parenthetical citations following the MLA documentation style. You do not place a comma between an author's name and a page number in a parenthetical reference, for example, nor do you use *p.* or *pp.* to indicate page(s), as in (*Jenkins 134*). (For advice on punctuating sentences containing parenthetical references, see pp. 651–652.)

STRATEGY

Use questions like these to help decide whether to make in-text citations general or specific and whether to make them parenthetical or part of the discussion.

- Am I trying to weave broad concepts into my own explanation or argument (general), or am I looking for precise ideas and details to support my conclusions (specific)?
- Will this part of my paper be clearer and more effective if I draw on the author's own words (specific) or if I merely point out that the author's text as a whole presents the concepts I am discussing (general)?
- Do I wish to highlight the source by naming the author (part of discussion), or to emphasize the information itself (parenthetical)?
- Will this passage be more concise, emphatic, or effective if I put the author's name in parentheses or if I work it into the discussion?
- Do I wish to refer to more than one source without distracting readers (parenthetical), or do the several sources I am citing need individual attention (part of discussion)?

Placement and Punctuation of Parenthetical Citations

In general, put parenthetical citations close to the quotation, information, paraphrase, or summary you are documenting. Place the parenthetical citation either at the end of a sentence (before the final punctuation) or at a natural pause in the sentence.

> Wayland Hand reports on a folk belief that going to sleep on a rug made of bearskin can relieve backache (183).

If the citation applies to only part of the sentence, put it after the borrowed material at the point least likely to disrupt the sentence.

> The folk belief that "sleeping on a bear rug will cure backache" (Hand 183) is yet another example of a kind of magic in which external objects produce results inside the body.

When you place an in-text parenthetical citation at the end of a long quotation set off as a block (see 35b), leave a space after the ending punctuation, and then add the citation.

> Many athletes are superstitious, especially baseball players, but perhaps the most suspicious of all are pitchers.
>
> > On the days they are scheduled to appear, many pitchers avoid activities that they believe sap their strength and therefore detract from their effectiveness, or that they otherwise generally link with poor performance. Many pitchers avoid eating certain foods on their pitching days. Some pitchers refuse to walk

continued

Placement and Punctuation of Parenthetical Citations
(continued)

> anywhere on the day of the game in the belief that every little exer-
> tion subtracts from their playing strength. One pitcher would never
> put on his cap until the game started and would not wear it at all
> on the days he did not pitch. (Gmelch 280)

If the material you are quoting contains quotation marks, use double
quotation marks to enclose the quotation as a whole and single quotation marks to enclose the interior quotation.

> According to Dubisch, "Being a 'health food person' involves more
> than simply changing one's diet or utilizing an alternative medical
> system" (61).

49b Creating MLA in-text citations

In-text citations following MLA documentation style may take
slightly differing forms depending on the number of authors, the number
of volumes in a work, and the number of works being cited. (For advice
on placing in-text citations within a passage and providing appropriate
punctuation, see the box beginning on page 651.)

Guide to MLA Formats for In-Text Citations

1. **One Author**
2. **Two or Three Authors**
3. **Four or More Authors**
4. **Corporate or Group Author**
5. **No Author Given**
6. **More than One Work by the Same Author**
7. **Authors with the Same Last Name**
8. **Indirect Source**
9. **Multivolume Work**
10. **Literary Work**
11. **Bible**
12. **Two or More Sources in a Single Citation**
13. **Selection in an Anthology**
14. **Electronic or Other Nonprint Sources**

1. One Author

Provide the author's last name in parentheses, or make either the full name or last name alone part of the discussion.

PARENTHETICAL — During World War II, government posters often portrayed homemakers "as vital defenders of the nation's homes" (Honey 135).

AUTHOR NAMED IN DISCUSSION — According to Maureen Honey, government posters during World War II often portrayed homemakers "as vital defenders of the nation's homes" (135).

2. Two or Three Authors

Give the names of all the authors in parentheses or in the discussion.

PARENTHETICAL — A century ago, whale oil was used not only for lighting but also for making soap, wool cloth, paint, rope, and leather; the bone was used not just for corsets but for making umbrellas, furniture, springs, fishing rods, and luggage (Norman and Fraser 209).

If the book had three authors, the citation would read (Norman, Fraser, and Jenko 209).

AUTHOR NAMED IN TEXT — As Norman and Fraser point out, a century ago, whale oil was used not only for lighting but also for making soap, wool cloth, paint, rope, and leather; the bone was used not just for corsets but for making umbrellas, furniture, springs, fishing rods, and luggage (209).

3. Four or More Authors

Supply the first author's name and the phrase *et al.* (meaning "and others") within parentheses. To introduce the citation as part of the discussion, use a phrase like "Britton and his colleagues point out. . . ."

Much of the writing that schoolchildren are required to do takes the form of tests or teacher-designed exercises (Britton et al. 24).

If you give all the authors' names rather than *et al.* in the works cited list, then give all the names in the in-text citation (660).

4. Corporate or Group Author

If an organization or government agency is named as the author, use its name (shortened, if cumbersome) in the citation.

Even in 1969, critics of the government's anti-communist policies were challenging the government's decision to divert money earmarked for education, health, and other "more fruitful programs" into "so-called national security" (American Friends 118).

"American Friends" is the shortened name of the American Friends Service Committee.

5. No Author Given

When no author's name is given, use the title instead (in a shortened version if it is long). Begin the abbreviated title with the word used to alphabetize the work in the list of works cited.

On January 1, 1993, the former state of Czechoslovakia split into two new states, the Czech Republic and the Slovak Republic (*Baedeker's* 67).

The shortened title refers to *Baedeker's Czech/Slovak Republics,* a book for which no author is given.

6. More than One Work by the Same Author

When the list of works cited includes more than one work by the same author, add the title in shortened form to your citation.

The members of some Protestant groups in the Appalachian region view the "handling of serpents" during worship "as a supreme act of faith" (Daugherty, "Serpent-Handling" 232).

"Serpent-Handling" is a shortened version of "Serpent-Handling as Sacrament." In a parenthetical citation, add a comma between the author's name and the title.

7. Authors with the Same Last Name

When the authors of different sources have the same last name, identify the specific author by giving the first initial (or the full first name, if necessary).

Although a number of Hebrew texts mention rebellious demons under the leadership of "Satanail" or "Satan" (D. Russell 110), the story of Satan and the rebellious angels gets its fullest development in Greek sources (J. Russell 192).

8. Indirect Source

When your source provides you with a quotation (or paraphrase) taken from yet another source, you need to include the phrase *qtd. in* (for "quoted in") to indicate the original source.

The play combines parts of two others, Shakespeare's *Hamlet* and Samuel Beckett's *Waiting for Godot,* in a manner Harold Bloom describes as a "kind of interlacing between an old play and a new one" (qtd. in Meyer 106).

Meyer is the source of the quotation from Harold Bloom.

When referring to an indirect source, you should generally include in your discussion the name of the person from whom the quotation is taken. If the same information were presented in a parenthetical citation— (*Bloom, qtd. in Meyer 106*)—some readers might mistakenly look for Bloom rather than Meyer in the list of works cited.

9. Multivolume Work

Give the volume number followed by a colon and a space, then the page number: (*Franklin 6: 434*). When referring to the volume as a whole, use a comma after the author's name and add *vol.* before the volume number: (*Franklin, vol. 6*).

In the classic Chinese novel *The Story of the Stone,* the character Xi-chun outwardly accepts her fate but secretly wishes for a different life: "If only I had been born into a different family! If only I were free to become a nun!" (Cao 4: 177).

The author's name is Cao, the volume number is 4, and the page number is 177.

10. Literary Work

When you refer to a literary work, consider including information that will help readers find the passage you are citing in any of the different editions of the work. Begin by giving the page number of the particular edition followed by a semicolon; then add the appropriate chapter, part, or section numbers.

In *Huckleberry Finn,* Mark Twain ridicules the exaggerated histrionics of provincial actors through his portrayal of the King and the Duke as they rehearse Hamlet's famous soliloquy: "So [the duke] went to marching up and down, thinking, and frowning horrible every now and then; then he would hoist up his eyebrows; next he would squeeze his hand on his forehead and stagger back and kind of moan; next he would sigh, and next he'd let on to drop a tear" (178; ch. 21).

Note that there is a semicolon after the page number, followed by *ch.* (for "chapter"). If you also include a part number, use *pt.* followed by a comma and the chapter number, as in (*386; pt. 3, ch. 2*). For a play, note the act, scene, and line numbers, if needed, as in this reference to *Hamlet*: (Ham. *1.2.76*). For poems, give line numbers (*lines 55–57*) or, if there are part divisions, both part and line numbers (*4.220–23*).

11. Bible

MLA style uses a period between the chapter and verse numbers (*Mark 2.3-4*). For parenthetical citations, employ abbreviations for names of five or more letters, as in the case of Deuteronomy: (*Deut. 16.21-22*).

12. Two or More Sources in a Single Citation

When you use a parenthetical citation to refer to more than one source, separate the sources with a semicolon.

Differences in the ways people speak, especially differences in the ways men and women use language, can often be traced to who has power and who does not (Tannen 83-86; Tavris 297-301).

13. Selection in an Anthology

If your source is a reprint of an essay, poem, short story, or other work appearing in an anthology, cite the work's author (not the editor of the anthology), but refer to the page number(s) in the anthology.

Andrew Holleran concludes that the AIDS epidemic has led many people to realize that "the most profound difference between men may be that between the sick and the well, but compassionate people try to reach across the chasm and bridge it" (552).

The selection appears on page 552 of the anthology *Patterns of Exposition*.

14. Electronic or Other Nonprint Sources

Provide the name of the author, the title, or any other information readers need to find the appropriate entry in your list of works cited. You need not include a page number for electronic sources a single page long or without page numbering. For numbered paragraphs, give the number and use the abbreviation *par(s)*.

In contrast, the heroine's mother in the film *Clueless* died in an ironic and contemporary fashion: the victim of an accident during liposuction.

49c Informative footnotes and endnotes

At times you may wish to comment on the usefulness or reliability of a source, provide some additional background details, or discuss a specific point at length. You recognize, however, that doing so would disrupt the flow of the discussion and would be useful for only a few readers. Informative footnotes (or endnotes) offer a solution. Place a number (raised slightly above the line of the text) at a suitable point in your discussion. Then provide the note itself, labeled with a corresponding number at the bottom of a page (for a footnote) or at the end of the paper on a page titled "Notes," coming before the list of works cited (for an endnote.)

[1]Anyone still inclined to question the intricacy of video games and the conceptual challenges they pose might consider investigating the numerous publications devoted to strategies for games like *Riven*, *Myst*, and even the various versions of *Doom*.

49d Creating an MLA list of works cited

In an alphabetized list titled "Works Cited," placed on a new page that follows the last page of your paper or report, provide readers with detailed information about the sources you have cited in the text. To indicate all the works you consulted, even if you did not cite them all, you may provide a list titled "Works Consulted."

In your list of works cited, alphabetize the entries by the author's last name or by last and first names for authors with the same last name. If a source does not identify an author, alphabetize by the first word in the title (other than *A, An,* or *The*).

Guide to MLA Formats for a List of Works Cited

1. Books and Works Treated as Books
1. One Author
2. Two or Three Authors
3. Four or More Authors
4. Corporate or Group Author
5. No Author Given
6. More than One Book by the Same Author
7. One or More Editors
8. Author and an Editor
9. Translator
10. Edition Other than the First
11. Reprinted Book
12. One or More Volumes of a Multivolume Work
13. Book in a Series
14. Book Published Before 1900
15. Book with a Publisher's Imprint
16. Anthology or Collection of Articles
17. Government Document
18. Title Within a Title

continued

**49d
MLA**

Guide to MLA Formats for a List of Works Cited *(continued)*

19. Pamphlet
20. Published Dissertation
21. Unpublished Dissertation
22. Conference Proceedings

2. ARTICLES AND SELECTIONS FROM BOOKS

23. Article in Journal Paginated by Volume
24. Article in Journal Paginated by Issue
25. Article in Weekly Magazine
26. Article in Monthly Magazine
27. Unsigned Article in Magazine
28. Article in Newspaper
29. Editorial or Letter to the Editor
30. Interview—Published
31. Review
32. Article from Encyclopedia
33. Selection in Anthology or Chapter in Edited Book
34. More than One Selection from Anthology or Collection (Cross-Reference)
35. Preface, Foreword, Introduction, or Afterword
36. Letter—Published
37. Dissertation Abstract

3. FIELD RESOURCES AND OTHER PRINTED RESOURCES

38. Interview—Unpublished
39. Survey or Questionnaire
40. Observations
41. Letter or Memo—Unpublished
42. Performance
43. Lecture
44. Map or Chart
45. Cartoon
46. Advertisement

4. MEDIA AND ELECTRONIC RESOURCES

47. Film or Videotape
48. Television or Radio Program
49. Recording
50. Artwork
51. Database: CD-ROM, Diskette, or Magnetic Tape
52. Online Source from Computer Service
53. Online Book
54. Online Journal Article
55. Online Magazine Article
56. Online Newspaper Article
57. Scholarly Project or Reference Database
58. Online Posting to Discussion Group
59. Synchronous Communication
60. Other Electronic Sources
61. FTP, Telnet, or Gopher Site
62. Work in an Indeterminate Medium
63. Email

1 Books and works treated as books

MODEL FORMAT FOR BOOKS AND WORKS TREATED AS BOOKS

period + space   period + space   colon + space
↓   ↓   ↓

Author(s). Title of Work. Place of Publication:

Publisher, Year Published.

↑   ↑   ↑
indent five spaces   comma + space   period

- **Author(s).** Give the author's last name first, followed by the first name (spelled out unless the author uses initials), any middle name or initial, and a period . Do not include titles like *M.D.* or *SJ*, but include other parts of a name, like *III* or *Jr.,* placing them at the end of the name preceded by a comma: *Valantasio, Louis, Jr.* (See Entries 2 and 3 on pp. 659–660 for sources with more than one author.)
- **Title of work.** Give the title of the work, including any subtitle. (Use a colon to introduce a subtitle unless the primary title ends with a question mark, dash, or exclamation point.) Capitalize the main words, and end with a period unless the title ends with some other mark of punctuation. Underline the title, but not the period.
- **Publication information.** After the title, provide the city where the work was published, followed by a colon and a single space. If not obvious, add the country (abbreviated, as in *Dover, Eng.*). If more than one place of publication appears in the work, use the first one in your citation. Then give the publisher's name (followed by a comma) and the date of publication (followed by a period). You may omit unnecessary words such as *Publisher, Inc.,* and *Co.* (For example, use just *McGraw,* not *McGraw-Hill, Inc.*) Substitute the letters *U* and *P* for the words *University* and *Press* where they appear in the publisher's name (for example, *U of Chicago P*). If any of the basic publication information is missing , use *n.p.* ("no place" or "no publisher") or *n.d.* ("no date").
- **Spacing.** Double-space all entries, and indent five spaces for the second and any additional lines in each entry. Leave spaces between each of the major elements in an entry (author's name, title of work, and publication information).

1. One Author

Twitchell, James B. ADCULTusa: The Triumph of
    Advertising in American Culture. New York:
    Columbia UP, 1996.

2. Two or Three Authors

Give the first author's name, starting with the last name, followed by the other names in regular order. Use commas to separate the names, and introduce the second of two names or the third name with *and.*

Kress, Gunther, and Theo van Leeuwen. Reading
    Images: The Grammar of Graphic Design.
    London: Routledge, 1996.

3. Four or More Authors

Use the first author's name and then the phrase *et al.* (meaning "and others"). You may choose to give all the names, but if you do, you must list them in any parenthetical citations (see p. 653).

> Bellah, Robert N., et al. <u>Habits of the Heart:</u>
>
> <u>Individualism and Commitment in American</u>
>
> <u>Life</u>. Berkeley: U of California P, 1985.
>
> All authors listed: Bellah, Robert N., Richard Madsen, William M. Sullivan, Ann Swidler, and Steven M. Tipton

4. Corporate or Group Author

Treat the corporation, organization, or government agency as the author, alphabetizing by the first main word of the organization's name. If the organization is also the publisher, repeat its name again, abbreviated if appropriate.

> International City/County Management
>
> Association. <u>The Municipal Year Book:</u>
>
> <u>1998</u>. Washington, DC: ICMA.

5. No Author Given

List the work alphabetically according to the first main word of its title.

> <u>Guide for Authors</u>. Oxford: Blackwell, 1985.

6. More than One Book by the Same Author

List multiple works by an author alphabetically by the first main word of the title. For the first entry, include the full name(s) of the author(s). For additional entries, use three hyphens in place of the name, followed by a period and a space, but only if the author or authors are *exactly* the same for each work. If the authorship differs in any way, include the name(s) in full.

> Tannen, Deborah. <u>That's Not What I Meant! How</u>
>
> <u>Conversational Style Makes or Breaks Your</u>
>
> <u>Relations with Others</u>. New York: Morrow,
>
> 1986.
>
> ---. <u>The Argument Culture: Moving from Debate</u>
>
> <u>to Dialogue</u>. New York: Random, 1998.

7. One or More Editors

Begin with the editor's name followed by a comma and the abbreviation *ed.* or *eds.*

Achebe, Chinua, and C. L. Innes, eds. African

Short Stories. London: Heinemann, 1985.

8. Author and an Editor

Begin with either the author's or the editor's name depending on whether you are using the text itself or the editor's contributions.

Weber, Max. The Theory of Social and Economic

Organization. Ed. Talcott Parsons. Trans.

A. M. Henderson and Talcott Parsons. New

York: Free, 1964.

9. Translator

Refer to the book by its author, not its translator, even though the English words are the translator's. Abbreviate the translator's title as *Trans.*

Baudrillard, Jean. Cool Memories II: 1978-1990.

Trans. Chris Turner. Durham: Duke UP,

1996.

10. Edition Other than the First

Give the edition number (*3rd ed.*) or description (*Rev. ed.* or *1998 ed.*, for example) after the title.

Cowie, Peter. Coppola: A Biography. Rev. ed.

New York: DaCapo, 1994.

11. Reprinted Book

Supply the original publication date after the title. If pertinent, include the original publisher or place of publication. Then follow with the publication information from the work you are using.

Ondaatje, Michael. The Collected Works of Billy

the Kid. 1970. Harmondsworth, Eng.:

Penguin, 1984.

12. One or More Volumes of a Multivolume Work

Indicate the total number of volumes after the title (or after the editor's or translator's name).

> Tsao, Hsueh-chin. <u>The Story of the Stone</u>.
>
> Trans. David Hawkes. 5 vols.
>
> Harmondsworth, Eng. Penguin, 1983-86.

If you are citing a particular volume instead of the whole work or several volumes from the whole work, supply only the particular volume number and publication information. Indicate the total number of volumes at the end of the entry.

> Tsao, Hsueh-chin. <u>The Story of the Stone</u>. Trans.
>
> David Hawkes. Vol. 1. Harmondsworth, Eng.:
>
> Penguin, 1983. 5 vols.

13. Book in a Series

Give the series name and any item number after the title of the work. Use abbreviations for familiar words in the name of the series (such as *ser.* for *series*).

> Hess, Gary R. <u>Vietnam and the United States:</u>
>
> <u>Origins and Legacy of War</u>. International
>
> History Ser. 7. Boston: Twayne, 1990.

14. Book Published Before 1900

For books published before 1900, include the publisher's name only if it is relevant to your research. Use a comma rather than a colon after place of publication.

> Darwin, Charles. <u>Descent of Man and Selection</u>
>
> <u>in Relation to Sex</u>. New York, 1896.

15. Book with a Publisher's Imprint

For a book issued with a special imprint name, give the imprint name first, followed by a hyphen and the main publisher's name.

> Sikes, Gini. <u>8 Ball Chicks: A Year in the</u>
>
> <u>Violent World of Girl Gangs</u>. New York:
>
> Anchor-Doubleday, 1997.

16. Anthology or Collection of Articles

To refer to an anthology or a collection of scholarly articles as a whole, supply the editor's name first, followed by *ed.*, and then the title of the collection.

> Zipes, Jack, ed. Don't Bet on the Prince:
>
> Contemporary Feminist Fairy Tales in North
>
> America and England. New York: Methuen, 1986.

To cite a selection within an anthology or collection, see Entries 33 and 34 on pp. 668–669.

17. Government Document

Begin with the government or agency name(s) or the author, if any. Start with *United States* for a congressional document or a report from a federal agency; otherwise, begin with the name of the government and agency or the name of the independent agency. For congressional documents, write *Cong.* (for *Congress*), identify the branch (*Senate* or *House*), and give the number and session (for example, *101st Cong., 1st sess.*). Include the title of the specific document and the title of the book in which it is printed. Use *GPO* for *Government Printing Office.*

> United States. National Research Council
>
> Committee on Global Change. Research
>
> Strategies for the U.S. Global Change
>
> Research Program. Washington: National
>
> Academy, 1990.
>
> United States. Cong. Senate. Committee on
>
> Environmental and Public Works.
>
> Subcommittee on Environmental Protection.
>
> Policy Options for Stabilizing Global
>
> Climate Hearing. 101st Cong., 1st sess.
>
> Washington: GPO, 1989.

18. Title Within a Title

When a book title contains another work's title, do not underline the title of the second work. If the second title would normally be enclosed in quotation marks, add them and underline the entire title.

MacPherson, Pat. <u>Reflecting on</u> Jane Eyre.

London: Routledge, 1989.

Golden, Catherine, ed. <u>The Captive Imagination:</u>

<u>A Casebook on "The Yellow Wallpaper</u>." New

York: Feminist, 1992.

19. Pamphlet

Use the same form for a pamphlet as for a book.

Vareika, William. <u>John La Farge: An American</u>

<u>Master (1835-1910)</u>. Newport: Gallery of

American Art, 1989.

20. Published Dissertation

Treat a published doctoral dissertation as a book. Include the abbreviation *Diss.*, the school for which the dissertation was written, and the year the degree was awarded.

Said, Edward W. <u>Joseph Conrad and the Fiction</u>

<u>of Autobiography</u>. Diss. Harvard U, 1964.

Cambridge: Harvard UP, 1966.

21. Unpublished Dissertation

Use quotation marks for the title; include the abbreviation *Diss.*, the school for which the dissertation was written, and the date of the degree.

Anku, William Oscar. "Procedures in African

Drumming: A Study of Akan/Ewe Traditions

and African Drumming in Pittsburgh." Diss.

U of Pittsburgh, 1988.

22. Conference Proceedings

Begin with the title unless an editor is named. Follow with details about the conference, including name and date.

<u>Environmental Impacts and Solutions</u>. Proc. of

the International Conference on

Residential Solid Fuels, 3-7 June 1981.

Beaverton: Oregon Graduate Center, 1982.

2 Articles and selections from books

MODEL FORMAT FOR ARTICLES AND SELECTIONS

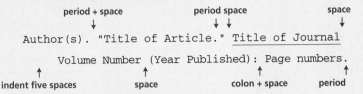

- **Author(s).** Give the author's last name first, followed by the first name, any initial, and a period. If the piece has more than one author, give subsequent names in regular order separated by commas with *and* preceding the final name.
- **Title of article.** Give the article's full title in quotation marks, concluding with a period unless the title ends with a question mark or an exclamation point.
- **Title of journal, periodical, or book.** Give the publication's title, underlined, but not including an opening *The, A,* or *An.* Do not end the title with a period.
- **Publication information.** Supply the volume number (and sometimes the issue number), the year of publication (in parentheses), and the page numbers for the full article or selection. The volume number is always found on the publication's cover or title page; even if it is in Roman numerals, use Arabic numerals for your entry. For a scholarly journal, you don't need to include the month or season (e.g. Winter). Introduce the page numbers with a colon.
- **Spacing.** Double-space all entries, and indent five spaces for the second and any additional lines in each entry. Leave a space between each of the major elements in an entry (author's name, article or selection title, and journal title along with publication information). Leave a space between the colon and the page number and also after the journal title and the volume number.

23. Article in Journal Paginated by Volume

Each volume consists of several issues, paginated continuously; that is, each issue begins where the preceding left off—at page 354, for example. Give the volume number after the journal's title.

Tobacyk, Jerome. "Superstitions and Beliefs
    About the Prediction of Future Events."
    Psychological Reports 68 (1991): 511-12.

24. Article in Journal Paginated by Issue

The issues making up a volume are paginated separately. Give the volume number first, followed by a period and the issue number.

```
Decker-Collins, Norma. "Freewriting, Personal

      Writing, and the At-Risk Reader." Journal

      of Reading 33.8 (1990): 654-55.
```

25. Article in Weekly Magazine

Put the day first, then the month (abbreviated except for May, June, and July), and then the year followed by a colon. Give inclusive page numbers. If the pages are not consecutive, give the first page with a plus sign (for example, 23+). (Treat biweekly magazines in a similar fashion.)

```
Wright, Robert. "The Power of Their Peers."

      Time 24 Aug. 1998: 67.
```

26. Article in Monthly Magazine

Treat a monthly or bimonthly magazine as a weekly magazine (Entry 25), but without listing the day.

```
Jacobson, Mark. "For Whom the Gong Tolls."

      Natural History Sept. 1997: 72+
```

27. Unsigned Article in Magazine

Begin with the title (ignoring *A*, *An*, and *The* when alphabetizing).

```
"Horseplay." New Yorker 5 Apr. 1993: 36-38.
```

28. Article in Newspaper

Treat a newspaper as a weekly magazine, including citation of pages (see Entry 25), but include the section number or letter with the page number. Omit *The*, *A*, or *An* at the beginning of a newspaper's name. For a local newspaper, give the city's name in brackets after the title unless the city is named in the title.

```
Pacelle, Mitchell. "When Blood Flowed Anew at

      Gettysburg, the Fur Flew, Too." Wall

      Street Journal 20 Aug. 1998: A1+.
```

29. Editorial or Letter to the Editor

Supply the title first for an unsigned editorial and the author's name first for a signed editorial. Identify with the word *editorial*.

```
"A False Choice." Editorial. Charlotte Observer
     16 Aug. 1998: 2C.
```

Use the word *letter* to identify a letter to the editor.

```
Varley, Colin. Letter. Archaeology May-June
     1993: 10.
```

30. Interview—Published

Treat the person interviewed, not the interviewer, as the author. For untitled interviews, include the word *Interview* (without underlining or quotation marks) in place of a title.

```
Stewart, Martha. "I Do Have a Brain." By Kevin
     Kelly. Wired Aug. 1998: 114.
```

31. Review

Give the title after the name of the reviewer. Cite an unsigned review by its title.

```
Honig, Alice Sterling. "Helping Children
     Problem-Solve." Rev. of I Can Problem
     Solve: An Interpersonal Cognitive Problem-
     solving Program, by Myrna Shure. Day Care
     and Early Education 21.1 (1993): 34-35.
```

For a review with no title, give the name of the reviewer followed by *Rev. of* ("Review of"), the work's title, a comma, the word *by*, and the author of the work.

```
Stuttaford, Genevieve. Rev. of Imaginary
     Homelands, by Salman Rushdie. Publishers
     Weekly 1 Mar. 1991: 61.
```

32. Article from Encyclopedia or Reference Volume

Begin with the author's name or with the article's title if no author is named. You need not include the publisher or place of publication for a common reference work or series; instead, note the edition and the date. If entries are arranged alphabetically, you need not note the volume or page(s).

Hansen, Klaus J. "Mormonism." The Encyclopedia

of Religion. Ed. Mircea Eliade. 20 vols.

New York: Macmillan, 1987.

"The History of Western Theatre." The New

Encyclopaedia Britannica: Macropedia. 15th

ed. 1987. Vol. 28.

33. Selection in Anthology or Chapter in Edited Book

List the author of the selection or chapter and give the title in quotation marks (but underline titles of novels, plays, and other works first published on their own). Next, provide the underlined title of the book containing the selection or chapter. If the collection has an editor, follow with the abbreviation *Ed.* and the name(s) of the editor(s) in regular order. Conclude with publication information and the selection's inclusive page numbers.

Atwood, Margaret. "Bluebeard's Egg."

"Bluebeard's Egg" and Other Stories. New

York: Fawcett-Random, 1987. 131-64.

If you are citing the original source for a selection reprinted in a collection, use the phrase *Rpt. in* ("Reprinted in") followed by information about the original source.

Atwood, Margaret. "Bluebeard's Egg."

"Bluebeard's Egg" and Other Stories. New

York: Fawcett-Random, 1987. 131-64. Rpt. in

Don't Bet on the Prince: Contemporary

Feminist Fairy Tales in North America and

England. Ed. Jack Zipes. New York: Methuen,

1986. 160-82.

34. More than One Selection from Anthology or Collection (Cross-Reference)

When you cite two or more works from an anthology or collection, include an entry for the collection and provide cross-references for individual selections.

Howard, Jean E., and Marion F. O'Connor, eds.
     <u>Shakespeare Reproduced: The Text in History</u>
     <u>and Ideology</u>. New York: Methuen, 1987.
Entry for collection.

Erickson, Peter. "The Order of the Garter, the
     Cult of Elizabeth, and Class-Gender
     Tension in <u>The Merry Wives of Windsor</u>."
     Howard and O'Connor 116-42.
Individual selection.

Goldberg, Jonathan. "Speculation: Macbeth and
     Source." Howard and O'Connor 242-64.
Individual selection.

35. Preface, Foreword, Introduction, or Afterword

Indicate whether the selection is a preface, foreword, introduction, or afterword. Give the title of the work and the name of its author, preceded by the word *By*.

Tomlin, Janice. Foreword. <u>The Complete Guide to</u>
     <u>Foreign Adoption</u>. By Barbara Brooke Bascom
     and Carole A. McKelvey. New York: Pocket,
     1997.

36. Letter—Published

Treat the letter writer as the author. Indicate the date or the collection number of the letter if the information is available.

Brevoort, Henry. "To Washington Irving." 9 July
     1828. Letter 124 of <u>Letters of Henry</u>
     <u>Brevoort to Washington Irving</u>. Ed. George
     S. Hellman. New York: Putnam, 1918.

37. Dissertation Abstract

For an abstract of a dissertation published in *Dissertation Abstracts International* (*DAI*) or *Dissertation Abstracts* (*DA*), follow the author's name and the title with the abbreviation *Diss.* (for "Dissertation"), the institution's name, and the date of the degree. Conclude with publication information for the particular volume of abstracts.

> Hawkins, Joanne Berning. "Horror Cinema and the
>
> Avant-Garde." Diss. U of California,
>
> Berkeley, 1993. <u>DAI</u> 55 (1995): 1712A.

3 Field resources and other printed resources

Use the following formats for sources other than books or articles.

38. Interview—Unpublished

Give the name of the person interviewed. Then indicate the type of interview: *Personal interview* (you did the interview in person), *Telephone interview* (you talked to the person over the telephone), or *Interview* (someone else conducted the interview, perhaps on a radio or television program). If a recorded or broadcast interview has a title, give it in place of the word *Interview*. Give the date of the interview or appropriate citation information for a broadcast or address (URL) for electronic source.

> Novak, Robert. Interview with Charlie Rose. <u>The</u>
>
> <u>Charlie Rose Show</u>. PBS. WGBH, Boston. 29
>
> Nov. 1993.
>
> Schutt, Robin. Personal interview. 7 Oct. 1998.

39. Survey or Questionnaire

MLA does not specify a form for these field resources. When citing your own field research, you may wish to use the following format.

> Arrigo-Nelson, Summer, and Jennifer Emily
>
> Figliozzi. Questionnaire on Student
>
> Alcohol Use and Parental Values.
>
> University of Rhode Island, Kingston. 15-
>
> 20 Apr. 1998.

40. Observations

MLA does not specify a form for this type of field research. You may wish to use the following form to cite your notes on field observations.

```
Williams, Keyshawn. Observations of ATM

        Patrons. Aurora, CO. 11 Mar. 1998.
```

41. Letter or Memo—Unpublished

Give the author's name, a brief description (for example, *Letter to Jane Cote*), and the date of the document. For letters addressed to you, use the phrase *Letter to the author*; for letters between other people, give the name and location of any library holding the letter in its collection.

```
Hall, Donald. Letter to the author. 24 Jan. 1990.
```

42. Performance

Following the title of the play, opera, dance, or other performance, supply the name of the composer, director, writer, theater or place of presentation, and city where the performance took place as well as the date (include actors when relevant).

```
For Colored Girls Who Have Considered

        Suicide/When the Rainbow is Enuf. Ntozake

        Shange. Dir. Ntozake Shange. New Federal

        Theater, New York. 20 July 1995.
```

43. Lecture

Identify speaker, title or type of presentation, and details of the meeting, sponsoring group, location, date; include electronic address, if any.

```
Dunkelman, Martha. "Images of Salome in Italian

        Renaissance Art." The Renaissance Woman,

        II. Sixteenth Century Studies Conf., Adams

        Mark Hotel, St. Louis. 11 Dec. 1993.
```

44. Map or Chart

If the source is electronic, conclude with its address (URL).

```
Arkansas. Map. Comfort, TX: Gousha, 1996.
```

45. Cartoon

Provide the cartoonist's name and the title, if any. Include the word *Cartoon* and publication information (or electronic address).

```
Guisewite, Cathy. "Cathy." Cartoon. Providence
     Sunday Journal 23 July 1995: F3.
```

46. Advertisement

Begin with the name of the subject of the advertisement (product, company, or organization). Include the electronic address (URL), if any.

```
Ford Mustang. Advertisement. Elle Sept. 1998:
     158-59.
```

4 Media and electronic resources

47. Film or Videotape

Alphabetize according to the title of the work. The director's name is almost always necessary; names of actors, producers, writers, musicians, or others are needed only if they are important to identification or to your discussion. Include the distributor, the date, and other relevant information including the URL for electronic sources.

```
Rosencrantz and Guildenstern Are Dead. Dir. Tom
     Stoppard. Perf. Gary Oldman, Tim Roth, and
     Richard Dreyfuss. Cinecom Entertainment,
     1990.
```

For a videotape, filmstrip, or similar resource, indicate the medium—*videocassette, videodisc,* and so forth. If the date of the original version is important, add this just before the description of the medium.

```
Rosencrantz and Guildenstern Are Dead. Dir. Tom
     Stoppard. Perf. Gary Oldman, Tim Roth, and
     Richard Dreyfuss. Videocassette. Buena
     Vista Home Video, 1990.
```

48. Television or Radio Program

Begin with the episode title, and use it to alphabetize the entry. Give the program's name and, if they are pertinent to the discussion, include names for writer, director, actors, or others. Use abbreviations for their roles, for example, *Writ.*, *Dir.*, *Prod.*, *Perf.*, *Cond.*, *Introd.*, or *Narr.* Conclude with the URL for an electronic source, if appropriate.

> "Louie and the Nice Girl." Taxi. Dir. James
>
> Burrows. ABC. 11 Sept. 1979.

49. Recording

You can begin the entry with the title of the recording or with the name of the person whose role in the recording you wish to emphasize, for example, the performer, the composer, the conductor, or the speaker. Underline the title of the compact disc, tape, or record. Put the name of a specific work in quotation marks unless the piece is identified by key, form, or number, such as *Symphony in A minor, no. 41.* Continue with performers or others involved, the manufacturer, and the year when the recording was issued. Indicate the medium if it is anything other than a compact disc (for example, *audiocassette,* or *LP* for a record).

> Short, Bobby. Late Night at the Cafe Carlyle.
>
> Telarc, 1987.
>
> Mozart, Wolfgang Amadeus. Symphony no. 40 in G
>
> minor. Vienna Philharmonic. Audiocassette.
>
> Cond. Leonard Bernstein. Deutsche
>
> Grammophon, 1984.

50. Artwork

Give the name of the artist, the title of the work, and the location of the work. Because many museum and gallery names are similar, indicate the city.

> Uccello, Paolo. Saint George and the Dragon.
>
> National Gallery, London.

51. Database: CD-ROM, Diskette, or Magnetic Tape

Databases containing information or texts come in portable forms (such as CD-ROM) or online. Begin entries with author and title, provide publication information about the printed source (if any); give the title of the database or service (underlined), the medium (e.g., *CD-ROM, Online*), the name of the vendor or computer service, and the publication date (for CD-ROM) or date of access (for online sources).

```
Shakespeare, William. All's Well That Ends

     Well. William Shakespeare: The Complete

     Works on CD-ROM. CD-ROM. Abingdon, Eng.:

     Andromeda Interactive, 1994.
```

For abstracts, include information about an article being summarized, the electronic version, and any printed version of the abstract.

```
Blich, Baruch. "Pictorial Representation and Its

     Cognitive Status." Visual Arts Research 15

     (1989): 68-75. Abstract. PsycLIT. CD-ROM.

     SilverPlatter. 3 Mar. 1996.
```

52. Online Source from Computer Service

If you use a source from a service (such as Dialog, Nexis, or Lexis) and the source has been published in print as well as online, cite the source according to the appropriate model (that is, journal, newspaper, or abstract). Add information on the online version, including the name of the database (underlined), the word *Online*, the name of the computer service, and the date of access. Give the elctronic address (URL) or the keyword or topic labels (path) you use to reach it. If you used a service to which a library subscribes (such as EBSCOhost), give the name of the database (underlined), the name of the service, the library, and the date you accessed the source. If you know the electronic address (URL), give it at the end.

```
Blich, Baruch. "Pictorial Representation and

     Its Cognitive Status." Visual Arts

     Research 15 (1989): 68-75. Abstract.

     PsycINFO. Online. Dialog. 9 Sept. 1995.
```

The following models demonstrate the guidelines for citing electronic sources according to the 1999 *MLA Handbook for Writers of Research Papers*. The MLA recommends the following general conventions.

- **Publication dates.** For sources taken from the Internet, include the date the source was posted or last updated or revised; give also the date the source was accessed.

- **Uniform resource locator.** Include a full and accurate **URL** for any source taken from the Internet (with access-mode identifier—*http*, *ftp*, *gopher*, or *telnet*). Enclose the URL in angle brackets ⟨ ⟩. When a URL continues from one line to the next, break it only after a slash. Do not add a hyphen.
- **Page numbering.** Include page or paragraph numbers when given by the source.

53. Online Book

Include the author's name and the title; the name(s) of any editor, compiler, or translator (if relevant); electronic publication information (sponsoring organization and date of publication if the online text has not been published before); information about print publication (if any); date of access; the scholarly project containing the work (if any) and date posted (see following example); and URL.

London, Jack. The Iron Heel. New York:

 Macmillan, 1908. The Jack London

 Collection. 16 Oct. 1996. Berkeley Digital

 Library SunSITE. 1 May 1998 ⟨http://

 sunsite.berkeley.edu/London/Writing/

 IronHeel/⟩.

54. Online Journal Article

Give the author; the title of the article (if any); the name of the periodical; details about the volume, issue, and item number; and date of publication (in parentheses). If the number of pages or paragraphs is available, place a colon after the parentheses containing the date and give the number. Finally, give your access date and add the electronic address in angle brackets.

Sheridan, Judith, and J. Devin McAuley. "Rhythm

 as a Cognitive Skill: Temporal Processing

 Deficits in Autism." Noetica 3.8(1998). 18

 Dec. 1998 ⟨http://www.cs.indiana.edu/

 Noetica/OpenForumIssue8/McAuley.html⟩.

55. Online Magazine Article

Supply the same information required for an online journal article.

```
Anderson, Christopher. "In Search of the
     Perfect Market" The Economist 14 Sept.
     1997. 5 Jan. 1998
     〈http://www.economist.com/
     editorial/freeforall/14-9-97/ec1.html〉.
```

56. Online Newspaper Article

When citing an editorial, a review, or a letter to the editor, indicate it as you would a similar print source. See Entries 29 and 31 for examples. Otherwise supply the author's name, the title of the article, the name of the online version of the newspaper followed by the date of publication, and the date of access and electronic address.

```
Warren, Jennifer. "Assembly Bill Requires
     Parental OK for Body Piercing." Los
     Angeles Times 28 May 1998. 5 Aug. 1998
     〈http://www.aegis.com/aegis/news/lat/
     lt11997/lt970517.html〉.
```

57. Scholarly Project or Reference Database

Begin with the title of the project or database and the name of its editor. (When citing specific material from the project, begin with the author and the title in quotation marks.) Follow with the name of the project or database. Include information such as version number, date of electronic publication or update, and name of any sponsoring institution. Conclude with date of access and electronic address.

```
"Imaging Radar." Ed. Robert Mah. Fact Sheets.
     Aug 1996. NASA Jet Propulsion Laboratory.
     3 Jan. 1999 〈http://www.jpl.nasa.gov/
     facts/〉.
```

58. Online Posting to Discussion Group

Give the name of the author, the title of the posting as in the subject line, and follow it with the label *Online posting*. Next give the date of posting and name of forum. Conclude with date of access and electronic address. For a forwarded posting, give the writer, title, and date of the document, then the phrase *Fwd. by* and the mname of the person forwarding it, followed by the phrase *Online posting,* the date of the posting, name of the forum, and electronic address.

> Harbison, Kimberly S. "Clic-liso Conference."
>
>   Online posting. 5 Mar. 1999. The Discourse
>
>   Studies List. 14 July 1999.
>
>   ⟨DISCOURS@LINGUIST.LDC.UPENN.EDU⟩.

Many discussion groups maintain archives. For your reader's convenience, cite archived versions whenever possible.

> Wooly, Simon. "Re: Hooked on Ebonics?" Online
>
>   posting. 24 Dec. 1996. Philadelphia
>
>   Online: Talk Show. 2 June 1998
>
>   ⟨http://interactive.phillynews.com/
>
>   talk-show/schools postings/199.html⟩.

When citing a Usenet newsgroup, give the information on the author, title, the phrase *Online posting,* and date of posting. Give the date of access. Next, in angle brackets, posting, give the name of the newsgroup, with the prefix *news.*

> Jarvilehto, Timo. "How Far Can Unity of the
>
>   Organism-Environment System Be Maintained?"
>
>   Online posting. 18 Dec. 1998. 19 Dec. 1998
>
>   ⟨news: sci.journals.psycoloquy⟩.

Again, citing an archived posting from a newsgroup is preferable. In that case, give the name of the group after the date of posting and follow the access date with the electronic address.

> Jarvilehto, Timo. "How Far Can Unity of the
>
>   Organism-Environment System Be Maintained?"
>
>   Online posting. 18 Dec. 1998. PSYCOLOQUY.
>
>   18 Dec. 1998 ⟨http://x2.dejanews.com/
>
>   =liszt/getdoc.xp?AN=424430517
>
>   .1&CONTEXT=915464904.1241448542&hitnum=0⟩.

59. Synchronous Communication

When citing material from a MUD, MOO, or other form of synchronous communication, begin with the speaker's name if you are citing only one. Give a description of the event, its date, its forum (e.g., *CollegeTownMOO*), and the date of access. End with the prefix *telnet://* and the electronic address in angle brackets.

```
Finch, Jeremy. Online debate "Can Proust Save

    Your Life?" 3 Apr. 1998. CollegeTownMOO. 3

    Apr. 1998 ⟨telnet://next.cs.bvc.edu.7777⟩.
```

For your readers' convenience, cite an archived version of material from a synchronous communication forum when possible. Provide the same information as above, but substitute the electronic address of the archived version for the electronic address of the forum at the end.

60. Other Electronic Sources

When citing electronic sources other than those explained above (such as a photo, work of art, film, or interview), adapt MLA models for their nonelectronic equivalents. Include the date of access and electronic address.

```
NASA/JPL. "Martian Meteorite." Photo. Views of

    the Solar System: Meteoroids and

    Meteorites. Ed. Calvin J. Hamilton. ⟨http://

    spaceart.com/solar/eng/meteor.htm#views⟩.
```

61. FTP, Telnet, or Gopher Site

For sources obtained through FTP (file transfer protocol), telnet, or gopher, supply information as you would for a similar source obtained via the World Wide Web, with the appropriate electronic address in angle brackets at the end.

```
Lewis, Deanna L., and Ron Chepesuik. "The

    International Trade in Toxic Waste: A

    Selected Bibliography." Electronic Green

    Journal 1.2 (1994). 29 Apr. 1996

    ⟨ftp://uiadaho.edupub/docs/pub/publications/

    EGJ⟩.
```

62. Work in an Indeterminate Medium

If the medium of your electronic source cannot be determined, give the description *Electronic* for the medium and list any information you can about its publication, the network, its sponsoring organization, and the date of access.

> "Red Scare." <u>Almanac of United States History</u>.
>
> Vers. 2.0. 1997. Electronic. Mount
>
> Pleasant Public Library, NY. 18 Dec. 1998.

63. Email

Begin with the writer's name and the title of the communication (in quotation marks), a description of the message including recipient, and the date.

> Smithee, Alan. "The Director Confesses."
>
> E-mail to the author. 17 Sept. 1995.

Note that *e-mail* is spelled with a hyphen in MLA citations.

Exercise

A. Rewrite the following sentences to add MLA-style in-text citations.

1. After the fact, however, Johanson and Edey admitted, "Neither of us was prepared for the explosion of interest that followed the formal disclosure of *afarensis* in print."

   The quotation is from page 294 of Donald Johanson and Maitland Edey's book *Lucy: The Beginnings of Humankind* (New York: Simon & Schuster, 1990).

2. In Samoa during the 1930s, girls separated socially from their siblings at about age seven and began to form close and lasting relationships with other girls their age.

   The reference is to Margaret Mead's discussion in *Coming of Age in Samoa,* originally issued in 1928 and reprinted in 1961 by Morrow Publishers in their Morrow Quill paperback series. It cites the general discussion in Chapter 5, "The Girl and Her Age Group," on pages 59 through 73 of the 1961 edition.

B. Create a list of works cited using MLA style, and include the following items.

1. An article reviewing books on Latin American families. The author is Elizabeth Anne Kuzenesof. Her review is titled "The History of the Family in Latin America." It appeared in the Spring 1989 issue

of *Latin American Research Review* on pages 168–189 (paginated by issue). This issue of the journal was number 2 in volume 24.

2. An interview of Donald Davis published in the October 1992 edition (volume 67) of the *Wilson Library Bulletin*. The interviewer was Judith O'Malley, and the interview appeared on pages 52 and 53. The periodical appears monthly.

3. A book of 280 pages by Vera Rosenbluth titled *Keeping Family Stories Alive*. The subtitle is *A Creative Guide to Taping Your Family Life and Lore*. It was published in 1990 by Hartley and Marks, a publisher in Point Roberts, Washington.

4. A collection of the stories of Shalom Aleichem titled *Around the Table: Family Stories of Shalom Aleichem*. The collection was edited by Aliza Shevron and translated by her. The book was illustrated by Toby Gowing. Scribner Publishers in New York issued the book in 1991. It contains 364 pages.

5. A scholarly article by Beverly Whitaker Long and Charles H. Grant III in volume 41 of the journal *Communication Education*. Volume 41 is dated 1992, and the article runs from page 89 to page 108. The title of the article is "The 'Surprising Range of the Possible': Families Communicating in Fiction."

49e Sample MLA paper

The following paper was written by a student using the MLA documentation style. The *MLA Handbook* recommends beginning a research paper with the first page of the text, using the format shown on Shane Hand's first page. Because his teacher required a title page and an outline as well, he prepared both of these, too. In the margins of the paper is a running commentary on the elements of the paper, from considerations of audience and purpose to organizational strategy, style, and format.

Title page optional

Title catches readers' attention

Place title one-third of the way down the page

```
Waste Disposal:
Have We Put Ourselves in Jeopardy?
```

Center and double-space all lines

```
by

Shane Hand
```

Double-space twice between groups of lines

```
Professor Charlotte Smith

English 1105


6 May 1999
```

Note form of date

Heading for all pages: last name, one space, page number (Roman numerals for outline, Arabic for paper) Hand i

Outline optional; check with instructor

Outline   Center heading
Double-space below heading

49e
MLA

Keep thesis statement short-one or two sentences

<u>Thesis statement</u>: Using landfills as a way to dispose of solid and hazardous wastes is no longer a valid option because we now know of the potential long-term dangers to our soil and groundwater that landfills represent. We must both find new technologies that safely dispose of waste and reduce our own consumption.

Outline uses sentences (rather than topics or phrases); ask instructor's preference

I. Mainly two types of waste pollute our environment: solid and hazardous (toxic).

  A. Most solid waste consists of packaging residues: aluminum cans, glass and plastic bottles, paperboard cartons, and wooden crates.

  B. Most hazardous waste consists of chemical toxins, by-products of manufacturing processes, or ingredients in a wide range of products.

II. Americans are finally becoming aware of the problems with dumping wastes in landfills.

  A. Space is the most obvious problem--people do not want a landfill in their local area.

  B. Pollution of soil and groundwater is a more threatening problem.

Hand ii

III. The key to solving the waste disposal problem
     is public commitment.
     A. People should take political action.
        1. They should urge politicians to pass
           recycling regulations.
        2. They should force businesses to become
Align all entries environmentally responsible.
of same level
        3. They should work to develop local and
           national recycling programs.
     B. People should change their own consumer
        habits.
 IV. A poll shows that most people already have
     changed their consumer habits.
  V. Along with public commitment, new waste
     disposal technologies must also be developed.
     A. Currently, landfills with clay and plastic
        linings reduce leakage into groundwater.
     B. Currently, incineration reduces the amounts
        and toxicity of hazardous wastes.
     C. New technology should not give anyone the
        excuse not to change consumption habits.
        Recycling is still the best approach to
        solving this problem.

1/2" from top

Hand 1

1" from top of page

↕ 1" from top of page

→ Shane Hand

Professor C. Smith

English 1105

6 December 1999

Put information here if you do not include title page

Double-space heading and paper

1" margin on each side

Waste Disposal: Have We Put Ourselves in Jeopardy?

Opens with attention-getting device; reader asks, "What is it?"

indent five spaces 1   A museum in New Jersey is dedicated to it. In California, artists use it to create high-priced sculpture. But no one, absolutely no one, wants to have garbage in his or her backyard. For decades we have buried it and hoped it would just disappear. But banishing it from sight did not get rid of it. Now our sins as a consumer society have come back to haunt us.

Uses we to identify with readers

2   There are many types of wastes polluting our environment. Simply put, they include municipal solid wastes and hazardous wastes. Both of these are a huge problem in the United States. They generally take up space or create a dangerous chemical imbalance. Sometimes both can happen, depending on the waste. Our soils are suffering from these pollutants, and we ourselves are in jeopardy.

Presents topic and stance

3   Solid waste, commonly known as garbage or refuse, is what for years we have calmly thrown away, confidently believing that, by some miracle, it will be collected and will disappear. A significant portion of the solid waste problem stems from packaging residues, specifically containers. Aluminum cans, glass and plastic bottles, paperboard cartons, and wooden crates are

Elaborates on ¶2 Adds definitions

1" bottom margin

thrown away in massive numbers, never to be used

Adds again. An average landfill today consists of six
facts and main types of trash. Paper takes up about 50 percent
statistics by volume; plastic covers are close to 10 percent;

metals take up 6 percent; glass holds 1 percent;

organic materials cover about 13 percent; and about

Cites 20 percent is miscellaneous substances (Rathje 116).
author
and page These numbers may seem meaningless, but when we

think about the nation's daily output of these

materials (500,000 tons), it becomes clear that the

landfills are filling very quickly, so fast that our

soils cannot degrade the waste fast enough to

balance the space with the input. In fact, some

pollutants never degrade.

Defines **4**   The average person assumes that hazardous
solid waste wastes account for a small percentage of today's
in larger environmental problems. However, hazardous wastes
context are generated by almost all sectors of the economy.

These wastes are a general consequence of the

industrialized society in which we live. They

reflect our need for packaging, appliances, cleaning

supplies, beauty aids, pharmaceuticals, and other

manufactured products. As with solid wastes, for

many years toxic wastes were considered safely gone

as soon as they were carted out of sight; as one

report reminds us, however, "As with other

environmental concerns, it is only within the past

twenty to thirty years that the possible adverse

environmental quality and health problems have been

Hand 3

Uses title in citation; author unknown

recognized and addressed" (<u>Hazardous Waste</u> 3). In
the past, hazardous waste disposal was accomplished
in the quickest and least costly manner, frequently
by open dumping and uncontrolled burning. These
practices have been found to present a hazard to
human health and the environment. The magnitude of
this problem can be best presented by totaling the
amount of hazardous wastes produced each year, which
the Office of Technology Assessment puts at about
250 million metric tons (5). As our industrial   *Cites source*
society grows, finding ways to eliminate these   *second time;*
                                                     page
wastes while allowing the same or an improved   *number only*
standard of living should be an overall goal.
                                                          Uses
5   When the land was young, it was wide-open and *generalization*
                                                   to shift from
unspoiled. Yet as the population grew, the spoilage *definitions to*
grew. But the problem has now reached such magnitude *argument*
that Americans are finally becoming concerned about
what happens to their refuse. To some extent this
concern is due to some misconceptions about the
viability of continued landfilling of municipal
solid wastes. One misconception is that the United
States is running out of landfill space. This does
not appear to be the case, as argued by a recent
study done on landfills. According to the study, "at
Uses expert source
     the current rate of landfilling, all the MSW *Uses brackets*
to make key point   *to set off*
[municipal solid waste] generated by the country   *added*
over the next thousand years could easily be   *explanation*
contained within a 30-by-30 mile area using current
landfill technology" (Wiseman 9). However, this does
                    Long quotation might have been paraphrased

not resolve the problem since this idea is impractical. The space problem is distinctly regional, and no one region will consent to be the site for such a landfill. And where landfill siting is most a problem--along the northeastern seaboard, for instance--it is more often due to political opposition than to a lack of available space. This opposition goes back to the "not in my backyard" syndrome.

Moves from topic of space to topic of environmental damage 6   Space is not the only problem these landfills have. There is a grave threat to the environment through the creation of leachate. Leachate is created when surface water contributes to the large amount of water already existing in solid waste. The water percolates through landfills, releasing toxic constituents and heavy metals into soil and groundwater. Leachate is not only dangerous but also expensive since it must be collected, conveyed, stored, treated, and disposed (Organic). It also has the potential to generate gases, including methane, that could have long-term environmentally destructive effects. A more immediate threat is that the gases could cause spontaneous explosions and fires. Even ordinary household items, once they are in landfills, can become hazardous wastes. A

Makes information "real" to readers seemingly innocent bottle of nail polish puts more than six toxic chemicals into a landfill. All of these toxic constituents take hundreds and even thousands of years to disappear.

Hand 5

7   The key to solving the waste problem once and for all is public commitment. The public should urge the politicians to pass recycling regulations and force businesses to become environmentally responsible. Public action must be taken to develop and institute recycling programs on the local and national level. Some may argue that recycling programs are expensive and thus not practical, but isn't our environment more important than a price tag? In other countries, such as Germany, recycling efforts have increased as much as 40 percent (Rathje 120). Funding for these programs comes from the government with the approval of the taxpayers (121). The public can also make a commitment even on a small scale. As seen in the above breakdown of a landfill's contents, at least 50 percent of a landfill's space is occupied by items that can be recycled. Reusing products and refusing to buy products that are not recyclable or do not contain recycled materials are two ways we as consumers can bring about change. All of these ideas will help control the space problem and relieve our soils. These kinds of efforts could be encouraged by local, state and federal governments by increased tax incentives akin to tax reduction programs in place that spur the cleanup and redevelopment of brownfields (Pennsylvania).

8   With these ideas in mind, I turned to the public to find out whether any of these ideas were

Presents one part of two-pronged proposal

Specifies public commitments

practiced or acceptable. I used a survey (Hand, see appendix) which consisted of a series of questions to find out people's habits and attitudes. My results are based on a collection of roughly three *Places* hundred responses. The participants in this survey *complete* were either from the Virginia Tech area or from a *survey form* *in appendix* subdivision in Upper Marlboro, Maryland (my *so it does* hometown). Their ages ranged from about seventeen to *not disrupt* *argument* fifty years old, which provided a wide range for the average consumer. Upon tabulating the responses, I obtained the following results.

Results *could also* *be in a* *table or* *graph*

Already Do

Use coffee mugs instead of polystyrene cups	55%
Reuse plastic wrap, foil, and plastic bags	64%
Recycle newspapers and magazines	46%
Recycle glass	57%
Recycle plastic containers	38%
Recycle aluminum cans	65%

Willing to Do

Take own bags to the store	66%
Shop at a store that's harder to get to but carries biodegradable products	59%
Recycle plastic containers	59%
Pay more for products in low-waste packaging	55%
Pay more for recycled paper	54%

9   It is important to remember that this survey represents only a small region of the United States.

Hand 7

These results could be different in other parts of
the country. It is also possible that my respondents
wanted to make themselves out to be more
environmentally responsible citizens than they
really are. Still, I was favorably surprised by my
results. It seems that many people do take some
steps to preserve the environment and are willing to
take other steps once they are made aware of them.
This demonstrates how important it is to educate the
public about the environment.

*Caution
about results
helps make
presentation
seem
balanced*

10   Of course, along with public commitment, there
must be technological improvement of waste disposal.
Space and toxicity problems in landfills can be
overcome or minimized by state-of-the-art landfill
technology. Landfills lined with clay interposed
between multiple layers of plastic sheeting greatly
reduce the risk of contaminating the groundwater,
especially if they are equipped with a system that
collects and treats the substances that filter to
the bottom of the landfill. Such a system does not
need continuous removal of the substance since
"landfills have an inherent capacity to lessen the
toxicity of the substances introduced or generated
in them" (Wiseman 9). This reduction in toxicity can
also be accelerated by maintaining landfills as
"biochemical" systems. As for the gases created,
they can be collected and even marketed as fuel.

*Presents
second
part of
proposal*

*Specifies
technology
that could
be developed
further*

11   The preferred method for management of
hazardous wastes is waste elimination. If wastes are
not generated as the result of residential,

*Reconnects to
first proposal*

commercial, and industrial actions, disposal is not
necessary. If waste is not eliminated, then steps
should be taken to reduce the amount generated. Due
to extensive research efforts in the past few years,

Specifies more is known about incineration technology than any
another of the other waste management alternatives. For one,
technology incineration provides a high level of toxic control.

The by-product--ash--takes up little space in a
landfill. On the other hand, when the ash by-product
of incineration is placed in a landfill, it returns
some heavy metals and other harmful organic
compounds to the soil (Montague). In addition to the
possible threat to the soil, many suspect that
incineration emissions may contribute to health
problems such as Down syndrome, asthma, and other
respiratory problems in humans as well as premature
deaths and deformaties in farm animals (Farley).
Without a doubt, incineration should play an
increasing role in hazardous waste management.

Repeats 12   Still, though new advances in waste management
need to technology are moving toward resolving this
change
habits in environmental problem, they do not give anybody the
conclusion excuse not to recycle since recycling is far more
beneficial to the environment than any technology.
We, as individuals, neighborhoods, and communities,
need to urge, by example and by political action,

Uses we the federal government to act now. Together, we can
and our to clean up our garbage mess so our country can once
strengthen
appeal to again be healthy and beautiful. We owe it to
readers ourselves as well as to future generations.

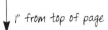

I" from top of page

First line of entry not indented Works Cited *Center heading*
Additional lines indented five spaces

Farley, Rose. "Bottom of the Ninth: Permit Hearings *List sources*
Begin in TXI's Quest to Become the Nation's *mentioned in paper*
Largest Toxic Waste Incinerator." 12-18 Feb. *Double-space*
1998. <u>Dallas News Observer</u>. 19 Jan. 1999
⟨http://www.dallasobserver.com/archives/1998/
021298/news2.html?cat=nfc&query =TXI⟩.

Hand, Shane. Questionnaire on Consumer Habits and
Attitudes Toward Recycling. Blacksburg, VA, and
Upper Marlboro, MD. 21-25 Feb. 1999.

<u>Hazardous Waste Incineration</u>. New York: American
Society of Mechanical Engineers, 1988.

Montague, Peter. "New Study Shows Incinerator Ash More
Dangerous Than We Realized." 29 Aug. 1988.
<u>Rachel's Hazardous Waste News</u> 92. 19 Jan. 1999
⟨http://www.enviroweb.org/pubs/rachel/rhwn092.htm⟩.

Organic Waste Technologies Inc. "Leachate
Evaporation." 19 Jan. 1999
⟨http://www.owtinc.com/leachate_1.htm⟩.

Pennsylvania Department of Environmental Protection.
"Brownfields Tax Incentive." 19 Jan. 1999
⟨http://www.dep.state.pa.us/dep/deputate/
airwaste/wm/landrecy/Tax/tas.htm⟩.

Rathje, William L. "Once and Future Landfills."
<u>National Geographic</u> May 1991: 116-34.

Wiseman, Clark A. "Impediments to Economically
Efficient Solid Waste Management." <u>Resources</u>
105 (1991): 9-11.

49e
MLA

Works Consulted

Brown, Kirk W. <u>Hazardous Waste and Treatment</u>.
        Woburn: Butterworth, 1983.

Bugher, Robert D. <u>Municipal Refuse Disposal</u>.
        Danville: Interstate, 1970.

Farley, Rose. "Bottom of the Ninth: Permit Hearings
        Begin in TXI's Quest to Become the Nation's
        Largest Toxic Waste Incinerator." 12-18 Feb.
        1998. <u>Dallas News Observer</u> 19 Jan. 1999
        ⟨http://www.dallasobserver.com/archives/1998/
        021298/news2.html?cat=nfc&query =TXI⟩.

Includes all works consulted even if not cited in the paper Flack, J. E. <u>Man and the Quality of His Environment</u>.
        Boulder: U of Colorado P, 1967.

Hand, Shane. Questionnaire on Consumer Habits and
        Attitudes Toward Recycling. Blacksburg, VA and
        Upper Marlboro, MD. 21-25 Feb. 1999.

<u>Hazardous Waste Incineration</u>. New York: American
        Society of Mechanical Engineers, 1988.

Montague, Peter. "New Study Shows Incinerator Ash
        More Dangerous Than We Realized." 29 Aug. 1988.
        <u>Rachel's Hazardous Waste News</u> 92. 19 Jan. 1999
        ⟨http://www.enviroweb.org/pubs/rachel/rhwn092
        .htm⟩.

Organic Waste Technologies Inc. "Leachate
        Evaporation." 19 Jan. 1999 ⟨http://www.owtinc
        .com/leachate_1.htm⟩.

Pennsylvania Department of Environmental Protection.
        "Brownfields Tax Incentive." 19 Jan. 1999

⟨http://www.dep.state.pa.us/dep/deputate/
airwaste/wm/landrecy/Tax/tas.htm⟩.

Rathje, William L. "Once and Future Landfills."
National Geographic May 1991: 116-34.

Van Tassel, Alfred J. Environmental Side Effects of
Rising Industrial Output. Lexington: Heath,
1970.

Wiseman, Clark A. "Impediments to Economically
Efficient Solid Waste Management." Resources
105 (1991): 9-11.

Appendix

Intro:

My name is Shane and I am taking a survey in order to study the habits of the average consumer. I am interested in seeing how your habits affect the environment. Please take a few moments to answer some questions.

Survey: *Includes clean copy of any survey, questionnaire, or other primary research document*

Do you . . .

Use coffee mugs instead of polystyrene cups?	Yes	No
Reuse plastic wrap, foil, and plastic bags?	Yes	No
Recycle newspapers and/or magazines?	Yes	No
Recycle glass?	Yes	No
Recycle plastic containers?	Yes	No
Recycle aluminum cans?	Yes	No

Are you willing to . . .

Take your own bags to the store?	Yes	No
Shop at a store that's harder to get to but carries biodegradable products?	Yes	No
Recycle plastic containers?	Yes	No
Pay more for products in low-waste packaging?	Yes	No
Pay more for recycled paper?	Yes	No

50

Documenting Sources: APA

The documentation style developed by the APA (American Psychological Association) identifies the source of information, ideas, or quotations by providing the author's name and the date of publication for the source within the parentheses. For this reason, APA style is often called a name-and-date style. The information in the parenthetical citation enables readers to locate more detailed information about the source in a **reference list** at the end of a paper or report.

Many writing situations call for either the APA style or a name-and-date style loosely based on the APA style but adapted to the needs of specific audiences. APA style can be easily modified and lends itself to informal uses; as a result, it is an important resource for writers looking for a direct, simple documentation system that does not disrupt the reading of a text with detailed information or by requiring readers to turn to a foot- or endnote.

Use **APA** Style in . . .

ACADEMIC SETTINGS

When writing in social science fields such as psychology, sociology, business, economics, education, and political science.

For publications or professional groups requiring use of APA style.

When writing papers for an instructor who requests documentation in a name-and-date style.

WORK AND PUBLIC SETTINGS

For readers whose professions are linked to academic fields in the social sciences (personnel managers, social workers, or school administrators, for example).

continued

> **Use APA Style in, *(continued)***
>
> When you are drawing heavily on research in the social sciences to
> support your paper.
>
> When writers or publications addressing audiences similar to yours
> regularly use APA style or a modified form of the style.
>
> **Consider Using APA Style (perhaps in a modified form) in . . .**
>
> **Work Settings**
>
> In business, because many business audiences prefer a name-and-date
> system, in part because it indicates how current the writer's sources
> are. (Professional audiences often have similar expectations.)
>
> **Public Settings**
>
> When you need a simple, direct system to identify your source and
> its date.

APA documentation style makes the year of publication part of an
in-text citation, as in (*Tannen, 1998*), and gives the date right after the author's name in a reference list to which the in-text citation refers.

> Tannen, D. (1998). The argument culture: Moving
>
>   from debate to dialogue. New York: Random
>
>   House.

For more detailed discussion of this documentation style, consult
the *Publication Manual of the American Psychological Association* (4th ed.,
1994).

50a Using in-text citations

The APA system provides parenthetical citations for quotations,
paraphrases, summaries, and other information in the text of a paper. For
advice on what to document and what not to document, see 46a. For an
APA in-text citation, you include the author's name and the year of publication, separating these items with a comma. You may choose to name the
author (and give the date) either within the parenthetical citation or
within your text.

Author's name inside parentheses. Include the author's name and the
year of publication inside parentheses, separating these items with a
comma. When you are documenting the source of a quotation, follow the
date with a comma, *p.* or *pp.*, and the page number on which the quoted
material appears in the source.

> One recent study points out that while "women radio news directors have exceeded the men in yearly salary, that may not be the case in other radio news positions" (Cramer, 1993, p. 161).

To indicate the specific location of information or the source of paraphrased or summarized material, give the page number of the source.

> In the mid-1960s, Tom Wolfe began writing unconventional and insight-filled essays about American popular culture. Despite his Ph.D. in American Studies from Yale, Wolfe and his work were at first ignored by most intellectuals, both inside and outside universities, who viewed serious or high-brow culture as far more important than popular culture (Aronowitz, 1993, p. 198).

Author's name as part of discussion. When you make an author's name part of the discussion, give the date of the source in parentheses after the name. For quoted or paraphrased material, provide the page number in the source within parentheses following the quotation or paraphrase.

> As Cramer (1993) points out, "Although women radio news directors have exceeded the men in yearly salary, that may not be the case in other radio news positions" (p. 161).

When you supply the author's name and the date in your text or in an in-text citation, your readers will be able to identify a source in the list of references you provide at the end of your paper.

50b Using content footnotes

Occasionally you may wish to expand information presented in the text or discuss a point further without making the main text of your paper more complicated or harder to follow. A content footnote allows you to do this, but you should use such footnotes sparingly because too many footnotes or long footnotes can distract your readers.

To prepare a content footnote, place a number slightly above the line of your text that relates to the footnote information. Make sure that you number the footnotes in your paper consecutively.

TEXT OF PAPER   I tape-recorded all the interviews and later transcribed the relevant portions.[1]

On a separate page at the end of your paper, below the centered heading "Footnotes," present the notes in the order in which they appear in your text. Begin each note with its number, placed slightly above the line. Indent five to seven spaces, the same as a paragraph, for the first line only of each footnote, and double-space all notes.

FOOTNOTE [1]Sections of the recordings were hard to hear and understand because of problems with the tape recorder or background noises. These gaps did not substantially affect information needed for the study.

Your instructor may prefer that you type any footnote at the bottom of the page with the text reference.

50c Creating APA in-text citations

> ### Guide to APA Formats for In-Text Citations
>
> 1. **One Author**
> 2. **Two Authors**
> 3. **Three to Five Authors**
> 4. **Six or More Authors**
> 5. **Corporate or Group Author**
> 6. **No Author Given**
> 7. **Specific Page or Section**
> 8. **Work Cited More than Once**
> 9. **Authors with the Same Last Name**
> 10. **Two or More Sources in a Citation**
> 11. **Personal Communications, Including Interviews and Email**

1. One Author

Supply the author's last name and the date of the publication in parentheses, separated by a comma and a space. If the author's name appears in the text, give only the date in parentheses. If both the name and the date are included in the text, no other information need be cited.

> Mallory's 1995 study of magnet schools confirmed several of the trends proposed earlier (Jacobson, 1989) and also updated the classification by Bailey (1991) based on district demographics.

2. Two Authors

Include both names in citations. In a parenthetical reference, separate the names by an ampersand (&); in the text, use the word *and*.

Part-time workers are usually paid an hourly wage rather than a salary (Mellor & Haugen, 1986). Durstan and Frank (1992) have reviewed the rates at which wages have increased in several major employment fields that include many part-timers.

3. Three to Five Authors

Include all the authors' names, separated by commas, for the first citation. For parenthetical citations use an ampersand (&) rather than *and*.

> Biber, Conrad, and Reppen (1998) point out that "the language you use to write a term paper is different from the language you use when talking to your roommate" (p. 135).

In the second and other following references, give only the first author's name followed by *et al.* (for example, "Biber et al. (1998) present evidence that . . .").

4. Six or More Authors

Give the name of the first author followed by *et al.* in all citations: (*Lichtenberg et al., 1998*). Supply the names of all authors in the reference list at the end of your report.

5. Corporate or Group Author

Spell out the name of an association, corporation, or government agency for the first citation, following with an abbreviation of a cumbersome name within brackets. You may use the abbreviation for later citations.

FIRST CITATION Depression has a number of different causes, some psychological and some physiological or organic (National Institute of Mental Health [NIMH], 1981.)

LATER CITATION The treatments for depressive disorders vary according to the duration and intensity of the condition (NIMH, 1981).

6. No Author Given

Give the title or the first few words of a long title (*The Great Utopia: The Russian and Soviet Avant-Garde, 1915–1932* might appear in a citation as *Great Utopia*).

> Art and design in 1920s Russia mixed aesthetically startling images with political themes and an endorsement of social change (*Great Utopia*, 1992).

7. Specific Page or Section

Indicate the part of the work you are citing: *p.* (for "page"); *chap.* ("chapter"), *fig.* ("figure"), for example. Spell out any words that may be confusing.

> Teenagers who survive suicide attempts experience stages of recovery, and these stages have distinct symptoms (Mauk & Weber, 1991, Table 1).

8. Work Cited More than Once

When you cite the same source more than once in a paragraph, repeat the source as necessary to clarify a specific page reference or show which information comes from one of several sources. If a second reference is clear, do not repeat the date.

> Personal debt has become a significant problem in the past decade. Much of the increase can be linked to the lack of restraint in spending people feel when using credit cards (Schor, 1998, p. 73). The problem is so widespread that "about one-third of the nation's population describe themselves as either heavily or moderately in financial debt" (Schor, p. 72).

9. Authors with the Same Last Name

When your reference list contains works by two different authors with the same last name, provide each author's initials for each in-text citation, both for works by a single author and for works by several authors.

> Scholars have looked in depth at the development of African American culture during slavery and reconstruction (E. Foner, 1988). The role of Frederick Douglass in this process has also been examined (P. Foner, 1950).

10. Two or More Sources in a Citation

If you are summarizing information found in more than one source, include all the sources—names and years—within the citation. Separate the authors and years with commas; separate the sources with semicolons. List sources alphabetically by author (as in your list of references; see p. 701), then oldest to most recent for several sources by the same author.

> Several researchers have found that work performance is affected by personality (Furnham, 1992; Gilmer, 1961, 1977).

11. Personal Communications, Including Interviews and Email

In your text, cite letters, memos, interviews, email, telephone conversations, and similar personal communications by giving the initials and last name of the person, the phrase *personal communication*, and the date. Readers probably will have no access to such sources, so you need not include them in your reference list.

AUTHOR NAMED IN TEXT	According to J. M. Hostos, the state has begun cutting funding for social services duplicated by county agencies (personal communication, October 7, 1995).
PARENTHETICAL REFERENCE	The state has begun cutting funding for social services duplicated by county agencies (J. M. Hostos, personal communication, October 7, 1995).

50d Creating an APA reference list

Immediately after the last page of your paper, you need to provide a list of references to enable readers to identify and consult the sources you have cited in your report.

- **Page format.** One inch from the top margin of a separate page at the end of your report's text (before notes or appendixes), center the heading "References" without underlining or quotation marks.
- **Alphabetizing.** List works cited in the report alphabetically by author or by the first main word of the title if there is no author. Arrange two or more works by the same author from the oldest to the most recent according to year of publication.
- **Spacing.** Double-space all entries and between entries.
- **Indentation.** Do not indent the first line, but indent five to seven spaces for the second and additional lines. *Note:* APA advises indenting the first line of a reference, not the following lines, if you are preparing a paper for publication because publications will adjust the indentation in the printed version. APA also suggests modifying this practice for student papers. We recommend indenting the second and subsequent lines for student papers because readers then can easily see the alphabetical order of the references. Be sure to check your instructor's preferences in academic settings or consider audience preferences when adapting the APA style to work or public settings.

Guide to APA Formats for References

1. BOOKS AND WORKS TREATED AS BOOKS
1. One Author
2. Two or More Authors
3. Corporate or Group Author
4. No Author Given
5. More than One Work by the Same Author
6. More than One Work by the Same Author in the Same Year
7. One or More Editors
8. Translator
9. Edition Other than the First
10. Reprint
11. Multivolume Work
12. Anthology or Collection of Articles
13. *Diagnostic and Statistical Manual of Mental Disorders*
14. Encyclopedia or Reference Work
15. Unpublished Dissertation
16. Government Document

2. ARTICLES AND SELECTIONS FROM BOOKS
17. Article in Journal Paginated by Volume
18. Article in Journal Paginated by Issue
19. Special Issue of Journal
20. Article in Popular Magazine (Weekly or Biweekly)
21. Article in Popular Magazine (Monthly)
22. Article with No Author Given

23. Article in Newspaper
24. Letter to the Editor or Editorial
25. Interview—Published
26. Review with a Title
27. Review Without a Title
28. Article from Encyclopedia or Reference Work
29. Chapter in Edited Book or Selection in Anthology
30. Dissertation Abstract

3. OTHER PRINTED AND FIELD RESOURCES
31. Report
32. Interview—Unpublished
33. Personal Communication
34. Paper Presented at a Meeting
35. Unpublished Raw Data

4. MEDIA AND ELECTRONIC RESOURCES
36. Film or Videotape
37. Television or Radio Program
38. Recording
39. Database or Information Service
40. Online Source or Archived Listserv
41. World Wide Web Page
42. Online Scholarly Article
43. Online Newspaper Article
44. Online Abstract
45. CD-ROM Abstract
46. Computer Program

1 Books and works treated as books

MODEL FORMAT FOR BOOKS AND WORKS TREATED AS BOOKS

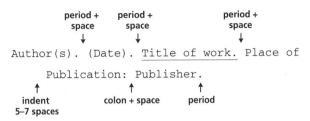

- **Author(s).** Give the author's last name followed by a comma and the initials of the first and middle names. For a book with more than one author, use the same inverted order for each author. Separate the names with commas, using an ampersand before the final name.
- **Date.** Provide the year of publication (in parentheses) followed by a period.
- **Title of work.** Give the title followed by a period, and underline both the title and the period. Use a capital only for the first word of the main title, the first word of any subtitle, and any proper nouns.
- **Publication information.** For U.S. publishers, give the city and state followed by a colon and a space; then supply the publisher's name, leaving out unnecessary words such as *Inc.* or *Publishers.* Abbreviate the name of the state using the standard postal abbreviation. You do not need to name the state for the following familiar publishing locations: Baltimore, Boston, Chicago, Los Angeles, New York, Philadelphia, and San Francisco. For publishers outside the United States, give the city and the abbreviated name of the country. No country is needed for these familiar locations: Amsterdam, Jerusalem, London, Milan, Moscow, Paris, Rome, Stockholm, Tokyo, and Vienna.
- **Spacing.** Double-space all entries, and indent five to seven spaces, the same indentation that you choose for paragraphing, for the second and any additional lines. Note that APA style advises indenting the first line of a reference, not the following lines, if you are preparing a paper for publication. Then the publication will adjust the indentation in the printed version. We recommend indenting lines following the first in your course papers because readers then can easily see the alphabetical order of the references. Be sure to ask your instructor's preferences and follow any specific directions carefully.

1. One Author

> Wilson, W. J. (1996). <u>When work disappears: The
>
> world of the new urban poor.</u> New York:
>
> Knopf.

2. Two or More Authors

List each author's last name first, followed by first and middle initials.

> Biber, D., Conrad, S., & Reppen, R. (1998).
>
> <u>Corpus linguistics: Investigating language</u>
>
> <u>structure and use.</u> Cambridge: Cambridge
>
> University Press.

3. Corporate or Group Author

Treat the organization or agency responsible for the work as an individual author, and alphabetize by the first main word. When author and publisher are the same, give the word *Author* following the place of publication instead of repeating the name.

> U.S. Department of Commerce. (1996). <u>Statistical</u>
>
> <u>abstract of the United States.</u> Washington,
>
> DC: U.S. Government Printing Office.

4. No Author Given

Give the title first, then the date. Use the first significant word of the title to alphabetize the entry.

> <u>Boas anniversary volume: Anthropological papers</u>
>
> <u>written in honor of Franz Boas.</u> (1906).
>
> New York: Stechert.

5. More than One Work by the Same Author

List works in chronological order. Include the author's name in each entry.

> Aronowitz, S. (1973). <u>False promises: The</u>
>
> <u>shaping of the American working class.</u> New
>
> York: McGraw-Hill.

Aronowitz, S. (1993) <u>Roll over Beethoven: The</u>
<u>return of cultural strife.</u> Hanover, NH:
Wesleyan University Press.

If the same lead author has works with different co-authors, alphabetize these entries based on the last names of the second authors.

6. More than One Work by the Same Author in the Same Year

List in alphabetical order works appearing in the same year by the same author. Add lowercase letters after dates (e.g., *1992a, 1992b*). Alphabetize by the first main word in the title. For in-text citations, provide both the date and the letter (*Gould, 1987b*).

Gould, S. J. (1987a). <u>Time's arrow, time's</u>
<u>cycle: Myth and metaphor in the discovery</u>
<u>of geological time.</u> Cambridge, MA: Harvard
University Press.

Gould, S. J. (1987b). <u>An urchin in the storm:</u>
<u>Essays about books and ideas.</u> New York:
Norton.
Alphabetized under *urchin,* **not** *An.*

7. One or More Editors

Include (*Ed.*) or (*Eds.*) after the name(s) of the editors.

Beckman, L., & Harvey, S. M. (Eds.). (1998).
<u>The new civil war: The psychology,</u>
<u>culture, and politics of abortion.</u>
Washington, DC: American Psychological
Association.

8. Translator

Include the translator's name, in normal order, after the title, followed by *Trans.*

Leontev, A. N. (1978). <u>Activity, consciousness,</u>
<u>and personality</u> (M. J. Hall, Trans.).
Englewood Cliffs, NJ: Prentice Hall.

9. Edition Other than the First

Include information about the specific edition in parentheses after the title (for example, *Rev. ed.* for "revised edition" or *3d ed.* for "third edition").

Gilmer, B. (1975). Applied psychology:

　　　Adjustments in living and work (Rev. ed.).

　　　New York: McGraw-Hill.

10. Reprint

Frankfort, H., Frankfort, H. A., Wilson, J. A.,

　　　Jacobsen, T., & Irwin, W. A. (1977). The

　　　intellectual adventure of ancient man: An

　　　essay on speculative thought in the

　　　ancient Near East. Chicago: University of

　　　Chicago Press. (Original work published

　　　1946)

11. Multivolume Work

Include the names of the editors or authors, making sure you indicate if they are editors. Then provide the inclusive years of publication. If the work is a revised edition or has a translator, give this information after the title. Then identify in parentheses the volumes you are using for your paper.

Strachey, J., Freud, A., Strachey, A., & Tyson,

　　　A. (Eds.). (1966-1974). The standard

　　　edition of the complete psychological works

　　　of Sigmund Freud (J. Strachey et al.,

　　　Trans.) (Vols. 3-5). London: Hogarth Press

　　　and the Institute of Psycho-Analysis.

12. Anthology or Collection of Articles

Give the name of the editor(s) first, followed by the abbreviation *Ed.* or *Eds.* in parentheses.

Cobley, P. (Ed.). (1996). The communication

　　　theory reader. London: Routledge.

Ghosh, A., & Ingene, C. A. (Eds.). (1991).

> Spatial analysis in marketing: Theory,
>
> methods and applications. Greenwich, CT:
>
> JAI.

13. *Diagnostic and Statistical Manual of Mental Disorders*

The manual known in short form as the *DSM-IV* is widely cited in fields such as psychology, social work, and psychiatry because its definitions and guidelines often have legal force and determine patterns of treatment. Because of the volume's importance, the APA *Publication Manual* recommends the following specific form for the entry.

American Psychiatric Association. (1994).

> Diagnostic and statistical manual of
>
> mental disorders (4th ed.). Washington,
>
> DC: Author.

In your text, following an initial full citation, you may use the standard abbreviations for this work: *DSM-III* (1980), *DSM-III-R* (1987), or *DSM-IV* (1994).

14. Encyclopedia or Reference Work

Kruskal, W. H., & Tanur, J. M. (1978).

> International encyclopedia of statistics
>
> (Vols. 1-2). New York: Free Press.

15. Unpublished Dissertation

Conrad, S. (1996). Academic discourse in two

> disciplines: Professional writing and
>
> student development in biology and
>
> history. Unpublished doctoral
>
> dissertation, Northern Arizona University,
>
> Flagstaff.

16. Government Document

```
Select Committee on Aging, Subcommittee on

     Human Services, House of Representatives.

     (1991). Grandparents' rights: Preserving

     generational bonds (Com. Rep. No. 102-

     833). Washington, DC: U.S. Government

     Printing Office.
```

2 Articles and selections from books

MODEL FORMAT FOR ARTICLES AND SELECTIONS

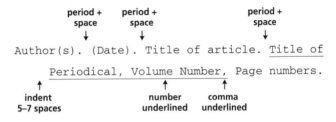

- **Author(s).** Give the author's last name and initials followed by a period and a space.
- **Date.** Supply the date in parentheses followed by a period and a space.
- **Title of article.** Give the article title, capitalizing only the first word (and the first word of any subtitle along with any proper names). Do not use quotation marks with the title. End with a period and a space.
- **Title of journal, periodical, or book.** Give the journal title (underlined, with all main words capitalized), the volume number (also underlined), and the page numbers. Use commas to separate these, and underline the comma following the title.
- **Spacing.** Double-space all entries, and indent five to seven spaces, the same indentation that you choose for paragraphing, for the second and any additional lines (see p. 701).

17. Article in Journal Paginated by Volume

You do not have to include the particular issue number because page numbers run continuously throughout the different issues making up a volume.

Eisenberg, A. R., & Garvey, C. (1981).
Children's use of verbal strategies in
resolving conflicts. Discourse Processes,
4, 149-170.

Iran-Nejad, A., McKeachie, W. J., & Berliner.
D. C. (1990). The multisource nature of
learning: An introduction. Review of
Educational Research, 60, 509-515.

Macklin, M.C. (1996). Preschoolers' learning of
brand names from visual cues. Journal of
Consumer Research, 23, 251-261.

Supply the names of all the authors in the entry in the reference list. In-text references should give only the name of the first author followed by *et al.*, as in (*Albertini et al., 1986*).

18. Article in Journal Paginated by Issue

When each issue of a journal begins with page 1, include the issue number in parentheses immediately (with no space) after the volume number. Do not underline the issue number.

Wurzbacher, K. V., Evans, E. D., & Moore, E. J.
(1991). Effects of alternative street
school on youth involved in prostitution.
Journal of Adolescent Health, 12(7),
549-554.

19. Special Issue of Journal

Begin with the special issue's editor (if other than the regular editor); otherwise, place the title at the beginning, then the date. Indicate in brackets that it is a special issue. You need not include page numbers.

Balk, D. E. (Ed.). (1991). Death and adolescent
bereavement [Special issue]. Journal of
Adolescent Research, 6(1).

20. Article in Popular Magazine (Weekly or Biweekly)

Supply the same information as you would for an article in a monthly magazine (see Entry 21), but add the specific date.

```
Adler, J. (1995, July 31). The rise of the
     overclass. Newsweek, 126, 33-34, 39-40,
     43, 45-46.
```
When an article is continued, list all the different pages, separated by commas.

21. Article in Popular Magazine (Monthly)

Include the month and year of the magazine. Spell out months. Add the volume number and pages. If there is no author, put the title first, before the date.

```
Dold, C. (1998, September). Needles and nerves.
     Discover, 19, 59-62.
```

22. Article with No Author Given

Begin the entry with the article's title, and alphabetize using the first main word in the title.

```
True tales of false memories. (1993, July/
     August). Psychology Today, 26, 11-12.
```

23. Article in Newspaper

Use *p.* or *pp.* to introduce the section and page numbers for newspaper articles. If no author is given, put the title first.

```
Murtaugh, P. (1998, August 10). Finding a brand's
     real essence. Advertising Age, p. 12.
```

24. Letter to the Editor or Editorial

Treat a letter to the editor like another newspaper article, but label it in brackets.

```
Bryant, K. (1995, July 16). Lawyers should push
     for early settlements of lawsuits [Letter to
     the editor]. San Jose Mercury News, p. 6C.
```

25. Interview—Published

Although APA does not specify a form for published interviews, you may wish to employ the following form, which is similar to other APA references.

> Kosek, J. (1993). A different type of
>
>   environmentalist: Ka-Kisht-Ke-Is (Chief
>
>   Simon Lucas) [Interview]. Cultural
>
>   Survival Quarterly, 17(1), 19-20.

26. Review with a Title

Following the title of the review, indicate in brackets the kind of work (*book, film, video program, television program,* and so on) and the title (underlined) of the work being reviewed.

> Stolarz-Fantino, S., & Fantino, E. (1985).
>
>   Cognition and behavior analysis [Review of
>
>   the book Judgment, decision, and choice].
>
>   Journal of the Experimental Analysis of
>
>   Behavior, 54, 317-322.

27. Review Without a Title

Begin with the name of the reviewer. If the review article does not have a title, substitute a description in brackets consisting of the phrase *Review* followed by the type of material and the title of the book, film, television show, or other topic of the review.

> Van Meter, E. J. (1994). [Review of the book
>
>   Preparing tomorrow's school leaders:
>
>   Alternative-designs]. Educational
>
>   Administration Quarterly, 30, 112-117.

28. Article from Encyclopedia or Reference Work

If no author is identified, begin with the title of the article. Use *In* before the work's title, and follow it with the volume and page numbers.

> Chernoff, H. (1978). Decision theory. In
>
>   International encyclopedia of statistics
>
>   (Vol. 1, pp. 131-135). New York: Free Press.

29. Chapter in Edited Book or Selection in Anthology

For a selection from an anthology, begin with the author's name, the year the book was published, and the title of the selection. Following the word *In,* cite the editors, the title of the collection, and the page numbers.

> Shepard, W. O. (1991). Child psychology:
>
> Identity and interaction. In J. H. Cantor,
>
> C. C. Spiker, & L. P. Lipsitt (Eds.),
>
> Child behavior and developmental training
>
> for diversity (pp. 236-257). Norwood, NJ:
>
> Ablex.

30. Dissertation Abstract

> Yamada, H. (1989). American and Japanese topic
>
> management strategies in business
>
> conversations. Dissertation Abstracts
>
> International, 50(09), 2982B.

If you consult the dissertation on microfilm, give the University Microfilms number at the end of the entry in parentheses: (*University Microfilms No. AAC--9004751*).

3 Other printed and field resources

31. Report

Begin with the name of the author, whether an individual or a group or government agency. If the agency also publishes the report, use the word *Author* in the publication information instead of repeating the group's name.

> Advisory commission to study the Consumer Price
>
> Index. (1996). Toward a more accurate
>
> measure of the cost of living. Washington,
>
> DC: Senate Finance Committee.

If the report has a number, give it in parentheses after the title with no punctuation between the title and parentheses. When several numbers are listed in the report, choose the one most likely to help readers obtain the document.

32. Interview—Unpublished

To refer to an interview you have conducted yourself, provide the information only as part of an in-text citation such as the following: (*R. Gelles, personal communication, September 14, 1993*). (See no. 33, below.)

33. Personal Communication

Letters, email, electronic discussion group postings, telephone conversations, and similiar communications cannot be consulted by your readers, so do not include them in your reference list. Instead, cite them in text. (See p. 701 and no.32, above for examples.)

34. Paper Presented at a Meeting

For an unpublished paper presented at a conference or symposium, include the month as well as the year, and list both the name and location of the meeting.

```
Nelson, J. S. (1993, August). Political
     argument in political science: A
     meditation on the disappointment of
     political theory. Paper presented at the
     annual meeting of the American Political
     Science Association, Chicago.
```

35. Unpublished Raw Data

When you use data from field observations, a survey, or similar kinds of research, briefly describe the contents of the data within brackets following the date. Conclude the entry with the phrase *Unpublished raw data*.

```
Williams, S. (1995). [Survey of student
     attitudes toward increased library fees].
     Unpublished raw data.
```

4 Media and electronic resources

36. Film or Videotape

Begin with the name or names of the people primarily responsible for the work, and indicate each person's role (for example, *Director* or *Producer*) in parentheses following the name. Underline the title, and then indicate the medium (for example, *film, videotape,* or *slides*) in brackets. At the end of the entry, within parentheses, indicate the location and name of the distributor (for example, *WGBH, Boston*). If the distributor is not well known, supply the address.

```
Simon, T. (Producer), & LeBrun, N. (Writer).

    (1986). Atocha: Quest for treasure

    [videotape]. (Available from Columbia

    Tristar Home Video, 3400 Riverside Drive,

    Burbank, CA 91505-4627)
```

37. Television or Radio Program

Begin the entry for a series of programs with the name of the script writer, the producer, the director, or any other person whose role you wish to indicate. Give the title of the program or series (underlined). Conclude with the location and name of the network or channel responsible for the broadcast.

```
Moyers, B. (Executive Editor). (1993). Bill

    Moyers' journal. New York: WNET.
```
Television series.

For a specific episode in a series, indicate the director in parentheses immediately following the title; then indicate the producer before the title of the series.

```
Moyers, B. A. (1993). A life together (D.

    Grubin, Director). In D. Grubin

    (Producer), Bill Moyers' journal. New

    York: WNET.
```
Single episode of television series.

38. Recording

Begin by giving the name of the writer and the date of copyright (in parentheses). Following the song title, supply the name of the recording artist in brackets, if this is someone other than the writer. Indicate the medium in brackets after the album title; include a number for the recording within the brackets if one is necessary for identifying the recording and obtaining a copy.

```
Freeman, R. (1994). Porscha [Recorded by R.

    Freeman & The Rippingtons]. On Sahara

    [CD]. New York: GRP Records.
```

50d
APA

39. Database or Information Service

Include the order number at the end of the citation.

Maher, F., & Tetreault, M. K. T. (1992). Inside
feminist classrooms: An ethnographic
approach. New Directions for Teaching and
Learning, 49, 57-74. (ERIC Document
Reproduction Service No. ED 443 234)

Schroeder, E. (1988). Therapy for the
chemically dependent family. Journal of
Chemical Dependency Treatment [On-line],
2(1). Available: DIALOG File: Journal
Chemical Dependency

Cite an abstract from an online information service (such as
Lexis/Nexis) according to the following model.

Sack, K. (1995, July 14). House panel to draft
bill requiring AIDS tests of newborns [On-
line]. The New York Times, p. A15.
Abstract from: Lexis/News/CURNWS

40. Online Source or Archived Listserv

Give the name of the author and in parentheses the date the message was posted, followed by a period. Next write the title of the message
from the subject line and in brackets a description of the message. Finally,
write the words *Retrieved from the World Wide Web* (or other Internet
source) with the date of retrieval, a colon, and the electronic address.

Morrison, A. (1998, September 11).
Chlorabucimil [Newsgroup posting].
Retrieved December 20, 1998, from the
World Wide Web: http://www.acor.org/lists/
cancer/ws/98/09/2/0078.html

41. World Wide Web Page

Include the information specified in Entry 40.

```
Ringertz, N. (1998, December 2). Alfred Nobel's
     health and his interest in medicine.
     [Essay posted on Web site The Electronic
     Nobel Museum Project]. Retrieved December
     31, 1998, from the World Wide Web: http://
     www.nobel.se/alfred/ringertz/index.html
```

42. Online Scholarly Article

Begin with the author(s) and the date of posting. Add the title, list the source with the volume and issue numbers, and list the page numbers if given. Then indicate the medium and the date of retrieval. Conclude with the availability information needed to find the source.

```
Sheridan, J., & McAuley, J. D. (1998). Rhythm
     as a cognitive skill: Temporal processing
     deficits in autism. Noetica, 3, 8.
     Retrieved December 31, 1998, from the
     World Wide Web: http://www.cs.indiana.edu/
     Noetica/OpenForumIssue8/McAuley.html
```

43. Online Newspaper Article

Begin with as much information as possible that would be provided for a printed source. Add the words *Retrieved from the World Wide Web* and give the date of retrieval, a colon, and the electronic address.

```
Sonner, S. (1998, December 31). Psychologist
     ponders horse killer. Washington Post
     Online [Newspaper, selected stories on
     line]. Retrieved December 31, 1998, from
     the World Wide Web: http://search
     .washingtonpost.com/wp-srv/WAPO/19981231/
     V000412-123198-idx.html
```

44. Online Abstract

For an abstract, give the source of the original work and the location of the abstract.

Globus, G. (1995, August). Quantum

    consciousness is cybernetic [Abstract].

    PSYCHE, 2(12). Retrieved January 8, 1998,

    from the World Wide Web:

    http://psyche.cs.monash.edu.au/ v2/

    psyche-2-12-curran.html

45. CD-ROM Abstract

Schroeder, E. (1988). Therapy for the

    chemically dependent family [CD-ROM].

    Journal of Chemical Dependency, 2, 95-129.

    Abstract from: SilverPlatter File: PsycLIT

    Item: 76-37924

46. Computer Program

In brackets after the title, identify the source as a computer program, a computer programming language, or computer software. If the program's author owns specific rights to it, begin the entry with the author's name. Otherwise, begin with the name of the material. Give the location and name of the organization producing the program. Add any version number or retrieval information at the end in parentheses unless it is part of the title.

Family tree maker [Computer software]. (1993).

    Fremont, CA: Banner Blue Software.

    (Windows version)

Exercise

A. Turn to Exercise A in Chapter 49. Rewrite the sentences supplied there to add in-text citations in APA style.

B. Turn to Exercise B in Chapter 49. Rewrite the items supplied there to create a list of references in APA style.

C. Working with a partner or a small group, compare your answers to Exercise A and B above. Correct any errors in your answers, using your handbook or your instructor's advice to resolve any differences of opinion.

50e Sample APA Paper

Supply abbreviated title (50 characters maximum) for heading

Running head: CYCLISTS

Cyclists 1

Number title page and all others using short title

Center title and all other lines

Competitive Cyclists: Who Are They?

Supply name and institution

Steven King

University of Rhode Island

Double-space twice between groups of lines

Ask your instructor if instructor's name, course name, and date are necessary

Professor Hasan Danesh

Sociology 150

Section 10

November 24, 1998

Use short title Cyclists 2
and page number

50e
APA

Center heading

Abstract

Supply one ¶ and do not indent

Cyclists at a race were asked to fill out a *Double-space abstract and* questionnaire about attitudes toward cycling, *rest of paper* demographics, and self-perception of social status. Responses to the questionnaire provided general *Summarize paper in no* support for an initial hypothesis regarding the low *more* level of women's participation in competitive *than about 120* cycling but not for a hypothesis regarding enjoyment *words* of extreme physical exertion and pain as a reason for undertaking competitive cycling. In addition, the responses suggested further hypotheses concerning the relative lack of participation by cyclists under 25 years old and the likelihood that people of different ages, marital status, and levels of education undertake competitive cycling for different reasons.

Besides the abstract, typical sections in an APA paper are Introduction, Method, Results, and Discussion

First part is introduction but no heading is used

↕ *1" top margin*

Indent ¶ five to seven spaces;

Repeat and center title

Competitive Cyclists: Who Are They?   *be consistent for ¶s and references*

Use introduction to present problem or subject, background information, and hypothesis or guiding question

1   Bicycle riding is the third most popular participant sport in the United States, with an estimated 55.3 million people riding a bike at least once a year (Interbike, 1992) for varying reasons and with widely differing perspectives (Worthington, 1998; Meyer, 1997; Zimberoff, 1996). Another report, from the Bicycle Institute of America (1990), estimates that 25 million American adults ride a bicycle an average of once a week. That same survey indicates that 220,000 adults took part in bicycle races during the year, or less than 1% of those who ride frequently.

Citation uses to no aut

1" margin each side

2   In this paper I report on a group of people who entered a particular bicycle race. I collected data through a survey taken at the race. The survey asked for demographic data as well as information about level of commitment and motivation. I then summarized and analyzed the data. Although the purpose of my study was primarily descriptive, I also was able to estimate the kind of support available for two hypotheses I developed before beginning the study. In addition, the study suggested several more hypotheses useful for further research.

[The introduction goes on to provide background information on competitive cycling as a sport.]

Explains how the study was carried out   Method   *Center section heading*

Follows general APA practice, discussing subjects, materials, and procedure for the study

3   I gathered the data for this paper at a bicycle race held in Westerly, Rhode Island, on Sunday, September 27, 1998. Called "The First Annual Charlestown 40 Kilometer Time Trial," the

↕ *1" bottom margin*

50e
APA

event consisted of each entrant riding the course individually "against the clock." The course was on smoothly paved roads and was relatively flat. There were 37 entrants, 34 male and 3 female. *Supplies cross-reference to survey in Appendix*

4   The respondents filled out a survey (see Appendix) after they had completed the event and were waiting for the results. I circulated through the parking area and asked the entrants to go to the registration table and complete the survey. My original plan was to have the entrants complete the survey prior to the race at registration. My goal was a 100% response. As it worked out, I achieved an 88% response rate (32 of 36 possible respondents; I was the 37th entrant).

5   The questionnaire requested basic demographic information including a question regarding self-perception of social status. It also asked respondents to rate their cycling ability and indicate how many years they had been active in cycling competition. A question about the distance traveled to get to the race was intended to provide some indication of the level of commitment to cycling competition. Traveling a substantial distance to the race involves a considerable time commitment and willingness to pay for transportation and meals in addition to race entry fees. A final open-ended question asked for three to five reasons why the respondent entered competitive cycling events.

50e
APA

Provides theoretical background for study and context for methods and conclusions; Literature Review section often follows Introduction

Literature Review

6   The factors motivating competitive cyclists do not appear to be a major issue in sociology or psychology at the present time. No journal articles that deal directly with the topic were found. Nonetheless, articles on body image, weight loss, and health risk-taking provide useful background for the present study.

7   In an article relating body image and exercise, David and Cowles (1991) make interesting comparisons between men and women and between younger and older men. Older men (over 25) and women of all ages are likely to desire to lose weight when asked to consider their own bodies. Women are far more dependent on dieting to lose weight than men, who seem more likely to exercise. Drewnowski and Yee (1987) also emphasize the tendency of women to turn to dieting and of men to turn to exercise in order to control weight. Schneider and Greenberg (1992) found that participants in individual sports such as swimming, jogging, tennis, and cycling tend to take fewer behavioral health risks in other aspects of their lives than do participants in team sports.

8   A physiological study of the determinants of endurance in well-trained cyclists found that cyclists with 5 or more years of cycling experience had superior endurance compared to similarly trained cyclists with 2 to 3 years of experience (Coyle, Coggan, Hopper, & Walters, 1988). This study suggests a link between performance and years of

Cite up to five authors in first reference to a work

cycling experience. Because responses to the survey were anonymous, this study was unable to test the hypothesis by linking experience to performance in the race.

Section added to discuss hypotheses in detail

Hypotheses

9   This study was intended to be descriptive and to produce hypotheses for further research rather than test them. Nonetheless, I began the study with two tentative hypotheses designed to help interpret the data. On the basis of my experience with cycling, I predicted that the percentage of women entrants in the race would be approximately 10% and would not exceed 20%. In addition, on the basis of my experience and my reading about cycling (Matheny, 1986), I predicted that a common response to the survey question on motivation would be a half-humorous suggestion of "love of pain" or "love of suffering." Pain and suffering in fact can be powerful if complex motivators in sport. Members of one bicycling group who race to remind the public about the effects of asbestos and toxic chemicals explain:

> We tell the public that the temporary pain
> we experience racing bicycles is nothing
> like the pain a mesothelioma or cancer
> patient faces every hour of every day. As
> bike racers, we choose to suffer swollen
> legs and burning legs when climbing
> mountains or sprinting for the win. We
> know that a terminal asbestos patient does

> not have this choice--his pain and anguish
> was [sic] forced upon him and his family.
> We do not take our health for granted!
> (Worthington, 1998)

This study aims to discover whether motivations of
this sort are widespread.

Provides detailed summary of
questionnaire responses

Results

10　　The gender split among respondents was 93.8%
male and 6.3% female. This closely matches the overall
registration proportion of 92.3% male and 7.7% female.
The mean age of respondents was 36.6 years, ranging
from a low of 16 to a high of 62. Only 1 entrant was
under 25 while 5 were over 50. Just under half (46.9%)
the respondents indicated they were married. No
respondents indicated a household size of 6 or more.
Education level was quite high middle class.

11　　The question rating level of cycling ability
brought about a respondent-created category. Three
respondents felt so torn between the intermediate
and advanced categories that they drew a large
circle around both. If only one person had done
this, I would have made an assignment based on other
criteria, but with 3 out of 32 choosing this option,
I decided to label it an additional category. There
was also one crossed-out and re-circled response to
this question, indicating that at least one more
person had difficulty with the distinction between
the two categories.

Detailed
information
could be
presented in table or chart

12　　The mean number of seasons involved with
competitive cycling was 4.2 years, ranging from 1 (5

cases) to 10 years (5 cases). Many of the athletes
probably had experience in other aerobic sports prior
to or overlapping with cycling. A high proportion
(71.9%) of the respondents traveled over 50 miles one
way to enter a race within the past year. Over two-
thirds (69.2%) of those who traveled this distance did
so with some frequency, four or more times during 1992.

13   The open-ended question regarding reasons for
entering bicycle races produced 22 different *Includes results*
that do not support
responses. The most popular cluster was enjoyment of *hypothesis*
competition at 75%, followed by enjoyment of
training at 59%, friendship with other cyclists at
40%, and health benefits of cycling at 31.3%.

Analyzes results and their Discussion
implications

14   In terms of the number of seasons of cycling
experience, those respondents older than the mean of
36.6 years averaged exactly twice as many years'
experience as those younger than the mean (5.8 years to
2.9 years). Only one cyclist (7%) over age 36 was in
the first year of competition, while four (22.2%) age *Might be*
organized
36 or under were in the first year. More of the young *more clearly*
riders traveled 50 miles to a race (77% to 64%), but *to correspond*
the older riders who did travel did so more frequently *with*
questionnaire
than their younger counterparts. Only 2 (11.2%) of the *items or*
younger group traveled 7 or more times, compared to 6 *previous*
discussion
(42.8%) of the older group. It seems that perhaps the
older group is more committed one way or the other--to
travel and compete regularly or to stay home.

15   Due to the low number of female
entrants/respondents, it is not appropriate to make

statistical comparisons between male and female respondents. I will say, though, that the responses of the 2 women who completed the survey show little to distinguish them from the male respondents. It may be that this particular survey did not bring out gender-based differences, or it may be that the cycling experience transcends gender. The data are too slim to support even a preliminary conclusion.

Explores relationships among answers, suggesting tentative conclusions and research issues

16   Drawing on the results, I compared married respondents to all others. I found that married racers tend to live in larger households, with 53.3% living in households of 3 or more versus 17.6% of the nonmarried group. Of interest is that there are no beginning-level cyclists among the married respondents but 25% among the nonmarried group. It is tempting to hypothesize that married people are less likely to take up a new competitive sport such as bicycle racing, but I'm restrained by personal knowledge of many cyclists who have started competing after being married. Married people also mentioned health benefits as a reason for competing more frequently than nonmarrieds (53.3% to 12.5%). Health benefits were also more important to older cyclists (42%) than younger cyclists (22%).

Continues discussion of relationships discovered through analysis of results

17   There was no apparent relationship between age and marital status. The mean age of the entire sample (36.635) and the mean age of the married cyclists (36.60) is within .035 years. When I controlled for marital status (married) and household size (3 or more), I discovered a drop in the percentage that

travel from 66.7% to 50%. Both respondents who
mentioned cycling as a stress release are married and
in a larger household. By the same token, there was
almost perfect agreement between these age and
marital status subgroups and the entire sample on the
two most popular reasons for competing, enjoyment of
competition and enjoyment of the training process.

18 Splitting the group on the basis of level of
education showed that 90% of those with no college
degree traveled 50 miles to a race at least once. But
only 1 (10%) mentioned racing for fun and only 1
(10%) mentioned racing for health benefits while 40%
mentioned competing to achieve personal goals. Health
(40%) and fun (31%) were both more important among
those with a college degree while achievement of
personal goals was relatively less important (13.6%).

[The discussion continues with a critique of the survey and its
administration. The writer raises questions about the representativeness
of the sample and the timing of the questionnaire's administration. He
also discusses some problems with the phrasing of individual questions.]

Conclusions   *Discusses whether the research*
supports hypotheses or answers guiding
19 This study had three goals: to describe the *questions*
group being studied, to test the viability of two
hypotheses, and to formulate additional hypotheses.
The survey responses provide a rough but interesting
description of competitive cyclists and suggest that
the group deserves further study.*Sums up goals of research and*
contributions to discussion of the subject
20 Of the two proposed hypotheses, the one
regarding the level of women's participation seems
likely to be supported by further research. This
research also needs to look at the reasons for the

relatively low level of women's participation,
perhaps beginning with the literature suggesting
that women in general tend to depend on diet rather
than exercise to control weight. Questions of body
image and the difficulty of cycling while
overweight may also be worth considering. Other
factors having nothing to do with weight may be
significant. For instance, women may be drawn to
mountain biking more than bicycle racing because of
more equitable distribution of sponsorships, media
coverage, and prize money (Meyer, 1996). Also,
women may perceive road training for bicycle racing
as more hazardous than other sporting activities
(Zimberoff, 1996) *Might consider whether family responsibilities limit women's participation*

21   The second hypothesis regarding "love of pain"
as a reason for cycling received little support from
the data. This response was not even among the top
10 on the questionnaire. *Suggests directions for further research*

22   Several new hypotheses emerged during the study.
One deals with the low number of male competitors
under 25 years of age. It may be the case that the
health and weight concerns of men under 25 and the
benefits of competitive cycling are contradictory.
Some hypotheses regarding reasons for competing seem
worth considering. It may be that people of different
ages, marital status, and education levels have
considerably different reasons for undertaking the
same activity, in this case, racing a bicycle. These
questions are certainly worth further study.

List sources alphabetically by last name of author

Cyclists 12

Center heading

**50e
APA**

References

Coyle, E. F., Coggan, A. R., Hopper, M. K., &   *Double-space*
First line Walters, T. J. (1988). Determinants of   *all entries*
of entry endurance in well-trained cyclists. Journal of
not indented   Applied Physiology, 64, 2622-2630.

David, C., & Cowles, M. (1991). Body image and
        exercise. Sex Roles, 25, 33-34.   *Additional lines indented*
                                            five spaces, like
Drewnowski, A., & Yee, D. K. (1987). Men and body   *paragraphs,*
        image: Are males satisfied with their body   *following*
                                                      instructor's
        weight? Psychosomatic Medicine, 49, 626-634. *directions*

Interbike 1992 directory. (1992). Costa Mesa, CA: *List source with*
                                                   no author by
        Primedia.   *title*

Matheny, F. (1986, February 5). Solo cycling. Volo
        News, 157.

Meyer, J. (1997). Alison Sydor, cyclist, on equity
        in cycling. Reprinted from ACTION, Winter 1994.
        Canadian Association for the Advancement of
        Women and Sport and Physical Activity.
        Retrieved November 9, 1998, from the World Wide
        Web: http://www.makeithappen.com/wis/readings/
        insydor.htm

Schneider, D., & Greenberg, M. (1992). Choice of
        exercise: A predictor of behavioral risks.
        Research Quarterly for Exercise and Sport, 9,
        231-245.

Worthington, R. G. (1998). Labor power racing: Lung
        busters, leg breakers. [Announcement posted on
        the World Wide Web]. Washington, DC. Author.
        Retrieved November 9, 1998, from the World

Wide Web: http://www.mesothel.com/pages/
labpower.htm

Zimberoff, B. F. (1996). Ocean to ocean on two
wheels: Harassment on the road. <u>Armchair World
NetEscapes.</u> Retrieved November 9, 1998, from
the World Wide Web: http://www.armchair.com/
escape/ bike7.html

*Center heading and name of
figure or material
Add A, B, and so on to heading
if more than one appendix*

Appendix

Survey

*Page numbers
continue*

50e
APA

Please take a minute or two to answer the following
questions for a University of Rhode Island study of
demographics and motivation of competitive athletes.

1. Sex (circle one) Male Female

2. Date of birth (month/day/year) __/__/__

3. Marital status (circle one)

    Married Single Divorced Widowed Other

4. Number of people in your household (circle one)

    1 2 3 4 5 6 or more

*Use clear material, retyped
or redrawn if necessary*

5. Education level (circle one)

    Haven't finished high school

    High school or equivalency degree

    Associate degree

    Bachelor's degree

    Master's degree

    Doctoral degree

6. In regard to family income, attitudes, and
   values, how do you view your social status?
   (circle one)

    Lower class   Lower middle class

    Middle middle class   Upper middle class

    Upper class

7. How do you rate yourself as a competitive
   cyclist? (circle one)

    Beginner Intermediate Advanced Expert

8. How many years have you been involved in
   competitive cycling? _____

9. Have you traveled more than 50 miles one way to
    enter a bike race, triathlon, or biathlon
    during 1992? (circle one) Yes No
    If you answered yes to the above question,
    approximately how many times did you travel
    that far to enter an event? _____

10. Please list a few (3 to 5) reasons why you
    enter competitive cycling events (including
    biathlons and triathlons).

    I. _____

   II. _____

  III. _____

   IV. _____

    V. _____

Thank you very much for completing this survey.

RIDE FAST!

Documenting Sources: CBE

One typical and widely used form of documentation in the natural sciences is the Council of Biology Editors (CBE) style.

USE CBE STYLE (IN ONE OF ITS VARIATIONS) IN . . .

ACADEMIC SETTINGS

When writing in natural science fields such as biology and related sciences

When writing for publications requiring use of CBE style

When writing papers for an instructor who requests CBE documentation or "some form of scientific documentation"

WORK AND PUBLIC SETTINGS

When addressing scientific issues for an audience that is reasonably expert in the field and expects you to provide current scientific knowledge

When writing for professional groups or company divisions that expect use of scientific documentation or require CBE documentation

---

CBE style tends to have more variations than the other styles, mainly because the papers written in the fields of natural science that employ **CBE documentation style** have different structural requirements. For this reason, it is important to check with your instructor or the publication or audience for which you are writing to find out which variations to use. The following discussion covers the two most common variations of CBE style. For more detailed information, see *Scientific Style and Format: The CBE Manual for Authors, Editors, and Publishers* (6th ed., 1994).

51a Creating CBE in-text citations

You can use one of two methods for CBE in-text references, the name-and-year method or the number method.

1 Use the name-and-year method

With this method, you include the name of the author or authors along with the publication year of the text. If you do not mention the author's name in the paper itself, include both the name and the year in parentheses; if you do mention the name, include only the year.

PARENTHETICAL REFERENCE

Decreases in the use of lead, cadmium, and zinc in industrial products have resulted in a "very large decrease in the large-scale pollution of the troposphere" (Boutron and others 1991, p 64).

AUTHOR NAMED IN TEXT

Boutron and others (1991) found that decreases in the use of lead, cadmium, and zinc in industrial products have resulted in a "very large decrease in the large-scale pollution of the troposphere" (p 64).

If you cite several works by the same author, all of which appeared in a single year, use letters (*a, b,* and so forth) after the date to distinguish them.

ONE OF SEVERAL APPEARING IN THE SAME YEAR

Decreases in the use of lead, cadmium, and zinc in industrial products have resulted in a "very large decrease in the large-scale pollution of the troposphere" (Boutron and others 1991a, p 64).

2 Use the number method

With this method, you use numbers instead of names of authors. The numbers can be placed in parentheses in the text or raised above the line as superscript figures. The numbers correspond to numbered works on your reference list. There are two ways to use the number method. In one style, you number your in-text citations consecutively as they appear in your paper and arrange them accordingly on the reference page.

Decreases in the use of lead, cadmium, and zinc in industrial products have reduced pollution in the troposphere (1).

In the second style, you alphabetize your references first, number them, and then refer to the corresponding number in your paper. Since only the number appears in your text, make sure you mention the author's name if it is important.

Boutron and others found that decreases in the use of lead, cadmium, and zinc in industrial products have reduced pollution in the troposphere (3).

51b Creating a CBE reference list

You may use "Cited References" or just "References" as the heading for your reference list. If your instructor asks you to supply references for all your sources, not just the ones cited in your text, prepare a second list called "Additional References," "Additional Reading," or "Bibliography."

The order of the entries in your reference list should correspond to the method you use to cite them within your paper. If you use the name-and-year method, for example, alphabetize the references according to the last name of the main author or by date of publication for works by the same author(s).

If you use the consecutive number method, the reference list will not be alphabetical but will be arranged according to which work comes first in your paper, which second, and so forth. If you use the alphabetized number method, arrange your list alphabetically, and then number the entries.

Following are some examples of the most commonly used formats for entries. Refer to *Scientific Style and Format: The CBE Manual* for further examples of documentation.

Guide to CBE Formats for References

1. BOOKS AND WORKS TREATED AS BOOKS

1. One Author
2. Two or More Authors
3. Corporate or Group Author
4. Editor
5. Translator
6. Conference Proceedings
7. Technical Report

2. ARTICLES AND SELECTIONS FROM BOOKS

8. Article in Journal Paginated by Volume
9. Article in Journal Paginated by Issue

10. Article with Corporate or Group Author
11. Entire Issue of Journal
12. Figure from Article
13. Selection in Anthology or Collection

3. ELECTRONIC RESOURCES

14. Patent from Database or Information Service
15. Online Article
16. Online Book
17. Online Abstract
18. CD-ROM Abstract

**51b
CBE**

1 Books and works treated as books

Formats for entries for the name-and-year method and the number method are the same except for the location of the year. The sample entries for a reference list follow the style for the number method, but model formats are shown for both methods.

MODEL FORMAT FOR BOOKS AND WORKS TREATED AS BOOKS

NAME-AND-YEAR METHOD

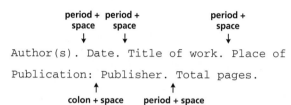

NUMBER METHOD

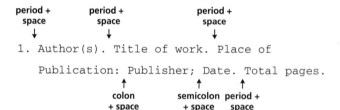

- **Author(s).** Give the author's name in inverted order, beginning with the last name and followed by *the initials only* (without periods or spaces) of the first and middle names, concluding with a period and a space. For more than one author, follow the same pattern for each author, and separate the names with a comma followed by a space. (Some scientific publications use full names for authors; check if this style is required for your paper.) If no author is given, begin with the word *Anonymous* in brackets.
- **Title of work.** Give the title followed by a period and a space. Do not underline the title, and capitalize only the first word and proper nouns or adjectives. Do not capitalize the subtitle following a colon.
- **Publication information.** Indicate the city, publisher, and date of publication. Put a colon after the city and a semicolon after the publisher. Conclude with a period. To avoid confusion between two cities with the same name or to identify cities likely to be unfamiliar, place a comma and a space after the city and include the abbreviated name of the state or the country.

- **Total pages.** Supply the total number of pages in the work, including the index, but do not add in any preliminary pages with Roman numerals.
- **Spacing.** Double-space your entries. For the name-and-year method, do not indent any lines. For the number method, begin the second and any later lines underneath the beginning of the opening word in the first line. If your instructor gives you other spacing directions, follow these carefully.

1. One Author

1. Simpson HN. Invisible armies: the impact of disease on American history. Indianapolis: Bobbs-Merrill; 1980. 239 p.

2. Two or More Authors

List each author's last name first, and use commas to separate the authors.

2. Freeman JM, Kelly MT, Freeman JB. The epilepsy diet treatment: an introduction to the ketogenic diet. New York: Demo; 1994. 180 p.

3. Corporate or Group Author

Treat an organization or government agency responsible for a work as you would an individual author. If the author is also the publisher, include the name in both places. You can use an organization's acronym in place of the author's name if the acronym is well known.

3. World Health Organization. Ataractic and hallucinogenic drugs in psychiatry: report of a study group. Geneva: World Health Organization; 1958. 179 p.

4. Editor

Identify the editor(s) by including the word *editor*(s) (spelled out) after the name.

4. Dolphin D, editor. Biomimetic chemistry. Washington: American Chemical Society; 1980. 437 p.

5. Translator

Give the translator's name after the title, followed by a comma and the word *translator.* If the work has an editor as well, place a semicolon after the word *translato*r and then name the editor and conclude with the word *editor.* Give the original title at the end of the entry after the words *Translation of* and a colon.

```
5. Jacob F. The logic of life: a history of
   heredity. Spillmann BE, translator. New
   York: Pantheon Books; 1982. 348 p.
   Translation of: Logique du vivant.
```

6. Conference Proceedings

Begin with the name of the editor(s) and the title of the publication. Indicate the name, year, and location of the conference, using semicolons to separate the information. Include the total number of pages at the end. You need not name the conference if the title does so.

```
6. Witt I, editor. Protein C: biochemical and
   medical aspects. Proceedings of the
   International Workshop; 1984 July 9-11;
   Titisee, Germany. Berlin: De Gruyter; 1985.
   195 p.
```

7. Technical Report

Treat a report as you would a book with an individual or corporate author, but include the total number of pages after the publication year. If the report is available through a particular agency—and it usually is—include the information a reader would need to order it. The report listed here can be obtained from the EPA department mentioned using the report number EPA/625/7-91/013. Enclose a widely accepted acronym for an agency in brackets following its name.

```
7. Environmental Protection Agency (US) [EPA].
   Guides to pollution prevention: the
   automotive repair industry. Washington: US
   Environmental Protection Agency; 1991; 46 p.
   Available from: EPA Office of Research and
   Development; EPA/625/7-91/013.
```

2 Articles and selections from books

MODEL FORMAT FOR ARTICLES AND SELECTIONS

NAME-AND-YEAR METHOD

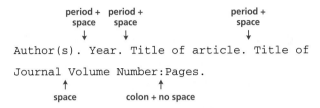

period +   period +   period +
space   space   space
↓   ↓   ↓
Author(s). Year. Title of article. Title of

Journal Volume Number:Pages.
               ↑   ↑
           space   colon + no space

NUMBER METHOD

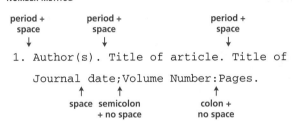

period +   period +   period +
space   space   space
↓   ↓   ↓
1. Author(s). Title of article. Title of

   Journal date;Volume Number:Pages.
               ↑   ↑   ↑
        space semicolon   colon +
               + no space   no space

- **Author(s).** Give the author's name in inverted order, beginning with the last name and followed by the initials only (without periods or spaces) of the first and middle names, concluding with a period and a single space. For more than one author, follow the same pattern for each author, and separate the names with a comma followed by a space. If no author is given, begin with *Anonymous,* placed in brackets.
- **Title of article and publication information.** Give the article name, journal name, date, volume number and issue number (in parentheses), and page numbers. Do not enclose the article title in quotation marks or underline the journal title. Capitalize only the first word and any proper nouns in an article's title; do not capitalize the first word in a subtitle. For journal titles, follow regular capitalization rules, but use abbreviations standard in the field (see below). Conclude the title of the article with a period and a space. Place a space but no punctuation between the title of the journal and the date. Do not include a space before or after the colon separating the volume number from the page numbers or between volume and issue numbers.

- **Pages.** Include the specific pages of the article or chapter.
- **Journal title (abbreviated).** Always abbreviate a journal title unless it is a one-word title. To find out how to abbreviate titles, notice the abbreviations used in your sources and ask your instructor which book lists abbreviations for your field.
- **Spacing.** Double-space all entries. Do not indent the first line or any subsequent lines (name and year); align second and later lines under the beginning of the initial word of the first line.

8. Article in Journal Paginated by Volume

8. Yousef YA, Yu LL. Potential contamination of groundwater from Cu, Pb, and Zn in wet detention ponds receiving highway runoff. J Environ Sci Hlth 1992;27:1033-44.

9. Article in Journal Paginated by Issue

Give the issue number within parentheses immediately (with no space) after the volume number.

9. Boutron CF. Decrease in anthropogenic lead, cadmium and zinc in Greenland snows since the late 1960's. Nature 1991;353(6340): 153-5, 160.

10. Article with Corporate or Group Author

Treat the corporate or group author as you would any author. If a person's name is part of the corporation, as in this example, do not transpose the first and last names. Alphabetize by the first main word in the corporation name, even if it is a first name.

10. Derek Sims Associates. Why and how of acoustic testing. Environ Eng 1991;4(1):10-12.

11. Entire Issue of Journal

Include the title of the main editor or compiler of the specific issue because this person will often be a guest editor.

11. Savage A, editor. Proceedings of the workshop on the zoo-university connection: collaborative efforts in the conservation of endangered primates. Zoo Biol 1989;1(Suppl).

12. Figure from Article

51b
CBE

Include the title of the figure (or table, chart, or diagram) and its number, as well as the page on which it appears. Use *p* in this context.

12. Kanaori Y, Kawakami SI, Yairi K. Space-time distribution patterns of destructive earthquakes in the inner belt of central Japan. Engng Geol 1991;31(3-4):209-30 (p 216, table 1).

13. Selection in Anthology or Collection

The first name and title refer to the article; the second name and title refer to the book from which the article is taken. Include the page numbers of the article at the end of the citation.

13. Moro M. Supply and conservation efforts for nonhuman primates. In Gengozian N, Deinhardt F, editors. Marmosets in experimental medicine. Basel: S. Karger AG; 1978. p 37-40.

3 Electronic resources

14. Patent from Database or Information Service

The sample below, from the inventors' names through the date, illustrates how to cite a patent. In this instance, information about electronic access is added at the end.

14. Collins FS, Drumm ML, Dawson DC, Wilkinson DJ, inventors. Method of testing potential cystic fibrosis treating compounds using cells in culture. US patent 5,434,086. 1995 July. 18 Available from: Lexis/Nexis/Lexpat library/ALL file.

15. Online Article

15. Grolmusz V. On the weak mod m representation of Boolean functions. Chi J Theor Comp Sci [serial online] 1995 July 21;100-5. 2 screens. Available from: http://www.csuchicago.edu/publication/cjtcs/ articles/1995/2/contents.html via the World Wide Web. Accessed 1996 May 3.

51b
CBE

16. Online Book

> 16. Darwin C. 1859. On the origin of species by
>   means of natural selection, or the
>   preservation of favoured races in the
>   struggle for life [book online]. London:
>   Down, Bromley, Kent. Available from:
>   ftp://sailor.gutenberg.org/pub/gutenberg/
>   etext98/otoos10.txt via the World Wide Web.
>   Accessed 1999 Feb 12.

17. Online Abstract

Use a form similar to that for journal articles, but give the word *abstract* in brackets following the title.

> 17. Smithies O, Maeda N. Gene targeting
>   approaches to complex genetic diseases:
>   atherosclerosis and essential hypertension
>   [abstract]. Proc Natl Acad Sci USA 1995;
>   92(12):5266-72. 1 screen. Available from:
>   Lexis/Medline/ABST. Accessed 1996 Jan 21.

18. CD-ROM Abstract

Indicate the medium (*CD-ROM*) in brackets following the title. Close the entry with the phrase *Available from,* followed by information about the source and retrieval number.

> 18. MacDonald R, Fleming MF, Barry KL. Risk
>   factors associated with alcohol abuse in
>   college students. Am J Drug and Alc Abuse
>   [CD-ROM]; 17:439-49. Available from:
>   SilverPlatter File: PsycLIT Item: 79-13172.

Exercise

 A. Turn to Exercise A in Chapter 49. Rewrite the sentences supplied there to add either form of in-text citations in CBE style. Prepare a corresponding list of references.

 B. Turn to Exercise B in Chapter 49. Rewrite the items supplied there to create a list of references following either form used in CBE style.

 C. Working with a partner or a small group, compare your answers to Exercises A and B above. Correct any errors in your answers, using your handbook or your instructor's advice to resolve any differences of opinion.

52

Documenting
Sources: CMS

The documentation style outlined in *The Chicago Manual of Style* (the CMS style) provides references in the form of endnotes or footnotes. Endnotes or footnotes are signaled by a superscript numeral in the text (for example,[1]) and a correspondingly numbered reference note at the end of the paper (an endnote) or, less often, at the bottom of the page (a footnote). A bibliography at the end of the paper provides a list of all the sources in alphabetical order. Endnotes and footnotes are less compact than parenthetical references, yet they offer you a chance to cite a source in more specific detail and to include brief explanatory material. Readers especially interested in your sources will find themselves repeatedly turning away from the text itself to consult the notes, however.

Use CMS Style in . . .

ACADEMIC SETTINGS

When writing papers in history and some other fields in the arts and sciences (check with your instructor)

When writing for publications and professional groups requiring use of CMS style or a footnote/endnote style

When writing papers for an instructor who requests documentation using "Turabian" or "Chicago Manual" style or who asks for footnotes or endnotes

WORK AND PUBLIC SETTINGS

When the audience you are addressing expects you to use footnotes/endnotes or when other writers addressing the audience generally use footnotes or endnotes

continued

> **USE CMS STYLE IN . . . *(continued)***
>
> **CONSIDER USING CMS STYLE (PERHAPS IN A MODIFIED FORM) IN . . .**
>
> **WORK AND PUBLIC SETTINGS**
>
> When you do not wish to distract readers by including author's names, page numbers, or dates of your sources throughout the text and when you recognize that your readers will not find it necessary to consult every note as they read

52a Using endnotes and footnotes

To indicate a reference in the body of your text, insert a number slightly above the line[2], making sure you number the references consecutively. Insert a number to indicate a reference to the source of a quotation, to alert readers to specific information and ideas borrowed from a source, or to specify the source of paraphrased or summarized material (see Chapter 46). At the end of the paper (in an endnote) or at the bottom of the page (in a footnote), provide detailed information about the source.

TEXT OF PAPER   To emphasize how isolated and impoverished his childhood neighborhood was, Wideman describes it as being not simply on "the wrong side of the tracks" but actually "under the tracks, if the truth be told—in a deep hollow between Penn and the abrupt rise of Bruston Hill."[1]

NOTE   1. John Edgar Wideman, Brothers and Keepers (New York: Penguin Books, 1984), 39.

1 Select endnotes or footnotes

Positioning footnotes between the body of the text and the bottom margin can be quite difficult and time-consuming. For this reason, even though it may be a bit easier for readers to look at the bottom of the page for a note than to turn to the end of the paper, you should generally employ endnotes. Most readers mark the page containing the endnotes so they can refer to notes with a minimum of disruption. Because readers may sometimes skip consulting a note unless they are particularly interested in your sources, you should make sure that you place all information necessary for understanding your argument or explanation in the body of your paper and not in the notes.

2 Consider content and explanatory notes

At times you may wish to supplement your text with material that may interest only a few readers. Notes are an appropriate place to do this, but don't make notes so detailed that they distract readers from the main text of the paper. You can also combine explanation with a source reference, though you need to make sure that a long and detailed discussion does not obscure the reference.

TEXT OF PAPER   Another potential source of conflict, or at least misunderstanding, in the contemporary workplace comes from differences in the ways men commonly give orders (directly) and the ways women give orders (indirectly, often in the form of requests or questions).[2]

NOTE   2. Deborah Tannen, "How to Give Orders Like a Man," <u>New York Times Magazine</u>, 18 August 1994, 46. It is sometimes easy to oversimplify the differences between the ways men and women use language. Tannen provides a detailed and balanced discussion in <u>Talking from 9 to 5</u> (New York: William Morrow, 1994).

52b Creating CMS notes

After you have placed a number slightly above the line of text[3] to indicate the presence of an endnote or footnote and have made sure that your numbering system maintains consecutive order, you need to prepare the note. A typical note provides the author's name in regular order, the title of the work being cited, publication information, and the page number(s).

Place endnotes at the end of a paper, after appendixes but before a bibliography. Supply notes on a separate page with the centered heading "Notes." Indent the first line six spaces. Start the note with the number, followed by a period and a space. Do not indent the second line or any others that follow. Double-space for ease of reading.

Guide to CMS Formats for Notes

1. BOOKS AND WORKS TREATED AS BOOKS
1. One Author
2. Two or Three Authors
3. Four or More Authors
4. No Author Given
5. Editor
6. Edition Other than the First
7. Multivolume Work

2. ARTICLES AND SELECTIONS FROM BOOKS
8. Article in Journal Paginated by Volume
9. Article in Journal Paginated by Issue
10. Article in Popular Magazine
11. Article in Daily Newspaper

12. Chapter in Book or Selection from Anthology

3. FIELD RESOURCES
13. Unpublished Interview

4. MEDIA AND ELECTRONIC RESOURCES
14. Audio or Video Recording
15. Electronic Information Service
16. CD-ROM
17. Online Book
18. Online Article

5. MULTIPLE SOURCES AND SOURCES CITED IN PRIOR NOTES
19. Multiple Sources
20. Book or Article Cited More than Once

1 Books and works treated as books

MODEL FORMAT FOR BOOKS AND WORKS TREATED AS BOOKS

```
   note                comma
 number             + space    space
   ↓                   ↓         ↓
   1. Author(s), Title (Place of Publication:
Publisher, Year), Page number(s).
                    ↑
               comma + space
```

- **Author(s).** Give the name of the author(s) in regular order followed by a comma and a space.
- **Title.** Give the title of the work being cited. Underline the title of a book and follow the title with a space. (See 38b-2 on capitalization of titles.)
- **Publication information.** Give all publication information within parentheses. Start with the city of publication, followed by a comma and an abbreviation for the state or country if this information is necessary to avoid confusion between two cities with the same name or to identify little-known places. Add a colon and a space; then give the publisher's name followed by a comma, a space, and the date of publication. Place a comma followed by a space after the closing parenthesis mark.
- **Page number(s).** Conclude with the specific page numbers containing the information being cited or the passage being quoted, paraphrased, or summarized.

1. One Author

> 1. Ruth Macklin, <u>Mortal Choices: Ethical Dilemmas in Modern Medicine</u> (Boston: Houghton Mifflin, 1987), 154.

2. Two or Three Authors

Separate the names of two authors with *and.* Separate those of three authors with commas as well as *and* before the name of the third author.

> 2. Mary Knapp and Herbert Knapp, <u>One Potato, Two Potato . . .: The Secret Education of American Children</u> (New York: W. W. Norton, 1978), 144.

> 2. Michael Wood, Bruce Cole, and Adelheid Gealt, <u>Art of the Western World</u> (New York: Summit Books, 1989), 206-10.

3. Four or More Authors

For works with more than three authors, give the name of the first author followed by *and others*. (Generally, all the names are supplied in the corresponding bibliography entry.)

> 3. Anthony Slide and others, <u>The American Film Industry: A Historical Dictionary</u> (New York: Greenwood Press, 1986), 124.

4. No Author Given

If the author is not known, begin the entry with the title.

> 4. <u>The Great Utopia: The Russian and Soviet Avant-Garde, 1915-1932</u> (New York: Guggenheim Museum, 1992), 661.

5. Editor

When a work has an editor, translator, or compiler (or some combination of these), give the name or names after the title preceded by a comma and the appropriate abbreviation, for example, *ed., trans.,* or *comp.*

> 5. Charles Dickens, <u>Bleak House</u>, ed. Norman Page (Harmondsworth, England: Penguin Books, 1971), 49.

Dickens is the author, and Page has prepared the particular edition of the work.

If you wish to emphasize the role of the editor, translator, or compiler, give his or her name at the beginning of the entry.

> 5. Donald M. Scott and Bernard Wishy, eds., <u>America's Families: A Documentary History</u> (New York: Harper & Row, 1982), 177.

The editors are responsible for assembling materials from a variety of sources.

> 5. Robert H. Ferrell, ed., <u>Dear Bess: The Letters from Harry to Bess Truman 1910-1959</u> (New York: W. W. Norton, 1983), 71-2.

The word *by* with the author's name (*Harry S. Truman*) would be appropriate following the title, but it is not necessary because the author's name appears in the title.

6. Edition Other than the First

Use an abbreviation following the title to indicate the particular edition, for example, *4th ed.* ("fourth edition") or *rev. and enl. ed.* ("revised and enlarged edition").

> 6. John D. La Plante, <u>Asian Art</u>, 3d ed.
> (Dubuque, Iowa: Wm. C. Brown, 1992), 7.

For a work that has been reprinted or appears in a special paperback edition, give information about both the original publication and the reprint.

> 6. Henri Frankfort and others, <u>The</u>
> <u>Intellectual Adventure of Ancient Man</u> (Chicago:
> University of Chicago Press, 1946; reprint,
> Chicago: University of Chicago Press, 1977),
> 202-4 (page citations are to the reprint
> edition).

7. Multivolume Work

A multivolume work can consist of volumes all by a single author (sometimes with different titles for each) or of works by a variety of authors with an overall title. If you are referring to the whole multivolume work, include the number of volumes after the title. To indicate volume and page number for a specific volume, use volume and page numbers separated by a colon and no space. Give the volume number and name for separately titled volumes after the main title and omit the volume number in the page reference.

> 7. Sigmund Freud, <u>The Standard Edition of</u>
> <u>the Complete Psychological Works of Sigmund</u>
> <u>Freud</u>, trans. James Strachey (London: Hogarth
> Press, 1953), 11:180.

2 Articles and selections from books

MODEL FORMAT FOR ARTICLES AND SELECTIONS

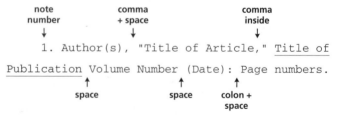

- **Author(s).** Give the author's name in regular order.
- **Title.** Put the title of the article or selection in quotation marks. Put a comma inside the closing quotation mark, and leave a space after the quotation mark.
- **Publication information.** Next give the title of the journal or book, underlined, and leave a space after it with no punctuation.

Supply the volume number and then the date of publication in parentheses, varying the information and style for different types of publications (see below). Place a colon after the final parenthesis, and leave a space.

- **Page number(s).** Supply the page numbers for the pertinent part of the article or selection.

8. Article in Journal Paginated by Volume

When the page numbers run continuously through the individual issues that make up a volume, give the volume number but do not include the month, season, or number of the individual issue containing the article. Give specific page numbers for the part of the article you are citing. If you wish to refer to the article as a whole, give inclusive page numbers for the entire article, for example, *98–114.*

> 8. C. Anita Tarr, "'A Man Can Stand Up': Johnny Tremain and the Rebel Pose," The Lion and the Unicorn: A Critical Journal of Children's Literature 18 (1994): 181.

9. Article in Journal Paginated by Issue

If each issue of a journal begins with page 1, give the volume number followed by a comma, the abbreviation *no.* (for "number"), and the issue number. If the issue is instead identified by month or season, include this information just before the year and within the same set of parentheses, for example (*Winter 1994*) or (*February 1996*). Give page numbers for the specific part of the article you are citing or inclusive page numbers for the entire article if you are referring to it as a whole.

> 9. Peter Smagorinsky and Pamela K. Fly, "A New Perspective on Why Small Groups Do and Don't Work," English Journal 83, no. 5 (1994): 54–55.

10. Article in Popular Magazine

Follow the name of the magazine with a comma and the date. Use this order for the date if it includes the day: *25 November 1995.* Place a comma at the end of the date before the page number, and give a page number for the specific part of the article you are citing or inclusive page numbers for the entire article if you are referring to it as a whole.

> 10. Deborah Tannen, "But What Do You Mean?" Redbook, October 1994, 57–58.

11. Article in Daily Newspaper

Identify newspaper articles by date (rather than volume number) following the title of the article and the name of the newspaper. Present the date in this order: *4 February 1996.* When the sections of a newspaper are separately paginated, provide the section number or letter and the page number—for example, *sec. B, p. 3*—using *p.* or *pp.* to introduce the page number(s).

```
      11. Debra West, "Stalking Weeds of Spring
for Traditional Meals," New York Times, 18 May
1995, sec. B, pp. 1, 7.
```

When an American newspaper's title does not include the city's name, give it at the start of the title (underlined). For less known newspapers, for those outside North America with the city not mentioned in the title, and for those from places easily confused with well-known cities, give the name of the state or country after the title or after the name of the city in the title: *Westerly (R.I.) Sun; Times* (London).

12. Chapter in Book or Selection from Anthology

For a selection from an anthology or for a book chapter, give the name of the selection or chapter in quotation marks followed by *in* and the name of book. If the book has an editor, follow the book's title with *ed.* and the editor's name.

```
      12. Fred Pfeil, "'Makin' Flippy-Floppy':
Postmodernism and the Baby-Boom PMC," in
Another Tale to Tell: Politics and Narrative
in Postmodern Culture (London: Verso, 1990),
107.
```
Chapter in a book.

```
      12. W. E. B. Du Bois, "The Call of
Kansas," in W. E. B. Du Bois: A Reader, ed.
David Levering Lewis (New York: Henry Holt,
1995), 173.
```
Selection from an edited collection of one writer's works.

```
      12. Julie D'Acci, "Defining Women: The
Case of Cagney and Lacey," in Private
Screenings: Television and the Female Consumer,
ed. Lynn Spigel and Denise Mann (Minneapolis:
University of Minnesota Press, 1992), 169.
```
Chapter in an edited collection of essays.

3 Field resources
13. Unpublished Interview

For unpublished interviews done by someone else, begin with the name of the person interviewed followed by a comma; then give the phrase *interview by,* the name of the interviewer, the date (in this order: *2 May 1978*), any file number, the medium (*tape recording* or *transcript,* for example), and the place where the interview is stored (such as *Erie County Historical Society, Buffalo, New York*). For interviews you conduct, provide the name of the person interviewed, the phrase *interview by author,* a description of the kind of interview, the medium, and the place and date of the interview.

> 13. Shawon Kelley, interview by author, tape recording, Los Angeles, Calif., 2 May 1995.

> 13. Morton Kosko, telephone interview by author, transcript, Scottsdale, Ariz., 22 January 1996.

4 Media and electronic resources
14. Audio or Video Recording

Start with the work's title unless the recording features a particular performer, composer, director, or writer. Give names and roles (if appropriate) of performers or others whose participation needs to be noted. Indicate the length of the recording (video), the company responsible, the recording number (audio), the date, and the medium (for example, *audiocassette* or *videocassette*).

> 14. <u>James Baldwin</u>, prod. and dir. Karen Thorsen, 87 min., Resolution Inc./California Newsreel, 1990, videocassette.

15. Electronic Information Service

For information and text you gather through an electronic information service, use whatever format would be appropriate for similar material available in printed form, but at the end of the entry provide the name of the service (such as *Dialog* or *ERIC*), the name of the vendor, and the accession or identifying numbers used by the service.

> 15. Mark Miller, "Two Beaked Whales Wash Up on Beach," <u>Daytona Beach News-Journal,</u> 20 January 1994, in Newsbank [database online] [cited 5 March 1995], ENV 3, G6.

16. CD-ROM

Supply information as you would for the print equivalent if it existed. After the title, indicate in brackets the type of medium: *[CD-ROM]*.

    16. William Shakespeare, All's Well That
    Ends Well. William Shakespeare: The Complete
    Works on CD-ROM [CD-ROM] (Abingdon, England:
    Andromeda Interactive, 1994).

17. Online Book

For a book that has been previously published in print, include all information as required by Entries 1–7. Indicate the medium of the source in brackets following the title: *[book online]*. With the original publication date, give the date you accessed the source. Finally, indicate the URL at which the book is available and the network in brackets: *[Internet]*.

    17. Charles Darwin, On the Origin of
    Species by Means of Natural Selection, or the
    Preservation of Favoured Races in the Struggle
    for Life [book online] (London: Down, Bromley,
    Kent, 1859 [cited 12 February 1999]); available
    from ftp://sailor.gutenberg.org/pub/gutenberg/
    etext98/otoos10.txt; [Internet].

18. Online Article

Include all information required in Entries 8 and 9. Following the publication information, indicate the medium of the source in brackets: *[journal online]*. Indicate the URL at which the book is available and the network in brackets: *[Internet]*. Include the date you accessed the source.

    18. Aaron Lynch, "Units, Events and
    Dynamics in Memetic Evolution," Journal of
    Memetics--Evolutionary Models of Information
    Transmission 2.1, June 1998 [journal online]
    [cited 12 February 1999]; available from
    http://www.cpm.mmu.ac.uk/jom-emit/1998/vol2/
    lynch_a.html; [Internet].

5 Multiple sources and sources cited in prior notes

19. Multiple Sources

When you wish to cite more than one source in a note, separate the references with semicolons and give the entries in the order in which they were cited in the text.

```
     19. See Greil Marcus, Mystery Train:
Images of America in Rock 'n Roll Music
(New York: E. P. Dutton, 1975), 119; Susan
Orlean, "All Mixed Up," New Yorker, 22 June
1992, 90; and Cornel West, "Learning to Talk
of Race," New York Times Magazine, 2 August
1992, 24.
```

20. Book or Article Cited More than Once

The first time you provide a reference to a work, you need to list full information about the source in the note. In later notes you need to provide only the last name of the author(s), a shortened title, and the page(s). Separate these elements with commas.

```
     21. Macklin, Mortal, 161.
     21. Wood, Cole, and Gealt, Art, 207.
```

If a note refers to the same source as the note before, you can use a traditional scholarly abbreviation, *ibid.* (from the Latin for "in the same place"), for the second note. *Ibid.* means that the entire reference is identical, but if you add a new page reference, the addition shows that the specific page is different.

```
     22. Tarr, "'A Man,'" 183.
     23. Ibid.
     24. Ibid., 186.
```

52c Creating a CMS bibliography

At the end of your paper you need to provide readers with an alphabetical list of the sources cited in your notes. CMS style calls for this list to be titled "Selected Bibliography" or "Sources Consulted" if it includes all the works you consulted. If you want to limit the list to the works appearing in your notes, you might call it "Works Cited," "References," or a similar title.

Place your bibliography on a separate page at the end of your paper, and center the title two inches below the upper edge. Continue the page numbering used for the text. Double-space entries for ease of reading. Do not indent the first line, but indent the second line and any subsequent lines five spaces. Alphabetize the entries according to the authors' last names or the first word of the title, excluding *A, An,* and *The,* if the author is unknown.

Guide to CMS Formats for Bibliography Entries

1. BOOKS AND WORKS TREATED AS BOOKS

1. One Author
2. Two or Three Authors
3. Four or More Authors
4. No Author Given
5. Editor
6. Edition Other than the First
7. Multivolume Work

2. ARTICLES AND SELECTIONS FROM BOOKS

8. Article in Journal Paginated by Volume
9. Article in Journal Paginated by Issue
10. Article in Popular Magazine

11. Article in Daily Newspaper
12. Chapter in Book or Selection from Anthology

3. OTHER PRINTED AND FIELD RESOURCES

13. Unpublished Interview

4. MEDIA AND ELECTRONIC RESOURCES

14. Audio or Video Recording
15. Electronic Information Service
16. CD-ROM
17. Online Book
18. Online Article

5. MULTIPLE SOURCES

19. Multiple Sources

1 Books and works treated as books

MODEL FORMAT FOR BOOKS AND WORKS TREATED AS BOOKS

period + space   period + space   colon + space

Author(s). Title. Place of Publication:
     Publisher, Date.

indent 5 spaces   comma + space

- **Author(s).** Give the author's last name followed by a comma, then the first and any middle names or initials followed by a period and a space.
- **Title.** Give the title of the work, underlined, ending with a period and space. Capitalize the main words of the title and any subtitle. Do not capitalize *a, an, the,* coordinating conjunctions (such as *and, or,* and *but*), and prepositions. Always capitalize the first and last words of any title or subtitle.
- **Place of publication.** Give the city where the work was published, followed by a comma and an abbreviation for the state or country if necessary to avoid confusion between cities with the same name or to identify little-known places. End with a colon and a space.

- **Publisher.** Give the publisher's name followed by a comma and a single space.
- **Date.** Give the date of publication followed by a period.

1. One Author

```
Macklin, Ruth. Mortal Choices: Ethical Dilemmas
     in Modern Medicine. Boston: Houghton
     Mifflin, 1987.
```

2. Two or Three Authors

```
Knapp, Mary, and Herbert Knapp. One Potato, Two
     Potato . . .: The Secret Education of
     American Children. New York: W. W. Norton,
     1978.
Wood, Michael, Bruce Cole, and Adelheid Gealt.
     Art of the Western World. New York: Summit
     Books, 1989.
```

3. Four or More Authors

```
Slide, Anthony, Val Almen Darez, Robert Gitt,
     and Susan Perez Prichard. The American
     Film Industry: A Historical Dictionary.
     New York: Greenwood Press, 1986.
```

4. No Author Given

```
The Great Utopia: The Russian and Soviet Avant-
     Garde, 1915-1932. New York: Guggenheim
     Museum, 1992.
```

5. Editor

```
Dickens, Charles. Bleak House. Edited by Norman
     Page. Harmondsworth, England: Penguin
     Books, 1971.
Ferrell, Robert H., ed. Dear Bess: The Letters
     from Harry to Bess Truman 1910-1959. New
     York: W. W. Norton, 1983.
Scott, Donald M., and Bernard Wishy, eds.
     America's Families: A Documentary History.
     New York: Harper & Row, 1982.
```

6. Edition Other than the First

```
Frankfort, Henri, H. A. Frankfort, John A.
     Wilson, Thorkild Jacobsen, and William A.
     Irving. The Intellectual Adventure of
     Ancient Man. Chicago: University of
     Chicago Press, 1946. Reprint, Chicago:
     University of Chicago Press, 1977.
La Plante, John D. Asian Art. 3d ed. Dubuque,
     Iowa: Wm. C. Brown, 1992.
```

7. Multivolume Work

```
Freud, Sigmund. The Standard Edition of the
     Complete Psychological Works of Sigmund
     Freud. Translated by James Strachey. Vol.
     11. London: Hogarth Press, 1953.
```

2 Articles and selections from books

MODEL FORMAT FOR ARTICLES AND SELECTIONS FROM BOOKS

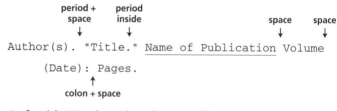

- **Author(s).** Give the author's last name followed by a comma, then the first and any middle names or initials followed by a period and a space.
- **Title.** Give the title of the article within quotation marks, and capitalize the main words of the title and of any subtitle. Do not capitalize *a, an, the,* coordinating conjunctions (such as *and* and *or*), and prepositions. Always capitalize the first and last words of any title or subtitle. If the article's title contains the title of a work that needs to be italicized or underlined, use underlining; if it contains a title that requires quotation marks, use single quotation marks to enclose the interior title.
- **Name of publication.** Give the title of the journal or magazine containing the article, and underline it.
- **Volume.** Give the volume number of the periodical; separate it from the name of the publication by a space without a comma or any other punctuation. Include the issue number only for certain kinds of publications.

- **Date.** Provide the year in which the article was published (within parentheses), but indicate the month or season only for certain kinds of publications.
- **Pages.** Follow the parentheses containing the date with a colon and a space; then give the inclusive pages on which the article appears.

8. Article in Journal Paginated by Volume

Tarr, Anita C. "'A Man Can Stand Up': Johnny Tremain and the Rebel Pose." The Lion and the Unicorn: A Critical Journal of Children's Literature 18 (1994): 178-189.

9. Article in Journal Paginated by Issue

Smagorinsky, Peter, and Pamela K. Fly. "A New Perspective on Why Small Groups Do and Don't Work." English Journal 83, no. 5 (1994): 54-58.

10. Article in Popular Magazine

Tannen, Deborah. "But What Do You Mean?" Redbook, October 1994, 57-58.

11. Article in Daily Newspaper

West, Debra. "Stalking Weeds of Spring for Traditional Meals." New York Times, 18 May 1995, sec. B, pp. 1, 7.

12. Chapter in Book or Selection from Anthology

D'Acci, Julie. "Defining Women: The Case of Cagney and Lacey." In Private Screenings: Television and the Female Consumer, edited by Lynn Spigel and Denise Mann, 169-201. Minneapolis: University of Minnesota Press, 1992.

Du Bois, W. E. B. "The Call of Kansas." In W. E. B. Du Bois: A Reader, edited by David Levering Lewis, 101-121. New York: Henry Holt, 1995.

Pfeil, Fred. "'Makin' Flippy-Floppy':
Postmodernism and the Baby-Boom PMC."
Chap. in <u>Another Tale to Tell: Politics
and Narrative in Postmodern Culture</u>.
London: Verso, 1990.

3 Other printed and field resources
13. Unpublished Interview

Kelley, Shawon. Interview by author. Tape
recording. Los Angeles, Calif., 2 May 1995.

Kosko, Morton. Telephone interview by the
author. Transcript. Scottsdale, Ariz., 22
January 1996.

4 Media and electronic resources
14. Audio or Video Recording

<u>James Baldwin</u>. Produced and directed by Karen
Thorsen. 87 min. Resolution
Inc./California Newsreel, 1990.
Videocassette.

15. Electronic Information Service

Miller, Mark. "Two Beaked Whales Wash Up on
Beach." <u>Daytona Beach News-Journal</u>, 20
January 1994. Database online. Available
from Newsbank, ENV 3, G6.

16. CD-ROM

Shakespeare, William. <u>All's Well That Ends
Well. William Shakespeare: The Complete
Works on CD-ROM</u> [CD-ROM]. Abingdon,
England: Andromeda Interactive, 1994.

17. Online Book

Darwin, Charles. <u>On the Origin of Species by
Means of Natural Selection, or the
Preservation of Favoured Races in the</u>

<u>Struggle for Life</u> [book online]. London:
Down, Bromley, Kent, 1859 [cited 12
February 1999]. Available from
ftp://sailor.gutenberg.org/pub/gutenberg/
etext98/otoos10.txt; [Internet].

18. Online Article

Lynch, Aaron. "Units, Events and Dynamics in
Memetic Evolution." <u>Journal of Memetics--
Evolutionary Models of Information
Transmission</u> 2.1, June 1998 [journal
online] [cited 12 February 1999].
Available from http://www.cpm.mmu.ac.uk/
jom-emit/1998/vol2/lynch_a.html; [Internet].

5 Multiple sources

19. Multiple Sources

When a note lists more than one source, list each one separately in
your bibliography, presenting them in alphabetical order among your
other sources.

Exercise

 A. Turn to Exercise A in Chapter 49. Rewrite the sentences supplied there to add note numbers in CMS style. Then prepare the
corresponding notes for these items.

 B. Turn to Exercise B in Chapter 49. Rewrite the items supplied
there to create a list of works cited in CMS style.

 C. Working with a partner or a small group, compare your answers
to Exercises A and B above. Correct any errors in your answers, using your handbook or your instructor's advice to resolve any differences of opinion.

53

Documenting
Sources: COS

Written in collaboration with Margaret M. Barber, University of Southern Colorado, and Janice R. Walker, Georgia Southern University

The World Wide Web (WWW) and Internet are quickly expanding as digital storehouses of books and articles previously available only on paper. Electronic databases and search engines allow researchers to locate sources to read onscreen or print out and read at leisure.

Electronic publication also permits new modes of authoring and creation of new kinds of text in which documentation styles developed for traditional materials are difficult to apply. Key ingredients needed for citations in MLA, APA, CMS, and CBE styles, such as names of authors, publication dates, and page numbers, may be missing from online texts; electronic addresses, critical for locating online sources, do not appear in traditional citation formats.

Columbia Online Style (COS) was developed by Janice R. Walker and Todd Taylor to respond to the need for ways to cite electronic sources in formats consistent with MLA, APA, CMS, CBE, or other traditional styles. Designed to be used in combination with one of these other styles, COS provides an efficient and flexible model for writers to adapt for citing materials found online.

If you have any doubt about what documentation style to use for electronic sources, find out what your instructor requires. The indexes in 53d and 53f cover the most common kinds of online sources. For other sources, see *The Columbia Guide to Online Style* by Janice R. Walker and Todd Taylor, published by Columbia University Press (1998) and updated on the Web at http://www.columbia.edu/cu/cup/cgos/.

USE **COS** FOR DOCUMENTATION OF ELECTRONIC SOURCES IN . . .

ACADEMIC SETTINGS

When you are already using MLA, CMS, APA, or CBE documentation style

When an instructor or editor does not specify another documentation style for online sources

WORK AND PUBLIC SETTINGS

For written memos or reports in which you use ideas or language from online sources, including email

When you can gain credibility by using authoritative sources found online, such as a letter to a newspaper editor

53a How to use COS for documentation

Before composing a rough draft, determine which documentation style you will be using in your paper—either MLA or CMS in the humanities or APA or CBE in the sciences—and study the chapter in this book that fully explains that style. Follow the chapter's guidelines for determining what to document, what not to document, when to use parenthetical citations, and when to use endnotes or footnotes.

Use two steps to document an electronic source with COS, just as you would with MLA, APA, or another style for print sources. First, place parenthetical citations at appropriate places within the text according to the style you are using in your paper, following the directions in 53b. Then, when you have finished the first draft, make a list of every source referred to in a parenthetical citation. Use this list to compile a list of citations (called a list of works cited in the humanities or a reference list in the sciences) following the directions in the chapter you are using for documenting print sources.

For material found online, study the basic format for citations in 53c. Then refer to the indexes in 53d (MLA/humanities) and 53f (APA/sciences) to locate the kind of electronic source you are citing. Use the numbered key to find instructions for devising each kind of citation. Your citation should conform to the example in terms of spacing, punctuation, use of capital and lowercase letters, italics, and parentheses. Combine your finished citations of print sources with those of online sources in one works cited or reference list, alphabetized by author, title, or other item that appears first in each citation.

53b Creating in-text citations

For MLA style, the typical citation for print sources will contain, in parentheses, the author's surname and the page number where the material used was found: (*Wiseman* 9). When using COS in the humanities, however, omit the page numbers in parenthetical citations unless they are provided in the electronic version. You will often find that online texts do not share the page-numbering conventions of print materials.

MLA IN-TEXT CITATION
A writing teacher explores an important lesson learned from baseball in his essay on teaching writing to a student who finds a way to "blend failure with hope and learning" (Hochman).

You may omit the parenthetical citation entirely if you work the author's name into the text.

AUTHOR'S NAME AS PART OF DISCUSSION
Will Hochman explores an important lesson learned from baseball in his essay on teaching writing to a student who finds a way to "blend failure with hope and learning."

GENERAL REFERENCE
Use only one citation at the end of a paragraph containing consecutive references to the same online source when no page numbers appear in parenthetical citations to indicate that different portions of the source were used. For material from several sources interspersed throughout a paragraph, indicate authorship for some sources in the text proper, where practicable, to minimize the need for parenthetical citations.

APA style in-text citations for print material includes the name, the date, and, when reference is to a specific passage, a page number or numbers.

APA IN-TEXT CITATION
(Jacobson, 1989, p. 22)

COS/scientific and CMS author-date styles use the same format as APA style, placing the author's last name and the date of publication in the citation.

COS/SCIENTIFIC IN-TEXT CITATION
(Hochman, 1998)

If you work the author's name into the text, the parenthetical reference needs to include only the date.

Will Hochman (1998) explores an important lesson learned from baseball in his essay on teaching writing.

NO AUTHOR GIVEN

In COS/humanities style, if the author's name is missing, use a shortened version of the title instead, placing the title in quotation marks, just as you would for print sources.

("Social Statistics")

For COS/scientific style, use the shortened version of the title, without quotation marks, and include the date of publication. If no publication date is indicated in an electronic source, provide the date of access, including the day, the month (abbreviated except for May, June, or July), and the year.

(Social statistics, 19 Dec. 1998)

If the electronic source uses only a nickname or an alias for an author's name, use the alias in your parenthetical citation. In COS/humanities style, just as with MLA style, if the author's name or alias is worked into your text, no parenthetical reference is needed. In COS/scientific style, however, a date of publication or access is placed in a parenthetical citation.

Vanessa, a new visitor to the Spanish language MOO, *Mundo Hispanico,* found that other students gently suggested word choices until they could understand her meaning (19 Dec. 1998).

If you use CMS for documentation, your endnotes or footnotes for online sources will include the distinctive elements in the works cited entries described below. Check with your instructor to determine whether or not to include a separate list of references, which is optional in different forms of CMS style. To create endnotes or footnotes for use with CMS style, find the section in the Form Index in 52c that corresponds with the type of electronic source you are citing. Follow COS guidelines, making any adjustments necessary to meet the basic requirements of CMS style.

53c Creating an entry for a works cited or reference list

Citations in humanities and scientific styles for print and online sources have key elements in common. Information on authorship, the titles of documents and complete works, names of publishers, and places and dates of publication allow a reader to determine the extent and quality of the author's research. Above all, such information permits the reader to identify and locate the original source. Major components of print and online materials, however, differ in some important ways that require variations in citation form.

- **Author.** Some online articles and Web sites have individually named authors. Others are designed by unidentified Webmasters or development teams working for organizations or corporations. Sites may be "compiled" or "maintained" by individuals who write some of the materials that appear but also organize material submitted by others and create links to documents housed at other sites. Using pseudonyms, a group of writers in the same room or building may create a single document by writing on computers connected by a local area network (LAN). Fiction writers using aliases may co-author stories by writing "synchronously" (at the same time) on MOOs. Others using made-up log-in names may join a newsgroup to discuss their common interest in a hobby or sport. Colleagues scattered around the globe in different time zones, usually using their own names, form email lists to discuss professional concerns in "asynchronous" conferences, reading and writing at different times that suit their convenience. Variations on ways to author online documents continue to proliferate.

For a citation using COS, list an individual, institutional, or corporate author if you can find one named. This information is often located at the bottom of the home page of a Web site. Cite an alias or log-in name if that is all you can find. Otherwise, refer to the examples in 53d or 53f for instructions on devising citations for sources without named authors.

- **Title.** The title of a document, such as an article, a poem, an essay, or a single Web page, appears after the individual or group author's name or, if no author is named, as the first item in the citation. The title of the complete work, such as an online journal or Web site, follows in italics. Italicize all titles of complete works when using COS. Use italics instead of underlining in the works cited or reference list to avoid confusion with uses of underlining specific to online publication, particularly the designation of hypertext links.

- **Publication information.** Citations for works previously published in print should contain the original publication information (city, publisher, year) followed by online publication information, including the title of the site where the document is stored; a file name or number, if applicable; the date of publication; and the electronic address, with path or directory names if there are any.

- **Electronic address.** The electronic address or URL (for uniform resource locator) is the single most essential piece of information for locating materials online. It must always be given in full and with precision, down to the last period or "dot." It begins with a protocol such as *http* (HyperText Transfer Protocol), *ftp* (file transfer protocol), *gopher,* or *telnet* in lowercase letters, followed by the main part of the address. In files accessed by using a Web browser, the address usually consists of the protocol with a colon and two slashes (for example, *gopher://*), a domain name (a unique identifier for an Internet host computer), any paths or directories needed to locate the material, and the file name. Do not use angle brackets around the electronic address or add punctuation at the end. Follow the URL with a single space and the opening parenthesis for the date of access.

- **Dates of publication and access.** An online document such as a Web page may be published without any indication of the date, or it may be revised periodically, even hourly, making a single date of publication impossible to determine. Provide the date of original publication, if available. COS follows the conventions of MLA and APA styles for providing dates. In addition, a date of last revision is included, if known.

The last term in the citation is the date of access, placed immediately after the electronic address and a single space. The date of access is always enclosed in parentheses. Include the day, month (abbreviated except for May, June, and July), and year you visited the site. Follow the closing parenthesis with a period, as in

> http://www.uscolo.edu (20 Dec. 1998).

The date of access indicates exactly when you visited the site. It is important because online sources are subject to change. When the date of publication and the date of access are identical, as with frequently updated sites, omit the date of publication. When the publication date is unknown, or when the date of revision is the same as the date of access, use the date of access instead. The date of access is never omitted.

53d Using COS in the humanities (with MLA, CMS)

The basic format for citing online sources in a works cited list is as follows.

```
Author's Surname, First Name. "Title of
    Document." Title of Complete Work. File or
    version number. Date of document or date
    of last revision. Protocol and address,
    access path, or directories (Date of
    access).
```

List the individual author of the site, last name first, followed by a comma, the first name or initial (whichever is required by the style you are using for print citations), a period, and a space. The title of the document or article, in quotation marks, is followed by a period placed inside the closing quotation mark. Capitalize words in the title as you would in an MLA or CMS entry. Give the title of a complete work such as an online journal or book, a site that organizes contributions by multiple authors, or a site that links together other sites (such as the *Virtual Jerusalem* "supersite" at http://www.virtualjerusalem.com). Follow with a period. Provide file or version numbers, if applicable.

Give the date the document was first published or, if available, the date of last revision, followed by a period. Omit these dates if they are identical to the date of access. Give the complete electronic address, including any path names or directories. Follow with a single space, the date of access in parentheses, and a period. If you cannot find one or more of these items, omit them, but always include an electronic address and date of access.

Brown, Mitchell C. "The Past: What Has Happened

Before." *The Faces of Science: African*

Americans in the Sciences. Rev. 31 Aug.

1998. http://www.lib.lsu.edu/lib/

chem/display/faces.html#Past (28 Dec. 1998).

Guide to COS/Humanities Formats for a List of Works Cited

1. CITATIONS FROM THE WORLD WIDE WEB (WWW)
1. WWW Site
2. WWW Site—Revised, Updated, or Modified
3. WWW Site—Authored by Group, Organization, or Institution
4. WWW Site—Corporate Author
5. WWW Site—Without Named Author, Group, or Title
6. WWW Site—Maintained or Compiled by Individual
7. WWW Site—Government
8. WWW Site—Printed Book Available Online
9. WWW Site—Electronic Book
10. WWW Site—Online Article
11. WWW Site—Article from News Service or Online Newspaper
12. WWW Site—Article from Archive (Previously Published in Print)
13. WWW Site—With Frames
14. WWW Site—Graphic or Audio File

2. EMAIL MESSAGES, DISCUSSION LISTS, OR NEWSGROUPS
15. Email—Personal
16. Email—Discussion List
17. Email—From Newsgroup
18. Email—From Message Archive

3. MATERIALS OBTAINED VIA GOPHER, FTP, OR TELNET
19. Via Gopher or FTP
20. Via Telnet

4. SYNCHRONOUS CONFERENCE RECORDS
21. MOOs, MUDs
22. LANs

5. REFERENCE TOOLS AND DATABASES
23. Entry in Online Dictionary
24. Article in Online Encyclopedia
25. Information on CD-ROM
26. Article from Online Database

6. SOFTWARE
27. Software/Video Game

1 Citations from the World Wide Web

1. WWW Site

```
Hochman, Will. "Beyond Exception: The Writer's

     Life." The Salt River Review 1.1 (1998).

     http://www.mc.maricopa.edu/users/cervantes/

     SRR/hochman.html (20 Dec. 1998).
```

2. WWW Site—Revised, Updated, or Modified

Before the electronic address, indicate the date the site was revised or modified, preceded by *Rev.* for "Revised" or *Mod.* for "Modified," depending on the terminology used on the page itself. Look for revision information in a side column or near the bottom of the page. Use the numeral for the day and an abbreviation for the month (unless it is May, June, or July), and give the year followed by a period. List the address and date of access.

```
AFL-CIO. "Facts About Working Women." Today's

     Unions. Rev. 7 Dec. 1998. http://www.aflcio.org/

     women/wwfacts.htm (19 Dec. 1998).
```

3. WWW Site—Authored by Group, Organization, or Institution

If a group, organization, or institution sponsors a site and no individual author is named, use the name of the group in place of the author.

```
International Olympic Committee. "Welcome to

     the Official Site of the International

     Olympic Committee." The Official Site of

     the International Olympic Committee.

     http://www.olympic.org (27 Dec. 1998).
```

4. WWW Site—Corporate Author

When a corporation serves as the author of a page, use its full name, and then give the page's title in quotation marks.

```
Goodwill Industries International, Inc.

     "Goodwill Career Links." Rev. 18 Dec. 1998.
```

```
http://www.goodwill.org/about/careerlk.htm
(19 Dec. 1998).
```

If the complete site has a title different from the name of the corporation used as author, place it after the title of the individual page, in italics.

```
LatinoLink Enterprises, Inc. "Job Bank."
    LatinoLink. 1998. http://www.latinolink .com/
    joblist.html (29 Dec. 1998).
```

5. WWW Site—Without Named Author, Group, or Title

When an author or authoring group is unnamed on a page, begin with the title in quotation marks or italics and follow with the Web address and date accessed.

```
"Social Statistics Briefing Room."
    http://www.whitehouse.gov/fsbr/ssbr.html
    (19 Dec. 1998).
```

If both author and title are omitted, begin with the file name.

```
chorusline.mpg. http://www.juggling.org/
    animations/chorusline.mpg (20 Dec. 1998).
```

6. WWW Site—Maintained or Compiled by Individual

A maintained site is one in which a Web designer organizes and posts information gathered from several sources, often including members of a sponsoring organization, much as a newsletter editor would do. The maintainer may also provide an index to material on other sites. For a maintained site, give the site's title first, and then the name of the maintainer, preceded by the abbreviation *maint.* For the author of a compiled site, one that consists primarily of links to other sites, use *comp.* for "compiler."

```
Southeast Colorado RC&D, Inc. Colorado
    Southeast Network. Comp. Alex Bray.
    http://www.ruralnet.net/~csn (17 Dec.
    1998).
```

If your reference is specifically to the work of the maintainer or compiler, give that name first, followed by *maint.* or *comp.*

Freeland, Cynthia, maint. *SWIP—The Society for*
  Women in Philosophy. Jan. 1997. http://
  www .uh.edu/~cfreelan/SWIP/ (17 Dec. 1998).

If the maintainer or compiler is not named, simply omit that information.

"Computers and Academic Freedom." *Academic*
  Freedom Policy Statements Archive. http://
  www.eff.org/pub/CAF/academic (27 Dec.
  1998).

7. WWW Site—Government

Use the name of the sponsoring government agency in place of the author. Note that for a site that is updated every few minutes, the date of publication is identical to the date of access.

U.S. Census Bureau. "POPClocks." *U.S. Census*
  Bureau: The Official Statistics.
  http://www.census.gov/main/www/popclock
  .html (27 Dec. 1998).

8. WWW Site—Printed Book Available Online

Many books first published on paper are now available online. To cite the online version, give the original print publication information, where available, followed by the electronic publication information, including the URL and date accessed. According to MLA style, when a book is published under a pseudonym, the author's real name is placed in brackets. If you know the name of the editor of the hypertext version, place it just before the Web address.

Twain, Mark [Samuel Langhorne Clemens]. *Innocents*
  Abroad: or, The New Pilgrim's Progress.
  Hartford: American, 1869. http://etext
  .virginia.edu/railton/innocent/iahompag
  .html (18 Dec. 1998).

9. WWW Site—Electronic Book

Electronic "books" might be more accurately described as hypertext narratives or interactive narratives. A site may have a single author using his

or her real name or multiple authors using pseudonyms and writing simultaneously at a MOO or contributing asynchronously to a developing text. Give
the primary author's name, if known; the title of the work in italics; the date
of publication or last revision; the electronic address; and the date of access.

> *The Company Therapist*. 1996. Rev. 19 Dec. 1998.
>
>   http://www.thetherapist.com/index.html
>
>   (21 Dec. 1998).

10. WWW Site—Online Article

List the author(s), followed by the article title in quotation marks
and the usual publication information. Include the volume and issue
numbers, if applicable, separated by a period. If both are included, place
the date of publication in parentheses.

> Palmquist, Mike, Will Hochman, Beth Kolko,
>
>   Emily Golson, Jonathan Alexander, Luann
>
>   Barnes, and Kate Kiefer. "Hypertext
>
>   Reflections: Exploring the Rhetoric,
>
>   Poetics, and Pragmatics of Hypertext."
>
>   *Kairos* 2.2 (1997). http://english.ttu.edu/
>
>   kairos/2.2/features/reflections/bridge
>
>   .html (16 Dec. 1998).

11. WWW Site—Article from News Service or Online Newspaper

Give the name of the author, if known, or the name of the news
source (for example, *Associated Press*); the title of the article in quotation
marks; the title of the news service or online newspaper in italics; and
other information as usual. When the date of publication is the same as
the date of access, use only the latter.

> Espy, David. "House Votes To Impeach Clinton."
>
>   *Yahoo! News*. http://dailynews.yahoo.com/
>
>   headlines/ap/washington/story.html?s+v/ap/
>
>   19981219/pl/ (19 Dec. 1998).

12. WWW Site—Article from Archive (Previously Published in Print)

Give the author's name; the title of the article in quotation marks;
the name of the journal in italics; the volume and issue numbers, if applic-

able; and the date of publication. List the name of the archive in italics, followed by the electronic address and the date accessed.

> Hauben, Michael F. "The Netizens and Community
>
> Networks." *Computer Mediated Communication*
>
> *Magazine* 4.2 (1997). *CMC Magazine Archive.*
>
> http://www.december.com/cmc/mag/1997/feb/
>
> hauben.html (16 Dec. 1998).

13. WWW Site—With Frames

For a document without its own URL, provide the italicized title of the page from which it was linked, the date of publication, and the electronic address of the main page, followed by a single blank space and the link(s) needed to reach the document.

> "Studies of Intermarriage Underway."
>
> *Communities in Transition* 1.1 (1995).
>
> http://www.hebrewcollege.edu/wilstein/
>
> index.html Wilstein Institute News (17
>
> Dec. 1998).

14. WWW Site—Graphic or Audio File

To cite a graphic or audio file alone, list the artist, photographer, or composer first; the title of the work, in italics if the work was first published separately, in quotation marks if it was first published as part of a larger work; the date it was produced; the address; and the date of access. To refer to the item within the context of a Web page, add the title of the page before the Web address.

> Seares, Robert. *Einstein with Young People.* 26
>
> Feb. 1931. "PhotoNet." *California*
>
> *Institute of Technology: Institute*
>
> *Archives.* http://www.caltech.edu/
>
> cgi-bin/arctohtml?1.8.1-12 (20 Dec. 1998).

2 Email messages, discussion lists, or newsgroups
15. Email—Personal

Always ask permission to cite a personal email message. Give the sender's real or log-in name and omit the email address. Use the subject line, in quotation marks, in place of a title; indicate that the message is personal email and follow with the date of the message.

```
Osborne, Paula. "Family Reunion." Personal
     email (19 Dec. 1998).
```

16. Email—Discussion List

Use the format for personal email, adding the name of the discussion list in italics between the date of the message and the address of the list. Unless the message has been retrieved from an archive, the date the message was sent serves as the date of access. Obtain permission from the sender to quote or use an email message in your work.

```
Kemp, Fred. "Digital Learning Communities."
     RHETNET. RHETNET-L@MIZZOU1.missouri.edu (4
     Sep. 1996).
```

17. Email—From Newsgroups

List the author's name or alias, the message's subject line in quotation marks, and its date if other than the date of access; give the name of the newsgroup in italics (if applicable), the newsgroup's protocol and address, and the date accessed.

```
Maffetone, Phil. "Re: Running and Carbohydrate
     Diet." 13 Dec. 1998. news:rec.running. (22
     Mar. 1999).
```

18. Email—From Message Archive

Give the author's real name or log-in name, the subject line of the message in quotation marks, the date of the post, the title of the discussion list (if known) in italics, and the list address. Then list the name of the archive in italics, the archive address of the post, and the date of access.

```
Caraveo, Shane. "New Stuff at NativeWeb." 20
     Aug. 1998. News, Announcements, and
     Information List. nw-news@nativeweb.org.
     Wotanging Ikche: Native American News
     Archives. http://www.nativeWeb.org/
     archives/news/9808/msg00000.html
     (21 Dec. 1998).
```

3 Materials obtained via gopher, ftp, or telnet
19. Via Gopher or FTP

Give the author's name, the title of the work, and original publication information if the work was previously published in print, including the city, publisher, and date. Then give complete information about the electronic version, including its title in quotation marks, any file or version numbers, the date of electronic publication or last revision, the title of database (if applicable) in italics, the protocol and address with any paths or directories, and the date accessed.

> Lewis, Sinclair. *Main Street*. New York:
>
>   Harcourt, 1920. "The Project Gutenberg
>
>   Etext of *Main Street,* by Sinclair Lewis."
>
>   Etext#543. May 1996. *Project Gutenberg*.
>
>   ftp://src.doc.ic.ac.uk/media/literary/
>
>   collections/project_gutenberg/gutenberg/
>
>   etext96/mnstr10.txt (14 Dec. 1998).

20. Via Telnet

Give the author of the document you are citing, if known; the title of the object or file in quotation marks; the name of the complete work or site, in italics, if applicable; the name of the maintainer of the site, if applicable; the protocol and complete address, including paths or commands needed to reach the document; and the date of access.

> "The Women's Collection of Electronic Texts."
>
>   Maint. Dene Grigar et al. *TWUMOO*. telnet://
>
>   205.165.53.14:8888 A EW WCET
>
>   (28 Dec. 1998).

4 Synchronous conference records
21. MOOs, MUDs

MOOs and MUDs function like chat rooms in many ways. Give the name or alias of the author of the message, if known; the type of message or the session title in quotation marks; the title of the site in italics; the protocol and full address, including paths or commands required for access; and the date of the exchange.

> Vanessa. Personal interview. *Mundo Hispanico*.
>
>   telnet://moo.syr.edu:8888 (28 Dec. 1998).

22. LANs

To cite a message in a conference created with software such as the InterChange feature of the Daedalus Integrated Writing Environment (DIWE), give the author's name or pseudonym as it appears in the transcript. Always ask the author's permission to quote or cite a message. Identify the software or LAN, as appropriate, and the date. For conference transcripts stored online, give the title and address of the location where the transcript can be found.

> "*Incidents in the Life of a Slave Girl*
>
>   InterChange." *DIWE*. University of Texas.
>
>   10 Apr. 1997. *E341L: Women's Popular*
>
>   *Culture InterChanges*. http://www.cwrl
>
>   .utexas.edu/~women/romance/interchanges/
>
>   incidents.html (27 Dec. 1998).

5 Reference tools and databases

23. Entry in Online Dictionary

Give the author's name, if available, or begin with the title of the entry in quotation marks. List the title of the dictionary in italics; give information about previous print publication, if applicable; give the date of publication of the online edition if different from the date of access; and list the electronic address and the date of access.

> Lapiaki, Jolanta A. "Network." *ASL Dictionary*
>
>   *Online*. http://dww.deafworldweb.org/
>
>   asl/n/network.html (17 Dec. 1998).
>
> **No separate publication date is given because the site is updated daily.**

24. Article in Online Encyclopedia

Name the author of the article, if available, or begin with the title of the article in quotation marks. After the italicized title of the encyclopedia, give information about the publisher (name and city); list a subscriber service, if applicable; give the copyright date; list the electronic address, including any applicable paths or directories; and give the date accessed.

> Hefner, Alan G. "The Legend of the Buffalo
>
>   Dance." *The Encyclopedia Mythica*. M. F.
>
>   Lindemans, 1998. http://www.pantheon.org/

```
mythica/articles/1/legend_of_buffalo
dance.html (17 Dec. 1998).
```

25. Information on CD-ROM

List the name of the author or editor, the title of the article or section in quotation marks, the title of the CD-ROM in italics, the version number preceded by *Vers.*, and the city, publisher, and year of publication. Omit the date of access.

```
Rose, Mark, ed. "Elements of Theater." The

    Norton Shakespeare Workshop CD-ROM. Vers.

    1.1. New York: Norton, 1997.
```

26. Article from Online Database

Give the author's name, the title of the article in quotation marks, and the italicized title of the journal or work in which the article originally appeared. List the version or edition number, if applicable; the date of publication; and the page numbers(s) in the original source. Give the name of the database or retrieval service in italics (or the complete electronic address), the file or article number, and the date of access.

```
Wittberg, Patricia. "Deep Structure in

    Community Cultures: The Revival of

    Religious Orders in Roman Catholicism."

    Sociology of Religion. Fall 1997: 239+.

    Searchbank: Expanded Academic ASAP,

    Article #A20245892 (18 Dec. 1998).
```

6 Software

27. Software/Video Game

Give the name of an individual or corporate author; the title of the software or video game in italics; the version number, if applicable; and the place, publisher, and date of publication.

```
Blair, C. Arthur. Black Quest: The Griot.

    Bladensburg, MD: Rediscovery Learning

    Works, 1997.
```

53e Sample COS/humanities-style works cited page

Works Consulted

Brown, Kirk W. *Hazardous Waste and Treatment.*
    Woburn: Butterworth, 1983.

Bugher, Robert D. *Municipal Refuse Disposal.*
    Danville: Interstate, 1970.

Farley, Rose. "Bottom of the Ninth: Permit

*Article from
archive of
an online
newspaper*

Hearings Begin in TXI's Quest to Become
    the Nation's Largest Toxic Waste
    Incinerator." *Dallas Observer Online.* 12
    Feb. 1998. *Dallas Observer Archives.*
    http://www.dallasobserver.com/archives/
    1998/021298/news2.html (19 Jan. 1999).

Flack, J. E. *Man and the Quality of His
    Environment.* Boulder: U of Colorado P,
    1967.

Hand, Shane. *Questionnaire on Consumer Habits
    and Attitudes Toward Recycling.*
    Blacksburg, VA, and Upper Marlboro, MD.
    21-25 Feb. 1999.

Hazardous Waste Incineration. New York:
    American Society of Mechanical Engineers,
    1988.

Montague, Peter. "New Study Shows Incinerator
    Ash More Dangerous Than We Realized."
    Rachel's Hazardous Waste News 92 (29 Aug
    1988). http://www.enviroweb.org/pubs/
    rachel/rhwn092.htm (19 Jan. 1999).

Organic Waste Technologies Inc. "Leachate
    Evaporation." 1998. *Corporate author, no individual
    author or site title*

```
    http://www.owtinc.com/leachate_1.htm (19
    Jan. 1999).
Pennsylvania Department of Environmental
    Protection. "Brownfields Tax Incentive." 1
    July 1998. http://www.dep.state.pa.us/
    dep/deputate/airwaste/wm/landrecy/Tax/
    tax.htm (19 Jan. 1999).
Rathje, William L. "Once and Future Landfills."
    National Geographic May 1991: 116-34.
Van Tassel, Alfred J. Environmental Side
    Effects of Rising Industrial Output.
    Lexington, MA: Heath, 1970.
Wiseman, Clark A. "Impediments to Economically
    Efficient Solid Waste Management."
    Resources 105 (1991): 9-11.
```

53f Using COS in the sciences (with APA, CBE)

The basic format for citing online sources in a reference list is as follows.

```
Author's Surname, Initial(s). (Date of document
    if different from date of last revision).
    Title of document. Title of complete work
    or site (file or version number). (Edition
    or date of last revision). Protocol and
    electronic address, access path, or
    directories (Date of access).
```

The author's last name is given first, followed by a comma and the initials of the first and middle names. If no single author is named, use the name of the sponsoring organization, if it appears on the page. If the document date is different from the date of access, place it in parentheses after the author's name, followed by a period and a space. Give the year first, followed by the month, if applicable, in unabbreviated form, and the day. COS/scientific style uses no quotation marks for titles and capitalizes only the first word of a title or subtitle and any proper nouns (except in journal titles, which are capitalized with APA style) follow with a period.

**53f
COS**

Italicize the title of the complete work or site. List the file, version, or edition number (in parentheses); the date of last revision or modification (in parentheses); the complete electronic address, and the date you accessed the site (in parentheses). For the revision date and date of access, list a numeral for day; an abbreviation for all months except May, June, and July; and the year (for example, *25 June 1942*). Although all of the above information may not apply or be available, provide as much of it as possible in your citation.

> Brown, M. C. (1997). The past: What has happened
>
> before. *The faces of science: African*
>
> *Americans in the sciences* (Rev. 31 Aug.
>
> 1998). http://www.lib.lsu.edu/lib/chem/
>
> display/faces.html#Past (28 Dec. 1998).

Guide to COS/Scientific Formats for a Reference List

1. CITATIONS FROM THE WORLD WIDE WEB (WWW)

28. WWW Site
29. WWW Site—Revised, Updated, or Modified
30. WWW Site—Authored by Group, Organization, or Institution
31. WWW Site—Corporate Author
32. WWW Site—Without Named Author, Group, or Title
33. WWW Site—Maintained or Compiled by Individual
34. WWW Site—Government
35. WWW Site—Printed Book Available Online
36. WWW Site—Electronic Book
37. WWW Site—Online Article
38. WWW Site—Article from News Service or Online Newspaper
39. WWW Site—Article from Archive (Previously Published in Print)
40. WWW Site—with Frames
41. WWW Site—Graphic or Audio File

2. EMAIL MESSAGES, DISCUSSION LISTS, OR NEWSGROUPS

42. Email—Personal
43. Email—Discussion List
44. Email—From Newsgroup
45. Email—From Message Archive

3 MATERIALS OBTAINED VIA GOPHER, FTP, OR TELNET

46. Via Gopher or FTP
47. Via Telnet

4. SYNCHRONOUS CONFERENCE RECORDS

48. MOOs, MUDs
49. LANs

5. REFERENCE TOOLS AND DATABASES

50. Entry in Online Dictionary
51. Article in Online Encyclopedia
52. Information on CD-ROM
53. Article from Online Database

6. SOFTWARE

54. Software/Video Game

1 Citations from the World Wide Web (WWW)

28. WWW Site

```
Hochman, W. (1998). Beyond exception: The
     writer's life. The Salt River review, 1
     (1) (Rev. Nov. 1998). http://www.mc
     .maricopa.edu/users/cervantes/SRR/hochman
     .html (20 Dec. 1998).
```

29. WWW Site—Revised, Updated, or Modified

If a date of last revision, updating, or modification is given on the site, indicate it in parentheses immediately after the title, preceded by the abbreviation *Rev.* or *Mod.*

```
AFL-CIO. (1998). Facts about working women.
     Today's unions (Rev. 7 Dec. 1998).
     http://www.aflcio.org/women/wwfacts
     .htm (19 Dec. 1998).
```

30. WWW Site—Authored by Group, Organization, or Institution

If a group, organization, or institution sponsors a site and no individual author is named, use the name of the group in place of an author.

```
International Olympic Committee. Welcome to the
     official site of the International Olympic
     Committee. The official site of the
     International Olympic Committee.
     http://www.olympic.org (27 Dec. 1998).
```

31. WWW Site—Corporate Author

When a corporation serves as the author of a page, use its full name; give the date of publication in parentheses if different from date of access, followed by a period and the page's title.

```
Goodwill Industries International, Inc. (1998).
     Goodwill career links (Rev. 18 Dec. 1998).
     http://www.goodwill.org/about/careerlk
     .htm (19 Dec. 1998).
```

If the complete site has a title different from the name of the corporation used as author, provide it, in italics.

```
LatinoLink Enterprises, Inc. (1998). Job bank.
     LatinoLink. http://www.latinolink.com/
     joblist.html (29 Dec. 1998).
```

32. WWW Site—Without Named Author, Group, or Title

When no author or authoring group is named on the Web page, begin with the title of the document, followed by the date of the document (if available), the electronic address, and the date accessed.

```
Social statistics briefing room.
     http://www.whitehouse.gov/fsbr/ssbr.html
     (19 Dec. 1998).
```

If no title is given, begin with file name and type.

```
chorusline.mpg [animated graphic file]. http://
     www.juggling.org/animations/chorusline
     .mpg (20 Dec. 1998).
```

33. WWW Site—Maintained or Compiled by Individual

A maintained site is one in which a Web designer organizes, indexes, and posts information gathered from several sources, often for a sponsoring organization. For a maintained site, give the group or author first, if applicable; the date of publication in parentheses; the title of the site; and, in parentheses; the name of the maintainer followed by the abbreviation *Maint.* For a compiled site that consists primarily of links to other sites, use *Comp.* after the name of the site's creator.

```
Southeast Colorado RC&D, Inc. Colorado Southeast
     network. (A. Bray, Comp.). http://www
     .ruralnet.net/~csn (17 Dec. 1998).
```

To make specific reference to the work of the maintainer or compiler, place that name first, followed by *Maint.* or *Comp.* in parentheses.

```
Freeland, C. (Maint.). (1997, January). SWIP—The
     Society for Women in Philosophy. http://www
     .uh.edu/~cfreelan/SWIP/ (17 Dec. 1998).
```

If the maintainer or compiler is not named, simply omit that information.

> Computers and academic freedom. *Academic*
>
>   *freedom policy statements archive.*
>
>   http://www.eff.org/pub/CAF/academic
>
>   (27 Dec. 1998).

34. WWW Site—Government

Use the name of the sponsoring government agency in place of the author; then proceed as usual. Note that for a site updated every few minutes, the date of publication is omitted because it is identical with the date of access.

> U.S. Census Bureau. POPClocks. *U.S. Census*
>
>   *Bureau: The official statistics.*
>
>   http://www.census.gov/main/www/popclock.
>
>   html (27 Dec. 1998).

35. WWW Site—Printed Book Available Online

An online version of a book first published on paper should be cited with as much original publication information as is available, including the date of publication, the name of the publisher, and the city where the publisher is located. For a book published under a pseudonym, give the real name in brackets. Place the name of the editor of the hypertext version, if you know it, just before the Web address.

> Twain, M. [S. L. Clemens]. (1869). *The*
>
>   *innocents abroad:* Or, *the new Pilgrim's*
>
>   *Progress.* Hartford: American.
>
>   http://etext.virginia.edu/railton/innocent/
>
>   iahompag.html (18 Dec. 1998).

36. WWW Site—Electronic Book

Electronic "books" vary in type. Some are more accurately described as hypertext narratives or interactive narratives. They may have multiple authors, who may be using pseudonyms and writing synchronously at a MOO or asynchronously, as in the case below. Give the primary author's name, if known; the date of publication in parentheses, if different from the date of last revision; the title of the work in italics; the date of last revision in parentheses; the electronic address; and the date of access.

```
The company therapist. (1996). (Rev. 19 Dec.

    1998). http://www.thetherapist.com/

    index.html (21 Dec. 1998).
```

37. WWW Site—Online Article

List the author(s) and give the date of publication in parentheses, the article title, and the usual publication information.

```
Palmquist, M., Hochman, W., Kolko, B., Golson,

    E., Alexander, J., Barnes, L., & Kiefer, K.

    (1997). Hypertext reflections: Exploring

    the rhetoric, poetics, and pragmatics of

    hypertext. Kairos, 2(2). http://english.ttu

    .edu/kairos/2.2/features/reflections/bridge

    .html (16 Dec. 1998).
```

38. WWW Site—Article from News Service or Online Newspaper

Give the name of the author, if known, or the name of the news source (for example, *Associated Press*); the title of the article; the title of the news service or online newspaper in italics; the electronic address; and the date accessed.

```
Espy, D. House votes to impeach Clinton. Yahoo!

    news. http://dailynews.yahoo.com/

    headlines/ap/washington/story.html?s+v/ap/

    19981219/pl/ (19 Dec. 1998).
```

39. WWW Site—Article from Archive (Previously Published in Print)

Give the author's name, the date of publication in parentheses; the title of the article; the name of the journal and the name of the archive, both in italics; the address; and the date accessed.

```
Hauben, M. F. (1997, February). The Netizens

    and community networks. Computer mediated

    communication magazine, 4(2). CMC magazine

    archive. http://www.december.com/cmc/

    mag/1997/feb/hauben.htm (16 Dec. 1998).
```

40. WWW Site—With Frames

For a document without its own URL, provide the italicized title of the page from which it was linked, then the electronic address of the main page, followed by a single blank space and the link(s) needed to get to the article.

```
Studies of intermarriage underway. (1995).

     Communities in transition, 1(1). http:/

     /www.hebrewcollege.edu/wilstein/index.html

     Wilstein Institute News (17 Dec. 1998).
```

41. WWW Site—Graphic or Audio File

Give the name of the artist, photographer, or composer; the date of production; the title of the work (in italics if first published separately); and original publication information. If you wish to refer to the item as part of a Web page, add the title of the page after the title of the file.

```
Seares, R. (1931, February 26). Einstein with

     young people. PhotoNet. California

     Institute of Technology: Institute

     archives. http://www.caltech.edu/

     cgi-bin/arctohtml?1.8.1-12 (20 Dec. 1998).
```

2 Email, discussion lists, or newsgroups

42. Email—Personal

Although scientific reference lists seldom include personal email, if you use it, include either the sender's name with the first initial or the log-in name; the date the message was sent, if different from the date of access, in parentheses; and the subject line. In brackets, indicate the kind of message. Always omit personal email addresses and ask the author for permission to use the post.

```
Osborne. P. Family reunion. [Personal email].

     (19 Dec. 1998).
```

43. Email—Discussion List

Provide the sender's real name or log-in name; the date the message was sent in parentheses; the subject line as the title; the name of the discussion list in italics; and the address of the list. Then give the name of the discussion list, its address, and the date of access.

```
Kemp, F. Digital learning communities. RHETNET.

    RHETNET-L@MIZZOU1.missouri.edu (4 Sep.

    1996).
```

44. Email—From Newsgroup

List the author's name or alias; the date the message was posted if other than the date of access; the subject line; the name of the newsgroup, if applicable, in italics; the protocol and address; and the date accessed.

```
Maffetone, P. (1998, December 13). Re: Running

    and carbohydrate diet. news:rec.running.

    (22 Mar. 1999).
```

45. Email—From Message Archive

Give the author's real name or log-in name; the date of posting in parentheses, if different from the date of access; the subject line of the message; the name of the discussion list in italics; and the list address. Then give the name of the archive in italics, the archive address of the post, and the date of access.

```
Caraveo, S. (1998, August 20). New stuff at

    nativeWeb. News, announcements, and

    information list. nw-news@nativeWeb.org.

    Wotanging Ikche: Native American news

    archives. http://www.nativeWeb.org/

    archives/news/9808/msg00000.html

    (21 Dec. 1998).
```

3 Materials obtained via gopher, ftp, or telnet

46. Via Gopher or FTP

Give the author's name; the date of original publication, if applicable, in parentheses; the title of the work (with book titles in italics); and, if previously published in print, the city and publisher. Give the title of the electronic version if it has been altered from the original; the file or version numbers, if applicable; the date of electronic publication or last revision in parentheses; the title of the database, if applicable, in italics; and the gopher or ftp protocol and address, paths or directories, and date accessed.

```
Lewis, S. (1920). Main Street. New York:
    Harcourt. The Project Gutenberg etext of
    Main street, by Sinclair Lewis.
    (Etext#543). (May 1996). Project
    Gutenberg. ftp://src.doc.ic.ac.uk/media/
    literary/collections/project_gutenberg/
    gutenberg/etext96/mnstr10.txt (14 Dec.
    1998).
```

47. Via Telnet

Give the author of the document you are citing, if known; the date of publication (in parentheses) if known and different from the date of access; the title of the work or object cited; the name of the complete work or site, in italics, if applicable; the date of publication, if known; the protocol and complete telnet address, followed by a single blank space and a list of any directories or commands needed to access the work; and the date of access.

```
The women's collection of electronic texts. (D.
    Grigar et al., Maint.). TWUMOO. telnet:/
    /205.165.53.14:8888 A EW WCET (28 Dec.
    1998).
```

4 Synchronous conference records

48. MOOs, MUDs

Give the name or alias of the author of the message, if known; the type of message or title of the session; the italicized title of the MOO or MUD site, if applicable; the protocol and complete address, including paths and any commands needed to access it; and the date of the exchange.

```
Vanessa. Personal interview. Mundo Hispanico.
    telnet://moo.syr.edu:8888 (28 Dec. 1998).
```

49. LANs

To cite a message in a conference created with software such as Daedalus InterChange, give the author's name or pseudonym as it appears in the transcript, the date of the session, and its title. Identify the software or LAN, as appropriate, and give the date. For transcripts stored online, give the title and address of the location where the transcript can be found. Always request the author's permission to quote an InterChange message.

> `Incidents in the life of a slave girl.`
>
> `InterChange. (1997, April 10). DIWE.`
>
> `University of Texas. E341L: Women's`
>
> `Popular Culture InterChanges. http://www`
>
> `.cwrl.utexas.edu/~women/romance/`
>
> `interchanges/incidents.html (27 Dec. 1998).`

5 Reference tools and databases

50. Entry in Online Dictionary

Give the author's name, if available, and the date of publication if different from the date of access; or begin with the entry as the title, followed by the date of publication. List the title of the dictionary in italics, and give information about previous publication, if applicable; give the electronic address and the date of access.

> `Lapiaki, J. A. Network. ASL dictionary online.`
>
> `http://dww.deafworldWeb.org/asl`
>
> `(17 Dec. 1998).`

No separate publication date is given because the dictionary is modified daily.

51. Article in Online Encyclopedia

Name the author of the article, if available, followed by the date of the document. If no author is named, begin with the title of the article, followed by the date. Give the title of the encyclopedia in italics; list the name of the publisher and information about print publication, if applicable; list the subscriber service, if applicable; give the electronic address, including paths or directories needed to reach the document; and add the date accessed.

> `Hefner, A. G. (1998). The legend of the buffalo`
>
> `dance. The encyclopedia mythica. M. F.`
>
> `Lindemans. http://www.pantheon.org/`
>
> `mythica/articles/l/legend_of_buffalo_dance`
>
> `.html (17 Dec. 1998).`

52. Information on CD-ROM

Give author's or editor's surname and initial(s), followed by *Ed.* in parentheses, if applicable. List the year of publication in parentheses, the title of the article or section of the disk cited, and the title of the disk in italics. Give the version number, preceded by the word *Version* in parentheses and followed by the publisher's city and name.

Rose, M. (Ed.). (1997). Elements of theater.

The Norton Shakespeare workshop (Version

1.1). New York: Norton.

53. Article from Online Database

Give the author's surname and initial(s); the date of publication in parentheses; the title of the article; original publication information, including the title of the publication; volume and file numbers, if applicable, in parentheses; the name of the database in italics; the article or file number in parentheses (or the complete electronic address); and the date of access.

Wittberg, P. (1997, Fall). Deep structure in

community cultures: The revival of

religious orders in Roman Catholicism.

Sociology of religion. 239+. *Searchbank:*

Expanded academic ASAP, Article #A20245892

(12 Dec. 1998).

6 Software
54. Software/Video Game

Blair, C. Arthur. (1997). *Black quest: The*

griot. Bladensburg, MD: Rediscovery

Learning Works.

53g Sample COS Reference List

References

Coyle, E. F., Coggan, A. R., Hopper, M. K., &

Walters, T. J. (1988). Determinants of

endurance in well-trained cyclists. *Journal of Applied Physiology, 64,* 2622-2630.

David, C., & Cowles, M. (1991). Body image and exercise. *Sex Roles, 25,* 33-34.

Drewnowski, A., & Yee, D. K. (1987). Men and body image: Are males satisfied with their body weight? *Psychosomatic Medicine, 49,* 626-634.

Interbike 1992 directory. (1992). Costa Mesa, CA: Primedia.

Matheny, F. (1986, February 5). Solo cycling. *Volo News,* 157.

Meyer, J. (1994, Winter). Alison Sydor, cyclist, on equity in cycling. *Action.* http://www.makeithappen.com/wis/readings/insydor.htm (9 Nov. 1998).

An article previously published in a periodical

Schneider, D., & Greenberg, M. (1992). Choice of exercise: A predictor of behavioral risks. *Research Quarterly for Exercise and Sport, 9,* 231-245.

Worthington, R. G. (1998). *Labor power racing: lung busters, leg breakers.* http://www.mesothel.com/pages/labpower.htm (9 Nov. 1998).

Citation for a Web site

Zimberoff, B. F. (1996). Ocean to ocean on two wheels: Harassment on the road. *Armchair World NetEscapes.* http://www.armchair.com/escape/bike7.html (9 Nov. 1998).

WRITING
STRATEGIES

CHAPTER

54

Writing Argumentative Papers Across the Disciplines

Some of the most common writing assignments in college courses, especially in the humanities and social sciences, are those that ask you to articulate and support a position or point of view. Such writing, including all forms of argument, is **point-driven writing.** Unlike purely informative writing, in which you play a neutral role and try to present information in an organized, objective, and readable way (see Chapter 56), **argumentative writing** is evaluative: it takes a stand. In argumentative writing, your own voice, attitudes, opinions, and values play an important role. As a result, you must attend carefully to the relationship between your ideas and your readers' potential responses.

Obviously, argumentative writing can't be separated entirely from informative writing. A grant proposal may need to educate a committee about existing research in the area being funded while it is also trying to persuade that committee to honor the financial request. But the *primary* goal of argumentative writing is to advance the writer's point of view, or to suggest a course of action to solve a problem. You want to say to your reader, rhetorically, "Try to see it my way," or "Here's a way to think about this, and here's why." In informative writing, you're more likely to imply, "Here's some new and interesting knowledge for you, but I'm just a reporter; don't confuse the message with the messenger."

This chapter presents some strategies for producing successful argumentative and other point-driven writing. The chapter also presents some sample argumentative papers written by college students, papers that take different approaches to persuading readers. Though the papers are effective, they also show how the writers struggled to meet the special demands of their assignments and what strategies of point-driven writing those assignments required. These sample papers also draw on a variety of sources for evidence that explains and supports the writer's perspective.

As you consider the Strategies for point-driven writing described and modeled in this chapter, remember that most writing is not formulaic. Do not think that to produce it you just need to remember a few rules. Even the simplest forms will vary according to your purpose, audience, and context.

54a Developing argumentative writing

54a
arg

In many classes you may be asked to write a short argumentative paper, often documented with outside sources. Unlike a full-scale "objective" research paper, this kind of writing documents and supports your own opinion, usually on one specific aspect of a particular topic. Because you must limit yourself to a narrow focus and get right to the point, you have to construct your argument carefully and efficiently.

1 Identify an issue

Your feelings about some things may be so strong that you want to argue with anyone who disagrees with your position. But what if no one really disagrees? What if no one thinks the subject is worth arguing about? To have an argument in a formal sense, you must begin with an **issue,** a subject about which there are two (or more) clearly differing opinions. No one, for example, is willing to say that driving while intoxicated is a good thing; anyone who tried to advance this opinion would be considered foolish, at best. Drunk driving is not an issue. However, reasonable people disagree about what policies are most likely to discourage people from driving while intoxicated—strict laws, harsh punishments, roadblocks, advertising campaigns, door-to-door public information programs, programs for high school students, and so on. For most readers this question is certainly an issue, and they would probably be glad to listen to differing opinions in hopes of discovering the best way to deal with the problem.

Use the following questions to help you determine whether you have chosen an issue worth pursuing in your writing.

1. *Is the issue clearly debatable?* A fact is something about which there can be no debate ("The world is round," "Mice are rodents," "President John F. Kennedy was assassinated on November 22, 1963"). The only facts that can be debated are those that might be reasonably challenged *as* facts. For example, it was widely held as "fact" that peptic ulcers were caused by excess acidity in the diet, and for years treatment involved changes in eating habits, antacids, or acid-inhibiting drugs. New evidence, however, now supports a theory that ulcers are caused by a bacterium able to be treated with antibiotics. The question "Are peptic ulcers caused by diet?" is, in light of this information, a much more debatable issue than the question "Does the earth have a moon?"

2. *Can you explore the issue with something more than pure speculation?* Claims that can't be verified often make for interesting philosophical discussion, but they don't lend themselves fully to argument. The question "Where do we go when we die?" is impossible to answer conclusively and therefore hard to develop into an arguable issue. Statements for which there is only tentative supporting evidence ("There may be life on other planets") also make difficult choices for argumentative writing.

3. *Is the issue more than a matter of pure taste or preference?* An author's own values and beliefs need to be supported in argumentative writing with sound reasoning or evidence. Statements such as "I hate anything with tomatoes in it" can't be supported with anything more than circular reasoning ("because I hate tomatoes"). However, evaluative statements based on comparisons or analyses, such as those found in reviews (see 54f), can become reasonable supporting evidence for a broader assertion ("The food at Alfredo's Restaurant is highly overrated").

4. *Does the issue avoid assumptions that are so deeply or universally held that they cannot be argued?* Although some of the most important social and political issues of our time seem like good topics for argumentative writing, they may seriously frustrate your writing process. Arguments about topics such as the right to die and capital punishment may invoke systems of belief, including religious belief, that can't be logically debated. Debates between nonreligious students and their fundamentalist peers rarely end in resolution or change—interesting or confrontational though the discussions may be. When you choose a topic, ask yourself whether and how it can be explored through the use of sound reasoning and evidence.

STRATEGY

Here are three ways to identify an issue of interest to you and of significance to your readers.

- In your journal or on a piece of paper, "talk" to yourself about problems, controversies, trends, or ideas that concern you or that affect the ways we all live. Try making a list, adding to each item a short (one- or two-sentence) summary of at least two different opinions on the subject.

- Interview friends and family about questions and problems that concern them and that inspire strong opinions. Keep a list of their responses, and add your own ideas. Identify subjects about which there are at least two reasonable and differing opinions. (If many of the issues you discover seem of limited or local concern—such as campus parking policies or a controversy over a garbage-fired incinerator—remember that a focused subject is often a better choice for writing than an overly broad one, even one of global concern.)

- Leaf through newsmagazines and opinion magazines (such as *The New Republic* and *National Review*); look at editorials in local and national newspapers (available in your library); and consult periodical indexes or databases like *Newsbank,* which provides newspaper editorials from the entire country (see 45d). List the issues that interest you, and write down any opposing opinions.

Exercise 1

A. Examine the following five issue statements. Decide which of the issues could be developed into argumentative papers and which would not lend themselves to such development. Explain why.

1. Banning campus visits by environmentally insensitive firms
2. The taste of fresh orange juice
3. The sale of pharmaceuticals (aspirin, sunscreen, condoms, tampons) in campus vending machines
4. Belief in the sacredness of cows
5. The reinstitution of chain gangs (prisoners shackled together at the legs) to do highway work

B. In a small group, compare your analysis of the items in Exercise 1A. Collectively choose two issue statements that would make good argumentative papers.

2 Articulate your stance

An **argument** is an attempt to resolve disagreement, not to defeat everyone who has an opinion other than yours. A good argument is positive: you attempt to persuade people to accept your opinion, but you don't attack them for having another point of view. In order to argue effectively, you first need a clear idea of your own opinion and the reasons why you hold it.

It is often easy to voice opinions in a lively discussion among friends—if another person disagrees, you can immediately defend or clarify what you have said or challenge the person with another point. In written argument, however, you don't have this luxury. Since your readers aren't responding to you "live," you need to anticipate their reactions and counterarguments.

STRATEGY

Here are several steps you can follow to begin articulating your stance and developing your arguments.

- Write informally (perhaps in your journal) about your intuitive reaction to your chosen issue. Does the issue make you feel scornful, pitying, fearful, or outraged? If the issue angers you, exactly what about it makes you angry?
- List the specific elements of the issue to which you have responded emotionally, and briefly summarize your responses. Add to this list other points that you may not react to emotionally but which, on an intellectual level, support your first reaction.
- Begin identifying facts, examples, and ideas that support your opinions. Also begin thinking about objections to your point of view. If you need to go outside your experience to provide support or to deal with opposing opinions, make a preliminary research plan identifying the kinds of information and ideas you may need to gather.

There are many other ways you can pinpoint your stance—for example, reading about the subject, talking with others, and listening to debates in person, on television, or on the radio. What is crucial, however, is that you make *writing* part of your attempt to develop your stand, not only because your final argument will be written but also because the act of writing pushes your thinking and reasoning.

3 Focus on a purpose and a thesis

As you begin identifying your point of view, try to limit the scope of your argument. If your issue is too broad, you will have a hard time covering it in a reasonable space and an equally difficult time persuading readers to agree with you. One good way to focus your effort is to ask yourself what kind of opinion you want to argue for. Do you want to argue that an activity, belief, or arrangement is good or bad (effective or ineffective, healthful or harmful, desirable or undesirable, and so on)? If so, you are asking readers to agree with a **value judgment.** Do you want to persuade readers that a particular course of action ought to be undertaken or avoided? If so, you are asking readers to agree with a particular **policy.** Do you want readers to agree that a particular explanation is correct or incorrect? If so, you are asking readers to endorse or reject an **interpretation.**

To construct an effective argument, you need to recognize your specific purpose for arguing and to focus on this purpose. For example, you may believe that stopping all cars on a highway to search for drunk drivers is a violation of civil liberties, so roadblocks should be replaced with another technique for keeping intoxicated people from driving. You need to recognize that this opinion commits you to arguing for both a value judgment (roadblocks violate civil liberties) and a policy (another technique for enforcing laws against drunk driving), so that your writing does not blur these points and the reasoning and evidence you use to support them.

STRATEGY

To organize your writing and to help readers focus on your opinion (and the evidence supporting it), state your outlook as a **proposition,** that is, as a thesis statement (see 5c) offering an opinion you want readers to adopt.

When you are planning and drafting a position paper, treat your proposition as a tentative thesis you will revise as you explore your reasoning in writing or as you identify supporting evidence and contrary arguments (see 5c-4). Check whether your tentative thesis blurs your specific purposes for arguing or is illogical.

BLURRED AND ILLOGICAL
Police should stop conducting unconstitutional roadblocks and substitute more frequent visual checks of erratic driving to identify people who are driving while intoxicated.

The value judgment and policy proposal are blurred in this thesis statement. In addition, the thesis is potentially illogical because the writer seems to assume that the roadblocks are unconstitutional and does not acknowledge that this value judgment needs to be argued (see "Begging the Question," 54c-5).

Make sure that your thesis either focuses on a single proposition or identifies two related propositions you will argue in an appropriate order.

SINGLE PROPOSITIONS
Roadblocks used to identify drunk drivers are unconstitutional.

Police should make more frequent visual checks of erratic driving to identify people who are driving while intoxicated.

RELATED PROPOSITIONS
The current practice of using roadblocks to identify drunk drivers is unconstitutional; therefore, police should use an alternative procedure such as instituting more frequent visual checks of erratic driving behavior.

Exercise 2

A. Examine the following propositions as possible thesis statements for argumentative essays. Decide whether each example provides an adequate thesis, and explain your judgments.

1. The United States should deregulate all mail service in order to increase competition and improve the quality of service.
2. Rap music, which is violent, vulgar, and sexist, should be banned from public consumption, and fines should be imposed on anyone listening to it in public places.
3. The demands for "computer literacy" (knowledge of how to use computers on the job, at home, and in all aspects of public life) will keep increasing with each generation; therefore, public schools should be required to have courses in computer literacy for all students.
4. All Americans select and wear their attire on the basis of a discriminatory class system which, in the schools, distracts students from their education; therefore, we should pass a federal law requiring all students in public schools to wear identical uniforms.
5. Arson is not a crime; it is a mental disease and should be treated as such.
6. If children read when they are growing up, they will become literate.
7. Orange juice tastes better than cranberry juice.
8. Recirculating the hot air from your clothes drier into your basement during the cold winter months can significantly reduce your heating costs.
9. Humanity's woes began when Eve tasted the forbidden fruit in the Garden of Eden.
10. The telephone resulted in a society less prone to writing, but email will likely lead us right back into the written word as a primary form of communication.

 B. In a small group, compare your responses to Exercise 2A. For any propositions that you all agree are inadequate, collaboratively draft a revised proposition that would make an acceptable thesis statement for a short argumentative paper.

4 Develop supporting evidence

As you think about an issue or do research on it, be alert for the different kinds of **supporting evidence,** including examples from your personal experience, examples from other people's experiences, quotations and ideas from recognized authorities on a subject, technical information and statistics, data from surveys and interviews (from your own research or someone else's), background and historical information, and comparisons to similar situations or problems.

As you collect evidence in support of an assertion, also examine the balance of different types of evidence. If all your evidence comes from your own experience, your reader might argue that because other people don't share those experiences, your argument is not entirely valid. Try to achieve a balance of facts and statistics, quotations from experts, and personal knowledge. Avoid relying too much on beliefs, especially from religious scripture, as supporting evidence.

Examples. Examples drawn from your own experience or from the experiences of others can be among the most persuasive kinds of evidence you can use for support. Events, people, ideas, objects, feelings, stories, images, and texts—all these and similar "instances" can be turned into examples to support a thesis and encourage readers to share your point of view.

Relying on examples is something we and our readers do every day. When we are trying to make a decision or form an opinion, we often call to mind our own experiences or those we have read or heard about. Almost without thinking, we then try to decide whether the experiences are representative or unique and whether they apply to the issue or situation we are considering.

In choosing to provide examples in support of an argument, therefore, you need to keep in mind both the readiness of readers to be persuaded by examples and the likelihood that they will approach examples critically. Remember, too, that the power of examples to persuade often rests in the concrete detail a writer provides. Detail serves to illustrate and explain the point being made as well as to support the writer's conclusions.

A fully developed example uses explanation to provide readers with the information they need if they are to come to agree with an opinion or judgment. It uses specific details to help persuade readers of the ethical or emotional importance of a proposition and of its relevance to the reader and to other people. The following extended example does these things by drawing on the writer's experiences.

> I am afraid to grow old—we're all afraid. In fact, the fear of growing old is so great that every aged person is an insult and a threat to the society. They remind us of our own death, that our body won't always remain smooth and responsive, but will someday betray us by aging, wrinkling, faltering, failing. The ideal way to age would be to grow slowly invisible, gradually disappearing, without causing worry or discomfort to the young. In some ways that does happen. Sitting in a small park across from a nursing home one day, I noticed that the young mothers and their children gathered on one side, and the old people from the home on the other. Whenever a youngster would run over to the "wrong" side, chasing a ball or just trying to cover all the available space, the old people would lean forward and smile. But before any communication could be established, the mother would take her child back to the "young" side.
>
> —Sharon Curtin, *Nobody Ever Died of Old Age*

54a
arg

Brief examples often serve more to explain than support, but by providing several related examples, you can often create a cluster of instances with considerable persuasive force, as in the following passage.

> The era of the modern family system had come to an end, and few could feel sanguine about the postmodern family condition that had succeeded it. Unaccustomed to a state of normative instability and definitional crisis, the populace split its behavior from its beliefs. Many who contributed actively to such postmodern family statistics as divorce, remarriage, blended families, single parenthood, joint custody, abortion, domestic partnership, two-career households, and the like still yearned nostalgically for the *Father Knows Best* world they had lost. —JUDITH STACEY, "The Family Values Fable"

54a arg

Quotations and Ideas from Authorities. By turning to the words or ideas of a recognized authority on a subject or issue, you can add to the reasons for readers to agree with your point of view. After all, we identify people as experts or authorities because we believe that they know more about a subject than we do, and the idea of expertise includes a general willingness to agree with the expert's opinion.

Most readers are nonetheless likely to maintain an intelligently critical attitude toward your use of ideas and quotations from experts. They will expect you to cite generally recognized authorities or to indicate why the person you are citing should be viewed as an authority. They may also reject the perspective of someone whose biases suggest a lack of fairness or balance, particularly if these biases differ from their own. As a result, you may need to present the words or ideas you are citing in ways that make clear that your source is both fair and authoritative, just as the writer of the following passage does.

> Another role of the [African-American] family is to pass along different kinds of successful coping strategies against racism. One strategy, the heightened sensitivity to the potential for exploitation by white persons, has been referred to by Grier and Cobbs in *Black Rage* as cultural paranoia. While this heightened sensitivity often has been pathologized by the dominant culture, it is a realistic and adaptive way of approaching situations that have frequently been antagonistic. Hopson and Hopson in *Different and Wonderful* suggest that another important coping strategy and a major source of psychological resilience is reflected in the sharing of African cultural derivatives with children while encouraging them to take pride in their ancestry. In *Long Memory*, Mary Berry and John Blassingame note that each generation of African Americans prepares the next for survival in a society that devalues them by passing along "searing vignettes" about what has preceded

them. They view this process as a long collective memory that is in and of itself an instrument of survival.
—BEVERLY GREENE, "African American Families: A Legacy of Vulnerability and Resilience"

Do not expect an authority to do all the work for you. After all, you cite an authority simply to add weight to your own thesis and perspective. You encourage readers to agree with you by pointing out that someone whose opinion carries considerable weight already agrees with you. For this process to be effective, you need to make sure that your words appear along with those of your source. This is important even when you include a quotation because you feel that your source makes a particular point more effectively and persuasively than you can. In the following paragraph, for example, the writer uses the final sentence to make sure readers see how the information he is citing fits his argument.

54a
arg

Accompanying this modern view of the nuclear family were the sentiments that enlivened it. The first of these was the sentiment, as described by Edward Shorter in *The Making of the Modern Family,* of *romantic love.* Beginning with nineteenth-century individualism, the belief arose that for each of us there is one other individual who was created as our perfect mate. Once we encountered that person, we would know it instantly and proceed to spend the rest of our lives forever "happily-ever-aftering." An essential condition of this romantic ideal was that a young woman would "save" herself for her fated partner. In this romantic context, [her] virginity was a valuable commodity that could be exchanged for a lifelong commitment to the relationship. Romantic love worked to keep couples together even when they were unhappy. **While this ideal was unfortunate for parents in unrewarding relationships, it often benefited children because parents stayed together and usually did not blame the children for the failure of the marriage.**
—DAVID ELKIND, "The Family in the Postmodern World"

As you search for examples to support your points, remember the importance of your own writing. No matter how well written your source, readers will ultimately be persuaded by what your own words say rather than by selected statements from someone else.

Detailed Information. The range of detailed information available to you on most issues is wide, including statistics, technical information, the results of surveys and interviews, background information, and historical detail. Which of these sources you choose and the role each plays in your writing will depend on the particular issue you are addressing, your point of view, and the views or knowledge of your intended readers. Be alert to these kinds of information as you think about an issue and undertake research, and consider the many different ways you can use the information to support your argument. Here are some examples of different kinds of detailed information used to support an author's thesis.

> Meanwhile, young people find it harder and harder to form or sustain families. According to an Associated Press report of April 25, 1995, the median income of men aged twenty-five to thirty-four fell by 26 percent between 1972 and 1994, while the proportion of such men with earnings below the poverty level for a family of four more than doubled to 32 percent. The figures are even worse for African American and Latino men. Poor individuals are twice as likely to divorce as more affluent ones, three to four times less likely to marry in the first place, and five to seven times more likely to have a child out of wedlock. — STEPHANIE COONTZ, "The Way We Weren't"

54a arg

Comparisons. One important way to arrive at a judgment is to compare a particular issue, problem, policy, or situation about which you are uncertain to one about which you are more certain. In trying to decide whether to expand a local recycling program, for example, you might reasonably look at the success of current efforts. In arguing for restrictions on television programs or for wider access to technical information gathered by governments or corporations, you might look at the success or failure of such practices in other countries.

Comparisons can be particularly useful when you are arguing for a particular policy. Your readers will be concerned about the consequences of a policy and its likelihood for success or failure. No one can predict the future, of course, but comparisons can help you persuade because they point to the probability of certain outcomes.

At the same time, you should expect readers to approach comparisons critically, being skeptical of those that are far-fetched or unreasonable and judging whether the comparison speaks directly to the issue at hand. Instead of asking a comparison to stand on its own, therefore, spend some time pointing out its applicability and answering possible objections to it. The author of the following passage, for example, uses comparison to argue for two-parent, child-centered families even though he acknowledges that one-parent families can raise children successfully.

> Infants and children need, at minimum, one adult to care for them. Yet, given the complexities of the task, childrearing in all societies until recent years has been shared by many adults. The institutional bond of marriage between biological parents, with the essential function of tying the father to the mother and child, is found in virtually every society. Marriage is the most universal social institution known; in no society has nonmarital childbirth, or the single parent,

been the cultural norm. In all societies the biological father is identified where possible, and in almost all societies he plays an important role in his children's upbringing, even though his primary task is often that of protector and breadwinner.

—DAVID POPENOE, "The American Family Crisis"

S T R A T E G Y

Develop a list of questions that can guide your search for facts, ideas, and experiences that support your proposition. Here are some possible questions.

54a
arg

- What are some good or bad consequences of this policy?
- What do experts say about solutions to the problem?
- What religious or moral values support my position on this issue?
- Are there any comparisons that might help readers understand my perspective?

Trying to answer these questions can help you decide whether you can use your own knowledge to support an assertion or whether you need additional facts, opinions, and information.

5 Recognize and respond to counterarguments

Traditional argumentation is like debate: you imagine an adversary, someone who doesn't go along with your ideas, and try to undermine that adversary's points or **counterarguments.** Most contemporary approaches to argument aren't quite as battle-like. Your point should be not so much to "win" as to acknowledge other people's perspectives yet still try to convince them of the validity of your views. With either kind of argument, however, you need to anticipate your readers' reactions.

S T R A T E G Y

Divide a sheet of paper into three columns. On the left, list the main points supporting your opinion. Write opposing points in the middle column. Put yourself wholly into the other position's point of view when you are listing opposing points. Pretend you are a person diametrically opposed to your original stance. Try to find weaknesses in the points in the left-hand column. Be as critical as possible.

In the rightmost column, list the possible defenses to the counterarguments you listed in the middle column. List any known or potential outside sources that would support your argument.

Sometimes it may be difficult to imagine any point of view other than your own. The process of inventing counterarguments may need to move beyond your own frame of reference and beliefs. This is where taking your thesis or position into a more public forum can help. Use various audiences as a "test" for your assertions. Put the idea forward tentatively, so that you will be seen as searching openly for differences of opinion. You might, for example, ask some friends or acquaintances, "What do you think about this issue?" or "Do you think that we ought to do *X* to solve *Y*?" Then listen carefully, and take note of the responses. You might gently extend your friends' reasoning by raising a subsidiary issue or counterargument: "But what about the fact that . . . ?" Again, listen.

Exercise 3

 A. Using the Strategy described in 54a-3, develop a workable thesis statement. List at least three pieces of supporting evidence or arguments for your assertion.

 B. In a small group, use the Strategy in 54a-5 to create a list of counterarguments against each member's main supporting arguments. In a discussion of each thesis statement, try collectively to respond to those counterarguments in ways that weaken the objections to the original arguments.

54b Developing a point: Argument in progress

Knowing that he had to begin writing a short argumentative paper, Zachary Carter began jotting ideas in his journal. As he walked through the student union on his way to a class, he noticed a group of students crowding around a table where several members of the Coalition on Animal Rights sat. Large posters on the wall showed cruelties allegedly inflicted on monkeys, dogs, and other animals as a result of medical experiments. The students and the Coalition members were carrying on a lively debate about the animal experiments. As Zachary listened, he knew that he had stumbled on an idea for his paper. He grabbed some leaflets and hurried to class.

1 Identify an issue

At lunch, Zachary glanced through the leaflets he had taken. He couldn't help feeling that they turned an enormous, undefined topic ("animal rights") into something very specific by focusing on only one issue (the morality of performing medical experiments on animals). He started writing about his own feelings on this subject in his journal.

> One day when I was little, I came across some neighborhood kids taunting a frog they'd found. They were kicking it, tossing it to each other, rolling it down the sidewalk. I was horrified, but the kids were a lot bigger than I was, so I just stood a few yards away, ready to run to my house if they turned on me. I found the frog's bashed-up body in the grass the next day.
>
> Animal rights. Maybe this violation was outrageous because there was no purpose but a sick pleasure for the kids. Experiments inflict pain, too, but we're supposed to think it's all for the good of human beings. I don't know. A frog, some experiments. These seem so small. The problem is so much bigger than this. It's humans as a species, multiplying, taking over the planet and pushing out other creatures.

54b
arg

On his way to class, Zachary continued to puzzle over the question of animal rights. The experimentation problem seemed like a complex argument, since people can claim that animal experiments have led to cures for dozens of diseases and thus made our lives better. At the same time, it seemed manageably narrow, since experiments can be studied, monitored, and controlled. But what about other aspects of animal rights? What about the destruction of rain forests, the wiping out of entire species by human development, or pollution killing off organisms by the thousands?

2 Investigate an Issue

The day after his encounter with the animal rights group, Zachary was checking his email messages on his computer when he decided to try out his thoughts on a listserv for students in his writing class.

> Hi, people. I've been thinking about animal rights. (I'm sure you saw the table in the student union.) I guess I'm more worried now than before about what happens to animals in experiments. But I keep thinking that the lab issue is missing the point. It seems so small compared to the huge injustices we keep doing to animals on the whole planet. If we stopped all the experiments in the world, animals still would have no rights because of what we are doing to their environment. What do you think?

Within a day, about a dozen students had posted responses. Several students offered sensible replies and even suggested where Zachary could get more information.

> In response to Zachary Carter's message: Take a situation like human hunger. Big problem, right? So some people create a food-shelf program in

one city, and it helps a few dozen families. It doesn't get rid of the problem, but it's a start. Same with taking care of our environment.

Zach Carter: Check out Richard Wagner's book <u>Environment and Man</u>, and while you're at it, Al Gore's <u>Earth in the Balance</u>.

3 Articulate a stance

After thinking about the listserv responses, Zachary knew that he had to work to articulate his stance. Was he concerned primarily about animal experiments? Or was his point more solution-based—that we should do something more fundamental about animal rights? But what was that something? Returning to his journal, he wrote a page exploring his ideas.

A day later, Zachary had narrowed his opinion into something approaching a thesis or proposition. In his brainstorming, he realized that he wanted to take a broader view of animal rights, and he settled on a tentative proposition for his paper.

> In considering the rights of animals, we must begin shifting our focus from small controversies such as animal experiments or the survival of a single species to the true injustice, the large-scale destruction of animals' habitat by humans.

Zachary felt generally satisfied with his focus but also knew that he really didn't have an argument, just a way of thinking about a problem. What exactly was he proposing—just that we should think more broadly, or that we should take some sort of action?

4 Find supporting evidence

Taking the advice of one of the listserv respondents, Zachary went to the library in search of the books by Wagner and Gore. He found that they dealt broadly with the issue of the environment. As he read, he was drawn again and again to passages dealing with the issue of human overpopulation. Was there a way to link animal rights to human overpopulation? Searching the electronic databases in his library, he located a series of books by Edward Abbey dealing with the environment. The anthology in his composition course also included a useful article titled "The End of Nature." There was plenty here, he thought, to help him support his ideas. He started jotting down some useful quotations.

> "Global warming, ozone depletion, the loss of living species, deforestation—they all have a common cause: the relationship between human civilization and the earth's natural balance."
> (Albert Gore, <u>Earth in the Balance</u>, p. 31)

Especially powerful for his paper were various proposals for reducing the human population, or at least keeping it from growing out of control. This one main argument, Zachary thought, could lay the foundation for an approach to animal rights in which the earth would be balanced between humans and animals in a harmonious ecosystem.

5 Recognize counterarguments

Because Zachary had already received some email objections to his original thoughts about animal rights, he decided to do most of his work on counterarguments by himself, trying to put himself in the shoes of people (including some of his friends) who would object to the idea. Using a listing strategy (see 54a-5), he divided a piece of paper into three columns, wrote down key supporting points, then imagined what people would say against his supporting points. After trying to come up with valid counterarguments, he looked for ways to defend his original supporting points. The result was a chart of ideas that he could develop in his paper.

**54b
arg**

Tentative thesis: In considering the rights of animals, we must begin shifting our focus from small controversies such as animal experiments or the survival of a single species to the true injustice, the large-scale destruction of animals' habitat by the overpopulation of humans

Supporting Points	Opposing Points	Defenses
Humans are pushing the balance of nature askew with their ever-increasing population.	We haven't yet mined the earth for all its resources, so we could support many more people in the future.	Mining all the earth's resources will inevitably destroy the existing ecosystem.
Large-scale tips in the balance of nature will cause a domino effect as interdependent species die off.	Entire species have gone extinct without major effects on ecology.	In the past, extinction has happened slowly and naturally because of changing conditions.
More humans need more water, leading to more dams, in turn leading to the destruction of submerged habitat.	Dams create lakes, which create new opportunities for plant and animal life.	Dams like the Glen Canyon Dam upset fragile ecosystems miles downstream.
Male sterilization can effectively curb overpopulation, as shown in Barbados, etc.	Sterilized men may change their minds about fathering children and then be unable to do so.	Semen can be collected prior to sterilization for later use in artificial insemination.

After creating this list, Zachary felt he was ready to begin more formal work on the structure of his paper in preparation for a preliminary draft. Note how he develops a complex argument that includes a definition of his key terms, adequate quotations from his sources to support his points, and a clear, crisp, readable style to engage his readers.

Animal Rights: The Big Picture

by Zachary Carter

1   The issue of animal rights is a multifaceted one, and, upon examination, it tends to make one follow a circle of logic which leads from one conclusion to the next, without the benefit of a final outcome or decision. But there is a way out of this circle, and that is to shift the focus of the issue away from small controversies such as animal experiments or the survival of a single species of tiny fish to the true injustice, the large-scale destruction of animals' habitat by the overpopulation of humans. Upon exploration, this particular avenue yields astonishing and interesting--even horrifying--results. Clearly an intense effort must be made to preserve the rights of animals (as defined later in this essay) for the benefit of every species involved, including the human race.

2   In order to examine this issue thoroughly, we must find a definition of both "animal" and "rights" and stick to them. So, for the purpose of this essay, "animal" will be defined as any creature that belongs to the kingdom Animalia, which includes reptiles, birds, insects, amphibians, and mammals (even humans). As for a concept of "rights," one must first look at what is most important for the

whole of nature. The earth is a vast, spinning
ecosystem, teeming with countless forms of life, all
in diverse conflict and chaos. Yet amid all the
confusion there is an order, a balance, an
underlying simplicity. The food chain,
photosynthesis, the Krebs cycle, the water cycle,
migratory patterns--all these things indicate the
presence of an underlying balance, a large-scale
cooperation of organisms, the purpose of which is to
promote life.

54b
arg

3   Al Gore tells of this in his book Earth in
Balance: "All its parts exist in a delicate balance
of interdependency" (50). This balance is important
to the continuation of life as we know it on earth
because "any interruption of this natural process
can have a magnified impact" (51). A large-scale tip
in this balance can result in devastating effects on
the lives of all creatures, Homo sapiens and other
species alike. It is apparent that the preservation
of this balance must be the paramount concern of any
society because all members in any society are
integral parts of nature. If the situation is viewed
in this light, then it becomes not only humanity's
right and every other species' right, but our duty
as well, for the very preservation of life and
nature as we know it, to live peacefully within the
balance of nature. Consequently, we arrive at the
most fundamental definition of "rights": the right
to exist within the balance of nature.

4   And now we come to the problem. Humans, driven
by natural instinct, are slowly pushing the balance
askew and, in the process, trampling on the rights

of other species to exist inside the balance. Because of the population boom, humans have spread across every continent, developing, settling, industrializing, mining, setting up agriculture, and so forth. Gore speaks of human intrusion into the balance: "Global warming, ozone depletion, the loss of living species, deforestation--they all have a common cause: the new relationship between human civilization and the earth's natural balance" (31).

5   The human race has destroyed vast areas of native habitat and cut down billions of trees which-- at that volume--are virtually irreplaceable. As Gore notes, "when we scrape the forests away, we destroy these crucial habitats along with the living species that depend on them" (116). Predatory species such as the wolf, coyote, and mountain lion, which are an important part of the ecosystem (because they dwell at the apex of the food chain), have been virtually wiped out in many areas. Deer and elk feel this loss through their subsequent boom in population, which in turn causes a demand for food which cannot be met. As a result, there are millions of starving deer and elk, all because of the destruction of a few predators.

6   These examples of habitat destruction and the killing of species are clearly a violation of animals' rights to exist within the balance. Another type of disruption is the damming of rivers, which not only submerges vast areas of habitat, but also upsets the fragile river ecology for hundreds of miles downstream. A prime example of this is the

former Glen Canyon in Utah, now under Lake Powell, a
result of the construction of Glen Canyon Dam. In
South America, huge amounts of the Amazon rain
forest are being burned, leaving billions, perhaps
trillions, of animals homeless if not killed.
Extinctions are on the rise: "living species of
animals and plants are now vanishing in the world at
a rate one thousand times faster than at any time in
the past 65 million years" (Gore 25). The
destruction of an entire species is an example of
another clear violation of the rights of animals to
exist within the balance. And there are more subtle
and terrifying problems than these: global warming,
the greenhouse effect, the rising of the oceans.
These, in the words of Bill McKibben, can lead us
"if not straight to hell, then straight to a place
with a comparable 'temperature'" (274). But the
underlying cause of all this injustice, the mother
of all problems, is overpopulation.

7   We face a future in which there is no longer
physical space on the earth for the human race, much
less the billions of other species that inhabit the
planet. In the words of Edward Abbey:

> The sea will be farmed, all deserts
> irrigated, whole mountains pulverized, the
> last forests turned to pulpwood
> plantations, in order to satisfy the ever-
> growing needs (no doubt as desperate as in
> the past) of a human population much
> larger than at present. (Down the River
> 117)

Richard Wagner, author of <u>Environment and Man</u>, states that "adding four billion more [people] staggers the imagination, for the earth is barely able to support its present population" (553). He also says that "overpopulation is one problem the entire world must share" (538). Clearly the population explosion must be stopped. This is the only way to make room for all species to have their rightful place within the balance, for the benefit of human beings and the whole of the natural world.

8   First, a move must be made to prevent future development of similar problems, and the only way to do this is to curb the population explosion. Several things can be used to this end. Abortion, while morally objectionable to many people, is a natural form of population reduction. Rabbits in the wild, for example, will abort their unborn fetuses if the local environment is insufficient for survival. If moral imperatives preclude the use of this method, then there are other equally effective chemical and mechanical methods, "but the most reliable method is sterilization" (Wagner 547). A simple operation performed on a man renders him unable to conceive offspring, and this does not affect sexual impulses. The irreversibility of this method can be combated by taking samples of semen before the operation. Then, at any time, the partner can be artificially inseminated (Wagner 547). A reduction in population <u>can</u> be achieved. This is demonstrated by the efforts of "Barbados, Taiwan, Mauritius, Hong Kong, Tunisia, Singapore, Costa Rica, Egypt, Chile, and South Korea," which have achieved a reduction (Wagner 554). This proposed reduction in population will help to prevent further encroachment upon the natural habitat of animal species by human expansion and exploitation.

9   As for the present, efforts should be made to develop new and streamline old technology in order to make more efficient use of resources. Gore says, "It is now an axiom in many fields of science that more new and important discoveries have taken place in the last ten years than in the entire previous history of science" (31). This trend is expected to continue, and, if so, efficiency of production and use of natural resources should be steered in that direction. Subsequently, waste disposal, energy production, and manufacturing should be improved significantly. Gore also says that "the transformation of the way we relate to the earth will of course involve new technologies, but the key changes will involve new ways of thinking about the relationship [between people and nature] itself" (35).

10   The first and most important imperative is that all individuals make a conscious effort to improve this relationship to the balance of nature, for the sake of animal rights, themselves, and their children. Without this effort to preserve the balance, all members of the human

54b arg

race are on a collision course with destruction,
taking millions of innocent species along with them:

> ...developers were bulldozing the last
> hundred acres of untouched forest in the
> entire area. As the woods fell away to
> make way for more concrete, more
> buildings, parking lots, and streets, the
> wild things that lived there were forced
> to flee. Most of the deer were hit by
> cars; other creatures--like the pheasant
> that darted into my neighbor's backyard--
> made it a little further. (Gore 25)

11   An effort to curb these injustices is in order
immediately, for the sake of the balance. For "the
earth, like the sun, like the air, belongs to
everyone--and to no one" (Abbey, Journey 88). And if
no effort is made...very well then...let the world
rot.

Works Cited

Abbey, Edward. "The Damnation of a Canyon." Beyond
      the Wall. New York: Holt, 1984.
---. Down the River. New York: Plume, 1991.
---. The Journey Home. New York: Plume, 1991.
Gore, Albert. Earth in the Balance: Ecology and the
      Human Spirit. New York: Houghton, 1992.
McKibben, Bill. "The End of Nature." The Informed
      Argument. Ed. Robert K. Miller. New York:
      Harcourt, 1992. 264-74.
Wagner, Richard H. Environment and Man. New York:
      Norton, 1978.

54c   Using critical thinking to strengthen your argument

When you plan and draft a position paper, try to assemble your opinions and supporting evidence in an order that reflects a chain of reasoning supporting your proposition (thesis statement). Some of the most effective ways to do this are using different strategies of argument (logical, emotional, imaginative, and ethical) and using data-warrant-claim (Toulmin) reasoning.

1 Build logical strategies

When you employ **logical strategies** for argument, you arrange your ideas and evidence in ways that correspond with patterns of thought that most people accept as reasonable and convincing. You do not have to provide absolute proof for your opinion; if you could, there would be no real need to argue. After all, arguments help to resolve disagreements precisely because an absolutely correct position cannot always be identified. In such a case, an argument helps readers choose among opinions that are reasonable alternatives.

Here are four of the most commonly used logical strategies.

Reasoning from consequences. You argue for or against an action, outlook, or interpretation, basing your argument on real or likely consequences (good or bad).

Reasoning from comparisons. You argue for or against a policy or point of view, basing your argument on similar situations, problems, or actions.

Reasoning from authority and testimony. You draw ideas and evidence to support your outlook from recognized experts or from people whose experience makes them trustworthy witnesses.

Reasoning from examples and statistics. You draw on events, situations, and problems presented as illustrations (examples) or in summarized, numerical form (statistics) to support your point of view.

Induction and deduction are other commonly used logical strategies. A **deductive argument** begins with an explicitly stated **premise** (or assertion or claim) and then goes on to support that premise. It uses **syllogistic reasoning** as the basic logical format. A **syllogism** includes a **major premise,** a **minor premise,** and a **conclusion.** Here is a simple truthful syllogism.

MAJOR PREMISE   All landowners in Clarksville must pay taxes.

MINOR PREMISE   Fred Hammil owns land in Clarksville.

CONCLUSION   Therefore, Fred Hammil must pay taxes.

54c
arg

Faulty syllogistic reasoning is easily illustrated in a flawed syllogism.

MAJOR PREMISE   All Ferraris are fast.

MINOR PREMISE   That car is fast.

CONCLUSION   Therefore, that car is a Ferarri.

In a complex argument, of course, these truthful and faulty kinds of reasoning are much more elaborate. You might begin an argumentative paper, for example, by saying something that your readers would generally hold to be true, go on to show that specific examples of that assertion must also be true, and end with your argumentative assertion. This basic sequence can be used to shape each paragraph as well as to frame the paper as a whole.

In contrast, an **inductive argument** does not explicitly state the premise; rather, it leads readers through an accumulation of evidence until they conclude what the writer wants them to. Such arguments usually begin with a **hypothesis,** which differs from an assertion in being tentative, an idea that the writer wants to consider but as yet has not reached any hard-and-fast conclusion about. Of course, in a finished written argument, this hypothesis is somewhat disingenuous since the writer *does* have a conclusion but withholds it until the readers are convinced by reading through all the supporting points.

This form of argument is effective when you are taking a controversial stand on an issue. If you asserted your stand explicitly at the beginning of the paper, you might put many of your readers on the defensive, ready to criticize your argument right from the start. However, if you hold off your assertion, your readers may also hold off their judgment.

Exercise 4

 A. Compose a simple proposition or thesis, and then try to support it with each of the four logical strategies described in 54c-1 (reasoning from consequences, reasoning from comparisons, reasoning from authority or testimony, and reasoning from examples and statistics). Invent authoritative statements or statistics if you wish.

EXAMPLE

Simple proposition: The student senate's proposal to allow alcoholic beverages to be served in the student union should not be passed.

Reasoning from consequences: The consumption of alcohol will increase crime on campus, especially personal assaults, drunk driving, and rape.

Reasoning from comparisons: Easy availability of alcohol deters students from their academic work; when a bar opened briefly three years ago near fraternity row, every fraternity experienced a drop in average grades.

Reasoning from authority and testimony: Having alcohol so easily available on campus may subvert our college's mission by contributing not to students' growth but to their deterioration. According to research conducted by Legman and Witherall, a large percentage of alcoholics over the age of thirty reported that their college binge drinking set a strong pattern for their later addiction.

Reasoning from examples and statistics: Bars on campus draw students away from more beneficial activities. Two years after Carmon College opened a wine and beer hall on campus, participation in lectures and special events had dropped by 26 percent; attendance at the film series declined by 18 percent; and weekend library usage between 5 p.m. and midnight dropped by 43 percent.

 B. In a small group, compare your theses and logical strategies. Discuss the strength of each strategy as it is used to support the thesis.

2 Draw on emotional strategies

In drawing on **emotional strategies,** you focus on the values, attitudes, belief systems, and emotions that guide people's lives and that are central to any decision-making process.

> **Values and beliefs.** You may present examples, ideas, or statements that confirm or contradict your readers' probable values.

> **Emotions and values.** You may present examples or use language that draws emotional responses (positive or negative) from your readers ("The consequence of this policy will be an increase in the already horrifying flood of bruised, battered, undernourished two- and three-year-olds brought into emergency rooms by parents who deny even the most obvious evidence of abuse").

Be aware that readers often see emotional strategies as weaker support for a point than reason or logic. In an argument against the use of animals for research, for example, an emotional appeal about cruelty to animals could be countered by an emotional appeal about the need for research to cure terrible diseases. A general emotional appeal about animal suffering is not as strong as specific, verifiable accounts of animals being subjected to unbearable pain in the name of research. Often the most powerful emotional appeals will be those directly linked to other forms of logical support.

Did You Know?

Some people think that the purpose of argument is to win a battle or to discredit the views of people with whom they disagree. A society that relied on such a view of argument to deal with problems and differing points of view would be a rather hostile place to live, however. Belgian scholar Chaim Perelman offers a different view of the aim of argument: to encourage or convince your audience to adhere to your point of view. In other words, argument creates agreement by encouraging people to come together in their beliefs and actions.

Chaim Perelman and L. Olbrechts-Tyteca, *The New Rhetoric* (South Bend: U of Notre Dame P, 1979).

---

3 Use data-warrant-claim (Toulmin) reasoning

In *The Uses of Argument* (1964), Stephen Toulmin proposes **data-warrant-claim reasoning,** which draws on several kinds of statements reasonable people usually make when they argue (statements of data, claims, and warrants), highlighting a way of relating these statements in order to convince readers.

Data corresponds to your evidence and *claim* to your conclusion. *Warrant,* however, is a more complex term; it refers to the mental process by which a reader connects the data to the claim. It answers the question "How?" Another way to understand this is to think of data as the indisputable facts and the warrant as the probable facts and assertions. As in an inductive argument, you present the data that lead to your claim, but you also present the warrants, the probable facts and assertions that will encourage readers to accept the validity of your claim.

For instance, as data, you might have the results of a detailed study establishing the likelihood of injury in each of the many different models of cars currently on the market. You could make a number of interpretive statements about the data (warrants) and point out patterns you see (probable facts—warrants) in order to provide reasoning that links the data to your claim: for the average consumer, buying a large car is a good way to reduce the likelihood of being injured in an accident.

To argue effectively, you need to show your readers *how* the data and the claim are connected. To warrant such a claim, you could say that there are small, medium, and large cars in the ratings and extend this warrant by pointing out that the large cars have a higher safety rating. To back up this warrant, you point out that although some of the smaller cars on each list are quite safe, in general, the large cars are the safest. You could extend the argument by citing further statistics (data) about safety along with arguments and reasoning from other sources (warrants).

DATA
Ratings of each car model according to likelihood of injury to driver and passenger (scale: 1 = low to 10 = high)

WARRANT
←——The cars in the ratings fall into three easily recognized groups: small, medium, and large.
Probable fact

WARRANT
←——The large cars as a group have a lower average likelihood of injury to passengers than either of the other groups.
Probable fact

**54c
arg**

WARRANT
←——Though some of the small and medium-sized cars have low likelihood of injury to passengers, almost all of the large cars seem quite safe.
Assertion and probable fact

WARRANT
←——Relatively few consumers will spend the time going over the crash ratings to determine which particular models get good or poor scores.
Assertion

CLAIM
For the average consumer, buying a large car is a good way to reduce the likelihood of being injured in an accident.

The data-warrant-claim approach to constructing an argument does not assume that an argument can provide absolute proof of a proposition. It aims instead at showing readers that an opinion or proposed action is plausible, grounded on good evidence and reasons, and worth their endorsement. Arguments that employ this kind of reasoning may sometimes seem more like purposeful dialogues than debates. If you employ this approach, you should take the attitude that your argument is open to other viewpoints, to compromise, and to negotiation.

4 Consider your audience and purpose

Remember that you won't write an effective argument if all you do is stridently voice your opinion on an issue. An argument is effective only if it's part of a relationship between you and your reader. Defining who your readers are, how you want them to perceive you, and what you want to convince them of is the essential first step to constructing an argument (see Chapter 5).

Your audience is partly determined by your topic and by your own stance. If you are writing about the abortion issue, for example, you need to be clear in your own mind whom you are addressing. Argument papers on this topic are often not well written because the audience is usually a vague "the other side." Remember, it is a fallacy to divide an issue into only two sides (see the discussion of the either/or fallacy in 54c-5). Likewise, it is ineffective to think of your readers as belonging to only one of two camps.

Rogerian argument, based on the theories of psychologist and group therapist Carl Rogers, provides a useful perspective for considering the responses of your audience. Rogers argued that people can more easily be changed when their opponent seems like an ally instead of an enemy. A highly combative or adversarial approach immediately puts a reader on the defensive, thus setting up a barrier to your ideas. The reader's psychological reaction is "Oh yeah? Well, let me tell you something, buster!" rather than "Hmmm, that's an interesting point worth considering."

Identifying Alternative Views. To practice Rogerian strategies, imagine for a moment that you share the views of someone who is opposed to your actual position or solution. What is your opponent's frame of reference? What assumptions might have led him or her to these views? Giving, for the moment, a charitable response that acknowledges someone else's right to hold an opinion you disagree with, what validity can you see in anything your opponent might say?

Rogers also found that a good way to understand someone's view is to try restating it rather than immediately countering it. When participants in a discussion negotiate their positions, sentences often begin not with statements of judgment or reaction ("Well, I think..." or "That point doesn't hold water."), but with statements of reflection and repetition: "What I hear you saying is....," or "It sounds to me like you're trying to...." This allows not only for mutual understanding of each person's points but for mutual respect for differences of opinion once those points are clearly articulated.

Making a Concession. When you understand your opponent's ideas, you may be prepared to work a **concession** into your argument. You make a concession when you acknowledge or consider a view opposed to one you are arguing. A concession does not have to be so strong that it undermines your entire argument. But placed strategically, it can help your reader to see that you have, in fact, tried to be fair-minded. A reader who recognizes that attitude will be more likely to trust your judgment and listen to you.

Concessions may appear briefly, embedded in the structure of a sentence, or they may be elaborate, sometimes taking one or more paragraphs to describe. Concessions embedded in single sentences often involve words like *although, while, while it may be true that, of course,* or *but.*

In a letter to the editor bemoaning the extinction of local, family-run hardware stores in the shadow of huge, warehouse-sized lumber centers,

Angie Krastaat made an extended concession that consumers may be attracted by the lower prices and large selection at the lumber centers, but then countered it with an anecdote that led to a generalization.

> Of course, the lumber centers do have their draws: paint in every color, discounted power tools, and items too large to fit into most small stores. But what they gain in selection and pricing they sorely lack in their robot-like relationship with their customers. Where else can you get a single nut, bolt or nail—just one—than a local hardware store? What large lumber center will replace that torn screen or broken window while you wait? Where can you find someone at Mega-Hardware who will work with you in the store to repair something, using ingenuity and bins full of single items?

54c arg

STRATEGY

To make your argument on "hot" issues more effective, try limiting your audience to a particular group of people concerned about the issue—on abortion, for example, focus on reaching sexually active teens, unmarried mothers, or the people who protest at abortion clinics. Also consider your image as an arguer. How do you want your readers to perceive you? Do you want to be perceived as erudite, rational, and coolly objective; as passionate and moving; as outraged; as reflective and forgiving?

---

5 Recognize misleading and illogical reasoning

A **fallacy** is a flaw in the reasoning of any persuasive work, whether it's an argumentative essay, an interpretation of a literary work, a report of the results of a study, or a review. Fallacies often show up in advertisements, stated directly in the copy and implied in the visual images. An ad for beer that shows attractive, bikini-clad women and muscular, handsome men romping on a California beach implies (illogically) that drinking the beer will get you that life-style. This example of faulty cause-effect reasoning implies that *because* you drink the beer, you'll be like the people in the ad. The same fallacy can be a problem in academic and professional writing as well but may not be as blatant. For instance, if you read an article that says legalizing marijuana will result in a dangerous increase in cocaine use, you ought to question how the writer demonstrates that cause-effect relationship and supplies evidence linking marijuana use to cocaine use.

Faulty Cause-Effect Relationship. This problem is also called *post hoc, ergo propter hoc* (Latin for "after this, therefore because of this") or just a **post hoc fallacy.** This flawed reasoning attempts to persuade you that just because one event happens after the other, the first event causes the second.

FAULTY CAUSE-EFFECT   The increase in explicit violence on television is making the crime rate soar.

> READER'S REACTION: This *may* be true, but no evidence is presented here linking the two situations.

False Analogy.   **Analogies** are comparisons between two things, often on the basis of shared characteristics. In a false analogy, the things may at first glance seem to be comparable but really are not. (See the discussion of the red herring and *ad populum* fallacies in this section.)

FALSE ANALOGY   Raising the national speed limit is like offering free cocktails at a meeting of recovering alcoholics.

> READER'S REACTION: I don't see the connection. Most drivers aren't recovering from an addiction to high-speed driving, and a legal limit is not the same thing as self-restraint.

Misleading Language/Misleading Evidence.   This fallacy is also called **equivocation** and **slanted statistics.** A writer can use misleading language by beginning with one definition of a term (usually one everyone agrees with), then shifting to another sense of the word, one that supports the writer's argument but that not all readers may agree with.

MISLEADING LANGUAGE   Everyone has the right of free speech, so censoring films by rating them Triple X is against one's constitutional rights.

> READER'S REACTION: This tries to pass off the *rating* of films as censorship (which it is not) and assumes that *free speech* and *censorship* are directly opposite terms (which they are not necessarily).

Misleading evidence includes statistics, survey results, and expert opinions stacked up in favor of only one side of the argument. For instance, someone who used an opinion poll to argue for the preservation of the spotted owl but polled only people at an environmental rally would have overwhelmingly favorable but misleading evidence.

Red Herring.   Similar to misleading evidence is the red herring fallacy. A red herring is something that distracts readers from the real argument.

RED HERRING   Gun control laws need to be passed as soon as possible to decrease the rate of domestic violence and home firearms accidents. The people who think guns should not be controlled are probably criminals themselves.

> READER'S REACTION: The second sentence doesn't logically follow from the first; it just attacks the people who would oppose the writer's argument instead of supporting the initial assertion.

Ad Populum.   *Ad populum* means "to the people" and refers to an argument that appeals to the audience's biases instead of using rational support.

54c
arg

AD POPULUM   All doctors should be tested for AIDS and should not be allowed to practice if they test HIV positive, so they don't spread the disease to their patients. Do you want to be one of those patients?

> READER'S REACTION: **This writer is obviously trying to invoke my fear of getting AIDS. The claim that HIV-positive doctors will pass on the disease to patients is not founded on valid research.**

Ad Hominem. Another faulty argument based on audience biases is the ad hominem fallacy, which means "to the man." This is a personal attack on the opponent rather than a debate on the issue.

54c
arg

AD HOMINEM   Of course Walt Smith would support a bill to provide financial assistance to farmers—he owns several large farms in the Midwest. Besides, how can he be a good senator after cheating on his wife?

> READER'S REACTION: **I'd like to hear reactions to Walt Smith's ideas, please. I don't really care whether he had an affair fifteen years ago.**

Bandwagon. This fallacy is also called *consensus gentium,* "consensus of the people." A **bandwagon argument** is one that tries to convince you everyone else agrees with the idea already, so you ought to join in.

BANDWAGON   Each year an increasing number of people are quitting smoking, so you ought to quit, too.

> READER'S REACTION: **This writer is trying to convince me to quit by saying that other people are doing it. Even though the assertion may be valid, the support is not.**

Begging the Question. This fallacy also is called **overgeneralization** or **hasty generalization.** An argument is begging the question when it presents assumptions as if they were facts, sometimes using words and phrases like *obviously, certainly, clearly, people always/never,* and even the seemingly innocuous *some people say.*

BEGGING THE QUESTION   Most people these days are trying to be more physically fit; obviously, they are afraid of getting old.

> READER'S REACTION: **No evidence is presented for either the claim that most people are trying to be more fit or the claim that they are afraid of getting old. On what basis are these stated as facts?**

Either/Or. An **either/or strategy** oversimplifies an issue, making it seem as if it has only two sides.

EITHER/OR   On the matter of abortion, there are two positions: either we support a human's right to life, or we allow women to have complete control over their bodies.

> READER'S REACTION: **Why can't someone endorse protecting life while also supporting the right to choose what happens to one's body?**

Circular Reasoning. Circular reasoning, also called **tautology,** is an attempt to support an assertion with the assertion itself.

CIRCULAR
REASONING

The university should increase funding of intramural sports because it has a responsibility to back its sports programs financially.

> READER'S REACTION: **All this really says is that the university should fund sports because it should fund sports.**

Exercise 5

 A. Choose a controversial topic you know something about—gun control, abortion, the death penalty, the right to die. Now choose any three of the fallacies described in 54c-5, and write one example of each fallacy to make claims about your topic. (Don't identify the names of the fallacies in your response.)

 B. In a small group, exchange copies of the fallacious arguments you wrote for Exercise 5A. Discuss each set of fallacies, trying to identify the logical problems and to suggest revisions or identify specific kinds of support needed.

Did You Know?

In a study of students who wrote dialogue journals (they swapped journal entries and responded to each other's ideas informally), researchers found the presence of considerable argument. But because the partners thought of themselves as carrying on a sustained conversation that required them to maintain their social link through the entries, they appeared to consider each other's views and present themselves in a nonconfrontational way.

Chris M. Anson and Richard Beach, "Argument in Peer Dialogue Journals," in Deborah Berrill, ed., *New Perspectives on Written Argument* (Cresskill, NJ: Hampton Press, 1995) 139–169.

54d The position paper

The short, often documented, **position paper** defines its issue, considers its audience, and draws on evidence and logical strategies to make its point.

1 Sample position paper

In the following paper, note how the writer frames her argument with an opening reference to the daily struggle of many people throughout the world to protect their limited food supply against spoilage and contamination. As you read, consider who the writer's audience is, what the main argument is, and how she constructs the support for the argument. What are the counterarguments, and how does she address them? What kind of support, if any, is missing? What fallacies, if any, do you detect?

Food Irradiation: An Idea Whose Time Has Come

by Stephanie Lewis

54d
arg

1   In almost every part of the world people struggle daily to protect their vital food supplies from spoilage. For most Americans, the threats of heat, damp, insect infestation, bacterial contamination, and rot may seem distant. Yet while there is no precise information on just how much of the world's food supply is lost to spoilage, it is clear that the losses are enormous, especially in less developed countries that can least afford the waste. In addition, many of these countries have warm climates that encourage the growth of organisms causing spoilage and that speed up the normal deterioration process (Thorne). Because the world's population is growing at a rapid pace, we need to find viable solutions to the problem of waste and decay.

Opens with background examples

2   The loss of edible food is only one part of the problem, however. Food-borne diseases are also some of the most common threats to human health. In particular, a fairly high percentage of raw animal meat is contaminated by bacteria, resulting in high levels of food-borne illness in most countries (Thorne).

Uses example plus authority

Supplies specific examples

3   Efforts to reduce the price the public pays for food wastage and food-borne disease began many years ago. The first methods for the preservation of food were sun drying, salting, smoking, canning, and cooking. (For people in developed countries, these are now often techniques of gourmet cooking.) Recently, however, scientists have developed a new method for food preservation, irradiation. In this method, food is exposed to measured amounts of ionizing radiation. Scientists have discovered that this form of food preservation can slow spoilage,

Supplies detailed information plus authority

reduce insect infestation, and prevent contamination by other harmful organisms that cause food-borne diseases (Food Safety). Food irradiation is a particularly promising way to help reduce the worldwide problems of waste and disease.

4   Nonetheless, the public in this country has not fully accepted the concept of food irradiation (Lamb). Because of a decades-long fear of thermonuclear war and well-publicized accidents involving nuclear power (Three Mile Island and *Supplies examples* Chernobyl), many people fear anything associated with radiation. This fear persists even if the radiation is used for a nonthreatening purpose such as the preservation of food. Often this feeling of apprehensiveness is due to a lack of knowledge and information on the subject of food irradiation. This is also due to some confusion between the phenomenon of radioactive contamination and the process of irradiation used in food preservation.

5   One main reason why food irradiation is not used widely is that governments are still unsure about consumer acceptance of irradiated products. Without such acceptance, food irradiation will be neglected in developing countries as well as in the developed world. Even though about thirty-four countries have given approval for the radiation process of some thirty products, the use of radiation has been slow to materialize. Nonetheless, there is clear evidence that food irradiation is safe and that it effectively controls spoilage. In addition, there is strong proof of its cost-effectiveness in controlling the organisms and bacteria that contribute to waste and reduced shelf life or storage time for food (Lamb).

Presents statistics and detailed information

Cites authority

54d arg

6   Even though radiation has been an aid to health in diagnosing and treating diseases and in sterilizing medical equipment and pharmaceutical products, many people are sincerely scared of anything that appears to raise the risk of radiation exposure. Perhaps the best way to deal with these fears is to address them directly.

7   Is irradiated food safe? The answer to this question is a clear <u>yes</u>. Irradiated food is not harmful because the treatment does not alter the food in any way that would be detrimental to people's health. Are irradiated foods still nutritious? <u>Yes</u>. Even though, as with all methods of food processing, the level of nutrients is lowered by irradiation, the food is still nutritious. It is important to remember that even storing food at room temperature after harvesting can reduce its nutritional value. Moreover, the loss of nutrients is generally unmeasurable or insignificant at low

Supplies detailed information

doses of radiation. So not only has it been
demonstrated that food irradiation is a safe form of
food preservation, it is also a method of preserving
the nutrition in food (Blumenthal).

Cites authority

8   Food irradiation could reduce the amount of
waste due to spoilage of the world's food supply.
With the world's population expected to double
during the next century, this form of food
preservation could aid in feeding this growing
number of people in a safe and healthful way at low
cost. This technology could improve the world we
live in and change for the better the lives of
millions of people.

[The paper ends with a list of works cited.]

2 Commentary on Stephanie Lewis's position paper

Lewis's focus is clear through most of the paper, even though she waits until the end of paragraph 3 to offer a thesis statement clearly presenting her proposition. She acknowledges sympathetically the fears many people have about food irradiation and offers some scientific evidence of its safety, but she might have offered even more. In her conclusion she speaks of the low cost of food irradiation, but she touches on this matter only indirectly earlier in the paper. Her paper would benefit from revision in these areas; nonetheless, it argues effectively in many ways.

54e The critique

A formal critique consists of two parts—a summary of the work being discussed, and a critical reaction to the work. The summary should objectively condense the whole work, including all of its main ideas. The critical response is your subjective reaction to the work, but this does not necessarily mean a negative reaction. Many students think a critique should tear a work apart, pointing out all its faults, but this is not true. A good critique attempts to explain *how* and *why* a work is written, although questioning both is often an important part of the critique. In writing a critique, you first understand a body of knowledge and opinion, then make a point about it that helps your reader to interpret it and see it from new perspectives.

1 Sample critique

This selection from a sample critique illustrates how the writer begins with an objective summary of Ortiz's speech and then adds his subjective reaction to Ortiz's ideas. Note the shift in tone as the student moves from summary to critique. Look for sentences that explain how and why Ortiz wrote the speech and for sentences that question Ortiz's ideas.

A Summary and Critique of Alfonso Ortiz's "Some Concerns Central to the Writing of Indian History"

by Reid Nelson

54e arg

1   In the speech "Some Concerns Central to the Writing of Indian History," Alfonso Ortiz addresses the inadequacies created when non-Native American historians write Native American histories. Ortiz feels there is a need for historians to develop "greater sensitivity toward, and respect for, tribal traditions, and of learning Indian languages" (20).

2   Ortiz says Indians place the significance of past traditions in the place where they originally occurred. Indians therefore think of the past as occurrences relating to a space and not as events that took place at a certain time as historians do. This makes specific dates in the past unimportant to Indians. Ortiz feels that this way of thinking is illustrated by the Pueblo peoples' saying "'When it has been four times,'" which unites a sense of time and space simultaneously by noting when a "distance of four days travel has passed" or "when a time span of four days has passed" (19).

3   Ortiz's dissatisfaction with historians is deepened by their tendency to change occurrences that happened in a particular space into events that took place at a certain time, a practice which does quite the opposite of that which Indians do.

Furthermore, some historians feel that Indian attempts to represent history in terms of space and to use metaphors to describe this history are only a process of mythologization. Ortiz feels that this is an unfortunate and inaccurate judgment because it precludes the possibility to better understand Native American cultures.

[The writer continues with three more paragraphs summarizing Ortiz's points.]

54e arg

7   In this speech Ortiz is both informing and persuading. Ortiz informs historians about the problems with the way they record Native American history and attempts to persuade them that their approach is detrimental to a better understanding of Native Americans.

8   Ortiz has presented his captive audience of historians with a very straightforward and simple argument. His speech utilizes neither complex theorizing nor bewildering vocabulary. Ortiz tells the audience the negative consequences that do occur when the situation goes unchanged, which are the continued misunderstanding of Native Americans and poor relations between the two groups, and strengthens this point by repeating it several times. The reception these ideas receive will depend on two things. It depends first on whether historians agree that there is a problem in the way they write history and second on whether they agree that Ortiz's proposals will benefit non-Native Americans' understanding of Indian history.

[The writer concludes with a summary paragraph and a full reference to the printed source for the speech.]

2 Elements of a critique

An effective critique includes the following elements.

- It does not confuse objective summary with subjective opinion.
- It summarizes all the text's main ideas and important subpoints.
- It expresses a critical opinion of the text fairly, stressing how and why the text works and balancing positive and negative points.
- It gives the reader a clear picture of the text's content, its writer's stance, and the strengths and weaknesses of its argument.

3 Commentary on Reid Nelson's critique

Nelson encountered a common problem with writing critiques—making the summary concise yet understandable. He tries to include everything in Ortiz's speech, which results in giving equal priority to every point. He could explain the main argument of the speech in more detail in the first paragraph; this would orient the reader more clearly. Nelson could be more concise by cutting out some of the lead-in phrases such as *Ortiz says* and *Ortiz feels* and by using active instead of passive voice. In the critique section, Nelson could more explicitly state the problems with Ortiz's ideas.

54f The review

A common academic writing assignment is the review. A **review** is a critical appraisal of an event, object, or phenomenon, such as an art show, a concert, a restaurant, or a book. People read reviews either to help them make a decision about attending or experiencing whatever is being reviewed or to test their own judgments of it against those of another person (usually an expert). When you write a review, you describe, analyze, and evaluate your subject from an informed but clearly opinionated perspective.

Reviews come in many forms and are written from many points of view, from fairly objective and descriptive to very judgmental. The most common reviews are those that describe and evaluate an artistic work or performance: a book, a movie, a concert, a ballet, an opera, an album or CD, an art exhibit, or a play. Reviews can also describe and evaluate objects, such as a new car, a computer program, or a stereo system; events, such as the gala opening of a store or a fashion show; or experiences, such as dining at a restaurant or touring an amusement park. You can review almost anything that can be experienced by others, although your choice of what to review may depend on the interests of your intended audience.

Reviews typically both describe and evaluate, but there is no formula for how to include these two perspectives. Some reviews use a simple two-part structure, with a description followed by an evaluation. Many reviews, however, begin with an evaluative point in a kind of thesis statement: such-and-such was or is a success or failure, good in these areas but poor in these, worth experiencing or a waste of time and money.

Despite the different formats for reviews, however, some important principles tie reviews together as one kind of point-driven writing. First, good reviews are *considered.* They don't just state an opinion but support it with specific information and details. Second, good reviews are *authoritative;* most professional reviewers have experienced whatever they review hundreds of times. In writing your own reviews, for example, try to choose something you have experienced before, such as a movie, book, or CD.

1 Sample review

This book review assignment asked the students to develop a thesis based on the book's contents; the thesis could agree or disagree with the book's author if the book took a position on an issue. As you read the review, note how the writer supports her evaluation with facts and details. Note also how her writing gives the impression that she is reasonably familiar with the topic of deaf culture and communication, adding to her credibility.

Laurent Clerc:

The Issue of Early Deaf Literacy

by Amy Braegelman

1   The preservation of a language, though the community that uses it may be small, is crucially important. Language is not just a communicative amenity--it is a reflection of (and an influence on) a specific culture. Not only does a language allow a culture to flourish, but it allows the people within that culture to flourish. In some cases, a language is particularly well suited to a specific culture because it is all that allows its users to function in society. To allow or force a language so tailored to die is to leave the culture with no effective means of communication, only whatever its people have managed to acquire, usually by bare necessity, of the surrounding, dominant language.

2   Cathryn Carroll's book Laurent Clerc: The Story of His Early Years (Washington, D.C.: Kendall Green Publications, 1991) gives the reader a broader

platform on which to base these convictions. Set in the early nineteenth century, Clerc examines the beliefs, stereotypes, and attitudes surrounding the deaf and their language. Like any culture that does not function within the mainstream, the deaf were heavily stigmatized historically; they were believed to be physically sick, mentally ill, or of low intelligence.

3   Of particular interest in Carroll's book is the account of Clerc's time at the Royal National Institute for the Deaf in Paris. The sadistic Dr. Itard, on the staff at the Institute during the first decades of the nineteenth century, dedicated all of his time and surgical background to the misguided endeavor of finding a cure for deafness. As Carroll points out, the school's students were the doctor's unfortunate subjects, and the consequences were "waste, folly, and pain" (86). Itard is a chilling representation of public sentiment at the time; the deaf were "sick" and needed to be cured. The cure, we know, was not available, and in Clerc we see how the deaf who were not used in experiments and were not part of the select few lucky enough to attend the Royal National Institute were treated: sent to live in filth in poorhouses, institutionalized in sanitariums, shunned as subhumans.

4   In this dramatic chronicle of deaf experience, Carroll goes on to show that even in the environment of the Royal National Institute, home and haven to men like Jean Massieu and Laurent Clerc--geniuses by any standards--the deaf were treated like an

54f
arg

attraction. Presentations were given to influential politicians and heads of state to display the talents of these deaf men and gain funding for the school. Audiences were free to ask Massieu and Clerc, positioned on stage like performers, any questions they liked. "What is eternity?" they asked, as if to test the relationship between the ears and the mind. "What is hope?" "Does God reason?"

5   Carroll's portrayal shows that among themselves, where they could be natural and talk freely, the deaf students at the Institute showed an open-minded insight that the hearing, for the most part, lacked at the time. Sign language allowed these students to form a community and a web of support in the hearing world. As Clerc recounts, "I wasn't only alone, I was deficient" (35), but in the deaf world, he finds he is not alone. Clerc illustrates the principle of literacy as power and control. On a trip to England, for example, Massieu and Clerc are accompanied by a hearing person, Abbé Sicard. Clerc recounts that "surrounded by people who spoke a language very different from his, our dear Abbé was completely at a loss. Massieu and I had no trouble getting around...we know how to use our bodies to ask for things." Carroll describes Sicard as a pompous, self-important man who thrives on the control he feels he can exert over the deaf, always under the guise of helpfulness. In England, where he cannot use his own language, he is powerless and is reduced to petty criticisms of the English language. Massieu and Clerc are used to

being surrounded by people who don't speak their language, and they adapt easily, feeling in control.

6   Carroll also devotes much of her book to explaining why the deaf were ostracized because of their lack of literacy and why it was often priests who undertook their education. Greater society felt that because the deaf could not learn about God, they were sinners and savages--and were damned. As Clerc puts it, "Abbé Sicard said we were savages. ... He said we were children with no thoughts, no feelings, no nothing. We were like statues until he, the great Abbé Sicard, woke us in his classroom.... He said that deafness doomed us to darkness and to hell" (75).

7   Carroll's fascinating book illustrates the folly of expecting one mode of communication, one language, to suffice for every member of society. Her book portrays the struggle of the deaf to gain equal standing in a greater society that had so much trouble accepting them. It is, finally, a grand illustration that not only does literacy enable us to function in society, it shapes the way that other people view us. The deaf students at the Royal National Institute for the Deaf were intelligent children, fully capable of functioning in society; many displayed potential to make valuable contributions to science, art, and literature. However, because they could not communicate with their mouths, it was socially acceptable to confine them to asylums and poorhouses rather than giving their language the status it deserved and elevating the deaf beyond the realm of human silence.

**54f
arg**

2 Elements of a review

An effective review includes the following elements.

* It clearly describes the subject of the review at the start, providing all the information a reader would need to share in the experience (if it is repeatable) or to know when and where it happened (if it was a "one-time" experience such as a one-night-only performance).
* It has a clear organization. Reviews of experiences and events (plays, movies, and so on) are sometimes chronologically arranged, whereas reviews of static objects such as books or art exhibits may focus on different aspects of the work in order of their importance.
* It offers a reasoned, supported evaluation of the subject's main elements. Movie reviews, for example, may evaluate the filming, acting, costuming, directing, special effects, script, plot, casting, length, or stunt work, or the adaptation of another work such as a novel.
* It is authoritative. A reviewer who discusses an actor's performance should probably know something about the actor's other work. A restaurant reviewer who judges the quality of the curry in an Indian restaurant should have some prior experience with Indian food.
* It is generally verifiable by its intended readers; that is, they should be able to see how one might arrive at the evaluation in the review, even though they may not entirely agree with that evaluation.

54g
arg

3 Commentary on Amy Braegelman's review

Amy's paper is a good example of a point-driven review, one that develops a thesis early on and then extends and supports that thesis with reference to the material found, in this case, in a nonfiction book. Her paper artfully treats the issue of deaf literacy, but its description of the book itself is sparse. Amy might have synthesized the book at the start or worked through its contents from beginning to end.

54g The point-driven essay exam

In many of your classes, teachers will use **essay exams** to evaluate your skills as a synthesizer of information and as a critical thinker, skills that cannot be seen from a true/false or multiple-choice test. Thus, merely listing information, facts, and quotes without discussing their significance or making connections among them is not acceptable. When you study for essay exams, you will need to move beyond memorization to thinking about what the information means and how it fits into a larger context. Writing these thoughts down in a journal will help you prepare. (See also 56h.)

When you begin the exam, *first read the question(s) carefully*. You have only a short time in which to write, even with a take-home exam. You need to write quickly and concisely, answering the question specifically and with as much support as possible. It is crucial to understand what kind of answer the teacher expects and to plan the essay before actually writing.

Next, decide what position you want to take or what point you will make in the essay. This will become your working thesis or proposition—a perspective or interpretation that you will support with evidence. Try creating a brief outline for your answer, even just a few lines or items listed on the facing page of the test booklet. Working from an outline will help you make your paper more focused, point-driven, and clearly organized.

1 Sample essay exam

This exam asked the student to identify and discuss a common theme running through a survey course in American literature and to show this theme in two stories. The students were allowed to use their books in class in order to find quotations. As you read selections from this answer, note how the writer focuses on one theme. Note, too, how he incorporates quotations to illustrate the theme.

> Moral Perfection in "Young Goodman Brown"
>
> and "The Birthmark"
>
> by Ted Wolfe

1   Hawthorne's "Young Goodman Brown" explores the conflict between good and evil. Young Goodman Brown has his religious faith tested during a journey into the woods. In what may or may not have been a dream, he is shown by the devil that everyone he believed to be good is evil.... When the devil is about to baptize him, Brown calls out for Faith, his wife, telling her to resist the temptation. He is really calling out for faith, as in faith in God. When he does this, the hellish vision passes, and he is alone in the woods. From this, I think we can conclude that Hawthorne believes that people should try to resist temptation and live moral lives.

2   But Goodman Brown is never the same after the experience, be it dream or reality. He becomes "a stern, a sad, a darkly meditative, if not a desperate man." In his heart he doubts the goodness of Faith/faith, Deacon Gookin, Goody Cloyse, and everyone else.... Symbolically, the experience in the woods caused him to give up his faith. The overriding message that Hawthorne is trying to convey is that one should try to keep one's faith, to believe in others' inherent goodness, and to try to live morally. If one doesn't, life becomes as barren and miserable as it became for Goodman Brown.

3   Hawthorne's "The Birthmark" also addresses the issue of morality....

[The answer continues with supporting detail from the second story.]

4   ... Hawthorne's point is that one should not get so caught up in trying to be morally perfect that it ruins one's life. People must learn to "find the perfect future in the present."

2 Elements of a point-driven essay exam

Although the specific criteria for an effective essay exam will vary from teacher to teacher and from course to course, an effective essay exam that makes and defends a point includes the following general elements.

- It addresses the exam question directly, taking into account all parts of the question.
- It uses references—quotes, facts, and other information—efficiently, supplying enough to illustrate or back up the writer's point without overloading the essay.
- It synthesizes material, makes connections among references, and discusses the significance of the material; it does not merely list information but interprets it and uses it to illustrate or document a point.

3 Commentary on Ted Wolfe's essay exam

Although Wolfe titles his essay "Moral Perfection," he digresses slightly to the themes of good and evil, faith, and living morally. These themes are all related to "moral perfection," but Ted could make the relationship clearer. His use of quotes is effective and using specific phrases rather than long passages conserved his time.

55

Reading and Writing About Literature

When you read a novel, see a play, or read (or listen to) a poem, you are encountering literature, or, more precisely, imaginative literature. The word *literature* has other meanings as well, some of them used in this book. The literature of a subject of academic study, for example, consists of all the things scholars have written about it. In addition, people often use the term *literature* to distinguish novels and plays that are well written, enjoyable, and worth taking seriously.

In most college courses, however, the term *literature* is applied to certain kinds of texts—fiction, poetry, and drama—that are meant to be read in a manner different from the way we read texts like biographies, histories, reports, scientific papers, or magazine articles. To read a work as literature means to pay attention both to the various meanings it conveys (its insights into human relationships, for example) and to the artistry with which these insights are conveyed (a lively and convincing portrait of a character, for example, or a passage whose vivid and original language evokes a strong emotional response or brings a scene to life in a reader's mind).

It is possible to read almost any kind of text with this dual attention. For instance, you might read a newspaper editorial with a simultaneous focus on the author's point of view and on the persuasive and artful way it is presented. Yet in those works regarded as imaginative literature, the author generally calls special attention to the techniques of presentation, techniques such as characterization, plot, symbolism, and figurative uses of language. In addition, imaginative literature often conveys its meanings through a fictional representation of some setting or human activity: the events of a story, a confrontation between characters, a monologue revealing thoughts and emotions, or a scene in which events take place. To understand the meaning of such texts, you need to read them with a different kind of attention than you give to other kinds of writing. Likewise, to present in writing your interpretation of and responses to literary texts, you need to employ some special strategies of explanation and support.

55a   Reading literary texts

When you read a novel, short story, or poem or view a drama or a film, you need to pay attention to both meaning and artistic technique. In doing this, however, you should be aware that there are many different strategies for reading and interpreting such works. Your choice of a reading strategy can determine the way you interpret a work's meaning and the way you respond to the writer's forms of expression. Your focus in reading can also dictate the strategies you should use in presenting your responses to a work. Your goal as a reader and writer concerned with meaning is to develop and present interpretations that your readers will consider insightful and convincing.

1 Read for meaning

For many critics and students of literature, to read for meaning is to read for theme. You can view **theme** as an idea, perspective, insight, or cluster of feelings that a work conveys or that permeates a work, organizing the relationships among its parts. Or you can view theme as the responses and insights readers are likely to derive from their experience of reading a work. In reading for meaning, therefore, you need to pay attention to theme, both as it is developed in a work and as it develops in your responses to the work.

S T R A T E G Y

As you read, write down any ideas, perspectives, insights or clusters of feelings the work seems to focus on. Pay attention to the various techniques writers generally employ for conveying meaning (see 55a-2): characterization and dialogue, events and conflicts, descriptions or scenes, and discussions of ideas and emotions (either by characters, the speaker, or the writer addressing readers directly). Write down potentially important ideas or themes in the margins (if you own the book), on a sheet of paper, or in a journal you keep while you read. You need not explore potential themes in depth; for a first reading, at least, an informal list can be very valuable.

Look especially for repetition and contrast as a key to importance. Repeated words and ideas, contrasting characters or events, and patterns of images can signal themes worth noticing.

In the following marginal notes on Anson Gonzalez's short poem "Little Rosebud Girl," for example, Sevon Randolf, a college student, indicates some repetitions and contrasts that reveal an important cluster of feelings and ideas (a theme) that she thinks the poem conveys.

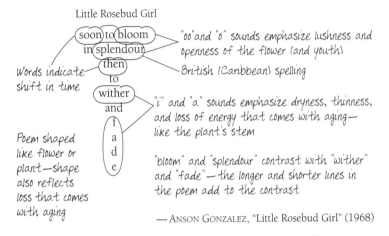

Little Rosebud Girl

soon to bloom
in splendour
then
to
wither
and
f
a
d
e

"oo" and "o" sounds emphasize lushness and openness of the flower (and youth)

British (Caribbean) spelling

Words indicate shift in time

"i" and "a" sounds emphasize dryness, thinness, and loss of energy that comes with aging— like the plant's stem

"bloom" and "splendour" contrast with "wither" and "fade"—the longer and shorter lines in the poem add to the contrast

Poem shaped like flower or plant—shape also reflects loss that comes with aging

— ANSON GONZALEZ, "Little Rosebud Girl" (1968)

55a
lit

The perspective you take as you read may suggest meanings and interpretations. If you know something about psychology, for instance, you might notice that the characters in a novel embody different psychological types or that the main character's actions can be explained as an attempt to overcome feelings of abandonment as a child. If you know something about history or political theory, you might be able to explain the events in a play as a reflection of an attempt to resolve contradictions affecting a particular society or culture. For example, you might be able to show that Shakespeare's plays *Macbeth* and *Henry IV* deal with questions of power and the proper form of government, major concerns in Elizabethan England. Finally, if you are familiar with contemporary feminist thought, you might note that the psychological and social portraits in a work seem to follow recognizable patterns of dominance and oppression and that the work seems to be designed as a commentary on the ways society has often distorted the lives of women. (Jennifer O'Berry's paper on "The Yellow Wallpaper" in 55c-2 draws on several such approaches.)

2 Read for technique

When you read for meaning, you inevitably read for technique. A writer cannot create events, portray characters, represent scenes, or elicit a reader's reactions without using techniques of characterization, plot, setting, or imaginative language. Nonetheless, because these techniques are such an important feature of every literary text, you may wish to focus on them as you read, either to understand a writer's artistry or to cite the writer's use of the techniques as evidence for your discussion of a work's meaning.

As you read, pay particular attention to the following elements of a novel, short story, poem, or drama and to the techniques the writer uses in creating these elements.

Did You Know?

If you look to contemporary literary critics for ways to analyze texts, you may notice that their work follows one or more "schools" of criticism. Some critics emphasize the formal techniques in a work (new criticism); others look for the way a text contradicts or undermines its explicit purposes (deconstruction). Still others pay attention to the historical context, either to explain a work's meaning (historicism) or to interpret it as a product of a specific social formation (new historicism). Some critics look at the many ways readers respond to a text (reader-response criticism); others are more concerned with the writer's mind or the way a text probes human psychology (psychological criticism). And some pay special attention to the role of gender in the reading and writing of literary texts (feminist criticism).

Steven Lynn, *Texts and Contexts: Writing About Literature with Critical Theory* (New York: HarperCollins, 1994).

Character. Identify the major and minor characters and their personality traits. Are they represented in depth with a variety of traits, even contradictions, or are they one-dimensional? Observe how the characters change and develop—or fail to change—in response to events. Note how self-aware the characters are. Which ones are presented positively, which negatively? Consider which characters, if any, represent values that the work (and the writer) seem to endorse.

Plot. Identify the order of events. Is it chronological, or have events been rearranged in some way? Decide what role conflicts play in developing the plot. Ask whether the events spring from the characters' personalities or serve primarily to reveal character traits. Is there a main conflict, a chain of conflicts, or a climax to which the work builds? Weigh the possibility that not all events are to be taken at face value. Watch for subplots alongside the main plot. Is the meaning of events clear to characters (and readers) from the start or only later? Pay attention to techniques of foreshadowing and suspense.

Setting. Note the time and place in which the events occur, along with any extended descriptions or background information relating to the place and time. Does the setting help explain the character's actions or reactions? Does it convey a mood that shapes the readers' reactions or the work's meaning?

If the work is from an earlier period, check for elements in the setting that require historical explanation.

Point of View. For novels and stories, decide who is telling the story. Stories can be narrated in the first person (*I*) either by a character in the narrative or by a narrative voice (sometimes representing the author). They can also be told in the third person by a narrator who speaks of the characters as *he* and *she* but does not identify himself or herself as *I*. Narrators may be limited in what they know, be omniscient (knowing and seeing things the characters cannot), or combine both in some way. Narrators may be reliable and truthful, be unreliable and deceptive, or mix these and other traits. The speaker in a poem may be a character or may be a persona, a voice that speaks for the poet.

55a
lit

Language. Look for special uses of language: similes, metaphors, understatement, paradoxes, ironic comments, and the like. Pay attention to vivid descriptive language that creates scenes and images (sight, sound, and the like). Look for unusual word choice and striking or emphatic arrangements of words. Be alert for rhythms in the wording and for patterns of sound and rhyme.

Genre. Pay attention to **genre**—the specific form or kind of work: novel, short story, poem, drama, or film. Be especially alert to the techniques and conventions characteristic of each form, and note how writers use these conventions to convey meanings and shape readers' reactions. Note instances in which the writer varies or alters conventions, perhaps by undermining them or developing them in unusual directions.

S T R A T E G Y

As you read a literary text, make notes on the large-scale techniques the writer uses to shape the work (genre, plot, and point of view, for example) and also on the smaller-scale techniques that appear to be important in a particular passage (language and character, for example). If you make your notes in the margins of your book, you can highlight passages you may wish to cite later in a paper. If you make notes in your journal, however, you will have more room to explore your responses and the ideas you may wish to develop in a paper. (Your journal entries also should note important passages for later use.)

Whenever possible, relate your observations on technique to your perceptions of a work's meaning. This will help you understand the purposes behind the techniques. It will also help you identify evidence for your interpretations of a work.

Note how T. J. Corini's marginal notes on the opening paragraph of John Edgar Wideman's novel *Philadelphia Fire* identify techniques and link them to meaning in a way that points toward a paper he might write.

first character—
a hero? an outlaw?

What's going on?

On a day like this the big toe of Zivanias had failed him Zivanias named for the moonshine his grandfather cooked, best white lightning on the island Cudjoe had listened to the story of the name many times. Was slightly envious. He would like to be named for something his father or grandfather had done well. A name celebrating a deed. A name to stamp him, guide him. They'd shared a meal once. Zivanias crunching fried fish like Rice Krispies. Laughing at Cudjoe. Pointing to Cudjoe's heap of cast-off crust and bones, his own clean platter. Zivanias had lived up to his name. Deserted a flock of goats, a wife and three sons up in the hills, scavenged work on the waterfront till he talked himself onto one of the launches jitneying tourists around the island. A captain soon. Then captain of captains. Best pilot, lover, drinker, dancer, storyteller of them all. He said so. No one said different. On a day like this when nobody else dared leave port, he drove a boatload of bootleg whiskey to the bottom of the ocean. Never a trace. Not a bottle or bone. *Whole ¶ presents contrasts of character, attitude, perspective, and detail*

55b
lit

The bones symbolize the contrast

His actions make him seem verbal, self-assured

Repetition and parallelism help emphasize his growing legend

2nd charact.
Cudjoe uncer of his manlin
Admires Z.?

2. self-sufficient?
of himself?
Characteriza—Z.'s actio and attitud contrast w/C contrast

Contrast

Exercise 1

 A. Choose a short text or part of a text you are planning to write about. Read it, making notes on the meaning and technique in the margins or in a journal.

 B. Ask a classmate to read the same text and make the same kind of notes that you made in Exercise 1A. (Return the favor by reading and annotating a text for your classmate.) Compare your notes, looking for points of agreement. Discuss any annotations or interpretations that need explanation or support.

55b Writing about literary texts

When you write about a literary text, you interpret and analyze an author's words and techniques. To do so, you must arrive at conclusions—

judgments and observations—with which another reader may agree or disagree. Consequently, you need to convince readers that your conclusions are both reasonable and well-founded. You can generally do this by offering evidence from the text or from secondary sources.

1 Write about meaning

In writing about the meaning of a literary work, you may explain and support your conclusions about its theme. Or you may focus on insights you develop by applying a particular perspective to the work (a historical perspective or a feminist perspective, for example).

Developing a Thesis. If you are writing about a work's theme, you need to make sure readers can easily identify your statement of the theme. Presenting your conclusion about the theme early in your paper in a thesis statement is a particularly effective strategy. In addition, if you develop a working thesis early in your drafting, you can revise it and use it to help focus your supporting paragraphs.

Selecting Evidence. Suppose you developed the following working thesis for a paper.

> In "Young Goodman Brown," Hawthorne focuses on the dangers to human relationships and community posed by excessive concern with the self.

For supporting evidence, you can turn to passages in the text itself, either those that seem to state this theme or those you can analyze and explain in ways that support your conclusion. Simply quoting passages from the work is not enough. You need to discuss and analyze them in detail in order to show readers why the passages support your interpretation. You can also cite or summarize other elements of a work, such as events, characters, and symbols, analyzing them in detail to show that the text and the techniques it employs are consistent with your interpretation. Finally, you can turn to the writing of critics and scholars, using it to support your thesis and your view of specific parts of a work.

Organizing. Because a paper about meaning focuses on your view of a text's theme or on your interpretation of all or part of the work, you need to organize the paper to explain and defend your perspective. There are two general ways to do this (with many variations, of course). One way is to separate your thesis into parts and take up each part in a different section of your paper. In writing about Hawthorne's "Young Goodman Brown," for instance, you might first demonstrate that the story deals with a character obsessed with the self, then look at what the story says about the consequences of this behavior. The other way to organize your paper is to divide it into parts corresponding to different segments of the work (beginning, middle, end) or different elements (characters, language, symbols), then show in sections of your paper how the particular part or element supports your thesis.

Writer's Tip

Follow these conventions for writing about literature.

- Use the present tense when summarizing literary texts ("In the next section of the play, Falstaff *acts* in a manner that calls into question the kind of morality he represents").
- Use the present tense for discussing what a writer does in a particular work or group of works ("Dickens *uses* descriptive passages in *Bleak House* to develop symbols that comment on the action and the characters").
- Use the past tense for discussing a work in historical context ("During the Vietnam War, Levertov's poetry *took* on a distinctly political tone").

---

2 Write about technique

In writing about technique, you explain the choices the author has made from the resources available for creating fiction, poetry, or drama. You also try to highlight the author's variations on the techniques, if any. Finally, you draw conclusions about the roles the techniques play in shaping the work's meaning and the likely responses of readers.

Developing a Thesis. Since your purpose in this kind of paper is to describe and analyze one or several techniques and then relate technique to meaning, your thesis statement should reflect this dual emphasis. In writing about the story "Young Goodman Brown," for example, you might say, "Hawthorne uses ambiguity in setting, symbolism, and characterization to suggest how excessive concern with the self can alter one's perception of everyday events."

Selecting Evidence. The primary evidence in a paper about technique is the text itself, presented either through quotations or through paraphrase and summary. But details from a text are not enough on their own to support your conclusions. You need to discuss the evidence, explaining the particular ways a technique is used and pointing out how this use supports your conclusions about the text's meaning. (The work of critics and scholars can also provide supporting evidence.)

Organizing. If you are examining a single technique, consider dividing your essay into parts corresponding to different sections of the work, demonstrating how the technique is employed in each section and for what purpose. (For a short work such as a poem, you might examine the work line by line or sentence by sentence, creating an **explication.**) If you examine more than one technique, you can divide your paper into parts, each concerned with the way a different technique is employed. Or you can take up each section of a work in turn, looking at the various techniques used there.

Writer's Tip

Stating your point in a thesis is a good start, but many promising papers still get bogged down in details, losing focus and losing the reader. One way to avoid this problem is to remind readers of your overall thesis each time you move to a new part of your essay, letting them know what section or technique you will discuss next and what you plan to conclude about it. This strategy can guide your drafting and your revision, helping you check the focus of your essay and pay attention to the needs of your readers.

55c
lit

Exercise 2

A. Choose a work you plan to write about. Read it, and write out a tentative thesis statement presenting your conclusions about the work's meaning and technique. Then prepare a list of particular passages or sections of the work you plan to use as evidence in your paper. Finally, create a rough outline or some other kind of plan for this paper.

B. Present your tentative thesis, list of evidence, and plan to a group of writers working on the same project. Discuss each writer's material, offering criticisms and suggestions to help each other prepare a draft. Draft your paper, and then share it with the same group for advice about revision. Take the group's advice into account as you revise and prepare the final draft.

55c The text analysis

A **text analysis** is a frequent assignment in many courses across the college curriculum. The first of the three examples here focuses on literary techniques in a poem. The second focuses on meaning in a short story. The third discusses visual strategies in a film.

1 Sample text analysis: Focus on technique

As you read the following paper, note how the writer goes through the poem line by line, accounting for nearly every image and phrase. This form of analysis is often called explication.

"Under Stars": A Portrait

by Chantele Giles

Under Stars

Tess Gallagher

The sleep of this night deepens
because I have walked coatless from the house
carrying the white envelope.
All night it will say one name
in its little tin house by the roadside.

I have raised the metal flag
so its shadow under the roadlamp
leaves an imprint on the rain-heavy bushes.
Now I will walk back
thinking of the few lights still on
in the town a mile away.

In the yellowed light of a kitchen
the millworker has finished his coffee,
his wife has laid out the white slices of bread
on the counter. Now while the bed they have left
is still warm, I will think of you, you
who are so far away
you have caused me to look up at stars.

Tonight they have not moved
from childhood, those games played after dark.

Again I walk into the wet grass
toward the starry voices. Again, I
am the found one, intimate, returned
by all I touch on the way.

                              1978

1   With the use of visual imagery in the poem
"Under Stars," Tess Gallagher paints a romantic, yet
lonely portrait of the relationship between the
speaker of the poem and her long-distance lover.
Although the speaker's emotional state is plagued
with images of loneliness, she projects the long-
distance romance as a positive relationship that is
warm and caring.

2   As Gallagher brushes "The sleep of this night
deepens" of the first stanza onto her canvas, her
poetry begins to take shape. The word "sleep"
implies that the relationship with her lover is
peaceful. Since the "night" personifies the
relationship, the phrase implies further that the
relationship is past the early stages and is
deepening with the "sleep" of the night. In the next
lines the speaker is walking "coatless from the
house / carrying the white envelope." She walks
"coatless" because she does not need to cloak the
relationship; she is neither afraid nor ashamed.
Since the "white envelope" connotes purity,
goodness, and truth, it symbolizes the relationship
as being true. The word "coatless" implies not only
that the speaker has nothing to hide, but that the
affiliation is warm and caring. If it were cold and
dysfunctional, the speaker would not be without a coat.

3   In the last two lines, Gallagher applies the final strokes to the first stanza. The first of the two lines implies that the speaker is consumed with thoughts of her lover. With the image of the "little tin house by the roadside," Gallagher suggests that the speaker's lover is some distance away, which implies that the speaker is trying to bridge the distance between the two of them. She accomplishes this by composing a letter and placing it in the "little tin house."

4   Since the second stanza exposes the inadequacies of the relationship, Gallagher applies a darker paint to her canvas. The "metal flag" suggests the cold reality of a long-distance relationship, since metal is cold to the touch; the flag's "shadow" implies that the relationship cannot be touched by the speaker. The association with her lover leaves only a lonely "imprint" on the speaker's heart, which is symbolized by the "rain-heavy bushes." The final three lines are painted a lighter color. With these lines, the speaker implies that the "shadow" of loneliness is not permanent. Since the "town a mile away" symbolizes the future, the speaker implies that the future is close at hand. The "few lights" of the town suggest that there is hope in the near future.

5   Gallagher allows the readers into the realm of the speaker's fantasy, as she begins the third stanza. The "millworker" and "his wife" represent her fantasy relationship. The warm atmosphere created by the "yellowed light" implies that the speaker's fantasy is cheerful and bright. In this

relationship, the couple reside and share their
meals together. The "white slices of bread" connote
food, nourishment, and sustenance. Since the "wife
has laid out the white slices of bread" for the
"millworker," the speaker implies that not only does
she want to be her lover's sustenance, but she also
wants to be consumed by him (the way the
"millworker" will consume the "bread").

55c
lit

6   The last lines of the third stanza illustrate
the speaker's need for closeness. Since the lover is
"so far away" and the speaker looks "up at the
stars," the speaker feels closer to her lover
because of the possibility that the lover may be
looking "up at the stars" also. This possibility
creates a connection between the speaker and her
lover. In the fourth stanza, Gallagher strokes onto
her portrait "Tonight they have not moved / from
childhood, those games played after dark." These
lines suggest that the distance between the speaker
and her lover has done little to change the
affection she feels for her lover. "Those games
played after dark" may refer to romantic liaisons;
since these liaisons involve intense feelings, the
speaker implies that the intensity of her feelings
"have not moved from [the] childhood" of the
relationship. Therefore, the speaker's connection to
her lover is permanent.

7   With "Again I walk into the wet grass,"
Gallagher demonstrates that the speaker looks "up at
the stars" on a regular basis, thus reinforcing the
various images of the poem such as walking coatless
and the "rain-heavy bushes." The "starry voices"

recall the images set forth in the third stanza and the first part of the fourth stanza. This line reinforces the images of the speaker's heavenly fantasy, as well as the feelings of permanence.

8   In the last lines, Gallagher displays the speaker's final analysis of the relationship. It is long-lasting and can survive the long-distance barrier. Since she considers herself to be "the found one," she implies that her lover is her one and only true love. She says further that her love is "returned by all" she touches, implying that their love is a powerful, all-encompassing natural force.

9   Tess Gallagher creates a gentle but stirring portrait of true love. Although the images suggest that the speaker endures the heartache of the separation, she does not succumb to the depression usually associated with it. Instead, she embraces the negative aspects of the situation and disempowers them through her fantasies and stargazing.

2 Sample text analysis: Focus on meaning

As you read, note how the writer backs up her interpretation with quotations from the story but does not let the quotations dominate the paper. If you have read this short story, consider other ways it could be interpreted; if you have not read the story, consider other ways the quotations used in this sample could be interpreted.

Images of Self in "The Yellow Wallpaper"

by Jennifer O'Berry

1   During the 1800s the idea of the "new woman" was appearing. Women began to realize that they were seen only as their husbands' and society's

"property." They began to pursue their independence and create their own identities. In Charlotte Perkins Gilman's short story "The Yellow Wallpaper," a nameless woman is searching for her personal identity and freedom from the oppressive childlike treatment inflicted on her by her doctor/husband. Gilman presents an elaborate metaphor about the images seen by the woman within the wallpaper found in her nursery/bedroom. This metaphor and the images the woman finds in the wallpaper play a significant role in the woman's achievement of finding her true self. Her state of insanity at the end of the story serves as a safe mask for her newly found freedom from alienation and oppression.

55c
lit

2   Gilman presents the woman in her story as a somewhat unstable character who believes that she is sick, although John, her doctor/husband, believes that she is only suffering from a "slight hysterical tendency" (416). This characterization seems intentional on the part of Gilman because it makes the reader see clearly that the woman's ideas are oppressed, even from the beginning, by her husband. John thinks that all his wife needs is a strict rest schedule in which she is "absolutely forbidden to 'work'" (416) until she is "well" again. Gilman seems to suggest, by putting work in quotes, that the duties of the woman, and all women at that time, were not truly considered work. She was forbidden to write and to have visitors. Early in the story, when the "rules" for her recovery are stated, the woman begins to comment on her disagreement with her husband, but she stops abruptly, as if she does not

dare to have such thoughts. She believes that she would more quickly recover if, instead of being quarantined and forbidden from such pleasures as her writing, she "had less opposition and more society and stimulus" (416).

3   The woman tells the reader that "Mary is so good with the baby" (417), implying that she herself does not want to spend time with the baby. The child is also never mentioned by the woman as being with her or spending time with her. This seems to suggest that she may actually be experiencing a type of postpartum depression, causing her to want to abandon her child. The thoughts that lead her to feel that she may be ill may actually be due to her desire to abandon her role of wife and mother which was so rigidly demanded by society at that time. She gets "unreasonably angry" (416) about the condition of things sometimes, but she blames this anger on her "nervous condition" (416). She tries to dismiss these thoughts because she feels that they are not proper. Therefore, she feels that she must be ill.

4   Gilman uses many images to enlighten the reader about the childlike treatment of the woman by her husband. The woman is directed by her husband to rest in a bedroom that used to serve as a nursery. Gilman chooses this room to show how John thinks of his wife. When referring to his wife, John commonly chooses names such as "blessed little goose" (418), "blessed child" (420), and "little girl" (421). This shows that he does not see his wife as an equal but rather as a helpless child who is solely dependent on him. As the woman begins to realize that she has

been a subject of this type of oppression, she begins to be "a little afraid of John" (422) and to "wish he would take another room" (424), which exhibits her awareness of this treatment and the desire to be free from it, and from him.

5   Because of her rigid rest schedule, the woman is forced to spend most of her time in her nursery/bedroom, where she begins to explore the "worst [wall]paper" (417) she has ever seen in her life. Since she is not allowed to do much else, she commits herself to "follow that pointless pattern to some sort of conclusion" (419). She finds many images in the pattern, all of which aid in her "improvement" (423) "because of the wallpaper" (423) out of her mother/wife roles. She describes the pattern as images that will "plunge off at outrageous angles, [and] destroy themselves in unheard-of contradiction" (417). These "contradictions" seem to be referring to the contradictory treatment of her by her husband and society's contradictory expectations of her to be the perfect wife and mother. She becomes entranced by the wallpaper and "follows the pattern about by the hour" (419). With each second, the images become more numerous and complex. She begins to see "a broken neck and two bulbous eyes" (418), a woman behind the pattern in wallpaper. This woman "is all the time trying to climb through...but nobody could climb through...it strangles so" (424). She begins to identify with the woman and decides that she will stop at nothing until the woman is released from her entrapment.

55c
lit

55c
lit

6   At the end of the story, the woman is simultaneously on the brink of self-identity and insanity. On the last night she is to stay in the house, she is left alone in the room where she finally frees the woman in the wallpaper. When the woman in the wallpaper begins to "crawl and shake the pattern" (425), the main character "[runs] to help her" (425). Through the night, the two women pull and shake the bars and are able to "peel off yards of that paper" (425). She breaks down some of these cultural bars with the help from the woman in the wallpaper. When morning arrives, there is only one woman—the two have merged, and the woman's true identity has been found. In the remaining wallpaper are "many of those creeping women" (426). This symbolically represents the great number of women who also desire to be freed from the bars put up by society. She wonders if those women will ever "come out of the wallpaper as [she] did" (426). This shows her symbolic escape and her desire for other women to experience this personal freedom.

7   John returns at the end of the story to discover his wife in a state of insanity. When he sees her as the woman in the wallpaper, creeping around the room, he faints. She "had to creep over him" (426) because he was blocking her path. This strongly symbolizes the conquering of her husband because of her dominant position over him. She tells him that he cannot "put [her] back" (426) because she is finally free. Her creeping, which is like that of an infant, seems to represent a birth of her

new self. At the same time, she has become
completely insane. It is rather ironic that she must
move into this state in order to be free from
oppression. This seems to represent society's view
of a liberated and self-identified woman. John
believes that his wife is not ill before she begins
her pursuit of self-discovery. When this discovery
is complete, he sees her as insane. The opposite is
true for the woman herself. She sees herself as ill
before her process of identification and fully
healthy afterward.

8   The woman in Gilman's short story uses the
yellow wallpaper as a tool to find her true self.
The color of the wallpaper itself seems to represent
the brightness and hope of a new horizon, yet at the
same time, it is a reminder of the "old, foul, bad
yellow things" (423), like a fungus that grows and
decays. This is representative of the woman's life.
She can never truly be free, because society's views
and ideas will never acknowledge that a liberated
woman can achieve her own identity.

3 Sample text analysis: Focus on technique (film)

As you read, notice how the writer organizes his paper and uses details
from the film to illustrate and support his points.

Realism and Visual Effect in Educating Rita

by Jason Fester

1   Educating Rita is a realistic film. It depicts
an older woman hairdresser who returns to college to
become educated. As a realistic film it presents
itself very conventionally with authentic sets,

vernacular dialogue, and routine eye-level shots with conversations consisting of medium two-shots and close-ups. Since the film concentrates on language and the interaction of characters, the other elements of cinematic technique seem secondary, and as a realistic film, this seems appropriate. "Realists . . . try to preserve the illusion that their film world is unmanipulated; an objective mirror of the actual world" (Giannetti 3). But the director inconspicuously uses color to parallel character development and contribute to the theme of his movie.

55c
lit

2   When Rita is first seen, she is light-skinned and has bleached blonde hair. She wears red lipstick, a thin white shirt, high heels, and a tight hot-pink skirt. The next time she is seen, she wears a white shirt, a bright red skirt, high heels, dangling silver earrings, and this time pink highlights adorning her hair. Rita is a vivacious, vivid woman, and the colors of her wardrobe reflect this. Her appearance presents her as sexual and corporeal.

3   The university, however, is a dull, colorless place. The building's walls are dirty white and gray stone. Frank's office is a dungeon of brown curtains, olive walls, and a drab red carpet, all bordered by a montage of tan, matte yellow, earth brown, and olive drab books. Everything associated with the university is plain, colorless, and somber. Frank's house continues the decorum of his office with brown curtains, muted yellow, and olive drab wallpaper. Frank wears suits exclusively in varying

tones of tan; his friend exists in the same gray
suit throughout the movie, and even Julia limits her
wardrobe to red-browns. There is no vividness to any
of these places or people. Everything, except Frank,
is sober.

4   This is the world to which Rita commits
herself, regardless of Frank's warning that she will
have to "suppress, perhaps even abandon altogether,
[her] uniqueness." Thus it is appropriate that at
the stage of her development when she has chosen to
commit to her education, saying "I want to change,"
she is wearing a tan jacket with a brown skirt.

55c
lit

5   With the advent of spring comes the next phase
of Rita's transformation: summer school. Here her
apparel consists of the light blues and greens of
the fertile season, suggesting that Rita herself is
flourishing and growing. Upon her return to
Cambridge, she responds to a compliment on her
appearance with "I got a whole new wardrobe." Her
appearance is now quite different from when she was
first introduced. Her hair is now her natural brown;
she is unadorned with jewelry or makeup; and she is
clothed in a blue blazer, loose-fitting white pants,
and a long white scarf. These neutral, asexual
colors and styles continue throughout this period of
her activities: light blues, greens, and soft grays
cause her to blend with the garments of her student
peers and the lusterlessness of the college.

6   Exceptions to this pattern are the
retrogressive Roaring Twenties outfits Rita wears
for the bistro. They consist of hot pinks,
turquoise, pink and blue leopard skins, and lime

greens arrayed in clashing ensembles. But these serve to mock her original style, for when she jokingly displays one outfit to Frank, he humourlessly replies, "Why can't you just be yourself?"

7   The end of the movie presents a Rita vastly different from the one introduced at the beginning. Rita is now merely Susan, a confused, unfulfilled woman. She is dressed in blue jeans, common and ordinary. She wears no makeup. Her long brown hair hangs limply on her shoulders. As she walks along, her blue clothes merge with the dreary blues and grays of the wet rained-on streets. She doesn't know where she's going; she doesn't know what she wants to do.

8   The director uses the colors of Rita's clothes contrasted against the colors of her environment to further express the character changes she undergoes. Even though this is a realistic film, the director surreptitiously manipulates one technique, color, in a way that affects the emotions and responses of the viewer.

Work Cited

Giannetti, Louis D. <u>Understanding Movies</u>. 6th ed.
    Englewood Cliffs: Prentice, 1993.

4 Elements of a text analysis

An effective text analysis includes the following elements.

- It presents a unified interpretation that attempts to convince its readers of one specific way of reading the text.

- It accounts for every idea, argument, image, or allusion; it does not overlook elements that don't fit into the interpretation.
- It does not try to hide behind a facade of objectivity, presenting opinions as absolute truths, but neither does it resort to the relativist plea that "one person's opinion is just as valid as another's."
- It attempts to add a new way of reading the text to the existing ways; it does not merely repeat what has already been written about the text.
- It assumes a dialogue with the reader.

5 Commentary on students' papers

Chantele Giles was faced with the problem typical of writing explications of poetry, that of making the explication as lively and as engaging as the poem itself. Knowing that she must account for every line and image of the poem, she starts at the beginning and moves line by line to the end. To add interest, she frames the explication with an analogy of the poet to a painter, but her prose still sounds too dry. She could enliven her paper by varying the organization, perhaps by using the analogy as a frame to begin and end the paper rather than to begin each paragraph. She could also alternate the line-by-line approach with an occasional comment on the overall meaning of the poem. And she could move beyond discussing the meaning of the poem to other ways of looking at it, such as analyzing its effect on her or other readers or comparing it to other poems.

Jennifer O'Berry uses quotations from the text well; she seems to have an intuitive sense of what is significant about them and how they relate to each other. She could improve the paper by discussing these quotations in more depth, explaining why they are significant in understanding how this story illustrates the ways women were oppressed. As the paper is now, the significance of the quotations is a bit unclear, mainly because Jennifer does not define the terms that she uses to explain their significance (terms such as *self-identity, true self, insanity,* and *oppression*). Defining these terms would help strengthen the connection between the quotations and the discussion.

Jason Fester assumes that readers will be familiar with the film he is discussing, and as a result, he does not adequately identify some of the characters, scenes, and relationships he discusses. At the same time, however, his discussion of Rita's appearance and its relationship to her character is especially clear. He organizes his discussion so that it follows the chronological order of the film. This is particularly appropriate not only because the organization aids him in demonstrating the pattern in Rita's changing dress but also because it allows him to draw parallels with Rita's changes in character and the themes developed through these changes. He also presents detailed evidence about the film's techniques so that he is able to show convincingly how the evidence supports his interpretations of the director's work.

CHAPTER

56

Writing Informative Papers Across the Disciplines

In many situations, your job as a writer may be primarily to convey information in a manner that is as clear, economical, and balanced as you can, serving the needs, interests, and curiosity of your readers. College writing assignments may ask you to gather and convey information—knowledge that you, as a student, have gained and are ready to convey to others. Unlike argument or other point-driven writing (see Chapter 54), **informative writing** doesn't aim primarily at supporting your opinion or your critical insights. Instead, informative writing asks you to adopt the stance of a careful reporter or an informed synthesizer.

Informative writing can describe a process or tell how to do something. It can report what others think about a topic or synthesize research findings. You can employ the strategies of informative writing to describe the components or structure of a natural object, to provide information that enables readers to arrive at informed judgments, or to record events.

Informative writing plays essential roles in business, government, research, and education. Most journalistic writing is also informative; reporters try to "tell it like it is" (or was). This chapter introduces some common uses for informative writing in college courses, and it outlines strategies you can employ in your informative writing in college and beyond.

56a Developing and presenting informative writing

Informative writing relies on thorough gathering of information, careful analysis and synthesis, and presentation shaped by both the subject matter and the readers' needs. Instead of thinking of readers as people to persuade, as in argumentative writing, you might think of them as clients who need information that you can supply in thoughtful, clear, and creative ways.

First, you need to offer your readers accurate information that is new, interesting, or useful to them. Your own values, attitudes, and opinions are less important than this information and its clarity and fairness. Though you, as a writer, are present everywhere in the text, as a source of personal opinions you may move to the background to let your readers focus on the details, ideas, and events that are your subject. Explanations of complicated ideas and phenomena may challenge readers, but the reading experience itself should be free from complications such as poor organization, inappropriate wording, or hard-to-follow sentences.

1 Analyze your readers' needs

56a
info

To provide an effective base for your informative writing, try to identify your readers and their purposes for wanting information. In academic settings, you can usually assume that you are providing a teacher and classmates with information related to the course work. Your classmates probably know relatively little about your topic; your teacher may have a fuller background but is reading both to learn something new and to discover what the presentation reveals about your knowledge and your insights.

S T R A T E G Y

Here are some ways to identify your readers' needs before you begin collecting and presenting information.

- In your journal or on a piece of paper, analyze your readers. How much background do they have in your subject? Are they experts, or do they represent a general, educated audience with no specialized knowledge? Are they merely curious about the topic, or will they do something with the knowledge (such as repair something, think differently about a subject, or seek more information)? (See also Chapter 5.)
- Find out what a friend or another trusted person would like to know about your topic, and list these questions or concerns.
- List information you already know about the topic. Then list questions you want to answer. If you ask and try to answer interesting questions, you are likely to share your involvement in the topic.

---

2 Collect information

Collecting expert material for an informative paper may involve probing your own memory or prior experiences; doing library research (see

Chapters 45 and 46); doing field research through interviews, observations, surveys, or questionnaires; or collecting physical material for analysis. For a complex paper, you may need information from several different sources, organized in a sequence so that each stage of such work can inform the others.

S T R A T E G Y

Here are some planning tips for informative writing. (See Chapter 44–48 for important guidelines for library and field research.)

- Create a list of possible information sources, and then order the sources in different possible sequences. In each sequence, note what information will likely come from each source and how it might affect the use of the next source. Also include notes about any practical issues in the collection of information. Choose the possible sequence that seems the most practical. Here is a sequence one writer chose for a paper on recent biological research in the South American rain forests.

  1. Interview with Prof. James ⟶ help me focus on which Amazonian areas are most relevant for my paper, and suggest possible sources
  2. General library research ⟶ background on rain forest research
  3. Biology library research ⟶ information on medicinal discoveries from rain forest plants
  4. Interview with Susan Shoulder ⟶ what she felt when discovering plants that have never been classified

- Keep copious and accurate notes. If you are observing, write down only what you are sure you are seeing. If you are conducting an interview, take accurate notes or use a tape recorder. If you feel you are reaching a conclusion during the interview, don't mix your conclusions into the notes as if they came from the person being interviewed. Instead, ask your interviewee whether your conclusion is justified.
- Go back to your source, if possible, to verify or extend your data. If you *think* you saw a picture of a controversial activist on the office wall of the mayor you interviewed, see if you can verify its presence before mentioning it in your paper. You might even ask the mayor about its significance. If something in your library research is unclear, go back for more information to clarify the issue or fill the gap.
- Remember that your readers expect you to be fair to your subject and its various interpretations. Begin with what you know to be true, based on facts and evidence; don't leap to unsupported interpretations. Represent accurately what you *see* in your observations and what you *hear* in your interviews. If you cannot be balanced in your research or presentation, change subjects, or change to a kind of writing (argument, for instance) that allows you to take a position.

3 Synthesize and "chunk" information

Informative writing relies on careful internal logic that helps readers to process and understand information. If you shift topics without an obvious plan, for example, readers will have trouble organizing information in their own minds and integrating it into their existing knowledge. In a paper about the relationship between diet and colon cancer in the United States, for instance, readers will be able to process the information more easily if you present it in logical categories rather than jumbling up disparate facts about colon cancer, the American diet, and the basic food groups.

S T R A T E G Y

56a
info

To find an internal logic to your information, try some informal grouping and outlining techniques (see also Chapter 3).

- **Chunks.** List the main areas your paper will cover. All the information you have gathered should fit into these "chunks." If something does not fit, reconsider your list. Perhaps you can create an additional category for this item (and for others already listed elsewhere).
- **Patterns.** Look for patterns in your information. For example, if you are **comparing** or **contrasting** two objects or phenomena, then your work will involve two main groups of details or ideas—perhaps dividing your paper into two large sections or into a number of subtopics, each discussed in terms of your two main subjects. If you use **classification,** however, you will organize your information in terms of groups, categories, or parts, each presented in its own section. (See also 8b on patterns in paragraphs.)
- Also consider a **sequential order** (organizing information in a pattern within a particular perspective or focus) such as a *spatial sequence* (describing physical features in relationship to each other), a *chronological sequence* (describing events in a series to explain a history or the stages in a process), or a *hierarchical sequence* (describing relationships and the relative importance of a subject's features or parts).

    In a complex paper, you may need to use more than one form of organization. A fairly long research paper about an artist might include chronological sequences about the artist's life and the development of his or her work, spatial sequences to describe and discuss specific works, and a hierarchical sequence in moving from least to most important works.

Exercise 1

 A. Choose a topic of interest to you. On the basis of your existing knowledge, select a potential organizing strategy to present some background information about the topic. Create a simple outline.

EXAMPLE Topic: Building a deck
Organizing strategy: Sequential
Outline:
1. Planning the location and style
2. Determining and obtaining the materials
3. Setting concrete piers
4. Building a supporting frame
5. Laying deck boards
6. Building stairs and rails
7. Finishing and trimming the deck

 B. Share your outlines in a small group. As you discuss the outlines, try to imagine an alternative organizing strategy based on the collective knowledge of the group.

56a info

4 Balance description with analysis or synthesis

In many kinds of informative writing, you will need to present information as a function of a careful **analysis** or **synthesis.** To analyze means to break a subject into its components and study the relationship among these parts—how they affect or relate to each other, how they work together, how they fit within a larger system, or how they are in turn divided into smaller systems. When you analyze, you look for connections, patterns, and relationships within the larger whole—for example, the "system" in a classroom rather than just the details describing it. On the other hand, synthesis involves combining separate elements into a unified whole, for example, bringing order to a "trend analysis" through an overview or general conclusion based on disparate studies or data.

S T R A T E G Y

Try the following ways to find a balance, when appropriate, among analysis, synthesis, and description.

- Collect as much descriptive or factual information as you can. Then look for connections and relationships in the factual information. Such relationships may be *causal* (*A* causes *B*), *sequential* (*A* comes before *B*), or *hierarchical* (*A, B,* and *C* are really parts of *X*). (Try some of the Strategies in Chapter 3 to help you see beyond simple facts.)
- Ask yourself whether your description or facts alone are enough to give your readers insight into your subject. Recounting the events in a homicide may be enough for a newspaper report, but a simple list of facts about oil consumption in the United States may not interest readers as much as a careful, objective analysis of the likely consequences of these facts.

---

5 Check your stance

While conveying information fairly may seem like an easy task, don't be deceived; even journalists acknowledge that it is very difficult to report anything without subtly conveying a "point" or opinion. Consequently, it is important for you to think carefully about your own stance in relation to your subject, one in which you are not invested in a particular finding, conclusion, or set of facts. If you decide in advance that you can't write in a balanced way about your subject, don't deceive your readers into believing that you are being nonjudgmental in your treatment.

S T R A T E G Y

- After writing a draft of an informative paper, ask yourself whether you are being true to the full range of information you discovered in your research. Ask yourself if you have left out information that might show your subject in a different and equally reasonable light. Responsible informative writing does not slant information but instead presents alternatives for readers to consider.
- Look carefully at any language in your draft that suggests an interpretation, such as *thus, therefore, as a result, consequently, it seems that,* or similar wording. Then ask whether that interpretation represents a fair conclusion in light of the information you gathered or whether it represents your particular opinion or bias.
- Locate and consider eliminating statements that carry strong personal opinions or judgments (such as *in my opinion, in my view, I believe,* or *I think*). Expletives like *it is clear that* and *there is evidence that* can also help convey values and opinions (see 9c). You need not eliminate all of your conclusions or opinions, but make sure they are identifiable as your own and do not unfairly shape the information you present.
- The personal pronoun *I* is more commonly used now in informative writing than in the past but may signal a stance that is too subjective or biased. Look carefully at any personal pronouns, and ask whether they help give a personal touch to your writing without adding bias.

Exercise 2

A. Indicate whether the following statements suggest a fair or biased stance on the topic. Write out a brief explanation of your conclusion.

EXAMPLE

After talking with about twenty mall shoppers, I am more convinced than ever that people who frequent malls are not avid readers.
Analysis: Suggests bias through the implication that the writer was convinced of the stated relationship before conducting the survey ("I am more convinced than ever").

1. These sixteen independent research reports indicate that people who live in the midst of suburban sprawl are just as likely to suffer from geographically related stress as people who live within city limits.
2. Although rural residents were not studied, I believe it is obvious that they are less stressed than urban and suburban residents.
3. Several studies showed conclusively that urban residents who spent at least one weekend a month at a rural retreat, such as a lakeside cabin, suffered from less stress than their counterparts who did not leave the city.
4. The results of most studies imply a lot about the relationship of stress to people's wealth. After all, if you're rich, you can afford to relieve your stress.
5. Three research studies also found that able people without jobs who lived in urban areas had less stress than their working counterparts. This fact shows that we must consider laziness when we think about stress.

 B. In a small group, compare your responses to Exercise 2A. Collectively revise any sentences that the group agrees imply a biased treatment of the subject.

56a
info

---

6 Present information clearly

Informative writing is highly sensitive to the ways readers understand and retain information. When you are working with many facts or statistics, for example, your readers may become confused, bored, or frustrated if you try to present all these in sentence form.

S T R A T E G Y

To help your readers learn efficiently from your informative writing without confusion or frustration, try employing the following strategies if they are appropriate for your subject and your audience. For more information on these strategies, see Chapter 13.

*   Use graphs, charts, tables, and figures. You can set off numerical data or words and short phrases elegantly in columns or boxes.
*   Use section markers. Longer informative papers can benefit from sections organized by numbers or subtitles.
*   Use graphic devices such as boldface, italics, or varied fonts (type styles) to help readers attend to specific terms or ideas that may be new. But be careful not to overuse such devices; too many different fonts, for example, can confuse readers more than help them.

- Use white space on the page. Too dense a text can tire your readers when you present a lot of information in long blocks. Break a discussion into shorter paragraphs, or use illustrations and tables.

Exercise 3

 A. Examine a chapter from one of your textbooks in a course such as psychology or biology. Write a brief informal description of strategies used in the textbook to make the information easy to learn and retain. Look for section markers, graphic devices, tables and charts, illustrations, and the use of white space to help "chunk" the text. Make a photocopy of one page to attach to your description.

 B. In a small group, compare textbook analyses. Observe any especially effective strategies for the presentation of information. Discuss how ineffective books or sections could be improved through the use of such strategies.

56b Developing an interview paper: Informative writing in progress

In his anthropology class, Brian Schwegler was assigned to write a paper about an interesting person, focusing particularly on the person's occupation. Examples his teacher offered were a mortician, a sky diver, and a female construction worker. The purpose of the assignment was to practice gathering information from sources other than library materials and to organize that information into an interesting, informative paper.

Brian remembered a performer at the boardwalk amusement area in a coastal resort town near his university campus. He decided that Dave "The Guesser" Glovsky would be a good subject. This person operated a guessing booth located near a striker hammer game. As a "guesser," Dave offers to guess people's ages, weights, occupations, and similar matters. When Dave agreed to give Brian an interview for his paper, Brian sketched this preliminary list of questions that could inform his final paper.

1. How do you guess? What do you do when you guess?
2. Do you do anything else besides guessing?
3. How did you get into this business?
4. What are some of your best guesses?
5. What types of people come to get guessed?

Arriving at the boardwalk armed with his questions and a tape recorder, Brian realized that he might be able to observe Dave at work as well as interview him. After spending about an hour with Dave doing both, Brian went home and began the long process of transcribing the tape-recorded session so he could accurately use quotations and details.

Below are the first few minutes of Brian's interview. Note how his list of preliminary questions helped to shape his interview without entirely controlling it. Also observe how accurately Brian created his transcript, even when other sounds on the tape drowned out a word or two.

**56b
info**

```
                    Dave Glovsky
        Palace Playland: Dave's Guessing Stand
                    July 8, 1999
                  Brian Schwegler
(Sound of game, "The Striker" hammer swing in
background for all of tape)
    First interchange between Brian Schwegler and
Dave Glovsky is inaudible, due to background noise.
BS: So, Dave, can you tell me a little something
about how you guess? Can you tell me how you guess?
DG: Ages? I read the lower lids. I read the lower
lid. It deteriorates as we get older. The more it
gets darker, they get older. Even children of
sixteen can fool me with the deterioration under the
eyes. They can have beautiful skin, but I don't
check the skin, I check the lower lid of their eyes.
BS: How about weight?
DG: Weight, well I just guess on the weight. You
know, I feel the arm, I feel the stomach. Not women
though, I don't touch the women. I just guess....
    [The interview continues until a customer arrives.]
DG: Hey come on in, have fun. What do you want me to
guess?
Female cust: My age.
```

DG: All right, that's a dollar. (Holds up one-dollar
bill) A hundred-dollar bill. Step into the office
here. (Points to a patch of pavement) Are you going
to tell me the truth?

Cust: Yeah.

DG: You wouldn't lie to me. You promise truly, yeah.
Smile, is that your father here. (Points to male
companion of similar age). I'm gonna say, look at
the beautiful girl. Look at the face on her. Let's
see if you are married. (Looks at hand to check for
rings) Nope, not married. Holy Cow! (Writes 22 on
pad) How old are you?

Cust: Eighteen.

DG: You got me, I got twenty-two.

Cust: Huh, yeah right.

DG: Well, the lower lid, the lower lid. What do you
want me to guess on now? (To female companion of
previous customer, who looks noticeably younger)

Cust 2: Age.

Cust: Twenty-two, I thought that you were going to
say twelve.

DG: Can't get them all. Smile. . . .

At the end of the interview, Dave invited Brian to his home the next morning to talk further. Brian also wondered what other workers thought about Dave, so he returned to Palace Playland as well.

As he analyzed the transcript, it occurred to Brian that Dave's success as a guesser may depend on establishing the right social relationship with his customers, getting them to offer information or behave in a way that reveals something about their ages or other characteristics. Instead of making Dave's technique obvious to readers, Brian chose to present Dave's methods without detailed commentary. This approach would allow his paper to be true to the facts but point readers to an analysis of those facts without forcing them to accept any particular conclusion.

Brian decided to organize his essay in sequential order, using a "blended" chronological sequence that weaves details about Dave's life (past) with details of events occurring during the interview (present). Brian also planned to use some spatial sequences throughout the paper in describing Dave's surroundings. But as he wrote, Brian realized that he had three main sources of information—the original interview and observation, his brief interviews with other fair workers, and his visit to Dave's house. Not wanting to explain too much in his paper about the various interviews, he decided to "chunk" the two interviews with Dave into a single temporal sequence. Here is how he diagramed the sequence in his planning notes.

Day 1:   Interview and observation session ⟶ blend in workers'
         comments ⟶ Dave's invitation to come to his house
Day 2:   Dave's house

Following are the first several pages of Brian's rough draft. Notice how Brian is able to maintain an objective, informative stance while still injecting some style and human interest into his account. Note also the artful balance of interview material and observational data, seamlessly blending information about Dave's life with the ongoing events in the present.

First Draft: Dave the Guesser

by Brian Schwegler

1   "Come on in, have some fun with the famous
guesser of Old Orchard," says Dave "The Guesser"
Glovsky. Relying on his voice and personality to
attract customers, he seems out of place in this
mechanized wonderland. Hand-painted signs covered
with cramped writing are his advertisement. I peer
at them and try to decipher the writing that is more
anxious than able.

          The Guesser Has Experience
                    Sex Appeal
               Personality   Try him, you'll
                             enjoy his humor
                             and guessing skill.

56b
info

Palace Playland's World Famous Guess Station:
Come in, fill up with fun--You'll be glad you did.

2   As I stand in front of his stand and read his
signs, a young woman approaches Dave.

3   "Hey, come on in, have fun. What do you want me
to guess?" Dave asks.

4   "My age," says the young woman.

5   "All right, that's a dollar." Holding up the
dollar bill that the woman gives him, Dave examines
it the way a jeweler examines a precious stone. "A
hundred dollar bill." Pointing to a space on the
pavement, Dave says, "Step into the office here."
Dave checks her out from all angles, looking for the
clue that will let him know her age within two
years, his margin of error. "Smile," he says while
peering into her face. Pointing to her boyfriend,
Dave asks, "Is that your father here?" Her face
erupts into a smile, and Dave has gotten some of the
information he needs to make his guess. "Let's see
if you are married," he says, looking for a wedding
ring. Seeing none, he smiles and winks at me. He
pulls a rumpled pad out of his pocket and a pen out
of nowhere and writes his guess on the paper. "How
old are you?"

6   "Eighteen."

7   "You got me, I got twenty-two." Turning to her
girlfriend, he says, "Can't get them all. Smile...."

8   Guessing is Dave's life, his living, his love.
While at his stand, he is an actor on a stage. He
not only wants to take people's money, he wants to
entertain his customers. A former Portland comedian,

56b
info

Dave once put on a show for Edwin Muskie while Muskie was governor. Talking about the people that he guesses, Dave says, "They like the fun that I give them. . . . I make them laugh." There doesn't seem to be much of a difference to Dave between being an actor and being a guesser. "I was a comedian anyways," he says with a shrug that tells me that is all that guessing is about.

**56b
info**

[The next two paragraphs further explain how Dave relates to people.]

11   Dave's guessing is a talent that he has worked on over the years. He has a system worked out for guessing the person's age. He relies on his knowledge of the human face, clinical knowledge tempered by forty-five years of experience. He explains it to me during a lull in our visit. I feel a kind of rush, excited to learn the secrets of the trade.

12   "Well, the way I guess ages, they don't realize that I check the lower lid of their eyes. And it's effective with eighty-five percent of the people. The eyes on the bottom deteriorate as we age. It gets darker and darker and wrinklier, and then at the age of, beginning at the age of thirty-nine, it starts to get a, getting a line up here, (on side of face). And then it gets deeper and deeper and deeper, and when it gets way up here (at top of cheeks), I really got to guess, fifty or sixty. And in the sixties, they start getting these things (loose skin on neck). So, through all of these years, I have accumulated all the knowledge of the human face."

[The next four paragraphs explain Dave's other types of guesses and his impact on customers.]

17   Other workers at Palace Playland recognize the role that Dave plays at the park. Chris McArthur, owner of Palace Groundz, a coffee stand, says, "There's a lot of people that come in here just to see him. And I've noticed people walk by and go, 'Oh my God, he's still alive, he's still here. I remember him when I was a little kid.'" . . .

[The paper continues for five more pages.]

56c   The short informative documented paper

In many courses, you may be asked to write an informative paper that draws on a few outside sources, most often those you have located in modest library research. Such papers do not argue a point but present information on a focused topic.

1 Sample short informative documented paper

As you read the following passages from David Aharonian's paper, note that even though it is informative, citing facts and statistics from four articles, it is not a paper without a thesis. Unlike an argumentative thesis (see 54a-3), however, David's thesis presents a conclusion based on his synthesis of research studies. Note, too, that his paper does not recommend a course of action, which would require taking a position; instead, it stops short of argument, allowing the reader to take the next step based on a considered response to the information David presents.

Desperate Times for Teachers

by David Aharonian

1   There is a major controversy regarding teacher salaries presently in this country. Many people feel that teachers are overpaid because they have summers off from work. They feel that teachers do not truly

work year round and therefore are either getting a fair rate of pay or getting too much. Many teachers, however, disagree with this assessment. They feel that they are underpaid for the work that they do. Most teachers find it very difficult just to make ends meet on a teacher's salary, and often they resort to moonlighting.

2   Moonlighting means that a person holds another job in addition to his or her career. . . .

[The next four paragraphs supply information and statistics on moonlighting teachers from two sources.]

7   But there really are no easy solutions to the problem. One obvious answer would be to increase teacher salaries (Alley 21). This would lead to less moonlighting and allow teachers to concentrate more on their primary occupation. But there are still plenty of people who oppose raising teacher salaries. Many times teachers may go two or three years without any raise in their pay. Then when the teachers do get their raises, it may only be 2 or 4 percent. This certainly lowers the morale of the teachers and can cause the teacher to become frustrated (Henderson 12). As one teacher in Oklahoma put it, "It's hard to look across the hall and see a teacher who's taught 14 years, making only $4,000 more than you are" (Wisniewski and Kleine 1).

[This paper ends with a list of works cited]

2 Elements of a short informative documented paper

An effective short informative documented paper includes the following elements.

- It concisely summarizes or synthesizes the views, research results, or positions of other writers.

- It presents information in the writer's own words but does so fairly, without bias.
- It may provide conclusions based on a reasoned consideration of the work it cites but usually allows the reader to decide what these conclusions mean for a course of action, set of beliefs, and the like.
- It is well organized and easy to read.

3 Commentary on David Aharonian's short informative documented paper

The writer does a good job of pulling together various research studies in an interesting short paper. His way of integrating the references into his own writing works nicely. If his paper had cited statistics more heavily, he could have presented them in a less narrative form, perhaps creating a box or chart. Although it ends with a direct quotation from a teacher, his paper seems to stop abruptly; he could have included a short paragraph summing up the material he cites. (For more information on research papers, see Chapters 44–48.)

56d
info

56d The literature review

The **literature review,** also sometimes called a survey paper or a review of the literature, is usually one section of a longer paper but may be assigned as a paper in itself. In a psychology paper reporting the results of an experiment, for instance, the literature review is the first section after the introduction. The purpose of a literature review is to synthesize the existing research on your topic—to describe the main points of comparison and disagreement in others' studies. As the first section of a longer paper presenting your own research, it provides a backdrop for your study. Your study generally would not repeat what another study has already done but might test the hypothesis or the methods of an earlier study, examine an aspect overlooked by previous researchers, or study a related aspect of the topic in order to add to the accumulated knowledge. A literature review, then, establishes a context for your own research.

Most literature reviews try to present the findings of others in a fair and balanced manner. Two or more studies may reveal major disagreements in a field, but your job in a literature review is to document those disagreements without judging the studies themselves, at least initially. Some kinds of literature reviews do judge the works being summarized; for example, an author of a medical research article may present the findings of previous studies while criticizing their methods. Such a review tends to be more point-driven (see Chapter 54) because the writer is laying the groundwork for a claim that his or her own methods are superior. In most general college courses requiring a literature review, however, you will be asked to summarize the literature instead of critique it. Your reviews will be informative, aiming at summary and synthesis.

> # Did You Know?
>
> College instructors often look for a thesis statement at the beginning of an academic paper as a guide to the line of reasoning and the kinds of evidence and arguments the student will present. Just as important for most instructors, however, are topic sentences and other statements in the body of a paper that guide readers through the steps in the reasoning and serve as reminders of the paper's overall purpose and direction. Students who do not include such reminders as they write may lose track of their own reasoning and produce disorganized papers. Even a well-organized paper can be hard to follow, however, if the writer does not provide readers with guidance throughout.
>
> Linda K. Shamoon and Robert A. Schwegler, "Sociologists Reading Student Texts: Expectations and Perceptions," *Writing Instructor* 8 (Winter 1988): 71–84.

1 Sample literature review

Turn to the research paper in 50e for a sample literature review in the context of a longer paper. As you read this sample, note how the writer connects his sources to each other and to his own study.

2 Elements of a literature review

An effective literature review includes the following elements.

- It accurately and concisely summarizes the results of other researchers.
- It synthesizes these other studies, combining results where they overlap, while giving credit to each researcher.
- It includes major points of disagreement among the other studies.
- It establishes a context for your own study.

56e The lab report

If you take courses in subjects like biology, chemistry, physics, or engineering, you may find yourself writing lab reports. Your teacher will want to read, quickly, what you did in an experiment, and you will need to make your report as concise and as clear as possible. Although the format of a lab report can help you organize the information clearly, you will still need to avoid ambiguous language and unclear references.

The **lab report** represents a kind of informative writing in its sharp focus on the objective description of causes and effects. It requires just the right balance between too little and too much detail. If certain aspects of an experiment or procedure are irrelevant to the cause-effect relationship, you need not include them. However, it is important to describe very clearly just what was done in the experiment and what happened as a result. The color of the counter in the lab is irrelevant information, but the size of the beaker used may be important both to the replication of the experiment and to the nature of the processes involved.

Lab reports follow different formats, depending on the discipline in which they are written and even the requirements of individual teachers. Some teachers value conciseness and require all lab reports to be no longer than two double-spaced pages. Others expect more detail and may stretch the length to five or ten pages. Check with your teacher about the format, style, and other requirements of the report, such as specific section numbers and headings. A typical structure begins with an overview or *abstract* of the experiment, including its focus or goal (why it was done), an *introduction* to the problem or principles involved (what it shows), a description of the *methods* used (how it was done), an explanation of the *results* (what happened), a *discussion* of the outcomes (what the results mean), and a *conclusion* (what the experiment shows). See the sample paper in 50e for a similar presentation of research results in the social sciences.

56e info

1 Sample lab report

Speed of Sound in Water

by Michael Perry

I. <u>Abstract</u>. This experiment was designed to measure the speed of sound in water and determine how changes in the properties of the water affect the speed of sound. First, the speed of sound in water at room temperature was measured using a "time of flight" method. Then the speed of sound was measured at different temperatures to determine the change in the speed with varying temperature. The speed of sound from part 1 of the experiment was 1479.7 m/s. In part 2 the speed of sound was found to vary from 1419.75 m/s at 10.8°C to 1581.03 m/s at 33.10°C.

II. <u>Introduction</u>. A wave traveling through a material causes quick compressions and expansions of the material. The pressure and density oscillate where these compressions and expansions take place. The speed of the wave is determined by how much the density changes with a given pressure change. Water is a liquid and is therefore less compressible than a gas, for example, air. So it takes a greater pressure in water to change density a given amount. We can therefore expect the speed of sound in water to be greater than that in air....

[The paper continues with the following sections: III Experimental, IV Results, V Discussion, and VI Conclusion.]

2 Elements of a lab report

An effective lab report includes the following elements.

- It strictly follows the lab report format required by your teacher.
- It does not digress into unnecessary commentary on the experiment.
- It uses specific terminology and unambiguous language.
- It presents data and results accurately, without distortion.

3 Commentary on Michael Perry's lab report

Some of the terms are specialized for the field, but this report is written to an audience that understands the jargon. Perry's report is for the most part clear and concise; however, he could have explained why the time of flight method was not accurate.

56f The abstract

Teachers may often ask you to submit an abstract along with your lab report, study, or other research paper. An abstract is a concise summary of your paper. It is entirely objective, restating the content of the paper without extraneous commentary. An abstract for a scientific study must include, at a minimum, a summary of the hypothesis, the method, the results, and the discussion sections of your paper. An abstract of the review of the literature might be needed as well. The reader of your abstract, with no familiarity with your paper, should be able to understand not only the gist of the paper but your method, stance (your theory or opinion), and conclusions.

1 Sample abstract

See the abstract in 56e, introducing a lab report, or in 50e, preceding a research study.

56g
info

2 Elements of an abstract

An effective abstract includes the following elements.

- It summarizes all the important sections of your paper.
- It defines any key terms used in unique or unusual ways.
- It is concise; all unnecessary words and phrases are eliminated.

56g The annotated bibliography

An **annotated bibliography** is just like a regular bibliography (see Chapters 49–53) except that each entry includes an annotation describing the aim, purpose, or content of the work cited. Its purpose is to provide a useful resource for readers who want to find out what has been written about a topic or to consult specific works themselves. Annotated bibliographies are also commonly assigned in college courses either to help students to survey and report on a body of scholarship or to help them prepare for a longer research paper.

Usually you begin with a brief introduction to the topic, perhaps highlighting the kinds of works covered in your bibliography. You then cite each work and follow it with an annotation, usually in a short paragraph or two. Annotations sometimes employ an abbreviated sentence structure like this: Summarizes research on the development of the Cherokee syllabary.

1 Sample annotations

The annotation below has been taken from Ian Preston's annotated bibliography, which consisted of an introduction to the topic followed by twelve entries. He prepared his bibliography for a writing class focusing on language and bilingualism in the United States.

```
          Annotated Bibliography on Bilingualism
                      by Ian Preston
Glazer, Nathan. "Where Is Multiculturalism Leading
     Us?" Phi Delta Kappan 75 (1993): 319-24. This
article describes the Center for the Study of Books
in Spanish for Children and Adolescents, an
organization that promotes the positive aspects of
bilingualism. Unlike other organizations that
portray their ethnic groups as victims, the Center,
Glazer argues, ought to be followed as a model of a
bilingual program.
```

2 Elements of an annotated bibliography

Effective annotated bibliographies usually include the following elements.

- An introduction which orients readers to the topic being covered in several paragraphs or pages, depending upon the complexity of the topic or the range of the citations.
- A list of references to the literature cited, each followed by a clear précis or summary of the work that briefly but accurately represents the work.
- Accurate references which readers often use to locate the works listed. (See Chapters 49–53 for help with accurate bibliographical entries.)
- An emphasis on summary in order to provide readers with an accurate depiction of what the work says or does, without unnecessary detail.
- Alphabetical organization, generally by the authors' last names. Long or complex annotated bibliographies are often organized into sections, sometimes chronologically ("Nineteenth-Century Studies," "Twentieth-Century Studies"), sometimes by general topic or focus ("Studies Using Quantitative Research Methods," "Studies Using Qualitative Research Methods"), but still alphabetically within each section.

3 Commentary on Ian Preston's entries

Preston successfully captures the gist of the work cited. Notice how he includes both the topic of the article and its author's point of view.

56h The informative essay exam

Essay exams can be divided into those in which you illustrate and defend a claim or point (see 54g) and those in which you provide clear and objective information. The latter, the informative essay exam, can be relatively short—a paragraph or two describing a phenomenon, for example—or longer, involving more elaborate descriptions and data.

Informative essay exams must be carefully organized, clearly written, and detailed. After receiving your exam question, spend a few minutes developing a simple outline; even a three- to five-paragraph structure can help you to chunk your information and move from point to point logically so that a teacher can quickly see whether the essay reflects adequate knowledge of the subject.

1 Sample informative essay exam

The short informative essay exam that follows was written in a general biology course in response to this assignment: "Define the concept of natural selection, being sure to explain its main features and how it affects behavior." Students were given thirty minutes to craft their answers.

```
          Natural Selection Essay Exam
                by Nicholas Branahan
     Natural selection is a process in which the
characteristics of an organism that best promote its
ability to reproduce are selected and the
characteristics which hinder it are weeded out. As
random gene mutations form new characteristics,
natural selection will select those that enhance the
organism's ability to reproduce. Ability to
reproduce depends on adaptability to the weather,
ability to find food, avoidance of predators, and
other aspects of survival.
```

[The answer continues in two more paragraphs.]

2 Elements of effective informative essay exams

An effective informative essay exam includes the following.

- It answers the question directly, without unnecessary padding.

- It is organized clearly and logically, with each paragraph focusing on a different aspect of the topic or question.
- It avoids obscure language or uninterpretable statements as a strategy for covering up an inability to answer the question.
- It includes, as possible, brief examples, cases, and references.

3 Commentary on Nicholas Branahan's informative essay exam

56h
info

Branahan's essay shows that he understands the concept of natural selection. The first paragraph provides a general definition of the concept of natural selection. The second paragraph answers the question about the ways in which natural selection may affect behavior. The third paragraph extends the concept by considering what happens to the organism when the environment changes. The writing is clear, concise, and error-free, but adding one or two brief examples would make the answer less abstract.

CHAPTER

57

Developing Business Writing

Enhanced by new communications technologies, communication between individuals is the critical factor in most business negotiations. Your personal success and the success of your work depend largely on how you represent yourself and communicate orally and in writing. Effective writers rapidly gain the respect and admiration of their colleagues, and writing ability often plays a role in professional advancement.

A complete discussion of business writing would take a book in itself. This chapter has a more modest goal: to acquaint you with some standard business writing styles and practices. Think of it as a preliminary guide to successful business writing. As you become more involved in professional activities during college you should add a complete business writing guide to your personal library. Such books offer sound advice on accepted business writing styles and present models of a number of business documents, such as letters, memos, proposals, reports, and résumés.

57a Using general strategies for successful business writing

Business writing is reader-centered: you're writing to persuade, inform, or meet the needs of your audience (see Chapter 5). Focus your effort on making your writing and the design of your document easily accessible to your readers. Keep in mind the general advice for writing found throughout Part I of this book, and pay special attention to the following composing strategies.

1 Plan to meet your readers' needs

Your main focus while planning business writing will be the relationship between your information and your audience. Sometimes your audience will be made up of different readers in different positions (for example, someone in the marketing department and someone else who handles shipments from the warehouse). Be sensitive to the needs and perspectives of your various intended readers.

Because your readers are likely to be busy and impatient—whether they are other people at work or members of the general public to whom you are writing in a professional capacity—you need to be especially careful in organizing your information.

57a
bus

Writer's Tip

Business documents should have a "friendly" design and layout, inviting the reader to read and to continue to read. Is there enough white space in your document to make it look uncluttered? Are your margins sufficient? What does the spacing of your document look like—are sections squeezed together, or have you left enough space to show blocks of information? Remember that a readable document is attractive and inviting, not tight and cluttered.

STRATEGY 1

Using the audience continuum in 5a, spend a few minutes writing about your intended readers. What do they know about the topic? How will they use the document? What do you know about their technical background, their level of education, their interest in the topic, and their need for what you have to offer?

STRATEGY 2

Write a precise outline of your information before you draft your document. In business writing, your reader should know what your document contains from the start, and its contents should have a logical and preconceived design. Outlines are especially effective (see Chapter 3).

2 Draft as clearly as possible

As you draft, remember to emphasize clarity. Effective business writing is easy to read—unambiguous, uncluttered, and direct.

STRATEGY

Instead of drafting with an eye to style, try to write the essential information as baldly and directly as you can. As you write, concentrate on exactly what you want to say. You can revise for a smoother and more appealing style after you've presented the main information directly.

---

3 Be sure to revise and edit

In some business settings you may be under pressure to write a document quickly—even more quickly, for example, than a paper due in two days for your composition class. Under these circumstances, it's easy to skip the revising process. Be especially careful not to fall into this trap. Reread *all* your documents. Plan your work so you have at least some time for revision and editing. Even a single badly chosen word, one garbled sentence, or a lone case of misinformation can be embarrassing.

In addition, set specific goals for your revising. Plan, for example, to eliminate wordy passages, extraneous information, and irrelevant facts. Or aim to avoid clichés, exaggeration, passive voice, and overly technical language. Try to choose vocabulary appropriate for your audience's level of expertise, and revise accordingly.

57b
bus

> ### Writer's Tip
> Business writing often makes use of graphics to present information clearly and concisely. When you use graphics, label them carefully, and mention them in the text of your document before they actually appear in the text. (See Chapter 13.)

57b Writing business letters

Good business letters follow some standard practices and established formats. Most business letters are presented in either block format or modified block format. In **modified block format,** which is often used for longer letters, the return address and the closing and signature are centered on the page, but the paragraphs are not indented from the left margin. (For an example, see 57g). In **block format,** often used for short letters, all paragraphs (including the greeting and signature) are flush at the left margin. In both styles, notations following the signature are flush left including initials for the writer and typist (RL: gw), *Enc.* or *Enclosure,* or *cc: Nancy Harris* (the name of a person sent a copy). Follow these additional guidelines for business correspondence.

- **Stationery.** The best is 25 percent or 50 percent white cotton bond paper. Avoid colors and fancy paper styles.
- **Print quality.** Check that your typewriter or word processor is in good repair. Use a laser printer or a letter-quality impact printer. Your credibility will be damaged and your readers may be frustrated by fuzzy or light print. Avoid nonstandard or stylized print styles—they are often hard to read.
- **Salutations.** Use the first name of your recipient only if you are already on a first-name basis. Use the full name if you don't know the person's gender. Avoid male-specific salutations such as "Dear Sir" or "Gentlemen"; they are not appropriate. If you do not know exactly to whom you are writing, use salutations such as these.

    Dear Accounts Department:

    Dear Credit Manager:
- **Longer letters.** Use plain paper of the same weight as the first page. Use letterhead stationery only for the first page.
- **Envelope.** Envelope paper should be the same color and weight as the letter, and the type style should match that of the letter. (See the sample envelope below for placement of information.)

```
Charisma Publishing, Inc.
757 First Street
Huntington, VA 24066



                        Mr. Elliott P. Buchanan
                        Driving Dynamics, Inc.
                        34 Westover Avenue
                        Lexington, MA 19046
```

57c Writing agendas

An **agenda** is a plan of action for a business meeting. Agendas are usually circulated in advance to those who will attend the meeting; however, occasionally an agenda may be presented at the start of a meeting to show the attendees how the meeting will be structured. Consider the following points when you create an agenda.

- List the date, location, time, and topic of the meeting at the top of the agenda.

- Clearly define the goals of the meeting.
- List in a logical order the issues to be discussed at the meeting; clearly show how the meeting will proceed.
- List any items to be discussed or introduced by specific individuals.

```
                      AGENDA

              Executive Committee
               February 5, 1999
               Conference Room B


1. Approve minutes of Jan. 8, 1999, meeting

2. President's report

3. Old business
   a. Fleet report (Ted Lakeland)
   b. Manufacturing division update (Rona Schwartz)
   c. Annual retreat (Tom Good)

4. Sales division report on expansion of sales
   territory

5. New committee and task force assignments
   a. Task force on sexual harassment
   b. Personnel committee

6. Recycling committee report (Kristen Danforth)

7. New business

8. Summary
```

57d Writing meeting minutes

Meeting minutes are a major form of organizational communication and often serve as a corporate "memory." You may also need to keep minutes for various school organizations and committees that are run in a businesslike manner. Minutes should be an impartial record of what occurred at a meeting, most of which will be dialogue and reports from attendees. Minutes may also describe visuals used at the meeting or documents circulated to participants.

For routine meetings, minutes can be brief, noting only the most important topics presented or discussed. In other cases, when significant topics are discussed in detail or when important individuals who did not attend the meeting will read the minutes and perhaps even make decisions based on their contents, more detailed minutes are required. Sometimes it is desirable to tape-record a meeting in order to write more detailed minutes. If you decide to tape a meeting, notify participants before the meeting starts. Meeting minutes should conform to the following guidelines.

- Consider who will be reading the minutes and for what purpose before determining how detailed the minutes should be.
- Carefully note the date, time, and location of the meeting.
- List the individuals who have participated in the meeting and, if it is not common knowledge, their positions in the organization or roles at the meeting. Note also those individuals whose attendance was expected but who did not attend. Always note who is chairing the meeting and who is taking minutes. The person taking the minutes should sign or initial the minutes next to his or her name. This person may be identified by *minutes* or by the term *secretary* or *recorder*.
- Always identify who said what, but *summarize* this information; include the most important points as accurately as you can. Try not to misquote or misinterpret anyone's remarks.
- Be impartial. Record as objectively as possible what transpired at the meeting. Editorializing in minutes is unprofessional.

Meeting identified by title

Driving Dynamics, Inc., Executive Committee Meeting

Minutes for January 8, 1999 *Date, location, and*
Boardroom, 9:00–10:05   *time*

Present: E. Buchanan (Chair), B. Kramer, M. Sun,
L. Whitlock, L. Hammond, E. Parker (minutes),
T. Perez, P. Straley, R. Allison, Mary Travis (state
police officer)   *Person taking minutes*

Absent: P. Pelligrino, L. Rosenberg

The next meeting of the executive committee will be
on Monday, February 5, at 4 p.m. in the boardroom.

Publicity--Publicity chairperson Tony Perez reported
that the new radio spots are nearly ready for
airing. Ads will be heard on WSPT-FM and WCAR-AM
four times each day starting January 23.

Hiring--Executive Committee chair Elliott Buchanan
announced that, beginning May 1, he will take a one-
Organ- year leave of absence from Driving Dynamics in order
ized by to complete a book on driving safety for which he
topic has contracted with a major publisher.

Recycling--Recycling Committee chair Lynn Rosenberg
sent in a written report. Company efforts to improve
recycling have been successful. New receptacles for
aluminum cans and glass bottles have been installed

in all lounge areas and in the main front and rear
entrance vestibules. Rosenberg suggested that more
efforts are needed for plain-paper recycling. The
Recycling Committee will investigate this issue and
give a report at the next meeting.

Because of lack of further business, the meeting
adjourned at 10:05.

57e Writing memos

Although some organizations provide employees with printed forms,
you should know how to write your own **memos.** These internal documents rarely circulate outside an organization. The organization's name
and logo, or letterhead, may appear at the top of the memo, but no address
is needed.

The words *to, from, subject,* and *date* appear on all memos, often in
this order. (The order is sometimes based on the filing system used in the
organization or business.) Spacing, notations for enclosures, additional
pages, and copies all follow the same pattern as in letters.

Reliable Book Wholesalers

To: Executive Committee members

From: Marilyn Caperton

Subject: Selection of new executive vice president

Date: January 29, 1999

   A meeting of the executive committee will be held
on February 4 to discuss the resignation of our
current vice president, Tracy Langer, and the
selection of a new vice president.

   Ms. Langer has taken a position with Rank,
Incorporated, of San Francisco and will leave her
position with us on March 15.

   We have several applications on file, and we need to
discuss the procedures we will follow to advertise the
position and hire a new vice president.

   Please come to the meeting with ideas or suggestions
for possible candidates.

Executive Committee Meeting
Presidential Boardroom
Friday, February 2, 3:30 p.m.

57f Writing résumés

Résumés and letters of application are the most important sales documents you will write; the "product" is, after all, yourself and everything you have accomplished. There are countless "right" ways to prepare these documents. This section offers some guidelines for the content, design, and construction of a résumé and letter of application. Take the time to write, revise, and edit your résumé so it will be attractive to a potential employer. Also be sure to visit your college placement service for help on résumé construction.

The purpose of a résumé and application letter is to get an interview, not a job. Few employers hire using only the information contained in a résumé and letter. When constructing your résumé and letter, concentrate on trying to create a professional identity for yourself. Don't brag, but highlight your skills or achievements clearly and objectively.

Potential employers favor job candidates who are motivated, mature, and responsible. You can't simply state these things; your résumé and letter must exemplify these traits. For instance, employers like applicants who know how to start and finish a project without help and who are self-motivated, capable, and willing to face challenges confidently. Describe your experiences not only in terms of what you have actually done but in terms of what you learned from the experiences and how they will help you in the future.

1 Begin with a résumé preparation checklist

Before you start to prepare your résumé, you need to reflect about both your career goals and your own qualifications and background.

STRATEGY

Write informally in response to the following questions. Jot down your ideas and as many examples from your background as you can remember. Later you can select the best ideas and examples for your purposes.

1. What kind of work do you want to do? What kind of job do you want?
2. What are your career goals?
3. What jobs have you held?
4. What volunteer positions have you held?
5. What are your skills, abilities, or interests, even if you have not been formally educated in these things?
6. What are the main features of your educational background? Consider the following points.
   a. College major, minor, and concentrations
   b. Special projects or research

c. Honors and awards

d. Memberships and offices in organizations

e. Volunteer positions

f. Special skills

g. Grade point average (overall and in major)

7. What other awards or special honors, if any, have you received (from work, volunteer efforts, or community organizations)?

8. Who might supply a good reference for you? Try to identify at least one former or current professor, one former job supervisor or employer, and one personal reference.

9. What makes you different from other applicants? Why should a prospective employer hire you rather than someone else?

57f
bus

2 Use categories to construct your résumé

After you've collected the information for your résumé, your task is one of construction—placing the information into appropriate categories, phrasing it concisely, and arranging it in a visually appealing way. Use the following advice as you work.

Career Objective. When you write your career objective, avoid empty phrases like *position of responsibility with a fast-growing firm.* Consider tailoring your objective to each position for which you apply.

Job Experience. When you get ready to describe your job experience, list all the duties you had, and then choose the ones you think might be most similar to those of the job you want. If you have had many jobs, don't list them all in your résumé. List only the ones you held the longest, the ones that are most similar to the job for which you are applying, or the ones that demonstrate your most employable characteristics. If you think that you have little job experience that relates to the job you seek, highlight other desirable job skills, such as handling responsibility, supervising others, working alone, or writing and public speaking. Don't simply state that you have these skills; provide examples from your experience.

Volunteer Experience. If you've held volunteer positions that may be attractive to a potential employer, list them; they're often considered important experience. Note that the position was voluntary, but handle the rest of the information just as you would for any other job. Don't use an apologetic tone here; the fact that you were not paid for the job doesn't mean it was not serious work that gave you valuable experience.

Sequence of Experience. Typically, jobs are listed in reverse chronological order (with your most recent job first). If your most important job experience is not your most recent, however, list that one first, and then list the others in chronological order.

Don't use "Résumé" here

Carol E. Westermeyer

College Address   *Full name,*   Home Address

Apt. 23 College Park   *address,*   7562 Galsworth Road
Greenville, Virginia 20205   *phone and*   Squires, Texas 30303
(804)555-3345   *email*   (512)555-7912
cwest@school.edu   *address*

Brief job objective

57f bus

OBJECTIVE   Entry-level position as a mechanical engineer

EDUCATION   B.S. Mechanical Engineering, May 1999   *Concise*
Virginia Polytechnic Institute and State *statement of*
University, Blacksburg, Virginia 24060   *education*
G.P.A.: 3.18/4.0 Minor: Economics

Reverse chronological order   *Dates and addresses included*

EXPERIENCE   <u>Technician/Assembler</u>, May 1995–September 1995
Communications Technology, Inc., Fairview, Virginia

Experience organized to show skills

- Developed cost analysis and designed prototype
  wireless communication products for Masters
  Mountain Laboratories.

Job titles underlined

- Built and tested various AF and RF products:
  transmitters, receivers, headsets, amplifiers,
  and antenna networks.

Past tense for job duties

- Served as company representative to demonstrate
  new generation of wireless radios at Atlanta
  National Radio Conference.

<u>Interoffice Administrator</u> (part time), 1994–present
Bergland Technology Associates, Lakeview, Virginia
- Updated and reorganized shop inventory control
  using office IBM software and hardware.

PROJECT   Member, Design Team for Formula Car, 1996–97
Virginia Tech Department of Mechanical
Engineering
- Drive train group duties included testing,
  tuning, and modeling constant velocity
  transmission (CVT) and coordinating data
  acquisition for CVT.

SKILLS   Computer: Finite Element (FEPC), Personal
Simulation Language (PSL)

Optional

Personal: Public speaking, technical writing

ACTIVITIES   President, Student Society of Engineers; Student
Engineering Council; Society of Automotive
Engineers; Gymnastics Club; <u>The Voice</u> (student
newspaper)

References available upon request

Centered

References. Unless the employer asks for specific references, use the general statement *References available upon request.* Few employers will want to look at your references unless they wish to interview you. You should have your references available, and you can print a separate page listing the names and addresses of three or four references to send out if you are so asked. (*Always* ask permission to use someone as a reference.) Most colleges have student placement services that will send out dossiers that include confidential references.

Writer's Tip: Using a Computer

Programs are now available for creating résumés on computers. Most such programs include several different formats for standard résumés as well as options for custommade résumés. The program prompts you for information in various categories. Once you've typed in this information, it is formatted according to the type of résumé you've selected. Résumé programs allow you to spend your time focusing on your background and accomplishments rather than spacing and layout. Try out several résumé formats to see which one will be the most appealing for the kind of job you want.

57g Writing letters of application

Your résumé and your application letter should be related documents; the topics named in both should be related and should work as a unit to make you appear organized and professional. Letters of application offer you a chance to discuss or highlight skills or experiences mentioned in your résumé or to add information not in your résumé. Your application letter should be concise—just a few well-written paragraphs. Remember that your readers may be considering many applicants and thus need to focus quickly on your main accomplishments and abilities. Wading through lots of irrelevant prose to locate this information will only frustrate them and compromise your application.

(See an illustration of a letter of application on the following page.)

1½" top margin

Apt. 23 College Park
Greenville, Virginia 20205
February 10, 1999

Uses business letter format

Writer's complete address

Dr. Grace Penland, Director
PKL Design, Inc.
232 Sturbridge Avenue
Fairfax, Virginia 20949

Recipient's complete address

1" side margins

Dear Dr. Penland:

Dear and name

**57g
bus**

I am interested in applying for a position as an entry-level
mechanical engineer at PKL Design, Inc. I found the position
advertised at the placement office at Virginia Tech. I will
graduate in May 1999 with a degree in mechanical engineering
and hope to start my career at that time.

Identifies job

Highlights job experience

Single-space text

During the past four years I have had a good deal of academic
experience in communications technology. As an active member
of the Formula Car drive train group, I learned much about the
practical challenges mechanical engineers face each day, and
about the complexities of collaborating and strategizing with
fellow team members. In my position with Communications
Technology, I was able to test and sharpen the skills I was
learning at school and use them on a regular basis. In
addition to the responsibilities noted in my résumé, I
designed an innovative software program that compiles data
used by other firms and interprets the results for the sales
division at Communications Technology.

Notes special skills

Double-space ¶s

My experience working with others has given me confidence
in my interpersonal skills and decision-making abilities,
particularly in the area of effective communication and
intellectual compromise. Making a contribution to an effort
goes much further than simply possessing skills; one must
have the ability to work toward a consensus everyone can
live with.

Tells how to reach applicant

I am available for an interview given a week's notice. I can
be reached by phone at (512)555-7912 between 3 p.m. and 5 p.m.
daily. Thank you for your time and consideration.

Sincerely,

Carol E. Westermeyer

Carol E. Westermeyer

Enclosure

Enclosure with letter noted

Three kinds of entries are found in this glossary: grammatical terms (such as *irregular verb*), rhetorical terms (such as *freewriting*), and words that writers frequently find confusing or difficult (such as *farther* and *further*). The latter entries, which deal with matters of usage, are indicated by an arrow (→).

→**a, an** When the word that follows the article *a* or *an* begins with a vowel, use *an*: *an apple, an outrageous film*. Use *a* before consonants: *a banana, a shocking film*. (*See 15-a*)

abridged dictionary Any type of abbreviated dictionary that does not aim to be exhaustive in its treatment of English vocabulary. (*See 29a*)

absolute phrase A phrase consisting of a noun, a pronoun, or a word group acting as a noun followed by a present or past participle and any modifiers; it is used to modify a noun or an entire clause. (*See 15c-2, 23d*)

Their lungs burning from the acrid smoke, the firefighters pressed ahead into the burning building.

abstract A concise summary of a paper, sometimes used as an overview or preface at the beginning of the paper itself. (*See 56f*)

academic community The interacting population of individuals involved in scholarly pursuits, from teachers to researchers to students, both within one institution and the broader arena available through publication and the Internet. (*See 1a*)

→**accept, except** Use *accept* to mean "to take or receive." Use *except* to mean "excluding."

She **accepted** the invitation.
Everyone finished the race **except** Larry.

acronym An abbreviation whose letters begin some or all of the words in the full version: *NASA* (National Aeronautics and Space Administration), *AIDS* (acquired immune deficiency syndrome). (*See 42 a-2*)

action statement In a writing assignment, the directions that specify the processes the writer should go through in completing the assignment.

action verb A verb that indicates an action or activity: *swim, analyze, dig, turn, negotiate*. (*See 15 a-3; compare* **linking verb**)

active voice The form of a verb in a sentence in which the doer (or agent) takes the position of the main subject, before the main verb. (*See 9c, 15a-3, 17d, 24c; compare* **passive voice**)

ad hominem A **fallacy** in which an argument is based on personal attack rather than rational support and evidence. (*See 54c-5*)

ad populum A **fallacy** in which an argument appeals to an audience's biases instead of using rational support. (*See 54c-5*)

adaptation The principle of adjusting writing style, organization, and language to the expectations of readers in particular settings.

adjective A word that modifies a noun, pronoun, or word group acting as a noun by answering such questions as "How many?" "What kind?" or "Which one?" (*See 15a-5, 19a, 19b*)

adjective clause (*See **relative clause***)

adjective phrase A phrase that modifies a noun. (*See 15d*)

adverb A word that modifies a verb, an adjective, an adverb, or an entire sentence by answering such questions as "When?" "Where?" "Why?" "How often?" "Which direction?" "What conditions?" and "What degree?" (*See 15a-6, 19a, 19b*)

adverb clause A clause that acts as an adverb. (*See 15d*)

→**adverse, averse** Someone opposed to something is *averse* to it; if conditions stand in opposition to achieving a goal, they are *adverse*.

Bill wasn't **averse** to going on the ski trip unless the warm temperature would be **adverse** to good skiing conditions.

→**advice, advise** *Advice* is a noun meaning "counsel" or "recommendations." *Advise* is a verb meaning "to give counsel or recommendations."

Professor Raul wanted to **advise** his students, but they believed they needed no **advice.**

→**affect, effect** *Affect* is a verb meaning "to influence." *Effect* is a noun meaning "a result." More rarely, *effect* is a verb meaning "to cause something to happen."

It is thought that CFCs **affect** the deterioration of the ozone layer. The **effect** of that deterioration on global warming is uncertain. Lawmakers need to **effect** changes in public attitudes toward our environment.

agenda A plan of action for a business meeting. (*See 57c*)

→**aggravate, irritate** *Aggravate* means "to worsen"; *irritate* means "to bother or pester."

He was **irritated** that the hotel had no humidifiers because the dry air **aggravated** his skin condition.

agreement The correct matching, in **person, number,** and **gender,** of subjects and verbs or pronouns and their antecedents. (*See Chapter 18*)

SUBJECT-VERB AGREEMENT	*The dog and the boy* **are running** in the field. *The dog* **is running** in the field.
PRONOUN- ANTECEDENT AGREEMENT	*A memo* should address the needs of **its** audience. *Memos* should address the needs of **their** audience.

→**ain't** Although widely used colloquially, *ain't* is inappropriate in formal writing. Use *am not, is not,* or *are not*; the contracted forms *aren't* and *isn't* are more acceptable than *ain't* but may still be too informal in some contexts.

all-purpose modifier A modifier such as *very, totally, major,* or *central* that adds little or no meaning to a sentence and often can be cut. (*See 30a-1*)

all-purpose word A filler word that carries little or no meaning and often can be cut: *factor, aspect, field, thing, kind.* (*See 30a-1*)

gloss

→**all ready, already** *All ready* means "prepared for"; *already* means "by that time."

Sam was **all ready** for the kickoff, but when he had climbed to his bleacher, the game had **already** started.

→**all right** This expression is always spelled as two words, not as *alright.*

→**all together, altogether** Use *all together* to mean "everyone"; use *altogether* to mean "completely."

We were **all together** on our decision to climb the cliff, but it was **altogether** too hard for us to leave Jennie behind.

→**allude, elude** Use *allude* to mean "hint at" or "refer to indirectly"; use *elude* to mean "escape."

Francis **alluded** to the time the refrigerator broke when he was on vacation; the rotten smell had **eluded** the house sitter, who never thought to open the refrigerator.

→**allusion, illusion** An *allusion* is a reference to something; an *illusion* is a vision or false belief.

Peter found an interesting **allusion** to UFOs in a government document. It turned out that the UFOs were just an **illusion.**

→**a lot** This expression is always spelled as two words, not as *alot.* Even when spelled correctly, *a lot* may be too informal for some academic writing. Use *many, much,* or some other modifier instead.

→**a.m., p.m.** These abbreviations may be capital or lowercase letters. (*See* 42a-3)

ambiguous reference A sentence in which a reader cannot identify a pronoun with its **antecedent.** (*See* 22a-1)

→**among, between** Use *between* to describe something involving two people, things, or ideas; use *among* to refer to three or more people, things, or ideas.

A fight broke out **between** the umpire and the catcher; then there was a discussion **among** the catcher, the umpire, and the team managers.

→**amount, number** Use *amount* to refer to a quantity of something that can't be divided into separate units. Use *number* when you want to refer to countable objects.

A large **number** of spices may be used in Thai dishes. This recipe calls for a small **amount** of coconut milk.

→**an, a** (*See* **a, an**)

analogy A comparison between two things, often on the basis of shared characteristics. (*See* 54c-5; see also **false analogy**)

analysis Writing that analyzes or "takes apart" a topic, often looking at how the parts relate to one another. (*See* 56 a-4)

analytical reading Reading that identifies ideas and information presented in a text. (*See* 46b)

analytical synthesis Bringing together summaries of several sources and pointing out their relationships in order to provide background information (*See* 46c-d)

analyze To divide or break something up into its constituent parts to examine their relationships. (*See* 4a-2)

gloss

→**and etc.** (*See* **etc.**)

→**and/or** Although widely used, *and/or* is usually imprecise and may distract your reader. Choose one of the words, or revise your sentence.

| IMPRECISE | The police **and/or** the fire department will usually arrive first when someone calls 911. |
| EDITED | The police **or** the fire department will usually arrive first when someone calls 911. |

anecdote A brief story or account of a personal experience, often used in an introductory paragraph to spark a reader's interest. (*See 8f-1*)

annotated bibliography A **bibliography** that includes annotations (short descriptions of each entry, sometimes with accompanying evaluative comments). (*See 56g*)

annotations Notes written about (or sometimes directly on) a draft or a published text. Annotations can include **interpretations,** questions, **counterarguments,** restatements, or **evaluations.** (*See 2a, 2b*)

→**ante-, anti-** Use *ante-* as a prefix to mean "before" or "predating"; use *anti-* to mean "against" or "opposed."

Some people experience strong **anti-racist** feelings when touring the slave quarters of **antebellum** Southern plantations that survived the Civil War.

antecedent The noun or pronoun to which another word (usually a **pronoun**) refers. (*See 15a-2, 18c, Chapter 22*)

antecedent   pronoun
Jean presented **her** proposal to the committee.

antithesis The use of parallelism to emphasize contrast within sentences. (*See 9d-4, 26b-2*)

antonym A word opposite in meaning to another word: *hot* and *cold.* (*See 29a; see also* **thesaurus**)

→**anyone, any one** *Anyone* as one word is an indefinite pronoun. Occasionally you may want to use *any* to modify *one*, in the sense of "any individual thing or person." (The same distinction applies to **everyone, every one;** *somebody, some body;* and *someone, some one.*)

Anyone can learn to parachute without fear. But the instructors are told not to spend too much time with **any one** person.

→**anyplace** Avoid using this term in formal writing; instead, use *anywhere* or revise your sentence.

→**anyways, anywheres** Avoid these incorrect versions of *anyway* and *anywhere.*

APA documentation style The style of documentation suggested by the American Psychological Association and described in its guide. (*See Chapter 50*)

application letter A brief letter of application for a job, usually accompanied by a **résumé.** (*See 57g*)

appositive A noun or pronoun that renames or stands for a preceding noun (*See 32c-3*)

appositive phrase A phrase consisting of an appositive (usually a noun) along with its modifiers, used to rename a noun in order to add information to a sentence. (*See 15c-3*)

Ken Choi and Stephanie Almagno, **my classmates,** won an award for their innovative packaging design.

gloss

→**apt, likely, liable** Use *apt* to mean "a tendency to." Use *likely* to mean "probable." Use *liable* only to imply risk, or, in a legal context, and obligation or responsibility.

Claude was **apt** to ski the most treacherous slopes when he was young, but he will **likely** keep to the moderate slopes now because he is **liable** to hurt himself again if he skis the expert slopes. The ski resort was **liable** for Claude's injuries because it did not mark the location of the cliff.

archaic word A word that is no longer in general use or is in the process of dropping from the language, such as *save* in the sense of "except." (*See 28b-4*)

argue To prove a point or persuade a reader to accept or entertain a particular position. (*See 4a-2; see also* **argument; argumentative writing**)

argument Not a disagreement, but the reasons, evidence, and explanations used in an attempt to resolve a disagreement by encouraging readers (listeners) to agree with the writer (speaker). (*See Chapter 54*)

argumentative writing Writing that presents and defends a position or point of view. (*See Chapter 54*)

article One of three words that precede a noun: *a, an,* or *the.* An *indefinite article* (*a* or *an*) precedes a general noun (one that does not refer to a specific thing). The *definite article the* precedes a specific noun. (*See 15a*)

artifacts Material objects characteristic of a group or culture. (*See 48a*)

→**as, like** Used as a preposition, *as* indicates a precise comparison. *Like* indicates a resemblance or similarity.

Remembered **as** a man of habit, Kant would take his walk at exactly the same time each day. He was **like** many other philosophers: brooding, thoughtful, and at times intense.

→**as to** *As to* is considered informal in many academic contexts and should be avoided.

INFORMAL	The media had many speculations **as to** the skater's involvement in the attack against her rival.
EDITED	The media had many speculations **about** the skater's involvement in the attack against her rival.

→**assure, ensure, insure** Use *assure* to imply a promise; use *ensure* to imply a certain outcome. Use *insure* only when you imply something legal or financial.

The surgeon **assured** the world-renowned pianist that his fingers would heal in time for the performance. To **ensure** that, the pianist could not practice for three weeks. In case of an even worse accident, the pianist had **insured** his hands with Lloyd's of London.

→**at** In any writing, avoid using *at* in direct and indirect questions.

COLLOQUIAL	Jones wondered where his attorney was **at.**
EDITED	Jones wondered where his attorney **was.**

atlas A book containing maps and related information.

audience The implied or intended readers for a particular piece of writing. (*See Chapters 5, 44*)

gloss

audiovisual collection A library collection of videotapes, films, audio recordings, and similar resources. (*See 45*)

auxiliary verb (*See* **helping verb**)

→**awful, awfully** Use *awful* as an adjective modifying a noun; use *awfully* as an adverb in verbal structures.

> Sanders played **awfully** at the U.S. Open Golf Tournament. On the sixth hole, an **awful** shot landed his ball in the pond.

→**awhile, a while** *Awhile* (as one word) functions as an adverb; it is not preceded by a preposition. *A while* functions as a noun (*while*) preceded by (*a*) an article and is often used in prepositional phrases.

> The shelter suggested that the homeless family stay **awhile.** It turned out that the children had not eaten for **a while.**

background information Information that helps readers understand the scope and substance of an issue, subject, or problem by providing knowledge of its history, context, or consequences. (*See 12b-2*)

→**bad, badly** Use *bad* as an adjective that modifies nouns or with a linking verb expressing feelings. Use *badly* as an adverb.

> The summit was scheduled at a **bad** time of year for some delegates. The British prime minister felt **bad** that some countries weren't represented. Several heads of state spoke **badly** of East-West relations.

balanced sentence A sentence built around pairs of parallel phrases and clauses, used to create emphasis. (*See 26b-2*)

bandwagon argument A **fallacy** in argumentative writing in which the writer tries to convince the reader that everyone else feels a particular way about a topic and that the reader ought to as well. (*See 54c-5*)

base form The present tense form of a verb. (*See* **tense**; *see 17a*)

→**because, since** In general, avoid using *since* in place of *because,* which is more formal and precise. Use *since* to indicate time, not causality.

INFORMAL	**Since** the meeting was canceled, Sam gave his nonrefundable plane tickets to a friend.
EDITED	**Because** the meeting was canceled, Sam gave his nonrefundable plane tickets to a friend.
CORRECT	**Since** then, Sam has avoided buying nonrefundable tickets for meetings.

begging the question In argument, a **fallacy** in which assumptions are presented as facts, sometimes using words like *obviously* or *clearly*. (Also known as *overgeneralization* or *hasty generalization*.) (*See 54c-5*)

→**being as, being that** Avoid using *being as* or *being that* in academic and other formal writing when you mean *because.*

→**beside, besides** Use *beside* as a preposition to mean "next to." Use *besides* as an adverb meaning "also" or an adjective meaning "except."

> Betsy placed the documents **beside** Mr. Klein. **Besides** being the best lawyer at the firm, Klein was also the most cautious.

gloss

→**better, had better** Avoid using *better* or *had better* in place of *ought to* or *should* in formal writing.

COLLOQUIAL	Fast-food chains **better** realize that Americans are more health-conscious today.
EDITED	Fast-food chains **ought to** realize that Americans are more health-conscious today.

→**between, among** (*See* **among, between**)

bibliographic sources Lists of resources you can consult in your research. **Bibliographies,** indexes, electronic databases, and catalogs all provide information about possible sources.

bibliographies Lists of library or other resources available in specific subject areas. (*See 45b-2, 46a*)

bibliography A list of the sources used by the writer of a research paper, an article, or a book, prepared so that a reader can easily find the same materials. (*See, for instance, the formats in Chapters 49–52; see also* **annotated bibliography**)

biographical sources Source materials that supply information about the lives and times of important people.

block format A format for short letters in which all the paragraphs are flush at the left margin. (*See 57b; compare* **modified block format**)

block quotation A quotation of sufficient length to justify separating it from the body of a text in an indented block of prose. (*See 35b*)

body The main section of a **paper** or written document. It is preceded by an **introduction** and followed by a **conclusion.** (*See 6a-2*)

Boolean logic An electronic search strategy whereby you use *and*, *or*, and *not* to link terms in a subject you are searching for; usage selected will expand or limit your search. (*See 45c*)

boundary statement A sentence at the start of a paragraph that acts as a bridge from the paragraph before. (*See 8d-2*)

brainstorming A technique for generating material for possible use in a written document. Brainstorming involves concentrating on a topic, thinking associatively, and finding connections among different ideas. (*See 2c-2*)

→**bring, take** *Bring* implies a movement from somewhere else to close at hand; *take* implies a movement in the opposite direction.

Please **bring** me a coffee refill, and **take** away these leftover muffins.

broad pronoun reference Using a pronoun to refer to an entire idea rather than a specific **antecedent.** (*See 22b-1*)

→**broke** *Broke* is the past tense of *break*; avoid using it as the past participle.

INCORRECT	The computer was **broke.**
EDITED	The computer was **broken.**

browser A computer software program, such as Netscape Navigator or Microsoftís Internet Explorer, allowing you access to Web sites. (*See 45c*)

→**burst, bursted** *Burst* implies an outward explosion. Do not use the form *bursted* for the past tense.

CORRECT	The gang of boys **burst** the balloon.

gloss

→**bust, busted** Avoid the use of *bust* or *busted* to mean "broke."

| COLLOQUIAL | The senator's limousine **bust** down on the trip to Washington. |
| EDITED | The senator's limousine **broke** down on the trip to Washington. |

→**but however, but yet** These are **redundant pairs;** choose one word of each pair, not both.

| INCORRECT | The medfly was a nuisance, **but yet** the state of California was finally able to control it. |
| EDITED | The medfly was a nuisance, **but** the state of California was finally able to control it. |

→**calculate, figure, reckon** These three terms are sometimes used informally to mean "imagine" or "think." When in doubt, avoid them.

| INFORMAL | John **figured** he had never seen such a large pike. |
| EDITED | John **thought** he had never seen such a large pike. |

→**can, may** *Can* implies ability; *may* implies permission or uncertainty.

Bart **can** drive now, but his parents **may** not lend him their new car.

→**can't hardly, can't scarcely** Use these pairs positively, not negatively: *can hardly* and *can scarcely,* or simply *can't.*

→**capital, capitol** *Capital* refers to a government center or to money; *capitol* refers to a government building.

Madison is the **capital** of Wisconsin.

card catalog A file of printed cards listing a library's books and other holdings. An individual work usually has several cards that list it by author, title, and subject area(s). (*See* **online catalog**)

case The grammatical role that a pronoun or noun plays in a sentence (as subject, object, direct object, and the like). *Subjective case* refers to the role played as the subject of a sentence. *Objective case* refers to the role played as the object of a sentence. *Possessive case* refers to the role played in a sentence to indicate possession or ownership. (*See 16a*)

cause-effect paragraph A paragraph explaining why something has occurred and exploring consequences (*See 8e*)

CBE documentation style The style of documentation suggested by the Council of Biology Editors and described in its guide. (*See Chapter 51*)

→**censor, censure** *Censor* means the act of shielding something from the public eye, such as a book or movie. *Censure* implies a punishment or critical labeling.

The school board **censored** *Catcher in the Rye,* but a group of parents **censured** the school by naming it on a list of "anti-intellectual" schools in the area.

→**center around** Something can't center *around* something else. Use *center on* or *focus on* instead, or reword as *revolve around.*

chain of reasoning In writing, the path a writer takes and asks others to follow. (*See 12b*)

→**chairman, chairperson, chair** The use of *chairman* is now considered sexist. *Chairperson* is an awkward but acceptable substitute. *Chair* is now a common nonsexist alternative.

SEXIST	Gayle is now **chairman** of the provost's academic standards council.
EDITED	Gayle is now **chair** of the provost's academic standards council.

character Any person, usually fictional, in a work of literature. (*See 55a-2*)

chat rooms Informal real-time communities hosted by private Internet services or available via the Internet Relay Chat (IRC) network. (*See 11c-3*)

→**choose, chose** Incorrect use of these terms often has its source in a simple spelling error. Use *choose* for the present tense form of the verb; use *chose* for the past tense form.

chronological order A pattern for structuring writing in which elements of an event are presented in the order in which they happened. (*See also* **sequential order**)

circular reasoning In argumentative writing, a **fallacy** in which an assertion is supported with the assertion itself. (Also known as *tautology.*) (*See 54c-5*)

→**cite, site** *Cite* means to acknowledge someone else's work; *site* means a place or location.

Phil decided to **cite** Chomsky's theory of syntax as evidence for his thesis. We chose the perfect **site** to pitch our tent.

claim (*See* **data-warrant-claim reasoning**)

clarifying sentence (*See* **limiting sentence**)

classification The organization of information into groups, categories, or parts. (*See 56a-3*)

classification paragraph A paragraph in which several subjects are sorted into groups based on their similarities or relationships. (*See 8e*)

cliché An overused or trite word or expression: *startling discovery, today's modern world, turn you on.* (*See 30b-1*)

→**climactic, climatic** *Climactic* refers to the culmination of something; *climatic* refers to the weather conditions.

climactic sentence order A sentence structured to build to a climax, often through the use of elements in a series. (*See 9c-2*)

What every truly modern home has, she said, is a dishwasher, a gas grill, a Jacuzzi, and a divorce.

clustering A planning strategy in which groups of ideas are related graphically to a kernel topic. (*See 3b-1*)

CMS documentation style The style of documentation described in *The Chicago Manual of Style.* (*See Chapter 52*)

code shifting Adjusting language to meet the expectations of particular communities. (*See 10a-4*)

coherence Writing in which each sentence or paragraph follows clearly from the one before and leads clearly to the next in a recognizable, easy-to-understand arrangement. (*See 8c*)

gloss

collaborative revision The process of working with one or more people in order to revise writing drafts. (*See 7c*)

collective noun A kind of noun that refers to a unit composed of more than one individual or thing: *group, board of directors, family.* Such nouns generally take a singular form even though they refer to more than one thing. (*See 15a, 18b, 18c, see also* **noun; count noun; mass noun**)

colloquialism A word or expression that is used informally (often in specific regions or among specific groups) but is not usually considered appropriate in formal and academic prose. (*28a-1*)

comma splice Two or more sentences (independent or main clauses) incorrectly joined with a comma. (*See Chapter 21, 32a; compare* **fused sentence**)

COMMA SPLICE	The human eye is not like that of the cat, it has many more color-sensitive cells.
EDITED	The human eye is not like that of the cat; it has many more color-sensitive cells.

common adjective Any adjective that is not **a proper adjective.** (*See 38b*)

common noun Any noun that is not **a proper noun.** (*See 15a-1, 38b*)

comparative form One of three forms taken by an adjective or adverb to indicate whether the noun or verb modified is being compared to something else. The comparative form adds *-er* or *more* to the adjective or adverb. (*See 19c; compare* **positive form** *and* **superlative form**)

ADJECTIVE	This oven is **cleaner** than mine. She is the **more imaginative** designer of the two.
ADVERB	Sometimes you can travel **faster** in Manhattan by foot than by car. Peggy designs **more imaginatively** than Horace.

→**compare to, compare with** Use *compare to* when you want to imply similarities between two things—the phrase is close in meaning to *liken to.* Use *compare with* when you want to imply both similarities and differences.

CORRECT	To help the little boy understand his virus, the doctor **compared** it **to** a tiny army in his body.
CORRECT	**Compared with** his last illness, this one was mild.

comparing and contrasting A technique for organizing an entire paper or for developing individual paragraphs or sentences. Opinions, characteristics, or objects are compared for similarities and differences, which often are presented in alternating form. (*See 8e; see 26b-2 on* **parallelism;** *see also* **point-by-point organization** *and* **subject-by-subject organization**)

complement A word (noun, pronoun, or adjective) or phrase tied by a linking verb to a subject. (*See 15b-2, 16b-2, 19b-2*). *A subject complement* "completes" the linking verb by describing the subject or renaming it. An *object complement* renames or describes the *direct object.*

→**complement, compliment** *Complement* means "an accompaniment"; *compliment* means "words of praise."

The diplomats **complimented** the ambassador on her choice of opera.

The theater's grand ceiling **complemented** the theme of the opera perfectly.

complete predicate (*See* **predicate**)

complete sentence A sentence that contains both a subject and a complete predicate and is therefore grammatical. (*See Chapter 20; compare* **sentence fragment**)

complete subject (*See* **subject**)

complex sentence A sentence with one **main clause** and one or more **subordinate clauses.** (*See 15e, 27b-1; compare* **compound sentence; compound-complex sentence; simple sentence**)

compound antecedent A group of words to which a pronoun or noun refers. (*See 22a; see also* **antecedent**)

compound-complex sentence A sentence with two or more **main clauses** and one or more **subordinate clauses.** (*See 15e; compare* **compound sentence; complex sentence; simple sentence**)

compound predicate A predicate that contains two or more complete verbs, usually connected with *and.* (*See 20c-1*)

The car **struck and injured** the bystander.

compound sentence A sentence with two or more **main clauses** and no **subordinate clauses.** (*See 15e, 27a; compare* **complex sentence; compound-complex sentence; simple sentence**)

compound subject Two or more subjects joined with *and* or *both . . . and.* (*See 16b, 18b-1*)

Jim and the rest of the Boy Scouts were responsible for the rescue.

conclusion The ending section of a paper, preceded by the **introduction** and **body** (*see 6a-2*), also the necessary consequence of a line of reasoning, especially in **deductive argument.** (*See 12b, 54c-1*)

conditional statement A sentence that expresses something improbable or hypothetical, often beginning with *if.* Conditional statements use the *subjunctive* form of the verb. (*See 17f*)

conjunction A word that joins two elements in a sentence. (*See 15a-8, 18b, 26b-2, 32a*) Coordinating conjunctions (*and, but, or, nor, for, yet,* and *so*) link grammatically equal elements such as parts of compound subjects, verbs, objects, and modifiers.

We analyzed **and** discussed the theory in class.

Fresh orange juice **or** grapefruit juice contain citric acid.

Subordinating conjunctions (*because, although, while, if,* or *since*) create a **subordinate** (or *modifying*) **clause.**

Because they were tired, they did not notice that the pot was boiling over.

conjunctive adverb An adverb such as *however, moreover, thus,* or *therefore* that joins sentences or elements within sentences and indicates a logical relationship between them. (*See 15a-6, 32b-3, 33a-2*)

connotation The associative or affective "shades of meaning" conveyed by a word, as opposed to its literal meaning. If someone is said to have *retreated* from a gathering, the word connotes that the person was feeling attacked or bewildered. (*See 28b-2*)

→**consensus of opinion** Avoid this redundancy by using *consensus.*

content The specific ideas or information presented in a piece of writing. (*See 5c*)

→**continual, continuous** *Continual* implies that something is recurring; *continuous* implies that something is constant and unceasing.

The **continual** noise of landing jets didn't bother the homeowners as much as the foul odor that drifted **continuously** from the landfill near the airport.

gloss

contraction A form in which two words are brought together, usually by eliminating one or more letters and adding an apostrophe to mark the omission(s): *it's, they're, can't.* (*See 34b-1*)

controlling idea (*See* **thesis statement**)

coordinate adjectives A pair of adjectives, each modifying a noun on its own and therefore separated by a comma. In *noncoordinate adjectives,* which are not separated by commas, the first adjective modifies the second, which modifies the noun. (*See 32f*)

coordinating conjunction (*See* **conjunction**)

coordination A sentence structure that links and equally weights main clauses using *coordinating conjunctions.* (*See 27a;* compare **subordination**)

> COORDINATE   These drawings present a **quick, simple** solution to the drainage problem.
>
> NONCOORDINATE We can use **flexible plastic** pipe to carry water away from the building.

correlative conjunctions Pairs of conjunctions (*not only . . . but also; either . . . or; neither . . . nor; both . . . and; whether . . . or*) that join sentence elements that are grammatically equal. (*See 15a-8; see 26b-2 on* **parallelism**)

→**could of, would of** These incorrect pairs are common because they are often pronounced as if they are spelled this way. Use the correct verb forms *could have* and *would have.*

> INCORRECT   I **could of** majored in psychology.
>
> EDITED   I **could have** majored in psychology.

count noun A type of noun that refers to individual ("countable") items: *chair, bean, cup.* A count noun can be made plural by the addition of an *-s.* (*See 15a-1; see also* **noun; collective noun; mass noun**)

counterargument A claim or opinion opposed to the one being supported in an argumentative paper. (*See 54a-5*)

→**couple, couple of** These terms are used colloquially; in formal writing, use *a few* or *two* instead.

> COLLOQUIAL   Watson took a **couple of** days to examine the data.
>
> EDITED   Watson took **a few** days to examine the data.
>
> EDITED   Watson took **two or three** days to examine the data.

criteria *Criteria* is the plural form of *criterion.* Make sure your verbs agree in number with this noun.

> SINGULAR   One **criterion** for winning the bonus <u>was</u> selling ten cars in two weeks.
>
> PLURAL   The **criteria** <u>were</u> too strict to follow.

critical notes Research notes that include comments, interpretations, or evaluations of a source. (*See 46b-2*)

critical reading Evaluating information and ideas presented by utilizing your own knowledge and insight, identifying unanswered questions, and interpreting sources. (*See Chapter 2, 46b*)

critical synthesis Brings together perspectives, opinions, interpretations, and evidence from a variety of sources and explores their potential connections. (*See 46d-2*)

gloss

critique A paper that summarizes and presents a critical reaction to a specific work, such as a speech or book. (*See 54e*)

cumulative sentence A sentence that begins with the main clause and then adds details and statements in the form of modifying phrases, clauses, and words. (*See 9c*)

→**curriculum** *Curriculum* is the singular form of this noun. For the plural, use either *curricula* or *curriculums,* but be consistent.

dangling modifier A sentence that contains no **headword** or **phrase** to which a modifier can be correctly linked. (*See Chapter 23; compare* **disruptive modifier** and **misplaced modifier**)

DANGLING	Staring from his study, **Paul's stomach** tied itself into knots.
EDITED	Staring from his study, **Paul** felt his stomach tying itself into knots.

→**data** Although now widely used for both the singular and plural, *data* technically is a plural noun; *datum* refers to a single piece of data. If in doubt, use the more formal distinction between the two, and make sure your verbs agree in number.

SINGULAR	This one **datum** is astonishing.
PLURAL	These **data** are not very revealing.

data-warrant-claim reasoning A reasoning or argumentative strategy in which data (indisputable facts) lead to a claim (or conclusion) through a mental process involving probable facts and assertions (warrants). Also called Toulmin reasoning. (*See 54c-3*)

database A computerized (CD-ROM or online) collection of resources available to researchers. Databases contain a wide variety of materials such as articles, graphics, bibliographies, and statistics and usually focus on a particular area of study or a particular topic. (*See 46a-3*)

declarative sentence A type of sentence that makes a statement. (*See 15e; compare* **exclamatory sentence; imperative sentence; interrogative sentence**)

The motor is making a rattling noise.

decorum Proper conduct and behavior; in writing, style and tone that fit the expectations of a particular social context. (*See 11a*)

deductive argument An argument that begins with an explicitly stated **premise** and goes on to support that premise, using **syllogism** as the basic logical format. (*See 54c-1 compare* **inductive argument**)

definite article (*See* **article**)

definition paragraph A paragraph designed to adequately introduce a term or concept to your readers. (*See 8e*)

demonstrative adjective (*See* **demonstrative pronoun**)

demonstrative pronoun A pronoun (*this, that, these,* or *those*), that points out or highlights an antecedent. (*See 15a-2, 18c-3*)

dependent clause (*See* **subordinate clause**)

description A kind of writing and a means of developing paragraphs that uses specific details to evoke images of places, objects, characters, or feelings. (*See also* **objective description** and **subjective description**)

desk dictionary A midsized dictionary suitable for most professional and academic contexts. (*See 29a*)

gloss

detailing list A prewriting and revision strategy for creating more detailed prose. (*See 3a-4*)

dialogue journal A kind of collaborative **working journal** in which partners swap journal entries and respond to each other's ideas.

diction The choice of words and phrases in a piece of writing. (*See Chapter 28*)

→**different from, different than** The subtle difference between these two phrases is marked by what follows them: use *different from* when an object follows, and use *different than* when an entire clause follows.

> Jack's quiche recipe is **different from** Marlene's, but his cooking method is **different** now **than** when he was an apprentice.

direct object (*See* **object**)

direct quotation A quotation that presents a speaker's or writer's ideas and feelings in the same words the speaker used, set off by quotation marks. (*See 24b-2, 24d*)

directions One type of process explanation in which the writer gives a step-by-step guide for assembling or creating something or for following a procedure.

→**discreet, discrete** *Discreet* means "reserved or cautious"; *discrete* means "distinctive, different, or explicit."

> Emmons was as **discreet** as an anthropologist could be, but he violated some of the **discrete** codes of research when he lived among the tribe.

discriminatory language Language that implies or reinforces racist or discriminatory views toward other cultures or groups. (*See 31b*)

discuss To provide an intelligent, focused commentary in a paper. (*See 4a-2*)

discussion list A type of electronic bulletin board with a specialized membership in a specific academic, work, or public community. (*See 44b*)

→**disinterested, uninterested** *Uninterested* implies boredom or lack of interest; *disinterested* implies impartiality or objectivity.

> It wasn't that Reagan was **uninterested** in environmental issues; he was simply a **disinterested** party when it came to special-interest groups.

disruptive modifier A sentence in which two closely connected elements such as a noun and a verb are inappropriately disrupted by a modifier. (*See 23c; compare* **dangling modifier** *and* **misplaced modifier**)

DISRUPTIVE	The engineer, **even though he could have lost his life if he had become trapped in the burning plant,** was able to shut off the gas valve and prevent millions of dollars in damage.
EDITED	**Even though he could have lost his life if he had become trapped in the burning plant,** the engineer was able to shut off the gas valve and prevent millions of dollars in damage.

division paragraph A paragraph in which a subject is split into its constituent parts so that the relationship between these parts can be highlighted or explained. (*See 8e-2*)

documentation The process of citing the source or reference for an idea, sentence, passage, or text in a research paper. (*See Chapters 49–53*)

domain name Locates an organization or other entity on the Internet. (*See 11b-2*)

→**done** Avoid using *done* as a simple past tense; it is a *past participle.* (*See 17d*)

> INCORRECT   The skater **done** the best she could at the Olympics.
>
> EDITED   The skater **did** the best she could at the Olympics.

→**don't, doesn't** These and other contractions may strike some academic readers as too informal. Check with your reader, or err on the side of formality (*do not, does not*) when in doubt.

double negative Avoid the incorrect use of two negative forms. (*See 19d*)

> INCORRECT   The state **hasn't** done **nothing** about it.
>
> EDITED   The state **has** done **nothing** about it.
>
> EDITED   The state **hasn't** done **anything** about it.

drafting The process of creating a preliminary but readable version of an essay or other text. (*See Chapter 6*)

draft thesis statement (*See* **tentative thesis statement**)

→**due to** When meaning "because," use *due to* only after some form of the verb *be.* Avoid *due to the fact that,* which is wordy.

> INCORRECT   The mayor collapsed **due to** campaign fatigue.
>
> EDITED   The mayor's collapse <u>was</u> **due to** campaign fatigue.
>
> EDITED   The mayor collapsed **because** of campaign fatigue.

editing The process of fine tuning a rough draft for problems in grammar, wording, style, sentence rhythm or length, and other details. (*See Chapter 14; compare* **proofreading** *and* **revising**)

→**effect, affect** (*See* **affect, effect**)

→**e.g.** From a Latin term meaning "for example," this abbreviation is common in much writing but should be avoided when possible.

> AWKWARD   Her positions on major issues, **e.g.,** gun control, abortion, and the death penalty, are very liberal.
>
> EDITED   Her positions on major issues **such as** gun control, abortion, and the death penalty are very liberal.

either/or strategy In argumentative writing, a **fallacy** in which an issue is oversimplified, usually into two sides or positions. (*See 54c-5*)

e-journals Scholarly journals published (or distributed) through electronic computer networks. (*See 45b-2*)

electronic community Writers and readers who participate in one of the many clusters of related sites that form and re-form on the Internet and World Wide Web. (*See Chapters 1, 44, 45*)

electronic indexes Computerized (CD-ROM or online) indexes to articles in magazines, newspapers, or scholarly journals. Indexes enable researchers to identify possible sources. (*See 45b-2; see also* **printed indexes**)

electronic research Research conducted using electronic media or technology, such as CD-ROM databases, online resources, or electronic card catalogs. (*See 45b-2; see also* **research**)

gloss

ellipsis A series of three or four evenly spaced periods telling a reader that something has been left out of a quotation. (*See 37d*)

As Fielding describes it, Squire Allworthy's house had "an Air of Grandeur in it, that struck you with awe . . . and it was as commodious within, as venerable without."

elliptical construction The omission of an otherwise repeated element in a sentence; appropriate omissions are not misleading or confusing. (*See 25b-2*)

LEFT IN	Some car owners invest lots of time caring for their cars; others **invest little time caring for their cars.**
OMITTED BUT CLEAR	Some car owners invest lots of time caring for their cars; **others invest little.**

email Mail exchanged through electronic computer networks. (*See 45c-3*)

embedded quotation A quotation used within a sentence you have written, as contrasted to a **block quotation.** (*See 47c*)

→**emigrate from, immigrate to** Foreigners *emigrate from* one country and *immigrate to* another. *Migrate* implies moving around (as in *migrant workers*) or settling temporarily.

emoticons Faces drawn with keyboard characters. (*See 11b-1*)

emotional strategy In argumentative writing, a focus on the values, attitudes, systems of beliefs, and emotions that guide people's lives and are central to most decision-making processes. (*See 54c-2*)

empty phrase A phrase that adds little or no meaning to a sentence and can be cut or reduced: *at this point in time, due to the fact that, each and every.* (*See 30a-1*)

e-newsletters Scholarly or professional newsletters containing current information and announcements, published (or distributed) through electronic computer networks. (*See 45c-3*)

→**ensure, assure, insure** (*See* **assure, ensure, insure**)

→**enthused** Avoid *enthused* to mean *enthusiastic* in formal writing.

equivocation (*See* **misleading language/misleading evidence**)

→**especially, specially** *Especially* implies "in particular"; *specially* means "for a specific purpose."

It was **especially** important that Nakita follow the workouts **specially** designed by her coach.

essay exam A test written out in essay form, either during a timed, in-class session or at home between class sessions. (*See 54g, 56h*)

→**etc.** Avoid this abbreviation in formal writing by supplying a complete list of items or by using a phrase like *so forth.*

INFORMAL	The Washington march was a disaster: it was cold and rainy, the protesters had no food, **etc.**
EDITED	The Washington march was a disaster: the protesters were cold, wet, and hungry.

ethnographic research Research that interprets the practices, behaviors, language, and attitudes of particular groups that are tied together by their interests or ways of understanding and acting in the world. (*See 48a*)

gloss

ethnography The written report of ethnographic research. (*See 48a*)

etymology The history of a word, including its source(s) and the changes it has undergone. (*See 29a*)

etymological dictionary (*See* **etymology**)

evaluation The process of deciding the relative worth of a source, phenomenon, or opinion, including the credibility or authority of a researched source. (*See 4a-2*)

evaluative summary (*See* **summary**)

→**eventually, ultimately** Use *eventually* to imply that an outcome follows a series of events or a lapse of events. Use *ultimately* to imply that a final or culminating act ends a series of events.

> **Eventually,** the rescue team managed to pull the last of the survivors from the wreck, and **ultimately** there were no casualties.

→**everyday, every day** *Everyday* is an adjective that modifies a noun. *Every day* is a noun modified by *every.*

> **Every day** in the Peace Corps, Monique faced the **everyday** task of boiling her drinking water.

→**everyone, every one** *Everyone* is a pronoun; *every one* is an adjective followed by a noun. (*See also* **anyone, any one**)

> **Everyone** was tantalized by **every one** of the items on the dessert menu.

evidence Information that gives readers reasons for accepting the accuracy, value, or importance of conclusions. (*See 12b-2*)

→**exam** In formal writing, some readers may be bothered by this abbreviation of the word *examination.*

→**except, accept** (*See* **accept, except**)

exclamatory sentence A type of sentence that expresses something emphatically. (*See 9d-2, 15d-2; compare* **declarative sentence; imperative sentence; interrogative sentence**)

> The car is on fire!

explanation A kind of writing that provides details on how a mechanism or procedure works.

expletive construction In indirect sentences, the use of opening expletives such as *there is, there are,* or *it is* to delay the actual subject until further into the sentence. (*See 9b, 30a-2*)

> **This is** the case in which the man bit the dog.

explication A line-by-line analysis of a text. (*See 55b-2*)

→**explicit, implicit** *Explicit* means that something is outwardly or openly stated; *implicit* means that it is implied or suggested.

> The conductors **explicitly** assured the passengers that they were traveling to a comfortable new life, but **implicit** in their voices was the Nazi menace that the Jews had come to recognize.

exploratory sources (*See* **preliminary sources**)

extend In writing assignments, to take an idea or concept and apply it more extensively. (*See 4a-2*)

fallacy Any flaw in reasoning, particularly in the context of persuasive or argumentative writing. (*See 54c-5*)

gloss

false analogy A **fallacy** in which two things that are presented as comparable are actually not. (*See 54c-5*)

→**farther, further** *Farther* implies a measurable distance; *further* implies something that cannot be measured.

The **farther** they trekked into the wilderness, the **further** their relationship deteriorated.

faulty cause-effect relationship A **fallacy** in which one event is assumed or implied to have caused another event. (*See 54c-5*)

faulty parallelism (*See* **parallelism**)

faulty predication A sentence in which the second part comments on or names a topic different from the one announced in the first part. (*See 25a-1; see* **shift**)

FAULTY	The **presence** of ozone in smog is **the chemical** that causes eye irritation.
EDITED	The **ozone** in smog is the **chemical** that causes eye irritation.

→**female, male** Use these terms only when you want to call attention to gender specifically, as in a research report. Otherwise, use the simpler *man* and *woman* or *boy* and *girl,* unless such usage is sexist. (*See Chapter 31*)

→**fewer, less** Use *fewer* for things that can be counted, and use *less* for quantities that cannot be divided.

Bush had **fewer** supporters for the bill than before, but there was much **less** media coverage this time.

field research (*See* **research**)

field resources Original documents, interviews, surveys, questionnaires, and personal observations gathered during the process of **research.**

figure, calculate, reckon (*See* **calculate, figure, reckon**)

→**finalize** Some readers object to adjectives and nouns that are turned into verbs ending in *-ize* (*finalize, prioritize, objectivize*). When in doubt, use *make final* or some other construction.

→**firstly** Use *first, second, third,* and so forth when enumerating points in writing.

INAPPROPRIATE	**Firstly,** I will compare Sartre's and Camus's versions of existentialism.
EDITED	**First,** I will compare Sartre's and Camus's versions of existentialism.

first person (*See* **person**)

five-paragraph theme A kind of academic paper that has a simple, clearly defined structure including an **introduction,** a **body** of three paragraphs each starting with a **topic sentence,** and a **conclusion.**

focus-imagine-choose strategy A strategy for choosing the correct case of pronouns: focus on the pronoun, imagine each possible choice, and choose the correct form. (*See 16b-1*)

focused freewriting Writing quickly, without stopping, about a particular idea or topic. (*See 3a-2; see also* **freewriting**)

focused paragraph (*See* **paragraph**)

gloss

format A general plan for the organization, such as length, level of formality, etc., or the actual appearance of a document. (*See 11a*)

→**former, latter** *Former* means "the one before" and *latter* means "the one after." They can be used only when referring to two things.

fragment (*See* **sentence fragment**)

freewriting A technique involving writing as quickly as possible without concern for style or grammar. Freewriting is often used to avoid writer's block, to "warm up" for more formal writing, or to generate ideas for a paper. (*See 3a-1; see also* **focused freewriting**)

→**freshman, freshmen** Many readers consider these terms sexist and archaic. Unless you are citing an established term or group (such as the Freshman Colloquium at Midwest University), use *first-year student* instead.

further, farther (*See* **farther, further**)

fused sentence Two or more complete sentences incorrectly joined without any punctuation. (*See Chapter 21; compare* **comma splice**)

FUSED	Frank Lloyd Wright's Robie House is a good example of his architectural principles it embodies the idea of "space, not mass."
EDITED	Frank Lloyd Wright's Robie House is a good example of his architectural principles; it embodies the idea of "space, not mass."

future perfect tense (*See* **perfect tense**)

future progressive tense (*See* **progressive tense**)

future tense (*See* **tense**)

gazetteer A dictionary of geographical places and cities.

gender Labeling of nouns and pronouns according to whether they are masculine, feminine, or neuter. Pronouns must agree in gender with the nouns to which they refer. (*See 15a-2, 16a*)

Harry put on **his** shirt.

general academic writing Writing typically found in introductory courses across the college curriculum, including term papers, essay exams, short reports, abstracts, summaries, and argumentative analyses.

general-interest magazines Magazines that appear monthly or weekly, with each issue paginated separately. (*See 45b-2*)

general pattern of development A type of paragraph development such as **narration, comparison,** or **cause-effect,** used to shape a paragraph's content and arrangement. (*See 8e-2*)

general reference A reference to the main ideas in a source or to information presented throughout the work, not in a single place. (*See 49a; compare* **informational reference** and **specific reference**)

general sources Books, indexes, databases, and nonspecialized periodicals used for background and to point the way to **specialized sources.** (*See Chapter 45*)

general-to-specific pattern (*See* **logical order**)

generalizations Conclusions reached on the basis of facts (*see 12b-2*) and summing up their meaning or qualities, or broad conclusions about what your research has to say about your topic. (*See 46d*)

gloss

genre The form, or category of discourse, to which a work conforms (e.g., poem, play, novel, novella, film). (*See 55a-2*).

gerund An *-ing* form of a verb that acts as a noun. (*See 15a-4, 16b-6; see also* **verbal phrase**)

Running can be enjoyable.

→**get** Avoid imprecise or frequent use of *get* in formal writing; use more specific verbs instead.

INFORMAL	Martin Luther King had a premonition that he would **get** shot; his sermons and speeches before his death **got** nostalgic at times.
EDITED	Martin Luther King had a premonition that he would **be** shot; his sermons and speeches before his death **waxed** nostalgic at times.

→**go, say** In very informal contexts, some speakers use *go* and *goes* colloquially to mean *say* and *says*. This usage is considered inappropriate in all writing.

INAPPROPRIATE	Hjalmar **goes** to Gregers, "I thought it best to make a clean break."
EDITED	Hjalmar **says** to Gregers, "I thought it best to make a clean break."

→**gone, went** Do not use *went* (the past tense of *go*) in place of the past participle form *gone*.

INCORRECT	The players **should have went** to their captain.
EDITED	The players **should have gone** to their captain.

→**good and** This is a colloquial term when used to mean "very" (*good and* tired; *good and* hot). Avoid it in formal writing.

→**good, well** *Good* is an adjective meaning "favorable" (a *good* trip). *Well* is an adverb meaning "done favorably." Avoid colloquial uses of *good* for *well*.

COLLOQUIAL	The Vikings played real **good** in the playoffs.
CORRECT	A **good** shot in the game of golf is not a hard-hit shot but a shot that is placed **well**.

→**got to** Avoid the colloquial use of *got* or *got to* in place of *must* or *have to*.

COLLOQUIAL	I **got to** improve my ratings in the opinion polls.
EDITED	I **must** improve my ratings in the opinion polls.

government documents Archives of congressional reports and documents issued by federal agencies as well as state and local governments. (*See 45b*)

→**great** In formal writing, avoid using *great* as an adjective meaning "wonderful." Use *great* in the sense of "large" or "monumental."

INFORMAL	Our trip to Stone Mountain was **great.**
APPROPRIATE	As you approach Stone Mountain, a **great** carving appears on the rock face.

gloss

guessing Unsure of the correct spelling of a word, and guessing on the basis of reason or similar sounding words. (*See 43a-1*)

guiding question In research, a specific question that helps to determine the kinds of sources to consult, the process of locating sources, and the possibilities for organizing the paper. (*See 44a-4*)

→**hanged, hung** Although the distinction between these terms is disappearing, some readers may expect you to use *hanged* exclusively to mean execution by hanging and *hung* to refer to anything else.

The convict was **hanged** at dawn.

The farmer **hung** the dead pheasant upside down for a day before cooking it.

hasty generalization (*See* **begging the question**)

→**have, got** (*See* **got to**)

→**have, of** (*See* **could of, would of**)

→**he, she, he or she, his/her** When you use gender-specific pronouns, be careful not to privilege the male versions. Look for ways to avoid awkward alternations of *he* and *she* or *his* and *her* by revising structures that require them. (*See 31a-3*)

headword The word a modifier refers to. (*See Chapter 23*)

helping verb The different forms of *be, do,* and *have* that link to main verbs and create complex verb forms. Helping verbs are sometimes called **auxiliary verbs** or **modal auxiliaries.** (*See 15a-3, 18b-1*)

> helping main
> verb   verb
> The tourist agency is planning to make a video of the local attractions.

homophones Words that sound like each other but are spelled differently (*accept/except; assent/ascent; principal/principle; stationary/stationery*). (*See 43b-4*)

→**hopefully** Although the word is widely used to modify entire clauses (as in "Hopefully, her condition will improve"), some readers may object. When in doubt, use *hopefully* only to mean "feeling hopeful."

Bystanders watched **hopefully** as the workers dug their way to the trapped spelunkers.

→**however, yet, but** (*See* **but however, but yet**)

→**hung, hanged** (*See* **hanged, hung**)

hypercorrection The phenomenon in which speakers using nonmainstream dialect unwittingly create a new error in trying to "repair" their speech. (*See 10b-4*)

hyphenated noun A single noun that consists of two or more words linked by hyphens: *father-in-law.* (*See 34a-3*)

hypothesis A tentative assertion to be explored in an argument. (*See 54c-1*)

idiom A common expression that typically means something different from its literal interpretation (e.g., *kick the bucket*). (*See 28b-5*)

→**if, whether** Use *if* before a specific outcome (either stated or implied); use *whether* when you are considering alternatives.

If holographic technology can be perfected, we may soon be watching three-dimensional television. But **whether** any of us will be able to afford it is another question.

illogical comparison (*See* **incomplete sentence**)

→**illusion, allusion** (*See* **allusion, illusion**)

→**immigrate to, emigrate from** (*See* **emigrate from, immigrate to**)

imperative mood (*See* **mood**)

imperative sentence A type of sentence that makes a request or command. (*See* 9d, 15e; *compare* **declarative sentence; exclamatory sentence; interrogative sentence**)

Do your chores immediately.

→**implicit, explicit** (*See* **explicit, implicit**)

inattention Knowing the correct spelling of a word but failing to use it. (*See* 43a-1)

incomplete comparison (*See* **incomplete sentence**)

incomplete sentence A sentence that fails to complete an expected logical or grammatical pattern. An *incomplete comparison* leaves out the element to which something is being compared. An *illogical comparison* is worded so that it seems to be comparing things that cannot be reasonably compared. (*See* 25b)

INCOMPLETE COMPARISON	The sound quality of the new digital audiotapes is much better.
EDITED	The sound quality of the new digital audiotapes is much better **than that of the old analog tapes.**

indefinite article (*See* **article**)

indefinite pronoun A pronoun that refers to people, things, or ideas in general rather than to specific antecedents. Indefinite pronouns include *all, another, any, anybody, anyone, anything, both, each, every,* and *everyone.* (*See* 15a-2, 16a)

independent clause (*See* **main clause**)

indicative mood (*See* **mood**)

indirect object (*See* **object**)

indirect question A sentence whose main clause is a statement and whose embedded clause asks a question. Such sentences usually behave as statements, not as questions. (*See* 36b-1)

Phil wondered whether it would be too much work to take on an additional course.

indirect quotation A quotation in which a writer reports the substance of someone's words but not the exact words the person used. Quotation marks are not needed. (*See* 24b-2, 24d)

inductive argument An argument that does not explicitly state a premise but leads the reader through an accumulating body of evidence to a conclusion. (*See* 54c-1; *compare* **deductive argument**)

inferences Conclusions reached on the basis of facts. (*See* 12b-2)

infinitive The "root," tenseless form of a verb. In English, infinitives are preceded by *to: to live, to perform, to abolish.* (*See* 15a-4, 15c-4; *see also* **split infinitive** and **verbal phrase**)

infinitive phrase A phrase that uses the *to* form of a verbal. It can be used as an adjective, an adverb, or a noun. (*See* 15c-4)

inform In a writing assignment, to tell the reader about some facts, views, or phenomena.

informants In field research, people interviewed or surveyed. (*See Chapter 48*)

informational notes Research notes that record facts, details, concepts, interpretations, and quotations from sources. (*See 46b-2*)

informational reference A reference that provides background information or material potentially useful for readers but too cumbersome to include in the text itself. (*Compare* **general reference** and **specific reference**)

informative writing Writing whose content and strategies are shaped by the purpose of conveying, explaining, or analyzing information (*See Chapter 56; see also* **point-driven writing**)

→**in regard to** Although it may sound sophisticated, *in regard to* is wordy and unnecessary. Use *about* instead.

WORDY	The cruise company was adamant **in regard to** its docking rights at Christiansted.
EDITED	The cruise company was adamant **about** its docking rights at Christiansted.

→**inside of, outside of** When you use *inside* or *outside* to mark locations, do not pair them with *of*.

INAPPROPRIATE	**Inside of** the hut was a large stock of rootwater.
EDITED	**Inside** the hut was a large stock of rootwater.

→**insure, assure, ensure** (*See* **assure, ensure, insure**)

intensifying phrase A phrase that is meant to make a sentence more forceful but carries little or no additional meaning; *for all intents and purposes, in my opinion, all things considered*. (*See 30a-1*)

intensive drafting Creating a preliminary version of an essay in collaboration with a close friend or colleague. (*See 6c*)

intensive pronoun A **reflexive pronoun** used to give emphasis to, or intensify, a sentence. (*See 15a-2, 16b-7*)

He was able to move the heavy refrigerator **himself.**
She **herself** was responsible for the mismanagement of the firm.

intentional fragment (*See* **partial sentence**)

interjection An emphatic word or phrase used to convey a strong reaction or emotion, such as surprise (*Hey!*) or disappointment (*Oh no!*). (*See 15a-9*)

interlibrary loans Systems that allow for the exchange of books, articles, and other resources between libraries to serve users of a library that does not have an item in its own holdings.

Internet Links computers of all kinds through email, discussion groups, resource sites, and the World Wide Web. (*See 45c*)

interpolation The introduction of your own words, marked with brackets, into a verbatim quotation from someone else. (*See 37b-1*)

Kent said, "Captain Sims **[the boat's owner]** has chosen a special place within two hours of Key West."

interpretation The process of reading into or adding your own understandings to a source, concept, or phenomenon. (*See 54a-3*)

interpretive reading A kind of **analytical reading** to determine the meaning, perspective, and purposes, both explicit and implicit of a text. (*See Chapter 2*)

gloss

interrogative pronoun The pronouns *who* and *which* when these are used to introduce questions. (*See 16a*)

interrogative sentence A type of sentence that poses a question. (*See 15e-2; compare* **declarative sentence; exclamatory sentence; imperative sentence**)

interrupters Parenthetical remarks such as *in fact* or *more importantly*. (*See 32d*)

interviews Conversations, verbal or written, with a person in order to gather information or ideas. (*See 48a, b*)

in-text citation In research writing, a citation that is placed within the text of the paper rather than at the end in a works cited page or bibliography. (*See 49b*)

intransitive verb A verb that is not followed by an **object** or **complement**. (*See 15b-2; compare* **transitive verb**)

verb   no object

The president **dreamed.**

introduction The first part of a paper or other document, often leading up to or containing a **thesis.** (*See 6a-2*)

invention A term from classical rhetoric referring to the process of generating and exploring ideas before writing a draft. (*See Chapter 3; see also* **brainstorming; planning; prewriting strategies**)

inverted sentence order A sentence in which the normal subject-verb-object/complement word order is shifted by placing a subsidiary element at the beginning of the sentence in order to call attention to it. (*See 9d-3*)

NORMAL	**The director's voice thundered** from the darkness near the rear of the auditorium with criticisms of our acting.
INVERTED	**From the darkness near the rear of the auditorium thundered the director's voice** with criticisms of our acting.

→**irregardless** Avoid this erroneous form of the word *regardless,* commonly used because *regardless* and *irrespective* are often used synonymously.

→**irregular verb** A verb that does not follow the usual pattern for distinguishing forms for the present, past, and past participle. (*See 17c*)

	Present	Past	Past participle
Regular Verb	bake	baked	baked
Irregular Verb	swim	swam	swum

→**irritate, aggravate** (*See* **aggravate, irritate**)

issue A subject about which there are two (or more) clearly differing opinions. (*See 54a-1*)

italic type Type that *slants to the right* and is the equivalent of <u>underlining</u> for emphasis or for some titles. (*See Chapter 39*)

→**its, it's** Use *its* as a possessive pronoun and *it's* as a contraction of *it* and *is.* (Some readers may also object to *it's* for *it is* in formal writing.) (*See 34b*)

The porcupine raised **its** quills threateningly. **It's** shame that dogs must learn about porcupines the hard way.

→**-ize, -wise** Some readers object to the process of turning nouns or adjectives into verbs by adding *-ize* at the end (*finalize, itemize, computerize*). When in doubt, opt for different verbs. Also avoid adding the suffix *-wise* to words, as in "Weather-*wise,* it will be a chilly night all over the region."

journalist's questions A set of questions (*who? what? when? where? why? how?*) used during the planning or prewriting process to generate or explore ideas or existing material.

key words Most **database** resources and other electronic sources of information such as an **online catalog** or **electronic indexes** allow researchers to retrieve information and listings by typing in important (key) words identifying the subject or some important ideas or details related to the subject.

→**kind, sort, type** These words are singular nouns; precede them with *this,* not *these.* In general, use more precise words.

→**kind of, sort of** Considered by most readers to be informal, these phrases should be avoided in academic and professional writing.

lab report A paper that summarizes the methods and results of a laboratory experiment. (*See 56e*)

→**latter, former** (*See* **former, latter**)

→**lay, lie** *Lay* is a transitive verb requiring a direct object (but not the self). *Lie,* when used to mean "place in a resting position," refers to the self but takes the form *lay* in the past tense. (*See 17i*)

INCORRECT	I was going to **lay** down for a while.
EDITED	I was going to **lie** down for a while.

→**less, fewer** (*See* **fewer, less**)

→**liable** (*See* **apt, likely, liable**)

library research (*See* **research**)

→**lie, lay** (*See* **lay, lie**)

→**like, as** (*See* **as, like**)

→**likely, apt, liable** (*See* **apt, likely, liable**)

limiting modifier A **modifier** such as *only, almost, hardly, just, scarcely, merely, simply, exactly,* or *even* that limits or qualifies a word, usually the one that follows it. (*See 23a-2*)

limiting sentence A sentence that limits, or narrows, the focus of a **topic sentence.** (*See 8b-2*)

link On a computer, a picture or icon or piece of text, usually shown in blue, that when clicked on takes you to another part of the Web page you are viewing, or to another site. (*See 3d*)

linking verb Verbs that express a state of being or an occurrence: *is, seems, becomes, grows.* Also known as **state-of-being verbs.** (*See 15a-3, 15b-2*)

listing A technique for exploring ideas by making a list of points, usually in preparation for writing a formal paper. (*See 3a-3*)

listserv The most common type of subscriber-based mailing list. (*See 11c-1*)

→**literally** Avoid using *literally* in a figurative statement (one that is not true to fact). Even when used correctly, *literally* is redundant because the statement will be taken as fact anyway.

INCORRECT	The visiting scholars **literally** died when they saw their accommodations.
REDUNDANT	The visiting scholars **literally gasped** when they saw their accommodations.
EDITED	The visiting scholars gasped when they saw their accommodations.

gloss

literature review A paper or part of a paper that provides a **synthesis** of existing literature or research on a specific topic. (*See 56d*)

logical order A pattern for paragraph development in which details and generalizations are arranged according to a *question-answer pattern,* a *problem-solution pattern,* a *general-to-specific pattern,* or a *specific-to-general pattern,* suggesting an internal logic to the flow of sentences and ideas.

logical strategies The arrangement of ideas and evidence in ways that correspond with patterns of thought that most people accept as reasonable and convincing. (*See 54c-1*)

looping A technique involving successively **freewriting,** reviewing the material produced from freewriting in order to find new ideas or concepts, and then freewriting on those ideas or concepts.

→**loose, lose** Commonly misspelled, these words are pronounced differently. *Loose* (rhyming with *moose*) is an adjective meaning "not tight." *Lose* (rhyming with *snooze*) is a present tense verb meaning "to misplace."

I was afraid that I would **lose** my ring because it was very **loose.**

→**lots, lots of, a lot of** (*See* **a lot**)

lurking Reading online without participating. (*See 11a-1*)

main clause A word group that contains a subject and a verb and can act as a complete sentence. Also called an *independent clause.* (*See 15c; compare* **phrase**)

main conclusion The end point of a chain of reasoning. (*See 12b-1*)

main verb The central or main verb (word showing action or state of being) in a sentence; it can stand alone or be accompanied by one or more **helping verbs.** (*See 15a-3*)

major premise (*See* **premise**)

major revision (*See* **revision**)

→**man, mankind** For many readers, these terms represent sexist usage when they refer to all humans. Use *people, humans, humanity,* or some other substitute. (*See Chapter 31*)

→**may, can** (*See* **can, may**)

→**maybe, may be** *Maybe* means *possibly; may be* is part of a verb structure.

The President **may be** addressing the nation tonight, so **maybe** we should turn on the news.

mass noun A kind of noun that refers to material that cannot be "counted," or divided into separate units to form a usual plural. (*See 15a-1; see also* **noun; collective noun; count noun**)

COUNT NOUNS	chair+s, cake+s, shadow+s, pea+s
NONCOUNT NOUNS	flour, rice, sugar, steel, sunlight, earth, water

→**media, medium** Technically, *media* is a plural noun requiring a verb that agrees in number. Many people now use *media* as a singular noun when referring to the press.

The **media** *is* not covering the story accurately.

Medium generally refers to a conduit or method of transmission.

The telephone was not a good **medium** for reviewing all the budget figures.

meeting minutes A report of the items discussed during a business meeting. (*See 57-d*)

memo A short, usually internal, note between or among people working in a business. (*See 57-e*)

microfiche A flat sheet of **microfilm** on which printed materials have been placed to save space. (*See* **microform collection**)

microfilm A type of film on which printed materials are recorded to save space. (*See* **microform collection**)

microform collection A library collection containing books, **periodicals,** newspapers, and unpublished documents in the form of **microfilm** or **microfiche.** (*See 45b-4*)

→**might of, may of** (*See* **could of, would of**)

→**mighty** Avoid this adjective in formal writing.

    INFORMAL   It was a **mighty** proud moment for NASA.

    EDITED   It was a **very** proud moment for NASA.

minor premise (*See* **premise**)

minor revision (*See* **revision**)

minutes (*See* **meeting minutes**)

misleading language/misleading evidence A **fallacy** in which a writer deceives a reader through the use of language or information. Using misleading language, the writer shifts the meaning of a term from one sense to another but still gives the erroneous impression of supporting the argument. Using misleading evidence, the writer uses faulty statistics, survey results, and other material slanted in favor of only one side of an argument. (*See 54c-5*)

misplaced modifier A modifier incorrectly placed relative to its intended **headword,** giving the impression that it modifies something else. (*See Chapter 23, compare* **dangling modifier** *and* **disruptive modifier**)

    MISPLACED   In *Walden,* Thoreau describes how he **simply** lived, conserving his resources.

    EDITED   In *Walden,* Thoreau describes how he lived **simply,** conserving his resources.

mixed sentence A sentence with mismatched topics or with a shifted grammatical structure. (*See 25a; see* **faulty predication**)

MLA documentation style The style of **documentation** suggested by the Modern Language Association and described in its guide. (*See Chapter 49*)

mnemonic An aid to memorization, for example, of correct spellings. (*See 43c-1*)

modal auxiliary verbs (*See* **helping verbs**)

moderator The person who decides which messages will be posted on a listserv. (*See 11c-1*)

modified block format A format for longer letters in which the return address and the closing and signature are indented but paragraphs are not. (*See 57b; compare* **block format**)

modifier A word or word group, functioning as an adjective or adverb, that qualifies or adds to a noun or verb. (*See Chapter 23*)

gloss

mood The verb form that indicates the speaker's attitude in a sentence. *Indicative mood* characterizes statements intended as truthful or factual. *Imperative mood* characterizes statements that function as commands. *Subjunctive mood* characterizes statements expressing uncertainty. Many **conditional sentences** require the subjunctive mood. (*See 17f, 24b-3*)

INDICATIVE MOOD	It will rain today.
IMPERATIVE MOOD	Beware of lightning!
SUBJUNCTIVE MOOD	Were it to rain, we would not play golf.

→**Ms.** To avoid the sexist labeling of women as "married" or "unmarried" (a condition not marked in men's titles), use *Ms.* unless you have reason to use *Miss* or *Mrs.* (for example, when giving the name of a character such as *Mrs. Dalloway*). Use professional titles when appropriate (*Dr., Professor, Senator, Mayor*). (*See Chapter 31*).

MUD (multi-user domain) A real-time venue used in academic and corporate settings, in which users learn a series of commands to communicate and move around in a carefully described text environment. (*See 11c-3*)

multiple-word noun A noun consisting of two or more words that are treated as a single unit when marking plurality or possession. (*See 34a-3*)

The **union leaders'** negotiations fell through.

→**must of, must have** (*See* **could of, would of**)

narrative A type of writing, or **genre,** in which the writer usually traces events in the past, present, or imagined future. Narratives tell stories about people, places, or events, often from the writer's own experience.

narrowing The process of taking a more specific perspective on a chosen topic. (*See 4c-1*)

neologism A word that has entered into general use very recently, sometimes not yet having been put into any dictionaries. (*See 28b-4*)

netiquette Commonsense guidelines that apply across nearly all Internet communities. (*See 11a-4*)

newsgroups A format for online communities in which the user chooses which individual posts to read. (*See 11c-1*)

nominalization A sentence in which a verb or adjective is (sometimes inappropriately) turned into a noun: *completion* (noun) from *complete* (verb), *happiness* (noun) from *happy* (adjective). (*See 9a-2, 30a-2*)

noncoordinate adjectives (*See* **coordinate adjectives**)

noncount noun (*See* **mass noun**)

nonrestrictive clause (*See* **restrictive modifier**)

nonrestrictive modifier (*See* **restrictive modifier**)

→**nor, or** Use *nor* in negative constructions and *or* in positive ones.

| NEGATIVE | Neither rain **nor** snow will slow the team. |
| POSITIVE | Either rain **or** snow may delay the game. |

→**nothing like, nowhere near** These are considered informal phases when used to compare two things (as in "Gibbon's position is **nowhere near as** justified as Carlyle's"). Avoid them in formal writing.

gloss

noun A word that names a person, place, or thing and is often preceded by an **article** (*a, an,* or *the*). (*See 15a-1; see also* **collective noun; count noun; mass noun**)

noun clause A clause that functions as a noun. (*See 15d*)

noun string A string of nouns used as modifiers (usually adjectives) of a main noun. Such strings are grammatically correct but may seem overly abstract or technical. (*See 9a-4*)

The **area computer network downlink access program** failed.

→**nowheres** *Use* nowhere *instead.*

number A grammatical concept referring to whether a noun or pronoun is singular or plural. Pronouns must agree in number with the nouns they modify, and subjects and verbs must also agree in number. (*See 15a-2, 15a-3, 16a, 17b, 18a*)

→**number, amount** (*See* **amount, number**)

object A noun, pronoun, or group of words functioning as a noun to which the action of a verb applies. *Direct objects* receive the action of **transitive verbs;** *indirect objects* are affected indirectly by the action of a transitive verb. (*See 15b-2; see also* **complement**)

object complement (*See* **complement**)

object of a preposition The noun or pronoun that follows a preposition. (*See 15b-2, 15c-1*)

object pronoun A pronoun that is the **object** of a verb. (*See 15c-1*)

objective case (*See* **case**)

objective description Description that emphasizes physical details. (*Compare* **subjective description**)

objective summary (*See* **summary**)

observation A kind of ethnographic research involving firsthand research (*onsite visiting and note taking*) of people, events, or settings. (*See 48a*)

→**of, have** (*See* **could of, would of**)

→**off of** *Use simply* off *instead.*

→**OK** When you write formally, use *OK* only in dialogue. If you mean "good" or "acceptable," use one of these terms.

→**on account of** Avoid this expression in formal writing. Use *because* instead.

online catalog A computerized listing of books, magazines, and other holdings in a library. A researcher can retrieve individual listings by author, title, or subject area. Many online catalogs list resources in more than one library and can be accessed through computer networks as well as by terminals in a library. (*See 45b; see also* **card catalog**)

online (electronic) periodicals Periodicals available through the Internet, with past issues or selected articles sometimes available in electronic archives. (*See 45b-2*)

outline A list, usually hierarchical, showing the main contents of a paper. (*See 3c-3*) A *working outline* shows the general sequence of information in a paper and the relationships between the segments of information. (*See 47b*)

→**outside of, inside of** (*See* **inside of, outside of**)

overblown language Diction that is too formal or technical for the writer's purpose and audience, often used out of a misguided attempt to impress the reader. (*See 30b-2*)

overgeneralization (*See* **begging the question**)

gloss

paragraph A unit of prose marked by an indent at the left margin and consisting of a **topic** and its **development.** A *focused paragraph* is one in which the topic, main idea, or perspective is evident and is maintained throughout the paragraph. A *unified paragraph* contains sentences that are clearly and directly related to the main idea. (*See Chapter 8*)

paragraph development The examples, facts, concrete details, explanatory statements, or supporting arguments that make a paragraph informative and give it a sense of structure. (*See Chapter 8*)

parallel drafting Preparing a preliminary version of a document by having each member of a group responsible for a specific section. (*See 6c*)

parallelism The expression of similar or related ideas in similar grammatical form. *Faulty parallelism* occurs when elements in parallel are given incorrect or unequal grammatical form (*See Chapter 26*). In paragraphs, parallelism refers to a technique in which grammatical structures are repeated in order to highlight similar or related ideas (*See 8c-d*).

paraphrase A rewriting of an original sentence or passage in your own words, preserving the essence and level of detail of the original. (*See 35a-2, 46c, 47d-2*)

partial sentence An effective sentence fragment used for emphasis. (*See 20d*)

participle The form a verb takes when it is linked to a helping verb. Verbs can take two participial forms, the *present participle* and the *past participle*. (*See 15a-4*)

particle (*See* **phrasal verb**)

passive voice The form of a verb in a sentence in which the doer (or agent) takes the position of the direct object. (*See 9c, 17h, 24c, 30a-2; compare* **active voice**)

    subject   verb
The ball was caught by the outfield

past participle (*See* **participle**)
past perfect tense (*See* **perfect tense**)
past progressive tense (*See* **progressive tense**)
past tense (*See* **tense**)

peer group A group of fellow writers, usually in a classroom, who participate in collaborative writing activities. (*See 5d-2*)

→**per** Use *per* only to mean "by the," as in *per hour* or *per day*. Avoid using it to mean "according to," as in "per your instructions."

→**percent, percentage** Use *percent* only with numerical data. Use *percentage* to imply a statistical part of something.

    INCORRECT   **A percentage** of my commute is through Tomkins State Park.

    CORRECT   Ten **percent** of the sample returned the questionnaire.

    CORRECT   A large **percentage** of the revenue from the parking meters was stolen.

perfect tense A tense used to indicate that something happens before something else happens. Three perfect tenses can be marked in verb phrases: present perfect, past perfect, and future perfect. (*See 17e*)

    PRESENT PERFECT   **I have reported** the fire already.

    PAST PERFECT   The fires **had burned** for an hour before the brigade arrived.

    FUTURE PERFECT   Nancy **will have finished** by the time the dentist is ready.

periodic sentence A sentence structured so that subsidiary phrases, clauses, or other elements are piled up at the beginning, delaying the sentence's main clause. (*See 9c-2*)

> Because she knows that inspired designs often spring from hard work, because she loves perfection yet fears failure, and because she believes that risk-taking ought to be accompanied by attention to detail, Janelle is working up to eighteen hours a day on the clothing for her fall collection.

periodical A recurring publication that contains articles by different authors. Periodicals include magazines, scholarly journals, and newspapers. (*See 45b-2*)

person The form that a noun or a pronoun takes to identify the subject of a sentence. *First person* is someone speaking (*I, we*); *second person* is someone spoken to (*you*); *third person* is someone being spoken about (*he, she, it, they*). Verbs must agree in person with their subjects. (*See 15a-3, 16a, 18a, 24a*)

persona The way a writer chooses to characterize himself or herself through the choice of words and phrases, voice, and other devices. (*See 10b, 28a-3*)

personal home page A category of Web page in which an individual author creates a place for herself online. (*See 11d*)

personal pronoun A pronoun that designates persons or things. (*See 15a-2, 16a*)

SINGULAR	I, me, you, he, him, she, her, it
PLURAL	we, us, you, they, them

personal voice In writing, the use of stylistic devices (such as personal pronouns, narration, or the expression of beliefs and opinions) that convey a strong sense of the writer's self. (*See 2c-3*)

phrasal verb A verb plus a closely associated word (**particle**) that looks like a **preposition** (*run down, burn up, call up, clear out*). Unlike prepositions, particles can be moved from a position after the verb to a position after a direct object. (*See 15a-3*)

BEFORE OBJECT	Mr. Sims **burned up** all the wood.
AFTER OBJECT	Mr. Sims **burned** all the wood **up.**

phrase A word group lacking one or more elements (such as a subject or predicate) that would make it a complete sentence. (*See 15c; compare* **main clause**)

plagiarism The unethical practice of claiming that another writer's words or text are your own, or citing another person's words or text without credit, thereby giving the illusion that that person's words are your own. (*See 47d*)

planning A set of writing strategies through which the writer generates material and makes decisions about the content, organization, and style of a piece of formal writing. (*See Chapter 3; see also* **brainstorming; prewriting; invention**)

planning paragraph A kind of transition paragraph used near the beginning of an essay or section of an essay in order to help readers understand the arrangement of a discussion. (*See 8c-2, 8f*)

plot The chain of events in a work of fiction. (*See 55a-2*)

gloss

→**plus** Avoid using *plus* as a conjunction joining two independent clauses.

> **INFORMAL**   The school saved money through its "lights off" campaign, **plus** it generated income by recycling aluminum cans.

> **EDITED**   The school saved money through its "lights off" campaign and also generated income by recycling aluminum cans.

Use *plus* only to mean "in addition to."

> **ACCEPTABLE**   The wearisome reelection campaign, **plus** the pressures from the media, exhausted the senator.

→**p.m., a.m.** (*See* **a.m., p.m.**)

pocket dictionary An abbreviated or abridged dictionary useful for quick checks on spelling or definitions. (*See 29a*)

point-by-point organization A strategy for arranging paragraphs that make use of **comparing and contrasting.** Comparable features of two different or opposed subjects are described one by one. (*See 8e-2; compare* **subject-by-subject organization**)

point-driven writing Writing whose content and strategies are shaped by the purpose of explaining the writer's ideas, interpretations, and perspectives and providing support for them. (*See 54g; see also* **informative writing**)

point of view The perspective from which something (particularly a work of fiction) is told. (*See 55a-2; see also* **person** and **persona**)

policy In argumentative writing, a position that a particular course of action is one that should be undertaken or avoided. (*See 54a-3*)

poll In fieldwork, research gathered by questioning a representative sample of people to obtain information or opinion. (*See 48c*)

position paper A short, often documented paper that defines an issue, considers an audience, and draws on evidence and logical strategies to make its point. (*See 54d*)

positive form One of three forms taken by an adjective or adverb to indicate whether the noun or verb modified is being compared to something else. The positive form is used when no comparison is indicated. (*See 19c; compare* **comparative form** and **superlative form**)

> **ADJECTIVE**   This is a **clean** oven.
> She is an **imaginative** designer.

> **ADVERB**   You can travel **fast** in Manhattan by foot.
> Peggy designs **imaginatively.**

possessive case (*See* **case**)

possessive noun A noun that expresses ownership. Possession is usually marked with an apostrophe to distinguish the form from a plural. (*See 34a*)

The bird's call is becoming fainter.

possessive pronoun A pronoun that shows ownership. (*See 15a-2*)

> **SINGULAR**   my, mine, your, yours, her, hers, his, its

> **PLURAL**   our, ours, your, yours, their, theirs

gloss

post hoc **fallacy** (*See* **faulty cause-effect relationship**)

→**precede, proceed** *Precede* means "come before"; *proceed* means "go ahead."

> The Mickey Mouse float **preceded** the mayor's car. The parade **proceeded** down Fifth Avenue.

predicate In a sentence, the word or words indicating an action, a relationship, consequences, or conditions. A predicate typically takes the form of a **verb phrase** preceded by the subject of the sentence. A *simple predicate* consists only of a verb or verb phrase; a *complete predicate* consists of a verb or verb phrase plus any modifiers and other words that receive action or complete the verb. (*See* 15b-2)

prefix An affix, such as *un-* in *unforgiving*, placed before a word. (*See* 43b-3)

preliminary sources Reference works (such as encyclopedias) or electronic sites (such as mail lists or bulletin boards) that you can consult early in a research project for background information or for issues and questions of current interest. Preliminary (or *exploratory*) sources help you explore broad topics and identify areas for further, more intensive research. (*See* 45a-3)

premise A claim or assertion that serves as the foundation of an argument. **Syllogistic reasoning** includes both *major* and *minor premises*—assertions or *claims* on which conclusions can be based. (*See* 54c-1)

preposition A word that indicates a location, direction, or time (for example, *to, from, with, under, in, over*). (*See* 15a-7; *see also* **object of a preposition**)

prepositional phrase A phrase, created from a preposition plus a noun phrase, that can add information to a sentence or make it more precise or detailed. (*See* 15a-7)

> A faint smell **of grilled onions** came **through the window.**

prereading strategies A set of reading strategies in which the reader previews, skims, and samples a reading before working through it more formally. (*See* 2a-1)

present participle (*See* **participle**)

present perfect tense (*See* **perfect tense**)

present progressive tense (*See* **progressive tense**)

present tense (*See* **tense**)

→**pretty** Avoid using *pretty* (as in *pretty good, pretty hungry, pretty sad*) to mean "somewhat" or "rather." Use *pretty* in the sense of "attractive."

prewriting strategies A set of writing strategies used to explore ideas and information in order to generate material for a formal paper. (*See* Chapter 3; *see also* **brainstorming; invention; planning**)

primary sources (*See* **research**)

→**principal, principle** *Principal* is a noun meaning "an authority" or "head of a school" or an adjective meaning "leading" ("a *principal* objection to the testimony"). *Principle* is a noun meaning "belief or conviction."

printed indexes Books listing articles that appear in magazines, newspapers, or scholarly journals. Indexes help researchers locate useful sources. (*See* 45b-2; *see also* **electronic indexes**)

problem-solution grid A planning strategy through which a variety of hypothetical solutions are generated to solve a specific problem. (*See* 3c-2)

problem-solution sequence A piece of writing in which a problem is presented followed by a proposal for one or more solutions, perhaps with their advantages and disadvantages. (*See* 3c-2)

gloss

→**proceed, precede** (*See* **precede, proceed**)

process Any kind of operation, mental or physical, including the specific steps and materials or mechanism involved in the operation. *(See 8e)*

progressive tense A tense used to show an ongoing action in progress at some point in time. Verb forms can show three types of progressive tense: *present progressive, past progressive,* and *future progressive. (See 17e)*

PRESENT PROGRESSIVE	The carousel **is turning** too quickly.
PAST PROGRESSIVE	The horses **were bobbing** up and down.
FUTURE PROGRESSIVE	The children **will be laughing.**

pronoun A word that takes the place of a noun, such as *them, his, she,* and *it.* Pronouns are often used to avoid repeating the nouns used in the sentence. *(See 15a-2, 18c)*

Jim changed **his shirt** after spilling gravy on **it.**

pronoun-antecedent agreement (*See* **agreement**)

pronoun reference The connection between a pronoun (*its, him, them,* etc.) and its **antecedent,** or the noun or person to which it refers. *(See Chapter 22)*

proofreading The process of reading a draft in order to identify and correct distracting and usually minor errors in spelling, punctuation, incorrect hyphenation, and word division. *(See 14d, Chapter 38–43; compare* **editing***)*

proper adjective An adjective derived from a proper noun, used to modify a noun: *Brazilian music, Dickensian portrait. (See 38b-1)*

proper noun A noun that refers to specific people, places, titles, or things and is capitalized: *Miss America, New Orleans, Xerox Corporation. (See 15a-1, 38b-1)*

proposition A **thesis statement** offering an opinion or conclusion that the writer wishes readers to accept or agree with. A proposition is supported or made convincing by an **argument.** *(See 54a-3)*

public community People linked by their interest in or participation in activities or organizations addressing the welfare or concerns of either the residents of a particular area or a clearly recognizable social group. A general, diverse population, rather than a specific one, such as a **work community.** *(See 1a)*

purpose The writer's rhetorical goals or aim for a piece of writing. *(See Chapter 4, 28a-2, 54a-3)*

purpose structure A series of statements briefly describing the function of each paragraph or section of a paper. *(See 4b-1)*

quantifier A word like *each, one,* or *many* that indicates the quantity of a subject. *(See 18b-1)*

query A question; more specifically, a string of words constructed to pose a "question" to the Internet, in a search. *(See 45c)*

question-answer pattern (*See* **logical order**)

questionnaire A printed set of questions used in a **survey** or often mailed to a large number of people, to extract information, possibly in-depth. *(See 48c)*

→**quote, quotation** Formally, *quote* is a verb and *quotation* is a noun. *Quote* is sometimes used as a short version of the noun *quotation,* but this may bother some readers. Use *quotation* instead.

→**raise, rise** *Raise* is a transitive verb meaning "to lift up." *Rise* is an intransitive verb (it takes no object) meaning "to get up or move up."

He **raised** his head from the newspaper and watched the fog **rise** from the lake.

→**rarely ever** Use *rarely* alone, not paired with *ever.*

| REDUNDANT | He **rarely ever** spoke about the gulag. |
| EDITED | He **rarely** spoke about the gulag. |

reader The intended or imagined **audience** for a piece of writing. (*See Chapter 5*)

→**real, really** Use *real* as an adjective modifying a noun; use *really* as an adverb.

Emmons drove **really** well in the race because for once she was in a **real** stock car.

real time Electronic discussions that take place without delay. (*See 11c-3*)

→**reason is because, reason is that** Avoid these phrases in formal writing; they are wordy and awkward.

reciprocal pronoun A pronoun (*one another, each other*) that enables a writer to refer to individual parts of a plural antecedent. (*See 15a-2*)

The two kinds of birds compete for territory by destroying **each other's** nests.

→**reckon, calculate, figure** (see **calculate, figure, reckon**)

red herring A **fallacy** in which some fact or information distracts a reader from the real argument. (*See 54c-5*)

redrafting Part of the revision process that involves writing unworkable material over again. (*See* **revision**)

redundancy The use of unnecessary or repeated words and phrases that can be reduced through **editing**. (*See 7a-4*). *Redundant pairs* are two words used when only one is needed: *aid and abet, one and only, part and parcel, kith and kin. Redundant phrases* say the same thing twice: *each individual, fresh news, free gifts.* (*See 30a-1*)

redundant pair (*See* **redundancy**)

redundant phrase (*See* **redundancy**)

reference chain A chain of pronouns whose antecedent is stated in the opening sentence of a passage. Reference chains can help to guide readers through a passage and remind them of the controlling topic. (*See 22a-3*)

reference list List of sources found at the end of a document. (*See Chapter 50*)

register In communication, the form language takes in a particular context, showing variations in pronunciation, grammar, or word choice. (*See 10b*)

reflexive pronoun A pronoun that enables a subject or doer of an action also to be the receiver of the action. (*See 15a-2*)

He paid **himself** for the work.

→**regarding, in regard, with regard to** (*See* **in regard to**)

→**regardless, irregardless** (*See* **irregardless**)

relative clause An adjective-like clause that modifies a noun or pronoun and begins with a **relative pronoun.** (*See 15a-2, 15d, 16c-1*)

Who bought the new minivan?
I reminisced about all the shellfish **that** I had bought in Seattle.

relative pronoun A pronoun (*who, whom, whose, which,* or *that*) introducing a subordinate clause that modifies or adds information to a main clause. (*See 15a-2, 15d, 16c-1, 18b-3, 27b-2*)

remote reference Placing a **pronoun** at a distance from its **antecedent.** (*See 22a-2*)

gloss

rereading The process of going back over a reading in order to review, summarize, or understand it. (*See 2a-2*)

research The process of investigating a topic, either through *primary sources* such as interviews or observations or through *secondary sources* such as other writers' books and articles on the same topic. *Library research* is conducted primarily using the print and electronic materials in libraries; *field research* is conducted in settings where the subject of the research can be found in primary form. (*See Chapter 44, 45a-1*)

research plan An anticipated sequence of activities that guides the work of a research paper. (*See 44c*)

research thread Recurring ideas, issues, or keywords that act as links between research sources. (*See 44a*)

→**respectfully, respectively** *Respectfully* means "with respect"; *respectively* implies a certain order for events or things.

The senior class **respectfully** submitted the planning document. The administration considered items 3, 6, and 10, **respectively.**

restrictive clause (*See* **restrictive modifier**)

restrictive modifier A midsentence clause that presents information essential to the meaning of a passage. In contrast, a *nonrestrictive modifier* adds information that is useful or interesting but not essential to the sentence's meaning. (*See 27b-2, 32c*)

RESTRICTIVE MODIFIER   The charts **drawn by hand** were hard to read.

NONRESTRICTIVE MODIFIER   The charts, **drawn by hand,** were hard to read.

résumé A synthesis (in one or two pages) of one's education and employment history, usually prepared for the purpose of applying for a job. (*See 57f*)

resumptive modifier A modifying clause or phrase used to extend a sentence that appears to have ended, adding new information or twists of thought. (*See 9d-4*)

People who are careful about what they eat may lead healthier lives, **healthier, though not necessarily longer.**

review A critical appraisal of an event, object, or phenomenon, such as an art show, a concert, or a book. Most reviews are both descriptive and evaluative. (*See 54f*)

revision The process of improving rough or preliminary versions of a document by making large-scale changes, additions, or deletions in the material. *Major revision* involves redrafting, reorganizing, adding, or deleting significant material; *minor revision* involves changes within paragraphs, often at the sentence level. (*See Chapter 7; see also* **editing** and **proofreading**)

rhetorical purpose (*See* **purpose**)

rhetorical question A question asked not in expectation of an answer but for the purpose of providing the answer. (*See 9d-2*)

rhyming dictionary A dictionary that gives rhymes for words. (*See 29a*)

→**rise, raise** (*See* **raise, rise**)

Rogerian argument A strategy for argument that calls for acknowledging the reasonableness of the opposing point(s) of view rather than strong opposition to alternative perspectives. (*See 54c-4*)

rough draft A preliminary version of a paper which will later undergo **revision.** (*See Chapter 6*)

gloss

run-in list A list whose items aren't placed on separate lines. Such lists can present items in full or partial sentences. (*See 38a-5; compare* **vertical list**)

run-on sentence (*See* **fused sentence**)

→**says, goes** (*See* **goes, says**)

scholarly journals Journals that appear approximately four times a year, with the page numbering running continuously throughout the separate issues making up an annual volume. (*See 45b-2*)

screen name A self-identifier the email user chooses. (*See 11b-2*)

search engines Software dedicated to indexing and sorting Web pages for user convenience. (*See 11d*)

search strategy A strategy for research papers in which you identify the type of research you are conducting, the sources you might consult, and the tasks you need to perform. (*See 45a*)

second person (*See* **person**)

secondary sources (*See* **research**)

semidrafting While creating a **rough draft,** the process of writing out full sentences interspersed with *etc.* or other words indicating that something needs to be added later. (*See 6b-3*)

sentence A group of words containing a complete subject and predicate. (*See also* **compound sentence; compound-complex sentence; declarative sentence; exclamatory sentence; imperative sentence; interrogative sentence; simple sentence**)

sentence adverb An adverb used to modify an entire sentence. (*See15a*)

sentence cluster A group of sentences that develop related ideas or information, often arranged using **parallelism.** (*See 26c-1*)

sentence fragment A part of a sentence incorrectly treated as a complete sentence with a capital letter at the beginning and a period at the end. (*See Chapter 20*)

FRAGMENT	They were able to get the pump started again. **By replacing the gas filter.**
EDITED	They were able to get the pump started again by replacing the gas filter.
	By replacing the gas filter, they were able to get the pump started again.

sequential order The organization of information into a specific sequence, such as *spatial* (the relationship of physical features), *chronological* (events in a series), or *hierarchical* (most to least important features). (*See 54a-3*)

→**set, sit** Set means "to place"; sit means "to place oneself."

The research assistant **set** the sample near the centrifuge and then **sat** down on the stool.

setting The physical and temporal context of a work of fiction. (*See 55a-2*)

sexist language Language that implies or reinforces unfair, misleading, or discriminatory stereotypes on the basis of gender. (*See 31a*)

shift An incorrect or inappropriate switch in **person, number, mood, tense,** or **topic.** (*See Chapter 24, 25a*)

→**should of** (*See* **could of, would of**)

show In a writing assignment, to demonstrate or provide evidence for something.

gloss

signal paragraph A type of transition paragraph used to alert readers to a major change in direction or the start of a new section of the discussion.

simple predicate (*See* **predicate**)

simple sentence A sentence with one main (independent) clause and no subordinate (dependent) clauses. (*See* 15d-1; *compare* **complex sentence; compound sentence; compound-complex sentence**)

simple subject (*See* **subject**)

→**since, because** (*See* **because, since**)

→**sit, set** (*See* **set, sit**)

site, cite (*See* **cite, site**)

slang New words not yet, possibly never to be, shared by the general population, but used by a limited social group. (*See* 10b)

slanted statistics (*See* **misleading language/misleading evidence**)

→**so** Some readers object to the use of *so* in place of *very*.

> **INFORMAL**   The filmmaker is **so** thoughtful about giving his films distinct themes.
>
> **EDITED**   The filmmaker is **very** thoughtful about giving his films distinct themes.

social context The social, cultural, generational, or economic circumstances of a writer; of an intended **audience;** or of a piece of writing. (*See* 5b)

→**somebody, some body** (*See* **anybody, any body**)

→**someone, some one** (*See* **anybody, any body**)

→**sometime, some time, sometimes** *Sometime* refers to an indistinct time in the future; *sometimes* means "every once in a while." *Some time* is an adjective (*some*) modifying a noun (*time*).

> The probe will reach the nebula **sometime** in the next decade. **Sometimes** such probes fail to send back any data. It takes **some time** before images will come back to us from Neptune.

→**sort, kind** (*See* **kind, sort**)

"sounding out" Trying to determine the correct spelling of a word by its sound. (*See* 43a-1)

spamming Sending unsolicited email to large groups. (*See* 11a-4)

spatial order In paragraph development, a pattern for arranging descriptive sentences based on the spatial or visual arrangement of a scene, work of art, person, mechanism, or phenomenon (left to right, top to bottom, and so on).

special collections Library collections that include rare books, manuscripts, and documents, including those of local historical interest. (*See* 45b)

specialized dictionary Dictionary that lists terms from a particular field or about a specific topic.

specialized sources Focused, often complex or technical resources for research that provide detailed information on narrow topics and often include the latest scholarly findings. Sources of this kind include research reports, scholarly articles, specialized electronic databases, and interviews with experts.

→**specially, especially** (*See* **especially, specially**)

specific pattern of development A preferred way of developing paragraphs reflecting reader and writer coming from a specific community; compare with **general pattern of development**. (*See* 8e-2)

specific pronoun reference Using pronouns to clearly specify the relationships between statements. (*See 22b*)

specific reference A reference that documents the exact location of a word, idea, or fact in a source (for example, on a specific page or in a chart or drawing). (*See 49a; compare* **general reference** and **informational reference**)

specific-to-general pattern (*See* **logical order**)

speculative writing Writing that explores and considers a topic without taking a position on it.

spelling dictionary A dictionary that gives the spellings of words but not their definitions or etymologies. (*See 29a*)

split infinitive An **infinitive** in which a word separates *to* from the verb. Some readers object to split infinitives. (*See 23c-3*)

SPLIT INFINITIVE	The office designer tried **to** respectively **address** each of the workers' concerns.
EDITED	The office designer tried **to address** each of the workers' concerns respectively.

squinting modifier A modifier that incorrectly appears to modify both the word or phrase that comes before it and the one that comes after it. (*See 23a-3*)

SQUINTING	Those who smoke **seldom** seem concerned about the potential health hazards.
EDITED	Those who **seldom** smoke seem concerned about the potential health hazards.

state-of-being verb (*See* **linking verb**)

→**stationary, stationery** *Stationary* means "standing still"; *stationery* refers to writing paper.

structure The arrangement of ideas, sections, or paragraphs in a paper or other text. (*See 5c-3; see also* **outline** and **purpose structure**)

structured observation Carefully planned and focused observation of events, people, or situations intended to produce research data from which conclusions can be drawn. (*See Chapter 48a*)

style The distinctive choice of words (**diction**), sentence structures, and **persona** in a piece of writing. (*See 5c-4*)

subject In a sentence, the doer or the thing talked about—typically the first noun phrase followed by a verb phrase. A *simple subject* consists of one or more nouns (or pronouns) naming the doer or the topic. A *complete subject* consists of the simple subject plus all its modifying words or phrases. (*See 15b-1*)

subject-by-subject organization A strategy for arranging paragraphs that make use of **comparing and contrasting.** The writer considers one subject in its entirety and then the other, instead of presenting one point for both and then the next point. (*See 8b; compare* **point-by-point organization**)

subject complement (*See* **complement**)

subject pronoun A pronoun that is the subject of a clause. (*See 15d*)

subjective case (*See* **case**)

subjective description Description that emphasizes the emotional impact of events or phenomena. (*See 8e; compare* **objective description**)

subject-verb agreement The verb agrees with the subject in grammatical form. (*See 18a*)

subjunctive mood (*See* **mood**)

gloss

subordinate clause A word group that contains both a subject and a predicate but cannot stand on its own as a sentence because it begins with a subordinating word such as *because, since, although, which,* or *that.* Also called a *dependent clause. (See 15a-8, 15d, 27b-1, 27b-2)*

subordinating conjunction (*See* **conjunction**)

subordination A sentence structure in which one clause modifies another, helping readers perceive the links between ideas and understand the relative importance of information. The **main clause** is accompanied by a **subordinate clause** that modifies, qualifies, or comments on the ideas or the information in the main clause. (*See 27b; compare* **coordination**)

→**such** Some academic readers will expect you to avoid using *such* without *that.*

INFORMAL	Anne Frank had **such** a difficult time living the life of a normal young girl.
EDITED	Anne Frank had **such** a difficult time growing up **that** her diary writing became her only solace.

suffix An affix added to the end of a word in order to form a derived word (*bold+ness*) or to provide a grammatical inflection (*talk+ing*). (*See 43b-3*)

summarize (*See* **summary**)

summary A précis in your own words of an original passage, preserving the essence of the original but boiling it down to its essential points. An *objective summary* focuses on the content of the original passage, without any authorial judgment or commentary. An *evaluative summary* contains the author's opinions and comments on the passage. (*See 35a-2, 47d*)

summary paragraph A transitional or concluding paragraph used to mark the end of a discussion or to help readers remember main points.

summative modifier A modifying phrase or clause that summarizes the preceding part of a sentence and then takes the sentence on a new course. (*See 9d-4*)

To protect your vegetables against harmful insects, you can use soap sprays, scatter insect-repelling plants among the beds, or introduce "friendly" insects like ladybugs and praying mantises—**three techniques** that will not leave a harmful chemical residue on the food you grow.

superlative form One of the three forms taken by adjectives and adverbs to indicate whether the noun or verb modified is being compared to something else. The superlative form adds *-est* or *-most* to the adjective or adverb and indicates a comparison of three or more objects or actions. (*See 19c; compare* **comparative form** and **positive form**)

ADJECTIVE	This is the **cleanest** oven I've seen.
	She is the **most imaginative** designer of the three.
ADVERB	You can travel **fastest** in Manhattan if you ride a bicycle.
	Peggy designs **most imaginatively** of the three.

supporting conclusions The links in the chain of reasoning. (*See 12b-1*)

supporting evidence Material that supports a central claim or **thesis,** including examples from personal experience, examples from other people's experience, quotations and ideas from recognized authorities, technical information and statistics, data from surveys and interviews, background and historical information, and comparisons to similar situations and problems. (*See 54a-4*)

gloss

supporting idea Material that supports an assertion or **thesis.** (*See 4c; see also* **supporting evidence**)

→**suppose to, supposed to** The correct form of this phrase is *supposed to;* the *-d* is sometimes mistakenly left off because it is not always heard in pronunciation.

→**sure, surely** In formal writing, use *sure* to mean "certain." *Surely* is an adverb; don't use *sure* in its place.

He is **sure** to pass the exam.
He has **surely** studied hard for the exam.

→**sure and, try and** *And* is sometimes used in place of *to* with *sure* and *try.* Write *sure to* and *try to* instead.

INCORRECT   We will be *sure and* bring our rackets.

CORRECT   Bob will *try to* win the match.

survey A research tool to obtain data for analysis, usually more complex than a **poll.** (*See 48c*)

suspended hyphen A hyphen used at the end of the first of two parallel modifiers (from which the noun is deleted). (*See 40b-2*)

The process is equally effective with **oil-** and **water-based** compounds.

syllabification The correct division of words into their syllables. (*See 29a*)

syllogism (*See* **syllogistic reasoning**)

syllogistic reasoning A kind of logical reasoning that includes a *major premise,* a *minor premise,* and a conclusion. (*See 54c-1; see* **premise**)

MAJOR PREMISE   All landowners in Clarksville must pay taxes.

MINOR PREMISE   Fred Hammil owns land in Clarksville.

CONCLUSION   Therefore, Fred Hammil must pay taxes.

synonym A word that is identical or nearly identical in meaning to another word: *ill* and *sick, large* and *big.* (*See 28b-2; see* **thesaurus**)

synthesis The combining or distilling of separate elements into a single, unified entity. Synthesizing source material for a research paper involves combining concepts and details from a variety of sources to form a unified discussion of a topic. (*See 56a-4*)

→**take, bring** (*See* **bring, take**)

tautology (*See* **circular reasoning**)

team drafting A method of preparing a preliminary version of a document in which one member of a group begins, then turns it over to a second, and so on; drafts are recirculated before revision. (*See 6c-2*)

tense The form a verb takes to indicate time—whether the verb's action occurred in the past (*past tense*) or the present (*present tense*). The present tense form is also called the **base form** of the verb. *Future tense* is marked with the use of **helping verbs.** (*See 15a-3, 17a, 17b, 24b-1, 24b-2*)

PAST   Her grandmother **made** possum stew.

PRESENT   Her friends **stop** to pick up "road kill."

FUTURE   Her children **will find** these old customs offensive.

tense sequence The pattern of tenses in a piece of writing. Incorrect tense shifts can annoy a reader. (*See 17g*)

tentative thesis statement A preliminary statement of your key ideas and purposes used to help focus planning for the drafting of a paper. (*See 47a-4*)

gloss

text analysis A paper that provides a close, analytical reading of a particular text, often a work of literature. The analysis can focus on elements of the text such as technique or meaning. (*See 55c*)

→**than, then** *Than* is a word used to compare something; *then* implies a sequence of events or a causal relationship.

> Gregorian chants are more lugubrious **than** other vocal music from that period. As a result, we were lulled by the Gregorian chants, but **then** the organ recital started.

→**that, which** Although the distinction between *that* and *which* is weakening in many contexts, formal academic writing often requires you to know the difference. Use *that* in a clause that is essential to the meaning of a sentence **(restrictive modifier)**; use *which* with a clause that does not provide essential information (*nonrestrictive modifier*).

> THAT   He has the report **that** will vindicate Clareson.
>
> WHICH   He has a penchant for emotionalism, **which** may help him win the jury's favor.

→**theirself, theirselves, themself** All these forms are incorrect; use *themselves* to refer to more than one person, *himself* or *herself* to refer to one person.

→**them** Avoid using *them* as a subject or to modify a subject, as in "*Them* are delicious" or "*Them* apples are very crisp."

theme In literary works, an idea, perspective, or cluster of feelings and insights conveyed to a reader through various fictional devices. (*See 55a-1*)

→**then, than** (see than, then)

→**there, their, they're** These forms are often confused in spelling because they all sound alike. *There* indicates location; *their* is a possessive pronoun; *they're* is a contraction of *they* and *are*.

> THERE   Look **over there.**
>
> THEIR   **Their** car ran out of gas.
>
> THEY'RE   **They're** not eager to hike to the nearest gas station.

thesaurus A dictionary of **synonyms** and **antonyms**—words similar or opposite in meaning to each other. (*See 28c-2, 29a*)

thesis or thesis statement A sentence, often at the conclusion of an essay's first paragraph, that establishes the point, main argument, or direction of a paper, giving the reader a sense of purpose and an understanding of the essay's contents. (*See 4c, 47a, 54a-3*)

third person (*See* **person**)

thread Continuing email discussion (*See 11b-2*)

→**thusly** Avoid this term; use *thus* or *therefore* instead.

→**till, until, 'til** Some readers will find *'til* and *till* too informal; use *until*.

time sequence A planning strategy, particularly for papers involving chronological or temporal structures, in which events are labeled along a timeline. (*See 3b-3*)

→**to, as** (*See* **as, to**)

gloss

→**to, too, two** Because these words sound the same, they may be confused. *To* is a preposition indicating location. *Too* means "also." *Two* is a number.

> The Birdsalls went **to** their lake cabin. They invited the Corbetts **too.**
> That made **two** trips so far this season.

topic The focus or subject of a piece of writing. (*See 4c-1*)

topic sentence A sentence, usually located at the beginning of a paragraph, which announces its main idea or perspective. (*See 8b*)

topic shift (*See* **faulty predication, shift**)

→**toward, towards** Prefer *toward* in formal writing. (You may see *towards* used in England and Canada.)

trace In a writing assignment, mapping out a history or chronology or identifying the origins of something. (*See 4a-2*)

transition (*See* **transitional expression**)

transitional expression Words or phrases (*in addition to, on the other hand, therefore, without a doubt*) that link one idea, sentence, or paragraph to the next, helping readers to see relationships among ideas by connecting them logically. (*See 8d-2, 32b-3 33a-z*)

transitive verb A verb followed by an **object** or **complement.** (*See 15b-2; compare* **intransitive verb**)

>   transitive verb   object
> The President **called** the British Prime Minister.

tree diagram A planning strategy in which a central idea (or trunk) generates many subsidiary or associative ideas (branches), which can branch off into even more subsidiary twigs. (*See 3b-2; compare* **clustering**)

→**try and, try to, sure and** (*See* **sure and, try and**)

→**ultimately, eventually** (*See* **eventually, ultimately**)

unabridged dictionary A full-size reference dictionary, generally available in a library, that has not been abbreviated to save space. (*See 29a*)

uncountable noun (*See* **noncount noun**)

unified paragraph (*See* **paragraph**)

→**uninterested, disinterested** (*See* **disinterested, uninterested**)

→**unique** Use *unique* alone; don't write *most unique* or *more unique* since the word indicates an absolute condition.

→**until, till** (*See* **till, until, 'til**)

URL Standing for Universal Resource Locator, a standardized notation specifying the address or location of files on the Internet. (*See 49d*)

→**use to, used to** Like *supposed to*, this phrase may be mistakenly written as *use to* because the *-d* is not always clearly pronounced. Write *used to.*

usenet newsgroups Electronic bulletin boards tending to attract diverse membership from many geographic regions and professions. (*See 44b*)

vague generalization A sentence or passage that offers so little specific information that it is not meaningful. (*See 30b-1*)

vague pronoun reference Using pronouns that refer to antecedents that are implied rather than stated, or pronouns that are not connected explicitly to a specific antecedent. (*See 22b*)

value judgment An argument that an activity, belief, or arrangement is desirable or undesirable. (*See 54a-3*)

gloss

verb   The word in a sentence that indicates the action that has occurred, is occurring, or will occur. (*See 15a-3*)

verb phrase   A phrase that consists of a main verb plus a helping verb. (*See 15a-3, 17b*)

verbals   Verbs or parts of verb phrases that are used to function as nouns, adjectives, or adverbs. The three kinds of verbals are **infinitives, participles,** and **gerunds.** (*See 15a-4, 15c-4*)

verbal phrase   A verbal plus its modifiers, object, or complements. (*See 15c-4*)

vertical file   A library file of clippings, pamphlets, and other useful materials.

vertical list   A list whose items are placed on separate lines. (*See 38a-5; compare* **run-in list**)

visuals   Drawings, photos, graphs, and other visual representations. (*See 47c-3*)

voice   (*See* **active voice, passive voice**)

→**wait for, wait on**   Use *wait on* only to refer to a clerk's or server's job; use *wait for* to mean "to await someone's arrival."

Julie **waited on** the customers while she **waited for** Melissa to arrive.

warrant   (*See* **data-warrant-claim reasoning**)

Web sites   Provide text and graphics with numerous links to related sites. (*See 45c*)

→**well, good**   (*See* **good, well**)

→**went, gone**   (*See* **gone, went**)

→**were, we're**   *Were* is the past plural form of the verb *was; we're* is a contraction of *we* and *are.*

We're going to the ruins where the fiercest battles **were.**

→**where . . . at**   (*See* **at**)

→**whether, if**   (*See* **if, whether**)

→**which, that**   (*See* **that, which**)

→**who, whom**   Although the distinction between these words is slowly disappearing from the language, many readers will expect you to use *whom* in the objective case. When in doubt, err on the side of formality. (Sometimes editing can eliminate the need to choose.) (*See 16c*)

QUESTIONABLE	The person **who** we chose to be the next board president was Harland Clasgow.
EDITED	The person **whom** we chose to be the next board president was Harland Clasgow.
EDITED	We chose Harland Clasgow to be the next board president.

→**who's, whose**   *Who's* is the contracted form of *who* and *is. Whose* indicates possession.

The man **who's** going to Frankfurt tried to find the man **whose** bag he mistakenly took at the airport.

→**wise, -ize**   (*See* **-ize, -wise**)

wordiness   Use of too many words. (*See Chapter 30*)

work communities   Groups of people or audiences that are involved in specific business or work environments, as well as governmental agencies. (*See 1a*)

working bibliography An in-progress bibliography or list of references kept during the **research** process. (*See 46a*)

working journal A place to explore ideas, develop insights, experiment with prose, write rough drafts, and reflect on reading. (*See 2c*)

working outline (*See* **outline**)

working thesis A statement of the major ideas to be covered in a paper, used to guide further planning and drafting. A working thesis often appears in a draft but is usually revised by the final version. (*See tk*)

works cited List of the works to which the writer makes reference in the body of a research paper, either through in-text (parenthetical) citations or through footnotes or endnotes. (*See 49b*)

→**would of, could of** (*See* **could of, would of**)

writer's commentary A writer's direct address of the reader or reference to himself or herself in prose that is not intended to convey personal feelings. (*See 30b-3*)

writing and reading community People with similar goals, preferences, and uses for both verbal and visual texts. (*See 1a*)

→**yet, however, but** (*See* **but however, but yet**)

→**your, you're** *Your* is a possessive pronoun; *you're* is a contraction of *you* and *are*.

If **you're** going to take physics, you'd better know **your** math.

gloss

CREDITS

*Anatomy of Anti-Comm*unism. New York: Hill and Wang, 1969, p. 118. The Holy Bible, Authorized King James Version. London: Oxford University Press, p. 397. "Bodybuilding" entry from *InfoTrac Academic Index.* Reprinted by permission of Information Access Co. Copyright © 1999 The Gale Group. "Bodybuilding" entry from *1991 Reader's Guide to Periodical Literature*, p. 271. Copyright © 1992. Reprinted by permission of H. W. Wilson Company. *The English Language*. London: Penguin Books, 1988, p. 69. "Exercise" entry from *1992 Reader's Guide to Periodical Literature*, p. 763. Copyright © 1993. Reprinted by permission of H. W. Wilson Company. "Exercise" entry from *1993 Social Sciences Index*, pp. 592–593. Copyright © 1993. Reprinted by permission of H. W. Wilson Company. *Merriam-Webster's Collegiate Dictionary.* Copyright © 1995 by Merriam-Webster Inc. By permission. "Sizing Up the Sexes" from *Time*, January 20, 1992. Copyright © 1992 by Time, Inc. Reprinted by permission. "The Stock Account" from *Prospectus*, College Retirement Equities Fund for Individual Retirement and Tax-Deferred Variable Annuity Certificates, March 1, 1990. Reprinted by permission. *Treasures of Tutankhamun*. National Gallery of Art, p. 13.

Edward Abbey, *Beyond the Wall*. New York: Holt, Rinehart & Winston, 1971, pp. 97, 98. **Edward Abbey,** *Down the River*. New York: Dutton, 1982, p. 117. **Edward Abbey,** *The Journey Home*. New York: Dutton, 1977, p. 88. **American Society of Mechanical Engineers**, 1988, "Hazardous Waste Incineration." **Robert A. Apostal and Carol Helland**, "Commitment to and Role Changes in Dual Career Families." *Journal of Career Development*, Volume 20, Winter 1993, p. 123. Reprinted by permission of Plenum Publishing Corp. and the author. **Francis Bacon**, *Essays, Civil and Moral and the New Atlantis*. New York: P. F. Collier & Son, 1937, p. 122. **Hanson W. Baldwin**, "R.M.S. Titanic." *Harper's Magazine*, 1933. **Albert C. Baugh and Thomas Cable**, *A History of the English Language*, 3rd ed. Englewood Cliffs, NJ: Prentice Hall, 1978, p. 243. **John Berendt**, "Class Acts." *Esquire*, 1991. **Wendell Berry,** *What Are People For?* Berkeley, CA: North Point Press, 1990. **Wm. Bingham,** *A. M., a Grammar for the English Langu*age. Philadelphia: E. H. Butler & Co., 1867, p. 98. **H. G. Bissinger,** *Friday Night Lights*. Reading, MA: Addison Wesley, 1990, pp. 176–177. **Louise Bogan,** "Old Countryside" from *The Blue Estuaries: Poems 1923–1968* by Louise Bogan. Copyright © 1968 by Louise Bogan. Copyright renewed © by Ruth Limmer. Reprinted by permission of Farrar, Straus & Giroux, LLC. **Claude F. Boutron et al.**, "Decrease in anthropogenic lead, cadmium and zinc in Greenland snows since the late 1960's." *Nature*, 1991. **Michael Bright**, *Animal Language*. Ithaca, NY: Cornell University Press, 1984. **Maurice Broner**, "Stand Up and Be Heard" from IEEE Trans. Eng. Writing Speech. Copyright © 1964, pp. 25–30. **J. Bronowski**, *The Ascent of Man*. Boston: Little, Brown, p. 213. **Marcia Brown**, *Stone Soup.* Copyright © 1947, copyright renewed © 1975 by Marcia Brown. Reprinted with the permission of Atheneum Books for Young Readers, an imprint of Simon & Schuster Children's Book Group. **Bill Bryson,** *The Mother Tongue*. New York: Morrow, 1990. **Jimmy Buffet**, *Where Is Joe Merchant?* Orlando, FL: Harcourt Brace & Company, 1992, p. 220. **Robert Burchfield**, *Points of View*. New York:Oxford University Press, 1992, p. 85. **Cathryn Carroll**, *Laurent Clerc: The Story of His Early Years*. Washington, D.C.: Gallaudet University Press, 1991. **Lorene Cary**, *Black Ice*. New York: Random House, 1991. **Wilkie Collins**, *The Woman in White*, New York: Dutton, 1969, p. 184. *Consumer Product Safety Review,* Fall, 1998 Issue, p. 2, Vol. 3, No.1, "Fast-Track Recalls." **Stephanie Coontz**, "The Way We Weren't." *National Forum: The Phi Kappa Phi Journal*, Volume 75, Number 3 (Summer 1995). Copyright © by Stephanie Coontz. By permission of the publishers. **Pamela J. Creedon**, *Women in Mass Communication*. Beverly Hills, CA: Sage, 1993. **Donna Woolfolk Cross**, *Mediaspeak*. Copyright © 1983 by Donna Woolfolk Cross. Reprinted by permission of The Putnam Publishing Group. **Sharon R. Curtin**, *Nobody Ever Died of Old Age*. Boston: Little, Brown. **Mary Lee Daugherty**, *"Serpent-Handling as Sacrament."* Theology Today, 1976. **Stephen Davis**, *Say Kids! What Time Is It? Notes form the Peanut Gallery*. Boston:

Little, Brown, p. 126. **Mike Davis,** "House of Cards." *Sierra*, 1995. **Joan Didion,** *After Henry.* Copyright © 1992 by Joan Didion. Reprinted with the permission of Simon and Schuster. **Annie Dillard,** *An American Childhood.* New York: HarperCollins, 1987. **A.H. Drummond, Jr.,** *The Complete Guide to Sailing.* New York: Fireside Books, p. 63. **Jill Dubisch,** "You Are What You Eat: Religious Aspects of the Health Food Movement. *The American Dimension: Culture Myths and Social Realities,* 1981. **Brad Edmondson,** "Making Yourself at Home: The Baby Boom Generation Yearns to Settle Down." Reprinted by permission. **Barbara Ehrenreich,** "What I've Learned from Men: Lessons for a Full-Grown Feminist." Reprinted by permission. **David Elkind,** "The Family in Postmodern World." *National Forum: The Phi Kappa Phi Journal,* Volume 75, Number 3 (Summer 1995). Copyright © by David Elkind. By permission of the publishers. **Melvin Feffer,** *Radical Constructionism.* New York: New York University Press, 1988. **Henry Fielding,** *The History Tom Jones: A Foundling,* ed. Fredson Bowers. Middletown, CT: Wesleyan University Press, 1975. **Florida Center for Environmental Studies Website,** www.ces.fav.edu. Reprinted by permission of CES, A State University System Research Center. **Adam Frank,** "In the Nursery of Stars." *Discover,* 1996. **Samuel J. Freeth,** "Incident at Lake Nyos." *The Sciences,* 1992. **Charles Gaines,** "Hulk Triumphant." *Esquire,* 1986. **Tess Gallagher,** *Amplitude.* St. Paul, MN: Graywolf Press, 1987. **Laurie Garrett,** *The Coming Plague.* New York: Penguin Books, 1994, p. 199. **Clifford Geertz,** *The Interpretation of Cultures.* New York: Basic Books, 1973, p. 413. **Louis Giannetti,** *Understanding Movies,* 6th ed., Englewood Cliffs, NJ: Prentice Hall, 1993. **Nikki Giovanni,** "Pioneers: A View of Home" from *Sacred Cows.* Copyright © 1988 by Nikki Giovanni. Reprinted by permission of William Morrow and Company, Inc. **Nathan Glazer,** "Where Is Multiculturalism Leading Us?" *Phi Delta Kappan,* 1993. **George Gmelch,** "Baseball Magic." *Transaction,* 1971. **Frank Goddio,** "San Diego: An Account of Adventure, Deceit, and Intrigue." *National Geographic,* 1994. **Daniel Goleman,** "Too Little, Too Late." *American Health,* 1992. **Anson Gonzalez,** "Little Rosebud Girl." Reprinted by permission. **Ellen Goodman,** "Religion in the Textbooks." Copyright © 1994. The Boston Globe Newspaper Co./Washington Post Writers Group. Reprinted with permission. **Al Gore,** *Earth in the Balance.* Boston:Houghton Mifflin, 1992, pp. 25, 31, 35, 50–51, 116. **Rick Gore,** "Dinosaurs." *National Geographic.* Reprinted by permission of the National Geographic Society. **Kenneth C. Green,** chart from *The Campus Computing Project.* Copyright © 1998 by Kenneth C. Green. Reprinted by permission. **Beverly Green,** "African American Families." *National Forum: The Phi Kappa Phi Journal,* Volume 75, Number 3 (Summer 1995). Copyright © by Beverly Green. By permission of the publishers. **Gerald Gross,** *Editors on Editing.* New York: Harper & Row, 1962, pp. 79, 81. **John Haines,** *The Stars, the Snow, the Fire.* New York: Simon & Schuster, 1977. **Donald Hall,** "A Small Fig Tree" from *Old and New Poems.* Copyright © 1990 by Donald Hall. Reprinted by permission of Ticknor & Fields/Houghton Mifflin Co. All rights reserved. **Pete Hamill,** "The Neverglades." Reprinted by permission of Janklow & Nesbit. **Thomas Harvey,** *A. M., a New English Grammar for Schools.* New York: American Book Company, 1900, p. 244. **Nathaniel Hawthorne,** *Young Goodman Brown* and *The Birthmark.* **Ernest Hemingway,** *The Old Man and the Sea.* New York: Scribner's 1952, p. 136. **E. Mavis Hetherington,** "Effects of Father Absence." *Developmental Psychology,* 1972. **Maureen Honey,** *Creating Rosie the Riveter.* Amherst: University of Massachusetts Press, 1984, p. 135. **J. N. Hook,** *The Appropriate Word.* Reading, MA: Addison Wesley, 1990, pp. 34, 180. **Zora Neale Hurston,** *Their Eyes Were Watching God.* New York: HarperCollins Publishers. Copyright © 1937, p. 4. **Robert Jastrow,** *The Enchanted Loom.* New York: Simon & Schuster, 1981. **Robert Jastrow,** *Journey to the Stars.* New York: Bantam Books, 1989, p. 91. **Donald Johnson and Maitland A. Edey,** *Lucy: The Beginnings of Humankind.* New York: Simon & Schuster, 1981, p. 294. **Frank Johnson,** "Public School Student, Staff, and Graduate Counts by State, School Year 1993–94." National Center for Education Statistics, U.S. Department of Education. **Lawrence E. Joseph,** "The Scoop on Ice Cream." *Discover,* 1992. **Simon Kerl,** *A. M., a Common-School Grammar of the English Language.* New York: Ivison, Blakeman, Taylor & Company, 1871, p. 337. **Maxine Hong Kingston,** *The Woman Warrior.* New York: Knopf, 1976, p. 8. **William Severini Kowinski,** *The Malling of America.* New York: Morrow, 1985. **Ann J. Lane,** *The Charlotte Perkins Gilman Reader.* New York: Pantheon Books, 1980. **Marsha Lesowitz et al.,** "School-based developmental facilitation groups for children of divorce." *Psychotherapy,* 1987. **Michael Lewis,** *Liar's Poker.* New York: Penguin Books, 1989, **James Y. Liu,** *Chinese Theories of Literature.* Chicago: University of Chicago Press, 1975. **Barry Lopez,** *Crossing Open Ground.* New York: Random House, 1988. **James Lundquist,** *Chester Himes.* New York: Random House, 1988. **T. R. Mayers,** "(snap) shots." Reprinted by permission of author. **Thomas R. McDonough,** "Is Anyone Out There?" *Discover,* November, 1992. Copyright © 1992 by

The Walt Disney Company. Reprinted with permission of Discover Magazine. **M. A. J. McKenna**, "Film provides 'Beauty'-ful role models." *Boston Herald*, 1991. **Bill McKibben**, *The End of Nature*. New York: Random House, 1989. **Ruth Macklin**, *Mortal Choices*. Boston: Houghton Mifflin, 1987, p.4. **Margaret Mead**, *Male and Female*. New York: Morrow, 1949, p. 251. **Hugh Merrill**, *The Blues Route*. New York: Morrow, 1990, p. 13. **Alfred Metraux**, *Haiti: Black Peasants and Their Religion*. London: Harrap, 1960. **Kinereth Meyer**, "It Is Written: Tom Stoppard and the Drama of the Intertext." *Comparative Drama*, 1989. **Mark Crispin Miller**, *Seeing Through Movies*. New York: Random House, 1990. **Margaret Mitchell**, *Gone with the Wind*. **Desmond Morris**, *Bodywatching*. New York: Crown, 1985, p. 39. **Paul Mongo and Bryan Clough**, "The Bulgarian Connection." **Ross C. Murfin**, *Joseph Conrad Heart of Darkness: A Case Study in Contemporary Criticism*. New York: St. Martin's Press, 1989, p. 84. **Edward R. Murrow**, *In Search of Light*. New York: Knopf, 1967, p. 36. **Bill Neal**, "How to Call a Pig." *Esquire*, 1991. **Kesaya Noda**, "Growing Up Asian in America," as appeared in Making Waves by Asian Women United. Reprinted by permission of the author. **Susan Orlean**, *Saturday Night*. New York: Random House, 1990. **Alfonso Ortiz**, "Some Concerns Central to the Writing of 'Indian' History." *The Indian Historian*. **Phil Patton**, "How a ridiculous idea mutated into a marketing star" *Smithsonian*, 1992. **Noel Perrin**, "About Men: The Androgynous Man." *The New York Times Magazine*, February 5, 1984. Copyright © 1984 by The New York Times Company. Reprinted by permission. **Brenda Peterson**, *Nature and Other Mothers*. New York: HarperCollins, 1992. **George Plimpton**. Reprinted by the permission of Russell & Volkening as agents for the author. Copyright © 1993 by George Plimpton. **Alexander Pope**. *Alexander Pope: Selected Poetry & Prose*. Orlando, FL: Holt, Rinehart & Winston, p. 78. **David Popenoe**, "The American Family Crisis." *National Forum: The Phi Kappa Phi Journal*, Volume 75, Number 3 (Summer 1995). Copyright © David Popenoe. By permission of the publishers. **Neil Postman**, *Amusing Ourselves to Death*. New York: Penguin Books, 1985. **Adrienne Rich**, *On Lies, Secrets and Silence*. New York: Norton, 1979, p. 13. **Mary Roach**, "Sunstruck" excerpted from an article by Mary Roach. *Health* © 1992. **Richard Rodriguez**, *Hunger of Memory*. Boston: David R. Godine, 1983. **Scott Rosenberg**, "The Genie-us of Aladdin." *San Francisco Examiner*, 1992. **Hubert Saal**, "Dylan Is Back" *Newsweek*, 1968. **Jan Sankey**, *ZEN and The Art of Stand-Up Comedy* . New York: Routledge. **Juliet B. Schor**, *The Overworked American*. New York: HarperCollins, 1991. **Brian Schwegler**, "Character Development Sketch: Davie 'The Guesser.'" *Salt Magazine*, August, 1994. Reprinted by permission of the author and SALT Center for Documentary Field Studies. **Mina P. Shaughnessy**, *Errors and Expectations: A Guide for the Teacher of Basic Writing*. New York: Oxford University Press, 1977, p. 7. **Philip Sidney**, "His Lady's Cruelty" from *The Oxford Book of English Verse 1250–1918*. London: Oxford University Press, 1973, p. 143. **Robert G. Sprackland, Jr.** *All About Lizards*. Neptune City, NJ: TFH Publications, 1977, p. 11. **Judith Stacey**, "The Family Values Fable." *National Forum: The Phi Kappa Phi Journal*, Volume 75, Number 3 (Summer 1995). Copyright © Judith Stacey. By permission of the publishers. **Elsie Myers Stainton**, *The Fine Art of Copyediting*. New York: Columbia University Press, 1991. **Jane Stern and Michael Stern**. *Roadfood*. New York: HarperCollins, 1992. **Andrew Sullivan**, "Muscleheads." *The New Republic*, 1986. **Deborah Tannen**, *You Just Don't Understand: Women and Men in Conversation*. New York: Morrow, 1990, p. 293. **Carol Tavris**, *The Mismeasure of Woman*. New York: Simon & Schuster, 1992. **Lewis Thomas**, *Late Night Thoughts on Listening to Mahler's Ninth*. New York: Penguin, 1982. **Larry A. Tucker**, "Effect of Weight Training on Self-Concept: A Profile of Those Most Influenced Most." *Research Quarterly for Exercise and Sport*, 1983. **Mark Twain**, Adventures of Huckleberry Finn. New York: HarperCollins, 1987. **Richard H. Wagner**, *Environment and Man*. New York: Norton, 1971, pp. 451, 454, 460. *Webster's Third New International Dictionary*. Copyright © 1993 by Merrian-Webster Inc., publisher of the Merriam-Webster dictionaries. By permission. **E. B. White**, "Late August" from *Writings from* The New Yorker 1927–1976. Copyright © 1949, © 1977 E. B. White. New York: Harper-Collins. **Walt Whitman**, "Song of Myself" from *Leaves of Grass*. New York: Norton, 1973, p. 28. **John Edgar Wideman**, *Brothers and Keepers*. New York: Random House, 1984. **John Edgar Wideman**, *Philadelphia Fire*. New York: Henry Holt, 1990, p. 3. **Ellen Willis**, "Rock, Etc." *The New Yorker*, 1974. **Clark A. Wiseman**, "Impediments to economically efficient solid waste management." *Resources for the Future*, 1991. **Richard Wisniewski and Paul Kleine**, "Teacher Moonlighting: An Unstudied Phenomenon." *ERIC*, 1983. **P. G. Wodehouse**, *The Mating Season*. New York: HarperCollins, 1949, p. 7. **Robert Wood**, "Advanced Algebra–McGuire Maps and Charts" in *Mathematical Knowledge*. Copyright © 1999 by Robert Wood. **Carl Zimmer**, "The Body Electric." *Discover*, February 1993. Copyright © 1992 by The Walt Disney Company. Reprinted with permission of Discover Magazine.

Note: Page numbers preceded by G- indicate terms in glossary.

index

index

index

index

index